READINGS IN RELIGIOUS PHILOSOPHY

MacGregor/Robb

Under the Editorship of
LUCIUS GARVIN
Macalester College

Readings in Religious Philosophy

GEDDES MACGREGOR
Dean, Graduate School of Religion
University of Southern California

J. WESLEY ROBB
Department of Religion
University of Southern California

HOUGHTON MIFFLIN COMPANY · BOSTON

Houghton Mifflin Company · Boston

Printed in the U.S.A.

Contents

PREFACE ix

SECTION ONE · *Introduction*

Alfred North Whitehead	*Definition of Religion*	3
George Galloway	*Philosophy, Theology, and the Philosophy of Religion*	5
Max Otto	*An Affirmative Faith in the Nonexistence of God*	14
W. Fraser Mitchell	*War Thoughts in Winter*	20
Miguel de Unamuno	*An Interpretation of the Nature of Religion*	21
Francis Thompson	*The Hound of Heaven*	26

SECTION TWO · *Basic Conceptions of God*

Lucretius	*On Nature*	32
Origen	*Faith and Reason*	43
	The Use of Allegory	44
	Evil Also Serves	45
Augustine	*Creation and Evil*	46
Josiah Royce	*The Larger Self*	50
Auguste Comte	*A Positivistic View of Religion*	64

SECTION THREE
The Traditional Case for Theism

Aristotle	*The Prime Mover*	68
Anselm	*The Ontological Argument*	75
Thomas Aquinas	*The Existence of God: The Five Ways*	81
René Descartes	*The Ontological Argument*	84
Gottfried Wilhelm Leibniz	*Monadology*	95
François Mauriac	*On Pascal*	103
Howard Albert Johnson	*On Kierkegaard*	112

SECTION FOUR · *Human Knowledge of God*

David Hume	*On Miracles*	132
Immanuel Kant	*Evil in Man*	136
Ignatius Loyola	*The Jesuit Method of Meditation*	145
John Henry Newman	*The Illative Sense*	149
Henri Bremond	*Against the Rationalist Obsession*	158
Paul Jury	*He Was Called Jesus*	165
	Jesus of Nazareth	170
Rudolf Otto	*The Numinous*	173
Anders Nygren	*The Centrality of Agape in the Christian Religion*	178
Austin Farrer	*The Freedom of the Will*	183

SECTION FIVE · *The Destiny of Man*

Plato	*The Immortality of the Soul*	194
F. C. S. Schiller	*A View of the Future Life*	199
Friedrich von Hügel	*The Meaning of Heaven and Hell*	208
W. E. Hocking	*On Living and Dying*	214
Donald MacKinnon	*Death*	221

SECTION SIX
Value-Experience and the Idea of God

Aristotle	*Love and Friendship*	226
W. R. Sorley	*Theism and Moral Values*	232
William James	*A Pragmatic Approach to the Moral Life*	241
Albert Schweitzer	*Reverence for Life*	246
Martin Buber	*The Response of Man to Man*	253

SECTION SEVEN · *The Mystery of Evil*

Job		258
Boethius	*Chance and Providence*	259
David Hume	*Nature Neither Good Nor Evil*	272
William Temple	*Finitude and Evil*	277
C. J. Ducasse	*The Problem of Evil and Some Attempted Solutions*	283
Bruce Marshall	*"All Glorious Within"*	292

SECTION EIGHT · *Religious Language*

A. J. Ayer	God *Is Meaningless*	304
A. D. Ritchie	*Errors of Logical Positivism*	310
A. C. Ewing	*Meaninglessness*	322
A. J. Ayer and F. C. Copleston	*Logical Positivism: Discussion between Professor Ayer and Father Copleston*	328
David Cox and Thomas McPherson	*Can the Verification Principle Be Applied to Christian Doctrines?*	356
Ernst Cassirer	*The Power of Metaphor*	369
Ronald W. Hepburn	*Demythologizing and the Problem of Validity*	377
F. W. Dillistone	*The Function of Metaphor*	386
W. Fraser Mitchell	*The Language of Religion*	392
H. D. Lewis	*Expression of the Experience of God*	399
INDEX		413

Preface

When my publishers asked me to compile an anthology of readings to complement my *Introduction to Religious Philosophy*, I saw at once that the task called for a collaborator such as Dr. Robb. He has borne the brunt of the labor, including the compilation of the Index. Except in the case of a few contributions arranged through the courtesy of my personal friends, I have done little more than suggest passages and write introductions and notes to them. The passages will seem to some readers curiously varied. The purpose of this variety is, of course, to introduce the student to some literary commonplaces and lively poetic byways as well as to the classical streams of religious philosophy.

The *Introduction to Religious Philosophy*, which appeared in both American and British editions, has been adopted as a standard text in many universities and colleges. Of course it has met with occasional hostility. Some have attacked it for being too Christian, while others have assailed it for being too atheistic in its approach. I account these criticisms, taken individually, a reproach to the author of a book on religious philosophy; taken together they constitute a compliment I can but hope to have deserved. At any rate, that quality in my book that evoked such picturesquely twin reactions is certainly reflected in the selection of the passages in this companion volume, which, whatever defects it may have, has been determined by anything other than the interests of any particular viewpoint. Perhaps only those who have engaged in similar work will appreciate the extent to which one's choice is restricted, in such a work, by practical considerations. I can but assure others that the task calls for more than jackdaw virtues.

GEDDES MACGREGOR

SECTION ONE

Introduction

Alfred North Whitehead

Whitehead (1861-1947) is one of the most distinguished figures in twentieth-century philosophy in the English-speaking world. Born in England, he came in his later years to a chair at Harvard. Educated at Trinity College, Cambridge, and influenced by mathematical philosophers such as Giuseppe Peano (1858-1932) and Gottlob Frege (1848-1925), he collaborated with Bertrand Russell in the epoch-making work Principia Mathematica. *His philosophy acquired, however, a speculative as well as an analytical side. Perhaps the best book for the beginner to read in order to appreciate both these aspects of Whitehead is his* Science and the Modern World. *His thought has had great influence on much modern religious philosophy, and the following is a passage from the beginning of his little book* Religion in the Making.

*Definition of Religion **

It is my purpose . . . to consider the type of justification which is available for belief in doctrines of religion. This is a question which in some new form challenges each generation. It is the peculiarity of religion that humanity is always shifting its attitude towards it.

The contrast between religion and the elementary truths of arithmetic makes my meaning clear. Ages ago the simple arithmetical doctrines dawned on the human mind, and throughout history the unquestioned dogma that two and three make five reigned whenever it has been relevant. We all know what this doctrine means, and its history is of no importance for its elucidation.

But we have the gravest doubt as to what religion means so far as doctrine is concerned. There is no agreement as to the definition of religion in its most general sense, including true and false religion; nor is there any agreement as to the valid religious beliefs, nor even as to what we mean by the truth of religion. It is for this reason that some consideration of religion as an unquestioned factor throughout the long stretch of human history is necessary to secure the relevance of any discussion of its general principles.

There is yet another contrast. What is generally disputed is doubtful, and what is doubtful is relatively unimportant — other things being equal. I am speaking of general truths. We avoid guiding our actions by general principles which are entirely unsettled. If we do not know what number is the product of 69 and 67, we defer any action pre-supposing the answer, till we have found out. This little arithmetical puzzle can be put aside till it is settled, and it is capable of definite settlement with adequate trouble.

But as between religion and arithmetic, other things are not equal. You *use* arithmetic, but you *are* religious. Arithmetic of course enters into your nature,

* A. N. Whitehead, *Religion in the Making* (New York: The Macmillan Co., 1927), pp. 13–18. Used by permission of Cambridge University Press, New York.

so far as that nature involves a multiplicity of things. But it is there as a necessary condition, and not as a transforming agency. No one is invariably "justified" by his faith in the multiplication table. But in some sense or other, justification is the basis of all religion. Your character is developed according to your faith. This is the primary religious truth from which no one can escape. Religion is force of belief cleansing the inward parts. For this reason the primary religious virtue is sincerity, a penetrating sincerity.

A religion, on its doctrinal side, can thus be defined as a system of general truths which have the effect of transforming character when they are sincerely held and vividly apprehended.

In the long run your character and your conduct of life depend upon your intimate convictions. Life is an internal fact for its own sake, before it is an external fact relating itself to others. The conduct of external life is conditioned by environment, but it receives its final quality, on which its worth depends, from the internal life which is the self-realization of existence. Religion is the art and the theory of the internal life of man, so far as it depends on the man himself and on what is permanent in the nature of things.

This doctrine is the direct negation of the theory that religion is primarily a social fact. Social facts are of great importance to religion, because there is no such thing as absolutely independent existence. You cannot abstract society from man; most psychology is herd-psychology. But all collective emotions leave untouched the awful ultimate fact, which is the human being, consciously alone with itself, for its own sake.

Religion is what the individual does with his own solitariness. It runs through three stages, if it evolves to its final satisfaction. It is the transition from God the void to God the enemy, and from God the enemy to God the companion.

Thus religion is solitariness; and if you are never solitary, you are never religious. Collective enthusiasms, revivals, institutions, churches, rituals, bibles, codes of behaviour, are the trappings of religion, its passing forms. They may be useful, or harmful; they may be authoritatively ordained, or merely temporary expedients. But the end of religion is beyond all this.

Accordingly, what should emerge from religion is individual worth of character. But worth is positive or negative, good or bad. Religion is by no means necessarily good. It may be very evil. The fact of evil, interwoven with the texture of the world, shows that in the nature of things there remains effectiveness for degradation. In your religious experience the God with whom you have made terms may be the God of destruction, the God who leaves in his wake the loss of the greater reality.

In considering religion, we should not be obsessed by the idea of its necessary goodness. This is a dangerous delusion. The point to notice is its transcendent importance; and the fact of this importance is abundantly made evident by the appeal to history.

George Galloway

When, in the nineteenth century, the influence of Hegel spread from Germany to other countries, it produced a peculiar and pervasive philosophical climate. While there was some sharp reaction in certain quarters against the absolutist system of Hegel, the age was characterized by a profuse variety of thought cast in a Hegelian mold. Though in Britain the philosophical tradition had been mainly empiricist, a Platonic tradition had continued to exert an influence in some circles, while writers such as Coleridge and Carlyle had also in some ways prepared the ground for an interest in Hegel. The Hegelian movement in British thought may be dated from 1865, when James Hutchison Stirling (1820-1909) interpreted Hegel's thought to British readers in The Secret of Hegel, *published that year. There were two types of Hegelianism, a left wing in which popular religion was roundly despised as mythology and a right wing whose adherents were ready to accept, in too facile a manner, everything in the religious tradition they happened to know. Both types, in their various forms, caused religion to be melted into a Hegelian mold where it was not replaced by a Hegelian mix. To many Hegelianism represented religion in a more "liberal" form. The more spiritualistic aspects of Hegel's teaching were developed in Britain by writers such as T. H. Green (1836-1882), W. Wallace (1844-1897), F. H. Bradley (1846-1924), and B. Bosanquet (1848-1923). John Caird (1820-1898) and his brother Edward (1835-1908) may be taken as interesting examples of the spirit of the movement as it affected religious thought: While both were imbued with Hegelian ideas, John was more orthodox in his Christianity and became Professor of Divinity at Glasgow University (later Principal); Edward, less orthodox, became Professor of Moral Philosophy.*

The term Religionsphilosophie *(philosophy of religion), though to be found in Germany in the last decade of the eighteenth century, is particularly associated with the Hegelian school. George Galloway, who died in 1933, is a good example of one of the later British exponents of a system so conceived. The following passage is taken from his book* The Philosophy of Religion, *for many years a standard work for students of the subject.*

Philosophy, Theology, and the Philosophy of Religion *

It will help to give greater definiteness to our conception of a Philosophy of Religion, if we consider briefly the relation in which it stands to Philosophy and

* George Galloway, *The Philosophy of Religion* (New York: Charles Scribner's Sons, 1922), pp. 41–53.

to Theology. The answer to the first question would seem at first sight to be quite simple: the Philosophy of Religion is just the application of philosophical principles and methods to religion regarded as a matter given. The speculative mind is directed to a certain aspect of experience, and reports the results of its examination. Formally this is clear enough, but in the practical working out of the problem a great deal will depend on our conception of the actual scope and powers of philosophical thought. If we maintain the possibility of a completed System of Philosophy, then we cannot concede to the Philosophy of Religion any independence of the System. Like a member of an organism, it has a well-marked place and function assigned to it, and its meaning essentially depends on its relation to the whole of which it is a part. Now it will probably be granted by most people that the aim of Philosophy is system: it seeks to rationalise, it strives to make manifest the systematic unity of the universe upon which the connexion and coherency of its elements rest. Accomplishment, however, may come short of intention; and it matters much in settling the question we have in mind whether a speculative system is an ideal, a regulative conception which we use to guide our thought, or is a realised fact. The latter, it is well known, was the belief of Hegel, though it is not likely that many thinkers in our own day would admit that Philosophy has achieved so much. Still his idea of the organic whole of the speculative sciences is of interest to us in the present connexion, for it is a profound and suggestive attempt to show the precise place which a Philosophy of Religion occupies in a fully articulated speculative System.

According to Hegel, Philosophy, in its dialectic movement or process of explicating itself, is also the explication of religion. The speculative System as well as the Philosophy of Religion has God for its object, God conceived as the Absolute. But the Philosophy of Religion differs from the other philosophical sciences in beginning with the idea of God instead of reaching it at the last: in the one case it is the *terminus a quo,* in the other the *terminus ad quem.* Again, while Philosophy treats the Absolute as primarily Logical Idea, the Philosophy of Religion regards it as object, the mind or spirit which appears or reveals itself. Religious doctrine presents the idea of the self-revealing God in the form of figurative thought: the Philosophy of Religion criticises and purifies these representations in order to raise them to the speculative form. To put the theory succinctly: the Philosophy of Religion shows that the truth of religion is the speculative Idea of God; while Philosophy shows us how the Idea or Absolute has differentiated itself in nature, in spirit, and in religion as a phase of the movement of spirit.

Without entering into detailed criticism, certain general remarks suggest themselves. There is, it appears to me, an element of truth in the Hegelian conception of the relationship now under review. A Philosophy of Religion depends on Philosophy: it is the application of philosophical thought to a specific phase or stage of experience in order to determine its general meaning and value. The explanation of any aspect of experience must be governed in its methods and principles by the methods and principles by which we explain experience as a whole. The idealistic interpretation of experience, for example, carries with it as a consequence a Philosophy of Religion constructed on idealistic lines. But the assertion that Philosophy can develop a complete System which gives a full and final meaning to each of its parts, must be subjected to serious qualifications. Reality can never be entirely absorbed in the process of rationalising it, and explanation itself rests in the end on postulates that cannot be transformed into logical elements in a system. We do not comprehend a thing by bestowing a name upon it; and the constant presence of unrationalised elements makes a final System an unattained ideal. We therefore deny that Philosophy has such a mastery over its materials, that it can exhibit in the light of a system the precise meaning and value of every aspect of experience. Owing to the presence in the universe of much which is unexplained, ultimate unification cannot be other than provisional. And if this be so, we must claim for the special philosophical disciplines a greater measure of independence than was conceded to them by Hegel. For each in its way is contributing to the development of a system rather than exactly determined by it. This is apparent enough in the case of religion. There is more in the religious consciousness than can be derived from any dialectic development of consciousness in general, and religious philosophy has the facts directly before it and handles them on its own responsibility. It should deal faithfully with the many and varied phenomena of religion, whether it succeed in giving them an adequate philosophical interpretation or no. The relation of the Philosophy of Religion to Philosophy is rather one of interaction and co-operation than of complete logical dependence. In practice at all events this is so; and it cannot be otherwise, since the idea of a completed philosophical System remains an ideal.

But the claim for a certain independence on the part of a Philosophy of Religion ought not to be pressed too far. The general standpoint from which it treats experience, and the forms and conceptions it uses in dealing with religious experience, are derived from Philosophy. It cannot arbitrarily create special forms and methods for its own service; it must draw them from the common speculative inheritance that has come down from the past. The dominant Philosophy of the age supplies the principles which men apply to religion in order to develop a theory of religious experience, and it determines in a general way the character of a religious philosophy. If the prevailing type of philosophical thought at a particular period be idealistic, dualistic, or realistic, it will be reflected in the way men interpret the meaning of religion. The Deistic notion of religion, for instance, is the reflexion of a general philosophical tendency or temper of mind: so likewise, the speculative theologies and religious philosophies of the post-Kantian epoch are deeply influenced by the far-reaching idealism which prevailed. It may be added that Idealism is the form of philosophical thinking which leads most readily to a philosophy of religion, inasmuch as mind or spirit is of primary value both for idealism and religion. Materialism, on the contrary, is a form of thought which is antagonistic to religion, and when it is accepted, it leaves no room for a philosophical theory of spiritual experience. The only task left for the materialist in respect of religion would be to demonstrate that it is and must be an illusion.

The difficulties of any attempt to isolate the Philosophy of Religion from Philosophy become plainer when we remember that the philosophical treatment of religion is not a simple process. It involves Psychology and Epistemology, Ethics and Metaphysics; and to suppose that a religious thinker can evolve principles for himself in each of these departments is absurd. In every case he is dependent on the work already done in these provinces, and this even when he tries, as he ought to do, to think things out for himself. Were he foolish enough to attempt to cut himself loose from the philosophical inheritance of his age, he could not entirely succeed in doing so. A purely religious philosophy, standing on its own ground, though it appeals to a certain type of mind, is not a workable conception; for it is not possible to dissever religious experience from other forms of experience, and in striving to understand religion it is also necessary to look beyond it.

The objection to a Philosophy of Religion which recognises a general dependence on Philosophy, has been urged from the side of Theology, and especially by theologians who are hostile to Metaphysics. The supreme truth of religion, it is held, is contained in Christianity, which is the revealed religion, and the most and best we can do is to explicate and state systematically the truths it contains. In recent times, Ritschl has given outspoken expression to this view, and has argued strongly against the intrusion of metaphysics into the sphere of religion. In his short work, *Theologie und Metaphysik* (1881), he takes his stand on Christianity as a historical revelation, and protests, not without force, against the fashion of importing into it metaphysical ideas which are alien to its substance. If men are resolved to philosophise about religion, he tells us, there is but one way to do so to any profit, and that is to set out from the Christian idea of God as scientifically valid, and to develop a world-view in dependence upon it. In other words, we cut the Philosophy of Religion clear from Philosophy by identifying it with a Philosophy of Christianity, and by developing our own religious categories and principles. This conception of a Christian Philosophy of Religion finds favour with some in our own day, and one can understand the desire for a kind of spiritual philosophy, preserving the religious interest throughout, and removed from the fluctuations of speculative opinion. Yet the conception does not appear to be tenable, and it would be hard to defend it successfully against various objections. We have already argued that it is impossible to develop a religious metaphysics which neither draws from nor depends on metaphysics in general. There is a fallacy in the notion that you can find the whole truth in any particular phase of experience, however important; and for a like reason no religion can be isolated from the rest without losing significance in consequence. It has been said that the man who knows no book but the Bible, does not even know it rightly; and it is the same with a religion. No single aspect of reality is "cut off with a hatchet" from the remainder, and to know any one thing you must see its relations to other things. Only to this large outlook do the characteristic elements in a given religion stand forth; and to understand the ethical and spiritual value of Christianity, one must recognise not merely its distinction from, but its relations to other religions. Christianity is supreme not because it is severely separate from all other types of religion, but because it is their goal and completion. Hence a Philosophy of Christianity, if it were to rise to the fulness of its task, would perforce widen out into a Philosophy of Religion. And the latter, in its turn, cannot successfully deal with religious experience in abstraction from the rest of experience. In other words, it must perform its work, recognising its relations to and receiving help from Philosophy as the universal Science. We cannot philosophise in compartments, and in the search for truth, breadth is necessary as well as concentration. The idea, then, of a Christian Philosophy of Religion which has its own form and content, while it is inspired by a sincere purpose, is not right in theory nor feasible in practice. We can either have a Christian Theology or a Philosophy of Religion, but we cannot properly combine the two. It is not possible at one and the same time to preserve the religious authority which is claimed for the one, and to maintain the freedom and largeness of vision which are demanded by the other.

We pass now to the second question, the relation in which the Philosophy of Religion stands to Theology. The two differ distinctly in their scope, and this is evident after the slightest examination. When we use the term *Philosophy of Religion,* there is no doubt about the field of study to which we refer. It is religion, as a universal phenomenon in human experience, which we are proceeding to examine. But the word *Theology,* used to denote a system of Dogmatics, is ambiguous. The further query will follow: What theology? Is it Jewish, Christian, or Mohammedan? If it be Christian, we have still to find out whether it is Roman Catholic or Protestant. The term therefore requires qualification ere we understand definitely what is meant. In its nature a theology is an articulated system of religious beliefs or doctrines which has been developed from some historic religion. In intention it is a statement of the truths which have proved themselves the working-values of a given religion: and it strives to present them in an intelligible form, so that they can be taught, and serve as a bond of union for a religious community or Church. The proper office of theology is not to criticise the religious experience out of which it grew, but rather to deal faithfully with that experience, and report what is implied in it. What is called "Speculative Theology," which seeks to raise religious doctrines to a philosophical form by exercising a free criticism upon them, is better ranked with religious philosophy.

The significance of theology in relation to religion will be better appreciated if we indicate briefly the process by which it comes to birth and develops. Theology always presupposes the existence of a living religion, and religions which have advanced to a certain stage naturally produce theological doctrines. Theology is anticipated and prepared for by tendencies which exist in the early forms of religion. The centre of a religion is the cultus, and the primitive way of explaining the traditional acts done in the cultus is to recite myths or legends about them. This was a crude though obvious plan of imparting a kind of meaning to religious usages handed down from the immemorial past, from the days when men moved in a world of instinctive beliefs, and reflective thought had not asserted its claims. With the great development of the personal consciousness which took place after the formation of national religion the rude form of reflexion passed into a higher form, and man began to make a conscious endeavour to explain and generalise the meaning of his religious rites and customs. The cultus is still the centre which offers a relatively stable material upon which reflexion is exercised and out of which religious doctrines are fashioned: these express the meaning and value which the community attaches to its religious activity. There are various causes which stimulate theological construction in a religious society: for instance, the expediency of presenting religious truth in a shape which can be taught; the need of defining what is true in opposition to rival religions and to heretical doctrines; and, finally, the felt obligation of meeting the demands which science and philosophy have made articulate. A decadent religion will not respond to these stimuli, but a vigorous faith will meet these needs and answer these demands by developing its doctrines and connecting them in a systematic way. Primarily, religious doctrines are designed to set forth the values of religious experience; but in the higher stages of culture, theology seeks to invest religious beliefs with a degree of reasonableness. It strives to become a system whose parts cohere with and mutually support each other. From the nature of the case, theology cannot be philosophy; yet in its maturer age, when science and philosophy are exercising an influence in the world around it, theology is prompted to enlarge its scope and to broaden out in the direction of a religious philosophy. The theologian passes beyond the original view of his office, which was to report faithfully the working conceptions and values implied in a given religion. He seeks now to unfold a world-view, based on religious postulates, but for which he also claims rationality. The motives that inspired this movement are not difficult to discern: the methods of explanation used in science and philosophy could not be altogether ignored by the theologian. Hence we find theology offering explanations of the nature of God, the creation and development of the world, and the origin of man. Doctrines bearing on these themes have entered into the structure of Christian Dogmatics, and have been embodied in the creeds of all the Christian Churches. When we consider the way in which theology was developed on these lines, we recognise that, in intention at least, it occupies a mediating position between faith on the one hand and reason on the other. Beginning with an explication of faith-experiences, it ends by offering what purports to be a rational view of the world. In this latter aspect of its development, however, Christian theology has become entangled in controversy, and has had to bear the brunt of criticism. Theology has failed to advance with scientific and philosophical culture, and in consequence its doctrines on the nature and origin of the world and man have fallen out of harmony with the knowledge of the age. Hence the so-called conflict between Science and Religion, about which so much was heard in the middle of last century. The dispute, when closely examined, was seen to gather round doctrines which theology had pushed forward under the shield of religious authority, but which really fell within the province of science. A dispute of the kind could only end in one way, theologians have been forced to resile from untenable positions, though time has shown the issues at stake were greatly magnified.

The controversy to which I have referred draws attention to a difficulty which attends an endeavour on the part of theology to mediate between faith and reason. The difficulty arises from presuppositions from which Christian theology set out in forming its doctrinal system. The Sacred Writings, it assumed, were an authoritative basis, and the truths which could be gathered from them were divinely sanctioned, and provided an assured ground for inference. The appeal in this instance was not to a continuous spiritual experience which could be examined, but to statements in documents of very different dates and character. When theology, therefore, building on statements taken as authoritative, proceeded to develop doctrines for which the claim of rationality was made, the position became insecure. The scientist refused to admit some of the premises from which the theologian set out: the latter retorted by declaring he took his stand on truths divinely revealed. The awkwardness of the theologian's position resulted from the double method he had employed: on the one hand claiming *rationality* for his doctrines, and on the other repelling criticism by an appeal to *authority*. He laid himself open to the objection that he ought to employ one method or the other, for it was impossible to use both consistently. And it must be granted that many of the difficulties which have beset theology in modern times are the result of an attempt to fuse together methods and principles which will not naturally blend. This remark applies to Protestant as well as to Roman Catholic theology.

If theology is to enter into some kind of organic relation with a Philosophy of Religion, and to prove a connecting link between faith and reason, the principle of authority which it invokes should be wider and more convincing than documentary evidences. In the end, the ground of authority must be the character of the spiritual experience itself, with the historic values which have grown out of it, and the faith which is its living expression. The degree of authority which attaches to Sacred Books is secondary and derivative: it depends upon the purity and fulness of the spiritual experience they embody and the worth they possess for the religious life. The authority of Christian theology centres in the intrinsic superiority of the spiritual values which it sets forth — values not for one age merely, but for every age.

It is not consistent to maintain that the sole sources for authoritative theological doctrines are spiritual, and yet to say they are limited to certain inspired periods and spiritual movements which lie in the distant past. And this not because such periods do not possess a supreme value for the religious development of man, but because every attempt by a later age to generalise the religious meaning of these great movements must be influenced by its own life and culture. Thus successive epochs of Christian history show us the Christian Church of the time reading, unconsciously often yet none the less really, its own temper and ideals into the primitive record of the origins of our faith. So it is that the Present steadily contributes, albeit without observation, to the meaning and value of the Past. Ignoring this truth, theologians imagined they could express the meaning of religion in doctrinal forms which would be valid for all time, and would serve from generation to generation as the authoritative embodiment of the Church's faith. Still fettered by these prejudices, theology in modern times has progressed with difficulty, and the modern religious consciousness is finding it increasingly hard to take the ecclesiastical creeds for the expression of its own meaning and aspirations. The Philosophy of Religion has thus to some extent displaced the older Dogmatics in the regard of thoughtful people, and in the circumstances the relations between it and ecclesiastical Theology are somewhat strained. Nor is it likely they will be until theology renounces the claim to finality and frankly accepts the e of doctrinal development.

ay be well to say at this point, that philosophy need have no quarrel with theology because the latter accepts postulates of faith made on grounds of value. The Christian experience, of which theology is the explication, ultimately rests on truths which are held on the assurance of faith, not on logical demonstration. No rational deduction, for instance, can give for its conclusion the Christian idea of God: faith makes it real, not logical proof. In view of the stress philosophy lays on the principle of rationality, it might seem that the presuppositions of theology were unfavourable to any close relation on its part with a Philosophy of Religion. This is true, no doubt, if the theologian takes faith in the narrow sense of beliefs held upon authority: it is not the case if he sets out from postulates of the religious life. Faith, conceived as postulates or demands which our inner life makes on the world, is by no means limited in its operation to religion. It pervades practical life, and neither science nor philosophy can dispense with it. The process of rationalising is never complete, and the exercise of reason rests in the last resort on postulates which cannot be rationally deduced. In this respect the difference between theology and religious philosophy is one of degree only: the one lays greater stress on faith, the other on reason; but reason cannot work without faith, and faith has its proper ally in reason.

The conclusions we draw may now be briefly stated. Theology is and must remain the exposition of the doctrines of a definite and historic religion. The principle of authority to which it appeals must not be external, but the enduring spiritual experience of which the religion is the practical and institutional expression. That experience, however, ought not to be arbitrarily limited to a particular epoch: it should not be conceived to begin at one point in history and to end at another. In other words, the theologian must take his stand on the development of religious experience, and he must abandon the idea that theological doctrines can assume a stereotyped and final form. This is only to give its due scope to the principle of the spirit leading the spiritually minded into fuller truth. But while thus enlarging its idea of experience, theology ought to abstain from excursions into the domain of metaphysics. It will not be denied that a good deal of metaphysics has found its way into Christian theology, and some of it, to say the least, is of questionable value. The objection to this intrusion is that theology is going beyond its legitimate sphere in developing metaphysical theories, for they stand in no direct and vital relation to the religious experience and the spiritual values of the religious life. Authority is not to be claimed for them, inasmuch as they cannot invoke the principle which alone would invest them with authority, the witness of spiritual experience. This is far from saying that religion ought not to be brought into contact with metaphysics at all; but it does mean that theology is not the proper science to deal with the metaphysical issues involved. Theology may be well content to leave the speculative problems of religion unanswered, and to hand them over for solution, if a solution be possible, to the Philosophy of Religion. The latter in virtue of its larger outlook is in a better position to deal with them; and so the religious philosopher comes in to complete the work of the theologian. The latter in consequence of the definitely limited task before him should be satisfied to allow others to handle the ultimate metaphysical problems connected with religion. Yet it is impossible for man, rationally constituted as he is, to set these problems aside, or to acquiesce in treating them as insoluble. And the growing importance of the Philosophy of Religion in the present day is partly due to the knowledge that it occupies ground on which the full and free discussion of these topics of perennial interest may properly take place.

In practice, it may be granted, it will sometimes be difficult to keep theology strictly apart from a Philosophy of Religion. For they deal with the same materials, and the exposition of the meaning of a theological dogma passes easily into a philosophical interpretation of it. And for the theologian who has no antipathy to metaphysics, the temptation to develop a speculative theory is not readily to be resisted. Nor will any harm ensue, provided his speculations are put forward as speculations, not as theological doctrines. What must be deprecated is an unwitting confusion of the two points of view. Hence it is right to insist that any speculative treatment of theological doctrines really belongs to the province of religious philosophy, and must be judged as such.

Max Otto

For many years Max Otto, born in 1876, was Professor of Philosophy at the University of Wisconsin. In his Science and the Moral Life *he upholds a position which is sometimes called "scientific humanism," but which some writers, following Windelband (1848-1915), prefer to call "hominism."*

The following passage from The Human Enterprise, *in which the same position is upheld, is selected as an expression of what Otto called "an affirmative faith in the nonexistence of God."*

An Affirmative Faith in the Nonexistence of God *

What has been the effect of turning away from hoped-for divine aid, and relying instead upon human initiative and effort?

Well, what is the answer? That in proportion as men have ceased to lean on God, they have not only learned to bend mechanical forces to good use and to control the physical conditions of human well-being, but they have opened up undreamed-of resources for the satisfaction of the noblest desires of which they are capable. In the securing of food, clothing, and shelter it has proved to be better to proceed as if the existence of God were irrelevant. The advance of medical science in safeguarding life, caring for bodily and mental health, and putting up a winning fight against diseases that had decimated mankind for centuries, is perhaps the most conspicuous example. It is not theism to which we must ascribe the development of medicine. Medical progress has had to fight against theistic prejudice. It was likewise theistic prejudice that stood in the way of a hopeful treatment of psychic disorders, of sex and population problems, of antisocial propensities, and similar difficulties.

Whenever men and women have been able to act as if there were no divinity to shape human ends, and have themselves assumed responsibility, they have discovered how to turn their abilities to good account. Is it likely that this process will be reversed in the future? I am convinced that we are nearer the beginning than the end of it, as helpless to change this general direction as we are to prevent ourselves from getting older. What we *can* do is to try to go forward intelligently, as in growing older we may try to grow wiser.

Not believing in God has worked well. It has worked better than believing did. It is responsible for a realistic acquaintance with our world and a better understanding of human nature. This would seem to furnish evidence, of a kind usually considered good, that there is no superhuman being who cares what becomes of mankind. And the vast majority of people have apparently

* From *The Human Enterprise*, by M. C. Otto. Copyright, 1940, F. S. Crofts & Co., Inc., pp. 323–334. By permission of Appleton-Century-Crofts, Inc.

been convinced. They show it by the way they live day in and day out. They go about their business from morning to night taking no counsel of God. True enough, they would not dream of admitting it and they are offended if anyone else does, but such paradoxical behavior is not unusual. Their refusal to be called unbelievers, like their continued attendance upon church services, though they do not subscribe to the church creed, merely shows that something holds them back from openly admitting what they take for granted six days of the week and most of the seventh. What is it that holds them back?

One thing that holds them back is human mortality. Much of the persisting theism is crisis theism. Many people, even of those who ordinarily give no thought to God, and who never lift a finger on behalf of the values of life most intimately associated with his name, are transformed into theists when confronted by the fact or thought of death. They cannot admit that death is the ruin of life, and since the existence of God is required to save it from being just that, a sufficient belief to meet the emergency lingers, though inert, in the background of their minds. I admit that it is a shallow belief, one that does not pervade their lives but comes forward only to attend funerals, weddings, and like occasions, yet it may be singularly genuine while it lasts. It lifts the believer for the moment, however temporary his belief, above the struggle for material advantage. He is made tender toward failure. A mood of reverence is awakened and a sense of the mystery of life. In a word, he lives for the time being in his better impulses. And when the theistic mood has retired again to the outermost fringe of interest, which it often does with shocking suddenness, the good words that were spoken for God in the interim echo and re-echo in memory. It is these echoes which hold many people back from accepting an explanation of the world which leaves out God, and makes them feel that anyone who faces death in the same nontheistic spirit as he faces life must be exceptionally hardhearted, if not downright vicious.

No one would claim, I trust, that belief in God is a necessity for creatures who know that they must die. For one thing, few people are called upon to undergo the ordeal of their own death. As a rule they are planning to be alive when unconsciousness overtakes them, and when they die they know nothing about it. Since men have foresight and imagination, however, it is not enough for them to know that they will not experience dying, if they also know that the time will come when they will be dead. It is usually taken for granted that unless they are supported by the hope of immortality it is a kindness not to allude to their last hours.

Statistical evidence is not available one way or the other. If it were, we could show, I believe, that a certain personal quality, more than any belief a man holds for or against theism, determines his behavior in the expectation of death. I wonder whether the commander of a regiment could tell by the behavior of soldiers under fire, who was a believer and who was not. I wonder whether a sea captain whose ship is sinking could divide his sailors into the two classes. I wonder whether the confirmed criminal who walks with a firm step to his execution is sustained by theistic faith or by the same psychic hardness, reckless nerve, and need for display which made a life of crime attractive.

And as for bravely bearing the death of others, I have never witnessed greater fortitude than that of devastated hearts for whom there was no balm in Gilead.

The crucial test of how a man will meet his own end is reserved for one who is snatched by the powerful arm of the law, and as he believes unjustly, out of active, sincere preoccupation with social reform and is condemned to die at a stated hour. By that test Bartolomeo Vanzetti, who was not upheld by faith in God, but by the vision of a social ideal for which he felt he was giving his life, and by the loyalty of friends, will bear comparison with Socrates. Since we are considering the possibility of meeting death without divine aid, it is well to recall the statement of Vanzetti when he was sentenced to die:

> If it had not been for these thing, I might have die unmarked, unknown, a failure. Now we are not a failure. This is our career and our triumph. Never in our full life could we hope to do such work for tolerance, for justice, for man's understanding of man as now we do by accident! Our words — our lives — our pains — nothing! The taking of our lives — lives of a good shoemaker and a poor fish-peddler — all! That last moment belongs to us — that agony is our triumph.

Another reason for the retention of theism is man's low opinion of himself as a moral being. Thousands who leave God out when engaged in practical pursuits, or in following the promptings of desire, are careful to keep him on hand for the sake of ideals. They feel that God is needed to validate and enforce the moral life. This they believe is especially true of "the masses." Without God, man is a purely natural creature and must act, so they think, like any other animal, though he may express his animality with superior shrewdness. A naturalistic attitude may suffice, indeed must suffice, when the need is one of feeding and housing men, keeping their bodies clean and healthy, increasing their efficiency as producers of material wealth; it can do nothing to make men decent human beings, and it is worse than useless in the attainment of moral character. Generosity, ethical idealism, civic-mindedness, interest in moral growth can be expected from none but those who are inspired by God.

To say it in another way, the higher life, however conceived, does not pay in its own terms, so that unless men believe in a God who makes good the losses incurred in living it, no one will find it attractive. A general acceptance of a nontheistic philosophy, so the argument runs, would "eat all nobility out of our conception of conduct and all worth out of their conception of life."

Here we have one of those persistent half-truths that manage to outlive repeated refutation. "But men are better," said Emerson, "than their theology. Their daily life gives it the lie. Every ingenuous and aspiring soul leaves the doctrine behind him in his own experience, and all men feel sometimes the falsehood which they cannot demonstrate." *Aspiration is much older than man's acquaintance with the gods, and it does not die when faith in them is lost.* A natural discontent with objects less perfect than they can be imagined, and the pursuit of idealized objects that stir the feelings, are the vital forces at work in men's upward striving. The visible results at a given time may seem slight; they are not slight when estimated over years and generations and centuries.

Evidence is everywhere about us, in the community where we live, in the street that runs by our door, in our own hearts. Men are aroused to adore supremely, to triumph over the cold hard misery of life, to serve and die without reward. I remember Justice Holmes and the Law, Jane Addams and World Peace, La Follette and the People. I think of Flaubert and his worship of Beauty, of "The Worst Journey in the World," made by three heroes to fill a gap in the evidence for Evolution. I stand with Captain Ahab on the deck of the *Pequod,* scanning the horizon for Moby Dick. I follow a lantern through the darkness and the churchyard to the tomb of the Capulets with its testimony to the power of romantic love. So my mind wanders on — for there is no end to the number and variety of examples of supreme devotion — wanders on until lost in the thicket of life. There I find devotion, heroism, self-sacrifice, loyalty to causes. What is it but this original virtue in human beings that faith in God draws upon to give itself vitality?

No; the conclusion cannot be withstood that greatness, from every point of view, has been achieved by individuals and by whole peoples in the absence of faith in God. Men can and do develop great conceptions of conduct, can and do devote themselves to social causes with enthusiasm and self-sacrifice, without counting on help from higher powers. Co-operative faith in the intelligent use of natural and human resources has provided a sufficient incentive to high-minded conduct.

The number of those who have adopted this platform as a working hypothesis for themselves, and are solicitous that it be tried on the largest possible scale, is growing. Say against these men and women what we please, we cannot truthfully say that they are the riffraff of human nature. In my judgment theirs is the only dependable type of idealism left to man in the modern world.

Perhaps the most plausible argument to be made against the foregoing considerations is that after all a study of the world in which we live discloses the slow working out of a great ethical purpose. And what can such a purpose be but the will of God? The evidence, however, does not, I think, support this interpretation.

In the first place, selection of the goal of natural events is premature. Suppose we were able to prove that a definite tendency is observable in the evolution of life on our globe, and suppose we could argue from tendency to *in*-tendency, neither of which we are in a position to do, we would still be unable to clinch the argument. We have not seen the drama to the end. Once it looked as if it were designed for fishes; then for reptiles; then for lower mammals. Now it may look as if designed for man. But the play is not over. The curtain has not dropped. How can we talk about the climax of a performance of which we have witnessed only the opening scenes?

What have we actually observed? Has everything moved in a steadily maintained direction toward man as the culminating goal? Evolution has been an incredible spendthrift of life. Highly organized creatures have been developed again and again only to be pushed up blind alleys and left there to die. If there is a God whose method has been Evolution, his slogan must have been, "We'll fight it out along this line if it takes a billennium!" But, unlike Grant, he has always surrendered.

In this maelstrom the human species, as Thomas Huxley said — and he knew something about the subject — "plashed and floundered amid the general stream of evolution, keeping its head above water as best it might, and thinking neither of whence or whither." If the great scene we look upon, with its waxing and waning of suns, its appearance and disappearance of plant worlds, its rise and fall of animal dynasties — if all this or any part of it is the working out of a divine purpose, "friendly to man's intellectual, moral and religious education," this purpose is well hidden.

What if we disregard Evolution and examine human history? Do we then observe the unfolding of a divine plan? Do we find demonstrable proof of a Power not ourselves that sides with the ethical best? Does it thwart the wrongdoer and circumvent the morally indifferent? Do we, or do we not, see "the wicked in great power and spreading himself like a green bay tree"? What happened to Socrates? To Jesus? According to the best authorities, they gave their lives to God and in the hour of their need he deserted them. They are conspicuous examples, but the fact which they illustrate is a commonplace of experience.

So far as the course of human life testifies, there is no indication that anything or anyone superhuman is bent upon the triumph of humane or ethical principles. *It seems to be up to us and us alone.* And since on the appearance of things man is forced to make shift with such powers as he can discover in himself and in his social and natural environment, why not be open and aboveboard at least about the appearances? Why not admit that for the practical realization of the good life we are obliged to act as we do in tilling the ground or baking bread, that is, to rely upon experimental knowledge to find out what it is we want and how to get it?

This surely offers a sufficient program for the most aspiring soul to work at. It has the added advantage of providing an escape from the chief risk of the ethical life, the danger of being victimized by our ideals. And we are less easily deceived by the type of leadership that would beguile our eyes from what we want to "higher things," in order that someone else may help himself to what he wants of things high or low.

If it is impossible to demonstrate the working presence of a divine ethical purpose in the world, there are, in the second place, certain demonstrable facts which make the existence of any such purpose very doubtful. I avail myself of a statement made by Bishop Ernest William Barnes in one of the profoundest books I have read, *Scientific Theory and Religion.* I do this because Bishop Barnes cannot be suspected of twisting the facts against the theistic position, and because his writings are sincere not only in the usual sense that he refuses to say what he does not believe to be true, but in the far more unusual sense of taking the trouble to assure himself that he is justified, in view of the evidence at hand, to say what he does. The statement is this:

> The whole process of creation now appears to be nonmoral. There is no evidence to lead us to infer that variations in the genes are directed towards ends which in our judgment are good. In such variations there seems, in fact, to be no ethical quality whatever. They have led to odious parasitism, to the carnage of the jungle, to the microbic diseases

which cause such suffering to humanity, to those animal appetites which are useful in the struggle for survival and are the basis of sin in man. This, the immoral, brutal, lustful side of creation is as characteristic as the parental self-sacrifice, the adventurous curiosity, the instinct for truth, the enthusiasm for righteousness, the beauty of form and the physical well-being which equally result from the evolving process.

In such facts as these "we are confronted," Bishop Barnes points out, "by a dilemma from which there is, at present, no escape." And he makes this further remark, which, coming from him, should have a salutary effect: "Verbal dexterity and the skilful use of those evasive phrases which are too common in modern theology might seem to offer escape to some: but to the man of science evasion is high treason against truth." To which I add that unless theism can find a solution for just this dilemma, the best we can in truth say for the cosmos is that up to date it has not prevented the human experiment from being tried. Anything more is too much.

For the reasons adduced in this chapter, and such as these, I have for myself arrived at an affirmative faith in the nonexistence of God. The affirmation is important. One may be *without* a belief in the *existence* of God or *have* a belief in the *nonexistence* of God. The two are not identical. Each is associated with distinctive further beliefs and distinctive individual and social commitments. What I desire to make clear, without taking space to elaborate the point, is the tentative, undogmatic, yet outspoken character of the belief in question. It is essentially a kind of faith, but the kind of faith we act on in daily life when we call a doctor or drive an automobile, in fact when we take any step whatever, a faith that is rooted in tested experience. It is militant, though not belligerent; convinced, but aware of difficulties in holding the position; an aggressive belief that is tempered by appreciative understanding of the motives and claims on the other side.

W. Fraser Mitchell

Fraser Mitchell is a contemporary British poet who, after distinguishing himself in his studies at the Universities of Edinburgh and Oxford, taught for many years at Reading University, England, and elsewhere. His poetic gifts were early recognized. The following poem, from the author's A Slim Volume, *reflects a Platonistic aspect in his deeply religious feeling and conviction. It expresses also, however, his very individualistic temper.*

War Thoughts in Winter *

The man who looks abroad and sees
Earth's chequer-board of black and white,
Whose pieces show like crystal trees
Rising from flames of aconite,
Knows that these transient things reveal
An inner world more surely real.

But he whose saddened gaze must trace
Mid camouflage and crude deceit
The deadly engines of our race
Is conscious of the soul's defeat;
Since neither form nor place can yield
The spirit pabulum or shield.

Yet, as the lark with burst of song
In silence of the guns recalls
Landscapes no wrath of man can wrong,
Where, scarcely marked, the twilight falls,
And on the instant breaks the spell
Holds mortals from their citadel;

So, from perversion of the sense
We must within the mind retire,
See inwardly, with gaze intense,
The thorn all snow, the gorse all fire —
Those hundred sights and one that serve
The soul to nurture and preserve.

* W. Fraser Mitchell, *A Slim Volume* (Huddersfield, England: Examiner Letterpress, 1960). Used by permission of the author.

Miguel de Unamuno

The life and thought of Unamuno (1864-1936) are so intimately connected with the circumstances of his Spanish environment that he has been inadequately appreciated elsewhere. His central interest in philosophy is the problem of man, and for him man is more than a "mind," as is man in the idealist tradition. Unamuno's conception of man has Biblical roots and his thought has affinities with that of St. Augustine, Pascal, and Kierkegaard. His thought, close to what is nowadays called existentialism, is properly to be associated with the older humanist tradition.

An Interpretation of the Nature of Religion *

A friend writes me from Chile saying that people there keep asking him this question, "Briefly, what is Mr. Unamuno's religion?" As this is not the first time I have been confronted with such a question, I am going to attempt, not to answer it, but to clarify the meaning of the question.

Peoples as well as individuals who are spiritually lazy — and spiritual laziness is wedded to extreme economic activity — whether they know it or not, desire it or not, seek it or not, lean toward dogmatism. Spiritual laziness flees from a critical or skeptical attitude.

I say skeptical, but taking the term skepticism in its etymological and philosophical sense, because skeptic means not one who doubts but one who investigates or searches carefully, as contrasted with one who affirms and believes that he has found out. There are those who scrutinize a problem, and there are those who give us a formula, whether it's the right one or not, as its solution.

In the realm of pure philosophical speculation it is precipitant to ask one for an exact solution, provided that he has furthered the clarification of a problem. When a long calculation turns out to be wrong, erasing what has been done and beginning again represents substantial progress. When a house threatens to fall or becomes completely uninhabitable, we tear it down, and we can't insist that another be built on its foundations. It is possible to build a new one with materials from the old, but only after tearing down the old one. Meanwhile the people can take refuge in a hut, if they don't have another house, or sleep in the open.

And we must not lose sight of the fact that in our daily life we rarely have to wait for definite scientific solutions. Men have lived, and still do, by hypotheses and very frail explanations, and even without any. In chastising a criminal, men don't stop to agree as to whether or not he had free will, just

* Miguel Unamuno, *Perplexities and Paradoxes* (New York: Philosophical Library, Inc., 1945), pp. 1–9. Used by permission.

as in sneezing one doesn't reflect about the harm that may come to him from the little obstacle in his throat that precipitates the sneeze.

To do them justice, I believe that men who maintain that if they didn't believe in the eternal punishment of hell they would sin, are mistaken. If they were to stop believing in penalties beyond the grave, not for this reason would they grow worse. They would merely seek another ideal justification for their conduct. The person who, being good, believes in a transcendental order, is not good so much because he believes in it as he believes in it because he is good. That this proposition will appear obscure and nonsensical to the over-inquisitive who are spiritually lazy, I am certain.

And I shall be asked, "What is your religion?" and I shall answer that my religion is to seek truth in life and life in truth, conscious that I shall not find them while I live; my religion is to struggle tirelessly and incessantly with the unknown; my religion is to struggle with God as they say Jacob did from earliest dawn until nightfall. I shall not admit the Unknowable and the Unrecognizable of which pedants write, nor any, "beyond this thou shalt not pass." I reject any eternal *ignorabimus.* In any event I wish to reach the inaccessible.

"Be perfect as your Father in Heaven is perfect," Christ said to us, and such an ideal of perfection is, beyond any doubt, unattainable. But He set the unattainable as the goal of our efforts. And he filled the gap, say the theologians, by supplying grace. I want to fight my battle without preoccupying myself about the victory. Are there not armies and even peoples headed for sure defeat? Do we not praise those who die fighting rather than surrender? Well, this is my religion.

Those who ask me this question are seeking a dogma, a restful solution for their lazy spirits. And they are not satisfied with this alone. They want to be able to place me in one of the pigeonholes where they keep their spiritual retinue, saying of me: he is a Lutheran, Calvinist, Catholic, atheist, rationalist, mystic, or any other of these labels of whose real meaning they are ignorant but which excuse them from further thinking. I do not wish to be pigeonholed because I, Miguel de Unamuno, like any other man who claims a free conscience, am unique. "There aren't illnesses, but sick people," some doctors say, and I say there aren't opinions, but opinionated people.

In religion there is hardly anything which rationally has a consequence, and since I haven't any I cannot rationally communicate it, because only what is rational is logical and transmissible. I do have in my affections, in my heart, and in my feelings, a strong leaning toward Christianity, without embracing the special dogmas of any Christian creed. All who invoke the name of Christ with love and respect I consider Christians, and the orthodox are odious to me, be they Catholic or Protestant — one is as intransigent as the other — who deny Christianity to those who do not interpret the Gospel as they do. I know a Protestant who refuses to admit that Unitarians are Christians.

I sincerely confess that the supposed rational proofs — the ontological, the cosmological, the ethical, etc., etc. — of the existence of God, do not convince me of anything: that all the reasons that can be given to prove that God exists seem to me to be fallacious and question-begging. On this subject I agree with Kant. And I am sorry that in dealing with it I cannot talk to shoemakers in shoemaking terms.

No one has been able to convince me rationally of the existence of God, but neither of his non-existence; the reasonings of the atheists seem to me even more superficial and futile than those of their opponents. And if I do believe in God, or at least believe that I believe in Him, it is principally because I want God to exist, and next, because He reveals Himself to me through my heart, in the Gospel, through Christ and through history. It is a matter of the heart.

Which means that I am not convinced of it as I am that two and two are four.

If we were dealing with something which did not concern the peace of my conscience and my consolation for having been born, I would pay scant attention to the problem; but since it involves all my inner life and motivates all my actions, I cannot satisfy myself by saying, "I do not know nor can I know." I do not know, and that is certain. Perhaps I can never know, but I *want* to. I want to, and that's enough.

I shall spend my life struggling with the mystery, even without any hope of penetrating it, because this struggle is my hope and my consolation. Yes, my consolation. I have become accustomed to finding hope in desperation itself. Let me not hear the superficial and crack-brained shouting, "Paradox."

I cannot imagine a cultured person without this preoccupation, and I expect very little from the realm of culture — and culture and civilization are not the same — that is, from those who are not interested in the metaphysical aspect of the religious problem, studying only its social or political aspect. I can hope for very little contribution to the spiritual treasure of mankind from those men or those peoples who, because of mental laziness, superficiality, scionism, or whatever it may be, ignore the great eternal problems of the heart. I expect nothing from those who say, "One shouldn't think about that." I expect even less from those who believe in a heaven and a hell like those we believed in as children, and still less from those who declare with a fool's conviction, "This is all nothing but fables and myths; those who die are buried and that's the end of it." I have hope only for those who do not know, but who are not resigned to being ignorant, for those who restlessly struggle to learn the truth and who are more concerned with the struggle than with the victory.

Most of my endeavor has always been to unsettle my neighbors, to rouse their hearts, to afflict them when I can. I said this before in my book, *The Life of Don Quixote and Sancho*, in which is found my fullest confession on this subject. Let them seek as I seek, struggle as I struggle, and between us all we shall extract one particle of the secret from God, and this struggle will at least increase our spiritual stature.

To further this work — religious work — I have found it necessary among peoples such as these Spanish-speaking ones, undermined by laziness and spiritual superficiality, half-asleep in the routine of Catholic or freethinking, socialistic dogmatism, I have found it necessary to appear at times impudent and indecorous, at others harsh and aggressive, and not rarely paradoxical and nonsensical. In our benighted literature one can scarcely be heard even if he forgets himself, screams and shouts from the depths of his heart. For a time the shout was almost unknown. Writers were afraid to appear ridiculous. It was and is with them as it is with many, who allow themselves to be insulted in mid-street, fearing the ridicule of being seen with their hats on the ground and in the custody of a policeman. Not I; whenever I have felt like shouting, I have shouted. Decorum has never checked me. And this is one of the things for which I have been most blamed by my fellow writers who are so correct and so polite even when they are espousing impropriety and inobedience. The literary anarchists are concerned, above all, about matters of style and syntax. When they raise protesting voices, they do it harmoniously; their discords tend to be harmonious.

Whenever I have felt a pain I have shouted and I have done it publicly. The psalms that appear in my volume of *Poems* are but cries from my heart, in which I have sought to start the grieving chords of others' hearts playing. If they have no such chords or if, having them, they are too rigid to vibrate, my cry will not make them resound, and they will affirm that is not poetry, beginning to examine it acoustically. One can also examine acoustically the cry of a man who suddenly sees his child fall dead, and he who lacks both a heart and children will never go beyond that.

Those psalms in my *Poems*, together with several other compositions which I have included, are my religion, my religion in song rather than in logical terms. And I sing it as best I can, with the voice that God has given me, because I cannot reason it. And if anyone sees more reasoning and logic and methods and exegesis than life in my verses, because in them there are no fauns, dryads, satyrs, water-lilies, greenish eyes or any other more or less modernistic affectations, let that be his lot, for neither with violin bow nor hammer am I going to touch his heart.

As from the plague I flee from being classified, hoping that I shall die hearing the spiritually lazy, who occasionally stop to listen to me, still asking, "What is that man?" The foolish liberals and progressives will consider me a reactionary and perhaps a mystic, without knowing, of course, what this means, and the foolish reactionaries and conservatives will consider me a kind of spiritual anarchist, and all of them a miserable, scatterbrained publicity-seeker. But nobody should care about what fools think of him, be they conservative or progressive, liberal or reactionary.

Since man is stubborn, however, and hates to learn, and usually returns to his former ways even after being lectured for hours, the busybodies, if they read this, will again ask me, "Fine, but what is your solution?" And to rid myself of them I will tell them if they are seeking solutions to go to the store across the street, because mine sells no such article. My intent has been, is, and will continue to be, that those who read my works shall think and meditate upon fundamental problems, and has never been to hand them completed thoughts. I have always sought to agitate and, even better, to stimulate, rather than to instruct. Neither do I sell bread, nor is it bread, but yeast or ferment.

I have friends, and very good friends too, who advise me to abandon this work and bend my efforts toward producing some objective work, something which, as they say, is definite, with something to it, lasting. They mean something dogmatic. I declare myself incapable of it, and demand my liberty, my holy liberty, even to contradict myself if it becomes necessary. I do not know whether anything that I have done or may do will endure for years, for centuries, after my death, but I do know that if one drops a stone in the shoreless sea the surrounding waves, although diminishing, will go on ceaselessly. To agitate is something, and if, due to this agitation, somebody else follows who does something which endures, my work will be perpetuated in that.

To awaken the sleeping and rouse the loitering is a work of supreme mercy, and to seek the truth in everything and everywhere reveal fraud, foolishness and ineptitude is a work of supreme religious piety.

Now you know, my good Chilean friend, what you must answer anyone who asks you what my religion is. Now then: if he is one of those fools who think that I show ill-will toward people or a country by speaking the truth to some of its unreflecting children, the best thing to do is not to answer him.

Francis Thompson

The English poet Francis Thompson (1859-1907) was intended for the Roman Catholic priesthood but turned to medical studies, which he pursued without success. He went to London, where for three years he lived in such destitution that he might have died of starvation but for the patronage of Wilfred Meynell, who discovered his poetic genius and befriended him. His poetry has some affinity with that of Donne. The Hound of Heaven, *published in 1893 in his first volume of poems, expresses with vivid and dramatic beauty the Pauline and Augustinian theme of the divine quest for man.*

The Hound of Heaven *

I fled Him, down the nights and down the days;
I fled Him, down the arches of the years;
I fled Him, down the labyrinthine ways
  Of my own mind; and in the mist of tears
I hid from Him, and under running laughter.
      Up vistaed hopes I sped;
      And shot, precipitated,
Adown Titanic glooms of chasmèd fears,
  From those strong Feet that followed, followed after.
      But with unhurrying chase,
      And unperturbèd pace,
    Deliberate speed, majestic instancy,
      They beat — and a Voice beat
      More instant than the Feet —
    "All things betray thee, who betrayest Me."

      I pleaded, outlaw-wise,
By many a hearted casement, curtained red,
  Trellised with intertwining charities;
(For, though I knew His love Who followèd,
      Yet was I sore adread
Lest, having Him, I must have naught beside).
But, if one little casement parted wide,
  The gust of His approach would clash it to.
  Fear wist not to evade, as Love wist to pursue.
Across the margent of the world I fled,
  And troubled the gold gateways of the stars,
  Smiting for shelter on their clangèd bars;
      Fretted to dulcet jars

* Used by permission of Sir Francis Meynell.

And silvern chatter the pale ports o' the moon.
I said to Dawn: Be sudden — to Eve: Be soon;
With thy young skiey blossoms heap me over
From this tremendous Lover —
Float thy vague veil about me, lest He see!
I tempted all His servitors, but to find
My own betrayal in their constancy,
In faith to Him their fickleness to me,
Their traitorous trueness, and their loyal deceit.
To all swift things for swiftness did I sue;
Clung to the whistling mane of every wind.
But whether they swept, smoothly fleet,
The long savannahs of the blue;
Or whether, Thunder-driven,
They clanged his chariot 'thwart a heaven,
Plashy with flying lightnings round the spurn o' their feet: —
Fear wist not to evade a Love wist to pursue.
Still with unhurrying chase,
And unperturbèd pace,
Deliberate speed, majestic instancy,
Came on the following Feet,
And a Voice about their beat —
"Naught shelters thee, who wilt not shelter Me."

I sought no more that after which I strayed
In face of man or maid;
But still within the little children's eyes
Seems something, something that replies,
They at least are for me, surely for me!
I turned me to them very wistfully;
But just as their young eyes grew sudden fair
With dawning answers there,
Their angel plucked them from me by the hair.
"Come then, ye other children, Nature's — share
With me" (said I) "your delicate fellowship;
Let me greet you lip to lip,
Let me twine with you caresses,
Wantoning
With our Lady-Mother's vagrant tresses,
Banqueting
With her in wind-walled palace,
Underneath her azured daïs,
Quaffing, as your taintless way is,
From a chalice
Lucent-weeping out of the dayspring."
So it was done:
I in their delicate fellowship was one —

Drew the bolt of Nature's secrecies.
I knew all the swift importings
On the wilful face of skies;
I knew how the clouds arise
Spumèd of the wild sea-snortings;
All that's born or dies
Rose and drooped with; made them shapers
Of mine own moods, or wailful or divine;
With them joyed and was bereaven.
I was heavy with the even,
When she lit her glimmering tapers
Round the day's dead sanctities.
I laughed in the morning's eyes.
I triumphed and I saddened with all weather,
Heaven and I wept together,
And its sweet tears were salt with mortal mine;
Against the red throb of its sunset-heart
I laid my own to beat,
And share commingling heat;
But not by that, by that, was eased my human smart.
In vain my tears were wet on Heaven's grey cheek.
For ah! we know not what each other says,
These things and I; in sound *I* speak —
Their sound is but their stir, they speak by silences.
Nature, poor stepdame, cannot slake my drouth;
Let her, if she would owe me,
Drop yon blue bosom-veil of sky, and show me
The breasts o' her tenderness:
Never did any milk of hers once bless
My thirsting mouth.
Nigh and nigh draws the chase,
With unperturbèd pace,
Deliberate speed, majestic instancy;
And past those noisèd Feet
A voice comes yet more fleet —
"Lo! naught contents thee, who content'st not Me."

Naked I wait Thy love's uplifted stroke!
My harness piece by piece Thou hast hewn from me,
And smitten me to my knee;
I am defenceless utterly.
I slept, methinks, and woke,
And, slowly gazing, find me stripped in sleep.
In the rash lustihead of my young powers,
I shook the pillaring hours
And pulled my life upon me; grimed with smears,
I stand amid the dust o' the moulded years —
My mangled youth lies dead beneath the heap.

My days have crackled and gone up in smoke,
Have puffed and burst as sun-starts on a stream.
Yea, faileth now even dream
The dreamer, and the lute the lutanist;
Even the linked fantasies, in whose blossomy twist
I swung the earth a trinket at my wrist,
Are yielding; cords of all too weak account
For earth with heavy griefs so overplussed.
Ah! is Thy love indeed
A weed, albeit an amaranthine weed,
Suffering no flowers except its own to mount?
Ah! must —
Designer infinite! —
Ah! must Thou char the wood ere Thou canst limn with it?
My freshness spent its wavering shower i' the dust;
And now my heart is as a broken fount,
Wherein tear-drippings stagnate, split down ever
From the dank thoughts that shiver
Upon the sighful branches of my mind.
Such is; what is to be?
The pulp so bitter, how shall taste the rind?
I dimly guess what Time in mists confounds;
Yet ever and anon a trumpet sounds
From the hid battlements of Eternity;
Those shaken mists a space unsettle, then
Round the half-glimpsèd turrets slowly wash again.
But not ere him who summoneth
I first have seen, enwound
With glooming robes purpureal, cypress-crowned;
His name I know, and what his trumpet saith.
Whether man's heart or life it be which yields
Thee harvest, must Thy harvest-fields
Be dunged with rotten death?

Now of that long pursuit
Comes on at hand the bruit;
That Voice is round me like a bursting sea:
"And is thy earth so marred,
Shattered in shard on shard?
Lo, all things fly thee, for thou fliest Me!
Strange, piteous, futile thing!
Wherefore should any set thee love apart?
Seeing none but I makes much of naught" (He said),
"And human love needs human meriting:
How hast thou merited —
Of all man's clotted clay the dingiest clot?
Alack, thou knowest not
How little worthy of any love thou art!

Whom wilt thou find to love ignoble thee,
    Save Me, save only Me?
All which I took from thee I did but take,
    Not for thy harms,
But just that thou might'st seek it in My arms.
    All which thy child's mistake
Fancies as lost, I have stored for thee at home:
    Rise, clasp My hand, and come!"

    Halts by me that footfall:
    Is my gloom, after all,
  Shade of His hand, outstretched caressingly?
    "Ah, fondest, blindest, weakest,
    I am He Whom thou seekest!
  Thou dravest love from thee, who dravest Me."

SECTION TWO

Basic Conceptions of God

Lucretius

Titus Lucretius Carus (ca. *99*- ca. *55* B.C.) *was a Roman philosophical poet. An Epicurean, he held that the universe came into being through the fortuitous concurrence of atoms, so that everything is built up by chance arrangement. Man is partly an exception, for he has free will. His soul, being composed of very rarefied matter, perishes with the body. Lucretius, with such a philosophy, has no place in his system for gods who are interested in or accessible to man. Pleasure and pain are the only guides in life; but by pleasure he means the serenity that proceeds from a quiet mind and the absence of fear. The work from which the following passage is taken is often accounted the greatest philosophical work written in classical Latin.*

On Nature *

Fear . . . holds . . . in check all mortals, because they see many operations go on in earth and heaven, the causes of which they can in no way understand, believing them therefore to be done by power divine. For these reasons when we shall have seen that nothing can be produced from nothing, we shall then more correctly ascertain that which we are seeking, both the elements out of which every thing can be produced and the manner in which all things are done without the hand of the gods.

If things came from nothing, any kind might be born of any thing, nothing would require seed. Men for instance might rise out of the sea, the scaly race out of the earth, and birds might burst out of the sky; horned and other herds, every kind of wild beasts would haunt with changing brood tilth and wilderness alike. Nor would the same fruits keep constant to trees, but would change; any tree might bear any fruit. For if there were not begetting bodies for each, how could things have a fixed unvarying mother? But in fact because things are all produced from fixed seeds, each thing is born and goes forth into the borders of light out of that in which resides its matter and first bodies; and for this reason all things cannot be gotten out of all things, because in particular things resides a distinct power. Again why do we see the rose put forth in spring, corn in the season of heat, vines yielding at the call of autumn, if not because, when the fixed seeds of things have streamed together at the proper time, whatever is born discloses itself, while the due seasons are there and the quickened earth brings its weakly products in safety forth into the borders of light? But if they came from nothing, they would rise up suddenly at uncertain periods and unsuitable times of year, inasmuch as there would be no first-beginnings to be kept from a begetting union by the unpropitious season. No nor would time be required for the growth of things

* Lucretius, *On the Nature of Things*, trans. H. A. J. Munro (London: G. Bell & Sons, 1886), pp. 4–9, 10–13, 18–20, 22–27. Used by permission.

after the meeting of the seed, if they could increase out of nothing. Little babies would at once grow into men and trees in a moment would rise and spring out of the ground. But none of these events it is plain ever comes to pass, since all things grow step by step [at a fixed time], as is natural, [since they all grow] from a fixed seed and in growing preserve their kind; so that you may be sure that all things increase in size and are fed out of their own matter. Furthermore without fixed seasons of rain the earth is unable to put forth its gladdening produce, nor again if kept from food could the nature of living things continue its kind and sustain life; so that you may hold with greater truth that many bodies are common to many things, as we see letters common to different words, than that any thing could come into being without first-beginnings. Again why could not nature have produced men of such a size and strength as to be able to wade on foot across the sea and rend great mountains with their hands and outlive many generations of living men, if not because an unchanging matter has been assigned for begetting things and what can arise out of this matter is fixed? We must admit therefore that nothing can come from nothing, since things require seed before they can severally be born and be brought out into the buxom fields of air. Lastly since we see that tilled grounds surpass untilled and yield a better produce by the labour of hands, we may infer that there are in the earth first-beginnings of things which by turning up the fruitful clods with the share and labouring the soil of the earth we stimulate to rise. But if there were not such, you would see all things without any labour of ours spontaneously come forth in much greater perfection.

Moreover nature dissolves every thing back into its first bodies and does not annihilate things. For if aught were mortal in all its parts alike, the thing in a moment would be snatched away to destruction from before our eyes; since no force would be needed to produce disruption among its parts and undo their fastenings. Whereas in fact, as all things consist of an imperishable seed, nature suffers the destruction of nothing to be seen, until a force has encountered it sufficient to dash things to pieces by a blow or to pierce through the void places within them and break them up. Again if time, whenever it makes away with things through age, utterly destroys them eating up all their matter, out of what does Venus bring back into the light of life the race of living things each after its kind, or, when they are brought back, out of what does earth manifold in works give them nourishment and increase, furnishing them with food each after its kind? Out of what do its own native fountains and extraneous rivers from far and wide keep full the sea? Out of what does ether feed the stars? For infinite time gone by and lapse of days must have eaten up all things which are of mortal body. Now if in that period of time gone by those things have existed, of which this sum of things is composed and recruited, they are possessed no doubt of an imperishable body, and cannot therefore any of them return to nothing. Again the same force and cause would destroy all things without distinction, unless everlasting matter held them together, matter more or less closely linked in mutual entanglement: a touch in sooth would be sufficient cause of death, inasmuch as any amount of force must of course undo the texture of things in which no parts at all were of an everlasting body. But in fact, because the fastenings of first-beginnings one with the other are unlike and matter is everlasting, things continue with body uninjured, until a force is found to encounter them strong enough to overpower the texture of each. A thing therefore never returns to nothing, but all things after disruption go back into the first bodies of matter. Lastly rains die, when father ether has tumbled them into the lap of mother earth; but then goodly crops spring up and boughs are green with leaves upon the trees, trees themselves grow and are laden with fruit; by them in turn our race and the race of wild beasts are fed, by them we see glad towns teem with children and the leafy forests ring on all sides with the song of new birds; through them cattle wearied with their load of fat lay their bodies down about the glad pastures and the white milky stream pours from the distended udders; through them a new brood with weakly limbs frisks and gambols over the soft grass, rapt in their young hearts with the pure new milk. None of the things therefore which seem to be lost is utterly lost, since nature replenishes one thing out of another and does not suffer any thing to be begotten, before she has been recruited by the death of some other.

Now mark me: since I have taught that things cannot be born from nothing, cannot when begotten be brought back to nothing, that you may not haply yet begin in any shape to mistrust my words, because the first-beginnings of things cannot be seen by the eyes, take moreover this list of bodies which you must yourself admit are in the number of things and cannot be seen. First of all the force of the wind when aroused beats on the harbours and whelms huge ships and scatters clouds; sometimes in swift whirling eddy it scours the plains and straws them with large trees and scourges the mountain summits with forest-rending blasts: so fiercely does the wind rave with a shrill howling and rage with threatening roar. Winds therefore sure enough are unseen bodies which sweep the seas, the lands, ay and the clouds of heaven, tormenting them and catching them up in sudden whirls. On they stream and spread destruction abroad in just the same way as the soft liquid nature of water, when all at once it is borne along in an overflowing stream, and a great downfall of water from the high hills augments it with copious rains, flinging together fragments of forests and entire trees; nor can the strong bridges sustain the sudden force of coming water: in such wise turbid with much rain the river dashes upon the piers with mighty force: makes havoc with loud noise and rolls under its eddies huge stones: wherever aught opposes its waves, down it dashes it. In this way then must the blasts of wind as well move on, and when they like a mighty stream have borne down in any direction, they push things before them and throw them down with repeated assaults, sometimes catch them up in curling eddy and carry them away in swift-circling whirl. Wherefore once and again I say winds are unseen bodies, since in their works and ways they are found to rival great rivers which are of a visible body. Then again we perceive the different smells of things, yet never see them coming to our nostrils; nor do we behold heats nor can we observe cold with the eyes nor are we used to see voices. Yet all these things must consist of a bodily nature, since they are able to move the senses; for nothing but body can touch and be touched. Again clothes hung up on a shore which waves break upon become moist, and then get dry if spread out in the sun. Yet it has not been seen in what way the moisture of water has sunk into them nor again in what way this has been dispelled by heat. The moisture therefore is dispersed into small particles which the eyes are quite unable to see. Again after the revolution of many of the sun's years a ring on the finger is thinned on the under side by wearing, the dripping from the eaves hollows a stone, the bent ploughshare of iron imperceptibly decreases in the fields, and we behold the stone-paved streets worn down by the feet of the multitude; the brass statues too at the gates shew their right hands to be wasted by the touch of the numerous passers-by who greet them. These things then we see are lessened, since they have been thus worn down; but what bodies depart at any given time the nature of vision has jealously shut out our seeing. Lastly the bodies which time and nature add to things by little and little, constraining them to grow in due measure, no exertion of the eyesight can behold; and so too wherever things grow old by age and decay, and when rocks hanging over the sea are eaten away by the gnawing salt spray, you cannot see what they lose at any given moment. Nature therefore works by unseen bodies.

And yet all things are not on all sides jammed together and kept in by body: there is also void in things. To have learned this will be good for you on many accounts; it will not suffer you to wander in doubt and be . . . distrustful of our words. If there were not void, things could not move at all; for that which is the property of body, to let and hinder, would be present to all things at all times; nothing therefore could go on, since no other thing would be the first to give way. But in fact throughout seas and lands and the heights of heaven we see before our eyes many things move in many ways for various reasons, which things, if there were no void, I need not say would lack and want restless motion: they never would have been begotten at all, since matter jammed on all sides would have been at rest. Again, however solid things are thought to be, you may yet learn from this that they are of rare body: in rocks and caverns the moisture of water oozes through and all things weep with abundant drops; food distributes itself through the whole body of living things; trees grow and yield fruit in season, because food is diffused through the whole from the very roots over the stem and all the boughs. Voices pass through walls and fly through houses shut, stiffening frost pierces to the bones. Now if there are no void parts, by what way can the bodies severally pass? You would see it to be quite impossible. Once more, why do we see one thing surpass another in weight though not larger in size? For if there is just as much body in a ball of wool as there is in a lump of lead, it is natural it should weigh the same, since the property of body is to weigh all things downwards, while on the contrary the nature of void is ever without weight. Therefore when a thing is just as large, yet is found to be lighter, it proves sure enough that it has more of void in it; while on the other hand that which is heavier shews that there is in it more of body and that it contains within it much less of void. Therefore that which we are seeking with keen reason exists sure enough, mixed up in things; and we call it void. . . .

. . . All nature then, as it exists by itself, is founded on two things: there are bodies and there is void in which these bodies are placed and through which they move about. For that body exists by itself the general feeling of mankind declares; and unless at the very first belief in this be firmly grounded, there will be nothing to which we can appeal on hidden things in order to prove anything by reasoning of mind. Then again, if room and space which we call void did not exist, bodies could not be placed anywhere nor move about at all to any side; as we have demonstrated to you a little before. Moreover there is nothing which you can affirm to be at once separate from all body and quite distinct from void, which would so to say count as the discovery of a third nature. For whatever shall exist, this of itself must be something or other. Now if it shall admit of touch in however slight and small a measure, it will, be it with a large or be it with a little addition, provided it do exist, increase the amount of body and join the sum. But if it shall be intangible and unable to hinder any thing from passing through it on any side, this you are to know will be that which we call empty void. Again whatever shall exist by itself, will either do something or will itself suffer by the action of other things, or will be of such a nature as things are able to exist and go on in. But no thing can do and suffer without body, nor aught furnish room except void and vacancy. Therefore beside void and bodies no third nature taken by itself can be left in the number of things, either such as to fall at any time under the ken of our senses or such as any one can grasp by the reason of his mind.

For whatever things are named, you will either find to be properties linked to these two things or you will see to be accidents of these things. That is a property which can in no case be disjoined and separated without utter destruction accompanying the severance, such as the weight of a stone, the heat of fire, the fluidity of water. Slavery on the other hand, poverty and riches, liberty, war, concord, and all other things which may come and go while the nature of the thing remains unharmed, these we are wont, as it is right we should, to call accidents. Time also exists not by itself, but simply from the things which happen the sense apprehends what has been done in time past, as well as what is present and what is to follow after. And we must admit that no one feels time by itself abstracted from the motion and calm rest of things. So when they say that the daughter of Tyndarus was ravished and the Trojan nations were subdued in war, we must mind that they do not force us to admit that these things are by themselves, since those generations of men, of whom these things were accidents, time now gone by has irrevocably swept away. For whatever shall have been done may be termed an accident in one case of the Teucran people, in another of the countries simply. Yes, for if there had been no matter of things and no room and space in which things severally go on, never had the fire, kindled by love of the beauty of Tyndarus' daughter, blazed beneath the Phrygian breast of Alexander and lighted up the famous struggles of cruel war, nor had the timber horse unknown to the Trojans wrapt Pergama in flames by its night-issuing brood of sons of the Greeks; so that you may clearly perceive that all actions from first to last exist not by themselves and are not by themselves in the way that body is, nor are terms of the same kind as void is, but are rather of such a kind that you may fairly call them accidents of body and of the room in which they severally go on.

Bodies again are partly first-beginnings of things, partly those which are formed of a union of first-beginnings. But those which are first-beginnings of things no force can quench: they are sure to have the better by their solid body. Although it seems difficult to believe that aught can be found among things with a solid body. For the lightning of heaven passes through the walls of houses, as well as noise and voices; iron grows red-hot in the fire and stones burn with fierce heat and burst asunder; the hardness of gold is broken up and dissolved by heat; the ice of brass melts vanquished by the flame; warmth and piercing cold ooze through silver, since we have felt both, as we held cups with the hand in due fashion and the water was poured down into them. So universally there is found to be nothing solid in things. But yet because true reason and the nature of things constrains, attend until we make clear in a few verses that there are such things as consist of solid and everlasting body, which we teach are seeds of things and first-beginnings, out of which the whole sum of things which now exists has been produced.

First of all then since there has been found to exist a two-fold and widely dissimilar nature of two things, that is to say of body and of place in which things severally go on, each of the two must exist for and by itself and quite unmixed. For wherever there is empty space which we call void, there body is not; wherever again body maintains itself, there empty void no wise exists. First bodies therefore are solid and without void. Again, since there is void in things begotten, solid matter must exist about this void, and no thing can be proved by true reason to conceal in its body and have within it void, unless you choose to allow that that which holds it in is solid. Again that can be nothing but a union of matter which can keep in the void of things. Matter, therefore, which consists of a solid body, may be everlasting, though all things else are dissolved. Moreover if there were no empty void, the universe would be solid; unless on the other hand there were certain bodies to fill up whatever places they occupied, the existing universe would be empty and void space. Therefore sure enough body and void are marked off in alternate layers, since the universe is neither of a perfect fulness nor a perfect void. There are therefore certain bodies which can vary void space with full. These can neither be broken in pieces by the stroke of blows from without nor have their texture undone by aught piercing to their core nor give way before any other kind of assault; as we have proved to you a little before. For without void nothing seems to admit of being crushed in or broken up or split in two by cutting, or of taking in wet or permeating cold or penetrating fire, by which all things are destroyed. And the more anything contains within it of void, the more thoroughly it gives way to the assault of these things. Therefore if first bodies are as I have shewn solid and without void, they must be everlasting. Again unless matter had been eternal, all things before this would have utterly returned to nothing and whatever things we see would have been born anew from nothing. But since I have proved above that nothing can be produced from nothing, and that what is begotten cannot be recalled to nothing, first-beginnings must be of an imperishable body, into which all things can be dissolved at their last hour, that there may be a supply of matter for the reproduction of things. Therefore first-beginnings are of solid singleness, and in no other way can they have been preserved through ages during infinite time past in order to reproduce things. . . .

. . . If all things are produced from four things and all again broken up into those things, how can they be called first-beginnings of things any more than things be called their first-beginnings, the supposition being reversed? For they are begotten time about and interchange colour and their whole nature without ceasing. But if haply you suppose that the body of fire and of earth and air and the moisture of water meet in such a way that none of them in the union changes its nature, no thing I tell you can be then produced out of them, neither living thing nor thing with inanimate body, as a tree; in fact each thing amid the medley of this discordant mass will display its own nature and air will be seen to be mixed up with earth and heat to remain in union with moisture. But first-beginnings ought in begetting things to bring with them a latent and unseen nature in order that no thing stand out, to be in the way and prevent whatever is produced from having its own proper being.

Moreover they go back to heaven and its fires for a beginning, and first suppose that fire changes into air, next that from air water is begotten and earth is produced out of water, and that all in reverse order come back from earth, water first, next air, then heat, and that these cease not to interchange, to pass from heaven to earth, from earth to the stars of ether. All which first-beginnings must on no account do; since something unchangeable must needs remain over, that things may not utterly be brought back to nothing. For whenever a thing changes and quits its proper limits, at once this change of state is the death of that which was before. Wherefore since those things which we have mentioned a little before pass into a state of change, they must be formed out of others which cannot in any case be transformed, that you may not have things returning altogether to nothing. Why not rather hold that there are certain bodies possessed of such a nature, that, if they have haply produced fire, the same may, after a few have been taken away and a few added on and the order and motion changed, produce air; and that all other things may in the same way interchange with one another?

"But plain matter of fact clearly proves," you say, "that all things grow up into the air and are fed out of the earth; and unless the season at the propitious period send such abundant showers that the trees reel beneath the soaking storms of rain, and unless the sun on its part foster them and supply heat, corn trees and living things could not grow." Quite true, and unless solid food and soft water should recruit us, our substance would waste away and life break wholly up out of all the sinews and bones; for we beyond doubt are recruited and fed by certain things, this and that other thing by certain other things. Because many first-beginnings common to many things in many ways are mixed up in things, therefore sure enough different things are fed by different things. And it often makes a great difference with what things and in what position the same first-beginnings are held in union and what motions they mutually impart and receive; for the same make up heaven, sea, lands, rivers, sun, the same make up corn, trees, and living things; but they are mixed up with different things and in different ways as they move. Nay, you see throughout even in these verses of ours many elements common to many words, though you must needs admit that the lines and words differ one from the other both in meaning and in the sound wherewith they sound. So much can elements effect by a mere change of order; but those elements which are the first-beginnings of things can bring with them more combinations out of which different things can severally be produced. . . .

Now mark and learn what remains to be known and hear it more distinctly. Nor does my mind fail to perceive how dark the things are; but the great hope of praise has smitten my heart with sharp thyrsus, and at the same time has struck into my breast sweet love of the muses, with which now inspired I traverse in blooming thought the pathless haunts of the Pierides never yet trodden by sole of man. I love to approach the untasted springs and to quaff, I love to cull fresh flowers and gather for my head a distinguished crown from spots whence the muses have yet veiled the brows of none; first because I teach of great things and essay to release the mind from the fast bonds of religious scruples, and next because on a dark subject I pen such lucid verses o'erlaying all with the muses' charm. For that too would seem to be not without good grounds: just as physicians when they purpose to give nauseous wormwood to children, first smear the rim round the bowl with the sweet yellow juice of honey, that the unthinking age of children may be fooled as far as the lips, and meanwhile drink up the bitter draught of wormwood and though beguiled yet not be betrayed, but rather by such means recover health and strength; so I now, since this doctrine seems generally somewhat bitter to those by whom it has not been handled, and the multitude shrinks back from it in dismay, have resolved to set forth to you our doctrine in sweet-toned Pierian verse and o'erlay it as it were with the pleasant honey of the muses, if haply by such means I might engage your mind on my verses, till you clearly perceive the whole nature of things, its shape and frame.

But since I have taught that most solid bodies of matter fly about for ever unvanquished through all time, mark now, let us unfold whether there is or is not any limit to their sum; likewise let us clearly see whether that which has been found to be void, or room and space, in which things severally go on, is all of it altogether finite or stretches without limits and to an unfathomable depth.

Well then the existing universe is bounded in none of its dimensions; for then it must have had an outside. Again it is seen that there can be an outside of nothing, unless there be something beyond to bound it, so that that is seen, farther than which the nature of this our sense does not follow the thing. Now since we must admit that there is nothing outside the sum, it has no outside, and therefore is without end and limit. And it matters not in which of its regions you take your stand; so invariably, whatever position any one has taken up, he leaves the universe just as infinite as before in all directions. Again if for the moment all existing space be held to be bounded, supposing a man runs forward to its outside borders and stands on the utmost verge and then throws a winged javelin, do you choose that when hurled with vigorous force it shall advance to the point to which it has been sent and fly to a distance, or do you decide that something can get in its way and stop it? for you must admit and adopt one of the two suppositions; either of which shuts you out from all escape and compels you to grant that the universe stretches without end. For whether there is something to get in its way and prevent its coming whither it was sent and placing itself in the point intended, or whether it is carried forward, in either case it has not started from the end. In this way I will go on and, wherever you have placed the outside borders, I will ask what then becomes of the javelin. The result will be that an end can no where be fixed, and that the room given for flight will still prolong the power of flight. Lastly one thing is seen by the eyes to end another thing; air bounds off hills, and mountains air, earth limits sea and sea again all lands; the universe however there is nothing outside to end.

Again if all the space of the whole sum were enclosed within fixed borders and were bounded, in that case the store of matter by its solid weights would have streamed together from all sides to the lowest point nor could anything have gone on under the canopy of heaven, no nor would there have been a heaven nor sunlight at all, inasmuch as all matter, settling down through infinite time past, would lie together in a heap. But as it is, sure enough no rest is given to the bodies of the first-beginnings, because there is no lowest point at all, to which they might stream together as it were, and where they might take up their positions. All things are ever going on in ceaseless motion on all sides and bodies of matter stirred to action are supplied from beneath out of infinite space. Therefore the nature of room and the space of the unfathomable void are such as bright thunderbolts cannot race through in their course though gliding on through endless tract of time, no nor lessen one jot the journey that remains to go by all their travel: so huge a room is spread out on all sides for things without any bounds in all directions round.

Again nature keeps the sum of things from setting any limit to itself, since she compels body to be ended by void and void in turn by body, so that either she thus renders the universe infinite by this alternation of the two, or else the one of the two, in case the other does not bound it, with its single nature stretches nevertheless immeasurably. [But void I have already proved to be infinite; therefore matter must be infinite: for if void were infinite, and matter finite] neither sea nor earth nor the glittering quarters of heaven nor mortal kind nor the holy bodies of the gods could hold their ground one brief passing hour; since forced asunder from its union the store of matter would be dissolved and borne along the mighty void, or rather I should say would never have combined to produce any thing, since scattered abroad it could never have been brought together. For verily not by design did the first-beginnings of things station themselves each in its right place guided by keen intelligence, nor did they bargain sooth to say what motions each should assume, but because many in number and shifting about in many ways throughout the universe they are driven and tormented by blows during infinite time past, after trying motions and unions of every kind at length they fall into arrangements such as those out of which this our sum of things has been formed, and by which too it is preserved through many great years when once it has been thrown into the appropriate motions, and causes the streams to replenish the greedy sea with copious river waters and the earth, fostered by the heat of the sun, to renew its produce, and the race of living things to come up and flourish, and the gliding fires of ether to live: all which these several things could in no wise bring to pass, unless a store of matter could rise up from infinite space, out of which store they are wont to make up in due season whatever has been lost. For as the nature of living things when robbed of food loses its substance and wastes away, thus all things must be broken up, as soon as matter has ceased to be supplied, diverted in any way from its proper course. Nor can blows from without hold together all the sum which has been brought into union. They can it is true frequently strike upon and stay a part, until others come and the sum can be completed. At times however they are compelled to rebound and in so doing grant to the first-beginnings of things room and time for flight, to enable them to get clear away from the mass in union. Wherefore again and again I repeat many bodies must rise up; nay for the blows themselves not to fail, there is need of an infinite supply of matter on all sides.

And herein, Memmius, be far from believing this, that all things as they say press to the centre of the sum, and that for this reason the nature of the world stands fast without any strokes from the outside and the uppermost and lowest parts cannot part assunder in any direction, because all things have been always pressing towards the centre (if you can believe that anything can rest upon itself); or that the heavy bodies which are beneath the earth all press upwards and are at rest on the earth, turned topsy-turvy, just like the images of things we see before us in the waters. In the same way they maintain that living things walk head downwards and cannot tumble out of earth into the parts of heaven lying below them any more than our bodies can spontaneously fly into the quarters of heaven; that when those see the sun, we behold the stars of night; and that they share with us time about the seasons of heaven and pass nights equal in length to our days. But groundless [error has devised such dreams] for fools, because they have embraced [false principles of reason.] For there can be no centre [where the universe is] infinite; no nor, even if there were a centre, could anything take up a position there [any more on that account] than for some quite different reason [be driven away.] For all room and space, which we term void, must through centre, through no-centre alike give place to heavy bodies, in whatever directions their motions tend. Nor is there any spot of such a sort that when bodies have reached it, they can lose their force of gravity and stand upon void; and that again which is void must not serve to support anything, but must, as its nature craves, continually give place. Things cannot therefore in such a way be held in union, o'er-mastered by love of a centre.

Again since they do not suppose that all bodies press to the centre, but only those of earth, and those of water, [both such as descend to the earth in rain] and those which are held in by the earth's body, so to say, the fluid of the sea and great waters from the mountains; while on the other hand they teach that the subtle element of air and hot fires at the same time are carried away from the centre and that for this reason the whole ether round bickers with signs and the sun's flame is fed throughout the blue of heaven, because heat flying from the centre all gathers together there, and that the topmost boughs of trees could not put forth leaves at all, unless from time to time [nature supplied] food from the earth to each [throughout both stem and boughs their reasons are not only false, but they contradict each other. Space I have already proved to be infinite; and space being infinite matter as I have said must also be infinite] lest after the winged fashion of flames the walls of the world should suddenly break up and fly abroad along the mighty void, and all other things follow for like reasons and the innermost quarters of heaven tumble in from above and the earth in an instant withdraw from beneath our feet and amid the commingled ruins of things in it and of heaven, ruins unloosing the first bodies, should wholly pass away along the unfathomable void, so that in a moment of time not a wrack should be left behind, nothing save untenanted space and viewless first-beginnings. For on whatever side you shall first determine first bodies to be wanting, this side will be the gate of death for things, through this the whole crowd of matter will fling itself abroad.

If you will thoroughly con these things, then carried to the end with slight trouble [you will be able by yourself to understand all the rest.] For one thing after another will grow clear and dark night will not rob you of the road and keep you from surveying the utmost ends of nature: in such wise things will light the torch for other things.

Origen

Origen (ca. 185- ca. 254 A.D.) was above all a Christian Biblical scholar. He upheld the divine inspiration of the Scriptures. This means anything other than that he was a literalist. Not only did his education and intelligence preclude this; his reverence for the Bible was too deep to permit him to have such an essentially irreligious attitude toward it. Seeing the world in Platonistic fashion as permeated by symbols and types of an invisible world of far greater importance and reality, Origen distinguished three modes of interpretation of Scripture: the literal, the moral, and the allegorical. Faith is useful as a steppingstone; but mystical knowledge supersedes it.

Central in his theology is the doctrine of the unity of God. In setting forth the mystery of the divine nature he was a Trinitarian. He departed, however, from the view of the Trinity that may be taken as the antecedent of the one that eventually prevailed in Christian orthodoxy.

The writings of Origen quoted here are from his work against Celsus, a pagan purporting to write as a detached observer of Christianity. Celsus' work, written about the year 178, is the earliest literary attack on Christianity of which we have any detailed information. Origen's reply to it is therefore interesting for this reason as well as for itself.

Faith and Reason *

[Faith is] useful for the multitude, and . . . we admittedly teach those who cannot abandon everything and pursue a study of rational argument to believe without thinking out their reasons. But . . . in practice others do the same. What man who is urged to study philosophy and throws himself at random into some school of philosophers, comes to do so for any reason except either that he has come across a particular teacher or that he believes some one school to be better than the rest? He does not wait to hear the arguments of all the philosophers and of the different schools, and the refutation of one and the proof of another, when in this way he chooses to be a Stoic, or a Platonist, or a Peripatetic, or an Epicurean, or a follower of some such philosophical school. Even though they do not want to admit it, it is by an unreasoning impulse that people come to the practice of, say, Stoicism and abandon the rest; or Platonism, because they despise the others as of lesser significance; or Peripateticism, because it corresponds best to human needs and sensibly admits the value of the good things of human life more than other systems. And some, who were alarmed at their first encounter with the argument about

* Origen, *Contra Celsum*, trans. Henry Chadwick (New York: Cambridge University Press, 1953). Book I, Chapter 10, p. 13; Book IV, Chapter 48, pp. 223, 224; Book IV, Chapter 70, pp. 239, 240. Used by permission.

providence based on the earthly circumstances of bad and good men, have too hastily concluded that providence does not exist, and have adopted the opinion of Epicurus and Celsus.

The Use of Allegory

Then, as though he [Celsus] had devoted himself only to hatred and hostility towards the doctrine of Jews and Christians, he says that *the more reasonable Jews and Christians allegorize these things.* He asserts that *because they are ashamed of them, they take refuge in allegory.* One might say to him that if any stories of myths and legends may be said to be shameful on the ground of their literal meaning, whether they were composed with a hidden interpretation or in any other way, what stories deserve to be so regarded more than those of the Greeks? In these divine sons castrate their divine fathers. Divine fathers swallow their divine sons. A divine mother gives a stone instead of a son to the father of men and gods. A father has sexual intercourse with his daughter. And a wife binds her husband, employing the brother of the person bound and his daughter to help her with the bonds. Why need I enumerate the outrageous stories of the Greeks about the gods which are obviously shameful even if they are to be interpreted allegorically? At any rate, in one place Chrysippus of Soli, who is considered to have adorned the Stoic school of philosophers by his many intelligent treatises, expounds the meaning of a picture at Samos, in which Hera is portrayed as performing unmentionable obscenities with Zeus. This honourable philosopher says in his treatises that matter receives the generative principles of God, and contains them in itself for the ordering of the universe. For in the picture at Samos matter is Hera and God is Zeus. It is because of these myths and thousands of others like them that we are unwilling to call the supreme God Zeus, or even to use the name, or to call the sun Apollo and the moon Artemis. But we practise a pure piety towards the Creator and praise the beautiful things which He has created, without defiling the things of God even by a name. We approve Plato's saying in the *Philebus,* when he refused to allow that pleasure was a god: "For my reverence, Protarchus," he says, "for the names of the gods is profound." Accordingly, we truly have reverence for the name of God and the names of the beautiful things which He has created, so that we do not accept any myth which might harm the young even if it is to be understood allegorically.

Evil Also Serves

Now Celsus has made the following remark about evils: *Even if something seems to you to be evil, it is not yet clear whether it really is evil; for you do not know what is expedient either for you or for someone else or for the universe.* This remark shows some discretion; but he suggests that the nature of evils is not entirely pernicious because something which is thought to be evil for a particular individual may possibly be of advantage to the universe. However, lest anyone should misunderstand my opinion and find in it an excuse for crime on the ground that his sin is, or at any rate could be, beneficial to the world as a whole, I will say that while God preserves the free will of each man He makes use of the evil of bad men for the ordering of the whole, making them useful to the universe; yet such a man is none the less guilty, and as such he has been appointed to perform a function which is repulsive to the individual but beneficial to the whole. It is, to take an illustration from cities, as though one said that a man, who had committed certain crimes and on that account was sentenced to do certain public services of benefit to the community, was doing something of benefit to the whole city, although he himself was engaged in a repulsive task and in a position in which no one even of slight intelligence would want to be.

Moreover, Paul the apostle of Jesus teaches us that even the very worst men may contribute something to the advantage of the whole, though in themselves they will be engaged in the most repulsive acts, while the very good men will be of most benefit to the whole and on their own account will be appointed to the best position. He says: "And in a great house there are not only vessels of gold and silver but also of wood and earthenware, and the one are to honour and the other to dishonour; therefore if any man cleanse himself, he will be a vessel unto honour, sanctified and meet for the master's use, prepared unto every good work."[1] I think it was necessary to quote this in reply to his remark: *Even if something seems to you to be evil, it is not yet clear whether it is evil; for you do not know what is expedient either for you or for someone else.* For I wanted to avoid giving anyone an excuse for sinning in what I have said on this subject, on the ground that he would be benefiting the community by his sin.

[1] II Tim. ii. 20–1.

Augustine

St. Augustine (354-430) was born at Tagaste in North Africa, of a pagan father and a Christian mother. Having studied rhetoric at Carthage with a view to following the profession of a lawyer, he gave himself up to literary pursuits. The pattern of his early life was pagan. An interest in philosophy and a passion for truth-seeking led him to follow the teachings of Mani, a Persian thinker whose system was one of the fashionable philosophies of the day. Passing through various more or less skeptical phases, he was attracted to Neo-Platonism. He became bitterly disappointed, however, by all such philosophies, not least because they seemed to do nothing for the lives of their adherents. Then, having come under the influence of an eloquent Christian preacher, St. Ambrose, Bishop of Milan, he found himself more and more impressed by the wonderful effects that Christianity seemed to have on many of those who embraced it. He noted, for instance, that ignorant Christian monks were able to fulfill their ideals, while he, a "golden" young man in a privileged position, had proved quite unable to realize his. At length came his dramatic conversion to Christianity, after which he wrote works that are among the most important of the Christian classics. These include his famous Confessions, *a work written in its entirety as a prayer addressed to God, and* The City of God, *in which we have a document that is highly important as the basis of a Christian philosophy of history. An intellectual giant of the most delicate spiritual perception, he is acknowledged by "Catholic" and "Protestant" alike as the writer without whom Christian theology could not have developed the richness it has attained. In the following passage from* Enchiridion *St. Augustine expounds his views on the problem of the existence of evil in a universe created by God.*

Creation and Evil *

Wherefore, when it is asked what we ought to believe in matters of religion, the answer is not to be sought in the exploration of the nature of things [*rerum natura*], after the manner of those whom the Greeks called "physicists."[1] Nor should we be dismayed if Christians are ignorant about the properties and the number of the basic elements of nature, or about the motion, order, and deviations of the stars, the map of the heavens, the kinds and nature of animals, plants, stones, springs, rivers, and mountains; about the divisions of space and

* *Augustine: Confessions and Enchiridion*, ed. Albert D. Outler, Vol. VII, Library of Christian Classics (Philadelphia: The Westminster Press, 1955). Used by permission.

[1] A famous example is Lucretius' *Περὶ φύσεως*, a passage from which is given earlier in the present volume. [Eds.]

time, about the signs of impending storms, and the myriad other things which these "physicists" have come to understand, or think they have. For even these men, gifted with such superior insight, with their ardor in study and their abundant leisure, exploring some of these matters by human conjecture and others through historical inquiry, have not yet learned everything there is to know. For that matter, many of the things they are so proud to have discovered are more often matters of opinion than of verified knowledge.

For the Christian, it is enough to believe that the cause of all created things, whether in heaven or on earth, whether visible or invisible, is nothing other than the goodness of the Creator, who is the one and the true God.[2] Further, the Christian believes that nothing exists save God himself and what comes from him; and he believes that God is triune, i.e., the Father, and the Son begotten of the Father, and the Holy Spirit proceeding from the same Father, but one and the same Spirit of the Father and the Son.

By this Trinity, supremely and equally and immutably good, were all things created. But they were not created supremely, equally, nor immutably good. Still, each single created thing is good, and taken as a whole they are very good, because together they constitute a universe of admirable beauty.

In this universe, even what is called evil, when it is rightly ordered and kept in its place, commends the good more eminently, since good things yield greater pleasure and praise when compared to the bad things. For the Omnipotent God, whom even the heathen acknowledge as the Supreme Power over all, would not allow any evil in his works, unless in his omnipotence and goodness, as the Supreme Good, he is able to bring forth good out of evil. What, after all, is anything we call evil except the privation of good? In animal bodies, for instance, sickness and wounds are nothing but the privation of health. When a cure is effected, the evils which were present (i.e., the sickness and the wounds) do not retreat and go elsewhere. Rather, they simply do not exist any more. For such evil is not a substance; the wound or the disease is a defect of the bodily substance which, as a substance, is good. Evil, then, is an accident, i.e., a privation of that good which is called health. Thus, whatever defects there are in a soul are privations of a natural good. When a cure takes place, they are not transferred elsewhere but, since they are no longer present in the state of health, they no longer exist at all.[3]

All of nature, therefore, is good, since the Creator of all nature is supremely good. But nature is not supremely and immutably good as is the Creator of it. Thus the good in created things can be diminished and augmented. For good to be diminished is evil; still, however much it is diminished, something must remain of its original nature as long as it exists at all. For no matter what

[2] This basic motif appears everywhere in Augustine's thought as the very foundation of his whole system.

[3] This [is a] . . . statement of a major motif which pervades the whole of Augustinian metaphysics. We see it in his earliest writings, *Soliloquies*, I, 2, and *De ordine*, II, 7. It is obviously a part of the Neoplatonic heritage which Augustine appropriated for his Christian philosophy. The good is positive, constructive, essential; evil is privative, destructive, parasitic on the good. It has its origin, not in nature, but in the will. Cf. *Confessions*, Bk. VII, Chs. III, V, XII–XVI; *On Continence*, 14–16; *On the Gospel of John*, Tractate XCVIII, 7; *City of God*, XI, 17; XII, 7–9.

kind or however insignificant a thing may be, the good which is its "nature" cannot be destroyed without the thing itself being destroyed. There is good reason, therefore, to praise an uncorrupted thing, and if it were indeed an incorruptible thing which could not be destroyed, it would doubtless be all the more worthy of praise. When, however, a thing is corrupted, its corruption is an evil because it is, by just so much, a privation of the good. Where there is no privation of the good, there is no evil. Where there is evil, there is a corresponding diminution of the good. As long, then, as a thing is being corrupted, there is good in it of which it is being deprived; and in this process, if something of its being remains that cannot be further corrupted, this will then be an incorruptible entity [*natura incorruptibilis*], and to this great good it will have come through the process of corruption. But even if the corruption is not arrested, it still does not cease having some good of which it cannot be further deprived. If, however, the corruption comes to be total and entire, there is no good left either, because it is no longer an entity at all. Wherefore corruption cannot consume the good without also consuming the thing itself. Every actual entity [*natura*] is therefore good; a greater good if it cannot be corrupted, a lesser good if it can be. Yet only the foolish and unknowing can deny that it is still good even when corrupted. Whenever a thing is consumed by corruption, not even the corruption remains, for it is nothing in itself, having no subsistent being in which to exist.

From this it follows that there is nothing to be called evil if there is nothing good. A good that wholly lacks an evil aspect is entirely good. Where there is some evil in a thing, its good is defective or defectible. Thus there can be no evil where there is no good. This leads us to a surprising conclusion: that, since every being, in so far as it is a being, is good, if we then say that a defective thing is bad, it would seem to mean that we are saying that what is evil is good, that only what is good is ever evil and that there is no evil apart from something good. This is because every actual entity is good [*omnis natura bonum est*]. Nothing evil exists *in itself*, but only as an evil aspect of some actual entity. Therefore, there can be nothing evil except something good. Absurd as this sounds, nevertheless the logical connections of the argument compel us to it as inevitable. At the same time, we must take warning lest we incur the prophetic judgment which reads: "Woe to those who call evil good and good evil: who call darkness light and light darkness; who call the bitter sweet and the sweet bitter."[4] Moreover the Lord himself saith: "An evil man brings forth evil out of the evil treasure of his heart."[5] What, then, is an evil man but an evil entity [*natura mala*], since man is an entity? Now, if a man is something good because he is an entity, what, then, is a bad man except an evil good? When, however, we distinguish between these two concepts, we find that the bad man is not bad because he is a man, nor is he good because he is wicked. Rather, he is a good entity in so far as he is a man, evil in so far as he is wicked. Therefore, if anyone says that simply to be a man is evil, or that to be a wicked man is good, he rightly falls under the prophetic judgment: "Woe to him who calls evil good and good

[4] Isa. 5:20.
[5] Matt. 12:35.

evil." For this amounts to finding fault with God's work, because man is an entity of God's creation. It also means that we are praising the defects in this particular man *because* he is a wicked person. Thus, every entity, even if it is a defective one, in so far as it is an entity, is good. In so far as it is defective, it is evil.

Actually, then, in these two contraries we call evil and good, the rule of the logicians fails to apply.[6] No weather is both dark and bright at the same time; no food or drink is both sweet and sour at the same time; no body is, at the same time and place, both white and black, nor deformed and well-formed at the same time. This principle is found to apply in almost all disjunctions: two contraries cannot coexist in a single thing. Nevertheless, while no one maintains that good and evil are not contraries, they can not only coexist, but the evil cannot exist at all without the good, or in a thing that is not a good. On the other hand, the good can exist without evil. For a man or an angel could exist and yet not be wicked, whereas there cannot be wickedness except in a man or an angel. It is good to be a man, good to be an angel; but evil to be wicked. These two contraries are thus coexistent, so that if there were no good in what is evil, then the evil simply could not be, since it can have no mode in which to exist, nor any source from which corruption springs, unless it be something corruptible. Unless this something is good, it cannot be corrupted, because corruption is nothing more than the deprivation of the good. Evils, therefore, have their source in the good, and unless they are parasitic on something good, they are not anything at all. There is no other source whence an evil thing can come to be. If this is the case, then, in so far as a thing is an entity, it is unquestionably good. If it is an incorruptible entity, it is a great good. But even if it is a corruptible entity, it still has no mode of existence except as an aspect of something that is good. Only by corrupting something good can corruption inflict injury.

But when we say that evil has its source in the good, do not suppose that this denies our Lord's judgment: "A good tree cannot bear evil fruit."[7] This cannot be, even as the Truth himself declareth: "Men do not gather grapes from thorns," since thorns cannot bear grapes. Nevertheless, from good soil we can see both vines and thorns spring up. Likewise, just as a bad tree does not grow good fruit, so also an evil will does not produce good deeds. From a human nature, which is good in itself, there can spring forth either a good or an evil will. There was no other place from whence evil could have arisen in the first place except from the nature — good in itself — of an angel or a man. This is what our Lord himself most clearly shows in the passage about the trees and the fruits, for he said: "Make the tree good and the fruits will be good, or make the tree bad and its fruits will be bad."[8] This is warning enough that bad fruit cannot grow on a good tree nor good fruit on a bad one. Yet from that same earth to which he was referring, both sorts of trees can grow.

[6] This refers to Aristotle's well-known principle of "the excluded middle."
[7] Matt. 7:18.
[8] Cf. Matt. 12:33.

Josiah Royce

Royce (1855-1916) was born in California and in 1882 became a professor at Harvard. His studies in Germany turned his attention successively to Kant, Schopenhauer, and Lotze. His compelling interest, however, was to find, in the philosophical idealism of his day, justification for moral and religious values. His personalistic absolutism might be said to lie between the absolute idealism of Hegel and the pragmatism of William James.

The Larger Self *

Idealism has two aspects. It is, for the first, a kind of analysis of the world, an analysis which so far has no absolute character about it, but which undertakes, in a fashion that might be acceptable to any skeptic, to examine what you mean by all the things, whatever they are, that you believe in or experience. This idealistic analysis consists merely in a pointing out, by various devices, that the world of your knowledge, whatever it contains, is through and through such stuff as ideas are made of, that you never in your life believed in anything definable *but* ideas, that, as Berkeley put it, "this whole choir of heaven and furniture of earth" is nothing for any of us but a system of ideas which govern our belief and our conduct. Such idealism has numerous statements, interpretations, embodiments. . . . In this aspect idealism is already a little puzzling to our natural consciousness, but it becomes quickly familiar, in fact almost commonplace, and seems after all to alter our practical faith or to solve our deeper problems very little.

The other aspect of idealism is the one which gives us our notion of the absolute Self. To it the first is only preparatory. . . .

I begin with the first and the less significant aspect of idealism. Our world, I say, whatever it may contain, is such stuff as ideas are made of. This preparatory sort of idealism is the one that, as I just suggested, Berkeley made prominent, and, after a fashion, familiar. I must state it in my own way, although one in vain seeks to attain novelty in illustrating so frequently described a view.

Here, then, is our so real world of the senses, full of light and warmth and sound. If anything could be solid and external, surely, one at first will say, it is this world. Hard facts, not mere ideas, meet us on every hand. Ideas any one can mould as he wishes. Not so facts. In idea socialists can dream out Utopias, disappointed lovers can imagine themselves successful, beggars can ride horses, wanderers can enjoy the fireside at home. In the realm of facts, society organizes itself as it must, rejected lovers stand for the time defeated, beggars are alone with their wishes, oceans roll drearily between home and the wanderer. Yet this world of fact is, after all, not entirely stub-

* Josiah Royce, *The Spirit of Modern Philosophy* (Boston: Houghton Mifflin Company, 1892), Lecture XI. Used by permission.

born, not merely hard. The strenuous will can mould facts. We can form our world, in part, according to our ideas. Statesmen influence the social order, lovers woo afresh, wanderers find the way home. But thus to alter the world we must work, and just because the laborer is worthy of his hire, it is well that the real world should thus have such fixity of things as enables us to anticipate what facts will prove lasting, and to see of the travail of our souls when it is once done. This, then, is the presupposition of life, that we work in a real world, where house-walls do not melt away as in dreams, but stand firm against the winds of many winters, and can be felt as real. We do not wish to find facts wholly plastic; we want them to be stubborn, if only the stubbornness be not altogether unmerciful. Our will makes constantly a sort of agreement with the world, whereby, if the world will continually show some respect to the will, the will shall consent to be strenuous in its industry. Interfere with the reality of my world, and you therefore take the very life and heart out of my will.

The reality of the world, however, when thus defined in terms of its stubbornness, its firmness as against the will that has not conformed to its laws, its kindly rigidity in preserving for us the fruits of our labors, — such reality, I say, is still something wholly unanalyzed. In what does this stubbornness consist? Surely, many different sorts of reality, as it would seem, may be stubborn. Matter is stubborn when it stands in hard walls against us, or rises in vast mountain ranges before the path-finding explorer. But minds can be stubborn also. The lonely wanderer, who watches by the seashore the waves that roll between him and his home, talks of cruel facts, material barriers that, just because they *are* material, and not ideal, shall be the irresistible foes of his longing heart. "In wish," he says, "I am with my dear ones, but alas, wishes cannot cross oceans! Oceans are material facts, in the cold outer world. Would that the world of the heart were all!" But alas! to the rejected lover the world of the heart *is* all, and that is just his woe. Were the barrier between him and his beloved only made of those stubborn material facts, only of walls or of oceans, how lightly might his will erelong transcend them all! Matter stubborn! Outer nature cruelly the foe of ideas! Nay, it is just an idea that now opposes him, — just an idea, and that, too, in the mind of the maiden he loves. But in vain does he call this stubborn bit of disdain a merely ideal fact. No flint was ever more definite in preserving its identity and its edge than this disdain may be. Place me for a moment, then, in an external world that shall consist wholly of ideas, — the ideas, namely, of other people about me, a world of maidens who shall scorn me, of old friends who shall have learned to hate me, of angels who shall condemn me, of God who shall judge me. In what piercing north winds, amidst what fields of ice, in the labyrinths of what tangled forests, in the depths of what thick-walled dungeons, on the edges of what tremendous precipices, should I be more genuinely in the presence of stubborn and unyielding facts than in that conceived world of ideas! So, as one sees, I by no means deprive my world of stubborn reality, if I merely call it a world of ideas. On the contrary, as every teacher knows, the ideas of the people are often the most difficult of facts to influence. We were wrong, then, when we said that whilst matter was stubborn, ideas could be moulded at pleasure. Ideas are often the most implacable of facts. Even my own ideas, the facts of my own inner life, may cruelly decline to be plastic to my wish. The wicked will that refuses to be destroyed, — what rock has often more consistency for our senses than this will has for our inner consciousness! The king, in his soliloquy in "Hamlet," — in what an unyielding world of hard facts does he not move! and yet they are now only inner facts. The fault is past; he is alone with his conscience.

What rests?
Try what repentance can. What can it not?
Yet what can it, when one cannot repent?
O wretched state! O bosom black as death!
O limëd soul, that, struggling to be free,
Art more engaged!

No, here are barriers worse than any material chains. The world of ideas has its own horrible dungeons and chasms. Let those who have refuted Bishop Berkeley's idealism by the wonder why he did not walk over every precipice or into every fire if these things existed only in his idea, let such, I say, first try some of the fires and the precipices of the inner life, ere they decide that dangers cease to be dangers as soon as they are called ideal, or even subjectively ideal in me.

Many sorts of reality, then, may be existent at the heart of any world of facts. But this bright and beautiful sense-world of ours, — what, amongst these many possible sorts of reality, does that embody? Are the stars and the oceans, the walls and the pictures, real as the maiden's heart is real, — embodying the ideas of somebody, but none the less stubbornly real for that? Or can we make something else of their reality? For, of course, that the stars and the oceans, the walls and the pictures have *some* sort of stubborn reality, just as the minds of our fellows have, our analysis so far does not for an instant think of denying. Our present question is, what sort of reality? Consider, then, in detail, certain aspects of the reality that seems to be exemplified in our sense-world. The sublimity of the sky, the life and majesty of the ocean, the interest of a picture, — to what sort of real facts do these belong? Evidently here we shall have no question. So far as the sense-world is beautiful, is majestic, is sublime, this beauty and dignity exist only for the appreciative observer. If they exist beyond him, they exist only for some other mind, or as the thought and embodied purpose of some universal soul of nature. A man who sees the same world, but who has no eye for the fairness of it, will find all the visible facts, but will catch nothing of their value. At once, then, the sublimity and beauty of the world are thus truths that one who pretends to insight ought to see, and they are truths which have no meaning except for such a beholder's mind, or except as embodying the thought of the mind of the world. So here, at least, is so much of the outer world that is ideal, just as the coin or the jewel or the bank-note or the bond has its value not alone in its physical presence, but in the idea that it symbolizes to a beholder's mind, or to the relatively universal thought of the commercial world. But let us look a little deeper. Surely, if the objects yonder are unideal and outer, odors and tastes and temperatures do not exist in these objects in just the way in which they exist in us. Part of the being of these properties, at least, if not all of it, is ideal and exists for us, or at best is once more the embodiment of the thought or purpose of some world-mind. About tastes you cannot dispute, because they are not only ideal but personal. For the benumbed tongue and palate of diseased bodily conditions, all things are tasteless. As for temperatures, a well-known experiment will show how the same water may seem cold to one hand and warm to the other. But even so, colors and sounds are at least in part ideal. Their causes may have some other sort of reality; but colors themselves are not in the things, since they change with the light that falls on the things, vanish in the dark (whilst the things remained unchanged), and differ for different eyes. And as for sounds, both the pitch and the quality of tones depend for us upon certain interesting peculiarities of our hearing organs, and exist in nature only as voiceless sound-waves trembling through the air. All such sense qualities, then, are ideal. The world yonder may — yes, must — have attributes that give reasons why these qualities are thus felt by us; for so we assume. The world yonder may even be a mind that thus expresses its will to us. But these qualities need not, nay, cannot resemble the ideas that are produced in us, unless, indeed, that is because these qualities have place as ideas in some world-mind. Sound-waves in the air are not like our musical sensations; nor is the symphony as we hear it and feel it any physical property of the strings and the wind instruments; nor are the ether-vibrations that the sun sends us like our ideas when we see the sun; nor yet is the flashing of moonlight on the water as we watch the waves a direct expression of the actual truths of fluid motion as the water embodies them.

Unless, then, the real physical world yonder is itself the embodiment of some world-spirit's ideas, which he conveys to us, unless it is real only as the maiden's heart is real, namely, as itself a conscious thought, then we have so far but one result: that real world (to repeat one of the commonplaces of modern popular science) is in itself, apart from somebody's eyes and tongue and ears and touch, neither colored nor tasteful, neither cool nor warm, neither light nor dark, neither musical nor silent. All these qualities belong to our ideas, being indeed none the less genuine facts for that, but being in so far ideal facts. We must see colors when we look, we must hear music when there is playing in our presence; but this *must* is a must that consists in a certain irresistible presence of an idea in us under certain conditions. *That* this idea must come is, indeed, a truth as unalterable, once more, as the king's settled remorse in Hamlet. But like this remorse, again, it exists as an ideal truth, objective, but through and through objective *for* somebody, and not *apart from* anybody. What this truth implies we have yet to see. So far it is only an ideal truth for the beholder, with just the bare possibility that behind it all there is the thought of a world-spirit. And, in fact, *so* far we must all go together if we reflect.

But now, at this point, the Berkeleyan idealist goes one step further. The real outside world that is still left unexplained and unanalyzed after its beauty, its warmth, its odors, its tastes, its colors, and its tones, have been relegated to the realm of ideal truths, what do you now *mean* by calling it real? No doubt it *is* known as somehow real, but *what* is this reality *known as* being? If you know that this world is still there and outer, as by hypothesis you know, you are bound to say *what* this outer character implies for your thought. And here you have trouble. Is the outer world, as it exists outside of your ideas, or of anybody's ideas, something having shape, filling space, possessing solidity, full of moving things? That would in the first place seem evident. The sound isn't outside of me, but the sound-waves, you say, are. The colors are ideal facts; but the ether-waves don't need a mind to know them. Warmth is ideal, but the physical fact called heat, this playing to and fro of molecules, is real, and is there apart from any mind. But once more, *is* this so evident? What do I *mean* by the shape of anything, or by the size of anything? Don't I mean just the idea of shape or of size that I am obliged to get under certain circumstances? What is the meaning of any property that I give to the real outer world? How can I express that property except in case I think it in terms of my ideas? As for the sound-waves and the ether-waves, what are they but things ideally conceived to explain the facts of nature? The conceptions have doubtless their truth, but it is an ideal truth. What I mean by saying that the things yonder have shape and size and trembling molecules, and that there is air with sound-waves, and ether with light-waves in it, — what I *mean* by all this is that experience forces upon me, directly or indirectly, a vast system of ideas, which may indeed be founded in truth beyond me, which in fact *must* be founded in such truth if my experience has any sense, but which, like my ideas of color and of warmth, are simply expressions of how the world's order must appear to me, and to anybody constituted like me. Above all, is this plain about space. The real things, I say, outside of me, fill space, and move about in it. But what do I mean by space? Only a vast system of ideas which experience and my own mind force upon me. Doubtless these ideas have a validity. They have *this* validity, that I, at all events, when I look upon the world, am bound to see it in space, as much bound as the king in Hamlet was, when he looked within, to see himself as guilty and unrepentant. But just as his guilt was an idea, — a crushing, an irresistible, an overwhelming idea, — but still just an idea, so, too, the space in which I place my world is one great formal idea of mine. That is just why I can describe it to other people. "It has three dimensions," I say, "length, breadth, depth." I describe each. I form, I convey, I construct, an idea of it through them. I know space, as an idea, very well. I can compute all sorts of unseen truths about the relations of its parts. I am sure that you, too, share this idea. But, then, for all of us alike it is just an idea; and when we put our world into space, and call it real there, we simply think one idea into another idea, not voluntarily, to be sure, but inevitably, and yet without leaving the realm of ideas.

Thus, all the reality that *we* attribute to our world, in so far as *we* know and can tell what we mean thereby, becomes ideal. There is, in fact, a certain system of ideas, forced upon us by experience, which we have to use as the guide of our conduct. This system of ideas we can't change by our wish; it is for us as overwhelming a fact as guilt, or as the bearing of our fellows towards us, but we know it only *as* such a system of ideas. And we call it the world of matter. John Stuart Mill very well expressed the puzzle of the whole thing, as we have now reached the statement of this puzzle, when he called matter a mass of "permanent possibilities of experience" for each of us. Mill's definition has its faults, but it is a very fair beginning. You know matter as something that either now gives you this idea or experience, or that would give you some other idea or experience under other circumstances. A fire, while it burns, is for you a permanent possibility of either getting the idea of an agreeable warmth, or of getting the idea of a bad burn, and you treat it accordingly. A precipice amongst mountains is a permanent possibility of your experiencing a fall, or of your getting a feeling of the exciting or of the sublime in mountain scenery. You have no experience just now of the tropics or of the poles, but both tropical and polar climates exist in your world as permanent possibilities of experience. When you call the sun 92,000,000 miles away, you mean that between you and the sun (that is, between your present experience and the possible experience of the sun's surface) there would inevitably lie the actually inaccessible, but still numerically conceivable series of experiences of distance expressed by the number of miles in question. In short, your whole attitude towards the real world may be summed up by saying: "I have experiences now which I seem bound to have, experiences of color, sound, and all the rest of my present ideas; and I am also bound by experience to believe that in case I did certain things (for instance, touched the wall, traveled to the tropics, visited Europe, studied physics), I then should get, in a determinate order, dependent wholly upon *what* I had done, certain other experiences (for instance, experiences of the wall's solidity, or of a tropical climate, or of the scenes of an European tour, or of the facts of physics)." And this acceptance of actual experience, this belief in possible experience, constitutes all that you mean by your faith in the outer world.

But, you say, Is not, then, all this faith of ours after all well founded? Isn't there really something yonder that corresponds in fact to this series of experiences in us? Yes, indeed, there no doubt is. But what if this, which so shall correspond without us to the ideas within us, what if this hard and fast reality should itself be a system of ideas, outside of our minds but not outside of every mind? As the maiden's disdain is outside the rejected lover's mind, unchangeable so far for him, but not on that account the less ideal, not the less a fact in a mind, as, to take afresh a former fashion of illustration, the price of a security or the objective existence of this lecture is an ideal fact, but real and external for the individual person, — even so why might not this world beyond us, this "permanent possibility of experience," be in essence itself a system of ideal experiences of some standard thought of which ours is only the copy? Nay, must it not be such a system in case it has any reality at all? For, after all, isn't this precisely what our analysis brings us to? Nothing whatever can I say about my world yonder that I do not express in terms of mind. *What* things are, extended, moving, colored, tuneful, majestic, beautiful, holy, *what* they are in any aspect of their nature, mathematical, logical, physical, sensuously pleasing, spiritually valuable, all this must mean for me only something that I have to express in the fashion of ideas. The more I am to know my world, the more of a mind I must have for the purpose. The closer I come to the truth about the things, the more ideas I get. Isn't it plain, then, that *if* my world yonder is anything knowable at all, it must be in and for itself essentially a mental world? Are my ideas to *resemble* in any way the world? Is the truth of my thought to consist in its *agreement* with reality? And am I thus capable, as common sense supposes, of *conforming* my ideas to things? Then reflect. What can, after all, so well agree with an idea as another idea? To what can things that go on in my mind conform unless it be to another mind? If the more my mind grows in mental clearness, the nearer it gets to the nature of reality, then surely the reality that my mind thus resembles must be in itself mental.

After all, then, would it deprive the world here about me of reality, nay, would it not rather save and assure the reality and the knowableness of my world of experience, if I said that this world, as it exists outside of my mind, and of any other human minds, exists in and for a standard, a universal mind, whose system of ideas simply constitutes the world? Even if I fail to prove that there is such a mind, do I not at least thus make plausible that, as I said, our world of common sense has no fact in it which we cannot interpret in terms of ideas, so that this world is throughout such stuff as ideas are made of? To say this, as you see, in no wise deprives our world of its due share of reality. If the standard mind knows now that its ideal fire has the quality of burning those who touch it, and if I in my finitude am bound to conform in my experiences to the thoughts of this standard mind, then in case I touch that fire I shall surely get the idea of a burn. The standard mind will be at least as hard and fast and real in its ideal consistency as is the maiden in her disdain for the rejected lover; and I, in presence of the ideal stars and the oceans, will see the genuine realities of fate as certainly as the lover hears his fate in the voice that expresses her will. . . .

What I have desired thus far is merely to give each of you, as it were, the sensation of being an idealist in this first and purely analytical sense of the word idealism. The sum and substance of it all is, you see, this: you know your world in fact as a system of ideas about things, such that from moment to moment you find this system forced upon you by experience. Even matter you know just as a mass of coherent ideas that you cannot help having. Space and time, as you think them, are surely ideas of yours. Now, what more natural than to say that *if* this be so, the real world beyond you must in itself be a system of somebody's ideas? If it is, then you can comprehend what its existence means. If it isn't, then since all you can know of it is ideal, the real world must be utterly unknowable, a bare *x*. Minds I can understand, because I myself am a mind. An existence that has no mental attribute is wholly opaque to me. So far, however, from such a world of ideas, existent beyond me in another mind, seeming to coherent thought essentially *un*real, ideas and minds and their ways, are, on the contrary, the hardest and stubbornest facts that we can name. *If* the external world is in itself mental, then, be this reality a standard and universal thought, or a mass of little atomic minds constituting the various particles of matter, in any case one can comprehend what it is, and will have at the same time to submit to its stubborn authority as the lover accepts the reality of the maiden's moods. If the world *isn't* such an ideal thing, then indeed all our science, which is through and through concerned with our mental interpretations of things, can neither have objective validity, nor make satisfactory progress towards truth. For as science is concerned with ideas, the world beyond all ideas is a bare *x*. . . .

There are problems soluble and problems insoluble in that world of ideas. It is a soluble problem if one asks what whole number is the square root of 64. The answer is 8. It is an insoluble problem if one asks me to find what whole number is the square root of 65. There is, namely, no such whole number. If one asks me to name the length of a straight line that shall be equal to the circumference of a circle of a known radius, that again, in the world of ideas, is an insoluble problem, because, as can be proved, the circumference of a circle is a length that cannot possibly be exactly expressed in terms of any statable number when the radius is of a stated length. So in the world of ideas, problems are definite questions which can be asked in knowable terms. Fair questions of this sort either may be fairly answered in our present state of knowledge, or else they could be answered if we knew a little or a good deal more, or finally they could not possibly be answered. But in the latter case, if they could not possibly be answered, they always must resemble the problem how to square the circle. They then always turn out, namely, to be absurdly stated questions, and it is their absurdity that makes these problems absolutely insoluble. Any fair question could be answered by one who knew enough. No fair question has an unknowable answer. But now, *if* your unknowable world out there is a thing of wholly, of absolutely problematic and inscrutable nature, is it so because you don't *yet* know enough about it, or because in its very nature and essence it is an absurd thing, an *x* that *would* answer a question, which actually it is nonsense to ask? Surely one must choose the former alternative. The real world may be unknown; it can't be essentially unknowable.

This subtlety is wearisome enough, I know, just here, but I shall not dwell long upon it. Plainly *if* the unknowable world out there is through and through in its nature a really inscrutable problem, this must mean that in nature it resembles such problems as, What is the whole number that is the square root of 65? Or, What two adjacent hills are there that have no valley between them? For in the world of thought such are the *only* insoluble problems. All others either may now be solved, or would be solved if we knew more than we now do. But, once more, *if* this unknowable is only just the real world as now unknown to us, but capable sometime of becoming known, then remember that, as we have just seen, only a mind can ever become an object known to a mind. If I know you as external to me, it is only because you are minds. If I can come to know *any* truth, it is only in so far as this truth is essentially mental, is an idea, is a thought, that I can ever come to know it. Hence, if that so-called unknowable, that unknown outer world there, ever could, by any device, come within our ken, then it is already an ideal world. For just that is what our whole idealistic analysis has been proving. Only ideas are knowable. And nothing absolutely unknowable can exist. For the absolutely unknowable, the *x* pure and simple, the Kantian thing in itself, simply cannot be admitted. The notion of it is nonsense. The assertion of it is a contradiction. Round-squares, and sugar salt-lumps, and Snarks, and Boojums, and Jabberwocks, and Abracadabras; such, I insist, are the only unknowables there are. The unknown, that which our human and finite selfhood hasn't grasped, exists spread out before us in a boundless world of truth; but the unknowable is essentially, confessedly, *ipso facto* a fiction.

The nerve of our whole argument in the foregoing is now pretty fairly exposed. We have seen that the outer truth must be, if anything, a "possibility of experience." But we may now see that a *bare* "possibility" as such, is, like the unknowable, something meaningless. That which, whenever I come to know it, turns out to be through and through an idea, an experience, must be in itself, before I know it, either somebody's idea, somebody's experience, or it must be nothing. What is a "possibility" of experience that is outside of me, and that is still nothing *for* any one else than myself? Isn't it a bare *x*, a nonsense phrase? Isn't it like an unseen color, an untasted taste, an unfelt feeling? In proving that the world is one of "possible" experience, we have proved that in so far as it is real it is one of actual experience.

Once more, then, to sum up here, *if*, however vast the world of the unknown, only the essentially knowable can exist, and *if* everything knowable is an idea, a mental somewhat, the content of some mind, then once for all we are the world of ideas. Your deepest doubt proves this. Only the nonsense of that inscrutable *x*, of that Abracadabra, of that Snark, the Unknowable of whose essence you make your real world, prevents you from seeing this.

To return, however, to our dilemma. *Either* idealism, we said, *or* the unknowable. What we have now said is that the absolutely unknowable is essentially an absurdity, a non-existent. For any fair and statable problem admits of an answer. *If* the world exists yonder, its essence is then already capable of being known by some mind. If capable of being known by a mind, this essence is then already essentially ideal and mental. A mind that knew the real world would, for instance, find it a something possessing qualities. But qualities are ideal existences, just as much as are the particular qualities called odors or tones or colors. A mind knowing the real world would again find in it relations, such as equality and inequality, attraction and repulsion, likeness and unlikeness. But such relations have no meaning except as objects of a mind. In brief, then, the world as known would be found to be a world that had all the while been ideal and mental, even before it became known to the particular mind that we are to conceive as coming into connection with it. Thus, then, we are driven to the second alternative. The real world must be a mind, or else a group of minds.

But with this result we come in presence of a final problem. All this, you say, depends upon my assurance that there is after all a real and therefore an essentially knowable and rational world yonder. Such a world would have to be in essence a mind, or a world of minds. But after all, how does one ever escape from the prison of the inner life? Am I not in all this merely wandering amidst the realm of my own ideas? *My* world, of course, isn't and can't be a mere *x*, an essentially unknowable thing, just because it *is my* world, and I have an idea of it. But then does not this mean that *my* world is, after all, forever just *my* world, so that I never get to any truth beyond myself? Isn't this result very disheartening? My world is thus a world of ideas, but alas! how do I then ever reach those ideas of the minds beyond me?

The answer is a simple, but in one sense a very problematic one. You, in one sense, namely, never *do* or can get beyond your own ideas, nor ought you to wish to do so, because in truth all those other minds that constitute your outer and real world are in essence one with your own self. This whole world of ideas is essentially *one* world, and so it is essentially the world of one self and *That art Thou*.

The truth and meaning of this deepest proposition of all idealism is now not at all remote from us. The considerations, however, upon which it depends are of the dryest possible sort, as commonplace as they are deep.

Whatever objects you may think about, whether they are objects directly known to you, or objects infinitely far removed, objects in the distant stars, or objects remote in time, or objects near and present, — such objects, then, as a number with fifty places of digits in it, or the mountains on the other side of the moon, or the day of your death, or the character of Cromwell, or the law of gravitation, or a name that you are just now trying to think of and have forgotten, or the meaning of some mood or feeling or idea now in your mind, — all such objects, I insist, stand in a certain constant and curious relation to your mind whenever you are thinking about them, — a relation that we often miss because it is so familiar. What is this relation? Such an object, while you think about it, needn't be, as popular thought often supposes it to be, the *cause* of your thoughts concerning it. Thus, when you think about Cromwell's character, Cromwell's character isn't just now *causing* any ideas in you, — isn't, so to speak, doing anything to you. Cromwell is dead, and after life's fitful fever his character is a very inactive thing. Not as the *cause*, but as the *object* of your thought is Cromwell present to you. Even so, if you choose now to think of the moment of your death, that moment is somewhere off there in the future, and you can make it your object, but it isn't now an active cause of your ideas. The moment of your death has no present physical existence at all, and just now causes nothing. So, too, with the mountains on the other side of the moon. When you make them the object of your thought, they remain indifferent to you. They do not affect you. You never saw them. But all the same you can think about them.

Yet this thinking *about* things is, after all, a very curious relation in which to stand to things. In order to think *about* a thing, it is *not* enough that I should have an idea in me that merely resembles that thing. This last is a very important observation. I repeat, it is *not* enough that I should merely have an idea in me that resembles the thing whereof I think. I have, for instance, in me the idea of a pain. Another man has a pain just like mine. Say we both have toothache; or have both burned our finger-tips in the same way. Now my idea of pain is just like the pain in him, but I am not on that account necessarily thinking about *his* pain, merely because what I am thinking about, namely my own pain, resembles his pain. No; to think about an object you must not merely have an idea that resembles the object, but you must *mean* to have your idea resemble that object. Stated in other form, to think of an object you must consciously aim at that object, you must pick out that object, you must already in some measure possess that object enough, namely, to identify it as what you mean. But how can you *mean,* how can you *aim at,* how can you *possess,* how can you *pick out,* how can you *identify* what is not already present in essence to your own hidden self? Here is surely a deep question. When you aim at yonder object, be it the mountains in the moon or the day of your death, you really say, "I, as my real self, as my larger self, as my complete consciousness, already in deepest truth possess that object, have it, own it, identify it. And that, and that alone, makes it possible for me in my transient, my individual, my momentary personality, to mean yonder object, to inquire about it, to be partly aware of it and partly ignorant of it." You can't mean what is utterly foreign to you. You mean an object, you assert about it, you talk about it, yes, you doubt or wonder about it, you admit your private and individual ignorance about it, only in so far as your larger self, your deeper personality, your total of normal consciousness already *has* that object. Your momentary and private wonder, ignorance, inquiry, or assertion, about the object, implies, asserts, presupposes, that your total self is in full and immediate possession of the object. This, in fact, is the very nature of that curious relation of a thought to an object which we are now considering. The self that is doubting or asserting, or that is even feeling its private ignorance about an object, and that still, even in consequence of all this, is *meaning,* is *aiming at* such object, is in essence identical with the self for which this object exists in its complete and consciously known truth.

So paradoxical seems this final assertion of idealism that I cannot hope in one moment to make it very plain to you. . . . But what I intend by thus saying that the self which thinks about an object, which really, even in the midst of the blindest ignorance and doubt concerning its object still means the object, — that this self is identical with the deeper self which possesses and truly knows the object, — what I intend hereby I can best illustrate by simple cases taken from your own experience. You are in doubt, say, about a name that you have forgotten, or about a thought that you just had, but that has now escaped you. As you hunt for the name or the lost idea, you are all the while sure that you mean just one particular name or idea and no other. But you don't yet know what name or idea this is. You try, and reject name after name. You query, "Was this what I was thinking of, or this?" But after searching you erelong find the name or the idea, and now at once you *recognize* it. "Oh, that," you say, "was what I meant all along, only — I didn't know what I meant." Did you know? Yes, in one sense you knew all the while, — that is, your deeper self, your true consciousness, knew. It was your momentary self that did not know. But when you found the long-sought name, recalled the lost idea, you recognized it at once, because it was all the while your own, because you, the true and larger self, who owned the name or the idea and were aware of what it was, now were seen to include the smaller and momentary self that sought the name or tried to recall the thought. Your deeper consciousness of the lost idea was all the while there. In fact, did you not presuppose this when you sought the lost idea? How can I mean a name, or an idea, unless I in truth am the self who knows the name, who possesses the idea? In hunting for the name or the lost idea, I am hunting for my own thought. Well, just so I know nothing about the far-off stars in detail, but in so far as I mean the far-off stars at all, as I speak of them, I am identical with that remote and deep thought of my own that already knows the stars. When I study the stars, I am trying to find out what I really mean by them. To be sure, only experience can tell me, but that is because only experience can bring me into relation with my larger self. The escape from the prison of the inner self is simply the fact that the inner self is through and through an appeal to a larger self. The self that inquires, either inquires without meaning, or if it has a meaning, this meaning exists in and for the larger self that knows.

Here is a suggestion of what I mean by Synthetic Idealism. No truth, I repeat, is more familiar. That I am always meaning to inquire into objects beyond me, what clearer fact could be mentioned? That only in case it is already I who, in deeper truth, in my real and hidden thought, *know* the lost object yonder, the object whose nature I seek to comprehend, that only in this case I can truly *mean* the thing yonder, — this, as we must assert, is involved in the very idea of *meaning*. That is the logical analysis of it. You can mean what your deeper self knows; you cannot mean what your deeper self doesn't know. To be sure, the complete illustration of this most critical insight of idealism belongs elsewhere. Few see the familiar. Nothing is more common than for people to think that they mean objects that have nothing to do with themselves. Kant it was, who, despite his things in themselves, first showed us that nobody really means an object, really knows it, or doubts it, or aims at it, unless he does so by aiming at a truth that is present to his own larger self. Except for the unity of my true self, taught Kant, I have no objects. And so it makes no difference whether I know a thing or am in doubt about it. So long as I really *mean* it, that is enough. The self that *means* the object is identical with the larger self that possesses the object, just as when you seek the lost idea you are already in essence with the self that possesses the lost idea.

In this way I suggest to you the proof which a rigid analysis of the logic of our most commonplace thought would give for the doctrine that in the world there is but *one* Self, and that it is *his* world which we all alike are truly meaning, whether we talk of one another or of Cromwell's character or of the fixed stars or of the far-off æons of the future. The relation of my thought to its object has, I insist, this curious character, that *unless* the thought and its object are parts of one larger thought, I can't even be *meaning* that object yonder, can't even be in error about it, can't even doubt its existence. You, for instance, are part of one larger self with me, or else I can't even be meaning to address you as outer beings. You are part of one larger self along with the most mysterious or most remote fact of nature, along with the moon, and all the hosts of heaven, along with all truth and all beauty. Else could you not even intend to speak of such objects beyond you. For whatever you speak of you will find that your world is meant by you as just your world. Talk of the unknowable, and it forthwith becomes your unknowable, your problem, whose solution, unless the problem be a mere nonsense question, your larger self must own and be aware of. The deepest problem of life is, "What is this deeper self?" And the only answer is, *It is the self that knows in unity all truth.* This, I insist, is no hypothesis. It is actually the presupposition of your deepest doubt. And that is why I say: Everything finite is more or less obscure, dark, doubtful. Only the Infinite Self, the problem-solver, the complete thinker, the one who knows what we mean even when we are most confused and ignorant, the one who includes us, who has the world present to himself in unity, before whom all past and future truth, all distant and dark truth is clear in one eternal moment, to whom far and forgot is near, who thinks the whole of nature, and in whom are all things, the Logos, the world-possessor, — only his existence, I say, is perfectly sure. . . .

Our whole idealistic analysis . . . from the beginning of this discussion, has been to the effect that facts must be facts for somebody, and can't be facts for nobody, and that *bare* possibilities are really impossible. Hence whoever believes, whether truly or falsely, about objects beyond the moment of his belief, is an organic part of a reflective and conscious larger self that has those objects immediately present to itself, and has them in organic relation with the erring or truthful momentary self that believes. . . .

Flee where we will, then, the net of the larger Self ensnares us. We are lost and imprisoned in the thickets of its tangled labyrinth. The moments are not at all in themselves, for as moments they have no meaning; they exist only in relation to the beyond. The larger Self alone is, and they are by reason of it, organic parts of it. They perish, but it remains; they have truth or error only in its overshadowing presence.

And now, as to the unity of this Self. Can there be many such organic selves, mutually separate unities of moments and of the objects that these moments mean? Nay, were there *many* such, would not their manifoldness be a truth? Their relations, would not these be real? Their distinct places in the world-order, would not these things be objects of possible true or false thoughts? If so, must not there be once more the inclusive real Self for whom these truths were true, these separate selves interrelated, and their variety absorbed in the organism of its rational meaning?

There is, then, at last, but one Self, organically, reflectively, consciously inclusive of all the selves, and so of all truth. I have called this self, Logos, problem-solver, all-knower. Consider, then, last of all, his relation to problems. In [a] previous lecture we doubted many things; we questioned the whole seeming world of the outer order; we wondered as to space and time, as to nature and evolution, as to the beginning and the end of things. Now he who wonders is like him who doubts. Has his wonder any rationality about it? Does he *mean* anything by his doubt? Then the truth that he means, and about which he wonders, has its real constitution. As wonderer, he in the moment possesses not this solving truth; he appeals to the self who can solve. That self must possess the solution just as surely as the problem has a meaning. The real nature of space and time, the real beginning of things, where matter was at any point of time in the past, what is to become of the world's energy: these are matters of truth, and truth is necessarily present to the Self as in one all-comprehending self-completed moment, beyond which is naught, within which is the world.

The world, then, is such stuff as ideas are made of. Thought possesses all things. But the world isn't unreal. It extends infinitely beyond our private consciousness, because it is the world of a universal mind. What facts it is to contain only experience can inform us. There is no magic that can anticipate the work of science. Absolutely the *only* thing sure from the first about this world, however, is that it is intelligent, rational, orderly, essentially comprehensible, so that all its problems are somewhere solved, all its darkest mysteries are known to the supreme Self. This Self infinitely and reflectively transcends our consciousness, and therefore, since it includes us, it is at the very least a person, and more definitely conscious than we are; for what it possesses is self-reflecting knowledge, and what is knowledge aware of itself, but consciousness? Beyond the seeming wreck and chaos of our finite problems, its eternal insight dwells, therefore, in absolute and supreme majesty. Yet it is not far from every one of us. There is no least or most transient thought that flits through a child's mind, or that troubles with the faintest line of care a maiden's face, and that still does not contain and embody something of this divine Logos.

Auguste Comte

Comte (1798-1857) who may be accounted the father of positivism in its modern forms and to whom the modern sociological sciences owe a special debt, claimed that a "religion of humanity" was needed to achieve the result he desired. Humanity replaces God as the Supreme Being. What is to be understood as "humanity" is not always clear, for in Comte's thought man seems to be little more than the meeting place of biological and sociological laws. Positivism, for Comte, is not merely a way of organizing the sciences; it represents, rather, a special attitude both to the sciences and to their use. In the following passage he indicates what he accounts the religious implications of his system.

A Positivistic View of Religion *

Positive religion brings before us in a definite shape the noblest of human problems, the permanent preponderance of Social feeling over Self-love. As far as the exceeding imperfection of our nature enables us to solve it, it will be solved by calling our home affections into continuous action; affections which stand half way between self-love and universal sympathy. In order to consolidate and develop this solution, Positivism lays down the philosophical and social principle of separation of theoretical from practical power. Theoretical power is consultative; it directs education, and supplies general principles. Practical power directs action by special and imperative rules. All the elements of society that are excluded from political government become guarantees for the preservation of this arrangement. The priests of Humanity who are the systematic organs of the moderating power, will always find themselves supported, in their attempts to modify the governing power, by women and by the people. But to be so supported, they must be men who, in addition to the intellectual power necessary for their mission, have the moral qualities which are yet more necessary; who combine, that is, the tenderness of women with the energy of the people. The first guarantee for the possession of such qualities is the sacrifice of political authority and even of wealth. Then we may at last hope to see the new religion taking the place of the old, because it will fulfil in a more perfect way the mental and social purposes for which the old religion existed. Monotheism will lapse like Polytheism and Fetichism into the domain of history; and will like them, be incorporated into the system of universal commemoration, in which Humanity will render due homage to all her predecessors.

* Auguste Comte, *System of Positive Polity* (London: Longmans, Green & Company, Ltd., 1875), pp. 319–321. Used by permission.

It is not then merely on the ground of speculative truth that Positivists would urge all those who are still halting between two opinions, to choose between the absolute and the relative, between the fruitless search for Causes and the solid study of Laws, between submission to arbitrary Wills and submission to demonstrable Necessities. It is for Feeling still more than for Reason to make the decision; for upon it depends the establishment of a higher form of social life.

Monotheism in Western Europe is now as obsolete and as injurious as Polytheism was fifteen centuries ago. The discipline in which its moral value principally consisted has long since decayed; and consequently the sole effect of its doctrine, which has been so extravagantly praised, is to degrade the affections by unlimited desires, and to weaken the character by servile terrors. It supplied no field for the Imagination, and forced it back upon Polytheism and Fetichism, which under Theology form the only possible foundation for poetry. The pursuits of practical life were never sincerely promoted by it, and they advanced only by evading or resisting its influence. The noblest of all practical pursuits, that of social regeneration, is at the present time in direct opposition to it. For by its vague notion of Providence, it prevents men from forming a true conception of Law, a conception necessary for true prevision on which all wise intervention must be based.

Sincere believers in Christianity will soon cease to interfere with the management of a world where they profess themselves to be pilgrims and strangers. The new Supreme Being is no less jealous than the old, and will not accept the servants of two masters. But the truth is, that the more zealous theological partisans, whether royalists, aristocrats, or democrats, have now for a long time been insincere. God to them is but the nominal chief of a hypocritical conspiracy, a conspiracy which is even more contemptible than it is odious. Their object is to keep the people from all great social improvements by assuring them that they will find compensation for their miseries in an imaginary future life. The doctrine is already falling into discredit among the working classes everywhere throughout the West, especially in Paris. All theological tendencies, whether Catholic, Protestant, or Deist, really serve to prolong and aggravate our moral anarchy, because they hinder the diffusion of that social sympathy and breadth of view, without which we can never attain fixity of principle and regularity of life. Every subversive scheme now afloat has either originated in Monotheism or has received its sanction. Even Catholicism has lost its power of controlling revolutionary extravagance in some of its own most distinguished members.

It is for the sake of Order therefore, even more than of Progress, that we call on all those who desire to rise above their present disastrous state of oscillation in feeling and opinion, to make a distinct choice between Positivism and Theology. For there are now but two camps: the camp of reaction and anarchy, which acknowledges more or less distinctly the direction of God: the camp of construction and progress, which is wholly devoted to Humanity.

The Being upon whom all our thoughts are concentrated is one whose existence is undoubted. We recognise that existence not in the Present only, but in the Past, and even in the Future: and we find it always subject to one fundamental Law, by which we are enabled to conceive of it as a whole. Placing our highest happiness in universal Love, we live, as far as it is possible, for others; and this in public life as well as in private; for the two are closely linked together in our religion; a religion clothed in all the beauty of Art, and yet never inconsistent with Science. After having thus exercised our powers to the full, and having given a charm and sacredness to our temporary life, we shall at last be for ever incorporated into the Supreme Being, of whose life all noble natures are necessarily partakers. It is only through the worship of Humanity that we can feel the inward reality and inexpressible sweetness of this incorporation. It is unknown to those who being still involved in theological belief, have not been able to form a clear conception of the Future, and have never experienced the feeling of pure self-sacrifice.

SECTION THREE

The Traditional Case for Theism

Aristotle

Aristotle (384-322 B.C.) was a member of the group that gathered in Athens around Plato. While in general sympathetic towards Plato's aims, he was a different sort of man — less the imaginative artist, more the empirical observer. His approach to the typical problems of his age was, as we should say, more "scientific" than that of his master, and he became, indeed, for many centuries the accepted authority on all matters that we should nowadays regard as scientific rather than philosophical or theological. Like the Greeks of his day generally, he felt the problem of change and motion to be one of the principal puzzles requiring solution. In Aristotle the concept of motion is abstract; in our day "process" would better convey what he meant. He regarded God as the cause (in several senses) of all motion and change. God is the Unmoved Mover of all things. An earlier Greek philosopher, Parmenides, had denied the reality of all that changes and moves. Aristotle, on the contrary, gave motion an ontological reality of its own; yet behind the world of change and motion he set an "ultimate" cause that is unique. Aristotle, rediscovered in the Middle Ages, was a challenge to men of all faiths, Muslims, Jews, and Christians, for his "scientific" teachings seemed to be at variance with Biblical and other religious conceptions. To Christian churchmen in the West he seemed at first, indeed, to represent the most formidable opposition to the traditional teaching of the Church, whose interpretation both of Scripture and of the Christian life had been deeply influenced by Platonic and Neo-Platonic notions. Many twelfth-century Christian churchmen no doubt felt toward Aristotle something of what many people in the nineteenth century were to feel toward Darwin; they thought there was an irreconcilable conflict between his "science" and their religion. The thirteenth-century Schoolmen, however, notably St. Thomas Aquinas, found it possible not only to reconcile Aristotle's system with the traditional faith of the Church, but to present a synthesis that eventually came to be accepted as a fuller and more systematic expression of the Faith in intellectual terms than anything previously devised. This synthesis still enjoys much prestige in the Roman Catholic Church.

The Prime Mover *

Motion, we say, is the fulfilment of the movable in so far as it is movable. Each kind of motion, therefore, necessarily involves the presence of the things that are capable of that motion. In fact, even apart from the definition of

* *The Basic Works of Aristotle*, ed. Richard McKeon (New York: Random House, 1941), pp. 355–359; 877–881. *Physics*, VIII, 1; *Metaphysics*, XII, 6–7. Used by permission of The Clarendon Press, Oxford, England.

motion, every one would admit that in each kind of motion it is that which is capable of that motion that is in motion: thus it is that which is capable of alteration that is altered, and that which is capable of local change that is in locomotion: and so there must be something capable of being burned before there can be a process of being burned, and something capable of burning before there can be a process of burning. Moreover, these things also must either have a beginning before which they had no being, or they must be eternal. Now if there was a becoming of every movable thing, it follows that before the motion in question another change or motion must have taken place in which that which was capable of being moved or of causing motion had its becoming. To suppose, on the other hand, that these things were in being throughout all previous time without there being any motion appears unreasonable on a moment's thought, and still more unreasonable, we shall find, on further consideration. For if we are to say that, while there are on the one hand things that are movable, and on the other hand things that are motive, there is a time when there is a first movement and a first moved, and another time when there is no such thing but only something that is at rest, then this thing that is at rest must previously have been in process of change: for there must have been some cause of its rest, rest being the privation of motion. Therefore, before this first change there will be a previous change. For some things cause motion in only one way, while others can produce either of two contrary motions: thus fire causes heating but not cooling, whereas it would seem that knowledge may be directed to two contrary ends while remaining one and the same. Even in the former class, however, there seems to be something similar, for a cold thing in a sense causes heating by turning away and retiring, just as one possessed of knowledge voluntarily makes an error when he uses his knowledge in the reverse way.[1] But at any rate all things that are capable respectively of affecting and being affected, or of causing motion and being moved, are capable of it not under all conditions, but only when they are in a particular condition and approach one another: so it is on the approach of one thing to another that the one causes motion and the other is moved, and when they are present under such conditions as rendered the one motive and the other movable. So if the motion was not always in process, it is clear that they must have been in a condition not such as to render them capable respectively of being moved and of causing motion, and one or other of them must have been in process of change: for in what is relative this is a necessary consequence: e.g., if one thing is double another when before it was not so, one or other of them, if not both, must have been in process of change. It follows, then, that there will be a process of change previous to the first.

(Further, how can there be any "before" and "after" without the existence of time? Or how can there be any time without the existence of motion? If, then, time is the number of motion or itself a kind of motion, it follows that, if there is always time, motion must also be eternal. But so far as time is concerned we see that all with one exception are in agreement in saying that it is

[1] I.e., by means of his knowledge he can be sure of giving a wrong opinion and thus deceiving some one.

uncreated: in fact, it is just this that enables Democritus to show that all things cannot have had a becoming: for time, he says, is uncreated. Plato alone asserts the creation of time, saying[2] that it had a becoming together with the universe, the universe according to him having had a becoming. Now since time cannot exist and is unthinkable apart from the moment, and the moment is a kind of middle-point, uniting as it does in itself both a beginning and an end, a beginning of future time and an end of past time, it follows that there must always be time: for the extremity of the last period of time that we take must be found in some moment, since time contains no point of contact for us except the moment. Therefore, since the moment is both a beginning and an end, there must always be time on both sides of it. But if this is true of time, it is evident that it must also be true of motion, time being a kind of affection of motion.)

The same reasoning will also serve to show the imperishability of motion: just as a becoming of motion would involve, as we saw, the existence of a process of change previous to the first, in the same way a perishing of motion would involve the existence of a process of change subsequent to the last: for when a thing ceases to be moved, it does not therefore at the same time cease to be movable — e.g., the cessation of the process of being burned does not involve the cessation of the capacity of being burned, since a thing may be capable of being burned without being in process of being burned — nor, when a thing ceases to be movent, does it therefore at the same time cease to be motive. Again, the destructive agent will have to be destroyed, after what it destroys has been destroyed, and then that which has the capacity of destroying *it* will have to be destroyed afterwards (so that there will be a process of change subsequent to the last), for being destroyed also is a kind of change. If, then, the view which we are criticizing involves these impossible consequences, it is clear that motion is eternal and cannot have existed at one time and not at another: in fact, such a view can hardly be described as anything else than fantastic.

And much the same may be said of the view that such is the ordinance of nature and that this must be regarded as a principle, as would seem to be the view of Empedocles when he says that the constitution of the world is of necessity such that Love and Strife alternately predominate and cause motion, while in the intermediate period of time there is a state of rest. Probably also those who, like Anaxagoras, assert a single principle (of motion) would hold this view. But that which is produced or directed by nature can never be anything disorderly: for nature is everywhere the cause of order. Moreover, there is no ratio in the relation of the infinite to the infinite, whereas order always means ratio. But if we say that there is first a state of rest for an infinite time, and then motion is started at some moment, and that the fact that it is this rather than a previous moment is of no importance, and involves no order, then we can no longer say that it is nature's work: for if anything is of a certain character *naturally*, it either is so invariably and is not sometimes of this and sometimes of another character (e.g., fire, which travels upwards naturally, does not sometimes do so and sometimes not) or there is a ratio

[2] Aristotle is thinking of a passage in the *Timaeus* (38 B).

in the variation. It would be better, therefore, to say with Empedocles and any one else who may have maintained such a theory as his that the universe is alternately at rest and in motion: for in a system of this kind we have at once a certain order. But even here the holder of the theory ought not only to assert the fact: he ought also to explain the cause of it: i.e., he should not make any mere assumption or lay down any gratuitous axiom, but should employ either inductive or demonstrative reasoning. The Love and Strife postulated by Empedocles are not in themselves causes of the fact in question, nor is it of the essence of either that it should be so, the essential function of the former being to unite, of the latter to separate. If he is to go on to explain this alternate predominance, he should adduce cases where such a state of things exists, as he points to the fact that among mankind we have something that unites men, namely Love, while on the other hand enemies avoid one another: thus from the observed fact that this occurs in certain cases comes the assumption that it occurs also in the universe. Then, again, some argument is needed to explain why the predominance of each of the two forces lasts for an equal period of time. But it is a wrong assumption to suppose universally that we have an adequate first principle in virtue of the fact that something always is so or always happens so. Thus Democritus reduces the causes that explain nature to the fact that things happened in the past in the same way as they happen now: but he does not think fit to seek for a first principle to explain this "always": so, while his theory is right in so far as it is applied to certain individual cases, he is wrong in making it of universal application. Thus, a triangle always has its angles equal to two right angles, but there is nevertheless an ulterior cause of the eternity of this truth, whereas first principles are eternal and have no ulterior cause. Let this conclude what we have to say in support of our contention that there never was a time when there was not motion, and never will be a time when there will not be motion.

. . . . .

Since [we have found that] there were three kinds of substance, two of them physical and one unmovable, regarding the latter we must assert that it is necessary that there should be an eternal unmovable substance. For substances are the first of existing things, and if they are all destructible, all things are destructible. But it is impossible that movement should either have come into being or cease to be (for it must always have existed), or that time should. For there could not be a before and an after if time did not exist. Movement also is continuous, then, in the sense in which time is; for time is either the same thing as movement or an attribute of movement. And there is no continuous movement except movement in place, and of this only that which is circular is continuous.

But if there is something which is capable of moving things or acting on them, but is not actually doing so, there will not necessarily be movement; for that which has a potency need not exercise it. Nothing, then, is gained even if we suppose eternal substances, as the believers in the Forms do, unless there is to be in them some principle which can cause change; nay, even this is not enough, nor is another substance besides the Forms enough; for if it is not to *act*, there will be no movement. Further, even if it acts, this will not be enough, if its essence is potency; for there will not be *eternal* movement, since that which is potentially may possibly not be. There must, then, be such a principle, whose very essence is actuality. Further, then, these substances must be without matter; for they must be eternal, if *anything* is eternal. Therefore they must be actuality.

Yet there is a difficulty; for it is thought that everything that acts is able to act, but that not everything that is able to act acts, so that the potency is prior. But if this is so, nothing that is need be; for it is possible for all things to be capable of existing but not yet to exist.

Yet if we follow the theologians who generate the world from night, or the natural philosophers who say that "all things were together,"[3] the same impossible result ensues. For how will there be movement, if there is no actually existing cause? Wood will surely not move itself — the carpenter's art must act on it; nor will the menstrual blood nor the earth set themselves in motion, but the seeds must act on the earth and the semen on the menstrual blood.

This is why some suppose eternal actuality — e.g., Leucippus[4] and Plato;[5] for they say there is always movement. But why and what this movement is they do not say, nor, if the world moves in this way or that, do they tell us the cause of its doing so. Now nothing is moved at random, but there must always be something present to move it; e.g., as a matter of fact a thing moves in one way by nature, and in another by force or through the influence of reason or something else. (Further, what sort of movement is primary? This makes a vast difference.) But again for Plato, at least, it is not permissible to name here that which he sometimes supposes to be the source of movement — that which moves itself;[6] for the soul is later, and coeval with the heavens, according to his account.[7] To suppose potency prior to actuality, then, is in a sense right, and in a sense not; and we have specified these senses.[8] That actuality is prior is testified by Anaxagoras (for his "reason" is actuality) and by Empedocles in his doctrine of love and strife, and by those who say that there is always movement, e.g., Leucippus. Therefore chaos or night did not exist for an infinite time, but the same things have always existed (either passing through a cycle of changes or obeying some other law), since actuality is prior to potency. If, then, there is a constant cycle, something must always remain,[9] acting in the same way. And if there is to be generation and destruction, there must be something else[10] which is always acting in different ways. This must, then, act in one way in virtue of itself, and in another in virtue of something else — either of a third agent, therefore, or of the first. Now it must be in virtue of the first. For otherwise this again causes the motion both of the second agent and of the third. Therefore it is better to say "the first." For it was the cause of eternal uniformity; and something else is the cause of

[3] Anaxagoras.

[4] Cf. *De Caelo*, iii. 300^b 8.

[5] Cf. *Timaeus*, 30 A.

[6] Cf. *Phaedrus*, 245 C; *Laws*, 894 E.

[7] Cf. *Timaeus*, 34 B.

[8] Cf. 1071^b 22–26.

[9] I.e., the sphere of the fixed stars.

[10] I.e., the sun. Cf. *De Gen. et Corr.* ii. 336^a 23 ff.

variety, and evidently both together are the cause of eternal variety. This, accordingly, is the character which the motions actually exhibit. What need then is there to seek for other principles?

Since (1) this is a possible account of the matter, and (2) if it were not true, the world would have proceeded out of night and "all things together" and out of non-being, these difficulties may be taken as solved. There is, then, something which is always moved with an unceasing motion, which is motion in a circle; and this is plain not in theory only but in fact. Therefore the first heaven[11] must be eternal. There is therefore also something which moves it. And since that which is moved and moves is intermediate, there is something which moves without being moved, being eternal, substance, and actuality. And the object of desire and the object of thought move in this way; they move without being moved. The primary objects of desire and of thought are the same. For the apparent good is the object of appetite, and the real good is the primary object of rational wish. But desire is consequent on opinion rather than opinion on desire; for the thinking is the starting-point. And thought is moved by the object of thought, and one of the two columns of opposites is in itself the object of thought; and in this, substance is first, and in substance, that which is simple and exists actually. (The one and the simple are not the same; for "one" means a measure, but "simple" means that the thing itself has a certain nature.) But the beautiful, also, and that which is in itself desirable are in the same column; and the first in any class is always best, or analogous to the best.

That a final cause may exist among unchangeable entities is shown by the distinction of its meanings. For the final cause is (*a*) some being for whose good an action is done, and (*b*) something at which the action aims; and of these the latter exists among unchangeable entities though the former does not. The final cause, then, produces motion as being loved, but all other things move by being moved.

Now if something is moved it is capable of being otherwise than as it is. Therefore if its actuality is the primary form of spatial motion, then in so far as it is subject to change, in *this* respect it is capable of being otherwise — in place, even if not in substance. But since there is something which moves while itself unmoved, existing actually, this can in no way be otherwise than as it is. For motion in space is the first of the kinds of change, and motion in a circle the first kind of spatial motion; and this the first mover *produces*.[12] The first mover, then, exists of necessity; and in so far as it exists by necessity, its mode of being is good, and it is in this sense a first principle. For the necessary has all these senses — that which is necessary perforce because it is contrary to the natural impulse, that without which the good is impossible, and that which cannot be otherwise but can exist only in a single way.

On such a principle, then, depend the heavens and the world of nature.

[11] I.e., the outer sphere of the universe, that in which the fixed stars are set.

[12] If it had any movement, it would have the first. But it produces this and therefore cannot share in it; for if it did, we should have to look for something that is prior to to the first mover and imparts this motion to it.

And it is a life such as the best which we enjoy, and enjoy for but a short time (for it is ever in this state, which we cannot be), since its actuality is also pleasure. (And for this reason[13] are waking, perception, and thinking most pleasant, and hopes and memories are so on account of these.) And thinking in itself deals with that which is best in itself, and that which is thinking in the fullest sense with that which is best in the fullest sense. And thought thinks on itself because it shares the nature of the object of thought; for it becomes an object of thought in coming into contact with and thinking its objects, so that thought and object of thought are the same. For that which is *capable* of receiving the object of thought, i.e., the essence, is thought. But it is *active* when it *possesses* this object. Therefore the possession rather than the receptivity is the divine element which thought seems to contain, and the act of contemplation is what is most pleasant and best. If, then, God is always in that good state in which we sometimes are, this compels our wonder; and if in a better this compels it yet more. And God *is* in a better state. And life also belongs to God; for the actuality of thought is life, and God is that actuality; and God's self-dependent actuality is life most good and eternal. We say therefore that God is a living being, eternal, most good, so that life and duration continuous and eternal belong to God; for this *is* God.

Those who suppose, as the Pythagoreans and Speusippus do, that supreme beauty and goodness are not present in the beginning, because the beginnings both of plants and of animals are *causes*, but beauty and completeness are in the *effects* of these,[14] are wrong in their opinion. For the seed comes from other individuals which are prior and complete, and the first thing is not seed but the complete being; e.g., we must say that before the seed there is a man — not the man produced from the seed, but another from whom the seed comes.

It is clear then from what has been said that there is a substance which is eternal and unmovable and separate from sensible things. It has been shown also that this substance cannot have any magnitude, but is without parts and indivisible (for it produces movement through infinite time, but nothing finite has infinite power; and, while every magnitude is either infinite or finite, it cannot, for the above reason, have finite magnitude, and it cannot have infinite magnitude because there is no infinite magnitude at all). But it has also been shown that it is impassive and unalterable; for all the other changes are posterior to[15] change of place.

[13] *Sc.*, because they are activities or actualities.

[14] I.e., the animal or plant is more beautiful and perfect than the seed.

[15] I.e., impossible without.

Anselm

St. Anselm (ca. 1033-1109), who was probably of royal descent on the maternal side, was born at Aosta in the region now known as Piedmont. In 1060 he took monastic vows at the Norman abbey of Bec, of which he became Abbot in 1078. In 1093 he was named Archbishop of Canterbury. His approach to a Christian philosophy is summed up in the phrase fides quaerens intellectum *(faith seeking understanding). While the distinguished contemporary Protestant theologian Karl Barth regards all of Anselm's work as essentially theological, the celebrated contemporary historian of medieval philosophy Étienne Gilson accounts him the father of medieval Scholasticism. At any rate, whether Anselm is considered primarily as a theologian or as a philosopher, his methods reflect a departure from earlier medieval ways of thought, although they represent Scholasticism only in its embryonic form.*

The Proslogium, *from which the following passage is taken, was written about 1077-1078. It may be regarded as the point of departure for all later medieval Christian thought. The Anselmic form of the ontological argument for the existence of God, which is developed here, is intended to show to unbelievers as well as believers the "necessity" of the existence of God. This is an extremely important document in the history of religious philosophy.*

The Ontological Argument*

Exhortation of the mind to the contemplation of God. — It casts aside cares, and excludes all thoughts save that of God, that it may seek Him. Man was created to see God. Man by sin lost the blessedness for which he was made, and found the misery for which he was not made. He did not keep this good when he could keep it easily. Without God it is ill with us. Our labors and attempts are in vain without God. Man cannot seek God, unless God himself teaches him; nor find him, unless he reveals himself. God created man in his image, that he might be mindful of him, think of him, and love him. The believer does not seek to understand, that he may believe, but he believes that he may understand: for unless he believed he would not understand.

Up now, slight man! flee, for a little while, thy occupations; hide thyself, for a time, from thy disturbing thoughts. Cast aside, now, thy burdensome cares, and put away thy toilsome business. Yield room for some little time to God; and rest for a little time in him. Enter the inner chamber of thy mind; shut out all thoughts save that of God, and such as can aid thee in seeking him; close thy door and seek him. Speak now, my whole heart! speak now to God, saying, I seek thy face; thy face, Lord, will I seek (Psalms xxvii. 8). And

* St. Anselm, *Proslogium,* trans. S. N. Deane (La Salle, Ill.: The Open Court Publishing Co., 1959), pp. 3–9; 158–161. Used by permission.

come thou now, O Lord my God, teach my heart where and how it may seek thee, where and how it may find thee.

Lord, if thou art not here, where shall I seek thee, being absent? But if thou art everywhere, why do I not see thee present? Truly thou dwellest in unapproachable light. But where is unapproachable light, or how shall I come to it? Or who shall lead me to that light and into it, that I may see thee in it? Again, by what marks, under what form, shall I seek thee? I have never seen thee, O Lord, my God; I do not know thy form. What, O most high Lord, shall this man do, an exile far from thee? What shall thy servant do, anxious in his love of thee, and cast out afar from thy face? He pants to see thee, and thy face is too far from him. He longs to come to thee, and thy dwelling-place is inaccessible. He is eager to find thee, and knows not thy place. He desires to seek thee, and does not know thy face. Lord, thou art my God, and thou art my Lord, and never have I seen thee. It is thou that hast made me, and hast made me anew, and hast bestowed upon me all the blessings I enjoy; and not yet do I know thee. Finally, I was created to see thee, and not yet have I done that for which I was made.

O wretched lot of man, when he hath lost that for which he was made! O hard and terrible fate! Alas, what has he lost, and what has he found? What has departed, and what remains? He has lost the blessedness for which he was made, and has found the misery for which he was not made. That has departed without which nothing is happy, and that remains which, in itself, is only miserable. Man once did eat the bread of angels, for which he hungers now; he eateth now the bread of sorrows, of which he knew not then. Alas! for the mourning of all mankind, for the universal lamentation of the sons of Hades! He choked with satiety, we sigh with hunger. He abounded, we beg. He possessed in happiness, and miserably forsook his possession; we suffer want in unhappiness, and feel a miserable longing, and alas! we remain empty.

Why did he not keep for us, when he could so easily, that whose lack we should feel so heavily? Why did he shut us away from the light, and cover us over with darkness? With what purpose did he rob us of life, and inflict death upon us? Wretches that we are, whence have we been driven out; whither are we driven on? Whence hurled? Whither consigned to ruin? From a native country into exile, from the vision of God into our present blindness, from the joy of immortality into the bitterness and horror of death. Miserable exchange of how great a good, for how great an evil! Heavy loss, heavy grief, heavy all our fate!

But alas! wretched that I am, one of the sons of Eve, far removed from God! What have I undertaken? What have I accomplished? Whither was I striving? How far have I come? To what did I aspire? Amid what thoughts am I sighing? I sought blessings, and lo! confusion. I strove toward God, and I stumbled on myself. I sought calm in privacy, and I found tribulation and grief, in my inmost thoughts. I wished to smile in the joy of my mind, and I am compelled to frown by the sorrow of my heart. Gladness was hoped for, and lo! a source of frequent sighs!

And thou too, O Lord, how long? How long, O Lord, dost thou forget us; how long dost thou turn thy face from us? When wilt thou look upon us, and hear us? When wilt thou enlighten our eyes, and show us thy face? When wilt thou restore thyself to us? Look upon us, Lord; hear us, enlighten us, reveal thyself to us. Restore thyself to us, that it may be well with us, — thyself, without whom it is so ill with us. Pity our toilings and strivings toward thee, since we can do nothing without thee. Thou dost invite us; do thou help us. I beseech thee, O Lord, that I may not lose hope in sighs, but may breathe anew in hope. Lord, my heart is made bitter by its desolation; sweeten thou it, I beseech thee, with thy consolation. Lord, in hunger I began to seek thee; I beseech thee that I may not cease to hunger for thee. In hunger I have come to thee; let me not go unfed. I have come in poverty to the Rich, in misery to the Compassionate; let me not return empty and despised. And if, before I eat, I sigh, grant, even after sighs, that which I may eat. Lord, I am bowed down and can only look downward; raise me up that I may look upward. My iniquities have gone over my head; they overwhelm me; and, like a heavy load, they weigh me down. Free me from them; unburden me, that the pit of iniquities may not close over me.

Be it mine to look up to thy light, even from afar, even from the depths. Teach me to seek thee, and reveal thyself to me, when I seek thee, for I cannot seek thee, except thou teach me, nor find thee, except thou reveal thyself. Let me seek thee in longing, let me long for thee in seeking; let me find thee in love, and love thee in finding. Lord, I acknowledge and I thank thee that thou hast created me in this thine image, in order that I may be mindful of thee, may conceive of thee, and love thee; but that image has been so consumed and wasted away by vices, and obscured by the smoke of wrong-doing, that it cannot achieve that for which it was made, except thou renew it, and create it anew. I do not endeavor, O Lord, to penetrate thy sublimity, for in no wise do I compare my understanding with that; but I long to understand in some degree thy truth, which my heart believes and loves. For I do not seek to understand that I may believe, but I believe in order to understand. For this also I believe, — that unless I believed, I should not understand.

Truly there is a God, although the fool hath said in his heart, There is no God.

And so, Lord, do thou, who dost give understanding to faith, give me, so far as thou knowest it to be profitable, to understand that thou art as we believe; and that thou art that which we believe. And, indeed, we believe that thou art a being than which nothing greater can be conceived. Or is there no such nature, since the fool hath said in his heart, there is no God? (Psalms xiv. 1). But, at any rate, this very fool, when he hears of this being of which I speak — a being than which nothing greater can be conceived — understands what he hears, and what he understands is in his understanding; although he does not understand it to exist.

For, it is one thing for an object to be in the understanding, and another to understand that the object exists. When a painter first conceives of what he will afterwards perform, he has it in his understanding, but he does not yet understand it to be, because he has not yet performed it. But after he has made the painting, he both has it in his understanding, and he understands that it exists, because he has made it.

Hence, even the fool is convinced that something exists in the understanding, at least, than which nothing greater can be conceived. For, when he hears of this, he understands it. And whatever is understood, exists in the understanding. And assuredly that, than which nothing greater can be conceived, cannot exist in the understanding alone. For, suppose it exists in the understanding alone: then it can be conceived to exist in reality; which is greater.

Therefore, if that, than which nothing greater can be conceived, exists in the understanding alone, the very being, than which nothing greater can be conceived, is one, than which a greater can be conceived. But obviously this is impossible. Hence, there is no doubt that there exists a being, than which nothing greater can be conceived, and it exists both in the understanding and in reality.

> God cannot be conceived not to exist. — God is that, than which nothing greater can be conceived. — That which can be conceived not to exist is not God.

And it assuredly exists so truly, that it cannot be conceived not to exist. For, it is possible to conceive of a being which cannot be conceived not to exist; and this is greater than one which can be conceived not to exist. Hence, if that, than which nothing greater can be conceived, can be conceived not to exist, it is not that, than which nothing greater can be conceived. But this is an irreconcilable contradiction. There is, then, so truly a being than which nothing greater can be conceived to exist, that it cannot even be conceived not to exist; and this being thou art, O Lord, our God.

So truly, therefore, dost thou exist, O Lord, my God, that thou canst not be conceived not to exist; and rightly. For, if a mind could conceive of a being better than thee, the creature would rise above the Creator; and this is most absurd. And, indeed, whatever else there is, except thee alone, can be conceived not to exist. To thee alone, therefore, it belongs to exist more truly than all other beings, and hence in a higher degree than all others. For, whatever else exists does not exist so truly, and hence in a less degree it belongs to it to exist. Why, then, has the fool said in his heart, there is no God (Psalms xiv. 1), since it is so evident, to a rational mind, that thou dost exist in the highest degree of all? Why, except that he is dull and a fool?

To Anselm's argument Gaunilon, a French monk, objected that it was plainly possible to conceive of a perfect island, more beautiful than any island one had ever seen, and that this would be no proof of its existence. Anselm replied to Gaunilon's criticism in the following observations.

> A criticism of Gaunilon's example, in which he tries to show that in this way the real existence of a lost island might be inferred from the fact of its being conceived.

But, you say, it is as if one should suppose an island in the ocean, which surpasses all lands in its fertility, and which, because of the difficulty, or rather the impossibility, of discovering what does not exist, is called a lost island; and should say that there can be no doubt that this island truly exists in reality, for this reason, that one who hears it described easily understands what he hears.

Now I promise confidently that if any man shall devise anything existing either in reality or in concept alone (except that than which a greater cannot be conceived) to which he can adapt the sequence of my reasoning, I will discover that thing, and will give him his lost island, not to be lost again.

But it now appears that this being than which a greater is inconceivable cannot be conceived not to be, because it exists on so assured a ground of truth; for otherwise it would not exist at all.

Hence, if any one says that he conceives this being not to exist, I say that at the time when he conceives of this either he conceives of a being than which a greater is inconceivable, or he does not conceive at all. If he does not conceive, he does not conceive of the non-existence of that of which he does not conceive. But if he does conceive, he certainly conceives of a being which cannot be even conceived not to exist. For if it could be conceived not to exist, it could be conceived to have a beginning and an end. But this is impossible.

He, then, who conceives of this being conceives of a being which cannot be even conceived not to exist; but he who conceives of this being does not conceive that it does not exist; else he conceives what is inconceivable. The non-existence, then, of that than which a greater cannot be conceived is inconceivable.

The difference between the possibility of conceiving of non-existence, and understanding non-existence.

You say, moreover, that whereas I assert that this supreme being cannot be *conceived* not to exist, it might better be said that its non-existence, or even the possibility of its non-existence, cannot be *understood.*

But it was more proper to say, it cannot be conceived. For if I had said that the object itself cannot be understood not to exist, possibly you yourself, who say that in accordance with the true meaning of the term what is unreal cannot be understood, would offer the objection that nothing which is can be understood not to be, for the non-existence of what exists is unreal: hence God would not be the only being of which it could be said, it is impossible to understand its non-existence. For thus one of those beings which most certainly exist can be understood not to exist in the same way in which certain other real objects can be understood not to exist.

But this objection, assuredly, cannot be urged against the term *conception,* if one considers the matter well. For although no objects which exist can be understood not to exist, yet all objects, except that which exists in the highest degree, can be conceived not to exist. For all those objects, and those alone, can be conceived not to exist, which have a beginning or end or composition of parts: also, as I have already said, whatever at any place or at any time does not exist as a whole.

That being alone, on the other hand, cannot be conceived not to exist, in which any conception discovers neither beginning nor end nor composition of parts, and which any conception finds always and everywhere as a whole.

Be assured, then, that you can conceive of your own non-existence, although you are most certain that you exist. I am surprised that you should have admitted that you are ignorant of this. For we conceive of the non-existence of many objects which we know to exist, and of the existence of many which we know not to exist; not by forming the opinion that they so exist, but by imagining that they exist as we conceive of them.

And indeed, we can conceive of the non-existence of an object, although we know it to exist, because at the same time we can conceive of the former and know the latter. And we cannot conceive of the non-existence of an object, so long as we know it to exist, because we cannot conceive at the same time of existence and non-existence.

If, then, one will thus distinguish these two senses of this statement, he will understand that nothing, so long as it is known to exist, can be conceived not to exist; and that whatever exists, except that being than which a greater cannot be conceived, can be conceived not to exist, even when it is known to exist.

So, then, of God alone it can be said that it is impossible to conceive of his non-existence; and yet many objects, so long as they exist, in one sense cannot be conceived not to exist. But in what sense God is to be conceived not to exist, I think has been shown clearly enough in my book.

Thomas Aquinas

Of the three famous thirteenth-century Christian Schoolmen, Thomas Aquinas (ca. 1225-1274) has exerted a greater influence than either Bonaventure or Duns Scotus. Of noble Italian birth and destined by his family for a Benedictine abbacy, he instead joined the Dominican Order of preaching friars, of which he has become the most distinguished son. Introduced by his teacher, Albertus Magnus, to Aristotle, whose writings had at that time been rediscovered, he developed the aim of trying to express in the philosophical idiom of Aristotle, who represented the thirteenth-century "challenge of science" to the Christian faith, a systematic Christian philosophy and theology. His work, whose extent is immense, did not go unopposed by ecclesiastical authorities, and it might well be said that he was a sort of thirteenth-century modernist. Eventually, however, he acquired such prestige that by the time of the Council of Trent (1545-1563) his system had become all but the official theology of the Roman Church.

St. Thomas held that it was possible to demonstrate the existence of God. It is possible, on the basis of sense perception, for the human intellect to develop arguments for this. He sets them forth in the following passage. These ways, known as the Quinque Viae, or Five Ways, are by no means independent of one another. They represent varieties of the Cosmological and Teleological Arguments. St. Thomas, while repudiating the Ontological Argument in the Anselmic form he knew, maintained that the existence of God could be in these other ways rationally shown.

The Existence of God: The Five Ways *

The existence of God can be proved in five ways.

The first and more manifest way is the argument from motion. It is certain, and evident to our senses, that in the world some things are in motion. Now whatever is moved is moved by another, for nothing can be moved except it is in potentiality to that towards which it is moved; whereas a thing moves inasmuch as it is in act. For motion is nothing else than the reduction of something from potentiality to actuality. But nothing can be reduced from potentiality to actuality, except by something in a state of actuality. Thus that which is actually hot, as fire, makes wood, which is potentially hot, to be actually hot, and thereby moves and changes it. Now it is not possible that

* *Basic Writings of St. Thomas Aquinas,* ed. A. C. Pegis (2 vols.; New York: Random House, 1945), I, pp. 22, 23. *Summa Theol.,* I, 2, 3. Used by permission.

the same thing should be at once in actuality and potentiality in the same respect, but only in different respects. For what is actually hot cannot simultaneously be potentially hot; but it is simultaneously potentially cold. It is therefore impossible that in the same respect and in the same way a thing should be both mover and moved, *i.e.*, that it should move itself. Therefore, whatever is moved must be moved by another. If that by which it is moved be itself moved, then this also must needs be moved by another, and that by another again. But this cannot go on to infinity, because then there would be no first mover, and, consequently, no other mover, seeing that subsequent movers move only inasmuch as they are moved by the first mover; as the staff moves only because it is moved by the hand. Therefore it is necessary to arrive at a first mover, moved by no other; and this everyone understands to be God.

The second way is from the nature of efficient cause. In the world of sensible things we find there is an order of efficient causes. There is no case known (neither is it, indeed, possible) in which a thing is found to be the efficient cause of itself; for so it would be prior to itself, which is impossible. Now in efficient causes it is not possible to go on to infinity, because in all efficient causes following in order, the first is the cause of the intermediate cause, and the intermediate is the cause of the ultimate cause, whether the intermediate cause be several, or one only. Now to take away the cause is to take away the effect. Therefore, if there be no first cause among efficient causes, there will be no ultimate, nor any intermediate, cause. But if in efficient causes it is possible to go on to infinity, there will be no first efficient cause, neither will there be an ultimate effect, nor any intermediate efficient causes; all of which is plainly false. Therefore it is necessary to admit a first efficient cause, to which everyone gives the name of God.

The third way is taken from possibility and necessity, and runs thus. We find in nature things that are possible to be and not to be, since they are found to be generated, and to be corrupted, and consequently, it is possible for them to be and not to be. But it is impossible for these always to exist, for that which can not-be at some time is not. Therefore, if everything can not-be, then at one time there was nothing in existence. Now if this were true, even now there would be nothing in existence, because that which does not exist begins to exist only through something already existing. Therefore, if at one time nothing was in existence, it would have been impossible for anything to have begun to exist; and thus even now nothing would be in existence — which is absurd. Therefore, not all beings are merely possible, but there must exist something the existence of which is necessary. But every necessary thing either has its necessity caused by another, or not. Now it is impossible to go on to infinity in necessary things which have their necessity caused by another, as has been already proved in regard to efficient causes. Therefore we cannot but admit the existence of some being having of itself its own necessity, and not receiving it from another, but rather causing in others their necessity. This all men speak of as God.

The fourth way is taken from the gradation to be found in things. Among beings there are some more and some less good, true, noble, and the like. But *more* and *less* are predicated of different things according as they resemble in their different ways something which is the maximum, as a thing is said to be hotter according as it more nearly resembles that which is hottest; so that there is something which is truest, something best, something noblest, and, consequently, something which is most being, for those things that are greatest in truth are greatest in being, as it is written [Aristotle] *Metaph.* ii. Now the maximum in any genus is the cause of all in that genus, as fire, which is the maximum of heat, is the cause of all hot things, as is said in the same book. Therefore there must also be something which is to all beings the cause of their being, goodness, and every other perfection; and this we call God.

The fifth way is taken from the governance of the world. We see that things which lack knowledge, such as natural bodies, act for an end, and this is evident from their acting always, or nearly always, in the same way, so as to obtain the best result. Hence it is plain that they achieve their end, not fortuitously, but designedly. Now whatever lacks knowledge cannot move towards an end, unless it be directed by some being endowed with knowledge and intelligence; as the arrow is directed by the archer. Therefore some intelligent being exists by whom all natural things are directed to their end; and this being we call God.

Descartes

René Descartes (1596-1650) is generally acclaimed the father of moder philosophic thought. His importance lies in his method, the cardinal principl of which was to accept no metaphysical proposition on authority but to doub all that could not be clearly and distinctly conceived as part of a logical an coherent whole. He was willing to doubt even his own existence; but he foun that in the very act of doubting his existence he was thinking, so that he coul go on to the conclusion Cogito, ergo sum *— "I think, therefore I exist." (Des cartes wrote in French:* Je pense, donc je suis. *The Latin text has:* Ego cogito ergo sum sive existo.) *Descartes maintained that as a finite mind looks beyon itself the first clear and distinct idea it perceives is that of God. How then is thi idea of God to be accounted for except on the supposition that God exists Descartes had more difficulty in determining whether the external world is, a we might say, a projection of our own minds, and this is a question he consider in relation to the idea of God.*

The Ontological Argument *

I will now close my eyes, I will stop my ears, I will turn away my sense from their objects, I will even efface from my consciousness all the images o corporeal things; or at least, because this can hardly be accomplished, I wil consider them as empty and false; and thus, holding converse only with my self, and closely examining my nature, I will endeavour to obtain by degree a more intimate and familiar knowledge of myself. I am a thinking (con scious) thing, that is, a being who doubts, affirms, denies, knows a few objects and is ignorant of many, — [who loves, hates], wills, refuses, — who imagine likewise, and perceives; for, as I before remarked, although the things which perceive or imagine are perhaps nothing at all apart from me [and in them selves], I am nevertheless assured that those modes of consciousness whic I call perceptions and imaginations, in as far only as they are modes of con sciousness, exist in me. And in the little I have said I think I have summe up all that I really know, or at least all that up to this time I was aware I knew Now, as I am endeavouring to extend my knowledge more widely, I will us circumspection, and consider with care whether I can still discover in mysel anything which I have not yet hitherto observed. I am certain that I am thinking thing; but do I not therefore likewise know what is required to rend me certain of a truth? In this first knowledge, doubtless, there is nothing tha gives me assurance of its truth except the clear and distinct perception of wha

* René Descartes, *The Method, Meditation, and Selections from the Principle* trans. John Veitch (Edinburgh: Blackwood & Sons, Ltd., 1899). Meditation II Used by permission.

I affirm, which would not indeed be sufficient to give me the assurance that what I say is true, if it could ever happen that anything I thus clearly and distinctly perceived should prove false; and accordingly it seems to me that I may now take as a general rule, that all that is very clearly and distinctly apprehended (conceived) is true.

Nevertheless I before received and admitted many things as wholly certain and manifest, which yet I afterwards found to be doubtful. What, then, were those? They were the earth, the sky, the stars, and all the other objects which I was in the habit of perceiving by the senses. But what was it that I clearly [and distinctly] perceived in them? Nothing more than that the ideas and the thoughts of those objects were presented to my mind. And even now I do not deny that these ideas are found in my mind. But there was yet another thing which I affirmed, and which, from having been accustomed to believe it, I thought I clearly perceived, although, in truth, I did not perceive it at all; I mean the existence of objects external to me, from which those ideas proceeded, and to which they had a perfect resemblance; and it was here I was mistaken, or if I judged correctly, this assuredly was not to be traced to any knowledge I possessed (the force of my perception).

But when I considered any matter in arithmetic and geometry, that was very simple and easy, as, for example, that two and three added together make five, and things of this sort, did I not view them with at least sufficient clearness to warrant me in affirming their truth? Indeed, if I afterwards judged that we ought to doubt of these things, it was for no other reason than because it occurred to me that a God might perhaps have given me such a nature as that I should be deceived, even respecting the matters that appeared to me the most evidently true. But as often as this preconceived opinion of the sovereign power of a God presents itself to my mind, I am constrained to admit that it is easy for him, if he wishes it, to cause me to err, even in matters where I think I possess the highest evidence; and, on the other hand, as often as I direct my attention to things which I think I apprehend with great clearness, I am so persuaded of their truth that I naturally break out into expressions such as these: Deceive me who may, no one will yet ever be able to bring it about that I am not, so long as I shall be conscious that I am, or at any future time cause it to be true that I have never been, it being now true that I am, or make two and three more or less than five, in supposing which, and other like absurdities, I discover a manifest contradiction.

And in truth, as I have no ground for believing that Deity is deceitful, and as, indeed, I have not even considered the reasons by which the existence of a Deity of any kind is established, the ground of doubt that rests only on this supposition is very slight, and, so to speak, metaphysical. But, that I may be able wholly to remove it, I must inquire whether there is a God, as soon as an opportunity of doing so shall present itself; and if I find that there is a God, I must examine likewise whether he can be a deceiver; for, without the knowledge of these two truths, I do not see that I can ever be certain of anything. And that I may be enabled to examine this without interrupting the order of meditation I have proposed to myself [which is, to pass by degrees from the notions that I shall find first in my mind to those I shall afterwards discover in it], it is necessary at this stage to divide all my thoughts into certain classes, and to consider in which of these classes truth and error are, strictly speaking, to be found.

Of my thoughts some are, as it were, images of things, and to these alone properly belongs the name *idea;* as when I think [represent to my mind] a man, a chimera, the sky, an angel, or God. Others, again, have certain other forms; as when I will, fear, affirm, or deny, I always, indeed, apprehend something as the object of my thought, but I also embrace in thought something more than the representation of the object; and of this class of thoughts some are called volitions or affections, and others judgments.

Now, with respect to ideas, if these are considered only in themselves, and are not referred to any object beyond them, they cannot, properly speaking, be false; for, whether I imagine a goat or a chimera, it is not less true that I imagine the one than the other. Nor need we fear that falsity may exist in the will or affections; for, although I may desire objects that are wrong, and even that never existed, it is still true that I desire them. There thus only remain our judgments, in which we must take diligent heed that we be not deceived. But the chief and most ordinary error that arises in them consists in judging that the ideas which are in us are like or conformed to the things that are external to us; for assuredly, if we but considered the ideas themselves as certain modes of our thought (consciousness), without referring them to anything beyond, they would hardly afford any occasion of error.

But, among these ideas, some appear to me to be innate, others adventitious, and others to be made by myself (factitious); for, as I have the power of conceiving what is called a thing, or a truth, or a thought, it seems to me that I hold this power from no other source than my own nature; but if I now hear a noise, if I see the sun, or if I feel heat, I have all along judged that these sensations proceeded from certain objects existing out of myself; and, in fine, it appears to me that sirens, hippogryphs, and the like, are inventions of my own mind. But I may even perhaps come to be of opinion that all my ideas are of the class which I call adventitious, or that they are all innate, or that they are all factitious, for I have not yet clearly discovered their true origin; and what I have here principally to do is to consider, with reference to those that appear to come from certain objects without me, what grounds there are for thinking them like these objects.

The first of these grounds is that it seems to me I am so taught by nature; and the second that I am conscious that those ideas are not dependent on my will, and therefore not on myself, for they are frequently presented to me against my will, — as at present, whether I will or not, I feel heat; and I am thus persuaded that this sensation or idea (*sensum vel ideam*) of heat is produced in me by something different from myself, viz., by the heat of the fire by which I sit. And it is very reasonable to suppose that this object impresses me with its own likeness rather than any other thing.

But I must consider whether these reasons are sufficiently strong and convincing. When I speak of being taught by nature in this matter, I understand by the word nature only a certain spontaneous impetus that impels me to believe in a resemblance between ideas and their objects, and not a natural light that affords a knowledge of its truth. But these two things are widely different; for what the natural light shows to be true can be in no degree doubtful, as, for example, that I am because I doubt, and other truths of the like kind; inasmuch as I possess no other faculty whereby to distinguish truth from error, which can teach me the falsity of what the natural light declares to be true, and which is equally trust-worthy; but with respect to [seemingly] natural impulses, I have observed, when the question related to the choice of right or wrong in action, that they frequently led me to take the worse part; nor do I see that I have any better ground for following them in what relates to truth and error. Then, with respect to the other reason, which is that because these ideas do not depend on my will, they must arise from objects existing without me, I do not find it more convincing than the former; for, just as those natural impulses, of which I have lately spoken, are found in me, notwithstanding that they are not always in harmony with my will, so likewise it may be that I possess some power not sufficiently known to myself capable of producing ideas without the aid of external objects, and, indeed, it has always hitherto appeared to me that they are formed during sleep, by some power of this nature, without the aid of aught external. And, in fine, although I should grant that they proceeded from those objects, it is not a necessary consequence that they must be like them. On the contrary, I have observed, in a number of instances, that there was a great difference between the object and its idea. Thus, for example, I find in my mind two wholly diverse ideas of the sun; the one, by which it appears to me extremely small, draws its origin from the senses, and should be placed in the class of adventitious ideas; the other, by which it seems to be many times larger than the whole earth, is taken up on astronomical grounds, that is, elicited from certain notions born with me, or is framed by myself in some other manner. These two ideas cannot certainly both resemble the same sun; and reason teaches me that the one which seems to have immediately emanated from it is the most unlike. And these things sufficiently prove that hitherto it has not been from a certain and deliberate judgment, but only from a sort of blind impulse, that I believed in the existence of certain things different from myself, which, by the organs of sense, or by whatever other means it might be, conveyed their ideas or images into my mind [and impressed it with their likenesses].

But there is still another way of inquiring whether, of the objects whose ideas are in my mind, there are any that exist out of me. If ideas are taken in so far only as they are certain modes of consciousness, I do not remark any difference or inequality among them, and all seem, in the same manner, to proceed from myself; but, considering them as images, of which one represents one thing and another a different, it is evident that a great diversity obtains among them. For, without doubt, those that represent substances are something more, and contain in themselves, so to speak, more objective reality [that is, participate by representation in higher degrees of being or perfection], than those that represent only modes or accidents; and again, the idea by which I conceive a God [sovereign], eternal, infinite, [immutable], all-knowing, all-powerful, and the creator of all things that are out of himself, — this, I say, has certainly in it more objective reality than those ideas by which finite substances are represented.

Now, it is manifest by the natural light that there must at least be as much reality in the efficient and total cause as in its effect; for whence can the effect draw its reality if not from its cause? and how could the cause communicate to it this reality unless it possessed it in itself? And hence it follows, not only that what is cannot be produced by what is not, but likewise that the more perfect, — in other words, that which contains in itself more reality, — cannot be the effect of the less perfect: and this is not only evidently true of those effects, whose reality is actual or formal, but likewise of ideas, whose reality is only considered as objective. Thus, for example, the stone that is not yet in existence, not only cannot now commence to be, unless it be produced by that which possesses in itself, formally or eminently, all that enters into its composition, [in other words, by that which contains in itself the same properties that are in the stone, or others superior to them]; and heat can only be produced in a subject that was before devoid of it, by a cause that is of an order, [degree or kind], at least as perfect as heat; and so of the others. But further, even the idea of the heat, or of the stone, cannot exist in me unless it be put there by a cause that contains, at least, as much reality as I conceive existent in the heat or in the stone: for, although that cause may not transmit into my idea anything of its actual or formal reality, we ought not on this account to imagine that it is less real; but we ought to consider that, [as every idea is a work of the mind], its nature is such as of itself to demand no other formal reality than that which it borrows from our consciousness, of which it is but a mode, [that is, a manner or way of thinking]. But in order that an idea may contain this objective reality rather than that, it must doubtless derive it from some cause in which is found at least as much formal reality as the idea contains of objective; for, if we suppose that there is found in an idea anything which was not in its cause, it must of course derive this from nothing. But, however imperfect may be the mode of existence by which a thing is objectively [or by representation] in the understanding by its idea, we certainly cannot, for all that, allege that this mode of existence is nothing, nor, consequently, that the idea owes its origin to nothing. Nor must it be imagined that, since the reality which is considered in these ideas is only objective, the same reality need not be formally (actually) in the causes of these ideas, but only objectively: for, just as the mode of existing objectively belongs to ideas by their peculiar nature, so likewise the mode of existing formally appertains to the causes of these ideas (at least to the first and principal), by their peculiar nature. And although an idea may give rise to another idea, this regress cannot, nevertheless, be infinite; we must in the end reach a first idea, the cause of which is, as it were, the archetype in which all the reality [or perfection] that is found objectively [or by representation] in these ideas is contained formally [and in act]. I am thus clearly taught by the natural light that ideas exist in me as pictures or images, which may in truth readily fall short of the perfection of the objects from which they are taken, but can never contain anything greater or more perfect.

And in proportion to the time and care with which I examine all those matters, the conviction of their truth brightens and becomes distinct. But, to sum up, what conclusion shall I draw from it all? It is this; — if the objective reality [or perfection] of any one of my ideas be such as clearly to convince me, that this same reality exists in me neither formally nor eminently, and if, as follows from this, I myself cannot be the cause of it, it is a necessary consequence that I am not alone in the world, but that there is besides myself some other being who exists as the cause of that idea; while, on the contrary, if no such idea be found in my mind, I shall have no sufficient ground of assurance of the existence of any other being besides myself; for, after a most careful search, I have, up to this moment, been unable to discover any other ground.

But, among these my ideas, besides that which represents myself, respecting which there can be here no difficulty, there is one that represents a God; others that represent corporeal and inanimate things; others angels; others animals; and, finally, there are some that represent men like myself. But with respect to the ideas that represent other men, or animals, or angels, I can easily suppose that they were formed by the mingling and composition of the other ideas which I have of myself, of corporeal things, and of God, although there were, apart from myself, neither men, animals, nor angels. And with regard to the ideas of corporeal objects, I never discovered in them anything so great or excellent which I myself did not appear capable of originating; for, by considering these ideas closely and scrutinising them individually, in the same way that I yesterday examined the idea of wax, I find that there is but little in them that is clearly and distinctly perceived. As belonging to the class of things that are clearly apprehended, I recognise the following, viz., magnitude or extension in length, breadth, and depth; figure, which results from the termination of extension; situation, which bodies of diverse figures preserve with reference to each other; and motion or the change of situation; to which may be added substance, duration, and number. But with regard to light, colours, sounds, odours, tastes, heat, cold, and the other tactile qualities, they are thought with so much obscurity and confusion, that I cannot determine even whether they are true or false; in other words, whether or not the ideas I have of these qualities are in truth the ideas of real objects. For although I before remarked that it is only in judgments that formal falsity, or falsity properly so called, can be met with, there may nevertheless be found in ideas a certain material falsity, which arises when they represent what is nothing as if it were something. Thus, for example, the ideas I have of cold and heat are so far from being clear and distinct, that I am unable from them to discover whether cold is only the privation of heat, or heat the privation of cold; or whether they are or are not real qualities: and since, ideas being as it were images, there can be none that does not seem to us to represent some object, the idea which represents cold as something real and positive will not improperly be called false, if it be correct to say that cold is nothing but a privation of heat; and so in other cases. To ideas of this kind, indeed, it is not necessary that I should assign any author besides myself: for if they are false, that is, represent objects that are unreal, the natural light teaches me that they proceed from nothing; in other words, that they are in me only because something is wanting to the perfection of my nature; but if these ideas are true, yet because they exhibit to me so little reality that I cannot even distinguish the object represented from non-being, I do not see why I should not be the author of them.

With reference to those ideas of corporeal things that are clear and distinct, there are some which, as appears to me, might have been taken from the idea I have of myself, as those of substance, duration, number, and the like. For when I think that a stone is a substance, or a thing capable of existing of itself, and that I am likewise a substance, although I conceive that I am a thinking and non-extended thing, and that the stone, on the contrary, is extended and unconscious, there being thus the greatest diversity between the two concepts, — yet these two ideas seem to have this in common that they both represent substances. In the same way, when I think of myself as now existing, and recollect besides that I existed some time ago, and when I am conscious of various thoughts whose number I know, I then acquire the ideas of duration and number, which I can afterwards transfer to as many objects as I please. With respect to the other qualities that go to make up the ideas of corporeal objects, viz., extension, figure, situation, and motion, it is true that they are not formally in me, since I am merely a thinking being; but because they are only certain modes of substance, and because I myself am a substance, it seems possible that they may be contained in me eminently.

There only remains, therefore, the idea of God, in which I must consider whether there is anything that cannot be supposed to originate with myself. By the name God, I understand a substance infinite, [eternal, immutable], independent, all-knowing, all-powerful, and by which I myself, and every other thing that exists, if any such there be, were created. But these properties are so great and excellent, that the more attentively I consider them the less I feel persuaded that the idea I have of them owes its origin to myself alone. And thus it is absolutely necessary to conclude, from all that I have before said, that God exists: for though the idea of substance be in my mind owing to this, that I myself am a substance, I should not, however, have the idea of an infinite substance, seeing I am a finite being, unless it were given me by some substance in reality infinite.

And I must not imagine that I do not apprehend the infinite by a true idea, but only by the negation of the finite, in the same way that I comprehend repose and darkness by the negation of motion and light: since, on the contrary, I clearly perceive that there is more reality in the infinite substance than in the finite, and therefore that in some way I possess the perception (notion) of the infinite before that of the finite, that is, the perception of God before that of myself, for how could I know that I doubt, desire, or that something is wanting to me, and that I am not wholly perfect, if I possessed no idea of a being more perfect than myself, by comparison of which I knew the deficiencies of my nature?

And it cannot be said that this idea of God is perhaps materially false, and consequently that it may have arisen from nothing, [in other words, that it may exist in me from my imperfection], as I before said of the ideas of heat and cold, and the like: for, on the contrary, as this idea is very clear and distinct, and contains in itself more objective reality than any other, there can be no one of itself more true, or less open to the suspicion of falsity.

The idea, I say, of a being supremely perfect, and infinite, is in the highest degree true; for although, perhaps, we may imagine that such a being does not exist, we cannot, nevertheless, suppose that his idea represents nothing real, as

I have already said of the idea of cold. It is likewise clear and distinct in the highest degree, since whatever the mind clearly and distinctly conceives as real or true, and as implying any perfection, is contained entire in this idea. And this is true, nevertheless, although I do not comprehend the infinite, and although there may be in God an infinity of things that I cannot comprehend, nor perhaps even compass by thought in any way; for it is of the nature of the infinite that it should not be comprehended by the finite; and it is enough that I rightly understand this, and judge that all which I clearly perceive, and in which I know there is some perfection, and perhaps also an infinity of properties of which I am ignorant, are formally or eminently in God, in order that the idea I have of him may become the most true, clear, and distinct of all the ideas in my mind.

But perhaps I am something more than I suppose myself to be, and it may be that all those perfections which I attribute to God, in some way exist potentially in me, although they do not yet show themselves, and are not reduced to act. Indeed, I am already conscious that my knowledge is being increased [and perfected] by degrees; and I see nothing to prevent it from thus gradually increasing to infinity, nor any reason why, after such increase and perfection, I should not be able thereby to acquire all the other perfections of the Divine nature; nor, in fine, why the power I possess of acquiring those perfections, if it really now exist in me, should not be sufficient to produce the ideas of them. Yet, on looking more closely into the matter, I discover that this cannot be; for, in the first place, although it were true that my knowledge daily acquired new degrees of perfection, and although there were potentially in my nature much that was not as yet actually in it, still all these excellences make not the slightest approach to the idea I have of the Deity, in whom there is no perfection merely potentially [but all actually] existent; for it is even an unmistakeable token of imperfection in my knowledge, that it is augmented by degrees. Further, although my knowledge increase more and more, nevertheless I am not, therefore, induced to think that it will ever be actually infinite, since it can never reach that point beyond which it shall be incapable of further increase. But I conceive God as actually infinite, so that nothing can be added to his perfection. And, in fine, I readily perceive that the objective being of an idea cannot be produced by a being that is merely potentially existent, which, properly speaking, is nothing, but only by a being existing formally or actually.

And, truly, I see nothing in all that I have now said which it is not easy for any one, who shall carefully consider it, to discern by the natural light; but when I allow my attention in some degree to relax, the vision of my mind being obscured, and, as it were, blinded by the images of sensible objects, I do not readily remember the reason why the idea of a being more perfect than myself, must of necessity have proceeded from a being in reality more perfect. On this account I am here desirous to inquire further, whether I, who possess this idea of God, could exist supposing there were no God. And I ask, from whom could I, in that case, derive my existence? Perhaps from myself, or from my parents, or from some other causes less perfect than God; for anything more perfect, or even equal to God, cannot be thought or imagined. But if I [were independent of every other existence, and] were myself the author of my being, I should doubt of nothing, I should desire nothing, and, in fine, no perfection would be awanting to me; for I should have bestowed upon myself every perfection of which I possess the idea, and I should thus be God. And it must not be imagined that what is now wanting to me is perhaps of more difficult acquisition than that of which I am already possessed; for, on the contrary, it is quite manifest that it was a matter of much higher difficulty that I, a thinking being, should arise from nothing, than it would be for me to acquire the knowledge of many things of which I am ignorant, and which are merely the accidents of a thinking substance; and certainly, if I possessed of myself the greater perfection of which I have now spoken, [in other words, if I were the author of my own existence], I would not at least have denied to myself things that may be more easily obtained, [as that infinite variety of knowledge of which I am at present destitute]. I could not, indeed, have denied to myself any property which I perceive is contained in the idea of God, because there is none of these that seems to me to be more difficult to make or acquire; and if there were any that should happen to be more difficult to acquire, they would certainly appear so to me (supposing that I myself were the source of the other things I possess), because I should discover in them a limit to my power. And though I were to suppose that I always was as I now am, I should not, on this ground, escape the force of these reasonings, since it would not follow, even on this supposition, that no author of my existence needed to be sought after. For the whole time of my life may be divided into an infinity of parts, each of which is in no way dependent on any other; and, accordingly, because I was in existence a short time ago, it does not follow that I must now exist, unless in this moment some cause create me anew as it were, — that is, conserve me. In truth, it is perfectly clear and evident to all who will attentively consider the nature of duration, that the conservation of a substance, in each moment of its duration, requires the same power and act that would be necessary to create it, supposing it were not yet in existence; so that it is manifestly a dictate of the natural light that conservation and creation differ merely in respect of our mode of thinking [and not in reality]. All that is here required, therefore, is that I interrogate myself to discover whether I possess any power by means of which I can bring it about that I, who now am, shall exist a moment afterwards: for, since I am merely a thinking thing (or since, at least, the precise question, in the meantime, is only of that part of myself), if such a power resided in me, I should, without doubt, be conscious of it; but I am conscious of no such power, and thereby I manifestly know that I am dependent upon some being different from myself.

But perhaps the being upon whom I am dependent, is not God, and I have been produced either by my parents, or by some causes less perfect than Deity. This cannot be: for, as I before said, it is perfectly evident that there must at least be as much reality in the cause as in its effect; and accordingly, since I am a thinking thing, and possess in myself an idea of God, whatever in the end be the cause of my existence, it must of necessity be admitted that it is likewise a thinking being, and that it possesses in itself the idea and all the perfections I attribute to Deity. Then it may again be inquired whether this cause owes its origin and existence to itself, or to some other cause. For if it be self-existent, it follows, from what I have before laid down, that this cause is God; for, since it possesses the perfection of self-existence, it must likewise, without doubt, have the power of actually possessing every perfection of which it has the idea, — in other words, all the perfections I conceive to belong to God. But if it owe its existence to another cause than itself, we demand again, for a similar reason, whether this second cause exists of itself or through some other, until, from stage to stage, we at length arrive at an ultimate cause, which will be God. And it is quite manifest that in this matter there can be no infinite regress of causes, seeing that the question raised respects not so much the cause which once produced me, as that by which I am at this present moment conserved.

Nor can it be supposed that several causes concurred in my production, and that from one I received the idea of one of the perfections I attribute to Deity, and from another the idea of some other, and thus that all those perfections are indeed found somewhere in the universe, but do not all exist together in a single being who is God; for, on the contrary, the unity, the simplicity or inseparability of all the properties of Deity, is one of the chief perfections I conceive him to possess; and the idea of this unity of all the perfections of Deity could certainly not be put into my mind by any cause from which I did not likewise receive the ideas of all the other perfections; for no power could enable me to embrace them in an inseparable unity, without at the same time giving me the knowledge of what they were [and of their existence in a particular mode].

Finally, with regard to my parents [from whom it appears I sprung], although all that I believed respecting them be true, it does not, nevertheless, follow that I am conserved by them, or even that I was produced by them, in so far as I am a thinking being. All that, at the most, they contributed to my origin was the giving of certain dispositions (modifications) to the matter in which I have hitherto judged that I or my mind, which is what alone I now consider to be myself, is enclosed; and thus there can here be no difficulty with respect to them, and it is absolutely necessary to conclude from this alone that I am, and possess the idea of a being absolutely perfect, that is, of God, that his existence is most clearly demonstrated.

There remains only the inquiry as to the way in which I received this idea from God; for I have not drawn it from the senses, nor is it even presented to me unexpectedly, as is usual with the ideas of sensible objects, when these are presented or appear to be presented to the external organs of the senses; it is not even a pure production or fiction of my mind, for it is not in my power to take from or add to it; and consequently there but remains the alternative that it is innate, in the same way as is the idea of myself. And, in truth, it is not to be wondered at that God, at my creation, implanted this idea in me, that it might serve, as it were, for the mark of the workman impressed on his work; and it is not also necessary that the mark should be something different from the work itself; but considering only that God is my creator, it is highly probable that he in some way fashioned me after his own image and likeness, and that I perceive this likeness, in which is contained the idea of God, by the same faculty by which I apprehend myself, — in other words, when I make myself the object of reflection, I not only find that I am an incomplete, [imperfect] and dependent being, and one who unceasingly aspires after something better and greater than he is; but, at the same time, I am assured likewise that he upon whom I am dependent possesses in himself all the goods after which I aspire, [and the ideas of which I find in my mind], and that not merely indefinitely and potentially, but infinitely and actually, and that he is thus God. And the whole force of the argument of which I have here availed myself to establish the existence of God, consists in this, that I perceive I could not possibly be of such a nature as I am, and yet have in my mind the idea of a God, if God did not in reality exist, — this same God, I say, whose idea is in my mind — that is, a being who possesses all those lofty perfections, of which the mind may have some slight conception, without, however, being able fully to comprehend them, — and who is wholly superior to all defect, [and has nothing that marks imperfection]: whence it is sufficiently manifest that he cannot be a deceiver, since it is a dictate of the natural light that all fraud and deception spring from some defect.

Leibniz

Gottfried Wilhelm Leibniz (1646-1716), the discoverer of the infinitesimal calculus, was a German philosopher whose outlook was much enlarged by his contacts with French scholars. A Protestant by upbringing, he corresponded with the celebrated French bishop and preacher Bossuet on the subject of Christian reunion. According to Leibniz the universe consists of an infinite number of indivisible and ever active monads. Every monad contains within itself the whole infinity of substance, so that it mirrors all existence in its own fashion, though restricted by its limitations. The whole universe is continuous, and the differences within it are relative. The monads form an ascending series, ranging from the lowest, which is next to nothing, to the highest, which is God. This system, which is thoroughly rationalist, is one that is not readily reconciled to Biblical emphases upon the divine transcendence.

Monadology *

Thus the final reason of things must be in a necessary substance, in which the variety of particular changes exist only eminently,[1] as in its source; and this substance we call *God.*

Now as this substance is a sufficient reason of all this variety of particulars, which are also connected together throughout, *there is only one God, and this God is sufficient.*[2]

* Gottfried Wilhelm Leibniz, *The Monadology*, trans. Robert Latta (Oxford, England: The Clarendon Press, 1898), pp. 38–60, 238–250. Used by permission.

[1] *Eminently* in contrast with *formally*. The terms are Scholastic and they were adopted by Descartes. Thomas Aquinas expresses the difference thus: "Whatever perfection is in the effect must also appear in the cause, after the same manner if the agent and the effect are of the same kind (*univocal*) (thus man begets man), or in a more *eminent*, that is to say excellent, way, if the agent is of another kind (*equivocal*)." Descartes says: "By the *objective reality of an idea*, I mean the entity or being of the thing represented by the idea, in so far as this entity is in the idea; and in the same way we may speak of an objective perfection or an objective design, &c. For all that we conceive as being in the objects of ideas is objectively or by representation in the ideas themselves. The same things are said to be *formally* in the objects of the ideas, when they exist in the objects just as we conceive them to exist; and they are said to be *eminently* in the objects, when they do not really exist as we conceive them, but when they are so great that their excellence makes up for this defect." *Réponses aux Deuxièmes Objections. Raisons qui prouvent l'existence de Dieu,* iii. and iv. . . .

[2] That is to say, all particular things are connected together in one system, which implies one principle, one necessary substance, one God. The argument is not merely from the existence of order in the world to the existence of an intelligence which produces this order, but from the fact that the whole forms *one* system to the existence of *one* ultimate sufficient reason of the whole. Otherwise there might be various "orders" or "disorders" in conflict with one another, each pre-supposing its own first principle or "God." This is Leibniz's form of the *Cosmological* proof of the existence of God.

We may also hold that this supreme substance, which is unique, universal[3] and necessary, nothing outside of it being independent of it, — this substance, which is a pure sequence of possible being, must be illimitable and must contain as much reality as is possible.[4]

Whence it follows that God is absolutely perfect; for perfection is nothing but amount of positive reality, in the strict sense, leaving out of account the limits or bounds in things which are limited. And where there are no bounds, that is to say in God, perfection is absolutely infinite.

It follows also that created beings derive their perfections from the influence of God, but that their imperfections come from their own nature, which is incapable of being without limits. For it is in this that they differ from God.[5] An instance of this *original imperfection* of created beings may be seen in the *natural inertia* of bodies.[6]

It is further true that in God there is not only the source of existences but also that of essences, in so far as they are real, that is to say, the source of what

[3] "Universal" in the sense of being equally the cause or first principle of *all* things. The whole spirit of Leibniz's philosophy is opposed to the supposition of a universal substance or spirit, of which all particular substances are merely *modes*. Thus in the *Considérations sur la Doctrine d'un Esprit Universel* (1702) he endeavours to refute the view that "there is but one spirit, which is universal and which animates the whole universe and all its parts, each according to its structure and according to the organs it possesses, as the same blast of wind produces a variety of sounds from different organ-pipes" or that "the universal spirit is like an ocean composed of an infinite number of drops, which are separated from it when they animate some particular organic body and which are reunited with their ocean after the destruction of the organism." This is "the view of Spinoza and of other similar authors, who will have it that there is only one substance, viz. God, who thinks, believes and wills one thing in me, and who thinks, believes and wills quite the opposite in some one else. . . ."

[4] As God is the sufficient reason of all, nothing is independent of Him. But if His possibility were in any way limited, it must be by some possibility outside and independent of Him. Consequently His possibility cannot be limited. And unlimited possibility means unlimited reality and unlimited existence. For that which is possible must be real, unless there is something else with which it is not compossible, that is to say, unless there is some other possible thing, whose nature limits it. . . . The argument in this and the following sections will become clear if we keep in view the idea which Leibniz seeks constantly to emphasize in every department of thought, namely that possibility or potentiality is never a mere empty capacity, a *tabula rasa*, a *potentia nuda*, but always, in however small a degree, a *tendency* to realization, which is kept back only by the other similar tendencies. This is what is meant by the "claims" and "aspirations" of the Monads. . . .

[5] Created beings must be essentially limited; otherwise they would not be created, but would be identical with God. In the *Théodicée* Leibniz (following the Scholastic principle, *bonum habet causam efficientem, malum autem deficientem*) uses this as a hypothesis by which to remove from God the responsibility for the existence of evil. The origin of evil is the essential imperfection of created substances; and God is the cause only of the perfection or positive reality of created things.

[6] This sentence . . . seems to have been added by Leibniz in revising the first copy of the *Monadology*. . . . The natural inertia of a body is its passivity or that in it which limits its activity. So far as the passivity of the body is real (i.e. not a mere appearance to us), it consists of confused perception. But God is *actus purus*, entirely without passivity, and His perceptions are all perfectly clear and distinct.

is real in the possible.[7] For the understanding of God is the region of eternal truths or of the ideas on which they depend,[8] and without Him there would be nothing real in the possibilities of things, and not only would there be nothing in existence, but nothing would even be possible.

For if there is a reality in essences or possibilities, or rather in eternal truths, this reality must needs be founded in something existing and actual, and consequently in the existence of the necessary Being, in whom essence involves existence, or in whom to be possible is to be actual.

Thus God alone (or the necessary Being) has this prerogative that He must necessarily exist, if He is possible. And as nothing can interfere with the possibility of that which involves no limits, no negation and consequently no contradiction, this [His possibility] is sufficient of itself to make known the existence of God *a priori*. We have thus proved it, through the reality of eternal truths. But a little while ago we proved it also *a posteriori*, since there exist contingent beings, which can have their final or sufficient reason only in the necessary Being, which has the reason of its existence in itself.

We must not, however, imagine, as some do, that eternal truths, being dependent on God, are arbitrary and depend on His will, as Descartes,[9]

[7] That is to say, God is not only the source of all actual existence, but also the source of all potential existence, of all that *tends* to exist. "What is real in the possible" is its tendency to exist. In a sense, "essences" or "possible" things are independent of God. He does not create them as essences. They are the objects of His understanding, and "He is not the author of His own understanding" (*Théodicée*, §380; E. 614 b; G. vi. 341). The nature of essences or possibilities is determined solely by the principle of contradiction. And yet, in another sense, they may be said to be dependent upon God, inasmuch as they are all expressions of His nature in one or another aspect or with particular limitations. His freedom, however, extends only to a choice of those which shall actually exist, and this choice is determined by His wisdom and His goodness, having regard to the nature of the "essences" themselves. "Without Him there would be nothing *in existence*," for the existence of things is the result of His will, His choice. "Without Him nothing would be *possible*," for all that is possible is the object of His understanding, and as His understanding is perfect (i.e. entirely free from confusion in its perceptions), its object must be the ultimate nature of things, that is, the very essence of God Himself. . . .

[8] Leibniz connects this part of his system with Plato's world of ideas. He mentions as one of the "many most excellent doctrines of Plato" that "there is in the Divine mind an intelligible world, which I also am wont to call the region of ideas."

[9] Cf. Descartes, *Lettre au Père Mersenne* (Cousin's ed., vol. vi., p. 109). "The metaphysical truths which you call eternal have been established by God and are entirely dependent upon Him, like all other created things. Indeed, to say that these truths are independent of God is to speak of God as a Jupiter or a Saturn and to subject Him to Styx and the Fates. . . . God has established these laws in nature, just as a king establishes laws in his kingdom." Cf. *loc. cit.*, p. 103. "We cannot without blasphemy say that the truth of anything precedes the knowledge which God has of it, for in God willing and knowing are one." Elsewhere he says that God was perfectly free to make it untrue that the three angles of a triangle should be equal to two right-angles. As early as 1671, in a letter to Honoratus Fabri, Leibniz writes: "If truths and the natures of things are dependent on the choice of God, I do not see how knowledge [*scientia*] or even will can be attributed to Him. For will certainly presupposes some understanding, since no one can will except in view of some good [*sub ratione boni*]. But understanding presupposes something that can be understood, that

and afterwards M. Poiret,[10] appear to have held. That is true only of contingent truths, of which the principle is *fitness* [*convenance*][11] or choice of the *best*, whereas necessary truths depend solely on His understanding and are its inner object.

Thus God alone is the primary unity or original simple substance, of which all created or derivative Monads are products and have their birth, so to speak, through continual fulgurations[12] of Divinity from moment to moment, limited

---

is to say, some nature. But if all natures are the result of will, understanding also will be the result of will. How, then, does will presuppose understanding?" (G. iv. 259). The point was much discussed by the Scholastics, with special reference to the question whether or not the moral law is independent of the will of God. Descartes's view is in harmony with that of Duns Scotus, while Leibniz follows Thomas Aquinas. For Descartes, the Divine and the human understanding differ in kind: for Leibniz they differ merely in degree.

[10] Pierre Poiret (1646–1719), a Calvinist minister, who held a charge in the Duchy of Zweibrücken, in the Rhine Palatinate. He was at first a Cartesian and published a book, *Cogitationes rationales de Deo, Anima et Malo,* which Bayle attacked. Afterwards he came under the influence of Antoinette Bourignon, the Dutch religious enthusiast, whose life he wrote and whose views he expounded at very great length. This influence led him to attack Cartesianism with much fervour, and he is now remembered as a mystic rather than as a philosopher.

[11] By *convenance* is meant mutual conformity, of such a kind that things "fit into" one another in the most perfect way. Thus the principle of *convenance* or of the *best* is what we should now call the idea of system. With Leibniz it is the same as the principle of sufficient reason, which is the principle of *conditioned,* as distinct from *unconditional* reality or truth.

[12] That is to say, "flashings" or "sudden emanations." "God is the primary centre from which all else emanates" (G. iv. 553). Cf. the Stoic *τόνος* which Cleanthes calls a "stroke of fire" (*πληγὴ πυρός*), Frag. 76. The relation of God to the other Monads is the crux of Leibniz's philosophy. He wishes to maintain both the individuality of the Monads and their essential unity with God. Thus he seems to take fulguration as a middle term between creation and emanation. "Creation" would mean too complete a severance between God and the other Monads; "emanation" would mean too complete an identity between them. "Fulguration" means that the Monad is not absolutely created out of nothing nor, on the other hand, merely a mode or an absolutely necessary product of the Divine nature, but that it is a possibility tending to realize itself, yet requiring the assistance, choice or will of God to set it free from the counteracting influence of opposite possibilities. As a possibility it has essential limits (i.e. it is not entirely perfect, *actus purus*); but it is ready to spring or "flash" into being, at the will of God. If there were no choice of God, possibilities would simply counteract one another. But His choice means no more than the removal of hindrances to development, in the case of certain "elect" possibilities. Creation adds no new being to the universe, and yet it is not emanation, in the sense of a mere modification of the one Eternal Being. Thus the "continual fulgurations" of Leibniz are to be distinguished from the "continual creation" of Descartes. According to Leibniz, conservation is not, as with Descartes, a miraculous renewal of the existence of things from moment to moment, an absolute re-creation constantly repeated; but it is the continuance of the activity, choice or will of God, by which certain possible things were set free to exist and through which alone they can persist. The successive states of any being are neither completely independent of one another, so that at each moment there is a new creation (Descartes), nor are they so absolutely dependent on one another that each proceeds from its predecessor by a logical or mathematical necessity (Spinoza), but they are connected together in a sequence which has its ground in the nature of the being, so that each is automatically unfolded from its predecessor ac-

by the receptivity of the created being, of whose essence it is to have limits.

In God there is *Power,* which is the source of all, also *Knowledge,* whose content is the variety of the ideas, and finally *Will,* which makes changes or products according to the principle of the best.[13] . . . These characteristics correspond to what in the created Monads forms the ground or basis[14] to the faculty of Perception and to the faculty of Appetition. But in God these attributes are absolutely infinite or perfect; and in the created Monads or the Entelechies . . . there are only imitations of these attributes, according to the degree of perfection of the Monad.

A created thing is said to *act* outwardly[15] in so far as it has perfection, and to *suffer* [or be *passive, pâtir*] in relation to another, in so far as it is imperfect. Thus *activity* [*action*] is attributed to a Monad, in so far as it has distinct perceptions, and *passivity* [*passion*] in so far as its perceptions are confused.

And one created thing is more perfect than another, in this, that there is found in the more perfect that which serves to explain *a priori* what takes place in the less perfect, and it is on this account that the former is said to act upon the latter.[16]

But in simple substances the influence of one Monad upon another is only ideal, and it can have its effect only through the mediation of God, in so far as in the ideas of God any Monad rightly claims that God, in regulating the others from the beginning of things, should have regard to it. For since one created Monad cannot have any physical influence upon the inner being of

---

cording to a regular law, provided that God chooses to allow this unfolding. The "continual fulgurations" are the continual exercise of God's will in allowing the Monads of the actual world to unfold or develop their nature.

[13] In the *Théodicée* (§150; E. 549 a; G. vi. 199) Leibniz hints at a connexion between this characterization of God's nature and the doctrine of the Trinity. "Some have even thought that there is in these three perfections of God a hidden reference to the Holy Trinity: that power has reference to the Father, that is to say, to the Godhead [*Divinité*]; wisdom to the eternal Word, which is called λόγος by the most sublime of the evangelists; and will or love to the Holy Spirit."

[14] Leibniz does not elsewhere discriminate three elements in the created Monad, and we must not suppose that the "ground or basis" is anything in itself, apart from the two "faculties." Leibniz wishes to emphasize the view that the Monad, whether created or uncreated, is essentially force or activity, manifesting itself in perception and appetition.

[15] Of course, no Monad really does act outside itself. This is merely Leibniz's explanation of what we mean when we speak of outward action, just as the Copernican system explains what we mean when we speak of "sunrise" and "sunset," though the sun neither "rises" nor "sets."

[16] Thus the explanation or reason of an event is its actual cause. This connects itself with Leibniz's view that the existence of a thing arises solely from the liberating of its essential activities, and that the Monads claim existence in proportion to their perfection, that is to say, to the distinctness of their perceptions. Cause and effect are relative: every created Monad is both at once. God alone is pure cause or reason (*actus purus*). Cause = relative activity = relative distinctness of perception. This may instructively be compared and contrasted with the views of Berkeley and Hume regarding cause and "necessary connexion." See Introduction, Part iii. p. 105. Cf. also Spinoza, *Ethics,* Part iii. Def. 1 and 2, and Prop. 1, 2 and 3.

another, it is only by this means that the one can be dependent upon the other.[17]

Accordingly, among created things, activities and passivities are mutual. For God, comparing two simple substances, finds in each reasons which oblige Him to adapt the other to it,[18] and consequently what is active in certain respects is passive from another point of view;[19] *active* in so far as what we distinctly know in it serves to explain [*rendre raison de*] what takes place in another, and *passive* in so far as the explanation [*raison*] of what takes place in it is to be found in that which is distinctly known in another.

Now, as in the Ideas of God there is an infinite number of possible universes, and as only one of them can be actual, there must be a sufficient reason for the choice of God, which leads Him to decide upon one rather than another.

And this reason can be found only in the *fitness* [*convenance*], or in the degrees of perfection, that these worlds possess,[20] since each possible thing has the right to aspire to existence in proportion to the amount of perfection it contains in germ.[21]

Thus the actual existence of the best that wisdom makes known to God is due to this, that His goodness makes Him choose it, and His power makes Him produce it.[22]

[17] We have here the principle of the Pre-established Harmony. It is a harmony or mutual compatibility in the very nature of things, anterior to their creation. Its perfection in the actual world is the ground of God's choice of that world; and thus it is not in any sense a created harmony. In this respect it differs from every form of Occasionalism.

[18] No two simple substances are exactly the same, yet all represent the same universe. Therefore a perception which is comparatively distinct in one must be comparatively confused in another or others, and whatever changes take place in one must be accompanied by corresponding changes in the others. Thus each fits into the others.

[19] Leibniz's expression here is *point de considération*. But he generally uses the phrase *point de vue*, which he introduced as a regular term in philosophical literature. . . . The term has a peculiar importance in Leibniz's philosophy.

[20] God is not compelled by an absolute, *metaphysical* necessity, but "inclined" by a *moral* necessity to create the world which, as one harmonious system, is the best. The distinction between moral necessity and absolute compulsion is of Scholastic origin. "Possible things are those which do not involve a contradiction. Actual things are nothing but the possible things which, all things considered, are the best. Therefore things which are less perfect are not on that account impossible; for we must distinguish between the things which God can do and those He wills to do. He can do everything, He wills to do the best." *Epistola ad Bernovllium* (1699). . . .

[21] This aspiration to existence is the tendency to pass into existence and to proceed from confused to distinct perceptions, which makes the "possible" things of Leibniz real essences as distinct from purely indeterminate capacities. Possibilities, according to Leibniz, are never quite empty: they are always realities in germ. . . . "From the very fact that there exists something rather than nothing, we must recognize that in possible things, or in possibility or essence itself, there is a certain need of existence [*exigentiam existentiae*] or (so to speak) a certain aspiration to exist, and, in a word, that essence by itself tends to existence. Whence it further follows that all possible things, i.e. things expressing essence or possible reality, tend with equal right to existence in proportion to the quantity of essence or reality they contain or to their degree of perfection; for perfection is nothing but quantity of essence."

[22] This section states briefly the principles of Leibniz's *Optimism*, which are fully

Now this connexion or adaptation of all created things to each and of each to all, means that each simple substance has relations which express all the others, and, consequently, that it is a perpetual living mirror of the universe.[23]

And as the same town, looked at from various sides, appears quite different and becomes as it were numerous in aspects [*perspectivement*]; even so, as a result of the infinite number of simple substances, it is as if there were so many different universes, which, nevertheless, are nothing but aspects [*perspectives*] of a single universe, according to the special point of view of each Monad.[24]

And by this means there is obtained as great variety as possible, along with the greatest possible order; that is to say, it is the way to get as much perfection as possible.[25]

Besides, no hypothesis but this (which I venture to call proved) fittingly exalts the greatness of God; and this Monsieur Bayle recognized when, in his *Dictionary* (article *Rorarius*[26]), he raised objections to it, in which indeed he

---

expounded and defended in the *Théodicée*. A world entirely free from evil would be indistinguishable from God Himself. The evil of the world arises entirely from the essential limitations of created things — their limitations as essences or possibilities. Consequently evil is not created by God; but He creates the universe in which there is the least amount of evil that is possible in any system of things.

[23] Cf. Nicholas of Cusa, *Dialogi de ludo globi* (1454–59), i. 157 a: "The whole is reflected in all the parts; all things keep their own relation [*habitudo*] and proportion to the universe." Also *De docta ignorantia* (1440), i. 11: "Visible things are images of the invisible, and the Creator can be seen and known by the creatures as in a mirror darkly [*quasi in speculo et aenigmate*]."

[24] The "point of view" of each Monad is its body. But we must not give a spatial meaning to the expression, as if the Monad's point of view depended on its having this or that position in space. For the Monad is absolutely non-spatial, and the nature of its body depends on the degree of confusedness (or distinctness) of its perceptions. Thus to say that the body is the point of view of the soul means simply that the particular way in which the soul represents or perceives the universe is determined by the degree of distinctness of its perceptions. Cf. *Théodicée*, §357 (E. 607 b; G. vi. 327). "The projections of perspective, which, in the case of the circle, are the same as the Conic Sections, show that one and the same circle can be represented by an ellipse, by a parabola and by a hyperbola, and even by another circle, by a straight line and by a point. Nothing seems more different, nothing more unlike, than these figures; and yet there is an exact relation between them, point for point. Thus it must be recognized that each soul represents to itself the universe, according to its point of view and by a relation peculiar to itself; but in this there always continues to be a perfect harmony."

[25] For Leibniz the highest perfection is the most complete unity or order in the greatest variety. The Monads have the most complete unity, because the essence of each consists in representing the same universe, while they have the greatest variety, because the points of view from which they represent it are infinitely various. . . .

[26] . . . Bayle compares Leibniz's theory to the supposition that a ship might be constructed of such a kind that entirely by itself, without captain or crew, it could sail from place to place for years on end, accommodating itself to varying winds, avoiding shoals, casting and weighing anchor, seeking a haven when necessary and doing all that a normal ship can do. He admits that the omnipotence of God could give such a power to a ship, but he maintains that the nature of the ship would make it impossible for it to receive such a power. And "however infinite be the knowledge and power of God, He cannot, by means of a machine which lacks a certain part, do that which requires the help of that part." Thus Bayle argues against the possibility of complete spontaneity in the Monads, and consequently maintains that the *Deus ex machina* is involved in Leibniz's Pre-established Harmony quite as much as in Occasionalism.

was inclined to think that I was attributing too much to God — more than it is possible to attribute. But he was unable to give any reason which could show the impossibility of this universal harmony, according to which every substance exactly expresses all others through the relations it has with them.

Further, in what I have just said there may be seen the reasons *a priori* why things could not be otherwise than they are. For God in regulating the whole has had regard to each part, and in particular to each Monad, whose nature being to represent, nothing can confine it to the representing of only one part of things; though it is true that this representation is merely confused as regards the variety of particular things [*le détail*] in the whole universe, and can be distinct only as regards a small part of things, namely, those which are either nearest or greatest[27] in relation to each of the Monads; otherwise each Monad would be a deity. It is not as regards their object, but as regards the different ways in which they have knowledge of their object, that the Monads are limited[28]. In a confused way they all strive after [*vont à*] the infinite, the whole[29]; but they are limited and differentiated through the degrees of their distinct perceptions.

[27] If the Monads are non-spatial, how can we speak of anything being nearest or greatest in relation to a Monad? Every Monad has a body of some kind and this body is confusedly perceived as spatial in itself and in relation to other bodies, though *really* it is nothing but an aggregate of non-spatial Monads. When therefore it is said that certain things are near or great in relation to a Monad, what is meant is that they are near or great in relation to the body of the Monad.

[28] That is to say, thought in the widest sense, conscious or unconscious, is limited only by itself: there can be nothing that is not an object of thought, more or less adequate. Contrast with this the position of Kant.

[29] Cf. Nicholas of Cusa, *Dialogus de Genesi* (1447) 72 b: "All things seek the same, which is something absolute."

François Mauriac

Blaise Pascal (1623-1662), mathematician and theologian, is one of the greatest of French geniuses. In the field of hydrodynamics, for example, his experiments led to the invention of the barometer. But the other side of Pascal's genius is even more interesting. A deeply religious person, he early concerned himself with the theological controversies of his day, in which he leaned strongly in the direction of Jansenism. In 1654 he underwent a definitive religious conversion in a mystical experience in which, he believed, he encountered "the God of Abraham, the God of Isaac, the God of Jacob, not of the philosophers and scholars." His famous Pensées *may be described as a scrapbook of reflections intended to vindicate Christianity to those to whom a more systematic argument would be made in vain. He emphasized the element of risk in the life of faith and speaks of the fact that "the heart has its reasons which 'reason' does not know." He has many affinities with modern Christian existentialists, not least in his emphasis on the role of the will in making a decision for or against God.*

In the passage that follows, François Mauriac, a great contemporary French Catholic writer, discusses some aspects of Pascal's life and thought.

On Pascal *

A young man of twenty-four, who had already proved himself the equal of the greatest mathematical geniuses, renounced science to devote himself exclusively to God — to God as He was being revealed by the disciples of the Bishop of Ypres, Jansenius, and whose doctrine the Abbé de Saint Cyran was spreading in France. This was Blaise Pascal. At the age of twenty-four he discovered that the rigorous method which he had brought to science was being used by others, the Jansenists, in the search for true religion.

If religious truth has once been revealed to us, reason, following Jansenius' teaching, must then be applied; all we need to do is to know the truth well and to live it.

Suffering physically, perhaps also humiliated by the starvation and deprivation of his adolescent senses, the young Pascal was — like all great and proud men — profoundly touched by the miserable state of mankind. The power which Jansenism exercised over certain minds stemmed from its clear, simple attitude toward corrupt nature. The wasting away of the flesh, disease, decrepitude, and final decay were, to the Jansenists, merely the image and reflection of the effect of concupiscence upon the lost soul. To perceive that once was to perceive it for all time.

* From *The Living Thoughts of Pascal,* presented by François Mauriac, edited by Alfred O. Mendel. Copyright, 1940, by David McKay Company, Inc. Courtesy of David McKay Company, Inc. Pp. 1–18.

Being tainted from birth we go inexorably toward evil, and Pascal learned from Saint Cyran that this inevitable downfall was punished by eternal castigation. Here he plunged headlong into heresy; he professed that we are condemned forever for following an invincible inclination, as though, in the material world, it were a crime for a man's body to have weight.

Believing in predestination, Pascal, nevertheless, did not despair. One hope remained: perhaps we are loved by God. Some of us are loved; the important thing was to belong to that small number, to be preferred above others. God drew the hearts of His loved ones toward Him, and the joy of His grace was all powerful. But since the sin of Adam, that grace was no longer our due. It was accorded only to those few who were chosen from all eternity — that is, divine mercy given freely, but irresistibly, by which the chosen few were rewarded.

We would not believe that such heresy could have attracted a young man if we did not know that the more terrible the doctrine, the greater the efforts of the believer to find reassurance. Calvin and Jansenius found their theology consoling. "They rob the Father to give to the Son," is Joubert's famous saying about the Jansenists. They hide from the Father to take refuge with the Son; they seek help from the Son against the terrifying image which they themselves created of the infinite Being.

But it is not by reason that they arrive at this concept. In order for Pascal at the age of twenty-four to give himself to Jesus Christ, bringing with him all his dearest ones, it was necessary that he should already be aware of Jesus Christ. He had not yet reached that famous night, eight years later, which was to see him, weeping out of sheer joy, in an ecstasy of love. The taste for sham perspectives has given rise to the legend that he underwent a first conversion, wholly intellectual, which a worldly period was to separate from the second conversion, wholly mystical. In point of fact, from 1646 on, Pascal probably experienced the equivalent of the night of the twenty-third of November, 1654. He himself hints as much; considerably later, speaking of that phase of his youth, he tells his sister Jacqueline that he must have had "horrible bonds" at that time to have resisted the grace which God offered him and the "emotions" with which He filled him. How could these "emotions" have manifested themselves except in tears of joy?

The era of these "horrible bonds" began in 1653, after glorious years, but years made wretched perhaps less by his own sickness than because of his beloved sister Jacqueline's entrance into the cloister at Port Royal. He did not openly deny any of the cloister's Christian principles, but during those years, in that silent atmosphere of God, in the complete abandonment of that way of life, the overperfect nuns and those "gentlemen" of Port Royal for whom the values of the world had no exchange price, were almost more than he could bear.

Suffering and abandoned, Pascal turned to those from whom he received applause, admiration, and friendship. The Jansenists refused to recognize the power of minds like his over inferior minds. But that which they scorned existed nevertheless.

M. Bourdelot, physician to Queen Christine of Sweden (to whom Pascal had dedicated his invention, the arithmetical machine, forerunner of all calculating machines), wrote to Blaise Pascal about this time: "You have the clearest, most penetrating mind I have ever seen. With your devotion to work, you will surpass both the ancients and the moderns . . ."

During this period, Pascal was admired, and also loved with that tenderness which in a young heart often accompanies admiration. Abandoned by his sister Jacqueline, Blaise found much pleasure in the enthusiastic friendship of the Duke de Roannez who, not content with being a fanatical admirer of Pascal's genius, became so personally attached to Pascal that he took him to the province of Poitou, which he governed. Blaise returned his affection, and when he was about to turn to God for the second time, it was the Duke who first prevented him from taking the final step. In order to retire from the world, Pascal had to obtain the Duke's consent, and this the Duke could not grant without tears.

As for Pascal's love-affairs, we know nothing of them. All that has been written about his relations with his friend's sister, Mademoiselle de Roannez, is absurd. If Pascal loved a woman, it would be precisely to her that he could not address such edifying letters as those written in the tone he uses toward Mademoiselle de Roannez. He would not have had the strength to use the tone of both devotee and theologian — what lover has ever had this courage?

We know nothing of Pascal in love, although he speaks of love like one who has suffered from it.

Is *The Discourse on the Passions of Love* entirely from his hand? The least one can say is that the tone of the *Pensées* runs through it. Perhaps Pascal was liked by some women — he was certainly admired by them. Above all, his conversation flattered them, uplifted them in their own eyes and in those of their admirers. But if he loved someone, she was assuredly neither a *précieuse* nor a scholar. The person he would have loved must have had a body as healthy as his own was ill, a youth as triumphant as his own youth was defeated and wounded. He could have cherished only this proud power of flesh and blood which had been denied to him. Everything that has been written about women, all the subtleties of professional psychologists are, where Pascal is concerned, not worth the simple and naked truth contained in seven words uttered by the painter Eugène Delacroix to explain his meagre success in society: "I am too pale and too thin."

In his *Discourse on the Passions of Love,* Pascal has unquestionably written just the contrary: "Women love to perceive a fastidiousness in men, and this is, it seems to me, the most vulnerable point whereby to win them." If he tried to make himself loved he succeeded only in making his spirit loved: "Love strengthens the spirit, and is nourished by the spirit. One needs spirit to love."

One would have to read the entire *Discourse* with real critical detachment in order to pass over the brilliant maxims, the after-dinner dissertations for the use of the ladies, and retain only the unwilling confession, the phrase that is never contrived, the cry of joy or of pain from which the heart is still bleeding.

However, his body betrays him; nothing demands more of health than does pleasure. The textbooks of literature and the encyclopedias give a carriage accident on the Pont de Neuilly as the reason for his conversion. But well before the day when the two horses took the bit in their teeth and leaped into the water, Pascal, surrounded by his strong, enthusiastic friends, must have experienced many times that deep weariness of a man who was different from other men and whose nature was inclined not toward diversion but toward concentration; yet who made a determined effort to turn away from himself, even though his whole spirit urged him to turn inward in order to know himself better.

Even if he had had no attachment of the heart, this life against the current would suffice to reveal his taste for eternal things. But if, in this atmosphere of pleasure, he had exhausted himself in the determined conquest of an indifferent female, to what degree could his pain not have reached? Later he was to write that the effects of love are "fearful." Pleasures no longer amused him; they did not prevent him from seeing himself, his wretchedness, and the death which was perhaps quite near.

It was on the night of the twenty-third of November, 1654, that Blaise Pascal sealed his definitive pact with God. Without the parchment which he always carried sewed into the lining of his doublet, and which was found at his death, we would know nothing of that joy, or of those tears of joy. This "memorial" is lost, but we have a copy from his hand.

From the time he renounced the world up to that unforgettable night, Pascal had turned with all his strength toward God, but it was with the illusion that only his reason had urged him to do so. Cut off from human relations, he could do nothing except wait for divine grace, filled with immense hope, because he had learned from his Jansenist teachers that God ultimately succeeds in drawing the heart of whomever He loves toward Him. Pascal had given up mundane pleasures — he hated them. This hate is the certain sign that he is loved by God; by that God whom he describes in his "memorial" as "the God of Abraham, the God of Isaac, the God of Jacob, *not of the philosophers and scholars.*"

The philosophers and the scholars felt the need for God, until Descartes began using Him only as a final, delicate gesture to set his universe into motion. After that, they learned to do without God who had become nothing but a word — a word: that is, to think of God now meant, for the most part, to think of nothing. How did Pascal find God by himself? This geometrician knew that "that which passes geometry surpasses us." And he knew that even in science no truth is held directly: "Man naturally recognizes only untruth and he must accept as truths only those principles whose opposite appears false to him."

How could Pascal reach God if God did not reach him? He could do nothing except wait and desire. Even this desire did not belong to him — it was the free gift of divine grace, the sign that heralded a miraculous election. And suddenly, on that night, God appeared. There was God — in person, the God of Abraham, Isaac, and Jacob, the God of loving kindness and consolation.

"*Certitude,*" Pascal writes in his "memorial," "*certitude, feeling, joy, peace, God of Jesus Christ.*" The unattainable is attained, and more than attained — possessed, loved, adored — by Jesus, in Jesus.

Everything outside of this is non-existent: — glory, the world. Jesus enters into a tainted creature. With what trembling of admiration does Pascal give us these simple words in the middle of the famous parchment: "*Grandeur of the human soul.*" And a little further on: "*Joy, joy, joy, tears of joy.*"

This man kneeling on the tiled floor of his chamber, weeping, has not reached this state by a tenacious effort of the will. There is nothing which the Christian soul disposes of less liberally than these outward signs.

Perhaps a saint would not have attached such great importance to that joy, to those tears of joy; he would have mistrusted them, for a saint does not seek joy, not even such joy, although he accepts it with humility when it is granted. The Jansenists reproach other Christians for giving too much to the free man and for reducing by that much the power of God. But in the last analysis, it is Jansenism which demands signs, and summons the Creator to console and reassure His creatures.

As one of those who receive salvation with fear and trembling, Pascal had need of joy to keep from losing heart. A time might come perhaps when he would no longer feel anything, when perhaps he could doubt the reality of that fire which, once consumed, leaves the heart cold and black. If then he could only touch the paper that he had sewed in his clothes — the tangible sign which proved there had been no illusion, that he had been visited, possessed soul and body, by living joy!

One should not separate the "memorial" found in the lining of the doublet from the meditation known as "The Mystery of Jesus" and published at the end of the *Pensées* — the meditation to which he undoubtedly devoted himself on that famous night. It was perhaps during that night that he heard the sublime words which he gives to Christ: "*Console thyself, thou wouldst not seek Me if thou hadst not found Me. I thought of thee in Mine agony; I have sweated such drops of blood for thee. . . . Dost thou wish that it always cost Me the blood of My humanity, without thy shedding tears?*"

These words are addressed to a sinner, who rises with difficulty, to a beginner who still stumbles, and it is this that gives them their unique ring. We know what Jesus says to His saints. But here is the way He speaks to the prodigal, to the sheep, lost and recovered. The present collection contains this dialogue between Pascal and Jesus: "*If thou knewest thy sins, thou wouldst lose heart.*" — "*I shall lose it then, Lord, for on Thy assurance I believe their malice. . . . Lord, I give Thee all.*" — "*I love thee more ardently than thou hast loved thine abominations.*"

By this word, abomination, shall we judge Pascal? Or should we accept what his elder sister, Gilberte Perrier, wrote: "But by the mercy of God he was always free from vice"? If he did indulge in vice, Gilberte learned nothing of it, nor did the rest of his family, except perhaps the younger sister, Jacqueline, who wrote to her penitent brother: "I am not astonished that God has shown you this grace, for it seems to me that, in many ways, you might still have been drawn toward the smell of the quagmire which you had embraced so eagerly." If purity had been natural to Pascal, he would not have experienced recovery with such power of feeling. "Without Jesus Christ," he wrote, "man must be in vice and misery."

But even a Christian, however fervent, can conceive of an honest life in the world. Nevertheless, Pascal still insisted, as a cured leper might, that "Apart from Him, there is but vice, misery, error, darkness, death, despair."

After the enlightenment of that famous night, Pascal might be precipitated into the Jansenists' battle against the Jesuits, and give himself up to the fury of the *Provincial Letters,* but he was never again to lose the peace that Christ gives to His loved ones. He might continue to astonish the world with his discoveries and by his works on Roulette, he might write treatises on solids of revolution, resolve the problems of integral calculus, and open the way for the creators of infinitesimal calculus. But he was always to remain anchored in God.

Let us try, then, to picture Blaise Pascal during the last years of his life. He carried the love of purity so far that even his pious sister was astonished — he would not allow a woman's beauty to be praised in his presence. Pascal's hatred for anything that might separate him from Jesus Christ — particularly his hatred for the gratification of the senses — is common to all saints, as is also the love of sickness and poverty. But with Pascal there is an added Jansenist terror of losing the grace he possesses. He feels himself more secure in illness, and blesses infirmity for putting him beyond all covetousness.

The poor occupy him more each day. Jesus identifies Himself with them; to serve them is to serve Him. While admiring the founders of hospitals, and those whom nowadays one calls public benefactors, he liked, as his sister Gilberte tells us, to "serve the poor in poverty." In other words, he liked to have a poor man near him, living beside him. And in as much as he wanted to feel that "such drops of blood had been sweated for him," he likewise wanted that poor man in particular to be his witness before the Saviour on the day when the word would be proclaimed: "I was hungry and you gave me to eat."

He developed a secret distrust of the purest affections, and tried in vain to convince Gilberte that she should no longer permit the caresses of her children. This is typical of that Jansenist mistrust of anything which might jeopardize — even from afar — the happiness of belonging to those chosen few who will never perish.

Not that he rejoiced egoistically in this happiness, since his last energies were used in writing the *Apologie,* of which the *Pensées* remain, and with which he wished to convert sinners. What is difficult to understand in this Jansenist is his hope of changing, by means of a single book, God's eternal pattern of the elect and the damned! Did he believe that the *Apologie* would change their respective numbers by even one unit? Undoubtedly he believed that "Faith embraces many truths that seem to contradict themselves. . . ." But it is strange that he could continue to believe in the God of Jansenius, who had damned a large part of the human race in advance, and that, at the same time, he could live united with the God of gentleness and consolation, the God of Jesus Christ, whose peace he describes in a sublime fragment which appears in this collection, the one beginning: "I love poverty because He loved it . . ."

Up to the end, Pascal struggled against his own heart. He had reflected on love as on everything else, according to his method, and he had arrived at clear principles to which he held fast. He execrated sentimentalism and esteemed only rational tenderness which consists, he said, "in participating in all that happens to our friends, in every way that reason tells us to, at the cost of our property, of our comfort, of our liberty, and even of our life should the object merit it." But the Jansenist in him still appeared in his demand that he should not be loved, in which he was futilely at odds with his own nature. He made a point of being harsh to poor Gilberte to turn her away from her attachment to him. He could not permit himself to be loved with personal attachment, undoubtedly because he naturally felt himself to be only too much inclined in that way. Saints do not know this terror. Pascal must have felt it greatly, and he must have had a strange mistrust of his own heart to have written on a paper which he always carried with him — in this case, not in his coat, as he had done with the "memorial," but within reach of his hand — and the state of which proves he often re-read: "It is unjust that men should attach themselves to me, even though they do it with pleasure and voluntarily. I should deceive those in whom I had created this desire; for I am not the end of any, and I have not the wherewithal to satisfy them. Am I not about to die? And thus the object of their attachment will die. Therefore, as I would be blamable in causing a falsehood to be believed, though I should employ gentle persuasion, and though it should give me pleasure; even so I am blamable in making myself loved. And if I attract persons to attach themselves to me . . . for they ought to spend their life and their care in pleasing God, or in seeking Him."

We have here the strongest proof that Pascal loved and that he was loved. This paper, always at hand, taken up at every temptation, re-read, meditated upon, this written promise that he had to be able to touch, to clasp in his hand whenever he went out of his way to be harsh, to be distant, to rebuff a cherished creature — what irrefutable testimony!

Although he was aware of his power over other minds, Blaise Pascal died without foreseeing that his most casual notes would be collected. Pascal's saintliness required that he should die without knowing this, that he should resign himself to this apparent defeat. Even his friends believed that none of his work would remain: "He will be little known to posterity," wrote the Jansenist Nicole [1625–95]. "What will remain of this great mind but two or three little works, of which there is already so much that is useless?"

Nicole, who was later to reproach the young Sévigné for admiring the *Pensées* too much, and who was to call Pascal a "collector of shells," had not understood that the genius of this man passed the barriers of his sect, that this river could not be contained within the narrow limits of Jansenism. The river was to flow, underground, across the century of Voltaire and Condorcet, and to reappear with greater power than ever in our own time.

After three centuries, Blaise Pascal is still involved in our quarrels; he is alive. His slightest thought troubles, or charms, or irritates, but he is understood instantly, before he has half begun. He is so obviously present that some people reply to him impatiently, ridiculing his eccentricities. Paul Valéry, for instance, calls him "the man who wastes his time sewing papers in his pockets."

This Jansenist is a son of Montaigne. Montaigne was his real teacher, not Jansenius, who taught him nothing about the human heart. Of course Pascal wrote: "It is not in Montaigne that I find everything that I see there, but in myself." But Montaigne served him as a guiding-mark. The valleys and heights of that identical nature and heart which Montaigne observed, were tragically illuminated by Pascal. His lightning rends the heavens and bathes with light the human landscape where the author of the *Essays* fearlessly walked.

An inconsistent Jansenist, Pascal does not resign himself to the chosen few. He knows that Montaigne is not Montaigne alone, but also a countless family of minds who feel that one can come to an understanding with nature — knowing it, they believe, in all its complexities, one can accept it as it is. Far from taking nature tragically, they install themselves in her midst and draw to themselves all the elements necessary to achieve a modest daily happiness. If they become contaminated, if they degrade themselves until their death, they accept that without flinching. Pascal was given the mission of disturbing them — he released a tempest of infinite love over the men of Montaigne.

If the sons of Montaigne deny that they are aware of this tempest, Pascal makes the effort to show them, even in their own nature, the traces of this love, the evidences of refusal, of reprobation, of redemption — just as the geologist deciphers the earth, and, by means of methodical excavations, reconstructs pre-historic life.

Pascal is in accord with Montaigne and with posterity in his desire to know man; he shares their passion for this study of the human heart to such an extent that he is more at home with his worldly friends, such as the Chevalier de Méré, or Miton, than with the austere Jansenists, MM. de Rebours and de Sacy. The more Pascal devotes himself to that knowledge of man, the greater becomes his admiration for the "*honnête homme*." This was the term he used to designate the man without pride, who cannot be called either a mathematician or a preacher, and in whom the world observes no outstanding quality except when there is need to make use of it. The Chevalier de Méré was undoubtedly referring to Pascal when he said: "I have a friend who would travel to India only to see an *honnête homme*."

When he writes his *Apologie*, it is this love for the "*honnête homme*" that incites Pascal to establish himself in the very heart of the natural man. And while the implacable Jansenist, M. de Sacy, sees in Montaigne the "object of demons and the pasture of worms," Pascal, on the other hand, utilizes the work of Montaigne (though apparently it had no such purpose) to convince unbelievers; it is Pascal who throws Montaigne into the current of redemption.

There lies one of the secrets of his power: he has no contempt for his adversary. Pascal declares that he will devote his energies toward the knowledge of himself. Even though "that will not serve to find the truth," it will "serve at least to order his life." Thus he accepts Montaigne's weapons.

Even after his conversion he cannot deny himself a grand indulgence toward the author of the *Essays*. "One can excuse," he notes, "his feelings — which are a bit free and sensual in certain encounters with life." Pascal's adversary is aware that he is faced by someone who does not misunderstand him, who goes so far as to recognize that the evil from which he recoils sometimes demands "an extraordinary grandeur of the soul." Pascal denies nothing that concerns man; he traverses all that is man in order to reach God.

It is admirable that this prodigious genius, century after century, could have been able to mingle with the crowd of restless beings, that he could have kept himself at their level, and, without ever lowering himself, could have put himself in the place of every one of us.

Every thinking man, even the free-thinker, joins Pascal as he joins Montaigne. Because of his passionate desire to know the singularities and the contradictions in the real man, the least of his *Pensées* touches a sensitive spot in us, and inevitably awakens a response. Pascal remains our equal in the most profound sense of the word, accepted as such by the most personal and individual part of ourselves. With real justification he can compare men to organs, the keys of which he knows and plays upon.

"Pascal possesses to the highest degree of intensity the feeling of the human person." This single phrase of Sainte-Beuve's defines the secret of his power. Geometrician that Pascal was, he ridiculed matter! Our mechanical civilization would perhaps have made this mechanician — who has stated that all the human bodies in the world are not worth man's slightest thought, and that all science and all philosophy are not worth the slightest sign of love — shrug his shoulders.

Pascal's Jansenist theology does not separate him from orthodox Christians. If Jansenius had condemned him to despair as he did so many other poor souls, Pascal would not have won posterity. But despair is a form of solitude from which he was saved. Taking a sharply turning path, he hoisted himself to the least solitary rock in the world — and there he has mingled with the crowd which has gathered about the Cross, waiting for all to be consummated.

It was not his prodigious mind through which he dominated inferior minds, that enabled him, above all else, to become a saint; it was not even his knowledge of man, that inexhaustible subject which the author of the *Pensées* explored to such lengths. Pascal's guiding force is his heart, the heart which he possesses in common with God's most humble creatures. Like them, he has clung with his two arms to the bloody Tree, and has not lifted his eyes much higher than the pierced feet of his Saviour.

A sinner, a convert is never alone. The great Pascal is the brother of all sinners, of all converts, of all wounded men whose wounds may reopen at any instant, of all whom Christ has pursued from afar, and who trust only in His love.

Howard Albert Johnson

Søren Aabye Kierkegaard (1813-1855) was a Danish religious thinker in some ways more poet than philosopher whose work is nevertheless of the greatest importance in the history of philosophic thought. Although he was largely ignored till about seventy years after his death, Kierkegaard's immense originality and profound significance has since been increasingly recognized. It is difficult to appreciate the significance of Kierkegaard without considerable knowledge of the philosophical and religious climate in which he was reared; nor is it easy even to understand him at all without reading at length in his works. The following essay, by Howard Albert Johnson, Canon Theologian at the Cathedral of St. John the Divine, New York City, and a distinguished interpreter of Kierkegaard, is provided by way of introduction to Kierkegaard's peculiar genius. It is based on an article by Canon Johnson in Theology Today *(January, 1945).*

On Kierkegaard *

There was a man in Denmark one hundred years ago, named Søren Kierkegaard, who felt terror at the age which was then coming to birth. It was the age in which man decided to build the Kingdom of God on earth.

This was everywhere hailed as a pious project, and was encouraged even by the Christian Church. But to Kierkegaard the undertaking was a sacrilege, based on the illusion of self-redemption.

What made the illusion difficult to dispel was the curious duplexity of the phenomenon itself. It had a sparing dose of Christianity in it. It was, in part, an expression of man's genuine longing for redemption, and the doctrine of progress itself had a Christian root. But Kierkegaard detected that, for all its calling upon God, it was a new and very subtle assertion of man's sovereignty against God. In place of the old trilogy, "Nature, Man, and God," life was more and more being thought of as the interplay between *two* entities, Nature and Mankind. Nothing more was needed than a greater exercise of the intelligence by which man would be able to alter and master the natural world. Thus, Utopia was assured. Kierkegaard could not shake off his impression that little by little God was being spirited away. In the churches God was accorded the deference due to a Rector Emeritus; meanwhile, a more vigorous administration held committee meetings to settle on policy. The policies discussed began on earth and ended on earth.

From its preachers, the age demanded a testimony (Goetheo-Hegelian) that man was well on the way of becoming holy and that the Kingdom of God was a simple human possibility. Naturally, it required considerable virtuosity

* Howard A. Johnson, *The Deity in Time.* Used by permission of the author.

on the part of exegesis to get the New Testament to say this, but it was accomplished, ingeniously enough, by dropping out original sin at the beginning and eschatology at the ending. If perhaps the ideal requirements seemed a little beyond man's reach, they were cunningly explained as having been made purposely hard — just as clocks are set forward in order to get us places on time! If this bore but scant resemblance to traditional Christianity, it seemed to trouble no one . . . except Kierkegaard, for where, in such an order of things, is there any need for a *saviour*? ". . . If the requirement is no greater, then a saviour, a redeemer, grace &c., become fantastic luxuries. . . . What Christianity presupposes — namely, the tortures of a contrite conscience, the need of grace, the deeply felt need, all these frightful inward conflicts and sufferings — what Christianity presupposes in order to introduce and supply grace, salvation, the hope of eternal blessedness, all this is not to be found, or is to be found only in burlesque abridgement . . ."[1]

The "burlesque abridgement" has received classic formulation, one hundred years later, in Richard Niebuhr's fine satiric sentence: "A God without wrath brought men without sin into a kingdom without judgment through the ministrations of a Christ without a cross."[2] It is Christianity with the bass register left out. The ancient and orthodox notion that between God and man there is an infinite difference of quality has here been abolished by the simple expedient of domesticating the Eternal and eternalizing the domestic. This is the definition of culture-religion, and S.K. branded "Christendom" as such. He saw it as a profane messianism, in which man himself was scheduled to be the messiah, and the goal — chiliasm *à la bourgeois*. He foresaw that the age, like Jeshurun of old, would wax fat . . . and then forsake God. When Jeshurun had become sleek, he "lightly esteemed the Rock of his salvation" and bowed himself down to "new gods that came up of late." The name of these? Progress, Science, Education, Humanity. These things gave us the Century of Progress, a century of progressive concern with the creature rather than the Creator. Kierkegaard knew that upon these things the wrath of God would fall. For God is love. And God will not tolerate idols because idols are not good for man.

When he warned that the skies were about to fall, his contemporaries dubbed him a misanthropic Chicken Little. In our day, however, the tragic consequences of finite self-sufficiency have become apparent. The idol's clay feet are breaking. Like the prophets of Israel, S.K. is read and heard only after the event. His apprehension at the beginning of the age is ours at its end. The warnings with which he tried to save us from our fate now help us to interpret our fate. Kierkegaard in the nineteenth century was trying to do what God in our century is doing by means of two world wars and the threat of a third.

The contemporary novelist Jacob Wassermann, for example, (in *The World's Illusion*) has understood in retrospect what Kierkegaard understood in prospect:

[1] *For Self-Examination* and *Judge for Yourselves!*, Oxford, 1941, p. 209.
[2] *The Kingdom of God in America,* Willet, Clark & Company, 1937, p. 193.

> Humanity to-day has lost its faith. Faith has leaked out like water from a cracked glass. Our age is tyrannised by machinery: it is a mob rule without parallel. Who will save us from machinery and from business? The golden calf has gone mad. The spirit of man kowtows to a warehouse. Our watchword is to be up and doing. We manufacture Christianity, a renaissance, culture, et cetera. If it's not quite the real thing, yet it will serve. Everything tends toward the external — toward expression, line, arabesque, gesture, mask. Everything is stuck on a boarding and lit by electric lamps. Everything is the very latest, until something still later begins to function. Thus the soul flees, goodness ceases, the form breaks, and reverence dies. Do you feel no horror at the generation that is growing up? The air is like that before the flood.

Having depicted S.K. as a prophet, I must at once remark that he did not wear a hairy mantle. Nor was he a grim and sour critic of human culture. In his own life he exemplified the maxim he asserted, that by the religious the aesthetic is not abolished but merely dethroned. He liked wine and good cigars and good company and the opera and long carriage rides into the country where he could enjoy the beauties of nature. The "aesthetic works," which were an important part of his literary production, demonstrate, as he meant them to do, his appreciation of the highest attainments of culture. These he opposed only when they cried, "Peace, peace; no evil shall come upon you."

Those who on the ground of his psychological peculiarities would dispense themselves from the necessity of heeding S.K. must at least recognize that he saw deeper into the human mind than more normal men have been able to see; and even the summary exposition of his thought which I essay to give here surely suffices to show that he was a cogent, consistent, and profound thinker, from whom one can escape, if at all, only by thinking more profoundly.

Existential Thinking

When Kierkegaard read the Hegelian philosophy, that vast system embracing all celestial and terrestrial knowledge, he had the impression that the whole world had been gained and the individual human soul lost. Compendious though this globe-girdling system was, it contained no ethic, no word of advice to an existing human being as to how he should live. It proudly deserted existence and left an ethical individual in the lurch.

Death was talked about with immense erudition . . . by men who spoke as if they themselves were somehow exempt from this dread experience. Immortality was everywhere learnedly discussed, yet faith in immortality (i.e. a belief in immortality that has retroactive power to transform one's mode of existence) everywhere declined. Christianity, too, came in for studious attention, not however as a demand upon men for experience and personal appropriation, but as a phenomenon whose historicity was first to be verified by unwearying philological research and whose place in the world-historical process was then to be assigned, so as to exhibit wherein it had been adumbrated in paganism and Judaism and to what extent it accorded with the eternal truths of pure reason. And of course not even God could escape the indignity of an explanation! He too had to pass before Reason's reviewing stand and report for inspection. His existence was more and more asserted . . . by proofs; less and less proved . . . by worship.

The old age sought to justify man before God and ended with faith in God alone. Our age sought to justify God to man and ended with faith in Man alone. Theodicy replaced theology.

Whenever you find men idly tinkering with the idea of God, you may be sure that they have no very clear conception of what they themselves are. In a voluptuous metaphysical dream, philosophers fumble after a conception of God without feeling any terror thereat. On the contrary, they plume themselves upon their gnostic proclivities. The whole procedure is a degenerate cleverness, an immoral *divertissement*, in which ethics is given the run-around. An exasperated Kierkegaard exclaims: "So rather let us sin, sin out and out, seduce maidens, murder men, commit highway robbery — after all, that can be repented of, and upon such a criminal God can still get a grip. But this proud superiority which has risen to such a height scarcely can be repented of, it has a semblance of profundity which deceives. So rather let us mock God out and out, as has been done before in the world — this is always preferable to the disparaging air of importance with which one would prove God's existence."[3]

Reflective thought, according to Kierkegaard, arrives only at the idea of God. Argument, at best, may make it probable that a God exists; but this Idea of God is only an *x*, itself unexplained, explaining nothing. Not one of the arguments for the existence of God can protect itself against the intrusion of dialectics. The ontological argument, for example, is a "deceptive movement of thought," an evasion of the real difficulty which is "to introduce God's ideal essence dialectically into the sphere of factual existence." The cosmological and teleological arguments are also beset with difficulties. "I contemplate the order of nature in the hope of finding God, and I see omnipotence and wisdom; but I also see much else that disturbs my mind and excites anxiety. The sum of all this is an objective uncertainty."[4]

After a naked dialectical analysis of the traditional proofs, Kierkegaard was forced to the conclusion that the "proofs" cannot give incontestable certainty. By a continued quantitative progression no new quality is produced; there can be no smooth and easy transition to faith. It is impossible, by successive logical steps, which involve no break in quality, to reason in the following manner: it is probable that there is a God, very probable, highly probable, exceedingly probable, *ergo:* God. Similarly, with regard to Christology, we cannot start with Jesus as a man who is so good, so very good, so excellently good, so preëminently good that *therefore* He is God. "God" is something

[3] *Concluding Unscientific Postscript*, Princeton, 1941, p. 485.

[4] *Postscript*, p. 182. There is in the *Postscript* at p. 298 a masterly analysis of the ontological argument. This is also dealt with, along with the physico-teleological proof, in Chapter III of the *Philosophical Fragments* (Princeton, 1936). Cf. the discourse, "What It Means to Seek God," in *Thoughts on Crucial Situations in Human Life* (Augsburg, 1941), and the discourse, "God Greater than Our Heart," in *Christian Discourses* (Oxford, 1939).

qualitatively different; our logic is guilty of a fallacy, a discontinuity, a *μετάβασις εἰς ἄλλο γένος*. God can be reached only by an act of faith, a leap.

When for every *pro*, reflection can suggest an equally cogent *contra*, so tha the thinker is run to a standstill and all he possesses is an objective uncer tainty, here, if he is willing to take the risk of committing himself to an error precisely here he can leap. The leap of faith is a passionate decision to believe in spite of the uncertainty. Were a man capable of proving God's existence objectively, he would not have to have *faith* that God is; he would *know* Precisely because he cannot know, he must believe or else suspend decision To believe in God is not to give intellectual assent to a proposition but to confide one's life to Him. Faith is a venture which chooses an objective un certainty with infinite passion, counting every delay a deadly peril.

Take a picture. A wader feels his way with his foot lest he get beyond hi depth. Shrewd and prudent, he wants probability, proof, demonstration tha the water will support him. He insists on keeping at least one toe on the bottom. Well, he can wade from now till doomsday, but so long as he wades he will never understand what swimming is. As a spectator standing knee deep, he can see others swimming and perhaps describe this phenomenon with complete scientific accuracy. But as for himself? Does *he* know wha swimming is like? This he can never know so long as he has not the faitl to entrust himself to the water. It is impossible to swim if you will not pu your life in jeopardy of drowning. You must launch out into the deep. With out risk there is no faith. Faith is swimming with seventy thousand fathom beneath you.

Where Do We Stand?

Thus does Kierkegaard make us aware of where we stand. We stand at the jumping-off place, for not by any logical construction can we span the gap The question is, will we jump? Not to jump is despair. To jump is faith This needs to be explained.

Let us first of all agree to be human beings. Let us start from our actua human situation and go in search of God. Mindful of our creatureliness, we shall eschew the pretension involved in trying to stand outside existence to look at things, including God, *sub specie aeterni*. We shall abandon the role of world-historic genius and *extraordinarius* admitted to fraternize with God in the royal box as spectator of universal history, and stand quite humbl where, in fact, we do stand: as finite, existing human beings, facing the futur in all its uncertainty, compelled to act in order to live. He who begins to tel us right off what God is in His own essence, what God was doing befor

[5] The "leap" (*Springet*) is a favorite subject for parody on the part of people wh have made up their minds beforehand not to like S.K. It will be well, then, to let Dr Walter Lowrie explain it. "It is by this metaphor that S.K. expresses his passionat repudiation of the smooth transition Hegel sought to effect by means of mediation S.K. protests that there is no real movement in logic, no genuine *becoming*, and tha in existence every movement which effects a real change is a "leap", an act of freedom This applies especially to faith, which is not attained by continuous and gradua approximation but by a resolution of the will, in 'the Instant' " (*Kierkegaard*, Oxford 1938, p. 628).

the creation of the world, etc., we shall quite summarily accuse of an attempt *à la* Munchausen.

Natural science and so also history can tell us something about the ground on which we stand. An archaeologist, returning from an expedition in the Near East, had this report to make. "We dug and dug until, at a depth of sixty feet, we uncovered the remains of a civilization 6000 years old. It had begun somehow, flourished for a while, and then had withered and died. It lay buried in its own dust. Immediately on top of that burial ground were the relics of another civilization, and so on. As I climbed out of that pit sixty feet deep, with each of my sixty steps I traversed one century of blood, sweat, and tears. There — layer upon layer — was a cross section of human history, 6000 years of it. And when, at the end of the day, I reached the top, look as I might in every direction, I could see nothing but vast, empty, barren, desert waste. And I said, Vanity of vanities. All is vanity."

We do not like this. We do not like it one bit. With the entire passion of our being we are opposed. We hunger to be freed from this futility that waits to engulf us. And do not give us the old song and dance that it is pride that makes us long for immortality. Not pride. At least, not pride alone. It is terror at the thought of extinction. It is protest against the insanity and injustice of a miserable merry-go-round that finally breaks down. We will not have it that our life is a "tale told by an idiot, full of sound and fury, signifying nothing."

But the evidence seems to be against us. A man is born, grows up, marries, begets children, becomes an alderman, takes sick, and dies — behold! these are his memoirs. Life is dog eat dog, and death takes not only the hindmost. Death takes us all.

This is man's situation. This is our predicament. Worse, it is *my* predicament. What then? Why then, three rival ways beckon to me: the aesthetic, the ethical, and the religious.[6]

Three "Stages" on Life's Way

If I want to I can sit myself down at an epicure's table to eat, drink, and be merry. But, as William James saw, no matter how merry the feasting, the skull will look in and grin at the banquet. Life lived in aesthetic categories may have an illusory brilliance, but it is nevertheless concealed despair, a desperate and unsuccessful fight against *ennui* and *angst*.[7]

There is no way to break this despair except by a leap. By an act of my own free choice, I can make the jump from aesthetic eudemonism to an ethical standpoint. If so, I brace myself stoically against my coming end; in the meantime, I grit my teeth and fight for personal integrity and the civic virtues. I

[6] There is, of course, a fourth possibility: world-and-life-negating mysticism. Here life is understood in terms of the σωμα-σημα pun. Release from the tragedy of life is sought by a retreat into eternity via recollection. For S.K., however, this is not a possibility; for the back door route to eternity by way of contemplation is barred by the fact of sin. Cf. *Fragments*, Ch. I; *Either/Or*, Vol. II, pp. 202 ff.

[7] *Angst:* anguished dread present in all human beings as the conscious or semi-conscious realization of the unsupported character of all existence. Our existence rests upon an abyss of nothingness. Hence, a dread of the future.

take up the position proposed by Sénancour: "Man is perishable. That may be; but let us perish resisting, and if it is nothingness that awaits us, do not let us so act that it shall be a just fate." Yet this again is despair, and few men are capable of living ethically, in heroic defiance of what Bertrand Russell has strikingly called "the trampling march of unconscious power." At best ethical endeavor is back-breaking labor. But here it is like polishing the brass of a sinking vessel. For all our exertion we do not budge from the place where destruction is. The real difficulty with "unyielding despair" is that, in most cases, finally it yields. In Kierkegaard's judgment, a purely humanistic ethic cannot maintain itself for long. It loses heart. It gets stifled by the tragic sense of life.

Atheistic ethical humanism, the position here described, belongs still to what Kierkegaard calls the aesthetic (or secular) sphere. It is, he says, "an ethical form of the aesthetic" and is part of "the perilous transition from the aesthetic to the [true] ethical"; but then, if the transition be not effected, it must be stigmatized as "a degenerate form of the ethical."

If the despair inherent in atheistic ethical humanism is to be broken, says Kierkegaard, it can be broken only by leaping again. This time to an ethico religious sphere. As Kierkegaard uses words, the authentic "ethical" means the standpoint of *theistic* ethical humanism. In certain respects, legalistic Judaism could be subsumed under this heading. So also Unitarianism. So also extremely liberal and moralistic versions of Christianity. So also, for example, Kantian ethical idealism. And so forth. Nearly every culture affords examples. By "ethical" Kierkegaard means any world-and-life-affirming ethic which rests on a theistic basis, with sanctions in an after-life.

Here we are conscious of ourselves as responsible beings, who are accountable to a Divine Law. "Thus and thus shalt thou do and thou shalt live." This is God's own truth. There is an eternal life in which wrongs will be redressed and justice done, a new world in which war shall be no more, neither tears nor sorrow nor death. Rejoice in it! Here is your absolute good, here is your *telos*. Now strive for it!

These words arouse my whole passion. I can be made free from sin and death! And this is what I want — mind, body, and soul. The bowels yearn for it. I feel a desperate need for it in the very marrow of my bones.

This is what Kierkegaard calls an existential problem. It concerns my existence both here and hereafter. It is, thus, a pathetic-dialectic problem. Pathetic, in that it involves all my passion, all my earnestness. Dialectic, in that it brings into play all my powers of thinking, attracting me and yet repelling me because it seems contrary to the evidence. Can I be indubitably sure that there really *is* such a good? No. Could it be proved incontestably? No. And yet I must venture absolutely everything for its sake? Yes. But is that not risky? Yes; this is *either/or*. *Either* despair/*or* the leap. Will you risk it? Then jump.

If I jump, venturing everything, I do not find myself transported to the seventh heaven or to any promised land or to a bed of roses. I find myself standing exactly where I stood before, but now I have a task. And that task is to relate myself to this conception of an eternal blessedness in such a way that it involves the reconstruction of my entire mode of existence. It must take hold of me in the very core of my being so as to bring the whole man into conformity with it. I give my life an absolute direction towards the absolute *telos.* And this is expressed in action through the transformation of my existence. All finite satisfactions are voluntarily relegated to the status of what may have to be renounced in favor of the eternal blessedness. The ethical task, accordingly, is simultaneously to sustain an absolute relationship to the absolute *telos* and a relative relationship to relative ends.[8]

The task is set. Now begin it . . . Aye, *just try!* On paper the task looks easy enough. Who is not a mighty man on paper? But in real life, as soon as I set out to relate myself absolutely to the absolute *telos* and relatively to the relative ends, I discover, to my dismay, that I am in the opposite situation: I am absolutely committed to relative ends! I am stuck fast in immediacy. Something is so wrong with me that I am not yet ready to essay the ideal task but must first of all do something else before the ideal task can even be begun. I must first begin by exercising myself in the far humbler task of renunciation. The relativities have got to be dethroned. But this is hard. It hurts to give up my many goods in order to strive absolutely for the absolute good. This is like being called upon to cut off the offending hand and pluck out the offending eye. Renunciation cuts to the quick. The one God summons me to a policy of iconoclasm, and alas! I am Icon No. 1. Self-annihilation is a fearful thing. And the truth of the matter is that I never quite succeed; the first annihilation is not thorough enough; I never get beyond the possibility of falling back; self-assertion returns in multiple ways; the danger does not diminish. I shall have to keep at the task of renunciation and mortification as long as I live, and this means the persistence of inward suffering my whole life long.[9]

Thus things go backward. The task is presented to me in existence, and just as I am ready at once to cut a fine figure and want to begin, it is discovered that a new beginning is necessary, the beginning upon the immense detour of dying from immediacy; and just when the beginning is about to be made at this point, it is discovered that there, *since time has meanwhile been passing,* an ill beginning is made, and that the actual beginning must be made by acknowledging that I am guilty. I awaken, not at birth, but as one who has already been alive — for a long time. All the while I was deliberating I was ethically responsible for my use of time. Even at the instant when the task was clearly set there has been some waste, for meanwhile time has passed, and the beginning was not made at once. I am a man with a history, a man with a bad past.

The consciousness of guilt is a man's first deep plunge into existence. Now the exister is in thorough distress, i.e. now he is truly in the medium of real life. It isn't that he sometimes fails. Essentially he always fails. If a man says he finds nothing to repent of, it is because he judges himself by human standards alone. He who justifies himself, denounces himself as one who no longer stands related to the ideal standard.

"If a man would have an essential understanding of his guilt, he must understand it through being alone, just he alone, alone with the Holy One who knows all. . . . The more profound the sorrow is, the more a man feels

[8] Cf. *Postscript,* pp. 347–385.

[9] Cf. *Postscript,* pp. 386–468.

himself to be nothing, less than nothing, and this diminishing self-esteem is the sign that the sorrowful is the seeker who is beginning to be conscious of God."[10]

Here he will discover that "confession is not merely an enumeration of particular sins, but is an understanding before God, of the continuity of sin in itself."[11] From his mistakes, his slips, he comes to understand the deeper malady: that sin is an unfathomable continuity, a *qualitative* determination His peccadillos, though they do not exactly shatter the world, bring the deeper malady to light. The little symptomatic mistakes exhibit his distance from God, so that now he understands himself under the total determinant: guilt This is the decisive expression for existential pathos in relation to God.

Slowly — imperceptibly, almost — Kierkegaard has led us from theistic ethical humanism to that which is, in fact, its opposite.

It was the happy presupposition of the ethicist that the personality is essentially sound. Basically man is all right. It was assumed that once the individual had accepted the moral task he could *of course* perform it. All he had to do was develop his own innate moral potentialities. The necessary strength, it was thought, lay immanent within the self. By individual self-discipline and determined self-effort, victory was assured.

It follows that, were the ethical ideal capable of realization, no scope would be found for the religious life in any deeper sense. To be sure, the ethicist has a religious vocabulary. He *speaks* of God and of immortality. But he does not enter into any personal relationship with God. God is *there,* simply as the background for the ethical life. He is there as Creator and as Lawgiver He is there to provide ultimate sanctions for morality. He is there as a God of justice and righteousness to undergird the universe and the ethical enterprise. And *after* this life, God will mete out appropriate rewards and punishments. But during *this* life, the ethicist has not in any decisive sense, a personal relationship with God. He merely accepts his duty from Him. Ethics then, means action, and the mood of the ethicist is victory.

But, in Kierkegaard's own experience, this mood of victory cannot endure for long if one takes the ethical requirements seriously. Actually, its requirement is so infinite that the individual always goes bankrupt.

In trying to conform his life to the ideal requirements, the ethicist begins to discover that there is something wrong with him. The more deeply this discovery is made, the more profound the sense of guilt and the sense of need What does it profit us that an eternal blessedness is promised the righteous when the Law makes it terrifyingly evident that we ourselves are *un*righteous

Thus, Kierkegaard has brought us — step by step — to what he calls *Religiousness* A. In formal content, Religiousness A is the same as the Kierkegaardian ethical stage, but psychologically and experientially the *mood* is different. *Religiousness* A arises when a man at last reaches the agonizing awareness of *incommensurability;* i.e., he sees with despair that he cannot measure up Alas! he does not have what it takes. After hearing the Commandments in all their severity, all he can do is confess his guilt and turn to the Lord with the cry: *Kyrie eleison!*

[10] *Crucial Situations,* p. 24 and p. 27.
[11] *Crucial Situations,* p. 30. Cf. *Postscript,* pp. 468–493.

This is *Religiousness* A, where self-esteem, self-trust, and the illusion of self-redemption are in process of destruction. It is a stage of ethical endeavor and failure, of redoubled exertion and renewed defeat, then of frantic striving and, finally, of despair. *Angst* in a new formation now seizes a man. The dreadful thing is no longer death and the encounter with nothingness; the dreadful thing is death and the encounter with God.

The ethical sphere, then, was only a transitional sphere. Its purpose was to develop a receptivity for religion. Its function was to develop within man a sense of need for God. Its highest expression is repentance as a negative action.

Who Can Be Saved?

Already the Old Testament understands that there are not many righteous, and the Apocrypha is beginning to wonder if there are any righteous enough to deserve salvation; then along comes Jesus of Nazareth who says, "With men it is impossible."

Now we are back again to that very precipice from which we tried to escape *via* ethical endeavor. We stand at the edge of the same abyss. Every ethical teaching of Jesus serves to point to this abyss, to remind us of the abyss, to show us how unbridgeable it is. Understand the Ten Commandments as Our Lord unveils them in the Sermon on the Mount, as referring not only to overt acts but to inward motive as well. Will we then be able to justify ourselves? Will we then be able to congratulate ourselves on being law-abiders? Or will we not rather find ourselves joining in the agonizing apostolic cry, "Who then *can* be saved?" This is the end of ethics as a way for men to go to God. *Religiousness* A, consisting in all those efforts, however various, by which a man tries to transform his existence to make it pleasing to God, ends in failure.

Like Paul, Kierkegaard sees it clearly. The Law is against us. He sees that we stand condemned, trapped, indefensible. The prisoner has been boxed. There is no escape. The verdict is *guilty*. The penalty, DEATH.

But now, something very curious happens. Does Paul, does S.K. hate the Law? No. They say, "The Law, although it slays us, is good. The Law is a schoolmaster to bring us to Christ." Is this not a curious *non sequitur*? What can they mean? They mean that *Religiousness* A is the necessary propaedeutic for *Religiousness B*. The Law is the "existential training school" in ethics which, by destroying self-trust and teaching the impossibility of self-justification, drives them out in search of a *saviour*. They no longer inquire, "What good thing shall *I* do to inherit life?" Now, prompted by utter need for help from beyond the self, they cry *de profundis*, "*Who* shall deliver me from this death?" The Law, by telling them the bad news about themselves, has made them attentive, for the first time, to the Good News about Jesus Christ.[12]

[12] Cf. *Postscript*, pp. 493–498; cf. *The Concept of Dread* (Princeton, 1944), pp. 13ff.: "Ethics points to ideality as a task and assumes that man is in possession of the condition requisite for performing it. Thereby ethics develops a contradiction, precisely for the fact that it makes the difficulty and the impossibility clear. What is said of the Law applies to ethics, that it is a severe schoolmaster, which in making a demand, by its demand only condemns, does not give birth to life."

To put this Good News as simply as possible, it is that God has done something in history on the basis of which sins are forgiven, redemption is received, the sharpness of death overcome, and the kingdom of heaven opened to all believers. The Deity has appeared in time "for us men and for our salvation." Since man could not go to God, God has come to man. The abyss has been closed from the divine side. Because He stood where we stood — in the dock — we no longer have to stand there. *Nostra assumsit, ut conferret nobis sua.* This is *Religiousness B.* It is the Absolute Paradox. It is the *Miracle.*[13]

Here we must supply, as Kierkegaard does, the whole Apostles' Creed, for it tells us how with God all things — even that most incredible of things, man's salvation — *is* possible. Kierkegaard prefers to explain this Divine Possibility in the form of a parable.[14]

The Divine Incognito

> There was a king who loved a humble maiden. No power on earth could stand in his way of accomplishing his purpose to marry her. But an anxious thought awoke in the heart of the king. Would she be happy in the life at his side? Would she be able to summon confidence enough never to remember what the king wished only to forget — that he was king and she, nothing but a peasant?
>
> The king mentioned this anxiety to no one; for if he had, each courtier would have said, "Your Majesty is about to confer a favor upon the maiden, for which she can never be sufficiently grateful her whole life long." But the king did not wish to have the maiden grovel before him

---

[13] *The Word became flesh.* "That that which in accordance with its nature is eternal, comes into existence in time, is born, grows up, and dies — this is the breach with all thinking" (*Postscript*, p. 513). This is Christianity's Absolute Paradox. Divinely, eternally theocentrically it may be no paradox, but no existing human being is able to look at it divinely, eternally, theocentrically. To him it is and remains a paradox. This is the sphere of faith. It can be believed altogether — against the understanding. If anyone imagines that he understands it, he can be sure he misunderstands it, having confounded Christianity with one or another pagan analogy. (Cf. *Postscript*, pp. 498–515.)

From the paradoxical character of the Miracle follow two important consequences:

(1) The paradox is related essentially to man as man, and qualitatively related to every man severally, whether he has much or little understanding. This is not esoteric *gnosis*. The simplest man can grasp the central fact, and the wisest man will never be able to exhaust it.

(2) Because the historical fact in question is not a simple fact, immediate contemporaneity is of no avail. Nor can learned historical inquiry help to annul the paradox so as to eliminate the risk it involves. There is no simple and direct transition from the reliability of an historical account to an eternal blessedness. In relation to the paradox we all stand equally close, equally distant. Whatever the century in which we live, whatever our varying intellectual endowments, these accidental circumstances have no power to differentiate our fortunes with respect to it. For it is a gamble, a risk, a leap. (Cf. *Fragments*. Cb. IV, Interlude, and Ch. V; cp. *Training in Christianity*, Oxford, 1941, pp. 66ff.)

[14] As quoted, it is abridged, paraphrased, and mutilated, from Chapter II of the *Fragments*. S.K. asks us to bear in mind that no analogy perfectly accords with the unique evangelic fact.

in abject gratitude all her life; he wanted her to be his equal, his wife, one with him in love.

It occurred to him that the union might be brought about by an *elevation* of the maiden. Make her a fine lady, give her a title and estates. The king could have done this secretly, and the maiden need never know how it was that her fortune was made. And the maiden might be greatly inclined to prize this. Intoxicated by her remarkable change of station, she might forget the old peasant days. Then could the king woo her. But the king, being a just man, perceived that such a method was deceitful. Not by deception can their love be made happy, except perhaps in appearance, for it would rest upon a falsification of the facts.

Another possibility occurred to the king. He might array himself in gorgeous robes of state and, coming suddenly to the maiden's cottage, overawe her with the pomp of his power. Seeing the regal apparition, she would have bowed down and quite forgotten herself in worshipful adoration. Alas! this might have satisfied the maiden, to give glory to the king, but it could not satisfy the king, because he desired not his own glorification but hers.

Here, then, is the king's dilemma: if he does not show himself to the maiden, his love for her would die, since it could have no chance to express itself; but if he shows himself to her in all his splendor, then the maiden will die — for she cannot be a wife who is totally prostrated with fear and awe.

There once lived a people who had a profound understanding of the divine. This people thought that no one could see God and live. Who grasps this contradiction of sorrow? Not to reveal oneself is the death of love, to reveal oneself is the death of the beloved!

Outwardly, this has been the story of a king who loved a maiden. Inwardly, it is the story of God's love for men. Moved by love, God is eternally resolved to reveal Himself, to communicate His own divine life to us. It may seem a small matter for God to make Himself understood to us, but this is not so easy of accomplishment as we may think. For God is God, and we are men and sinful men. The inequality between the king and the maiden is only a poor human symbol of the inequality between God and us men. Here there is an endless qualitative difference. And the nobility of the king in not wishing to deceive the maiden or strip her of free choice in the matter is but a meagre token of the nobility of God in not wishing to deceive us and strip us of our freedom.

We have seen how the king's love of the maiden was doomed to defeat if the king deceived her by enriching her with titles and estates. Even so, God might conceivably elevate sinful man, take him up into Himself, transfigure him, fill his cup with millennial joys, and let the sinner forget himself in tumultuous ecstasy. And the sinner might call this happiness, but it would not be the real happiness that God longs to give man: full personal communion.

We have seen how the king thought of appearing to the maiden in monarchical pomp, so that the maiden might forget herself in reverent admiration. Even so, God might reveal Himself to us in all His effulgent majesty; and, at the sight of Him, we would prostrate ourselves and worship Him. And that would satisfy us, but it could not satisfy God. For God does not desire His glorification but ours. God will do anything to win us to His love — anything but coerce us.

Therefore, the union must be brought about in some other way. Since we found that it could not be brought about by an elevation of the maiden (or the sinner, let us say now), it must be attempted by a *descent* on the part of the king (or let us say God now). Let the sinner be called *x*. In this *x* we must include the lowliest man on earth. For God does not make a distinction here; all have sinned and come short of the glory of God. In order that the union may be brought about, God must therefore descend to become the equal of such a one, and so He will appear in the likeness of the humblest. But the humblest in our world is one who must serve others, and God will therefore appear in the form of a *servant*. But this servant form is no mere outer garment, like the beggar-cloak in which the king thought to disguise himself. For when the king descended to the maiden masqueraded in peasant attire, this was after all a kind of deceit. But when God assumed the form of a servant, it was His true form and figure. The true God became true Man.

Behold where he stands — God! There; do you not see him? He is God. Which one? Surely not the one girt with a towel who is washing feet? Why, that man was born in a stable; there was no room for him at the inn, nor has there ever been any room for him in the world: he simply cannot be fitted in to our way of doing things. And tomorrow he is to be put out of the way once and for all. He is a blasphemer, you know; he is a sinner, for he takes his meals with publicans, he converses with harlots, he touches lepers. And you say *he* is God! Pah! — do not mock me! I have better sense than that! Say rather he is a megalomaniac or someone terribly deceived or a scoundrel or a demon (who knows? — perhaps it is by Beelzebub, the prince of demons, that he casts out demons). What an outrageous claim you make for him. It offends me to the quick!

You see, the servant-form was no mere outer garment; and therefore, God must suffer all things, endure all things, make experience of all things. He must suffer hunger in the desert, he must thirst in the time of his agony, he must be forsaken in death, absolutely like the humblest — behold the man!

His is a passion-story from birth until death. His suffering consists in bearing the burden that mankind may misunderstand his love and take offence at him. This God-Man, this Suffering Servant. who hath no form nor comeliness, who hath not beauty that we should desire him, anxiously says to each man: "Behold, I stand at the door of your humble cottage and knock; if you will open unto me, I shall come in and sit down and sup with you."

It is less terrible to fall to the ground when the mountains tremble at the Voice of God than it is to sit at table with him as an equal; and yet it is God's concern precisely to have it so.

What kind of talk is this? Gods do not besmirch themselves by going through the messiness of human birth. Gods do not get themselves crucified. A theophany, that I could understand. A Docetic appearance, even that, perhaps, I could accept. But if you tell me that ultimate Deity has appeared in time in flesh and blood, I will tell you that you are talking nonsense. This is more than paradoxical. This is absurd.

To this the Christian assents. Indeed it is absurd, and yet "the foolishness of God is wiser than men." For the Christian has a sort of double-vision: as thinker, he knows all the dialectical contradictions: as believer, he embraces them as Gospel truth. To the Jew in me this is a scandal — that one so lowly (stable-born) should give himself out to be so high and mighty; or that one so lofty (the Son of God) should permit himself to be so deeply abased; it is paradox either way.[15] To the Greek in me this is folly — for the eternal *logos* is timeless, disembodied, dwelling above in the realm of pure form; but here I am confronted, with rude directness, by a carpenter, who says that *he* is the *logos*, embodied, incarnate, and that no one can come to the *logos* but by him.[16]

As Jew, I had expected a Messiah who would vindicate me and crown my endeavours with good things and length of days. Instead I get a Messiah who accuses me not only of habitual sinning but of active, positive hostility towards God. He says that all my evolution, all my progress, all my self-made righteousness ends in . . . crucifixion.

As Greek, I had assumed that I was my own Christ, that in spite of all my imperfection I nevertheless possessed intact a divine something (*nous, pneuma,* spark) which gave me access to the eternal *logos*. By going deep into my own soul, I could mount to the heights. The maximum of my need I imagined to be a teacher who, by questioning me, would awaken in me that self-activity which would enable me to take myself into eternity by way of recollection. It matters not at what moment or at whose instigation I begin to remember that I am eternal; the historical is a matter of indifference. But here is a teacher who says, "Without me ye can do nothing. Your proposed retreat to eternity *via* recollection is barred by the fact of sin. Because of sin, there is no longer any immanent fundamental kinship between you and the eternal."[17]

Thus does Christianity begin by profoundly humiliating a man. It strips him of every intellectual and moral pretension. It drives him naked and trembling to the throne of God. And here, if a man will but confess that God's judgment upon him is just and will sue for mercy, here precisely is the miracle of acquittal, of forgiveness, of reconciliation. He has Christ for his clothing when he confesses himself naked, Christ for his resurrection when he acknowledges himself dead.

"Becoming a Christian is then the most fearful decision of a man's life, a struggle through to attain faith against despair and offense, the twin Cerberuses that guard the entrance to a Christian life."[18]

Faith is the most disputable of things while in process of approximation; but when reflection is called to a halt by a resolution of the will (the leap), doubt is excluded and "the peace of God which passeth understanding" becomes the supreme reality of his life.

Now we are in a position to understand Kierkegaard's succinct statement of the problem: "The eternal blessedness of the individual is decided in time through the relationship to something historical, which is furthermore of such a character as to include in its composition that which by virtue of its essence

[15] Cf. *Training in Christianity,* Part II.
[16] Cf. *Fragments,* Ch. I.
[17] Cf. *Postscript,* pp. 184 ff., 505–508, 516–518.
[18] *Postscript,* p. 333.

cannot become historical, and must therefore become such by virtue of the Absurd."[19]

The perfection of Christianity is not a doctrine or a code or a law or a philosophy. It is a Person. Christianity is the fact that God has existed as a particular man. It rests its whole claim on Jesus as the point where eternity has intersected time. The object of faith is the reality of this God-Man, that He really exists. The answer of faith is therefore unconditionally yes or no. For it does not concern a doctrine, as to whether the doctrine is true or not; it is the answer to a question concerning a fact: "Do you or do you not suppose that He has really existed?" And the answer, be it noted, is with infinite passion. The dialectical difficulties react upon passion to intensify it and enflame it, like oil upon fire. One's eternal blessedness is at stake — but is it not a painful contradiction to base one's blessedness upon something historical? Is it not madness to require the greatest possible subjective passion, to the point of hating father and mother, and then to put this together with an historical knowledge, which at its maximum is only a sketchy approximation?

Here is something historical, the story of Jesus Christ.

But now is the historical fact quite certain? To this one must answer: even though it were the most certain of all historical facts it would be of no help, there cannot be any *direct* transition from an historical fact to the foundation upon it of an eternal blessedness. That is something qualitatively new.

"How then do we proceed? Thus. A man says to himself . . . : here is an historical fact which teaches me that in regard to my eternal blessedness I must have recourse to Jesus Christ. I must certainly preserve myself from taking the wrong turning into scientific inquiry and research, as to whether it is quite certainly historical; for it is historical right enough: and if it were ten times as certain in all its details it would still be no help: for *directly* I cannot be helped.[20]

[19] *Postscript*, p. 345.

[20] *Historismus* leads at most to the perception, historically motivated, that Christianity has certain advantages over paganism, Judaism, etc. Meanwhile, *historismus* is in danger of falling into a "philological occupation-complex" in which decision for Christ, personal commitment to Him, is forever postponed. We all await the publication of the latest commentary, the unearthing of a new codex, by which the remaining obscurities, it is hoped, will be cleared up. Thinking to eliminate the risk, we become stuck in a "learned parenthesis." Let the scholar labor ever so assiduously, he will not in this way become a Christian — he only becomes erudite. (Cf. *Postscript*, Book I, and *Training in Christianity*, pp. 26–39.) In the *Fragments*, p. 87, S.K. puts it like this: "If the contemporary generation had left nothing behind them but these words: 'We have believed that in such and such a year God appeared among us in the humble figure of a servant, that he lived and taught in our community, and finally died,' it would be more than enough. The contemporary generation would have done all that was necessary; for this little advertisement, this *nota bene* on a page of universal history, would be sufficient to afford an occasion for a successor, and the most voluminous account can in all eternity do nothing more." With good reason, the Kierkegaardian pseudonym, Johannes Climacus, is here putting the case as emphatically and as extremely as is possible, and I believe that, if worst comes to worst, he is right. At the same time, however, I agree with Kierkegaard who believes, personally, that we have — and must have — something more concrete to go on than the naked declaration, lacking specific content, that "the Word became flesh." But for this S.K. assigns a reason

"And so I say to myself: I choose; that historical fact means so much to me that I decide to stake my whole life upon that *if*. Then he lives; entirely full of the idea, risking his life for it: and his life is the proof that he believes. He did not have a few proofs, and so believed and then began to live. No, the very reverse.

"That is called risking; and without risk faith is an impossibility. . . ."[21]

The salvation that is offered is free, and yet, after all, it is bought *à tout prix*, for it involves nothing less than the total surrender of the self. "Lord, I believe; help thou mine unbelief!"

Christianity as Adoration and Imitation

What, then, will life be like if one takes this risk?

The Christian relates himself to the God-Man as one whom he adores and seeks to imitate. The first and foremost thing is adoration, and it is only through adoration of so gracious a Redeemer that there can be any question of being like Him. Christ Himself must help the one who is to imitate Him. And in one respect no one can be like Him, nor even think of wishing to imitate Him, *in so far as He is our saviour and atoner.*

When we compare ourselves to Christ, we discover that we never succeed in being like Him. Not even in what we call our best moments. Christ, as the Example, is He who makes endless demands upon us, and we feel terribly the unlikeness. Then we flee *to* the Example, and He has mercy upon us. Thus, the Example is He who most sternly and endlessly condemns us — and at the same time it is He who, as Redeemer, has mercy upon us. Kierkegaard expresses this dialectic in a noble prayer:

"Help us all and everyone, Thou who art both willing and able to help, Thou who art both the Pattern and the Redeemer, and again both the Redeemer and the Pattern, so that when the striver sinks under the Pattern, then the Redeemer raises him up again, but at the same instant Thou art the Pattern, to keep him continually striving. Thou, our Redeemer, by Thy blessed suffering and death, hast made satisfaction for all and for everything; no eternal happiness can be or shall be earned by desert — it has been deserved. Yet Thou didst leave behind Thee the traces of Thy footsteps, Thou the Holy pattern of the human race and of each individual in it, so that, saved by Thy redemption, they might every instant have confidence and boldness to will to strive to follow Thee."[22]

---

we were perhaps unprepared for. Something of what the Word made flesh actually *did* in the flesh is required — in order that the Incarnate Lord may not only constitute a specific revelation of God but also may appear before us in definite lineaments as the pattern, the paradigm, the model whom we are required to follow. (Cf. e.g. *Papirer*, X^5 A-45.) It is evident that, for Kierkegaard, Christ as Example, as embodiment of the Will of God, plays the same role as is played, for St. Paul and Luther, by the Law. The function of the Law or of Christ, as full-length portrait of the Law carried out in flesh and blood, is to crack human pride and to drive men to Christ as Redeemer.

[21] *Journals*, Oxford, 1938, §1044.

[22] *Judge for Yourselves!*, p. 161. Cp. the Collect for Easter II.

Thus does ethics have a paradoxical reinstatement — an ethics on the far side of conversion, on the basis of grace.[23] Grace is Christianity's first, last, and always — but not in such a way as to abrogate ethics. Justification by grace through faith means not antinomianism but a new relation to the Law. Works are done not in the frantic exertion of saving our lives but in glad gratitude to Him who *has* saved our lives. This is obedience to a living Lord, not to an impersonal Law. The love of God, made manifest in Christ, constrains us, impels us to move out toward neighbor and the world in works of love. Nor do we do to this task unaided. Through prayer and sacrament the Risen and Ascended Christ empowers us for the task by communicating to us the power of His own deathless life.[24] Thus, good works appear as the fruit of fellowship. The ethical task, although it may involve painful collision with the world, is joyously undertaken under the guidance and inspiration of the Holy Ghost.

Perhaps now we can welcome Kierkegaard's brilliant distillation: "An unlimited humiliation, the boundless grace of God, and a striving born of gratitude: these three things constitute Christianity."[25]

This, too, Kierkegaard explains in a parable for Pentecost:[26]

> Once upon a time there was a rich man who ordered from abroad at a high price a pair of entirely faultless and high-bred horses which he desired to have for his own pleasure and for the pleasure of driving them himself. Then about a year or two elapsed. Anyone who previously had known these horses would not have been able to recognize them again. Their eyes had become dull and drowsy, their gait lacked style and decision, they couldn't endure anything, they couldn't hold out, they hardly could be driven four miles without having to stop on the way, sometimes,

[23] Cf. especially S.K.'s profound remarks about "the second ethics" in *The Concept of Dread*, pp. 16 ff. A pity there is no time to explore the fact that there is also, for Kierkegaard, a second aesthetics — a proper appreciation of beauty, of the arts, of food and wine — also on the basis of grace. This is part of what S.K. means by the concept "repetition." "Everything comes back — transfigured," he says. In faith, by virtue of the absurd, the man who has infinitely renounced everything now makes the second movement of infinity by which everything renounced is received a second time cleansed and restored, raised to the second power, and employed and enjoyed eucharistically.

[24] While it is true that S.K. died in the midst of a violent attack on the Church only the most perverse will fail to understand that what he was attacking was not *ecclesia* as such but the empirical Church of Denmark, the Establishment, as he knew it in his day, when to be a Dane was tantamount to being a Christian — i.e. one was born that way. Although it would be folly to maintain that S.K. had a proper appreciation of the Church, if we accept the New Testament conception as definitive, it would also be foolish to suppose that he was utterly lacking ecclesiologically. So far was he from doing away with the Church, he simply *presupposed* it. Of course there would be the assembly of the brethren for prayer and praise, sermon and sacrament. To convince ourselves of this, we have only to read his moving "Discourses on the Communion for Fridays." And, as I have shown elsewhere, when S.K. stresses the *individual*, it is not the individual against *ecclesia* he stresses but the individual against the *masses*, against *das Man* of Heidegger, the de-personalized convention-ridden collectivism of our time.

[25] *Papirer*, X³ A 734.

[26] *For Self-Examination*, pp. 104 ff.

they came to a standstill as he sat for all he was worth attempting to drive them, besides they had acquired all sorts of vices and bad habits, and in spite of the fact that they of course got fodder in over-abundance, they were falling off in flesh day by day. Then he had the King's coachman call. He drove them for a month — in the whole region there was not a pair of horses that held their heads so proudly, whose glance was so fiery, whose gait was so handsome, no other pair of horses that could hold out so long, though it were to trot for more than a score of miles at a stretch without stopping. How came this about? It is easy to see. The owner, who without being a coachman pretended to be such, drove them in accordance with the horses' understanding of what it is to drive; the royal coachman drove them in accordance with the coachman's understanding of what it is to drive.

So it is with us men. Oh, when I think of myself and of the countless men I have learned to know, I have often said to myself despondently, "Here are talents and powers and capacities enough — but the coachman is lacking." Through a long period of time, we men, from generation to generation, have been, if I may so say, driven (to stick to the figure) in accordance with the horses' understanding of what it is to drive, we are directed, brought up, educated in accordance with man's conception of what it is to be a man. Behold therefore what we lack: exaltation, and what follows in turn from this, that we only can stand so little . . .

Once it was different. Once there was a time when it pleased the Deity (if I may venture to say so) to be Himself the coachman; and He drove the horses in accordance with the coachman's understanding of what it is to drive. Oh, what was a man not capable of at that time!

Think of to-day's text! [Acts 2:1–12] There sit twelve men, all of them belonging to that class of society which we call the common people. They had seen Him whom they adored as God, their Lord and Master, crucified; as never could it be said of anyone even in the remotest, it can be said of them that they had seen everything lost. It is true, He thereupon went triumphantly to heaven — but in this way also He is lost to them: and now they sit and wait for the Spirit to be imparted to them, so that thus, execrated as they are by the little nation they belong to, they may preach a doctrine which will arouse against them the hate of the whole world — and that on the most terrible terms, against its will.

It is Christianity that had to be put through. These twelve men, they put it through. They were in a sense men like us — but they were well driven, yea, they were well driven!

SECTION FOUR

Human Knowledge of God

David Hume

Hume (1711-1766), a Scotsman and probably the most influential of all British philosophers, tried to show how all our knowledge is derived from sense experience, except for "relations of ideas." "If we take in our hand any volume; of divinity or school of metaphysics, for instance; let us ask, Does it contain any experimental reasoning concerning quality or number? No. Does it contain any experimental reasoning concerning matter of fact and substance? No. Commit it then to the flames: for it can contain nothing but sophistry and illusion."

In the following passage Hume presents his argument on the subject of miracles. It should be noted that Hume, like others who have taken a similar point of view, considers a miracle to be a breach of what is supposed to be a natural law. Newtonian mechanics had shown the general regularity of matter in motion. Hume examines the whole question of miracles in this context. The New Testament conception arises in a different context: A miracle is a sign of God's power; it is an event through which God speaks. Its significance does not lie in the event's inexplicability by present or future sciences; it lies, rather, in a showing forth of the power of God. It might be said therefore that Hume's argument rests upon a mistake; nevertheless, this is a classic passage on the subject, and, though it was written in a context different from that of today, the argument can very easily be brought up to date in terms of modern scientific findings. It presents, in a convenient form, the familiar objection to the notion of the miraculous as the miraculous is commonly understood.

On Miracles *

Our evidence . . . for the truth of the *Christian* religion is less than the evidence for the truth of our senses; because, even in the first authors of our religion, it was no greater; and it is evident it must diminish in passing from them to their disciples; nor can any one rest such confidence in their testimony, as in the immediate object of his senses. But a weaker evidence can never destroy a stronger; and therefore, were the doctrine of the real presence ever so clearly revealed in scripture, it were directly contrary to the rules of just reasoning to give our assent to it. It contradicts sense, though both the scripture and tradition, on which it is supposed to be built, carry not such evidence with them as sense; when they are considered merely as external evidences, and are not brought home to every one's breast, by the immediate operation of the Holy Spirit.

Nothing is so convenient as a decisive argument of this kind, which must at least *silence* the most arrogant bigotry and superstition, and free us from

* *The Philosophical Works of David Hume* (4 vols.; Boston: Little, Brown & Co., 1854), IV, pp. 124–139. Used by permission.

their impertinent solicitations. I flatter myself, that I have discovered an argument of a like nature, which, if just, will, with the wise and learned, be an everlasting check to all kinds of superstitious delusion, and consequently, will be useful as long as the world endures. For so long, I presume, will the accounts of miracles and prodigies be found in all history, sacred and profane.

Though experience be our only guide in reasoning concerning matters of fact; it must be acknowledged, that this guide is not altogether infallible, but in some cases is apt to lead us into errors. One, who in our climate, should expect better weather in any week of June than in one of December, would reason justly, and conformably to experience; but it is certain, that he may happen, in the event, to find himself mistaken. However, we may observe, that, in such a case, he would have no cause to complain of experience; because it commonly informs us beforehand of the uncertainty, by that contrariety of events, which we may learn from a diligent observation. All effects follow not with like certainty from their supposed causes. Some events are found, in all countries and all ages, to have been constantly conjoined together: Others are found to have been more variable, and sometimes to disappoint our expectations; so that, in our reasonings concerning matter of fact, there are all imaginable degrees of assurance, from the highest certainty to the lowest species of moral evidence.

A wise man, therefore, proportions his belief to the evidence. In such conclusions as are founded on an infallible experience, he expects the event with the last degree of assurance, and regards his past experience as a full *proof* of the future existence of that event. In other cases, he proceeds with more caution: He weighs the opposite experiments: He considers which side is supported by the greater number of experiments: to that side he inclines, with doubt and hesitation; and when at last he fixes his judgement, the evidence exceeds not what we properly call *probability*. All probability, then, supposes an opposition of experiments and observations, where the one side is found to overbalance the other, and to produce a degree of evidence, proportioned to the superiority. A hundred instances or experiments on one side, and fifty on another, afford a doubtful expectation of any event; though a hundred uniform experiments, with only one that is contradictory, reasonably begets a pretty strong degree of assurance. In all cases, we must balance the opposite experiments, where they are opposite, and deduct the smaller number from the greater, in order to know the exact force of the superior evidence.

To apply these principles to a particular instance; we may observe, that there is no species of reasoning more common, more useful, and even necessary to human life, than that which is derived from the testimony of men, and the reports of eye-witnesses and spectators. This species of reasoning, perhaps, one may deny to be founded on the relation of cause and effect. I shall not dispute about a word. It will be sufficient to observe that our assurance in any argument of this kind is derived from no other principle than our observation of the veracity of human testimony, and of the usual conformity of facts to the reports of witnesses. It being a general maxim, that no objects have any discoverable connexion together, and that all the inferences, which we can draw from one to another, are founded merely on our experience of their constant and regular conjunction; it is evident, that we ought not to make an exception to this maxim in favour of human testimony, whose connexion with any event seems, in itself, as little necessary as any other. Were not the memory tenacious to a certain degree; had not men commonly an inclination to truth and a principle of probity, were they not sensible to shame, when detected in a falsehood: Were not these, I say, discovered by *experience* to be qualities, inherent in human nature, we should never repose the least confidence in human testimony. A man delirious, or noted for falsehood and villainy, has no manner of authority with us.

And as the evidence, derived from witnesses and human testimony, is founded on past experience, so it varies with the experience, and is regarded either as *proof* or a *probability*, according as the conjunction between any particular kind of report and any kind of object has been found to be constant or variable. There are a number of circumstances to be taken into consideration in all judgements of this kind; and the ultimate standard, by which we determine all disputes, that may arise concerning them, is always derived from experience and observation. Where this experience is not entirely uniform on any side, it is attended with an unavoidable contrariety in our judgements, and with the same opposition and mutual destruction of argument as in every other kind of evidence. We frequently hesitate concerning the reports of others. We balance the opposite circumstances, which cause any doubt or uncertainty; and when we discover a superiority on one side, we incline to it; but still with a diminution of assurance, in proportion to the force of its antagonist.

This contrariety of evidence, in the present case, may be derived from several different causes; from the opposition of contrary testimony; from the character or number of the witnesses; from the manner of their delivering their testimony; or from the union of all these circumstances. We entertain a suspicion concerning any matter of fact, when the witnesses contradict each other; when they are but few, or of a doubtful character; when they have an interest in what they affirm; when they deliver their testimony with hesitation, or on the contrary, with too violent asseverations. There are many other particulars of the same kind, which may diminish or destroy the force of any argument, derived from human testimony.

Suppose, for instance, that the fact, which the testimony endeavours to establish, partakes of the extraordinary and the marvellous; in that case, the evidence, resulting from the testimony, admits of a diminution, greater or less, in proportion as the fact is more or less unusual. The reason why we place any credit in witnesses and historians, is not derived from any *connexion*, which we perceive *a priori*, between testimony and reality, but because we are accustomed to find a conformity between them. But when the fact attested is such a one as has seldom fallen under our observation, here is a contest of two opposite experiences; of which the one destroys the other, as far as its force goes, and the superior can only operate on the mind by the force, which remains. The very same principle of experience, which gives us a certain degree of assurance in the testimony of witnesses, gives us also, in this case, another degree of assurance against the fact, which they endeavour to establish; from which contradiction there necessarily arises a counterpoize, and mutual destruction of belief and authority.

I should not believe such a story were it told me by Cato, was a proverbial saying in Rome, even during the lifetime of that philosophical patriot. The incredibility of a fact, it was allowed, might invalidate so great an authority.

The Indian prince, who refused to believe the first relations concerning the effects of frost, reasoned justly; and it naturally required very strong testimony to engage his assent to facts, that arose from a state of nature, with which he was unacquainted, and which bore so little analogy to those events, of which he had had constant and uniform experience. Though they were not contrary to his experience, they were not conformable to it.

But in order to increase the probability against the testimony of witnesses, let us suppose, that the fact, which they affirm, instead of being only marvellous, is really miraculous; and suppose also, that the testimony considered apart and in itself, amounts to an entire proof; in that case, there is proof against proof, of which the strongest must prevail, but still with a diminution of its force, in proportion to that of its antagonist.

A miracle is a violation of the laws of nature; and as a firm and unalterable experience has established these laws, the proof against a miracle, from the very nature of the fact, is as entire as any argument from experience can possibly be imagined. Why is it more than probable, that all men must die; that lead cannot, of itself, remain suspended in the air; that fire consumes wood, and is extinguished by water; unless it be, that these events are found agreeable to the laws of nature, and there is required a violation of these laws, or in other words, a miracle to prevent them? Nothing is esteemed a miracle, if it ever happen in the common course of nature. It is no miracle that a man, seemingly in good health, should die on a sudden: because such a kind of death, though more unusual than any other, has yet been frequently observed to happen. But it is a miracle, that a dead man should come to life; because that has never been observed in any age or country. There must, therefore, be a uniform experience against every miraculous event, otherwise the event would not merit that appellation. And as a uniform experience amounts to a proof, there is here a direct and full *proof,* from the nature of the fact, against the existence of any miracle; nor can such a proof be destroyed, or the miracle rendered credible, but by an opposite proof, which is superior.

The plain consequence is (and it is a general maxim worthy of our attention), "That no testimony is sufficient to establish a miracle, unless the testimony be of such a kind, that its falsehood would be more miraculous, than the fact, which it endeavours to establish; and even in that case there is a mutual destruction of arguments, and the superior only gives us an assurance suitable to that degree of force, which remains, after deducting the inferior." When anyone tells me, that he saw a dead man restored to life, I immediately consider with myself, whether it be more probable, that this person should either deceive or be deceived, or that the fact, which he relates, should really have happened. I weigh the one miracle against the other; and according to the superiority, which I discover, I pronounce my decision, and always reject the greater miracle. If the falsehood of his testimony would be more miraculous, than the event which he relates; then, and not till then, can he pretend to command my belief or opinion.

Immanuel Kant

Kant (1724-1804) is one of the greatest figures in the history of Western thought. His importance lies as much in his empirico-rationalist solution to the problem of knowledge as in his peculiar contribution to ethical theory. While he found no room for a theology that had pretensions to rational proof, he believed that the truth of religious ideas could be otherwise established. "I had to remove knowledge," he said, "to make room for faith." Miracles are of no particular significance for religion. Our religious assurances must spring, rather, from our moral consciousness and the voice of duty. There must be a God to vindicate the claims of duty and justice. Kant's interpretation of Christianity is a very moralistic one: He has no concern for a mystical religion, but only for what he calls "religion within the limits of reason alone." This is the theme of the following passage.

Evil in Man *

. . . The proposition, man is *evil,* can mean only, he is conscious of the moral law but has nevertheless adopted into his maxim the (occasional) deviation therefrom. He is evil by *nature,* means but this, that evil can be predicated of man as a species; not that such a quality can be inferred from the concept of his species (that is, of man in general) — for then it would be necessary; but rather that from what we know of man through experience we cannot judge otherwise of him, or, that we may presuppose evil to be subjectively necessary to every man, even to the best. Now this propensity must itself be considered as morally evil, yet not as a natural predisposition but rather as something that can be imputed to man, and consequently it must consist in maxims of the will which are contrary to the law. Further, for the sake of freedom, these maxims must in themselves be considered contingent, a circumstance which, on the other hand, will not tally with the universality of this evil *unless* the ultimate subjective ground of all maxims somehow or other is entwined with and, as it were, rooted in humanity itself. Hence we can call this a natural propensity to evil, and as we must, after all, ever hold man himself responsible for it, we can further call it a *radical* innate *evil* in human nature (yet none the less brought upon us by ourselves).

That such a corrupt propensity must indeed be rooted in man need not be formally proved in view of the multitude of crying examples which experience *of the actions* of men puts before our eyes. If we wish to draw our examples from that state in which various philosophers hoped preëminently to discover the natural goodliness of human nature, namely, from the so-called *state of*

* Immanuel Kant, *Religion within the Limits of Reason Alone,* trans. T. M. Green and H. H. Hudson (Chicago: The Open Court Publishing Company, 1934), pp. iii, iv; 27–39. Used by permission.

nature, we need but compare with this hypothesis the scenes of unprovoked cruelty in the murder-dramas enacted in Tofoa, New Zealand, and in the Navigator Islands, and the unending cruelty (of which Captain Hearne[1] tells) in the wide wastes of northwestern America, cruelty from which, indeed, not a soul reaps the smallest benefit,[2] and we have vices of barbarity more than sufficient to draw us from such an opinion. If, however, we incline to the opinion that human nature can better be known in the civilized state (in which its predispositions can more completely develop), we must listen to a long melancholy litany of indictments against humanity: of secret falsity even in the closest friendship, so that a limit upon trust in the mutual confidences of even the best friends is reckoned a universal maxim of prudence in intercourse; of a propensity to hate him to whom one is indebted, for which a benefactor must always be prepared; of a hearty well-wishing which yet allows of the remark that "in the misfortunes of our best friends there is something which is not altogether displeasing to us"; and of many other vices still concealed under the appearance of virtue, to say nothing of the vices of those who do not conceal them, for we are content to call him good who is *a man bad in a way common to all;* and we shall have enough of the vices of *culture* and civilization (which are the most offensive of all) to make us rather turn away our eyes from the conduct of men lest we ourselves contract another vice, misanthropy. But if we are not yet content, we need but contemplate a state which is compounded in strange fashion of both the others, that is, the international situation, where civilized nations stand towards each other in the relation obtaining in the barbarous state of nature (a state of continuous readiness for war), a state, moreover, from which they have taken fixedly into their heads never to depart. We then become aware of the fundamental principles of the great societies called *states*[3] — principles which flatly contradict their

[1] Samuel Hearne (1745–1792), an English traveller, in the service of the Hudson Bay Company. His *Account of a Journey from Prince of Wales's Fort in Hudson's Bay to the Northwest* was published in 1795. Kant evidently had read the brief account of Hearne's travels in Douglas's Introduction to *Cook's Third Voyage*, London, 1784.

[2] Thus the war ceaselessly waged between the Arathapescaw Indians and the Dog Rib Indians has no other object than mere slaughter. Bravery in war is, in the opinion of savages, the highest virtue. Even in a civilized state it is an object of admiration and a basis for the special regard commanded by that profession in which bravery is the sole merit; and this is not without rational cause. For that man should be able to possess a thing (*i.e.*, honor) and make it an end to be valued more than life itself, and because of it renounce all self-interest, surely bespeaks a certain nobility in his natural disposition. Yet we recognize in the complacency with which victors boast their mighty deeds (massacres, butchery without quarter, and the like) that it is merely their own superiority and the destruction they can wreak, without any other objective, in which they really take satisfaction.

[3] When we survey the history of these, merely as the phenomenon of the inner predispositions of mankind which are for the most part concealed from us, we become aware of a certain machine-like movement of nature toward ends which are nature's own rather than those of the nations. Each separate state, so long as it has a neighboring state which it dares hope to conquer, strives to aggrandize itself through such a conquest, and thus to attain a world-monarchy, a polity wherein all freedom, and with it (as a consequence) virtue, taste, and learning, would necessarily expire. Yet this monster (in which laws gradually lose their force), after it has swallowed all its neighbors, finally dissolves of itself, and through rebellion and disunion breaks up into

public pronouncements but can never be laid aside, and which no philosopher has yet been able to bring into agreement with morality. Nor (sad to say) has any philosopher been able to propose better principles which at the same time can be brought into harmony with human nature. The result is that the *philosophical millennium,* which hopes for a state of perpetual peace based on a league of peoples, a world-republic, even as the *theological millennium,* which tarries for the completed moral improvement of the entire human race, is universally ridiculed as a wild fantasy.

Now the ground of this evil (1) cannot be placed, as is so commonly done, in man's *sensuous nature* and the natural inclinations arising therefrom. For not only are these not directly related to evil (rather do they afford the occasion for what the moral disposition in its power can manifest, namely, virtue); we must not even be considered responsible for their existence (we cannot be, for since they are implanted in us we are not their authors). We are accountable, however, for the propensity to evil, which, as it affects the morality of the subject, is to be found in him as a free-acting being and for which it must be possible to hold him accountable as the offender — this, too, despite the fact that this propensity is so deeply rooted in the will that we are forced to say that it is to be found in man by nature. Neither can the ground of this evil (2) be placed in a *corruption* of the morally legislative reason — as if reason could destroy the authority of the very law which is its own, or deny the obligation arising therefrom; this is absolutely impossible. To conceive of oneself as a freely acting being and yet as exempt from the law which is appropriate to such a being (the moral law) would be tantamount to conceiving a cause operating without any laws whatsoever (for determination according to natural laws is excluded by the fact of freedom); this is a self-contradiction. In seeking, therefore, a ground of the morally-evil in man, [we find that] *sensuous nature* comprises too little, for when the incentives which can spring from freedom are taken away, man is reduced to a merely *animal* being. On the other hand, a reason exempt from the moral law, a *malignant reason* as it were (a thoroughly evil will), comprises too much, for thereby opposition to the law would itself be set up as an incentive (since in the absence of all incentives the will cannot be determined), and thus the subject would be made a *devilish* being. Neither of these designations is applicable to man.

But even if the existence of this propensity to evil in human nature can be demonstrated by experiential proofs of the real opposition, in time, of man's will to the law, such proofs do not teach us the essential character of that propensity or the ground of this opposition. Rather, because this character concerns a relation of the will, which is free (and the concept of which is therefore not empirical), to the moral law as an incentive (the concept of which, likewise, is purely intellectual), it must be apprehended *a priori* through the

many smaller states. These, instead of striving toward a league of nations (a republic of federated free nations), begin the same game over again, each for itself, so that war (that scourge of humankind) may not be allowed to cease. Although indeed war is not so incurably evil as that tomb, a universal autocracy (or even as a confederacy which exists to hasten the weakening of a despotism in any single state), yet, as one of the ancients put it, war creates more evil men than it destroys.

concept of evil, so far as evil is possible under the laws of freedom (of obligation and accountability). This concept may be developed in the following manner.

Man (even the most wicked) does not, under any maxim whatsoever, repudiate the moral law in the manner of a rebel (renouncing obedience to it). The law, rather, forces itself upon him irresistibly by virtue of his moral predisposition; and were no other incentive working in opposition, he would adopt the law into his supreme maxim as the sufficient determining ground of his will; that is, he would be morally good. But by virtue of an equally innocent natural predisposition he depends upon the incentives of his sensuous nature and adopts them also (in accordance with the subjective principle of self-love) into his maxim. If he took the latter into his maxim *as in themselves wholly adequate* to the determination of the will, without troubling himself about the moral law (which, after all, he does have in him), he would be morally evil. Now, since he naturally adopts *both* into his maxim, and since, further, he would find either, if it were alone, adequate in itself for the determining of the will, it follows that if the difference between the maxims amounted merely to the difference between the two incentives (the content of the maxims), that is, if it were merely a question as to whether the law or the sensuous impulse were to furnish the incentive, man would be at once good and evil: this, however, (as we saw in the Introduction) is a contradiction. Hence the distinction between a good man and one who is evil cannot lie in the difference between the incentives which they adopt into their maxim (not in the content of the maxim), but rather must depend upon *subordination* (the form of the maxim), *i.e., which of the two incentives he makes the condition of the other.* Consequently man (even the best) is evil only in that he reverses the moral order of the incentives when he adopts them into his maxim. He adopts, indeed, the moral law along with the law of self-love; yet when he becomes aware that they cannot remain on a par with each other but that one must be subordinated to the other as its supreme condition, he makes the incentive of self-love and its inclinations the condition of obedience to the moral law; whereas, on the contrary, the latter, as the *supreme condition* of the satisfaction of the former, ought to have been adopted into the universal maxim of the will as the sole incentive.

Yet, even with this reversal of the ethical order of the incentives in and through his maxim, a man's actions still may prove to be as much in conformity to the law as if they sprang from true basic principles. This happens when reason employs the unity of the maxims in general, a unity which is inherent in the moral law, merely to bestow upon the incentives of desire, under the name of *happiness,* a unity of maxims which otherwise they cannot have. (For example, truthfulness, if adopted as a basic principle, delivers us from the anxiety of making our lies agree with one another and of not being entangled by their serpent coils.) The empirical character is then good, but the intelligible character is still evil.

Now if a propensity to this does lie in human nature, there is in man a natural propensity to evil; and since this very propensity must in the end be sought in a will which is free, and can therefore be imputed, it is morally evil.

This evil is *radical*, because it corrupts the ground of all maxims; it is, moreover, as a natural propensity, *inextirpable* by human powers, since extirpation could occur only through good maxims, and cannot take place when the ultimate subjective ground of all maxims is postulated as corrupt; yet at the same time it must be possible to *overcome* it, since it is found in man, a being whose actions are free.

We are not, then, to call the depravity of human nature *wickedness* taking the word in its strict sense as a disposition (the subjective *principle* of the maxims) to adopt evil *as evil* into our maxim as our incentives (for that is diabolical); we should rather term it the *perversity* of the heart, which, then, because of what follows from it, is also called an *evil heart*. Such a heart may coexist with a will which in general is good: it arises from the frailty of human nature, the lack of sufficient strength to follow out the principles it has chosen for itself, joined with its impurity, the failure to distinguish the incentives (even of well-intentioned actions) from each other by the gauge of morality; and so at last, if the extreme is reached, [it results] from looking only to the squaring of these actions with the law and not to the derivation of them from the law as the sole motivating spring. Now even though there does not always follow therefrom an unlawful act and a propensity thereto, namely, *vice*, yet the mode of thought which sets down the absence of such vice as being conformity of the *disposition* to the law of duty (as being virtue) — since in this case no attention whatever is paid to the motivating forces in the maxim but only to the observance of the letter of the law — itself deserves to be called a radical perversity in the human heart.

This *innate* guilt (*reatus*), which is so denominated because it may be discerned in man as early as the first manifestations of the exercise of freedom, but which, none the less, must have originated in freedom and hence can be imputed, — this guilt may be judged in its first two stages (those of frailty and impurity) to be unintentional guilt (*culpa*), but in the third to be deliberate guilt (*dolus*) and to display in its character a certain *insidiousness* of the human heart (*dolus malus*), which deceives itself in regard to its own good and evil dispositions, and, if only its conduct has not evil consequences — which it might well have, with such maxims — does not trouble itself about its disposition but rather considers itself justified before the law. Thence arises the peace of conscience of so many men (conscientious in their own esteem) when, in the course of conduct concerning which they did not take the law into their counsel, or at least in which the law was not the supreme consideration, they merely elude evil consequences by good fortune. They may even picture themselves as meritorious, feeling themselves guilty of no such offenses as they see others burdened with; nor do they ever inquire whether good luck should not have the credit, or whether by reason of the cast of mind which they could discover, if they only would, in their own inmost nature, they would not have practised similar vices, had not inability, temperament, training, and circumstances of time and place which serve to tempt one (matters which are not imputable), kept them out of the way of those vices. This dishonesty, by which we humbug ourselves and which thwarts the establishing of a true moral disposition in us, extends itself outwardly also to falsehood and deception of others. If this is not to be termed badness, it at least deserves the name of worthlessness, and is an element in the radical evil of human nature, which (inasmuch as it puts out of tune the moral capacity to judge what a man is to be taken for, and renders wholly uncertain both internal and external attribution of responsibility) constitutes the foul taint in our race. So long as we do not eradicate it, it prevents the seed of goodness from developing as it otherwise would.

A member of the British Parliament[4] once exclaimed, in the heat of debate, "Every man has his price, for which he sells himself." If this is true (a question to which each must make his own answer), if there is no virtue for which some temptation cannot be found capable of overthrowing it, and if whether the good or evil spirit wins us over to his party depends merely on which bids the most and pays us most promptly, then certainly it holds true of men universally,[5] as the apostle said:[6] "They are all under sin, — there is none righteous (in the spirit of the law), no, not one."[7]

Concerning the Origin of Evil in Human Nature

An origin (a first origin) is the derivation of an effect from its first cause, that is, from that cause which is not in turn the effect of another cause of the same kind. It can be considered either as an *origin in reason* or as an *origin in time.* In the former sense, regard is had only to the *existence* of the effect; in the latter, to its *occurrence,* and hence it is related as an event to its *first cause in time.* If an effect is referred to a cause to which it is bound under the laws of freedom, as is true in the case of moral evil, then the determination of the will to the production of this effect is conceived of as bound up with its determining ground not in time but merely in rational representation; such an effect cannot be derived from any *preceding* state whatsoever. Yet derivation of this sort is always necessary when an evil action, as an *event* in the world, is referred to its natural cause. To seek the temporal origin of free acts as such (as though they were operations of nature) is thus a contradiction. Hence it is also a contradiction to seek the temporal origin of man's moral character, so far as it is considered as contingent, since this character signifies the ground of the *exercise* of freedom; this ground (like the determining ground of the free will generally) must be sought in purely rational representations.

[4] Sir Robert Walpole. What he said, however, was not so universal: "All those men" (referring to certain "patriots") "have their price."

[5] *allgemein*

[6] Cf. Romans, III, 9–10.

[7] . . . Experience . . . never can reveal the root of evil in the supreme maxim of the free will relating to the law, a maxim which, as *intelligible act,* precedes all experience. Hence from the singleness of the supreme maxim, together with the singleness of the law to which it relates itself, we can also understand why, for the pure intellectual judgment of mankind, the rule of excluding a mean between good and evil must remain fundamental; yet for the empirical judgment based on *sensible conduct* (actual performance and neglect) the rule may be laid down that there *is* a mean between these extremes — on the one hand a negative mean of indifference prior to all education, on the other hand a positive, a mixture, partly good and partly evil. However, this latter is merely a judgment upon the morality of mankind as appearance, and must give place to the former in a final judgment.

However the origin of moral evil in man is constituted, surely of all the explanations of the spread and propagation of this evil through all members and generations of our race, the most inept is that which describes it as descending to us as an *inheritance* from our first parents; for one can say of moral evil precisely what the poet said of good:[8] *genus et proavos, et* quae non fecimus ipsi, *vix ea nostra puto*.[9] Yet we should note that, in our search for the origin of this evil, we do not deal first of all with the propensity thereto (as *peccatum in potentia*); rather do we direct our attention to the actual evil of given actions with respect to its inner possibility — to what must take place within the will if evil is to be performed.

In the search for the rational origin of evil actions, every such action must be regarded as though the individual had fallen into it directly from a state of innocence. For whatever his previous deportment may have been, whatever natural causes may have been influencing him, and whether these causes were to be found within him or outside him, his action is yet free and determined by none of these causes; hence it can and must always be judged as an *original* use of his will. He should have refrained from that action, whatever his temporal circumstances and entanglements; for through no cause in the world can he cease to be a freely acting being. Rightly is it said that to a man's account are set down the *consequences* arising from his former free acts which were contrary to the law; but this merely amounts to saying that man need not involve himself in the evasion of seeking to establish whether or not these consequences are free, since there exists in the admittedly free action, which was their cause, ground sufficient for holding him accountable. However evil a man has been up to the very moment of an impending free act (so that evil has actually become custom or second nature) it was not only his duty to have been better [in the past], it is *now* still his duty to better himself. To do so must be within his power, and if he does not do so, he is susceptible of, and subjected to, imputability in the very moment of that action, just as much as though, endowed with a predisposition to good (which is inseparable from

[8] Ovid, *Metamorphoses*, XIII, 140–141: "Race and ancestors, and those things *which we ourselves have not made*, I scarcely account our own."

[9] The three so-called "higher faculties" (in the universities) would explain this transmission of evil each in terms of its own specialty, as *inherited disease, inherited debt*, or *inherited sin*. (1) The *faculty of medicine* would represent this hereditary evil somewhat as it represents the tapeworm, concerning which several naturalists actually believe that, since no specimens have been met with anywhere but in us, not even (of this particular type) in other animals, it must have existed in our first parents. (2) The *faculty of law* would regard this evil as the legitimate consequence of succeeding to the *patrimony* bequeathed us by our first parents, [an inheritance] encumbered, however, with heavy forfeitures (for to be born is no other than to inherit the use of earthly goods so far as they are necessary to our continued existence). Thus we must fulfil payment (atone) and at the end still be dispossessed (by death) of the property. How just is legal justice! (3) The *theological faculty* would regard this evil as the personal participation by our first parents in the *fall* of a condemned rebel, maintaining either that we ourselves then participated (although now unconscious of having done so), or that even now, born under the rule of the rebel (as prince of this world), we prefer his favors to the supreme command of the heavenly Ruler, and do not possess enough faith to free ourselves; wherefore we must also eventually share his doom.

freedom), he had stepped out of a state of innocence into evil. Hence we cannot inquire into the temporal origin of this deed, but solely into its rational origin, if we are thereby to determine and, wherever possible, to elucidate the propensity, if it exists, *i.e.*, the general subjective ground of the adoption of transgression into our maxim.

The foregoing agrees well with that manner of presentation which the Scriptures use, whereby the origin of evil in the human race is depicted as having a [temporal] *beginning*, this beginning being presented in a narrative, wherein what in its essence must be considered as primary (without regard to the element of time) appears as coming first in time. According to this account, evil does not start from a propensity thereto as its underlying basis, for otherwise the beginning of evil would not have its source in freedom; rather does it start from *sin* (by which is meant the transgressing of the moral law as a *divine command*). The state of man prior to all propensity to evil is called the state of *innocence*. The moral law became known to mankind, as it must to any being not pure but tempted by desires, in the form of a *prohibition* (Genesis II, 16–17). Now instead of straightway following this law as an adequate incentive (the only incentive which is unconditionally good and regarding which there is no further doubt), man looked about for other incentives (Genesis III, 6) such as can be good only conditionally (namely, so far as they involve no infringement of the law). He then made it his maxim — if one thinks of his action as consciously springing from freedom — to follow the law of duty, not as duty, but, if need be, with regard to other aims. Thereupon he began to call in question the severity of the commandment which excludes the influence of all other incentives; then by sophistry he reduced[10] obedience to the law to the merely conditional character of a means (subject to the principle of self-love); and finally he adopted into his maxim of conduct the ascendancy of the sensuous impulse over the incentive which springs from the law — and thus occurred sin (Genesis III, 6). *Mutato nomine de te fabula narratur.*[11] From all this it is clear that we daily act in the same way, and that therefore "in Adam all have sinned"[12] and still sin; except that in us there is presupposed an innate propensity to transgression, whereas in the first man, from the point of view of time, there is presupposed no such propensity but rather innocence; hence transgression on his part is called a *fall into sin*; but with us sin is represented as resulting from an already innate wickedness in our nature. This propensity, however, signifies no more than this, that if we wish to address ourselves to the explanation of evil in terms

[10] All homage paid to the moral law is an act of hypocrisy, if, in one's maxim, ascendancy is not at the same time granted to the law as an incentive sufficient in itself and higher than all other determining grounds of the will. The propensity to do this is inward deceit, *i.e.*, a tendency to deceive oneself in the interpretation of the moral law, to its detriment (Genesis III, 5). Accordingly, the Bible (the Christian portion of it) denominates the author of evil (who is within us) as the liar from the beginning, and thus characterizes man with respect to what seems to be the chief ground of evil in him.

[11] Horace, *Satires*, I, 1. "Change but the name, of you the tale is told." (Conington).

[12] Cf. Romans V, 12.

of its *beginning in time,* we must search for the causes of each deliberate transgression in a previous period of our lives, far back to that period wherein the use of reason had not yet developed, and thus back to a propensity to evil (as a natural ground) which is therefore called innate — the source of evil. But to trace the causes of evil in the instance of the first man, who is depicted as already in full command of the use of his reason, is neither necessary nor feasible, since otherwise this basis (the evil propensity) would have had to be created in him; therefore his sin is set forth as engendered directly from innocence. We must not, however, look for an origin in time of a moral character for which we are to be held responsible; though to do so is inevitable if we wish to *explain* the contingent existence of this character (and perhaps it is for this reason that Scripture, in conformity with this weakness of ours, has thus pictured the temporal origin of evil).

But the rational origin of this perversion of our will whereby it makes lower incentives supreme among its maxims, that is, of the propensity to evil, remains inscrutable to us, because this propensity itself must be set down to our account and because, as a result, that ultimate ground of all maxims would in turn involve the adoption of an evil maxim [as its basis]. Evil could have sprung only from the morally-evil (not from mere limitations in our nature); and yet the original predisposition (which no one other than man himself could have corrupted, if he is to be held responsible for this corruption) is a predisposition to good; there is then for us no conceivable ground from which the moral evil in us could originally have come. This inconceivability, together with a more accurate specification of the wickedness of our race, the Bible expresses in the historical narrative as follows.[13] It finds a place for evil at the creation of the world, yet not in man, but in a *spirit* of an originally loftier destiny. Thus is the *first* beginning of all evil represented as inconceivable by us (for whence came evil to that spirit?); but man is represented as having fallen into evil only *through seduction,* and hence as being *not basically* corrupt (even as regards his original predisposition to good) but rather as still capable of an improvement, in contrast to a seducing *spirit,* that is, a being for whom temptation of the flesh cannot be accounted as an alleviation of guilt. For man, therefore, who despite a corrupted heart yet possesses a good will, there remains hope of a return to the good from which he has strayed.

[13] What is written here must not be read as though intended for Scriptural exegesis, which lies beyond the limits of the domain of bare reason. It is possible to explain how an historical account is to be put to a moral use without deciding whether this is the intention of the author or merely our interpretation, provided this meaning is true in itself, apart from all historical proof, and is moreover the only one whereby we can derive something conducive to our betterment from a passage which otherwise would be only an unfruitful addition to our historical knowledge. We must not quarrel unnecessarily over a question or over its historical aspect, when, however it is understood, it in no way helps us to be better men, and when that which can afford such help is discovered without historical proof, and indeed must be apprehended without it. That historical knowledge which has no inner bearing valid for all men belongs to the class of *adiaphora,* which each man is free to hold as he finds edifying.

Ignatius Loyola

Ignatius Loyola (ca. 1491-1556), founder of the Society of Jesus (Jesuits), wrote out of his mystical experiences at Manresa, Spain, the Ejercicios *or "Spiritual Exercises" as a guide to his followers. Conceiving his mission as that of a soldier of Christ, he established his organization on military lines, and the* Ejercicios *became, accordingly, a sort of manual-at-arms for his Christian soldiers. It contains definite rules designed to enable souls to conquer their passions and so give themselves to the efficient service of Christ. The most striking feature of the manual is a peculiar combination of sense impressions and the use of imagination and understanding in moving the will. The full course was designed to extend for about a month, but is often compressed within a considerably shorter period. The following illustrates the method.*

The Jesuit Method of Meditation *

Meditation consists in calling to mind some dogmatic or moral truth, and reflecting on or discussing this truth according to each one's capacity, so as to move the will and produce in us amendment.

Thus, if you have to meditate on the sin of the angels, you will call to mind how they, having disobeyed their Creator, forfeited grace and were cast out of heaven into hell. You will then reflect attentively on this subject, so as to feel confounded by and blush at the multitude of your sins, compared to this one single sin which ruined the rebel angels. In fine, you will conclude that you have often merited the same punishment as they, since you too have so often sinned.

To meditate usefully, observe well the following rules:

Before Meditation

1. The subject should be divided into two or three points, that the meditation may be rendered more easy by a division which is natural and easy to remember.

2. Before beginning, we must by a preparatory prayer beg of God by His grace to direct all the powers and operations of our souls to His service and glory alone.

3. The heart having taken this proper and generous resolution, the faithful soul must impress the subject proposed on the mind, the imagination, and the will.

If the subject of the meditation is a history, — for example, that of the Prodigal Son, — the *memory* must recall the principal facts. This is the first prelude as generally used, particularly during the second and following weeks.

* Ignacio de Loyola, *The Spiritual Exercises of St. Ignatius* (New York: Frederick Pustet Company, Inc., 1914), pp. 54–61. Used by permission.

The *imagination* seizes its object by placing it in a certain spot which the mind represents to itself. This has caused the name of "composition of place" to be given to the second prelude. If the meditation is on some visible object, such as the birth of Jesus Christ, we must figure to ourselves the place where this mystery was accomplished, — the stable at Bethlehem, the manger, &c. If the mind is occupied by a truth purely intellectual, — for example, the misery of sin, — we may assist ourselves by a picture of a soul imprisoned in the body, banished among animals in this vale of tears. The object of this prelude is to give the soul the impression that would be produced upon it by the sight of a picture representing exactly the subject of meditation; or, still better, by the sight of the place where the mystery occurred. We must avoid in this, even more than in other points, all violent efforts of the mind, or loss of time. Since every person's imagination is not sufficiently lively and docile to succeed easily in this prelude, it must be set aside if it prove an embarrassment.

The *will* is exercised in soliciting a grace according to the mystery: for example, contrition, sorrow, joy, &c.

During the Meditation

1. We must endeavour to understand and feel inwardly the truth on which we meditate, rather than think much on it.

2. If facility and consolation are experienced, we must beware of vain satisfaction. We must never make a vow lightly or without advice. Our reflections and sentiments must always be directed towards our own amendment.

3. In times of dryness and desolation we must be patient, and wait with resignation the return of consolation, putting our trust in the goodness of God. We must animate ourselves by the thought that God is always with us, that He only allows this trial for our greater good, and that we have not necessarily lost His grace because we have lost the taste and feeling of it.

4. Meditations should be ended by one or several *Colloquies*. These are familiar conversations in which we speak to God like a son to a father, a servant to a master, one friend to another, a criminal to a judge; sometimes acknowledging our faults, sometimes exposing our wants, sometimes asking graces. These colloquies are addressed to the Blessed Virgin, to our Saviour, or to God the Father, sometimes to all three successively. This is the part of the meditation requiring the most liberty and confidence, but also the most respect. They must be concluded either by the "Ave Maria," the "Anima Christi," or the "Pater," according to the person to whom they are addressed. These colloquies may take place not only at the end, but at the beginning, or in the course of the meditation, as devotion may inspire. When we address ourselves to Jesus Christ, and beg Him to intercede for us before God, it must be understood that we consider Him, not simply as God, but in His human nature as our Mediator and Advocate.

After Meditation

When two meditations have been made, it is customary to repeat them once or twice. This method is very useful, for it often happens that the first view of a mystery offers food chiefly to the *curiosity* of the mind; but, this desire of knowledge once satisfied, the soul returns calmly to its first impressions, and can more easily give free course to its affections; for it is in the affections of the heart that the fruits of an exercise consist. In these repetitions we must avoid all long reasonings, and only replace before our eyes, and run over, so to say, our first thoughts, dwelling on them with our will and heart. The use of the colloquies should be more frequent during the repetitions than during the Exercises.

Additional Recommendations

in the form of resolutions, which will assist us in making the exercises well, and obtaining from God what we ask of Him

1. On lying down, before going to sleep, during the short time which will suffice for repeating the "Hail Mary," I will fix the hour of my rising, and review in my mind the points of my meditation.

2. On awakening, immediately excluding all other thoughts, I will apply my mind to the truth on which I am going to meditate; at the same time I will excite in my heart suitable sentiments. For example, before the Exercise on the "triple sin," I will say to myself while I dress, "And I, loaded with so many graces, the object of predilection to my Lord and King, I stand convicted of ingratitude, of treason, of rebellion, before His eyes and those of His whole court." Before the Exercise on personal sins, "Behold me, a criminal deserving death, led before my Judge loaded with chains." These sentiments must accompany the act of rising, and will vary according to the subject of meditation.

3. Standing a few paces from the spot where I am going to make my meditation, I must recollect myself, raise my mind above earthly things, and consider our Lord Jesus Christ as present and attentive to what I am about to do. Having given to this preparation the time required to say the "Our Father," I will offer the homage of my soul and body to our Saviour, assuming an attitude full of veneration and humble respect.

4. I will then begin my meditation, if I am alone in my chamber or elsewhere without witnesses, in the posture most suitable to the end I propose to myself, sometimes with my face bowed to the earth, sometimes standing, sometimes sitting; only observing that if I obtain what I seek kneeling, or in any other attitude, I ought to remain so without seeking anything better. In the same way, if any particular point causes me to experience the grace which I am seeking, I must remain there calmly until my devotion is satisfied, without caring for anything more.

5. After having finished the Exercise, I will either walk about or sit still, and examine how it has succeeded. If it has not, I will ascertain the cause, sincerely repent, and make firm resolutions for the future. If the success has been satisfactory, I will make acts of thanksgiving, and resolve to follow the same method for the future.

6. I will lay aside during the first week all joyful thoughts, such, for instance,

as the glorious resurrection of Jesus Christ. This thought would dry up the tears which I ought at this period to shed over my sins. I must rather call up thoughts of death and judgment, in order to assist my sorrow.

7. For the same purpose, I will shut out the daylight, only allowing sufficient light to enter my room to enable me to read and take my meals.

8. I will carefully avoid all laughter, or any thing which can lead to it.

9. I will not look at any one, unless obliged to salute them or say adieu.

10. [This recommendation relates to penance, of which there are two kinds: (*a*) interior, consisting of grief for one's sins, and (*b*) exterior, consisting of self-chastisement. Severe restraint in matters of food and sleep is recommended, and also the further mortification of the body by the infliction upon it of inconvenience and pain. All such penance is to be more unpleasant than is temperance, yet it must never be so severe as to injure one's health. G. MacGregor.]

John Henry Newman

Newman (1801-1890) is from perhaps every point of view the most remarkable figure in English church life in the nineteenth century. The leader of the Tractarian party in the Church of England and by far the most influential churchman at Oxford, he was eventually received, in 1845, into the Roman Church. Less popular in Vatican circles than was his English contemporary, Cardinal Manning, Newman was a churchman of the deepest personal conviction and the finest scholarship, and his writings exhibit an exceptionally acute insight into the nature of religious faith. In 1879 Pope Leo XIII named him a Cardinal of the Roman Church, a recognition that many felt to be very belatedly conferred. In 1870 Newman published his Grammar of Assent, *in which he developed the notion of the "illative sense," the faculty of judging from given facts by processes outside the limits of ordinary reasoning — a faculty that he accounted of immense importance in reaching religious certitude. The illative sense is not a feeling or emotion; rather, it is the faculty which, underlying the ratiocinative faculty, compels assent.*

*The Illative Sense **

Certitude is a mental state: certainty is a quality of propositions. Those propositions I call certain, which are such that I am certain of them. Certitude is not a passive impression made upon the mind from without, by argumentative compulsion, but in all concrete questions (nay, even in abstract, for though the reasoning is abstract, the mind which judges of it is concrete) it is an active recognition of propositions as true, such as it is the duty of each individual himself to exercise at the bidding of reason, and, when reason forbids, to withhold. And reason never bids us be certain except on an absolute proof; and such a proof can never be furnished to us by the logic of words, for as certitude is of the mind, so is the act of inference which leads to it. Every one who reasons, is his own centre; and no expedient for attaining a common measure of minds can reverse this truth; — but then the question follows, is there any *criterion* of the accuracy of an inference, such as may be our warrant that certitude is rightly elicited in favour of the proposition inferred, since our warrant cannot, as I have said, be scientific? I have already said that the sole and final judgment on the validity of an inference in concrete matter is committed to the personal action of the ratiocinative faculty, the perfection or virtue of which I have called the Illative Sense, a use of the word "sense" parallel to our use of it in "good sense," "common sense," a "sense of beauty," &c.; — and I own I do not see any way to go further than this in

* John H. Newman, *A Grammar of Assent* (New York: Longmans, Green & Co., Inc., 1906), pp. 344–362; 371–383.

answer to the question. However, I can at least explain my meaning more fully; and therefore I will now speak, first of the sanction of the Illative Sense, next of its nature, and then of its range.

The Sanction of the Illative Sense

We are in a world of facts, and we use them; for there is nothing else to use. We do not quarrel with them, but we take them as they are, and avail ourselves of what they can do for us. It would be out of place to demand of fire, water, earth, and air their credentials, so to say, for acting upon us, or ministering to us. We call them elements, and turn them to account, and make the most of them. We speculate on them at our leisure. But what we are still less able to doubt about or annul, at our leisure or not, is that which is at once their counterpart and their witness, I mean, ourselves. We are conscious of the objects of external nature, and we reflect and act upon them, and this consciousness, reflection, and action we call our rationality. And as we use the (so called) elements without first criticizing what we have no command over, so is it much more unmeaning in us to criticize or find fault with our own nature, which is nothing else than we ourselves, instead of using it according to the use of which it ordinarily admits. Our being, with its faculties, mind and body, is a fact not admitting of question, all things being of necessity referred to it, not it to other things.

If I may not assume that I exist, and in a particular way, that is, with a particular mental constitution, I have nothing to speculate about, and had better let speculation alone. Such as I am, it is my all; this is my essential stand-point, and must be taken for granted; otherwise, thought is but an idle amusement, not worth the trouble. There is no medium between using my faculties, as I have them, and flinging myself upon the external world according to the random impulse of the moment, as spray upon the surface of the waves, and simply forgetting that I am.

I am what I am, or I am nothing. I cannot think, reflect, or judge about my being, without starting from the very point which I aim at concluding. My ideas are all assumptions, and I am ever moving in a circle. I cannot avoid being sufficient for myself, for I cannot make myself anything else, and to change me is to destroy me. If I do not use myself, I have no other self to use. My only business is to ascertain what I am, in order to put it to use. It is enough for the proof of the value and authority of any function which I possess, to be able to pronounce that it is natural. What I have to ascertain is the laws under which I live. My first elementary lesson of duty is that of resignation to the laws of my nature, whatever they are; my first disobedience is to be impatient at what I am, and to indulge an ambitious aspiration after what I cannot be, to cherish a distrust of my powers, and to desire to change laws which are identical with myself.

Truths such as these, which are too obvious to be called irresistible, are illustrated by what we see in universal nature. Every being is in a true sense sufficient for itself, so as to be able to fulfil its particular needs. It is a general law that, whatever is found as a function or an attribute of any class of beings, or is natural to it, is in its substance suitable to it, and subserves its existence, and cannot be rightly regarded as a fault or enormity. No being could endure, of which the constituent parts were at war with each other. And more than this; there is that principle of vitality in every being, which is of a sanative and restorative character, and which brings all its parts and functions together into one whole, and is ever repelling and correcting the mischiefs which befall it, whether from within or without, while showing no tendency to cast off its belongings as if foreign to its nature. The brute animals are found severally with limbs and organs, habits, instincts, appetites, surroundings, which play together for the safety and welfare of the whole; and, after all exceptions, may be said each of them to have, after its own kind, a perfection of nature. Man is the highest of the animals, and more indeed than an animal, as having a mind; that is, he has a complex nature different from theirs, with a higher aim and a specific perfection; but still the fact that other beings find their good in the use of their particular nature, is a reason for anticipating that to use duly our own is our interest as well as our necessity.

What is the peculiarity of our nature, in contrast with the inferior animals around us? It is that, though man cannot change what he is born with, he is a being of progress with relation to his perfection and characteristic good. Other beings are complete from their first existence, in that line of excellence which is allotted to them; but man begins with nothing realized (to use the word), and he has to make capital for himself by the exercise of those faculties which are his natural inheritance. Thus he gradually advances to the fulness of his original destiny. Nor is this progress mechanical, nor is it of necessity; it is committed to the personal efforts of each individual of the species; each of us has the prerogative of completing his inchoate and rudimental nature, and of developing his own perfection out of the living elements with which his mind began to be. It is his gift to be the creator of his own sufficiency; and to be emphatically self-made. This is the law of his being, which he cannot escape; and whatever is involved in that law he is bound, or rather he is carried on, to fulfil.

And here I am brought to the bearing of these remarks upon my subject. For this law of progress is carried out by means of the acquisition of knowledge, of which inference and assent are the immediate instruments. Supposing, then, the advancement of our nature, both in ourselves individually and as regards the human family, is, to every one of us in his place, a sacred duty, it follows that that duty is intimately bound up with the right use of these two main instruments of fulfilling it. And as we do not gain the knowledge of the law of progress by any *à priori* view of man, but by looking at it as the interpretation which is provided by himself on a large scale in the ordinary action of his intellectual nature, so too we must appeal to himself, as a fact, and not to any antecedent theory, in order to find what is the law of his mind as regards the two faculties in question. If then such an appeal does bear me out in deciding, as I have done, that the course of inference is ever more or less obscure, while assent is ever distinct and definite, and yet that what is in its nature thus absolute does, in fact, follow upon what in outward manifestation is thus complex, indirect, and recondite, what is left to us but to take things as they are, and to resign ourselves to what we find? that is, instead of devising, what cannot be, some sufficient science of reasoning which may compel certitude in concrete conclusions, to confess that there is no ultimate test of truth besides the testimony born to truth by the mind itself, and that this phenomenon, perplexing as we may find it, is a normal and inevitable characteristic of the mental constitution of a being like man on a stage such as the world. His progress is a living growth, not a mechanism; and its instruments are mental acts, not the formulas and contrivances of language.

We are accustomed in this day to lay great stress upon the harmony of the universe; and we have well learned the maxim so powerfully inculcated by our own English philosopher, that in our inquiries into its laws, we must sternly destroy all idols of the intellect, and subdue nature by co-operating with her. Knowledge is power, for it enables us to use eternal principles which we cannot alter. So also is it in that microcosm, the human mind. Let us follow Bacon more closely than to distort its faculties according to the demands of an ideal optimism, instead of looking out for modes of thought proper to our nature, and faithfully observing them in our intellectual exercises.

Of course I do not stop here. As the structure of the universe speaks to us of Him who made it, so the laws of the mind are the expression, not of mere constituted order, but of His will. I should be bound by them even were they not His laws; but since one of their very functions is to tell me of Him, they throw a reflex light upon themselves, and, for resignation to my destiny, I substitute a cheerful concurrence in an overruling Providence. We may gladly welcome such difficulties as are to be found in our mental constitution, and in the interaction of our faculties, if we are able to feel that He gave them to us, and He can overrule them for us. We may securely take them as they are, and use them as we find them. It is He who teaches us all knowledge; and the way by which we acquire it is His way. He varies that way according to the subject-matter; but whether He has set before us in our particular pursuit the way of observation or of experiment, of speculation or of research, of demonstration or of probability, whether we are inquiring into the system of the universe, or into the elements of matter and of life, or into the history of human society and past times, if we take the way proper to our subject-matter, we have His blessing upon us, and shall find, besides abundant matter for mere opinion, the materials in due measure of proof and assent.

And especially, by this disposition of things, shall we learn, as regards religious and ethical inquiries, how little we can effect, however much we exert ourselves, without that Blessing; for, as if on set purpose, He has made this path of thought rugged and circuitous above other investigations, that the very discipline inflicted on our minds in finding Him, may mould them into due devotion to Him when He is found. "Verily Thou art a hidden God, the God of Israel, the Saviour," is the very law of His dealings with us. Certainly we need a clue into the labyrinth which is to lead us to Him; and who among us can hope to seize upon the true starting-points of thought for that enterprise, and upon all of them, who is to understand their right direction, to follow them out to their just limits, and duly to estimate, adjust, and combine the various reasonings in which they issue, so as safely to arrive at what it is worth any labour to secure, without a special illumination from Himself? Such are the dealings of Wisdom with the elect soul. "She will bring upon him fear, and dread, and trial; and She will torture him with the tribulation of Her discipline, till She try him by Her laws, and trust his soul. Then She will strengthen him, and make Her way straight to him, and give him joy."

The Nature of the Illative Sense

It is the mind that reasons, and that controls its own reasonings, not any technical apparatus of words and propositions. This power of judging and concluding, when in its perfection, I call the Illative Sense, and I shall best illustrate it by referring to parallel faculties, which we commonly recognize without difficulty.

For instance, how does the mind fulfil its function of supreme direction and control, in matters of duty, social intercourse, and taste? In all of these separate actions of the intellect, the individual is supreme, and responsible to himself, nay, under circumstances, may be justified in opposing himself to the judgment of the whole world; though he uses rules to his great advantage, as far as they go, and is in consequence bound to use them. As regards moral duty, the subject is fully considered in the well-known ethical treatises of Aristotle. He calls the faculty which guides the mind in matters of conduct, by the name of *phronesis*, or judgment. This is the directing, controlling, and determining principle in such matters, personal and social. What it is to be virtuous, how we are to gain the just idea and standard of virtue, how we are to approximate in practice to our own standard, what is right and wrong in a particular case, for the answers in fulness and accuracy to these and similar questions, the philosopher refers us to no code of laws, to no moral treatise, because no science of life, applicable to the case of an individual, has been or can be written. Such is Aristotle's doctrine, and it is undoubtedly true. An ethical system may supply laws, general rules, guiding principles, a number of examples, suggestions, landmarks, limitations, cautions, distinctions, solutions of critical or anxious difficulties; but who is to apply them to a particular case? whither can we go, except to the living intellect, our own, or another's? What is written is too vague, too negative for our need. It bids us avoid extremes; but it cannot ascertain for us, according to our personal need, the golden mean. The authoritative oracle, which is to decide our path, is something more searching and manifold than such jejune generalizations as treatises can give, which are most distinct and clear when we least need them. It is seated in the mind of the individual, who is thus his own law, his own teacher, and his own judge in those special cases of duty which are personal to him. It comes of an acquired habit, though it has its first origin in nature itself, and it is formed and matured by practice and experience; and it manifests itself, not in any breadth of view, any philosophical comprehension of the mutual relations of duty towards duty, or any consistency in its teachings, but it is a capacity sufficient for the occasion, deciding what ought to be done here and now, by this given person, under these given circumstances. It decides nothing hypothetical, it does not determine what a man should do ten years hence, or what another should do at this time. It may indeed happen to decide ten years hence as it does now, and to decide a second case now as it now decides a first; still its present act is for the present, not for the distant or the future.

State or public law is inflexible, but this mental rule is not only minute and particular, but has an elasticity, which, in its application to individual cases, is, as I have said, not studious to maintain the appearance of consistency. In old times the mason's rule which was in use at Lesbos was, according to Aristotle, not of wood or iron, but of lead, so as to allow of its adjustment to the uneven surface of the stones brought together for the work. By such the philosopher illustrates the nature of equity in contrast with law, and such is that *phronesis*, from which the science of morals forms its rules, and receives its complement.

In this respect of course the law of truth differs from the law of duty, that duties change, but truths never; but, though truth is ever one and the same, and the assent of certitude is immutable, still the reasonings which carry us on to truth and certitude are many and distinct, and vary with the inquirer; and it is not with assent, but with the controlling principle in inferences that I am comparing *phronesis*. It is with this drift that I observe that the rule of conduct for one man is not always the rule for another, though the rule is always one and the same in the abstract, and in its principle and scope. To learn his own duty in his own case, each individual must have recourse to his own rule; and if his rule is not sufficiently developed in his intellect for his need, then he goes to some other living, present authority, to supply it for him, not to the dead letter of a treatise or a code. A living, present authority, himself or another, is his immediate guide in matters of a personal, social, or political character. In buying and selling, in contracts, in his treatment of others, in giving and receiving, in thinking, speaking, doing, and working, in toil, in danger, in his recreations and pleasures, every one of his acts, to be praiseworthy, must be in accordance with this practical sense. Thus it is, and not by science, that he perfects the virtues of justice, self-command, magnanimity, generosity, gentleness, and all others. *Phronesis* is the regulating principle of every one of them.

These last words lead me to a further remark. I doubt whether it is correct, strictly speaking, to consider this *phronesis* as a general faculty, directing and perfecting all the virtues at once. So understood, it is little better than an abstract term, including under it a circle of analogous faculties, severally proper to the separate virtues. Properly speaking, there are as many kinds of *phronesis* as there are virtues: for the judgment, good sense, or tact which is conspicuous in a man's conduct in one subject-matter, is not necessarily traceable in another. As in the parallel cases of memory and reasoning, he may be great in one aspect of his character, and little-minded in another. He may be exemplary in his family, yet commit a fraud on the revenue; he may be just and cruel, brave and sensual, imprudent and patient. And if this be true of the moral virtues, it holds good still more fully when we compare what is called his private character with his public. A good man may make a bad king; profligates have been great statesmen, or magnanimous political leaders.

So, too, I may go on to speak of the various callings and professions which give scope to the exercise of great talents, for these talents also are matured, not by mere rule, but by personal skill and sagacity. They are as diverse as pleading and cross-examining, conducting a debate in Parliament, swaying a public meeting, and commanding an army; and here, too, I observe that, though the directing principle in each case is called by the same name, — sagacity, skill, tact, or prudence, — still there is no one ruling faculty leading to eminence in all these various lines of action in common, but men will excel in one of them, without any talent for the rest.

The parallel may be continued in the case of the Fine Arts, in which, though true and scientific rules may be given, no one would therefore deny that Phidias or Rafael had a far more subtle standard of taste and a more versatile power of embodying it in his works, than any which he could communicate to others in even a series of treatises. And here again genius is indissolubly united to one definite subject-matter; a poet is not therefore a painter, or an architect a musical composer.

And so, again, as regards the useful arts and personal accomplishments, we use the same word "skill," but proficiency in engineering or in ship-building, or again in engraving, or again in singing, in playing instruments, in acting, or in gymnastic exercises, is as simply one with its particular subject-matter, as the human soul with its particular body, and is, in its own department, a sort of instinct or inspiration, not an obedience to external rules of criticism or of science.

It is natural, then, to ask the question, why ratiocination should be an exception to a general law which attaches to the intellectual exercises of the mind; why it is held to be commensurate with logical science; and why logic is made an instrumental art sufficient for determining every sort of truth, while no one would dream of making any one formula, however generalized, a working rule at once for poetry, the art of medicine, and political warfare?

This is what I have to remark concerning the Illative Sense, and in explanation of its nature and claims; and on the whole, I have spoken of it in four respects, — as viewed in itself, in its subject-matter, in the process it uses, and in its function and scope.

First, viewed in its exercise, it is one and the same in all concrete matters, though employed in them in different measures. We do not reason in one way in chemistry or law, in another in morals or religion; but in reasoning on any subject whatever, which is concrete, we proceed, as far indeed as we can, by the logic of language, but we are obliged to supplement it by the more subtle and elastic logic of thought; for forms by themselves prove nothing.

Secondly, it is in fact attached to definite subject-matters, so that a given individual may possess it in one department of thought, for instance, history, and not in another, for instance, philosophy.

Thirdly, in coming to its conclusion, it proceeds always in the same way, by a method of reasoning, which, as I have observed above, is the elementary principle of that mathematical calculus of modern times, which has so wonderfully extended the limits of abstract science.

Fourthly, in no class of concrete reasonings, whether in experimental science, historical research, or theology, is there any ultimate test of truth and error in our inferences besides the trustworthiness of the Illative Sense that gives them its sanction; just as there is no sufficient test of poetical excellence, heroic action, or gentleman-like conduct, other than the particular mental sense, be it genius, taste, sense of propriety, or the moral sense, to which those subject-matters are severally committed. Our duty in each of these is to strengthen and perfect the special faculty which is its living rule, and in every case as it comes to do our best. And such also is our duty and our necessity, as regards the Illative Sense.

The Range of the Illative Sense

Great as are the services of language in enabling us to extend the compass of our inferences, to test their validity, and to communicate them to others, still the mind itself is more versatile and vigorous than any of its works, of which language is one, and it is only under its penetrating and subtle action that the margin disappears, which I have described as intervening between verbal argumentation and conclusions in the concrete. It determines what science cannot determine, the limit of converging probabilities and the reasons sufficient for a proof. It is the ratiocinative mind itself, and no trick of art, however simple in its form and sure in operation, by which we are able to determine, and thereupon to be certain, that a moving body left to itself will never stop, and that no man can live without eating.

Nor, again, is it by any diagram that we are able to scrutinize, sort, and combine the many premisses which must be first run together before we answer duly a given question. It is to the living mind that we must look for the means of using correctly principles of whatever kind, facts or doctrines, experiences or testimonies, true or probable, and of discerning what conclusion from these is necessary, suitable, or expedient, when they are taken for granted; and this, either by means of a natural gift, or from mental formation and practice and a long familiarity with those various starting-points. Thus, when Laud said that he did not see his way to come to terms with the Holy See, "till Rome was other than she was," no Catholic would admit the sentiment: but any Catholic may understand that this is just the judgment consistent with Laud's actual condition of thought and cast of opinions, his ecclesiastical position, and the existing state of England.

Nor, lastly, is an action of the mind itself less necessary in relation to those first elements of thought which in all reasoning are assumptions, the principles, tastes, and opinions, very often of a personal character, which are half the battle in the inference with which the reasoning is to terminate. It is the mind itself that detects them in their obscure recesses, illustrates them, establishes them, eliminates them, resolves them into simpler ideas, as the case may be. The mind contemplates them without the use of words, by a process which cannot be analyzed. Thus it was that Bacon separated the physical system of the world from the theological; thus that Butler connected together the moral system with the religious. Logical formulas could never have sustained the reasonings involved in such investigations.

Thus the Illative Sense, that is, the reasoning faculty, as exercised by gifted, or by educated or otherwise well-prepared minds, has its function in the beginning, middle, and end of all verbal discussion and inquiry, and in every step of the process. It is a rule to itself, and appeals to no judgment beyond its own; and attends upon the whole course of thought from antecedents to consequents, with a minute diligence and unwearied presence, which is impossible to a cumbrous apparatus of verbal reasoning, though, in communicating with others, words are the only instrument we possess, and a serviceable, though imperfect instrument.

One function indeed there is of Logic, to which I have referred in the preceding sentence, which the Illative Sense does not and cannot perform. It supplies no common measure between mind and mind, as being nothing else than a personal gift or acquisition. Few there are, as I said above, who are good reasoners on all subject-matters. Two men, who reason well each in his own province of thought, may, one or both of them, fail and pronounce opposite judgments on a question belonging to some third province. Moreover, all reasoning being from premisses, and those premisses arising (if it so happen) in their first elements from personal characteristics, in which men are in fact in essential and irremediable variance one with another, the ratiocinative talent can do no more than point out where the difference between them lies, how far it is immaterial, when it is worth while continuing an argument between them, and when not.

Henri Bremond

Henri Bremond (1865-1933) was a French writer on the spiritual life, a passage from whose twelve-volume opus maximum, *the* Histoire littéraire du sentiment religieux en France, *is here reproduced in translation (though no translation could do justice to his remarkable French style). Bremond, who entered the Society of Jesus in 1882, was ordained priest in 1892; but he left the Society in order to devote himself entirely to his literary work. His labors, unrecognized by the Roman Church, were crowned by the French Academy. Bremond's central interest lay in the seventeenth-century French spiritual writers, in whom he found a cohesive tradition springing from the thought and influence of St. Francis of Sales (1567-1622). What he admired in this tradition was the absence of the rigorism of the more ascetical writers on the spiritual life and an emphasis on what he called* pur amour, *the disinterested love of God. In the passage here quoted he characteristically attacks a writer, Pierre Nicole (*supra, *page 109), whom he terms an "anti-mystical rationalist" and in contrast to whom he offers a more mystical account of our knowledge of God.*

Against the Rationalist Obsession *

We reproach them for that lack of imagination which prevents them from supposing a case where they could not shift for themselves.

—— M. Barrès,
Méditation sur Sainte-Beuve

A small village in the Alps, almost inaccessible, whose inhabitants practically never leave it, and where, from father to son, everyone has goiter. Sunday worship. Enter the church a lost traveler. People turn around; they nudge each other, and soon wild laughter breaks out over all the pews. He does not have goiter! From the height of his pulpit, the pastor, himself caught by the infection, nevertheless tries to bring his sheep back to a more tolerant attitude. "After all, if this good man is not made like us, he is only the more to be pitied. Let us not further insult his strange infirmity." — This fable symbolizes marvelously the anti-mystic rationalism of Nicole and many other people. The goiter is the rational knowledge which they have of God, and which seems to them to be the only appropriate, the only possible, kind. As means of communication between him and us, they allow only the abstract way of reasoning, images, *distinct* ideas, and the feelings which these same ideas arouse. Man, they say, is a rational animal. No angel then. An animal, he has senses

* Henri Bremond, *Histoire littéraire du sentiment religieux en France* (12 vols.; Paris: Bloud et Gay, 1925), IV, "La conquête mystique," pp. 550–560. English translation by Sarah Ann Caner.

by which external objects penetrate him in some way, or at least make him feel, as it were, their presence. The flame burns him; a thorn lacerates him; a soft hand caresses him. Rational, he manipulates in his way the data of the senses, aided in this by a curious little torch, which encourages him to compare these data with each other, to give suitable names not only to a single flame, to a single thorn, but to all; then, to conceive of other invisible and intangible objects, e.g., the soul, souls, and God. These last objects escape, by definition, all immediate, direct (in a word, sensible) apprehension; they escape experience. One comes to represent them, however, for better, for worse, and so well that one can write folios on them, rich in clear and distinct ideas: God the Creator, Providence; omniscience, omnipotence, goodness, justice, and so forth. It is understood that by these concepts we do not attain to God himself, but only to a certain image of him, clear enough, moving enough, however, to excite veneration, obedience, and love in our will and in our affective faculties. In heaven we will see him face to face; here below in the reflection of a reflection.

The mystics claim to reach God by another way, more obscure as to the truth, but, on the other hand, more direct. When they want to describe this way, they are embarrassed. Words fail them. For want of anything better, they generally have recourse to words which give the impression, confused but strong, which sensible objects make on us — heat, taste, grasp, for example — but they warn us that these words must not be taken in the proper sense: God is not a flame, he is not a fruit, he has no hands. In short, their mystical knowledge, their *contemplation,* is distinguished from both rational and sensible knowledge; it is knowledge like the former, but indistinct; it is contact like the latter, but spiritual. According to St. John of the Cross, "Mystical theology is the mysterious and supernatural knowledge of God." "Contemplation," writes St. Francis of Sales, "is nothing else than a loving, *simple,* and permanent attention of the spirit to divine things."[1] And M. Saudreau: "What makes the basis, the essential, of contemplation is an intimate union of the heart with God, a loving union, due not to precise and reasoned considerations, but to a general and indistinct knowledge of God."[2]

These courageous definitions call for a remark which Nicole, to his misfortune, could not make — the lack of which, in my opinion, resolves the debate. Do you not feel, indeed, that the mystics must be very sure of themselves and of the treasure they flatter themselves that they possess, to expose themselves thus, right from the threshold of their works, to the irony of the learned? Think of the unfavorable sense which practically all the words one has just read first suggest, of the calm avowal of impotence and poverty that they conceal: "mysterious" — in other words, inexplicable, unintelligible; "simple" — in other words, devoid of concepts; "general" — in other words, vague, confused; finally, "irrational, imprecise, indistinct." Does one ever see the inventor

[1] Lamballe, *La contemplation, ou principes de théologie mystique* (Paris, 1916), p. 47 ff.

[2] Saudreau, *Les degrés de la vie spirituelle* (Paris, 1912), II, p. 37. Knowledge and love, the one involving the other; but, as we are discussing here the rationalist prejudice, we speak above all of "knowledge."

of any new philosophy entice the gallery by such hollow promises? Ordinarily, more light is promised us; here, on the contrary, more darkness. But the mystics are not fools; many of them have read Aristotle, St. Thomas, even Descartes and the *Port-Royal Logic*, where they learned, if it was necessary, that confusion in itself is not a merit. It must be, then, that their confusion, since they hoist it so high, is not a confusion like the confusion of others; it must be that, in their thought, the epithets which they use do not have the pejorative and degrading sense they would have were they applied to other objects; finally, it must be that the experience which they present to us appears to them of such value, of such splendor, that the idea of comparing it to the cryings of childhood or to the uncertain lights of the narrow-minded could occur to no one. They well expect to find unbelievers, but intelligent and critical ones, who will treat such a grave discussion seriously. One usually thinks twice before imputing to anybody too glaring absurdities and the negation of first principles.

Thus when a man, accounted wise, preaches the folly of the Cross, one understands without difficulty that this folly is not like other follies, and one does not run to denounce the hysteria of the preacher to the police. Nevertheless, do not expect such an elementary wisdom either from Nicole or from most of the other anti-mystics. With these ill-sounding, "confused," "indistinct" epithets scarcely understood, their rationalism sees red, so to speak, it throws itself headlong on these horrible syllables, it rips them up with its horns, it stamps endlessly on the shameful remains in the arena. I do not apologize for my ridiculous metaphors. All exasperations are permitted to him who has read (alas, and reread) the *Refutation of the Errors of the Quietists*. Try for yourself.

In this accursed book, everything is brought back to one argument a hundred times repeated: It is absurd to prefer a confused *idea* to a clear *idea*, or, if you will, a stone to the vine in flower, a centime to a louis,[3] a grub to a beautiful butterfly. Obviously, that is absurd; moreover, the mystics, and Mme. Guyon herself, have never maintained any such thing. They do not compare, they do not prefer, this *idea* to that *idea*, but, what is entirely different, this order of *knowledge* to that order. To the rational knowledge which is formed from *ideas* and which reasons upon them, they oppose mystical knowledge, contemplation, that is, a direct, immediate means — not of *conceiving* God, which would make no sense, but of embracing Him in some way and possessing Him. The question then is not of knowing whether a confused idea of God is worth more or less than a clear idea, but whether the experience of God, present to the interior of our soul, and making its presence sensible, is worth more or less than the theological conceptions of a scholar, or, again, of knowing whether the chemical analysis of our food is more nourishing than a good meal. But one will ask, is this mystical knowledge of God possible? For the moment, I know nothing about it, and indeed I reproach Nicole with not having clearly asked, frankly discussed, this question, the only question. Fundamentally, I am sure that he did not dare to declare that such knowledge is impossible; but his entire discussion implies that it is. Bent upon conceiving only a single

[3] *Louis d'or*, a gold coin.

order of knowledge, rational knowledge, he constantly holds as demonstrated precisely that which he ought to demonstrate, namely, that there is only this order of knowledge. Such is, unless I am mistaken, what in good logic one calls begging the question, not to use a more shocking expression.[4] So with a reunion of scholars to which at the time of M. Thiers one would have submitted the plan of an airplane. One can fly, they would have said, only with the living wings of bird or angel. But, by your own confession, not only have you no wings, but besides, your man-bird would move only the tips of his fingers.

The second sin, equally mortal, is against method, against the light. Malaval, Guilloré, and Bernières have not invented the definitions that one has just recalled; they have them from the great mystics, from St. Theresa, from John of the Cross, both canonized by the Church. But these Nicole is formally forbidden to discuss. A genuflection, and he passes by. Lack of courage, of logic, of integrity? That's for him to look to. It remains no less evident that, when Malaval, Guilloré, and Bernières say exactly the same things as St. Theresa, if the former are absurd, the latter is also. Let us come to the proof:

> One must confess that there have never been enthusiasms (extravagances) comparable to those into which these mystics are carried away, when their imagination is excited, and I cannot refrain from relating here a remarkable example, of the aforesaid Malaval, which has been adopted by the Abbé of Estival as very fine:
>
> "This contemplation," he says . . . , "is not the *consideration* of the works of nature or of grace, nor a *reflection* on passages of sacred Scripture or the Fathers . . . , nor the *meditation* on the life or the death of the Saviour . . . , nor a lofty *speculation* on the attributes of God. It is not a *diversity* of *reasons* in the *understanding*, nor a *multitude of affections* in the *will*, nor a *remembrance* of pious things in the *memory*, nor an *invention* of images and forms in the *imagination*. Finally, it is neither tenderness, nor sweetness, nor *sensibility;* but a *simple and loving vision* of God, stayed upon faith, which is everywhere. We see God and we *contemplate* him by this *simple* look in a very profound silence, in a very simple and supereminent vision of an impenetrable and ineffable being . . . , which deprives us of every other *conception* and *expression*, and in a rapture of the will so sweet that it is not at all concerned with *finding the motive* of its love, which is God alone, and which is effected by a *vision of faith wholly simple and unreflecting*. . . . It is here that the soul finds a delicious *rest*, which establishes it above loftiness and baseness, above delights and ecstasies; above the most beautiful *manifestations*, *notions*, and divine *speculations* (on God); above all tastes and all drynesses. Thus words, voices, and tongues, *intellectual* as well as physical, cease, and yield to a very profound, very loving, very intimate silence, in which men can come into the presence of God."

[4] One could equally well say that all Nicole's syllogisms have four terms — the term *knowledge* having at least two senses, and very different ones (rational, mystical); whence a perpetual ambiguity. Thus: The *serpent* is a musical instrument; now the viper is a serpent. Therefore . . . [In French the word *serpent* has two meanings: (*a*) a scaly, limbless reptile, and (*b*) an obsolete wind instrument. Hence the pun. G. MacGregor.]

> Do not think that this author means what he says or that he has any distinct idea. That would be contrary to his principles. The souls he claims to describe have neither manifestations, nor notions, nor speculations, nor tastes, nor delights, nor ecstasies. What do they have then? They *know* nothing about it, he says; he who speaks about it knows nothing either. However, after having silenced intellectual and physical voices, he has not been able to silence his own; and, cost what it may, he must speak of that which he professes *not to understand.*[5]

Does Malaval also profess not to *experience* it? That is the whole question. Nevertheless, laugh if you please, but have the courage of your irony and laugh at St. Theresa.

> Thus this great God [she writes] shows that he listens to the soul that speaks to him, *suspending her understanding, stopping her thoughts,* calling back, as one says, the word from her lips, so that she cannot utter anything without a painful effort. She knows the divine Master instructs her without *sound of words,* holding her powers suspended, because their activity, *far from being of some help to her, could then only hinder her.* Each of the powers enjoys its divine object, but in a way which is *incomprehensible* to her. The soul feels herself inflamed by love without *knowing how she loves.* She knows she enjoys what she loves while not knowing how she enjoys it. But her enjoyment, she understands, goes altogether beyond the range of natural desire. . . . And that, my daughters, is perfect contemplation. Now you can know in what way it differs from mental prayer.[6]

Exactly, now we have come to the point, rejoins Nicole. In mental prayer, one understands something, and nothing at all in contemplation. Contemplation consists, it is said,

> in a confused, general, and indistinct knowledge of God. What is there so excellent in this? Just the means of conceiving God more feebly? All the least spiritual men conceive God in this way when they speak of Him.[7]

Moreover, this rudimentary intelligence forms some idea of God, but contemplation "teaches nothing."[8] So far as knowledge is concerned, it is difficult to conceive anything more scanty. God is not even known in a Christian and Catholic way.[9]

If we are to believe Malaval, who, let us repeat, does not speak otherwise than St. Theresa, "the Siamese and the Chinese would be in spirituality the

[5] Nicole, *Réfutation des principales erreurs du quiétisme* (Paris, 1695), p. 175 f.

[6] In Lamballe, *op. cit.,* p. 24 f. Cf. Nicole: "If the soul herself does not know what she is doing, what chance is there that the Abbé of Estival should know it and be in a position to tell us? And can one take all he relates about it for anything other than pure imaginings?" (*Réfutation,* p. 173 f.)

[7] *Réfutation,* p. 167 f.

[8] *Ibid.,* p. 335.

[9] *Ibid.,* p. 310. The mystics continually repeat that contemplation supposes faith: that their "simple vision" is "a vision of faith."

most sublime people in the world; for Europeans are very far from carrying as far as they the strange desire for inactivity of body and mind."[10]

And, more doctorally (more *ex cathedra*): "One does not increase in light by renouncing all light."

The mystics do not renounce all light but only the incontestably very wretched, very "scanty" lights which our *reason* gives us on God. Nicole insists: "One does not grow in the love of God in not representing God under any *idea* which can make one love Him, and that is what would happen in this way."[11]

And likewise one is in no danger of being burned in not forming any scientific *idea* of flame and in contenting oneself with holding one's finger over the flame of a candle.

Or again:

> Indeed, there is nothing very edifying in . . . [this mystical] knowledge, which is neither capable of cultivating the mind, nor of moving the heart. But even though this knowledge should be a thousand times higher, it would do nothing to exalt the merit of this prayer. One cannot possess God at all in this life by mere knowledge.[12]

By mere intellectual knowledge, certainly. But indeed it is a question of knowing whether contemplation, which, furthermore, is knowledge and love at the same time, does not put us in the state of possessing God. It is always the same paralogism, and if the rationalist gets momentarily tired of pawing the ground far from the question, the moralist returns to the attack. . . . All the same it is good to see Pierre Nicole propose to inflict his *Essays on Moral Philosophy* on St. Theresa. Good, provided one does not have too sensitive nerves. For the moment comes when one is tempted to say, like Sainte-Beuve exasperated by the enormities of the great Arnauld: "How stupid all this is!" According to my way of thinking, at any rate, this moment has already come. Then learn — it is to St. Theresa, John of the Cross, and Francis of Sales that this speech is addressed — learn that there is a "part of the duties of the Christian life which consists in avoiding evil. *Diverte a malo.*" (This Latin will frighten them!) And learn that in order to avoid evil, one must not take it for the good, and that one strongly risks falling over this obstacle "if one does not know DISTINCTLY the good and the evil." From which already follows "the need for a crowd of distinct thoughts," for the lack of which St. Theresa herself, with all her simplicity, never knew whether she was allowed to lie or not. But there is a second part "of the duties of the Christian life," that "which obliges us to do the good, *et fac bonum* . . ." But

> . . . this good ought not to be done by chance; a great many rules must be devised for it . . . one must prefer actions of duty and obligation to other actions, and for this one must discern them by *distinct* enlightenments. . . . Not only must one practice charity; one must vary its order. One must prefer more important actions to less important ones. One must suit one's actions to a *great many* circumstances; one must avoid many faults. All this can be known only through distinct ideas. Confused ideas can only produce confusion.

[10] *Ibid.*, p. 311. [11] *Ibid.*, p. 212. [12] *Ibid.*, p. 171.

David likewise warns Solomon against the mystical illusion: *ut intelligas universa quae agis*. In short, as these two duties (*diverte a malo; fac bonum*) "fill all life, I do not know where one is to place contemplation and simple attention."[13]

Enough, enough! Let us flee these drunken Bacchanalia. When good sense raves it is just too tiresome.

However, let us not complain about Nicole. No one excels as he does in not understanding. The anti-mystics are generally much more irritating; they grope, they are afraid of going astray, they avoid declaring themselves unambiguously. Their fundamental mistake (plain enough, indeed) is less glaring, less intelligent — there is no other term for it — than that of the clear Nicole. They all fall into the same snare, but Nicole cheerfully from head to foot. . . .

Contemplation, say the mystics, is indeed a knowledge, but of a particular kind, and one which takes after sensible experience, after a fashion. By means of it "man has the feeling of entering . . . into immediate contact — without images, without discourse, but not without enlightenment — with an infinite goodness." It is "a quasi-experimental perception of God" accompanied by "a kind of immediate, indisputable, imposing evidence."[14] It is, in a word, a mysterious grace, which does not make us conceive through intelligence, but, rather, makes us grasp, taste, realize the presence of God in our inmost being. Let us hear St. Theresa:

> The feeling of the presence of God then suddenly seized me. It was absolutely impossible for me to doubt that he was within me or that I was not wholly swallowed up in him. *It was not a vision*; it is, I believe, what is called mystical theology.[15]

"Not a vision"; a "something" more confused, less distinct, but also more delicious, more captivating, more profound. Nothing but a *feeling*, but what a feeling! Nothing but a presence, but what a presence! Here, I will recall that a feeling is not an idea, and that the *idea* of a presence is singularly different from the *feeling* of that same presence.[16]

[13] *Ibid.*, pp. 329–334.

[14] Léonce de Grandmaison, *Études*, 5 mai, 1913, p. 323 f.

[15] Lamballe, *op. cit.*, p. 40.

[16] "*Sentiment*" in French conveys more than does "*feeling*" in English; it means also *sense, impression,* etc. [G. MacG.]

Paul Jury

Paul Jury was born in Bergerac, Dordogne, France, in 1878. The atmosphere in which he was nurtured till the age of nine was one that he has described as "deliberately without religion." He later received some Protestant catechetical instruction. Although he had never even been inside a Roman Catholic church till his early teens, he eventually entered the novitiate of the Society of Jesus, in which he was ordained to the priesthood. In 1923 he was permitted to leave the Society for the secular priesthood. At that time he had no animosity against the Jesuits, feeling rather, he tells us, an astonishment that men of such mediocrity should have been able to acquire such great repute either for good or for evil.

In his early forties, however, he began to lose his faith in Christianity. The beginning of what proved to be his lifelong interest in Freudian psychology did not appear until he was at least forty-five. While writing privately against the Church, he continued to wear the cassock and perform his priestly functions, a course of action which in his journals he essayed to justify. He predicted with irony that he should probably be given the Last Rites of the Church before he died. After his death in 1953 it was publicly stated that he had received Extreme Unction; but his close friend André Michel later ascertained, through the testimony of Jury's sister, that this was not the case.

His unpublished papers were left in the hands of this gifted young writer and professeur de lycée, *André Michel, who edited and published some of them under the title* Journal d'un prêtre *(Paris: Gallimard, 1956). The following, hitherto unpublished, is a translation by André Michel, revised by Geddes MacGregor, of two notes written by Jury in 1941 and 1942, in which he fiercely attacks what he takes to be a mainspring of the Christian claim.*

While they would be entirely out of place in an anthology strictly confined to philosophical critiques of religion, they are included in the present anthology (which is more broadly conceived for the purpose of introducing the student to as wide a range as possible of treatments of religious concerns, including therefore literary appreciation and psychological revolt as well as philosophical analysis) on the basis of a twofold interest. In the first place, Jury's thought is largely independent of the main stream of modern New Testament scholarship. He probably knew little of its technicalities, and he was writing out of a tradition in which, in his generation, such investigations were discouraged. In the second place, they are of considerable psychological interest in reflection upon and discussion of the very intricate problem of the conditions of faith in God.

He Was Called Jesus *

He was called Jesus. About that, no dispute. One may deny this or that about him; one may think he did one thing or another, but one knows for certain that he was called Jesus. This is the solid kernel; this is the foundation stone.

The Jews, because of Isaiah, were persuaded that the Messiah would be called *Emmanuel.* Isaiah had perhaps not thought so. Isaiah's opinion was probably of no importance. The idea had gained ground, however, that the witness, the messenger of God, would be called Emmanuel.

The first Christians could have contested this starting point. It is a fact that they accepted it — indeed, they accepted it much more than did the Jews. Thus one day came — and they had already accepted and proclaimed in Jesus the fulfillment of the prophecies — when this objection arose: But Jesus was not called Emmanuel! What is the meaning of this?

Jesus' being called Jesus and not Emmanuel had great, decisive consequences: Jesus, at least on one point, a delicate point, did not answer the description of the Messiah. A ticklish difficulty, for whether you fail to fill the mold at a hundred points or at one, it proves that the mold does not fit you at all, that you are not the person who is called for. Among the God-candidates, *all* come near more or less; otherwise they would not be candidates. They come sometimes very, very near to the model, to the required formula. But *one only* answers *all* the requirements, failing nowhere. "Those who fail, even for want of one point, lose their donkey"[1] — or their title. *Jesus fails at least on this point.* That is certain and quite sufficient.

But, when one looks closer, one sees that it is not a question of detail, but on the contrary an irreducible kernel. An enormous knot of vipers is there squeezing or coiling, as you please.

Let us see the proof of it.

In order that the God-candidate should be called Emmanuel, what was necessary? Only this trifle: that his parents ought to have thought about it, have reasons to think, *from his birth,* that the fruit of their marriage would be the Messiah, and at any rate name him *in that prospect.* But how could they have had that prospect?

The simplest solution is that, desiring — since it is said that all the women of Israel desired to give birth to the Messiah and therefore made haste to become pregnant — desiring, then, to give the Emmanuel to the world, and taking, as it happens, their desire for a beginning of reality, a way to force fortune, his parents would then, at all events and to begin with, have called him Emmanuel.

One may wonder whether this incomparable name — at least in its meaning of the Messiah, who had to be unique — was not set apart, whether a

* Written November 5, 1941.

[1] Note by the editor André Michel: A French saying, meaning that an important matter may fail because of the slightest adverse circumstance.

Jew would have dared to give it to his son, whether he would not have shrunk from the offence to public opinion: Who are you, to dare to pretend to have him as a son? What do you ground yourself on? And, in front of a newborn infant, slobbering and soiling its swaddling clothes, the father would have stood nonplused.

However, a king or a magnate, relying on his prestige and the temporal blessings already received, and expecting for his son a still greater fortune than his own, may have thought of forming his son with a view to such a future: He will reform and save his people. Who knows, after all, if God will not confirm my hope? More wonderful things have happened.

But those are dreams of the rich, of the powerful.

The parents of Jesus were nothing; they could not lull themselves with any such delusion. These unambitious parents would have called their child Emmanuel only if this child were extraordinary from birth. Their child was extraordinary indeed, but he became so eventually; he was not so *in his cradle, from his birth*. No! It was necessary that at the circumcision, on the eighth day, when the name was imposed, the child was already so remarkable that it represented *a future*.

Look at an eight-day-old infant, and dare to prophesy! One would have to be as stupid as Paterne Berrichon repeating the fancies of Rimbaud's sister (who was not there) to tell us that the poet was extraordinary *from birth*! People venture such assertions only in connection with kings' sons. For in that case they think they are sure. But even then they make royal mistakes. But for anyone to say of a baby who is not the son of a Louis XIV or a Napoleon that he will be a great man is going rather far. So far that it never happens.

We know what Vergil predicted for the son of Pollion; after all, he was the son of Pollion. Well, being the son of a consul and being cherished by an emperor did not prevent that royal-fated tadpole from being a nobody. Similarly, Louis XIV's son, the Dauphin who from his cradle was hailed as a god, turned out to be a fool and did not even reign. The young Napoleon was supposed to climb over the skies and to outdo his father. Yet, born with the title King of Rome, he never ruled Rome, was not even a king, fathered no princes, and did not even succeed his father. And as for Louis-Napoleon, who would have laid any stake on him? Yet that ninny became an emperor and held sway over Europe for eighteen years.

Clearly it is impossible to foresee the future of a fragile new life, which perhaps will not reach maturity, which perhaps will be only a fool, or which perhaps will be ousted from his birthright by someone weaker than himself and held in little esteem.

To prophesy that a child will be Emmanuel, nothing less suffices than parents informed from heaven: Your child is the one everyone is waiting for, he will fulfill the role. In the light of such knowledge they would have only to obey, to give him his sacred name, his free pass against all people, despite appearances and contradictions. *And it is precisely that which the parents of Jesus neither dared to do nor even thought of doing.* Oh, if only Jesus instead of being called Jesus had been called Emmanuel, he would hold a trump card! To be what he was, to do what he did, and, on top of all that, to be called Emmanuel in reality would be proof that his parents were *in on the secret of the future,* that they were *expecting* it, an important indication! Why not say that they had been inspired by the Almighty? But since they did not give the indispensable stamp, we must rightly conclude that they had not received any special enlightenment. And that is enough to upset everything. By naming their child Jesus and not Emmanuel they proved that no angel had spoken to Joseph. Much less to Mary. *Jesus was the son of an ordinary couple, who suspected nothing.*

Approaching the question from another angle, one might say: For Jesus to be the Messiah he would have to be called Emmanuel; and for him to be called Emmanuel his parents would have to be in on the secret — the child's name depending not on the child, but on the parents. In calling their son Jesus, without thinking further, they provide irrefutable evidence that there was neither angelic announcement nor any other kind of revelation at the birth of the one who was called the Messiah, that this one became Messiah *solely by his own will and action* and not by the will and preparation of God.

So all that we are told about Jesus before his baptism turns out to be a legend, invented at a later period, and indeed after Mark wrote, for he does not mention it and has no inkling of it. That is really remarkable!

The Christians were aware of the breach and tried to fill it in. They said to themselves: Being the Messiah, he must have always known it. *At least his family* must have known it; for a being does not come from heaven without the family's being aware of it! So let us describe his parents as being in on the secret. Then they thought up the convenient story of Joseph's being informed by an angel in his sleep. Sleep is a broad-shouldered pretence; it is well known that in dreams everything is possible, even angels! A dream provides a way of introducing the supernatural without breaking up everything and without exposing oneself to too many contradictions. Who cannot dream that he is a king? Who cannot dream that heavenly voices are speaking to him? People are so hungry for the miraculous that no more is needed. A Joseph was invented informed thus: You will have a son; he will be the Messiah.

This is all very well. But why did they not add: *And you shall call him Emmanuel?* They did not say it simply because there is not, during his whole life, the slightest indication that Jesus was ever called Emmanuel. Therefore it was *not possible* to instruct Joseph to give his son a name which in fact he never bore. This suffices to show that the ingenious invention is not ingenious enough, is even crude, and badly fits the rigid facts.

Jesus never called himself Emmanuel during his lifetime, not even in the rapture of triumph. Not only his parents; neither he himself nor his followers ever thought of claiming this title for him. Jesus is Jesus for eternity and he is simply Jesus. That is the stumbling block. It was only when the Jews had discovered the objection, when the Christians had pieced together the prophecies about the Messiah with a view to applying them to Jesus, that an attempt was made to make the New Testament agree with the Old, Jesus with the Prophets, and history with the sacred legend. It was only when they thought it necessary to deck him out in the style of the Ancients, anoint him and make a mystagogue of him, that the question of Emmanuel suddenly came up. But then it was too late: The die was cast and was on the table. All they could do was piece things together, compensate, and engage in endless discussions. Too many documents were lying around with the revealing and denunciating word: Jesus of Nazareth!

One wanted at least the name Jesus to be heaven-sent. By a stroke of luck, the name Jesus meant Saviour. A beautiful name: one full of boundless possibilities!

Nothing could be easier than to say that it was heaven-sent. Just imagine, Saviour! It has been said: He will save his people! Then, when he had not saved anything, they specified, saviour of his people from their sins; then, when there were more pagans than Jews among his followers, saviour of mankind from sin.

That was how Joseph's dream was thought up — a dream inspired by God, as is shown by the angel and the fine words he utters, which the future could easily fulfill, since the prophecy was made some sixty or seventy years at least after the event. In this way the name Jesus was given greater and more spiritual significance *to support the belief that it was equivalent to Emmanuel.*

This is so patently the goal toward which this arrangement was aimed that the Evangelist — a completely unsystematic rogue — writes: And he shall be called Emmanuel, as the Prophet has said. Hey presto! Yet, my dear friend, the facts you produce say nothing of all that. Jesus is still not Emmanuel. There is only one way to call someone Emmanuel: It is at first not to call him Jesus: It is to give him from the eighth day the reserved and incommunicable name.

Conclusion:

Parents not informed! So no angel or miraculous conception. So no God who watched over the child or announced him to his parents from birth as he had announced him to his people, long before, by Isaiah.

This suffices to show that a piecing together took place in the Gospels, which, contrary to commonplace judgment, are not pure, but tortuous, pettifogging, and extremely shortsighted. This suffices to establish that Jesus does not accord with the expectation. He is anything you like, even the most remarkable of men, but he is not the "Expected," "Announced," "Fulfillment of the Old Testament," the *Messiah.*

Perhaps this does not affect the real greatness of Jesus. It is enough for us to reject all Christian mythology and say with serenity: On the day Jesus was born there was no angel, no special star, no message of peace. The heavens did not open, intervene, or speak on that day any more than they do any other time!

Jesus of Nazareth *

Had he been the Messiah, Jesus would have had to be born at *Bethlehem.* But he was simply called Jesus *of Nazareth,* because that was where he came from, and — whatever one may do — the only place he came from. Now, can a Messiah come from Nazareth?

As in the case of Emmanuel, an attempt was made to mitigate Nazareth. Alas, nothing could be done about it!

In twenty places, whenever Jesus is mentioned, the Homeric epithet of Nazareth springs up. And not only the epithet! Many characteristic and decisive episodes unexpectedly and undeniably recall this degrading origin. They stick to his skin like the tunic of Nessus. If only Nazareth could have been removed! But impossible: It was a part of him. So recourse was had to subterfuge.

And what in a smarting way confirms the fact that Jesus was from Nazareth and not Bethlehem is that *no one ever even once* mentioned Bethlehem in this connection. This is a very strong argument. For, after all, if he were from Bethlehem and not from Nazareth, sometime or other it would have been mentioned; it would have been known. This is paramount and decisive confirmation of the true title, Jesus *of Nazareth.*

Now, if Jesus is not from Bethlehem, Micah (V, 1–5) spoke in vain, or else Jesus did not fit the bill. In either case the heavens were mistaken or, which is more likely, did not speak.

To get around this difficulty the evangelist who signs himself Matthew invents a fantastic story, which is worthy of examination. Matthew, who recounts the beautiful legend of Jesus, Saviour of his people, imagines that he was called the Nazarean[1] *not because he was from Nazareth but because he was a Nazarene.* And he was a Nazarene *to fulfill the Scriptures.* Better still, that this title might be given to him more easily, he went to live at Nazareth! This is a shameless pack of lies, which deserve the whipping post and allow us to grasp a fact which has been carefully disguised and colored: The Gospel of Matthew, which is supposed to be the Jewish gospel par excellence, was written by a man who knew nothing whatever about Palestine for a public equally ignorant. Its Jewish appearance is an artifice, a trick, glue to catch simpletons.

This is what Matthew says (II, 22–23):

> Χρηματισθεὶς δὲ κατ' ὄναρ ἀνεχώρησεν εἰς τὰ μέρη τῆς Γαλιλαίας, καὶ ἐλθὼν κατῴκησεν εἰς πόλιν λεγομένην Ναζαρέτ· ὅπως πληρωθῇ τὸ ῥηθὲν διὰ τῶν προφητῶν ὅτι Ναζωραῖος κληθήσεται.

* Written February 27, 1942.

[1] Whereas in English the words *Nazarite, Nazarene,* and *Nazarean* are used indiscriminately with the various meanings of "from Nazareth" and "belonging to an ancient Hebrew sect," the French text uses "Nazaréen" for the first meaning and "Naziréen" for the second one. We translate "Nazaréen" by *Nazarean* and "Naziréen" by *Nazarene.* [A. Michel]

"And, being warned in a dream, he turned aside into the parts of Galilee. And he came and dwelt in a city called Nazareth, that it might be fulfilled which was spoken by the prophets, he shall be called a Nazarene."

First, no prophet — and that's something! — prophesied that the Messiah would be a Nazarene; that is, that he would never cut his hair or beard, that he would never drink alcohol, that he would take the vows taken by Samson, Samuel, John the Baptist, and so many others (or, at any rate, taken for them).

Matthew would be hard put to supply any reference for his statement. Well-trained commentators and apologists have exhausted themselves there in vain. So the infallible Matthew (evangelists, like apostles — and Matthew is both — are infallible) is mistaken, or, rather, he is lying, for his statement is biased and deliberate. That is the first point. Here is the second:

Jesus was never at any time a Nazarene. *He was indeed the very opposite.* This can most easily be proved from Matthew himself, who has left lying about in his dossier texts and facts to disprove him.

In Chapter XI, 16–19, he writes:

> But whereunto shall I liken this generation?
>
> It is like unto children sitting in the markets, and calling unto their fellows,
>
> And saying: We have piped unto you, and ye have not danced;
>
> We have mourned unto you, and ye have not lamented.
>
> For John came neither eating *nor drinking,* and they say: He hath a devil. [This was to call him insane. *John* was a Nazarene; that is why he did not drink.]
>
> The Son of Man came eating *and drinking,* and they say: Behold a man gluttonous, and *a winebibber,* a friend of publicans and sinners!

So Jesus *drank like anyone else,* just like those who were not regarded as particularly abstemious or devout —sinners and publicans. He was not in any way a Nazarene.

If one wants to develop this theme, "friend of publicans and sinners," it will be easy to accumulate from Matthew himself texts which depict this type and in many ways draw it more precisely: Jesus was so much the opposite of a Nazarene that he was found excessive on that score. Let us take for example (Matthew IX, 9) just the episode of the vocation of Levi, who has mistakenly been identified with Matthew. And this is the man Matthew would have us believe was a Nazarene!

The Greek term, *Ναζωραῖος,* has the double meaning of "inhabitant of Nazareth" and "person pledged to Nazareneship." But *nazir* and *Nazareth* do not stem from the same root. These words are related to each other by a pun rather than by kinship. One can be assured that the Jews never confused the two and that it is not from Nazareneship that Nazareth and its inhabitants derive their name.

Jesus was from Nazareth. That was why he was called Ναζωραῖος on the cross. It was not because he was a Nazarene. Matthew, do you think you can make us swallow the contrary?

Yet he could do it, because he was writing outside Palestine and because he was writing for people who were quite at sea — who knew neither the Scripture nor things Jewish. A likeness of words was sufficient for them. And I maintain furthermore that Matthew could have launched this absurd explanation only because he did not know much more than his readers and therefore did not realize its grotesqueness: It would have stuck in the throat of a real Palestinian Jew, no matter how much he might have wanted to overcome the objection.

So however we understand the name Jesus of Nazareth, whether by Jesus or by Nazareth, we come back to irrefutable evidence that Jesus is not the Messiah. He should have been Emmanuel of Bethlehem; he is not, and no trickery on the part of his partisans will change the fact.

Rudolf Otto

The central theme of Das Heilige, *the best-known work of the German Protestant theologian Rudolf Otto (1869-1937), is that there is a special* kind *of* experience, sui generis, *peculiar to the religious consciousness. This he calls "the numinous." It is to be distinguished from ethical and aesthetic experience, for example, and is expressed in words such as* holy, *which do not refer to art or morals but to an experience that is unique. In his interpretation of the nature of religion, Otto shows in a marked degree the influence of Schleiermacher (1768-1834), whose famous* Reden über die Religion *he edited.*

The Numinous *

"Holiness" — "the holy" — is a category of interpretation and valuation peculiar to the sphere of religion. It is, indeed, applied by transference to another sphere — that of Ethics — but it is not itself derived from this. While it is complex, it contains a quite specific element or "moment," which sets it apart from "the Rational" . . . and which remains inexpressible — an ἄρρητον or *ineffable* — in the sense that it completely eludes apprehension in terms of concepts. The same thing is true (to take a quite different region of experience) of the category of the beautiful.

Now these statements would be untrue from the outset if "the holy" were merely what is meant by the word, not only in common parlance, but in philosophical, and generally even in theological usage. The fact is we have come to use the words *holy, sacred* (heilig) in an entirely derivative sense, quite different from that which they originally bore. We generally take "holy" as meaning "completely good"; it is the absolute moral attribute, denoting the consummation of moral goodness. In this sense Kant calls the will which remains unwaveringly obedient to the moral law from the motive of duty a "holy" will; here clearly we have simply the *perfectly moral* will. In the same way we may speak of the holiness or sanctity of Duty or Law, meaning merely that they are imperative upon conduct and universally obligatory.

But this common usage of the term is inaccurate. It is true that all this moral significance is contained in the word "holy," but it includes in addition — as even we cannot but feel — a clear overplus of meaning, and this is now our task to isolate. Nor is this merely a later or acquired meaning; rather, "holy," or at least the equivalent words in Latin and Greek, in Semitic and other ancient languages, denoted first and foremost *only* this overplus: if the ethical element was present at all, at any rate it was not original and never constituted the whole meaning of the word. Anyone who uses it to-day does undoubtedly always feel "the morally good" to be implied in "holy"; and ac-

* Rudolf Otto, *The Idea of the Holy,* trans. John W. Harvey (London: Oxford University Press, 1926), pp. 5–11. Used by permission.

cordingly in our inquiry into that element which is separate and peculiar to the idea of the holy it will be useful, at least for the temporary purpose of the investigation, to invent a special term to stand for "the holy" *minus* its moral factor or "moment," and, as we can now add, minus its "rational" aspect altogether.

It will be our endeavour to suggest this unnamed Something to the reader as far as we may, so that he may himself feel it. There is no religion in which it does not live as the real innermost core, and without it no religion would be worthy of the name. It is pre-eminently a living force in the Semitic religions, and of these again in none has it such vigour as in that of the Bible. Here, too, it has a name of its own, viz. the Hebrew *qādôsh,* to which the Greek ἅγιος and the Latin *sanctus,* and, more accurately still, *sacer,* are the corresponding terms. It is not, of course, disputed, that these terms in all three languages connote, as part of their meaning, *good, absolute goodness,* when, that is, the notion has ripened and reached the highest stage in its development. And we then use the word "holy" to translate them. But this "holy" then represents the gradual shaping and filling in with ethical meaning, or what we shall call the "schematization," of what was a unique original feeling-response, which can be in itself ethically neutral and claims consideration in its own right. And when this moment or element first emerges and begins its long development, all those expressions (*qādôsh,* ἅγιος, *sacer* &c.) mean beyond all question something quite other than "the good." This is universally agreed by contemporary criticism, which rightly explains the rendering of *qādôsh* by "good" as a mistranslation and unwarranted "rationalization" or "moralization" of the term.

Accordingly, it is worth while, as we have said, to find a word to stand for this element in isolation, this "extra" in the meaning of "holy" above and beyond the meaning of goodness. By means of a special term we shall the better be able, first, to keep the meaning clearly apart and distinct, and second, to apprehend and classify connectedly whatever subordinate forms or stages of development it may show. For this purpose I adopt a word coined from the Latin *numen. Omen* has given us *ominous,* and there is no reason why from *numen* we should not similarly form a word "*numinous.*" I shall speak then of a unique "numinous" category of value and of a definitely "numinous" state of mind, which is always found wherever the category is applied. This mental state is perfectly *sui generis* and irreducible to any other; and therefore, like every absolutely primary and elementary datum, while it admits of being discussed, it cannot be strictly defined. There is only one way to help another to an understanding of it. He must be guided and led on by consideration and discussion of the matter through the ways of his own mind, until he reach the point at which "the numinous" in him perforce begins to stir, to start into life and into consciousness. We can co-operate in this process by bringing before his notice all that can be found in other regions of the mind, already known and familiar, to resemble, or again to afford some special contrast to, the particular experience we wish to elucidate. Then we must add: "This X of ours is not precisely *this* experience, but akin to this one and the opposite of that other. Cannot you now realize for yourself what it is?" In other words our X cannot, strictly speaking, be taught, it can only be evoked, awakened in the mind; as everything that comes "of the spirit" must be awakened.

The reader is invited to direct his mind to a moment of deeply-felt religious experience, as little as possible qualified by other forms of consciousness. Whoever cannot do this, whoever knows no such moments in his experience, is requested to read no further; for it is not easy to discuss questions of religious psychology with one who can recollect the emotions of his adolescence, the discomforts of indigestion, or, say, social feelings, but cannot recall any intrinsically religious feelings. We do not blame such a one, when he tries for himself to advance as far as he can with the help of such principles of explanation as he knows, interpreting "Aesthetics" in terms of sensuous pleasure, and "Religion" as a function of the gregarious instinct and social standards, or as something more primitive still. But the artist, who for his part has an intimate personal knowledge of the distinctive element in the aesthetic experience, will decline his theories with thanks, and the religious man will reject them even more uncompromisingly.

Next, in the probing and analysis of such states of the soul as that of solemn worship, it will be well if regard be paid to what is unique in them rather than to what they have in common with other similar states. To be *rapt* in worship is one thing; to be morally *uplifted* by the contemplation of a good deed is another; and it is not to their common features, but to those elements of emotional content peculiar to the first that we would have attention directed as precisely as possible. As Christians we undoubtedly here first meet with feelings familiar enough in a weaker form in other departments of experience, such as feelings of gratitude, trust, love, reliance, humble submission, and dedication. But this does not by any means exhaust the content of religious worship. Not in any of these have we got the special features of the quite unique and incomparable experience of solemn worship. In what does this consist?

Schleiermacher has the credit of isolating a very important element in such an experience. This is the "feeling of dependence." But this important discovery of Schleiermacher is open to criticism in more than one respect.

In the first place, the feeling or emotion which he really has in mind in this phrase is in its specific quality not a "feeling of dependence" in the "natural" sense of the word. As such, other domains of life and other regions of experience than the religious occasion the feeling, as a sense of personal insufficiency and impotence, a consciousness of being determined by circumstances and environment. The feeling of which Schleiermacher wrote has an undeniable analogy with these states of mind: they serve as an indication to it, and its nature may be elucidated by them, so that, by following the direction in which they point, the feeling itself may be spontaneously felt. But the feeling is at the same time also qualitatively different from such analogous states of mind. Schleiermacher himself, in a way, recognizes this by distinguishing the feeling of pious or religious dependence from all other feelings of dependence. His mistake is in making the distinction merely that between "absolute" and "relative" dependence, and therefore a difference of degree and not of intrinsic quality. What he overlooks is that, in giving the feeling the name "feeling of dependence" at all, we are really employing what is no more than a very close analogy. Any one who compares and contrasts the two states of mind introspectively will find out, I think, what I mean. It cannot be expressed by means of anything else, just because it is so primary and elementary a datum in our psychical life, and therefore only definable through itself. It may perhaps help him if I cite a well-known example, in which the precise "moment" or element of religious feeling of which we are speaking is most actively present. When Abraham ventures to plead with God for the men of Sodom, he says (Genesis xviii. 27): "Behold now, I have taken upon me to speak unto the Lord, which am but dust and ashes." There you have a self-confessed "feeling of dependence," which is yet at the same time far more than, and something other than, *merely* a feeling of dependence. Desiring to give it a name of its own, I propose to call it "creature-consciousness" or creature-feeling. It is the emotion of a creature, abased and overwhelmed by its own nothingness in contrast to that which is supreme above all creatures.

It is easily seen that, once again, this phrase, whatever it is, is not a *conceptual* explanation of the matter. All that this new term, "creature-feeling," can express, is the note of self-abasement into nothingness before an overpowering, absolute might of some kind; whereas everything turns upon the *character* of this overpowering might, a character which cannot be expressed verbally, and can only be suggested indirectly through the tone and content of a man's feeling-response to it. And this response must be directly experienced in oneself to be understood.

We have now to note a second defect in the formulation of Schleiermacher's principle. The religious category discovered by him, by whose means he professes to determine the real content of the religious emotion, is merely a category of *self*-valuation, in the sense of self-depreciation. According to him the religious emotion would be directly and primarily a sort of *self*-consciousness, a feeling concerning one's self in a special, determined relation, viz. one's dependence. Thus, according to Schleiermacher, I can only come upon the very fact of God as the result of an inference, that is, by reasoning to a cause beyond myself to account for my "feeling of dependence." But this is entirely opposed to the psychological facts of the case. Rather, the "creature-feeling" is itself a first subjective concomitant and effect of another feeling-element, which casts it like a shadow, but which in itself indubitably has immediate and primary reference to an object outside the self.[1]

[1] This is so manifestly borne out by experience that it must be about the first thing to force itself upon the notice of psychologists analysing the facts of religion. There is a certain naïveté in the following passage from William James's *Varieties of Religious Experience* (p. 58), where, alluding to the origin of the Grecian representations of the gods, he says: 'As regards the origin of the Greek gods, we need not at present seek an opinion. But the whole array of our instances leads to a conclusion something like this: "It is as if there were in the human consciousness *a sense of reality, a feeling of objective presence,* a *perception* of what we may call *'something there,'* more deep and more general than any of the special and particular 'senses' by which the current psychology supposes existent realities to be originally revealed." ' (The italics are James's own.) James is debarred by his empiricist and pragmatist standpoint from coming to a recognition of faculties of knowledge and potentialities of thought in the spirit itself, and he is therefore obliged to have recourse to somewhat singular and mysterious hypotheses to explain this fact. But he grasps the fact itself clearly enough and is sufficient of a realist not to explain it away. But this "feeling of reality," the feeling of a "numinous" *object* objectively given, must be posited as a primary im-

Now this object is just what we have already spoken of as "the numinous." For the "creature-feeling" and the sense of dependence to arise in the mind the "numen" must be experienced as present, a "numen praesens," as in the case of Abraham. There must be felt a something "numinous," something bearing the character of a "numen," to which the mind turns spontaneously; or (which is the same thing in other words) these feelings can only arise in the mind as accompanying emotions when the category of "the numinous" is called into play.

The numinous is thus felt as objective and outside the self. We have now to inquire more closely into its nature and the modes of its manifestation.

---

mediate datum of consciousness, and the "feeling of dependence" is then a consequence, following very closely upon it, viz. a depreciation of the *subject* in his own eyes. The latter presupposes the former.

Anders Nygren

The Greek word agape *is believed to have been coined by Biblical writers in order to avoid the sensual implications of the ordinary Greek word for love,* eros. *St. Paul speaks of* agape *as the greatest of the Christian virtues. Translated into Latin as* caritas, *it became, in the older versions of the English Bible, "charity," which is now misleading. The relation between* agape *and* eros *is one that gives rise to much dispute: Are the two entirely different, and, if they are not, how precisely are they related? In any case, what exactly is* agape? *In the following passage the Swedish theologian Anders Nygren attempts an answer.*

The Centrality of Agape in the Christian Religion *

. . . The idea of love occupies a central place in Christianity. That is so obvious a fact that it would hardly seem to need any special investigation. But it is also a fact that the idea of Agape in Christianity constitutes the answer to certain quite definite questions; and, obviously, we can only understand the full force of an answer if we are clear about the question that is being answered. The same idea can have very different meanings, according as it represents the answer to one question or another. Hence it is by no means superfluous to inquire more closely into the question or questions to which the idea of Agape is intended as the answer. In this way the idea of Agape will be placed in its proper setting, related to its context.

We have indicated the central importance of love in Christianity by describing it as a Christian "fundamental motif"; but this term can be variously understood and we have still to define it. We raised, but did not answer, the two following questions: (1) What do we mean by describing anything as a fundamental motif? (2) What right have we to ascribe to the idea of Agape, which is after all only one among other characteristically Christian ideas, such fundamental significance as to call it a fundamental motif? These questions must now receive a definite answer.

First, then, what do we mean by calling anything a fundamental motif? The primary associations of the term are perhaps with the realm of art. The fundamental motif is that which makes a work of art into a unified whole, determines its structure, and gives it its specific character. It is the theme that constantly recurs in new variations, imparting its own tone and colour to the whole. But broad and indefinite statements like these are insufficient to show the precise sense in which we are using the term "fundamental motif". For this purpose the following definition may be given: A *fundamental motif is that which forms the answer given by some particular outlook to a question of such a fundamental nature that it can be described in a categorical sense*

* Anders Nygren, *Agape and Eros* (Philadelphia: The Westminster Press, 1953), pp. 41–48. Used by permission.

as a fundamental question. To develop the full meaning of this statement we should have to go into the whole doctrine of the categories, for which this is naturally not the place. All we can do here is to touch on the most necessary points.

If we take the broadest possible survey of human thought, we get a lively impression of the truth of the old saying that there is nothing — or very little — new under the sun. There are a certain few themes which constantly recur in fresh variations and combinations, but in such a way that the old theme can still be recognised in the new forms. Quite early in the history of thought we find the great fundamental questions asked concerning the True, the Beautiful, the Good, and — to crown them all — the Eternal. For our Western civilisation the formal statement of these questions was the work of Plato, though the materials for it were in existence long before his time. And great as the changes may be which these questions have undergone since, we can none the less say that we are still occupied ultimately with these same great questions today when we speak of the problems of Knowledge, of Æsthetics, of Ethics and of Religion. Indeed, we might very well describe the whole development of civilised thought as a constantly renewed attempt to state these questions and fix their meaning. It happens, however, from time to time in the historical process that the meaning of one or other of these questions is completely altered. This is the way in which new developments take place with respect to the great fundamental questions of humanity. It is not that a traditional question is set aside and a new question substituted for it, but rather that a new meaning is unexpectedly discovered in the old question. The form of the question remains unchanged, but its content is different; it does not *mean* the same; the frame is old but the picture is new.

When we speak of a fundamental motif we are moving in the realm of those comprehensive, ultimate questions which we have just mentioned. The fundamental motif is the answer given by some particular type of outlook to one or more of these questions. This answer need by no means take the form of a theoretical proposition; it can equally well be a general, underlying sentiment which involves a certain attitude towards these questions or — more passively — a certain reaction to them. There is thus a close connection between fundamental motifs and fundamental questions of the "categorical" kind we have described; but it is of the greatest importance to maintain a clear distinction between them. They differ as a question and an answer differ, and this difference cannot safely be ignored.

In all ages it has been the conscious or unconscious endeavour of metaphysics to blur this distinction. Men have believed that by philosophical analysis the answer could be deduced from the question. At this point there is an obvious difference between the metaphysical systems and every religious outlook. Even though the two types may state their answer (often for emotional reasons) in very similar language, yet the difference always remains. The metaphysician always tries in one way or another to deduce his answer as "necessary," while the religious mind firmly refuses to do so, but insists on its answer as axiomatic and thus maintains a synthetic relation between question and answer.

In the case of two of these great fundamental questions, the ethical and the religious, Christianity has brought a revolutionary change not only with regard to the answers but with regard to the questions themselves. It has so altered the way of putting both these questions that they no longer have the same meaning as before, and it has also given them both a new answer. This change, in respect both of questions and answers alike, is essentially bound up with the idea of Agape.

It is not difficult to see how the meaning of the *ethical* question has changed in the course of history. Most of the problems treated as ethical by the ancient philosophers fall for us entirely outside the ethical sphere, while what we regard as quite central in ethics is not treated by them at all. For this change the ethical contribution of Christianity is chiefly responsible. Yet we can see also how the original form of the question survives even when it has acquired a new content; for ethical discussion is still occupied with the problem of the Good. But this problem clearly has a quite different meaning according as it is looked at from an individualistic point of view or conceived in terms of fellowship or personal relationships. Ancient ethics were individualistic. The problem of the Good was therefore the problem of a "Highest Good" — that is, of something which could in every respect satisfy the individual. The dominant question was that of *eudæmonia,* happiness; and although different answers might be given — the answer of Hedonism, that happiness is the pleasure of the moment; or of Aristotle, that it consists in activity and the attainment of perfection; or of Stoicism, that it is *ataraxia,* independence and indifference towards the external vicissitudes of life — yet the statement of the question remains always the same.

Now it is just in respect of this question that Christianity makes a revolutionary change; for Christianity consistently makes fellowship the starting-point for ethical discussion. The question of the Good is no longer envisaged from the point of view of the isolated individual, but rather from that of man in society, man in his relation to God and to his fellow-men. Here we see the influence of the idea of Agape. Agape, or love, is a social idea which as such has nothing in common with individualistic and eudæmonistic ethics; and when the question of the Good is approached from the point of view of social relationships it takes on an entirely new meaning. It becomes dissociated from eudæmonism and utilitarianism and turns into the entirely independent question of "the Good-in-itself."[1]

Equally far-reaching is the change that Christianity has brought with regard to the *religious* question, the question of the Eternal or of man's fellowship with God. The meaning of this question must clearly vary according as the centre of gravity in the religious relationship is placed in man's ego or in the Divine: in the former case we get an egocentric, in the latter a theocentric religion. In both cases we speak of "religion," because both involve a relation between man and God; yet we have really two quite separate questions here

[1] This question is discussed in detail in my *Etiska grundfrågor,* 1926, where the first chapter deals with "The Independence of the Ethical Judgment" and the second with "The Concept of the Good."

for it makes all the difference whether we are interested in God as the One who can satisfy all the needs and desires of the ego, or as the sovereign Lord who has absolute authority over the ego. In so far as the religious question has now come to be envisaged from a theocentric rather than an egocentric point of view, it is chiefly due to Christianity that the change has come about. Doubtless there is scarcely any religion from which the theocentric tendency is wholly absent; but it has nowhere else been able to overcome those contrary influences that appeal to man's natural tendency to take everything around him into his own service, and to judge and value everything according as it advances or retards his own interests. The study of the underlying motifs of the different religions shows that there is always a dominant group of motifs of an egocentric character. It is in Christianity that we first find egocentric religion essentially superseded by theocentric religion. We shall see later on that this revolution, too, is intimately connected with the idea of Agape.

It follows that Christianity takes a unique place as a creative force in the history of human thought. It has revolutionised the treatment of the fundamental questions of religion and ethics, and the very way in which it puts these questions reveals a creative power of the highest order. The reason why it has been equally creative in both religion and ethics is that these, from a Christian point of view, are not strictly two separate things, but are so interwoven with one another as to be really two different aspects of the same thing. Christianity knows nothing either of a non-ethical fellowship with God or of non-religious ethics. The Christian Religion is a thoroughly ethical religion and its ethic is a thoroughly religious ethic.

The fundamental motif of an outlook is its answer to a fundamental question of a "categorical" nature. We have observed that human thought concentrates on a few such questions. There are a certain few great questions, first raised long ago, which recur with extraordinary persistence throughout history demanding an answer. When men grapple with these questions their concern as a rule is simply to find an answer to them; they rarely think of the questions themselves — that is, the way in which they are stated — as a matter for investigation. The questions are simply taken over from tradition as something given and once for all established. But a question has an extraordinary power of suggestion and constraint. It directs our attention to the different possible answers and so seems to leave all the different possibilities open; yet the number of possible answers may be seriously limited by the very way in which the question is put. To a wrongly stated question there can be no right answer. The question thus indirectly influences the answer. It is in this way, above all, that a fundamental question stated in a certain way can hold the minds of men in bondage for centuries, not to say millennia. What men seek is a better way of answering the question, while the question itself is passed on unaltered. Modifications of the fundamental questions, therefore, generally take place more or less unawares, and it is only rarely that a really radical revolution occurs. When this happens it is the result of a new total attitude to life in general.

Two of these extremely rare revolutions — that which has turned the religious question from an egocentric into a theocentric question, and that which has freed the ethical question from eudæmonism and turned it into the question of "the Good-in-itself" — have resulted, as we have seen, from the contribution made by Christianity. But the creative significance of Christianity is not exhausted in the restatement of questions. It is manifested even more clearly in the answer that Christianity gives to the fundamental religious and ethical questions thus restated. Here we find also that characteristically Christian interpenetration of religion and ethics of which we spoke above, for to both these questions Christianity gives precisely the same answer. To the religious question, now stated in theocentric terms, What is God? Christianity replies with the Johannine formula: God is ἀγάπη. And to the ethical question, What is the Good, the "Good-in-itself"? the answer is similar: The Good is ἀγάπη, and the ethical demand finds summary expression in the Commandment of Love, the commandment to love God and my neighbour.

We have therefore every right to say that ἀγάπη is the centre of Christianity, the Christian fundamental motif *par excellence*, the answer to both the religious and the ethical question. Agape comes to us as a quite new creation of Christianity. It sets its mark on everything in Christianity. Without it nothing that is Christian would be Christian. Agape is Christianity's own original basic conception.

Austin Farrer

Austin Marsden Farrer, a distinguished contemporary English theologian, was for many years Fellow of Trinity College, Oxford, and is now Warden of Keble. A rigorous, penetrating, and most unusual thinker, he is well known for the versatility of his work, which ranges from metaphysical treatises to highly original methods and theories of modern Biblical criticism. The passage quoted here is from a philosophical essay on the problem of the freedom of the will, a traditional puzzle to which much modern scientific discovery about behavior is plainly relevant and which is therefore of interest to many modern philosophers, whether they happen to care about theological questions or not. In the passage quoted, however, Farrer considers the question not only from the point of view of a modern philosopher but also in its relation to theological difficulties and insights. His treatment of the subject has evoked much criticism and stimulated considerable discussion among contemporary philosophers. It is important for this reason as well as for its own sake.

The Freedom of the Will *

The time has come to survey the question of voluntary freedom with a wider sweep. . . . Let us stop arguing about the freedom of the will, and ask ourselves why, after all, it matters. Let us beg the question of liberty, and say: Supposing that we have a voluntary freedom, what is the use of making the fact clear, or stripping away the sophistries which obscure it? For, as even determinists admit, men must be allowed to think as though they were freely inventing, and to make choices as though they were freely deciding. Will not the libertarian and the determinist, therefore, live and act in an identical way? If there is a difference between them, it is that the determinist hopes to perform a feat of which the libertarian despairs. For the determinist thinks that, reflecting after the event on his neighbour's conduct or his own, he should be able to descry in it the structure of reason, the lineaments of necessity; whereas the libertarian renounces any such hope. And so it may seem that the practical value of libertarianism is nil; it makes a metaphysical fuss about deciding and inventing, things which the sensible man does as he goes along, with no fuss at all. Whereas the practical value of determinism is tangible; it holds before us the hope of causal explanation; it gives us a programme to work upon.

The determinist claim which we have just stated contains an implicit admission, which the counter-argument will seize. What is determinism? It is not a hypothesis, it is a hope. Whatever patterns or regularities are to be

* Austin Farrer, *The Freedom of the Will* (London: Adam & Charles Black, Ltd., 1958), pp. 297–309. Used by permission.

found in human behaviour, a libertarian is just as free to recognise, study and profit by them, as a determinist can be. The determinist is in no position actually to plot out the most part of human conduct, as the simple exemplification of established uniformities, whether before or after the conduct occurs. He is singular merely in holding the hope, the pious hope, that under ideal conditions it could be done. Now where we have a general and pious hope entertained about what can be done, we may postulate, as the counterpart to it, a pious faith about the way things are. If some form of action or achievement is held to be in general an ideal possibility, it is surely held to be so in consequence of the general nature of things. If we hope that we will reduce conduct to causal explanation, we believe conduct is such as to be causally explicable. The hope and the belief belong together, and they share the same pious character. If the hope is a pious hope, the belief is a pious belief; not the sort of belief I have when I believe Viet-Minh to be a republic, but the sort I have when I believe the Yellow Race to be a messianic people.

Once it has been seen that determinism is a faith, the way is open to consider libertarianism as a faith also. Now the determinist attack which we were just now considering, amounted to saying that bare libertarianism is an empty faith; it makes a fuss over assuring people of their freedom to do what they will do in any case — contrive, invent, decide. The point ought to be conceded. Bare libertarianism is an empty faith; and if we cast fate out of liberty-hall only to keep the rooms empty, swept and garnished, the demon will return with reinforcements. For the patterns of necessity play so large a part in our thinking, they will always encroach on empty ground. Bare libertarianism is an empty faith; but then libertarianism need not be, and commonly is not, held as an isolated conviction. It is supported by other beliefs, beliefs which both give it significance, and themselves borrow significance from it. We will recall two of them: about creativity, and about responsibility, the believer in freewill has his own way of thinking. We will take the two terms in order.

It may be true that, for practical purposes, the doctrine of necessity concedes the felt freedom of our acts; but it teaches us, when we reflect on them, to view them as the expressions of a natural inevitability. And (the libertarian complains) such a teaching cannot but undermine in us the seeming importance of what we do. For it tells us that there is some nature of things, or of ourselves, in accordance with which we are bound to act; whose tendencies our decision merely applies to the case, and, as it were, precipitates. To employ again the gross metaphor we have used — the statute-laws of our universe, or of our kind, are fixed; our decisions are, at the best, those of judges; our discretion is limited to an application of law to instance. By contrast, the libertarian may see himself as making law. Within the limits which physical and psychological facts prescribe, man may have the sheer liberty to make himself the sort of creature he chooses to be, by adopting a certain sort of life, and building up the customs and aptitudes required for it. No doubt our power to make ourselves is much restricted; by the time we take the task in hand, our elders have done so much to us already. But they have done it, and we shall do the like to our children, pupils or charges. The fact that man-making by men is exercised on others, not on one's self, does not diminish the portentousness of the undertaking. Any one of us, it is true, will overestimate his importance, if he supposes that he alone, in independence of other individuals or of the social mould, can shape any single soul, his child's or his own. Nevertheless, according to the libertarian belief, the total moulding force will be a function of the number (whatever it be) of free agencies; whether aware, or unaware of their freedom; whether employing it to carve a destiny, or asleep on it, in a nest of convention.

Certain existentialist thinkers on the Continent have carried self-creation to the limit, and have boldly proclaimed (without, in their own eyes, discrediting their doctrine) that liberty is so absolute, it topples over into an absurdity. It may amuse us to compare Sartre's estimate of our condition with Pope's mockery of man. "Go, wondrous creature," says the poet to the featherless biped, "teach Providence to rule; then drop into thyself, and be a fool." Yet, according to Pope, we need not resign ourselves to cosmic folly, for we need not undertake to play providence. We can play the fool in a corner, and it will not be calamitous; *dulce est desipere in loco.* Whereas according to the existentialist philosopher, the sceptre of Providence is forced into our fingers; if we do not play providence to ourselves, no one will; there is no other God. The ordeal of Phaeton is ours; the reins are in our hands, the doors of dawn are open, and we must guide the chariot of the Sun. We must — but it's absurd; our ignorance, our liability to passion, the mutual frustration of our aims, present the spectacle of forty Phaetons drunk, driving wild on the Place de la Concorde.

"Now, my child," they used to say to me, marking the end of a penal silence, "Now you can say what you like." My young lips were struck dumb by so portentous an option; and so it is, when existentialism throws my life into my lap, and says "Be yourself, my boy, and make it up as you go along." The effect is like a paralytic stroke. I come to again, however, at last, and begin to remember — with what consolation to remember — my responsibilities. There will, no doubt, be occasions for sheer personal option, but thank heaven I have not to meditate *in vacuo* on what to make of myself, as the God of Leibniz meditates on what to make of the world. Thank heaven I have this lecture to write, and beyond that, my pupils to see to; and ah, beyond that, if I dare to look, there is Lazarus on the doorstep, covered with sores.

What is it, then? I must, by my effort, and invention, and fidelity, make my life; but always responsibly. Now we talked of responsibility in a previous chapter. We saw that the notion derived from the law-court, and might, even in morals, have a very limited application. The flattest determinism could allow that we are, through the operation of fairly obvious motives, swayed by a social code, for the keeping of which we feel responsibility. But we suggested in our discussion that the most interesting extension of the notion is that which stretches it furthest, and makes us responsible for acting or not acting on our basic valuations; and it is this extended sense of responsibility that we shall consider in the present chapter.

Here, then, is our trinity of notions, our libertarian battlecry, Liberty, Creativity, Responsibility — or death! We are free, and free to make our lives, but always in response to claims; claims which we may be psychologically free, but are not morally free, to ignore. What is it, then, that ultimately exerts these claims upon us? The philosophy of "How we think" may point out with complacency that we do not commonly trace our responsibilities to a higher source than the custom of our kind, or cite an authority superior to the American way of life. And doubtless a Gallup poll, say of the Civil Service and other black-coated workers, would do much to support the contention; especially if the questionnaire were suitably framed. *Vox Gallupi vox Dei;* still, we must be careful not to misinterpret so august an oracle. It may be that people are content to find their authority in custom; but authority for what? Not, ultimately, for what they should do, but for what they should prize. The man who follows the American way of life does not see in the customs of the tribe obligatory performances, which are their own justification; he takes them both to express, and to be inspired by, a respect for humanity.

The citizen is found, then, to have two objects of respect; and he can easily be reduced to that bewilderment produced by Socratic queries in the common breast, if we ask him which is supreme, humanity, or the American way of life? Let Socrates clear up the confusion Socrates has caused. It is plain to the philosopher that humanity, and the American way of life, are not objects of respect on the same level, or so as to be possible rivals to one another. We may respect the American way of life as a sound indicator, pointing out to us what there is in humanity most deserving of respect, as well as how that respect may in practice be paid. Humanity we respect absolutely, if once we can see it straight; and this respect obliges us; we hold ourselves responsible for acting, or failing to act, in accordance with it.

We say that our respect is payable to humanity. The world is almost too convenient; indeed, to the modern ear it is an actual equivocation. It means mankind, and it means the characteristic excellence of human nature. Both are objects of respect, or of regard. But so far from coinciding in practice, they are inclined to tug us in different directions, and, on occasion, to tear us apart. To regard mankind is to accept men as they are, to spare them frustration, to give them their will and pleasure. To regard humanity, in the other sense, is to look for what a believer calls the divine image in us, and the unbeliever the human ideal. It is to censure vice or folly, and push against the tide of appetite, as well in other men, as in ourselves.

To all working moral systems, or ways of life deserving the name, some respect for humanity in both senses is common ground. All direct us to accept mankind as it is, and all uphold a standard of what it should be. And all, no doubt, have their practical ways of dealing with the tension which results; of squaring (if we are to take the Christian example) the law Christ delivers on the Mount, with the indulgence he manifests to sinners. The perplexity is a practical perplexity; it cannot be exorcised by logical analysis. It is no use telling us that there is no rivalry between our two aims; that the human ideal, or divine similitude in us is no concrete entity, let alone person, capable of competing for our attention against John Robinson or Robert Jones; that it is merely a way of conceiving what either of these characters has it in him to aspire after. Such philosophical solutions offer no practical consolation, because the perplexity concerns our action. We have either to accept our children as they are, or (however tactfully) edge them towards what they should be.

The modern world has not even yet got over the antique method of reconciling our two aims; a method reflected in that equivocation in the word "humanity," on which we have just remarked. To the Greek philosopher it was no equivocation at all. Just as, to the old-fashioned botanist, a spotted orchid was simply a specimen of the kind, more or less perfect, the teleology of nature being single-mindedly bent on making it as typical as circumstance allowed; so equally, to the Greek thinker, human individuals were simply specimens of mankind, in each of whom the form of the species was, as it were, doing its best to realise itself. To the great scandal of the modern student, everything distinctive of a person, all that makes the individuality of a character, was written off by the Greek as accidental to the essential man, and irrelevant to the teleology of existence. "Be human, my son" was the supreme moral injunction; "Be a Man with a large M." What we call the pull of the ideal was simply the self-realisation of the natural species *man*, on all the levels of being or action; and especially, of course, on the highest. A bad man was a bad specimen, limited, frustrated, warped, unhappy. The art of felicity and the art of virtue were one, and to respect men as they are was the same thing as to respect what they should be. For what are they, it was asked, what have they in them capable of moving respect, besides their human nature, struggling to be itself? Who could seriously respect in a man what was accidental to his being?

Ideal humanity was to the Aristotelian a timeless form of natural substance, a typical object of natural science, engraved in the order of the world, and unalterable as long as heaven revolves. It was conceivable — though God forbid! — that a concentration of disastrous accident might exterminate us, like the dodo; but nothing could change our essence. Had dodos survived, they would have remained incurably (or, I suppose we should say, triumphantly) dodonian. While men survive, they will be as human as ever.

How hopelessly the Greek position has been shot to pieces is a thrice-told tale: shot to pieces by individualism in ethics, historicism in sociology, and evolutionism in biology. It is not this that we wish to dwell upon, but upon the fact that the Greek did at least know what he was regarding, and towards what he held himself responsible, when he set up the common human essence against the trivial claims of individual deviation. He was respecting a form of nature, timeless and virtually divine. He and his metaphysical faith are gone into limbo, never to return. But what do we, we Anglo-Saxon intellectuals, respect, when we balance regard for the human ideal against our regard for mankind?

The answer of "We think" philosophy to this question is not always mere academic mumbling. There are the forthright prophets who declare: "We learn to have confidence in our volitions," our aspirations for the future of mankind. It is too hasty a dismissal which rejoins: "And did not Stalin have confidence in *his* volitions, when he collectivised the farms, and several million farmers died?" For Stalin's trouble was practical miscalculation. The Socialist utopia was only just round the corner, when the Germans began engaging him in an arms-race — was not it a pity? Otherwise the tears of the peasants would soon have dried, in the dawn of a glorious day. Anyhow, we are not marxist doctrinaires — we have not got ideas into our heads; we keep them at arm's length, and scrutinise them. So we may have confidence in our volitions, our directives for the moulding of mankind; as, according to an ancient myth, God had confidence in his volitions, when he made us this being that we are, and surveying it, called it very good.

Let us pause for a moment, and see what has happened to us. Alarmed by the existentialist predicament, unattracted by the task of being Phaeton and running amok with the horses of the Sun, we took refuge in responsibility. We would create our lives, perhaps, but responsibly, in answer to the claims of mankind, and the truth of our nature. But has not responsibility proved a broken reed? If we are responsible, after all, to our own volitions, are we not back in the car with Phaeton, making up our minds which way to drive? What advantage have we over the most self-intoxicated existentialist, except a sort of cautious collectivism? We are not Stalin, we are the Civil Service; *we* are to have confidence in *our* volitions; not *I* in *mine*. And the volitions in which we have confidence are not the dramatic decisions which existential novel-writing, and historical disaster, throw into relief, they are policies somehow settled, and acquiesced in, by a communal complacency. It is this that does duty for "the truth of human nature," when the philosophy of "we think" expands into the field of "we approve" and "we decide."

We have been moving too rapidly and shouting too loud. Let us sit down and consider carefully what is at stake. Our philosophers will point out to us that whether we believe in Aristotle's truth of human nature, or whether we put our confidence in their and our volitions, there is no getting round the sheer fact of approval and disapproval, in either case. It is on this indicator that we must rely, for determining what belongs to the human good, and what does not. We have seen that Aristotle himself, however confident in nature as providing the rule of right, defined "good" as "whatever any sort of being is after." The definition is general, covering the good for animals and plants, and even, to our amused delight, the good for stones; they find it in cuddling down as near as they can to the earth's centre. If we are speaking of man, and his moral good, we may wish to specialise the verb, and say that "being after" on our level has the name of "aspiration." So what human nature aspires after is determined, according to Aristotle, by the lineaments of nature herself; but that is only a metaphysical belief. In practice there is no way to discover what humanity aspires after, but experiencing or observing the aspiration. If our good is that towards which aspiration naturally jumps, there is no way of knowing what it is, save by dropping the cat on the floor, and seeing in what direction it does jump.

Even then, merely to observe in what direction our neighbours' aspiration jumps, will not convince us of the good. After learning all we can from others, and sympathising with them as much as we are able, we may still wonder whether they are not the victims of a common perversity, so long as our aspiration fails to jump with theirs. No good can convince us, that does not win us; the good being defined as what attracts, it cannot be seen as good unless it is felt as attractive; always bearing in mind that we are not now talking of any and every attraction, but of that serious attraction only which can draw our total aspiration.

Well then (say our philosophers) since in practice the human good is known as that which we aspire after, why not leave it at that, and cut away the dead wood, the metaphysical part of Aristotle's doctrine? What use does it serve, to allege that the direction of a healthy aspiration is laid down in the unalterable nature of things, if all we can in practice do is follow our aspiration whither it leads? Why regret the collapse of Aristotelian dogmatism, as though some other dogmatism were needed in its place, which we cannot supply? No substitute is needed, when a chimera has been exploded.

Those who are familiar with this type of debate will see immediately to what issue we have brought the question down: the issue between positivism and natural faith. Not in this question only, but over a whole range of questions, positivists have wished to restrict belief to what a practical test can verify. As with morals, so (for example) with physics. We have no way of discovering physical being outside us, except through its interferences with our bodies, or our instruments; and a strict positivism would reduce physical doctrine to a systematisation of such interferences, actual or potential. But natural faith, including the natural faith of physicists, rebels. It may be (we protest) that we do not know the physical world, except as that which we sound by our interferences with it. But we believe that what we are sounding is a mass of energies carrying on business out there in space, on their own account and, as it were, under their own names, whether any soundings of them are taken or not. There is no circumventing or bypassing the soundings, to reach a direct acquaintance with the physical-in-itself; yet we believe it is something in itself, and if we are theological as well as physical believers, we attribute to God a simple knowledge of it.

It is much the same with natural faith and positivist reduction, in the matter of the good. We cannot bypass aspiration, so as to grasp the good after which it aspires; we can only grasp it through aspiring after it. Yet we cannot cease to believe that there is a true or proper good after which aspiration "feels, if perchance she may find it." For aspiration is always endeavouring to be right aspiration, and to respond to objects, or pursue aims, intrinsically meriting it. Divorced from this endeavour, aspiration is no longer aspiration. If we have confidence in our aspirations, or, in the phrase we previously took up, confidence in our volitions, it is that they are sound, healthy or right; that is to say, that they are after the proper objectives. There is, of course, a striking difference between our natural faith in physical realities, and our natural faith in genuine goods. Physical things would be ideally definable without reference to any soundings of them; goods would not, even ideally, be definable without reference to any aspirations after them; the good being nothing but the proper object of aspiration.

Let us be clear, anyhow, of this: that what Aristotelianism offered, and what positivists have rejected, was a metaphysical, not a directly practical, conviction. Aristotle did not tell us, even if he sometimes thought he did, any other means of descrying the good than approval, aspiration, love. He claimed to tell us what, in its general bearings, that good was, to which these sentiments or attitudes were the natural pointers. It was all that served or expressed the due expansion of an eternal essence, human nature. "Well," it may be asked, "and what was the use of the metaphysical belief, even while men could still believe it? It did not direct their aim." No; but it grounded their faith. To reverence, to worship our own volitions, though backed by those of the Civil Service, is flat idolatry. Whereas nature was divine perfection to the Greeks; and even to Christian Hellenists she was a divine ordinance.

Well, but (we shall be told) this is scarcely news. Who does not know that metaphysical belief, the world over, supplies men with something to adore? But our philosophers will tell us that the wish has everywhere been father to the thought; the pathetic, the essentially childish or recessive desire for an object of unqualified reverence, disappointed by every empirical reality, creates a metaphysical one. The Greeks virtually deified an immanent perfection, supposed to be working itself out in the transience of event. Christians have set their divine perfection further back, a creative will behind, rather than within, the cosmic process. If you want something to worship, this is the sort of thing. We deny ourselves the childish luxury.

"We deny ourselves. . . ." Such language is damaging, if it is not ironical. We cannot take seriously men who talk as though they were free to entertain metaphysical beliefs, or not to entertain them; to say (in the extreme case) "No, I don't think we will have God, thank you" or to say "Yes, let's have him." For either we believe or we do not. What pattern of conviction about the basis of action can we in fact entertain? If we have wrestled with the sophistries of determinism, it was only to clear or to liberate an actual conviction of our power, in some measure, to make ourselves. But if we indeed have the conviction, have we a conviction complementary to it — the conviction of our responsibility for the exercise of this power? The questionnaire proceeds: Responsibility to what? And desiring to voice a common agreement, and to steer clear of metaphysics, we answer, Responsibility to mankind, in others and in myself. What I do with my life, what I do to my neighbours, comes under the claim of something I cannot but hold sacred, their humanity, my integrity. But leave me out of the picture; even if I am free to damn myself, I am not free to betray or outrage them.

So far, surely, we have been drawing out practical convictions which we actually entertain. Do we, then, desert the path of moral realism and begin to chase wild metaphysical geese, when we take a step further and ask, what it is in any man, that demands this practical reverence? It is not just what he happens to think or to desire, that is sacred to me. I am not to respect the villainy of villains, nor to forward the self-dehumanisation of the perverse. I may say that I respect what they have it in them to be, their proper destiny. But this may not be anything that they want, even in the depth of their hearts; and simply to say that it is what I want for them, that my volition about them commands my limitless regard, does not satisfy me; by which I mean, that I cannot believe it. Can you?

Well, what am I to do about it? What alternative is there? It is too late, surely, to hanker after Aristotelianism, or hope to reinstate the timeless essence of man, the identical shaping everywhere at work in different qualities of clay, the one way of growing right, as against twenty thousand ways of growing wrong. It is too late to reinstate the changeless rule of essence, for reasons we have named already: individualism in ethics, in sociology historicism, and in biology evolution. No, if we are to believe an objective rule of human good, it must be a flexible rule; and they are surely right who say, there is nothing for us to put our confidence in, which has not the inventiveness of volition. Only, whose? Whose will do I respect, as a will expressed in the facts and possibilities, the hopes and the claims represented by my neighbours' existence — or, indeed, by my own?

So, then, when it is said that theological belief is morally irrelevant, because after all, God or no God, we have to explore the facts to decide a policy of action, and in deciding, trust our aspiration, we make answer that moral policies are at the service of reverence and love, and that as soon as we consider what we reverence, what we love, the practical bearing of theology appears. For it is no trifling difference, whether we value our neighbour simply for what he is, or for the relation in which he stands to the will of God; a will establishing his creation, and intending his perfection. Those that are so minded reverence not a single, but a double object, God in their neighbour, and their neighbour in God. The divine is not far removed from them, but touches them as nearly as physical things touch them. For the physical is known to us by the way it conditions our physical motion; and the divine will, which is God himself, is known to us in limiting or evoking our dutiful action, through all the persons with whom we have to do.

SECTION FIVE

The Destiny of Man

Plato

Plato (427-347 B.C.), generally accounted the most influential philosopher in the history of Western thought, incorporated into his philosophy many ancient ideas, not least on the subject of the immortality of the soul. Contrary to the prevailing popular opinion of his own day, and in keeping with the Pythagorean doctrine to which he was indebted, he taught that the soul is by its own nature essentially immortal.

The passages set forth here are classic texts in the history of thought upon the subject of immortality.

The Immortality of the Soul *

The soul through all her being is immortal, for that which is ever in motion is immortal; but that which moves another and is moved by another, in ceasing to move ceases also to live. Only the self-moving, never leaving self, never ceases to move, and is the fountain and beginning of motion to all that moves besides. Now, the beginning is unbegotten, for that which is begotten has a beginning; but the beginning is begotten of nothing, for if it were begotten of something, then the begotten would not come from a beginning. But if unbegotten, it must also be indestructible; for if beginning were destroyed, there could be no beginning out of anything, nor anything out of a beginning; and all things must have a beginning. And therefore the self-moving is the beginning of motion; and this can neither be destroyed nor begotten, else the whole heavens and all creation would collapse and stand still, and never again have motion or birth. But if the self-moving is proved to be immortal, he who affirms that self-motion is the very idea and essence of the soul will not be put to confusion. For the body which is moved from without is soulless; but that which is moved from within has a soul, for such is the nature of the soul. But if this be true, must not the soul be the self-moving, and therefore of necessity unbegotten and immortal? . . . .

. . . . .

And now, O my judges, I desire to prove to you that the real philosopher has reason to be of good cheer when he is about to die, and that after death he may hope to obtain the greatest good in the other world. And how this may be, Simmias and Cebes, I will endeavour to explain. For I deem that the true votary of philosophy is likely to be misunderstood by other men; they do not perceive that he is always pursuing death and dying; and if this be so, and he has had the desire of death all his life long, why when his time comes should he repine at that which he has been always pursuing and desiring?

* *The Dialogues of Plato,* trans. Benjamin Jowett (2 vols.; New York: Random House, 1937), I. *Phaedrus,* 245b; *Phaedo,* 64a–68a. Used by permission of The Clarendon Press.

Simmias said laughingly: Though not in a laughing humour, you have made me laugh, Socrates; for I cannot help thinking that the many when they hear your words will say how truly you have described philosophers, and our people at home will likewise say that the life which philosophers desire is in reality death, and that they have found them out to be deserving of the death which they desire.

And they are right, Simmias, in thinking so, with the exception of the words "they have found them out"; for they have not found out either what is the nature of that death which the true philosopher deserves, or how he deserves or desires death. But enough of them: — let us discuss the matter among ourselves. Do we believe that there is such a thing as death?

To be sure, replied Simmias.

Is it not the separation of soul and body? And to be dead is the completion of this: when the soul exists in herself, and is released from the body and the body is released from the soul, what is this but death?

Just so, he replied.

There is another question, which will probably throw light on our present enquiry if you and I can agree about it: — Ought the philosopher to care about the pleasures — if they are to be called pleasures — of eating and drinking?

Certainly not, answered Simmias.

And what about the pleasures of love — should he care for them?

By no means.

And will he think much of the other ways of indulging the body, for example, the acquisition of costly raiment, or sandals, or other adornments of the body? Instead of caring about them, does he not rather despise anything more than nature needs? What do you say?

I should say that the true philosopher would despise them.

Would you not say that he is entirely concerned with the soul and not with the body? He would like, as far as he can, to get away from the body and to turn to the soul.

Quite true.

In matters of this sort philosophers, above all other men, may be observed in every sort of way to dissever the soul from the communion of the body.

Very true.

Whereas, Simmias, the rest of the world are of opinion that to him who has no sense of pleasure and no part in bodily pleasure, life is not worth having; and that he who is indifferent about them is as good as dead.

That is also true.

What again shall we say of the actual acquirement of knowledge? — is the body, if invited to share in the enquiry, a hinderer or a helper? I mean to say, have sight and hearing any truth in them? Are they not, as the poets are always telling us, inaccurate witnesses? and yet, if even they are inaccurate and indistinct, what is to be said of the other senses? — for you will allow that they are the best of them?

Certainly, he replied.

Then when does the soul attain truth? — for in attempting to consider anything in company with the body she is obviously deceived.

True.

Then must not true existence be revealed to her in thought, if at all?

Yes.

And thought is best when the mind is gathered into herself and none of these things trouble her — neither sounds nor sights nor pain nor any pleasure, — when she takes leave of the body, and has as little as possible to do with it, when she has no bodily sense or desire, but is aspiring after true being?

Certainly.

And in this the philosopher dishonours the body; his soul runs away from his body and desires to be alone and by herself?

That is true.

Well, but there is another thing, Simmias: Is there or is there not an absolute justice?

Assuredly there is.

And an absolute beauty and absolute good?

Of course.

But did you ever behold any of them with your eyes?

Certainly not.

Or did you ever reach them with any other bodily sense? — and I speak not of these alone, but of absolute greatness, and health, and strength, and of the essence or true nature of everything. Has the reality of them ever been perceived by you through the bodily organs? or rather, is not the nearest approach to the knowledge of their several natures made by him who so orders his intellectual vision as to have the most exact conception of the essence of each thing which he considers?

Certainly.

And he attains to the purest knowledge of them who goes to each with the mind alone, not introducing or intruding in the act of thought sight or any other sense together with reason, but with the very light of the mind in her own clearness searches into the very truth of each; he who has got rid, as far as he can, of eyes and ears and, so to speak, of the whole body, these being in his opinion distracting elements which when they infect the soul hinder her from acquiring truth and knowledge — who, if not he, is likely to attain to the knowledge of true being?

What you say has a wonderful truth in it, Socrates, replied Simmias.

And when real philosophers consider all these things, will they not be led to make a reflection which they will express in words something like the following? "Have we not found," they will say, "a path of thought which seems to bring us and our argument to the conclusion, that while we are in the body, and while the soul is infected with the evils of the body, our desire will not be satisfied? and our desire is of the truth. For the body is a source of endless trouble to us by reason of the mere requirement of food; and is liable also to diseases which overtake and impede us in the search after true being: it fills us full of loves, and lusts, and fears, and fancies of all kinds, and endless foolery, and in fact, as men say, takes away from us the power of thinking at all. Whence come wars, and fightings, and factions? whence but from the body and the lusts of the body? Wars are occasioned by the love of money, and money has to be acquired for the sake and in the service of the body; and by reason of all these impediments we have no time to give to philosophy; and, last and worst of all, even if we are at leisure and betake ourselves to some speculation, the body is always breaking in upon us, causing turmoil and confusion in our enquiries, and so amazing us that we are prevented from seeing the truth. It has been proved to us by experience that if we would have pure knowledge of anything we must be quit of the body — the soul in herself must behold things in themselves: and then we shall attain the wisdom which we desire, and of which we say that we are lovers; not while we live, but after death; for if while in company with the body, the soul cannot have pure knowledge, one of two things follows — either knowledge is not to be attained at all, or, if at all, after death. For then, and not till then, the soul will be parted from the body and exist in herself alone. In this present life, I reckon that we make the nearest approach to knowledge when we have the least possible intercourse or communion with the body, and are not surfeited with the bodily nature, but keep ourselves pure until the hour when God himself is pleased to release us. And thus having got rid of the foolishness of the body we shall be pure and hold converse with the pure, and know of ourselves the clear light everywhere, which is no other than the light of truth." For the impure are not permitted to approach the pure. These are the sort of words, Simmias, which the true lovers of knowledge cannot help saying to one another, and thinking. You would agree; would you not?

Undoubtedly, Socrates.

But, O my friend, if this be true, there is great reason to hope that, going whither I go, when I have come to the end of my journey, I shall attain that which has been the pursuit of my life. And therefore I go on my way rejoicing, and not I only, but every other man who believes that his mind has been made ready and that he is in a manner purified.

Certainly, replied Simmias.

And what is purification but the separation of the soul from the body, as I was saying before; the habit of the soul gathering and collecting herself into herself from all sides out of the body; the dwelling in her own place alone, as in another life, so also in this, as far as she can; — the release of the soul from the chains of the body?

Very true, he said.

And this separation and release of the soul from the body is termed death?

To be sure, he said.

And the true philosophers, and they only, are ever seeking to release the soul. Is not the separation and release of the soul from the body their especial study?

That is true.

And, as I was saying at first, there would be a ridiculous contradiction in men studying to live as nearly as they can in a state of death, and yet repining when it comes upon them.

Clearly.

And the true philosophers, Simmias, are always occupied in the practice of dying, wherefore also to them least of all men is death terrible. Look at the matter thus: — if they have been in every way the enemies of the body, and are wanting to be alone with the soul, when this desire of theirs is granted, how inconsistent would they be if they trembled and repined, instead of rejoicing at their departure to that place where, when they arrive, they hope to gain that which in life they desired — and this was wisdom — and at the same time to be rid of the company of their enemy. Many a man has been willing to go to the world below animated by the hope of seeing there an earthly love, or wife, or son, and conversing with them. And will he who is a true lover of wisdom, and is strongly persuaded in like manner that only in the world below he can worthily enjoy her, still repine at death? Will he not depart with joy? Surely he will, O my friend, if he be a true philosopher. For he will have a firm conviction that there, and there only, he can find wisdom in her purity. And if this be true, he would be very absurd, as I was saying, if he were afaid of death.

F. C. S. Schiller

Ferdinand Canning Scott Schiller (1864-1937), after teaching at Cornell, was a Fellow of Corpus Christi College, Oxford, for nearly thirty years. He spent the last few years of his life as professor at the University of Southern California. He was a close friend of William James, though the philosophical positions they held differed considerably. In his humanistic pragmatism Schiller expounded a theory of the real as pure actuality that contains within itself all theoretical possibilities. In the following passage he considers the conception of a future life in the light of his general philosophical position.

A View of the Future Life *

The philosopher, as the genius of Plato long ago perceived,[1] is a very strange being. He is in the world, but not of it, residing mainly in a "Cloud-cuckoo-dom" of his own invention, which seems to have no relation to the actual facts of life, and makes no difference to anything or anybody but the philosopher himself. Its sole function seems to be to make the philosopher himself feel happy and superior to everybody who does not understand his philosophy enough to enter into it, that is, to everybody else in the world.

But even so the philosopher is not happy in his paradise — of sages. He is terribly worried by all the other philosophers, each of whom is quite as cantankerous and cranky as himself, and wants to carry him off into his own private Nephelococcygia. And as he will not, and indeed cannot, enter into it, they all get very angry. They get so angry that they cannot even laugh at each other. But when they get a little calmer (not that there is really such a thing as calm among philosophers any more than among *cirrus* clouds — only they live so far aloof and aloft that people cannot see how they behave) they fall to criticizing. And so when one of them has built himself a nice new Nephelococcygia high up in the clouds, the rest all try to pull to pieces the abode of his soul, and bombard him with buzzing chimeras bottled in vacuum tubes and riddle him with sesquipedalian technicalities. In this they are usually successful, for, though so perverse, they are immensely clever, and their critical acumen is as wonderful as their unconsciousness of their own absurdity. And so, one after the other, each loses his scalp, and is buried in the ruins of his system.

Or rather he is *not*; for the burial customs of philosophers are as strange as the rest of their behaviour, and unlike those of any other tribe of men. Among the Scientists, for instance, there are also savage wars, and they practise vivisection. But the Scientists are not head-hunters. They forget the errors of

* F. C. Schiller, *Humanism* (London: Macmillan and Company, Ltd., 1912), pp. 351–374. Used by permission of Dr. Charles Reginald Schiller Harris.

[1] *Republic*, 490.

their vanquished warriors and bury their remains, preserving only the memory of the work they did for Science. And thus do they keep clean the face of Science, and every morning wash away every bloodstain and every speck of error in the waters of Lethe, so that the many may believe that Science is infallible and its history is one unbroken progress; which is both more Christian and more worldly-wise.

But not so the philosophers. They still believe in the discipline of dirt, and keep the face of the fair goddess they profess to worship like unto the face of Glaucus the sea-god,[2] and the thicker grow the incrustations of historic error the better they are pleased. For they are simply devoted to the memory of ancient errors. They venerate them and collect them and dry them (in their histories of philosophy), and label them and exhibit them in glass cases with the scalps of their authors. They compile whole museums of such antiquities, and get themselves appointed the curators thereof. One of our universities is popularly believed to have appointed about two dozen such curators of the relics of the great fight between Aristocles, the son of Ariston, and Aristoteles, the son of Nicomachus. And the cause thereof was not Argive Helen, if you please, but the transcendence of the universal! Verily philosophic immortality is as terrible a thing and as hard to bear as that of Tithonus!

Such, I cannot help suspecting, are the real sentiments of intelligent men of the world concerning philosophers, though only a philosopher could be rude enough to set them down in black and white. But calumny, like murder, will out, and only so can it be met. And so those who, like Plato, have had the deepest faith in the value of philosophy have ever also been the readiest to admit and to confront the allegations of detractors.

And yet, at bottom, this was never quite an easy thing to do. The weaknesses of philosophy are manifest; its obscurity, its flimsiness, its intense individuality, its remoteness and uselessness for the ordinary purposes of life, cannot but catch the public eye. Its virtues (if any) are hidden out of sight. It seems safer, therefore, on the whole, for the sage to flaunt his shame and to assume its burden; boldly to disavow all purpose to better or instruct the world, cynically to confess that whether or not his astounding feats of conceptual prestidigitation can entertain the gaping crowd, they do at least amuse himself, honestly to disclaim the search for some more subtle service springing from his exercises. It may have happened here and there that the prescience of some wild and philosophic guess outstripped the plodding march of science. It may have happened now and then that in some reflective soul the conduct of life has been improved by study of its theory. But over most men habit bears such sway that this would be a marvel, and such precarious incidents are not enough to prove the useful nature of philosophy.

And yet if it were permitted to appeal to the philosophic heresy which just now is stirring up in all the bottled chimeras a buzzing fit to burst their vacuum tubes, if we might argue as pragmatists, it would seem obvious that even philosophy must have some use. For if it had not, society would scarce continue the endowment of philosophy, whose professors might thereupon find themselves reduced to breaking stones instead of systems. It is quite true

[2] Cp. Plato, *Republic*, 611 D.

that there is always a flavour of impertinence about the intervention of a philosopher in a subject of scientific research. For he cannot, as such, be trusted to make original contributions to the facts, and when he makes an attempt to criticize the contributions of others, it is quite true that he is terribly prone to do so from the *a priori* basis of some far-fetched cosmic theory which nobody else in the world besides himself believes in or even understands, and so achieves a comic rather than a cosmic interest. If, again, he contents himself with ponderously pondering on the accepted facts of a science he becomes a bore, consuming time and getting in the way of more practical workers.

It must be admitted, therefore, that the usefulness of a philosopher is very limited. It is undeniable only in cases where he is needed to clear out of the way other philosophers who have become obstreperous and obstructive; but such occasions do not occur frequently, and no really vigorous movement pays much heed to what philosophers are saying.

Nevertheless philosophy seems to me to have also a more important function, which may enable it to be scientifically suggestive and serviceable, at all events at a certain stage in the development of a science.

The function in question is that of discussing the working methods of a science, of exhibiting their full scope and logical implications and connexions, and considering the merits of the alternative ways of treating the subject. Such a critical *methodology* of a science is necessarily dull, but, perhaps, on that account, all the better adapted for philosophic discourse. And in view of the intellectual myopia which scientific specialism engenders, there are, perhaps, few things more salutary, as an unpleasant medicine is salutary, than for a science to become conscious of the working assumptions, or methodological postulates, on which it proceeds.

In the case of Psychical Research, in particular, the discussion of such methodological assumptions seems to be more novel, easier and more useful than in disciplines which have already reached a more assured position among the sciences. It is likely to be more novel, because of the novelty of the whole subject. It is likely to be easier to dissect out and contemplate in abstraction the methodological assumptions of an inchoate and infant science, because its organism is not so strongly knit and the flesh of fact does not so closely shroud the bone of method by which it is supported; it is still in a low stage of organization in which the whole may be taken to pieces and put together without much injury to the vitality of its parts. An advanced science, on the other hand, is far more difficult to handle: it imposes on the philosophic critic by its very mass of coherent and consistent interpretation; it appeals to him by its noble record of service to the human race; it crushes him by the sheer weight of immemorial authority. In it facts and theories have long been welded together into so indissoluble a union that the former can no longer be questioned, while the latter have for the most part risen to the dignity of indispensable "necessary truths" implied in the very nature of the human mind and underlying the whole structure of human knowledge. We gain little help therefore from the assumptions of sciences like mathematics and mechanics in considering what assumptions should be made in a new subject like Psychical Research; we learn little about the making of a science from sciences which can neither be unmade nor remade, and in whose case it requires a considerable effort of philosophic thought to realize the methodological character of their fundamental postulates. More might perhaps be learnt from the assumptions of *parvenu* sciences which have but recently obtained full recognition, but for the fact that a critical dissection of their methods is decidedly dangerous. For the "*arbor scientiae*" seems in their case to have developed a symbiotic arrangement greatly resembling that whereby certain trees protect themselves; just as any attack on the latter is ferociously resented by a host of ants which the tree provides with food and shelter, so any interference with such a science is sure to draw down upon the mildest critic the onslaught of an infuriated professor who lives upon the science. In Psychical Research, on the other hand, no such danger is to be apprehended; we have not yet developed any professionals whose mission it is, as William James has wittily remarked, to kill out the layman's general interest in the subject, and hence the philosopher may proceed at his leisure to observe how the science is made and to try instructive experiments with its working methods, without fear of offending vested interests.

Again, a philosophic discussion of possible methods is likely to be more useful in Psychical Research because such methods are still plastic cartilage, as it were, which has not yet grown into rigid bone, and may be moulded into a variety of forms. Hence by reflecting betimes upon the advantages of alternative methods, the philosopher may flatter himself that he can be of real service in guiding the course of investigation, or at least in helping it to avoid certain pitfalls. Not, of course, that even here he would be wise to presume to lay down the law *a priori* as to the actual working and merits of the various methods; he should content himself with expounding the logical characteristics which sound methods in Psychical Research must possess, and explaining why exactly they must possess them.

I do not propose, however, on this occasion to discuss the methodological value of the assumptions made in Psychical Research generally, but only in so far as they affect the question of a future life. The reasons for this are obvious. The possibility of a future life provides much of the motive force in such inquiries. Most of the active members of the Society[3] are probably interested in this question, and whether they desire or fear a future life, they agree in wanting to know what chance or danger there is of it. It is true that the S.P.R. is unique in aiming to solve this problem in a scientific way, but though we are scientific, we may yet be honest — in avowing the existence of a practical motive. If attacked on this score, let us meet our critics with the doctrine that in this respect at least we are *not* unique, inasmuch as in the end all true science is inspired by practical motives, and that it is the fear, no less than the hope, of a future life that renders its possibility so urgent a subject for scientific consideration. Moreover, just now the evidence in connexion with Mrs. Piper's trances[4] seems to have brought this possibility well

[3] The Society for Psychical Research was established in London in 1882 on the initiative of a Dublin physicist, Sir William Barrett. [Eds.]

[4] Mrs. Leonore E. Piper of Boston, Massachusetts, was one of the most celebrated mediums of the early days of the S.P.R. After the death of F. W. H. Myers (1843–

above the horizon of the S.P.R., while at the same time much confusion and prejudice still seem to prevail about it which philosophic criticism may help to dissipate. For a comprehensive statement of the new evidence and new interpretations of old evidence which render it the bounden duty of the philosopher to readjust himself and his formulas to the growth of knowledge, I can now (1903) point to Frederic Myers' valuable work on *Human Personality and its Survival of Bodily Death.*

I may begin by passing over with a merely formal mention the assumptions which are required for every scientific investigation. As a matter of course we must assume that the phenomena under investigation are knowable and rational in the sense of being amenable to determinable laws. The need for this assumption is so plain that *a priori* attacks on Psychical Research on the score of undermining the fundamental principle of all scientific research can hardly be put down to anything but voluntary or involuntary ignorance of the grossest kind.

Next we must enunciate a methodological axiom with which at first sight few will be disposed to quarrel, viz. that we must proceed to the unknown from what is known to us. The remark is Aristotle's,[5] and I may be suspected of quoting it merely because Oxonians can but rarely resist a temptation of quoting Aristotle. But in reality it is not such a truism as it appears, at least in the meaning I propose to put upon it. It means in this connexion that, both psychologically and logically, we must interpret any supposed future life by the knowledge we have acquired of our present life. It is a methodological necessity, in other words, that we must project this world into the next, if ever we purpose scientifically to know it. Our assumption may be wrong in the sense that it may be wrecked on barrier reefs of impenetrable fact — possibly it will be — but, right or wrong, we can work with no other at the outset. As we go on we shall no doubt detect the initial crudities of our assumptions, and correct them as our knowledge grows. But whatever differences we may discover between the two worlds must rest upon the postulate of a fundamental identity, in default of which our reason would be merely paralysed. From a complete otherness of the other world nothing would follow; a future life in which everything was utterly different would mean nothing to us, and in proportion as the difference grows the practical efficacy and theoretical knowableness of the conception diminish.

Now this, I venture to think, is a philosophic result of no small practical importance.

(1) It goes a long way toward explaining the anomaly of the feebleness of most people's religious beliefs about the future life. For the heavens and hells of the various religions, in spite of their pretensions to evoke forces which should utterly dwarf the threescore years and ten of our mortal life, are found

1901), an English pioneer in the field whose work was widely respected, not least by William James, an examination was made of the scripts of four women who had developed a facility in automatic writing, to see whether there was evidence of any communication by Myers after his death. Mrs. Piper was one of this group, which also included Rudyard Kipling's sister, under the pseudonym "Mrs. Holland." [Eds.]

[5] *Eth. Nic.* i. 3. 5.

in practice to constitute motives so weak that they are continually routed and set aside by the trivial temptations of the moment. The reason is that they have ordinarily been conceived as differing too radically from the known conditions of life to excite the same serious belief, to require the same matter-of-fact forethought as, *e.g.*, next year's crops or to-morrow's money market. And so the belief in a future life, even where it has not been degraded into a merely verbal assent to a traditional formula, has commonly lacked that intimacy of association with the ordinary concerns of life which is needed to render it psychologically efficacious as a stimulus to action.

(2) Again, it turns out that the spiritists were by no means wrong in principle when they proceeded to construe the future life, of which they believed themselves to possess cogent evidence, very much on the lines of our earthly life. Their constructions may in detail be as crude and absurd as their adversaries allege — I am neither familiar enough with the literature to discuss this point nor convinced that they are — but it is a mistaken prejudice to reject such accounts *a priori* as too trivial or undignified to be ascribed to the inhabitants of another world. Owing, no doubt, to the unduly tragic view we have come to take of death, the prejudice that the decease of Brown, Jones, and Robinson must instantly transmute them into beings of superhuman powers and tastes, and transport them into regions where they are initiated into the uttermost ecstasies and agonies of the scheme of things, has become inveterate. Indeed, I have often been amused to see how strongly this notion influences people who are really entire disbelievers in the possibility of any future life; while scorning everything "supernatural," they reject the spiritist's version thereof as *not supernatural enough*, because they are quite sure that if there were a future life at all, it would have to be as full of angels and demons as what they would call "the traditional mythologies." In a more respectable form the same feeling shows itself in the large number of persons who refuse to accept the evidence, *e.g.*, in the Piper case, because they think they would not like the sort of life to which it seems to point. This may seem a somewhat naïve *ignoratio elenchi*, but the psychical researcher can hardly afford to smile at it, for he is continually having it impressed upon him how very serious are the obstacles which prejudices of this sort form to the discovery and recognition of the facts, and how manifestly the "will to believe" is the *ratio cognoscendi* of truth. Hence a systematic challenge of the whole assumption that another world must be as different as is conceivable (or rather inconceivable) from this, is needed to clear the atmosphere.

And inasmuch as the groundlessness of a false assumption is never revealed more clearly than by a request for the reasons on which it rests, I should like, for my own part, to add to the general challenge a particular request, asking philosophers to show cause why a hypothetical "other" world must necessarily be conceived as out of time and out of space. The conviction that this must be so underlies, I am sure, much of the high philosophic scorn of empirical spiritism and popular theology, but I do not think it would be easy to support it by a valid and cogent philosophic argument. For so long as temporality and spatiality form indispensable characteristics of the only real world we experience, the presumption surely is that they will pervade also any other, until at least a definite method has been suggested whereby they may be transcended.

(3) Thirdly, it must be recognized that the methodological principle of interpreting the unknown by the known tells strongly in favour of the simpler, and *prima facie* easier, theory of the agency of personal spirits as against the more complex and unfamiliar notions of an impersonal clairvoyance, or subliminal consciousness, or non-human modes of cognition by gods, devils, or cosmic principles of a more or less unknowable kind. I am very far from thinking that we should in such matters hastily commit ourselves to the interpretation which *prima facie* seems the most plausible, or, indeed, to any definitive theory whatsoever, and I should be sorry to see the ingenious attempts to provide a non-spiritistic explanation of the phenomena in question prematurely abandoned — if only on account of their excellence as mental gymnastics — but I cannot admit that such attempts are one whit less anthropomorphic in principle than the "spiritist" hypothesis (they only stray further from their human model), while I cannot help admitting that methodologically they are more cumbrous and so considerably inferior. The spirit hypothesis has the same kind of initial advantage over its rivals as the "solid" atom has in physics over the "vortex ring" or the "ether stress." And while our knowledge remains in its rudiments this advantage is considerable, though, as the parallel shows, it may easily become problematical.

Admitting, therefore, that as a working theory the hypothesis of the persistence after death of what we call the human personality possesses considerable advantages over rival theories, let us inquire further by what methods, resting on what postulates, that theory may be verified.

(1) We may rule out once more the notion that such a future life is essentially supernatural in character. This notion has been a favourite with believers, but it is easily turned into a terrible weapon in the hands of their adversaries. For the supernatural is, as such, conceived to be insusceptible of investigation, and belief in it must be mere faith, exposed to every doubt and jeer, if, indeed, it can be even that, seeing that a real faith must be nourished by at least partial and prospective verification in fact. Hence the answer to this notion is simply this: that if the future life be really "supernatural" in the sense of having no connexion of any sort with nature, there could not possibly be any evidence of it, and it would have to be for us non-existent; while if there be evidence of it, this would *ipso facto* include it in the widest conception of nature, and render the nature of the connexion between this world and the next a legitimate subject for scientific research. If, therefore, the connexion be rare and precarious, the reason cannot possibly be that from time to time some audacious spirit has impiously achieved the impossible by breaking through the natural order; it must lie in the peculiarities of the natural order itself. Or, to sum up in a single phrase a discussion which would long have become needless but for the persistence of attempts to dispose of an inconvenient investigation into facts by logical quibbles about words, if "supernature" is to be retained, it must not be in the sense of something alien and hostile to "nature," but strictly as meaning a higher department or aspect of nature itself.

(2) We must suppose a certain continuity of psychological constitution in

the human spirit throughout every phase of its existence. Without this we should not know ourselves again after death. This does not imply that death may not be a great event, involving a great gain (or loss) in the intensity and extent of consciousness and memory; it asserts only that if we are to have knowledge of a future life at all, we must assume that the general characteristics of mental life will persist. Without this, too, there could be no proof of "spirit-identity" to others: without "spirit-identity" there could be no proof of a future life. Unfortunately, however, this assumption of ours would lead us to expect that the proof of "spirit-identity" would be difficult. For it is psychologically far more probable that the moral character and the feelings would traverse the shock and change of death unshaken, than that little bits of knowledge about terrestrial affairs would persist in equal measure. Yet it is these latter that afford the best tests of "spirit-identity," and it is suggestive that whereas at first Mrs. Piper's "G.P."[6] communications abounded in such tests, they have gradually grown rare.

(3) As we must try to explain all the facts by principles already known to be valid, we must account for the remarkable dissociation between this world and the next by the principle of psychological continuity. That such dissociation must exist will hardly be denied by any one who has realized how very rare an experience a "ghost" is, even with the most expert of ghost seers and in its most favoured haunts. But it would seem that if the departed still retained their personality and psychical continuity, "ghosts" ought to be more plentiful than blackberries, and unhedged by that divinity which makes people so reluctant to make a clean breast of their ghost stories. *Prima facie*, therefore, it requires explanation that in spite of psychic continuity so much dissociation should prevail.

Nevertheless it may, I think, be shown that the assumption of psychical continuity would be quite compatible with the prevalence of an almost complete dissociation between this world and the next. For any great event tends to dissociate us from our past, and this would apply *a fortiori* to an event like death, which *ex hypothesi* launches us into a new world. A new world, moreover, would engross us not only by its novelty, but also by the practical need of accommodating ourselves to new conditions of existence. Hence the psychological conditions for great concern about the world we had left behind us would hardly be present. This argument, moreover, could be considerably strengthened by psychological observations with regard to the interest which is taken in the affairs of our world by the aged. For it would be unlikely that an interest which had already grown faint should effectively maintain itself amid the distractions of a new life.

And even if the desire to communicate were felt, it could hardly be assumed that the knowledge and power to do so would at once be at the disposal of the newcomer, who, for aught we know, might find that, as upon his entry upon this scene, a period of helplessness and dependence analogous to infancy had to be passed through.

It would seem probable, therefore, that to render communication effective, quite as systematic and sustained an effort would be needed on the other side

[6] George Pelham. This was a pseudonym given to a supposed communicator. [Eds.]

as is being made by the S.P.R. on this, while the self-regarding motives for making it would be indefinitely less potent. For while each of us *ought to have* the strongest personal interest in determining what his prospects may be after death, no such case could be made out for a retrospective interest of the departed in our world. And in their world the prevalent social sentiment might esteem it better to leave us in our present doubt and discourage attempts to pry into the possibilities of communication with another world. That would only be to suppose that their social sentiment is the same as ours. Only it would in their case be more reasonable. For why should they incommode themselves to impart to us a knowledge which each one of us is bound to gather for himself within a few years more? And this suggestion will appear the more probable when we remember that, according to the principle of psychic continuity, the *same* people will be making the same sentiment in both cases. Nevertheless, it is conceivable that some day a fortunate coincidence of the efforts of an infinitesimal minority on both sides should succeed in establishing spirit-identity and forcing upon the reluctant masses of men the scientific fact of a future life which they did not in the least desire to have so established. Even then, however, we should still be very far from any definite and detailed knowledge of the nature of the future life in itself, the difficulties of transmitting which would increase enormously in proportion as the dissociation between the two spheres of existence became greater.

Thus the general upshot of our discussion so far would be that a future life which was accessible to scientific methods of proof would necessarily appear to be of a somewhat homely and humdrum character, displeasing to spiritual sensationalists. Broadly speaking, our conceptions of it would rest on the assumption of social and psychic continuity, and they would tend to suppose that the reward and punishment of the soul consisted mainly in its continuing to be itself, with the intrinsic consequences of its true nature revealed more and more clearly to itself and others. Hence there would be but little scope for epic flights of a lurid imagination, and those who hanker after the ecstasies of the blessed and the torments of the damned would have to go, as before, to the preachers and the poets. We may, however, trust these latter to work up a more copious material into pictures quite as edifying and thrilling as those of Homer, Dante, and Milton.

Friedrich von Hügel

Baron Friedrich von Hügel (1852-1925) is one of the most remarkable theolo gians of recent times. Born in Florence, he received a cosmopolitan educatio before settling in England in 1867. As a Roman Catholic layman sympatheti to the French modernists, he was more influential outside the Roman Catholi Church than within it, for his thought was anything but typical of that o Roman theologians of his day. His lay status protected him from the eccle siastical censure he might have suffered had he been a priest. His opus maxi mum, The Mystical Element in Religion as Studied in St. Catherine of Geno and her Friends, *is one of the most profound studies ever written on Christia mysticism. The following passage, from his* Essays and Addresses on the Philos ophy of Religion, *illustrates his thoughts on the notions of heaven and hell.*

The Meaning of Heaven and Hell *

We stand now before the problem of Heaven and Hell properly so called the final supernatural alternatives of the supernaturally awakened soul. Yet here again, we must first clear away three very prevalent objections and mis apprehensions. Let us move from the more general to the more particula difficulties.

First and foremost, then, we have to confront the opinion, increasingl prevalent in Western Europe since the beginning of the eighteenth century one which now pervades fairly all the non-religious, and even much of th religious, thought of our day — that the conception of Heaven is, in substance beautiful, or at least true, or at the very least harmless; but that any and ever conception of Hell is essentially hideous, or at all events unreasonable, or a the very least most dangerous and noxious. Thus serious scholars attempt t prove that our Lord's utterances as to Hell are all due to misconceptions o His disciples, or even to amplifications by writers who had not heard Hi words; or, again, that these utterances, if really proceeding from our Lor Himself, only continue, without any special verification or emphasis, certai already prevalent opinions — that they have no organic connexion with th roots of His revelation and message. Thus, too, otherwise helpful religiou philosophers reduce Hell to a long Purgatory, or simply to a rhetorical o emotional expression (perceived or not perceived by our Lord Himself to b only such) for a correct and indeed noble sense of the intrinsic difference be tween right and wrong and of the correspondingly intrinsic differences be tween the respective consequences of right and of wrong — differences whic

* Friedrich von Hügel, *Essays and Addresses on the Philosophy of Religion* (Ne York: E. P. Dutton and Co., Inc., 1926), pp. 205–208, 215–220. Reprinted by pe mission of E. P. Dutton and Co., Inc.

are really outside of time and space, but which can only be described, at all vividly, in temporal and spatial pictures. The net result of all such teachings (quite apart from the still more prevalent and insidious Pantheistic tendencies of our time) is at the least to emphasise the conviction of Mother Julian of Norwich that "all will be well," whilst the teaching of Christ and of His Church will nevertheless turn out to have been true; or, more boldly, to welcome back, as alone satisfactory, the notions, not of Origen himself, but of some Origenists, as to the eventual Restitution of All Things — of all souls; or, again, quite generally, to treat as a barbarous, impertinent irruption into our superior insight and humanity, not only the applications and details, but the very substance, of the convictions of Tertullian, St. Augustine and Dante. What can we adduce against such a denial?

We must first of all remember our discrimination — that the question concerning the final destination of man, as such, is not identical with the question concerning the final condition of particular human beings. Hence it is quite beside the mark to bring up the cases of little children, of idiots, of pure savages. We must also not forget that there need be no real question of Hell even for the majority of the supernaturally awakened souls, if there actually exists a state and process of purgation in the Beyond, as there undoubtedly exists such a state and process here. Yet these provisos do not eliminate the real possibility of Hell, as the general rule, wheresoever is a real possibility of Heaven; they leave Heaven and Hell as a generally inter-related couple.

We must next try vividly to realise the fact that it is not Hell which is so much more difficult to believe in than is Heaven; but that it is the entire specifically spiritual conception of man, of his deepest self, which is difficult, as contrasted with the naturalistic view of these same things. The purely naturalistic view of man conceives him as a mere superior animal, which projects its own largely fantastic wishes on to the void or the unknown, and which then wishes them back as objective realities distinct from itself their true creator. And this view is the more plausible, the more quickly statable, the more vividly picturable, the alone readily transmittable, view. But then, the view has all these qualities, precisely because it stops short at the surface-impressions of things, and remains utterly inadequate to all the deeper and deepest implications, requirements and ends of knowledge in general, and of art, ethics, philosophy and religion in particular. Yet as soon as we hold the difference between various kinds of human acts and dispositions to be always potentially, and often actually, of essential, of ultimate, of more than simply social, simply human importance, we are insisting upon values and realities that essentially transcend space and even time. Every at all noble, every even tolerably adequate, outlook always possesses some such more than merely empirical, simply contingent, or purely material and mechanical character. Plato, the Stoics, Plotinus possess this outlook, although in very different degrees; it ruled the Western world, during the Christian Middle Ages; and, after the largely negative rationality of most of the Renaissance, it gave its note of pathetic distinction and splendour to the great spirit of Spinoza, gravely cramped by Pantheism though it was in its speculation. In Kant it again reappears in a more theistic setting, and with the deep perception of that deep fact — radical evil — of man's frequent declaring, willing and doing what he well knows to be false and bad, but pleasant; in Schopenhauer it relieves the general pessimistic oppression with glimpses of a Beauty abiding and all-sustaining. And now, in these our times, we are again coming, in different lands and from different experiences and starting-points, to schemes really adequate, indeed deeply friendly, to this Transcendence present in all our nobler aspirations, acts and ends. Thus every profound search after, or belief in, the fundamental truth or essential beauty or satisfying goodness of anything — when we press it duly home and sincerely and delicately analyse it — overflows the ordinary, superficially obvious, requirements of man's knowledge, action, life. In each case we get a scheme that looks too big and too ambitious for us little men, and that involves alternatives too wide and deep for the average moments of the average mortal.

We have then, for our purpose, only to ask whether the alternatives — Heaven, Hell — are like or are unlike these ultimate implications of man's deepest needs and aspirations, elevations and falls. And the answer will assuredly be: "They are not unlike, but like."

. . . . .

We are at last face to face with the special subject-matter of our quest. And we must, consequently, attempt to find and to describe the characteristics of our deepest experiences; and, in each instance, to contrast the fully willed and bliss-bringing acceptance, and the full refusal, with its pain and contraction, of this our profoundest call.

Our deepest spiritual experiences appear always to possess some or all of four qualities. And the contrasted effects, as respectively within the right disposition and the wrong disposition, seem to be as follows:

In our deepest moments here below, our experiences are least changeful and most constant; they are, in those moments, least successive and most nearly simultaneous. They thus come nearest to the character of God, and to an apprehension of that character. God is Pure Eternity, Sheer Simultaneity; the animal man is almost Pure Succession, indeed all but mere change; the spiritual man is, in proportion to his spirituality, More or Less Simultaneous.

We have every reason, then, to hold that these experiences, and their differences, apply also to the supernaturally awakened souls in the Beyond. The saved spirits will thus, according to the degree of their supernatural call and of their supernatural establishment within it, be quasi-simultaneous in their intelligence, feeling, volition, acts, effectuations. This their life will, at any one moment of its slow succession, be too rich and varied to require much succession for the unravelling of its capacities and acts. Indeed, this richness will be actually the richer for this quasi-simultaneity of its contents and gains; since thus the many connexions and contrasts between these many things will be very largely present together with the things themselves.

The lost spirits will persist, according to the degree of their permanent self-willed defection from their supernatural call, in the all but mere changingness, scatteredness, distractedness, variously characteristic of their self-elected earthly life. And owing to their past experience of the opposite conditions, and to their (still extant although diminished) consciousness of the supernatural call, they will feel the unsatisfactoriness of this their permanent non-recollection more than they felt it upon earth.

In our deepest moments here below, again, our greatest expansion and delight arises from our sense of contact, more or less close and vivid, with Realities not ourselves; in such moments we not simply reach truth — something abstract, something which we predominantly refer to the already developed tests and standard of our own minds — but Reality, some deeply concrete and living thing which enlarges our experiences of fact and indeed our thus experiencing souls themselves.

We have then, again, every reason to hold that these experiences, and their contrasted differences, will persist, greatly heightened, in the Beyond. The saved spirits will thus, according to the degree of their supernatural call and of their supernatural establishment, be supported, environed, penetrated by the Supreme Reality and by the keenest sense of this Reality. This sense of God, — of God as distinct from, previous to, independent of, our apprehension of Him — of God as self-revealing and self-giving, will evoke continuous acts and habits — an entire state — of a responsive self-givingness in the soul itself. The great Divine Ecstasy will evoke and be met by the little human ecstasy. Not primarily, this, a self-consciousness of the soul, with a more or less dim or even hypothetic reference to, or assumption of, God derivatively attached thereto; but the sense of God and of the joy in Him, central and supreme, and the sense of the self, chiefly as of the channel for, the recipient of, and the response to, all this Divine Reality, Joy and Life.

The lost spirits will persist, according to the degree of their permanent self-willed defection from their supernatural call, in the varyingly all but complete self-centredness and subjectivity of their self-elected earthly life. But now they will feel, far more fully than they ever felt on earth, the stuntedness, the self-mutilation, the imprisonment involved in this their endless self-occupation and jealous evasion of all reality not simply their own selves.

In our deepest moments, once more, we reach the fullest sense of our membership of the social human organism, of our possessing a fruitful action upon it precisely because of this our glad acceptance of our special little place within the great family of the thinkers, workers, sufferers, achievers amongst our fellows in the long past and in the wide present. We have, then, no reason to doubt that, in the Beyond, these experiences and their contrasted differences will obtain — and in still greater measure.

The saved spirits, then, will receive, exercise, enjoy, aid, and complete a richly various, deep and tender, social life with fellow souls. And as the intercourse of these spirits with God is not simply mental or abstractly contemplative, but quite as much emotional, volitional, active, efficacious; so also this their intercourse with the fellow souls is mental, emotional, volitional, active, efficacious. And the quasi-simultaneity, and the deep sense of and delight in realities, which we have already found so strongly to characterise these saved spirits, will doubtless penetrate and enrich this their social joy. For thus they will profoundly perceive, feel and will themselves as just parts, special parts, of this great social whole; and they will profoundly see, feel and will themselves, as greatly surpassed in sanctity by innumerable other souls. The joy in the rich interconnexion and various supplementation between these countlessly different souls, and the joy in reality — realities other and far fuller than themselves, will thus add to the bliss and the fruitfulness, outwards and inwards, which spring from the social experience and activity of the saved.

The lost spirits will persist, according to the degree of their permanent defection, in their claimfulness and envious self-isolation, in their niggardly pain at the sight or thought of the unmatchable greatness and goodness of other souls. But now the disharmony of all this with their own past better experiences and their own still present sense of the supernatural call, becomes more fully and more unintermittently conscious within them than it was wont to be in them on earth.

And lastly, our deepest moments are assuredly often, perhaps always, shot through, in their very joy, with suffering — even though this suffering be only the birth-pangs of a fuller spiritual life and fruitfulness. Our profoundest happiness here below always possesses something of the heroic; and the heroic appears impossible without obscurity met by faith, pain borne by patience, risk and loss faced and transformed by the magic of self-immolation. Thus our fullest nobility and its unique joys appear as though, after all, reserved for this our earth alone. But not so.

The saved spirits in the Beyond will doubtless no further know suffering and pain, temptation and risk and fall, within themselves, such as we poor little men now know them upon earth. And yet it is not difficult to find, within the deepest characteristics of the human soul even upon earth and the most certain and most dominant conditions of the Other Life, operative causes for the continuance in Heaven itself of the essentials in the nobility furnished by devoted suffering and self-sacrifice here below. For the saved spirits in the Beyond indeed see God as He is — but this doubtless only in so far as their finite natures, indefinitely raised and expanded by Supernature though they be, can do so. What they see is indeed the very Reality of God; what they feel and will, and what they act with and for, is in very truth this Reality itself. Nevertheless, they are not themselves Gods; they are finite, God is infinite; they are more or less successive, God is purely simultaneous; they exist through Him, He is self-existent; and thus contrastedly in many other ways. And yet it is God, as He is in Himself, and not as He is only partially seen by them, whom these spirits desire to comprehend, to love, to will and to serve. Hence, even in Heaven, there remains, for the saved soul, room and the need to transcend itself, to lose itself, that it may truly find itself. Here is an act possessed of an element of genuine darkness, of real tension, succeeded by an accession of further light and wider expansion. St. Catherine of Genoa from her own spiritual experiences, vividly conceived and finely pictured, in the souls destined to Purgatory, their joyous acceptance of, their freely willed plunge into, this intrinsically necessary bath of purgation; and their escape, by means of this pain, from the now far greater suffering produced within them by their clear perception of the stains and disharmonies still present in their own souls. Such souls thus taste an ever-increasing bliss and peace within their ever-decreasing pain, whilst those impurities and hardenings are slowly surely, sufferingly yet serenely, purified, softened and willed away. We can, *mutatis mutandis,* similarly picture to ourselves the soul's acts in confrontation of God, even in Heaven, as, in a sense, plunges, away from the quite clear yet limited vision, into a wider, but at first dimmer, experience of the great Reality. And thus such plunges of the soul there into God, and the somewhat similar goings-out there of the same soul to its fellow souls (whom also it will hardly see as completely as it wills to love and serve, and to learn from them) are the equivalents there of men's heroic plunges here away from sin and self, or from quite clear sense-impressions and pictures of the visible world into the suffering and sacrifice which accompany the fidelity to the instincts and intuitions (as yet relatively obscure) of a fuller love and service of God and men.

The lost souls are left to the pain of stainedness and self-contraction; they do not attain to, since they do not really will, the suffering of purification and expansive harmonisation. For man, once he is supernaturally awakened, cannot escape pain; he can only choose between the pain of fruitful growth, expansion, tension — the throes of spiritual parturition, — the pangs of the wide-open welcome to the pressing inflow of the fuller life, and the aches of fruitless stunting, contraction, relaxation, the dull and dreary, or the angry and reckless, drifting in bitter-sweet unfaithful or immoral feelings, acts, habits, which, thus indulged, bring ever-increasing spiritual blindness, volitional paralysis and a living death. Only in Heaven and in Hell is the will finally determined as between the solicitations of the pain within the joy of the right, and of the pleasure within the dreariness of the wrong. Yet even in Heaven there is a certain analogue to the genuine cost in the real gain traceable within the deepest acts of the human soul whilst here on earth. And hence, correspondingly, the very pains of Hell consist largely in the perception by the lost soul of how unattainable is that fruitful suffering which would furnish the one escape from the fruitless pangs now actually endured.

W. E. Hocking

William Ernest Hocking was born in 1873. A distinguished American exponent of an idealistic philosophy, he was impressed by the importance of the notion of immortality. His first book on the subject, Thoughts on Death and Life, *was published in 1937.* The Meaning of Immortality in Human Experience, *from which the following passage is taken, appeared in 1957 as an enlarged and revised edition of his earlier work. Disclaiming religious or cultural boundaries, he felt himself to be in sympathy with the religious life of both East and West. In* The Coming World Civilization *he applied his principles to the world situation.*

On Living and Dying *

Analysis is not solution: it offers truth, but something short of *the* truth. Its function is, not to replace intuitive persuasions regarding life and death, but to cure the vagrancy of a feeling-driven imagination, ready to substitute itself for truth. The deeper the hold of feeling on any issue, the sterner must be the resolve that feeling be disciplined by analysis, and not only for the sake of truth, but for the sake of feeling. For feeling has its own truth and falsity and the *truthfulness of feeling,* quite as much as of thought, is an issue of life and death which a self-indulgent civilization has not yet begun to fathom. Without truth, feeling is corrupt: but conversely, without feeling, truth is barren. A true analysis must still seek its full truth in its organic unity with feeling.

Our analysis has turned on certain familiar concepts — the self, physical nature, freedom, reality, creativity. The term "creativity" became for us a token of reality, on the ground that that which only conserves cannot so much as explain its own presence in the universe. But "creativity" as a descriptive concept presents a trap, as a fallacious attempt to naturalize a primitive wildness and give it the decor of scientific standing. Let us be clear that as an impersonal principle of world-process creativity falls lifeless: there is *no creativity in the universe without feeling* — or more specifically, without a subjective factor, an inner urge, whose nature is akin to what we call "love."

If this is the case, human destiny turns on the nature and potency of love: and love, in its most general sense, as the life of our own creativity — that is to say, of ourselves — needs less to be defined than to be recognized in self-consciousness, in immediate experience. We have only to confirm, as primary authorities, what Plato or the depth-psychologists, as secondary authorities, may tell us: that there is a *total élan* of our being toward an undefined goal; that the various impulses welling up in us through the subconscious tend to

* William E. Hocking, *The Meaning of Immortality in Human Experience* (New York: Harper & Brothers, 1957), pp. 245–255. Used by permission.

merge in a single self-sublimating Eros. And this central and pervasive longing presents to us images of total fulfillment, as it has to the race through all reflective history.

There are two great symbols of such fulfillment, that of the Beatific Vision of "The Good," and that of Creating through vesting our total *élan* in specific objects, the love of things, beings, persons. The beatific vision, putting an end to striving, dissolves time itself as individual experience. Creating-through-love is within the time-field and portends continued creation in time. Broadly speaking, the classic Orient (together with the neo-Platonic strain) tends to find fulfillment in the time-transcending vision; the West, in the continued working of love through time.

Our further understanding of human survival will depend on referring this issue to experience — experience of two kinds, first that of love itself, and then that of death. We shall briefly carry out this self-consulting inquiry: we shall find, I believe, that *Immortality involves both* modes of fulfillment.

The Experience of Creative Love

Love, as we commonly mean it, is specific: it is of things, beings, persons. Its horizon is indeed beyond them, it is *toward* something universal discerned in and through these particulars — the undefined object of our *total élan.* Love as a passion tends to vest its total fulfillment in individual objects, as the theme of its most tangible creativity.

The first impulse of specific love — and I include in love the response of the mind to beauty — appears less like a will to create than like a will to hold, to detain, as a step toward possession: *Verweile doch, du bist so schön.* But even this primitive impulse is the reverse of a state of repose: it is a haunting drive to know that being through and through, to grasp in thought the secret of its being, to obliterate its otherness and merge with it. Not literally to possess — though that term is used — for the free being is not to be destroyed in its freedom; but to be possessed in thought, and so to be reproduced, for we fully conceive *only what we make.* (This is the primitive motive of honest art — not imitation, not invention, but an ever-continuing appropriation of the real through one's own begetting.)

And thus to love is to treat the loved being as worthy of permanence. The impulse of caring is to hold that being forever above the accidents of time and death — as if one could! The miracle of love is that it so spontaneously forgets its own limitations: it assumes its right to act *in loco Dei* — and with the right assumes also its capacity! The pathetic folly of human affection? Or is it the reverse, a point at which human finitude rises to the point of participating in deity? I propose that here, in willing to confer immortality on another mortal, the self is in that moment reaching a deeper self-consciousness, an intimation of its own destiny.

Even so, the will to immortalize is not the whole of what we mean by the creative power of love. Nor is it limited to biological begetting. Human loves in their biological symbols of overcoming death achieve only the transfer of mortality, a possibly endless series of ending lives. Creative love does not leave the loved being unchanged: here the remoter horizon of the total *élan* or eros is to be remembered. It is this universal's fulfillment that is to be realized in the particular: in the savage-prophetic words of Nietzsche, "All great love is the beloved to create; and all creators *are hard*." What is loved, whether in persons or in nature, is never static perfection: in persons it is "the pilgrim soul," led on by that same vision — an unrealized self, striving toward what it *is* not, but has potency for. The life of the lover — aware not alone of what is, but of what is unborn possibility in the beloved — is in bringing that possibility to birth under the egis of the shared (though undefined) goal. Thus love becomes the energy of a continuous creativity in time.

And since the unrealized but germinal self has the dimension of infinitude, the *mission of love in time is never done.* Unless such love holds in itself an assurance of its own perpetuity, it moves under the shadow of a cosmic deceit.

We turn to inquire whether the experience of dying can throw any light on the field of this potential shadow.

The Experience of Dying

We are not without ability to follow this experience for part of its course. There is the empathic observation, definitely perilous from the standpoint of truth, of the *witness* of dying; there is the report of persons who have gone *part way* into death and have returned; there is a broad stream of *tradition* from alleged seers, whose credentials we ourselves must judge.

As observers, we have to recognize the fact that when death is drawing its outline to a life, there is often on the part of the dying person an *apparent welcome* to terminus. Occasionally there is a more affirmative attitude, a certain "being in love with death" as if the dying were attracted toward nescience; such reversal of the will to live may invade life even before death approaches — as with Mozart, or Rilke, or O'Neill. There is such a thing as a normal will to die.

In the Orient, voluntary relinquishment of life has a respected place. A former student of mine, Dr. N. N. Sen Gupta, psychologist at Lucknow, gave me in 1931 an account of his uncle's predicted, and presumably controlled, death during a morning dhyana. Throughout Yoga-land one meets such accounts; Norman Hall relates some of them in his South Sea stories. Among us of the West, there is no such recognized art of purposefully stilling breath and heartbeat by direct will-control. But the foreknowledge and acceptance of the coming end, as by instinctive dismissal of *élan vital,* is not unknown. A friend tells of the farewell-to-life of her father's father:

> As a very old man, he was accustomed to ask one of the children to stay home from work, to be with him, on days when he felt he needed care. One day he said a good-bye to each child, in a little ceremonious way which he had. Next day, on being asked whom he would like to have stay with him, he answered, "Nobody: I want to be alone today." In the evening, we found him as if asleep in his chair, dead.

In our world-region, for most of us, young or old, death arrives in the midst of concerted efforts to fend it off, efforts accepted as obligatory and unquestioned. Yet, in my judgment, this is seldom the whole inwardness of the event for the dying. So far as I have been able to observe the approach of death, or to follow the observations of others, it has seemed possible to detect on the part of the dying person, in the later stages, a complicity with nature, as if, before dying were finished one became a consenting party. The following account appears to be fairly typical of death from disease:

> The patient was dying of TB. He had been unconscious, had reverted to a period of clear awareness, and had sunk back into coma. The physician said, "This is the last time: he will not come back." The nurse said, "Yes: he will come back." He came back twice — the second time only a moment or two before his breathing stopped. X was with him then, and he knew. Then without struggle he dropped away, as if in a deep welcoming of peace. When breathing and heartbeat stopped, the face composed itself into a beauty not to be described.

Such dismissal, if not reversal, of the will-to-live is independent of any judgment on the part of the dying that his work is finished: there are few who can say that. The dismissal supervenes on completed tasks, but also on broken-off labors — as with the King of Siam in the play, upon an "etcetera" — and on the deaths of the young. It seems to record a swift, infinitely relieving perception that *agenda are not the essence of living*; and that in some sense endings *should be* broken off. Otherwise one would regard his position in the universe as that of a spent Roman candle. Let the ever-seeking Faust but arrive at his goal, and — if it is the total goal — he has no future. The peace that comes to the dying is not that of terminus: it is — as I interpret it — the peace of *handing-on*, and of reverting to origins, with the felt opening of a perspective more profoundly valid.[1]

There are many reports of experience from persons who have returned from a part-way passage into death — and I have now in a minor way joined that company — reports which tend to confirm these conjectures. Gerald Heard will allow me to quote from a letter of May, 1951:

> I believe the account given in Leo Tolstoy's remarkable short story, *The Death of Ivan Ilyitch*, is based on, and gives a vivid account not only of an actual experience, but of the experience which, in its main outline, will be ours when we "emerge" — when, as the Sanskrit text puts it, the grass core is drawn out from its sheath. That we do relinquish our restricted contact with the sensory world and pass into another frame of reference, I feel no doubt, both from my own experience and from those of others.

Drawing together these fragmentary data of experience, direct and indirect; and passing over a considerable body of literary evidence to the effect that

[1] But whether from a broken-off ending or from a sense of tentative conclusion, let me here record my conviction that though we of the West may have lost the power of relinquishing life by inner control, the normal will-to-die should be respected. With that will there also arrives the *right to die*, often cruelly denied or delayed, through a mistaken view of duty, abetted by the necessities of law.

death has a double aspect, that of enemy and that of friend;[2] we may interpret the experience of dying in its usual course somewhat as follows:

After the earlier stages of detachment from identity with the body (in its socially expressive character), there occurs a sort of coming-forth into light, as in passing through a tunnel, an unshelling or emergence like the relief of a diver coming to the surface. The change which often comes over the features — an erasure of the marks of anxiety or suffering, a transfiguring into nobility and peace, a cosmic dignity — this visible change very probably registers a phase of the inwardly felt transition. Even before that point, we must distinguish between the experience of the dying person and the interpretations of the witness, based on normal expressive signs, except at moments of the dying person's return to recognition. There is ground to believe that the dying one tends early to separate his own being-in-the-world from that of his body, as if to say "Where art thou, pain?" And while the welcoming of death has in it a certain natural acquiescence in the growing weariness of a failing organism, a physically conditioned immense relief on "entering into rest"; this welcoming appears to be typically far more affirmative, as if new elements of experience and insight had entered consciousness.

The Beatific Vision as Fulfillment

There is much in what we have noted to suggest that death brings a cessation of experience in time, whether as eternal absorption of the person in the One, as in the concept of Nirvana, or some other type of the beatific vision, consummatory and terminal.

The Hindu conception has its profound insights, based on its legitimate demand that religion and philosophy must found themselves on experience, a "direct awareness of the ground of existence."[3] The essence of this view is not in the notion of Karma — for Karma as the transmission of defective action through successive rebirths is not true immortality. "The real self,

[2] Much could be recorded of the widespread recognition in all cultures of the friendliness of death. Schubert's *Death and the Maiden,* with its terminal assurance, "*Bin Freund, und komme nicht zu strafen,*" may illustrate. And even in the more terrible forms of death, the note persists. A striking instance is found in the execution — some say the crucifixion — of the Persian mystic Al Hallaj in Baghdad, March, 922 A.D., done to death for blasphemy because he said "I am the Real." Al Hallaj had anticipated his fate, and had written:

> Slayer, I hail thee with my dying breath,
> Victor, I yield the fortress of my heart.
> The doors fly open, and the poor lips part
> Once more, and then no more, world without end.
> The cup is poison, and the thought is death;
> And He that gives them,
> is not He the Friend?

This was his faith; it was also his deed. "During his execution," says Nicholson, "which was carried out in a barbarous manner, Hallaj displayed the utmost fortitude." He left upon his tormentors an undying impression of inner elevation.

[3] Swami Asashananda, "Hindu View of Immortality," in *Prabuddha Bharata,* February, 1957, 51 ff. The following quotations in this paragraph are from the same article, recording an address given at Northwest Philosophical Conference, U.S.A., 1956.

which is eternal and universal, does not undergo change." Its innate identity with the One cannot be discarded, though it is disguised and hidden under empirical conditions: its ultimate aim is to recover self-awareness. As Vivekananda inclined to put the matter, "Nature . . . takes the self-forgetting soul by the hand . . . bringing him higher and higher . . . till his lost glory comes back, and he remembers his own nature." The clamorous ego, insisting on its separateness from others and the One, is finally "cut away": after this consummation, no more experience-in-time.

There is no lack of spontaneous agreement with this outlook in western literature, so far as it, too, is based on direct experience, rather than on traditional imagery. Consider this plea of Siegfried Sassoon in *Sequences:*

> I think
> If through some chink in me could shine
> But once — O, but one ray
> From that all-hallowing and eternal day,
> Asking no more of Heaven,
> I would go hence.

In that summary "go hence," what powerful quitclaim of all lien upon the continuing universe! And yet without surrendering the claim of right, upon which I have insisted, as against the world that has produced us, the right to understand! Then willingly cease?

The Union of Vision and Time

I recur to my suggestion that the two symbols of fulfillment *belong together,* and cannot truly be conceived in separation. As indicating how this is possible, let me point out that in fact the two modes of experience occur together in this life.

For the course of common living is not without its occasional "rays from that eternal day." Recall the experiences of "illumination" of which John Masefield speaks. . . . They come — I believe to everyone in some degree — into our most desperate gropings: they offer — for an hour, a day, a group of days — a vision of the meaning of things: "Now, for the first time, I *see*!" Such in-lighting is not a termination: it is a new beginning. The glow vanishes, but the enlightenment remains, unbanishable. And the life-action that follows is lifted and directed by a unique sense of initiation — as if by a new hold on an *a priori* one should always have been living by — an awakening that knows its own awakeness — no completed truth, but an anticipation of ultimate attainment.[4]

This, if I am not mistaken, is the true sense of the Hindu Jivanmukta, release within present existence. For the true eternity is time-inclusive, not time concluding. It spans the future, but *also the past.* Its insight often arrives (as does every valid *a priori*) with a sense of recollection, as if one were recurring to a past perception, long forgotten. The forward-looking longing

[4] William E. Hocking, *The Meaning of God in Human Experience* (New Haven, Conn.: Yale University Press, 1922), 30 f.

transforms itself into a nostalgia. Plotinus has marvelously expressed this double time-reference of the impact of physical beauty:

> perceived at the first glance,
> it is evident that there is such a quality,
> recognized by the soul as something long familiar,
> arresting and beckoning. [Ennead I, vi, 2]

So if, in death, some fragment of the beatific vision should be our lot, arresting and beckoning the passing spirit — one who had already known love in its truthfulness — it would be indeed a glimpse of eternity, and a oneness with the One: but not a terminus of time in eternal changelessness. For the time which can be untimed, *at a time,* is not ended. It would be at once self-recovery, remembrance, and the continued lure to create through love in ongoing time. Our oneness with the One is participation, not in fixity, but in partnership with him that continually labors and creates, world without end . . .

Donald MacKinnon

Professor Donald MacKinnon, an Anglican layman, is a contemporary philosopher who, after a distinguished career at Oxford and Aberdeen, now holds a professorial chair at the University of Cambridge. The paper that follows is one originally given on the British Broadcasting Corporation's Third Programme.

Death *

To many contemporary philosophers it seems that claims to survive death must be described as nonsense statements, and that the philosopher's job is to lay bare their nonsensical character, and uncover the violations of syntactical propriety they contain. Of course, we do talk regularly of people surviving catastrophes and *escaping* death. We may even in certain unusual circumstances be justified in speaking of dead men as not really dead: in cases of catalepsy, and so on. But death itself is not something we can significantly speak of surviving. If we say we survive death, we do not know what we are saying. For we cannot stretch our lines of connection with ordinary usage far enough to establish the sense of it. The words are combined in a way that, if we attend to them closely, defies the possibility of our attaching sense to them.

When something is proposed to us for assent or dissent, we demand almost as a condition that we should have some idea of the sort of arguments relevant to establishing it. And, of course, such arguments must be internally sound — that is, they must not be self-contradictory, nor entail the denial of what we hope to establish by means of them. Now if it can be shown that arguments for the survival of bodily death, all of them, sooner or later take for granted the absence of the very condition of bodily death, then they can have no power to establish survival. If it is the case that in order to think survival of bodily death, one has got to think bodily death away, then what one is thinking is not survival but simply the absence of the condition one is supposed to survive. To work this out in detail would involve the description of a whole series of arguments: to show how here in one way, there in another the reference to the body as something still there was allowed to creep back. There is no substitute for such pains. One would have to take some more or less traditional treatise on immortality and track out in the arguments the recurrence of references to some shadowy, ghostly counterpart of bodily existence: or the unacknowledged takings-for-granted of the continuance of the conditions of such existence.

* A. Flew and A. MacIntyre (eds.), *New Essays in Philosophical Theology* (New York: The Macmillan Co., 1955), pp. 261–266. Used by permission of The Macmillan Co. and Student Christian Movement Press, Ltd.

One cannot, if one is honest, ignore the extent to which metaphysical arguments, like those concerning immortality, have gained plausibility from a refusal to attend to the logic of our language. How much indeed does our glib talk about survival owe to our refusal to reflect on the very significance of the pronoun "I" itself. "I survive" — but what is "I"? Do I suppose that "I" is the name of a kind of ultimate substrate of qualities, clad with its states much as a clothes-horse is draped with towels, shirts, etc.? Do I think that I am related to my biography in that kind of way? Yet much of our superficial talk about survival suggests that we do. Whether we think of the survival, or of the survivor, we are at once plunged into bewilderment. What exactly are we talking about?

One can certainly put a question-mark against almost every stage in the fabric of traditional argumentation on this issue. And yet one is somehow sure that that is not the end of the matter. I have already mentioned the importance of description, the description of arguments, the description of instances of proof, and so on. How odd it is that philosophers, who, where the exact sciences are concerned, are insisting more and more that we eschew the general formula and concentrate on the individual instance, should, where metaphysics is concerned, ignore their own rubric! Metaphysical arguments are so often treated as if they could be exhaustively set out in a formal scheme; whereas, of course, of all arguments they are surely the ones that require the most detailed and individual treatment. For in them, surely, so much more is set out, albeit indirectly, of the inwardness of the person whose arguments they are.

To put it very crudely, just what is it that is at stake for a person in this matter of immortality? What is it that is bothering him? Of course, you can show the queerness, the confusedness of the way in which the bother is expressing itself, when it does so by means of the traditional language of survival, and so on. You can discredit this means of expression by showing the logical confusions into which it plunges: but does that settle the perplexity, the issue in the mind of the bewildered person? Now I am not suggesting for one moment that when we think, there is a ghostlike something called our thought that tries now one form of expression, now another; rather like a stout man trying on suits off the peg, and discarding them one by one. The relation of thought to its expression isn't a bit like that. But isn't there something which we all of us know, a kind of confused knowing that we haven't said what we mean but that if we persevere, we might get the sense of what we are after through the criticism of what we've said?

Put it another way. Death is a clinical phenomenon. You can learn a great deal about it from text-books of pathology, medical jurisprudence and so on. But is it only that? Do we regard death as something about which we could learn everything we have to learn through a mere extension of the sort of information we can already pick up from the kind of text-books I have mentioned? Or have we anything to learn from poetry, from the language of religion and so on? Or are we to say that anything we find conveyed only by such language as religious persons use is somehow merely peripheral . . . the merest expression of private feeling and as such ultimately insignificant?

You see how the issue under discussion has been turned round. It is no longer a stretching or straining after inconceivable states of being. It has rather become a question of the way we regard the term of human life. Is it or is it not true that those who still mouth the logical vulgarities of traditional arguments concerning immortality do so because in the end they just cannot allow that the clinician has said or can say all that is to be significantly said about death?

Again, I know my description is not nearly detailed enough. How can it be when to make it so would involve me in a vast multiplication of individual instances? To understand the issue of immortality, you must look at the ways people talk of death: the ways they talk when they are defending a theory, the ways they talk when they are off guard and speak to themselves freely.

This issue, of course, does not stand alone. For all its intimacy to the individual, it cannot be isolated in the way the aim of an experiment can be. By translating the problem into terms of our human attitude to death, one does more than merely bring it down to earth in the sense of perhaps uncovering a little what is in people's minds when they bother about it. One relates the issue to all those manifold other issues that touch our relation to our neighbour. Such issues are only made explicit to us by means of language: so, too, the continually besetting problem of their place in the scheme of things.

Suppose we were as a kind of exercise simply to look at things people have said or written about death in relation to their lives as human beings. One could avert attention from all concern with speculation about what comes after, concern oneself with death as a factor in human life. One could call it a study of the logic of poetic and religious expression on the subject. It might be that such an exercise would open our minds a little to what drives people to speak so hazardously about survival and immortality. Such an enterprise would call for sympathetic imagination — for a readiness perhaps to widen our horizons. But I can see no other way to get at the inwardness of this problem than a readiness to take the strain of such a widening.

Of course, the question will remain how such expression is related to that of the sciences and their commonsensical basis: the problem I referred to when I mentioned the place of human relations in the scheme of things. But at least one will have taken an important step towards curing oneself of the illusion that the stumbling speech of those who speak of immortality and survival (I except here the psychical researchers) is expressive of an attempt to gain knowledge of fact without the discipline of experiment and reflective analysis. One will have begun to track the language to its human source, to plot the experience of which it is the expression. The experience, indeed, *which takes shape through such expression.*

But what of proof? How does one prove, for instance, that the agony of a person suddenly, and as it seems to him irrationally, bereaved is not a bubble on the surface of things? How does one confer on grief itself the dignity of validity? The jargon is repulsive: but in the end perhaps just *this* is the real issue. I spoke of the bereavement as seeming irrational: I spoke of the protest. At such a moment a person may be simultaneously conscious of life as having form, direction, meaning. And yet as having no form, no direction, no meaning. The violence of the disturbance is due to the fact, not that meaning has never been found, but that suddenly it has been taken away — as if by a malignant practical joker. Some philosophers insist with good reason that such a phrase as "the meaning of life" is empty of sense. But if they are altogether right, then the very anguish of spirit I have been describing is shown up as trivial and empty. And is this something we can allow? It is less a pinchbeck survival than the place of man in the world that is at issue. Almost we would beg the world that it does not treat our agonies as nothings.

Christian theology, which did so much to transform men's attitude to the after-life, speaks less of immortality than of resurrection, less of personal survival than of the life of the world to come. It speaks less of assurance that something will survive as of hope that "all manner of thing will be well." To develop this theme properly belongs not to philosophy but to theology, and above all to Christology, the pivot and centre of characteristically Christian theology. Indeed sometimes the man who is at all trained in this theology must be impatient of discussions of immortality, which studiously refrain from referring to the *event* of the death and resurrection of Christ. Clearly, however, that issue cannot be raised here.

But this at least can be said without prolonged invasion of the theological field. There is no escape at any point in life from the fear that our very seriousness about ourselves is sound and fury signifying nothing. The medieval schoolmen would have said: inevitably so, for man is poised between being and not being; he draws his existence wholly from the self-existent God. The movement of human thought must reflect man's situation in being. Because he is so poised between being and not being, he will never see his existence as something assured. Again and again, in taking stock of himself, he will not find easily the arguments which will assure him that his standing is secure. At their wisest the schoolmen would never allow that by a formula we could somehow escape the most fundamental conditions of our existence. In the end they would have said: the proof of the pudding is in the eating; a necessary implication of their insistence on the primacy of being over thought. And perhaps we must say the same. There is no other proof possible that a seriousness in life is justified than is found in living. One cannot by any magic escape the conditions of humanity, assume the absolute perspective of God. If it is better to arrive than to travel, we are still inescapably travelling *in statu viae,* to use the old phrase. And our perspectives are necessarily those of travellers, at least for most of the time. But there still remains a difference between the traveller who takes the measure of his road and the one who seeks to be oblivious of its windings.

SECTION SIX

Value-Experience and the Idea of God

Aristotle

In the following passage Aristotle (see also page 68) considers, in the context of his ethical system, the nature of friendship.

Love and Friendship *

The kinds of friendship may perhaps be cleared up if we first come to know the object of love. For not everything seems to be loved but only the lovable, and this is good, pleasant, or useful; but it would seem to be that by which some good or pleasure is produced that is useful, so that it is the good and the useful that are lovable as ends. Do men love, then *the* good, or what is good for *them*? These sometimes clash. So too with regard to the pleasant. Now it is thought that each loves what is good for himself, and that the good is without qualification lovable, and what is good for each man is lovable for him; but each man loves not what is good for him but what seems good. This however will make no difference; we shall just have to say that this is "that which seems lovable." Now there are three grounds on which people love; of the love of lifeless objects we do not use the word "friendship"; for it is not mutual love, nor is there a wishing of good to the other (for it would surely be ridiculous to wish wine well; if one wishes anything for it, it is that it may keep, so that one may have it oneself); but to a friend we say we ought to wish what is good for his sake. But to those who thus wish good we ascribe only goodwill, if the wish is not reciprocated; goodwill when it *is* reciprocal being friendship. Or must we add "when it is recognized"? For many people have goodwill to those whom they have not seen but judge to be good or useful; and one of these might return this feeling. These people seem to bear goodwill to each other; but how could one call them friends when they do not know their mutual feelings? To be friends, then, they must be mutually recognized as bearing goodwill and wishing well to each other for one of the aforesaid reasons.

Now these reasons differ from each other in kind; so, therefore, do the corresponding forms of love and friendship. There are therefore three kinds of friendship, equal in number to the things that are lovable; for with respect to each there is a mutual and recognized love, and those who love each other wish well to each other in that respect in which they love one another. Now those who love each other for their utility do not love each other for themselves but in virtue of some good which they get from each other. So too with those who love for the sake of pleasure; it is not for their character that men love ready-witted people, but because they find them pleasant. Therefore those who love for the sake of utility love for the sake of what is good for

* *The Basic Works of Aristotle*, ed. Richard McKeon (New York: Random House, 1941), *Nichomachean Ethics*, Book VIII, Chapters 2–5; Book IX, Chapters 11, 12; pp. 1059–1064, 1092, 1093. Used by permission of The Clarendon Press, Oxford, England.

themselves, and those who love for the sake of pleasure do so for the sake of what is pleasant to *themselves,* and not in so far as the other is the person loved but in so far as he is useful or pleasant. And thus these friendships are only incidental; for it is not as being the man he is that the loved person is loved, but as providing some good or pleasure. Such friendships, then, are easily dissolved, if the parties do not remain like themselves; for if the one party is no longer pleasant or useful the other ceases to love him.

Now the useful is not permanent but is always changing. Thus when the motive of the friendship is done away, the friendship is dissolved, inasmuch as it existed only for the ends in question. This kind of friendship seems to exist chiefly between old people (for at that age people pursue not the pleasant but the useful) and, of those who are in their prime or young, between those who pursue utility. And such people do not live much with each other either; for sometimes they do not even find each other pleasant; therefore they do not need such companionship unless they are useful to each other; for they are pleasant to each other only in so far as they rouse in each other hopes of something good to come. Among such friendships people also class the friendship of host and guest. On the other hand the friendship of young people seems to aim at pleasure; for they live under the guidance of emotion, and pursue above all what is pleasant to themselves and what is immediately before them; but with increasing age their pleasures become different. This is why they quickly become friends and quickly cease to be so; their friendship changes with the object that is found pleasant, and such pleasure alters quickly. Young people are amorous too; for the greater part of the friendship of love depends on emotion and aims at pleasure; this is why they fall in love and quickly fall out of love, changing often within a single day. But these people do wish to spend their days and lives together; for it is thus that they attain the purpose of their friendship.

Perfect friendship is the friendship of men who are good, and alike in virtue; for these wish well alike to each other *qua* good, and they are good in themselves. Now those who wish well to their friends for their sake are most truly friends; for they do this by reason of their own nature and not incidentally; therefore their friendship lasts as long as they are good — and goodness is an enduring thing. And each is good without qualification and to his friend, for the good are both good without qualification and useful to each other. So too they are pleasant; for the good are pleasant both without qualification and to each other, since to each his own activities and others like them are pleasurable, and the actions of the good *are* the same or like. And such a friendship is as might be expected permanent, since there meet in it all the qualities that friends should have. For all friendship is for the sake of good or of pleasure — good or pleasure either in the abstract or such as will be enjoyed by him who has the friendly feeling — and is based on a certain resemblance; and to a friendship of good men all the qualities we have named belong in virtue of the nature of the friends themselves; for in the case of this kind of friendship the other qualities also[1] are alike in both friends, and that which is good

[1] I.e., absolute pleasantness, relative goodness, and relative pleasantness, as well as absolute goodness.

without qualification is also without qualification pleasant, and these are the most lovable qualities. Love and friendship therefore are found most and in their best form between such men.

But it is natural that such friendships should be infrequent; for such men are rare. Further, such friendship requires time and familiarity; as the proverb says, men cannot know each other till they have "eaten salt together"; nor can they admit each other to friendship or be friends till each has been found lovable and been trusted by each. Those who quickly show the marks of friendship to each other wish to be friends, but are not friends unless they both are lovable and know the fact; for a wish for friendship may arise quickly, but friendship does not.

This kind of friendship, then, is perfect both in respect of duration and in all other respects, and in it each gets from each in all respects the same as, or something like what, he gives; which is what ought to happen between friends. Friendship for the sake of pleasure bears a resemblance to this kind; for good people too *are* pleasant to each other. So too does friendship for the sake of utility; for the good are also useful to each other. Among men of these inferior sorts too, friendships are most permanent when the friends get the same thing from each other (e.g. pleasure), and not only that but also from the same source, as happens between ready-witted people, not as happens between lover and beloved. For these do not take pleasure in the same things, but the one in seeing the beloved and the other in receiving attentions from his lover; and when the bloom of youth is passing the friendship sometimes passes too (for the one finds no pleasure in the sight of the other, and the other gets no attentions from the first); but many lovers on the other hand are constant, if familiarity has led them to love each other's characters, these being alike. But those who exchange not pleasure but utility in their amour are both less truly friends and less constant. Those who are friends for the sake of utility part when the advantage is at an end; for they were lovers not of each other but of profit.

For the sake of pleasure or utility, then, even bad men may be friends of each other, or good men of bad, or one who is neither good nor bad may be a friend to any sort of person, but for their own sake clearly only good men can be friends; for bad men do not delight in each other unless some advantage come of the relation.

The friendship of the good too and this alone is proof against slander; for it is not easy to trust any one's talk about a man who has long been tested by oneself; and it is among good men that trust and the feeling that "he would never wrong me" and all the other things that are demanded in true friendship are found. In the other kinds of friendship, however, there is nothing to prevent these evils arising.

For men apply the name of friends even to those whose motive is utility, in which sense states are said to be friendly (for the alliances of states seem to aim at advantage), and to those who love each other for the sake of pleasure, in which sense children are called friends. Therefore we too ought perhaps to call such people friends, and say that there are several kinds of friendship — firstly and in the proper sense that of good men *qua* good, and by analogy the other kinds; for it is in virtue of something good and something akin to what is found in true friendship that they are friends, since even the pleasant is good for the lovers of pleasure. But these two kinds of friendship are not often united, nor do the same people become friends for the sake of utility and of pleasure; for things that are only incidentally connected are not often coupled together.

Friendship being divided into these kinds, bad men will be friends for the sake of pleasure or of utility, being in this respect like each other, but good men will be friends for their own sake, i.e. in virtue of their goodness. These, then, are friends without qualification; the others are friends incidentally and through a resemblance to these.

As in regard to the virtues some men are called good in respect of a state of character, others in respect of an activity, so too in the case of friendship; for those who live together delight in each other and confer benefits on each other, but those who are asleep or locally separated are not performing, but are disposed to perform, the activities of friendship; distance does not break off the friendship absolutely, but only the activity of it. But if the absence is lasting, it seems actually to make men forget their friendship; hence the saying "out of sight, out of mind." Neither old people nor sour people seem to make friends easily; for there is little that is pleasant in them, and no one can spend his days with one whose company is painful, or not pleasant, since nature seems above all to avoid the painful and to aim at the pleasant. Those, however, who approve of each other but do not live together seem to be well-disposed rather than actual friends. For there is nothing so characteristic of friends as living together (since while it is people who are in need that desire benefits, even those who are supremely happy desire to spend their days together; for solitude suits such people least of all); but people cannot live together if they are not pleasant and do not enjoy the same things, as friends who are companions seem to do.

The truest friendship, then, is that of the good, as we have frequently said;[2] for that which is without qualification good or pleasant seems to be lovable and desirable, and for each person that which is good or pleasant to him; and the good man is lovable and desirable to the good man for both these reasons. Now it looks as if love were a feeling, friendship a state of character; for love may be felt just as much towards lifeless things, but mutual love involves choice and choice springs from a state of character; and men wish well to those whom they love, for their sake, not as a result of feeling but as a result of a state of character. And in loving a friend men love what is good for themselves; for the good man in becoming a friend becomes a good to his friend. Each, then, both loves what is good for himself, and makes an equal return in goodwill and in pleasantness; for friendship is said to be equality, and both of these are found most in the friendship of the good.

. . . . .

Do we need friends more in good fortune or in bad? They are sought after in both; for while men in adversity need help, in prosperity they need people

[2] 1156^b 7, 23, 33, 1157^a 30, ^{b}4.

to live with and to make the objects of their beneficence; for they wish to do well by others. Friendship, then, is more necessary in bad fortune, and so it is useful friends that one wants in this case; but it is more noble in good fortune, and so we also seek for good men as our friends, since it is more desirable to confer benefits on these and to live with these. For the very presence of friends is pleasant both in good fortune and also in bad, since grief is lightened when friends sorrow with us. Hence one might ask whether they share as it were our burden, or — without that happening — their presence by its pleasantness, and the thought of their grieving with us, make our pain less. Whether it is for these reasons or for some other that our grief is lightened, is a question that may be dismissed; at all events what we have described appears to take place.

But their presence seems to contain a mixture of various factors. The very seeing of one's friends is pleasant, especially if one is in adversity, and becomes a safeguard against grief (for a friend tends to comfort us both by the sight of him and by his words, if he is tactful, since he knows our character and the things that please or pain us); but to see him pained at our misfortunes is painful; for every one shuns being a cause of pain to his friends. For this reason people of a manly nature guard against making their friends grieve with them, and, unless he be exceptionally insensible to pain, such a man cannot stand the pain that ensues for his friends, and in general does not admit fellow-mourners because he is not himself given to mourning; but women and womanly men enjoy sympathisers in their grief, and love them as friends and companions in sorrow. But in all things one obviously ought to imitate the better type of person.

On the other hand, the presence of friends in our *prosperity* implies both a pleasant passing of our time and the pleasant thought of their pleasure at our own good fortune. For this cause it would seem that we ought to summon our friends readily to share our good fortunes (for the beneficent character is a noble one), but summon them to our bad fortunes with hesitation; for we ought to give them as little a share as possible in our evils — whence the saying "enough is *my* misfortune." We should summon friends to us most of all when they are likely by suffering a few inconveniences to do us a great service.

Conversely, it is fitting to go unasked and readily to the aid of those in adversity (for it is characteristic of a friend to render services, and especially to those who are in need and have not demanded them; such action is nobler and pleasanter for both persons); but when our friends are prosperous we should join readily in their activities (for they need friends for these too), but be tardy in coming forward to the objects of their kindness; for it is not noble to be keen to receive benefits. Still, we must no doubt avoid getting the reputation of kill-joys by repulsing them; for that sometimes happens.

The presence of friends, then, seems desirable in all circumstances.

Does it not follow, then, that, as for lovers the sight of the beloved is the thing they love most, and they prefer this sense to the others because on it love depends most for its being and for its origin, so for friends the most desirable thing is living together? For friendship is a partnership, and as a man is to himself, so is he to his friend; now in his own case the consciousness of his being is desirable, and so therefore is the consciousness of his friend's being, and the activity of this consciousness is produced when they live together, so that it is natural that they aim at this. And whatever existence means for each class of men, whatever it is for whose sake they value life, in *that* they wish to occupy themselves with their friends; and so some drink together, others dice together, others join in athletic exercises and hunting, or in the study of philosophy, each class spending their days together in whatever they love most in life; for since they wish to live with their friends, they do and share in those things which give them the sense of living together. Thus the friendship of bad men turns out an evil thing (for because of their instability they unite in bad pursuits, and besides they become evil by becoming like each other), while the friendship of good men is good, being augmented by their companionship; and they are thought to become better too by their activities and by improving each other; for from each other they take the mould of the characteristics they approve — whence the saying "noble deeds from noble men." — So much, then, for friendship; our next task must be to discuss pleasure.

W. R. Sorley

The influence of Kant on nineteenth-century English religious thought was such that proof of the existence of God was characteristically sought in moral values. In the Hegelian climate that prevailed in the latter part of the century some religious thinkers felt the need to go beyond both metaphysical dualism and Hegel's monistic absolutism. One of the most persuasive of these English thinkers was William Ritchie Sorley (1855-1935), whose book of Gifford Lectures, Moral Values and the Idea of God, *published in 1911, remained a standard work on the subject for many years as one of the best representatives of the method it used and the point of view it upheld. The following passage contains one of its most important chapters.*

Theism and Moral Values *

As we have seen, neither pluralism nor monism is able to give an interpretation of reality in which both the moral order and the order of nature are adequately recognised. The failure of the latter theory was mainly due to its refusal to admit the ideas of purpose and of freedom into its account. And its rejection of these ideas was due to the requirements of its theory rather than to an unprejudiced study of the facts. We have found that, even if experience does not compel us to admit the reality of purpose in nature and of individual freedom, at least it does not exclude these ideas, and it justifies our acceptance of them as postulates in the formation of a comprehensive view of reality as a whole.

We must therefore return to the point which was reached in examining the moral argument. The result of that examination had about it — I am willing to admit — a certain air of paradox. If we were asked to state the strongest objection to the theistic view of the world which is felt at the present time, we should reply without hesitation that it lies in the existence and power of evil in the world. The dilemma of Epicurus is still with us: If God wishes to prevent evil but cannot, then he is impotent; if he could but will not, he is malevolent; if he has both the power and the will, whence then is evil? If the world had been so constructed that only good appeared in it and no evil, then (it is supposed) the theistic interpretation might hold; but it fails to account for a world like this of mingled good and evil. The paradox of which I have been guilty consists in taking this very fact of evil and founding upon it a theistic argument. Had everything in the world been harmonious, had there been no discord, pain, or evil, had all actual events brought forth moral values and been examples of moral law, then it might have seemed as if, in

* W. R. Sorley, *Moral Values and the Idea of God* (London: Cambridge University Press, 1921), pp. 446–449, 456–468. Used by permission.

our explanation of the universe, we need not go beyond this one universal law, at once natural and moral, which would be displayed by all things and at all times. Now, such an explanation will not fit our world, just because of the discord between nature (including man) and morality. But the moral order, as well as the order of nature, is of the essence of reality; and they can be harmoniously united in one universe only when nature is understood not merely in its present appearance but as working out a purpose — that purpose being or including the making of moral beings. To repeat what has been already said, "If we do not interpret the world as purposive, our view of it cannot find room for both the natural order and the moral order. If we do interpret it as purposive, we must attribute an idea and purpose of good to the ground of the world": that is to say, our view will be an ethical theism. If the purpose be the production of finite selves who will freely realise goodness, we have a point of view from which it is possible to explain, in general terms, both the slow stages and frequent lapses in their moralisation, and also the nature of the medium in which this moralisation has to be achieved. Epicurus's dilemma has made an assumption in formulating its alternatives. It regards goodness as something that can be produced by compulsion. It overlooks the possibility that the will to goodness means the creation of beings who will achieve goodness freely and whose freedom needs experience of all sorts of circumstances that it may develop into secure harmony with the moral order.

If we look at the theistic interpretation of reality from this point of view, we shall see that certain modifications have to be made in that doctrine of the unity of the world which led to and was expressed in the monistic theory. In the first place, the time-process as a whole, that is to say, the course of the world or system of nature, will have to be regarded as purposive. Taking it at any moment, we cannot say that it is perfect or a complete expression of a divine meaning: that divine meaning can only be gathered from its course as a whole, or from insight into the purpose which determines its course as a whole. And, in the second place, the finite individuals, in whom the spiritual nature of reality is manifested, must be acknowledged as agents in the accomplishment of the world-purpose, as possessing a real though limited power of initiative, and therefore a certain measure of independence. The time-process is the means whereby this freedom and independence are made contributory to complete ethical harmony or unity.

This ethical unity, be it noted, could not be arrived at in any other way, if the view is correct that the realisation of moral values requires freedom. At the same time, the attainment of this ethical unity, just because it requires freedom, involves in its process a certain modification of the doctrine of the actual unity of the universe. It is impossible to take any and every particular situation or event, especially those involving human factors, and to say "here the divine is manifested," or "the perfection of the universe required just this act; anything else would have been inconsistent with the completeness of the whole." Yet in this way the monist must interpret things. In practice, he may be as ardent as any reformer in discussing the good and evil of conduct in contemplation, and in preferring good to evil; but, looking at the matter as a philosopher, he must regard the event as inevitable: anything else would have contradicted the nature of things, which is also the nature of God: to regret it or wish it undone is to quarrel with that which alone is — to sin against the holy ghost of logic. Now, unity of this sort is inconsistent with a due appreciation of the moral aspect of reality. The ethical unity of the universe is a unity to be attained. It does not belong in its completeness to any particular stage of the time-process, but only to its realised purpose. In its working out ethical unity requires a very real diversity, for it needs the cooperation of free individuals. We cannot identify these individuals with God or refer each action of theirs to the divine nature as its cause. As possessing in himself the purpose, or an idea of the purpose, of the whole time-process, God must be regarded as transcending the process itself; as communicating freedom to the individual minds whose being depends upon his, he must be regarded as transcending them also, for their actual volitions may be alien to his nature; and we may have to interpret this transcendence as self-limitation.

. . . . .

How then are we to conceive the world in the light of the idea of God? We have discarded the pantheistic answer to the question, which identifies the world with God; and we have equally rejected the deistic view which regards God as a being external and aloof. But the positive conception is more difficult to define. It must be something intermediate between the two impossible extremes. Neither identity on the one hand, nor complete distinction, on the other hand, will satisfy our quest for a view of the relation of the world to God. It would seem, therefore, that we are forced to adopt a principle of selection amongst the facts of the world; and selection is an awkward business and hard to apply without arbitrariness, still harder to apply without the appearance of arbitrariness. Yet arbitrariness must be avoided. We may not say "I see God's hand here, in the providence that saved my fall, when ruin encompassed others; but I cannot see it there, where misfortune awaited myself." If there is to be selection it must be in accordance with a definite principle, and that principle must be well grounded.

Where can we find a guiding principle? Is there anywhere in the world a standard for discriminating the divine from that which is not divine, so that we may lay hold of the standard and by means of it get a point of view from which reality as a whole may be seen as a revelation of God? If there is any such, we must find it in one or other of the realms into which we have found the real in our experience to divide itself — in the realm of nature and its laws, or in that of finite selves and their wills, or in that of intrinsic values. But the first will not serve, for we have seen that imperfection clings to it. For the same reason the second region — that of finite selves — is an insecure guide; and besides, we have attributed to these selves a freedom which is inconsistent not indeed with their dependence upon God, but with their being regarded as a true mirror of the divine nature. There remains then the realm of values — an ideal realm, very imperfectly realised in our experience, and only incompletely conceived in our consciousness. It is possible for us to mistake the true meaning of these ideal values; but the possibility of error does not affect the validity of truth when discovered. The values are there, and in our apprehension of them we have at least a guide which gives us a principle for selecting between the worthy and the unworthy, and enables us to attain a certain insight into the purpose of the whole.

Is it a misleading instinct which has lead men almost uniformly to use the adjective "divine" in speaking of these higher values — of beauty and truth and goodness? The poets and artists have used this language in speaking of beauty; and though they may not have meant to convey a dogma by it, they intended it to express their admiration of what was highest. The philosophers have often employed similar language, when their theory allowed them to see more in the world than mechanical law and to regard the quest for truth as of greater significance than dialectical dispute. And to the moralist it has often been almost an axiom that goodness and God mean the same thing. Of the other values I will not speak, for my topic is the moral values and their bearing on our interpretation of reality.

Now of the moral order of the universe we have discovered that it does belong to the order of reality, and further that it cannot be fitted into a pantheistic conception of that order. Its distinction from, and yet intricate relation to, the natural order, and its implication of freedom in the lives which it claims to rule, forbid the easy solution that the All is simply One. But if the moral order is not altogether sundered from the natural order, if the universe is really a universe and not a multiverse, then we must hold that the moral order is the order of that one mind whose purpose nature and man are slowly fulfilling. Here therefore we have a key to the theistic interpretation of the world. The moral order expresses the divine nature; and things partake of this nature in so far as they conform to that order or manifest goodness.

This gives us the principle of which we are in search. The theistic universe is fundamentally ethical. The central point in our idea of God is not the pantheistic conception of a substance of infinite attributes or an Absolute free from all determinations; nor is it the deistic conception of an external Creator or First Cause. Neither "Own Cause" nor "First Cause" will be our conception, but — if we must speak of cause at all — then it will be Final Cause. And Final Cause must mean the purpose of realising goodness. The difficulty of the conception of Creation is mixed up with the difficulty of the relation of the time-process as a whole to ultimate reality; and with that difficulty I am not making any attempt to deal. But the notion of Creation involves a more essential point than the idea either of a beginning *in* time or of a beginning *of* time. It involves the idea of God as the ground or support of the world — not merely its beginning — for without him it could not at any moment exist. For this reason, while we may not see God in each natural event, we must yet look through nature to God and see his mind in its final purpose.

I have already spoken of nature as the medium for the production and perfection of goodness in finite minds. This interpretation we may give — indeed, we must give — if we accept the moral and the natural orders as belonging together. But it does not follow that it will explain everything in nature. It would be too proud an assumption to assert that the whole of nature, of which we know only the barest fragment, has no other purpose than this one which concerns ourselves. Omniscience is a foible against which the modest philosopher should be on his guard. What other purposes than this there may be in the wealth of worlds which people space, or even in the small world known to ourselves, we cannot tell; and, except as a matter of speculative interest, it does not concern us to know. On such questions the only safe attitude is one of provisional agnosticism. But these doubtful issues do not interfere with our interpretation of our own consciousness and the world which environs it. The certainty of the moral law is not affected by anything that lies hidden among the unexplored recesses of the starry heavens.

The same conception of purpose, which guides the theist in the explanation of the world of nature, must serve him also in the interpretation of the realm of finite spirits. They too must be interpreted through their purpose, and this purpose will be, as before, the realisation of goodness. But there is this difference. Nature is a medium only; *through* it the end is to be reached. But minds are not a mere medium: it is *in and by* them that values are to be realised. They must themselves attain these values and not merely receive them. To nature we can ascribe no power or freedom of its own; each of its operations must be regarded as prescribed for it. But finite spirits themselves either contribute to working out the world-purpose or else oppose their wills to it.

The question of freedom has been already discussed, and the validity of the idea defended. And I may now venture to express the opinion that it is essential to the theistic interpretation of reality. So many theists are convinced determinists, that this statement may have an appearance of arrogance. Yet no other view seems to me really open. If there is no freedom in man's volition, and each act is rigidly determined by his inherited disposition and his environment, then it is plain that every act of man is really caused by that being who is the author at once of his nature and of the world in which he lives. To his Creator, and only to his Creator, it ought to be imputed. And, if this is so, we are left without any kind of hypothesis by which to explain the preference of the worse to the better course, or to render that preference consistent with the goodness of God. On the determinist theory, as on the assumption of freedom, man and nature may be purposive, and in the end harmony may be established and goodness triumph. But, on the former theory, we can think of no reason why goodness should not have been established from the outset, or why men should have been formed with dispositions that led them to sin. The evil in the world has to be referred to God as its author; and ethical theism falls to the ground.

If ethical theism is to stand, the evil in the world cannot be referred to God in the same way as the good is referred to him; and the only way to avoid this reference is by the postulate of human freedom. This freedom must be a real freedom, so that it may account for the actual choice of evil when good might have been chosen. We have therefore to face the inference that there is a limitation of the divine activity: that things occur in the universe which are not due to God's will, though they must have happened with his permission, that is, through his self-limitation. Nor does this view justify the objection that we are making the divine nature finite; for, if it is conceived as limited, it is not limited by anything outside itself. Rather we may say that a higher range of power and perfection is shown in the creation of free beings than in the creation of beings whose every thought and action are pre-determined by their Creator.

On the other hand, individual freedom is not, and cannot be, unlimited: otherwise each free being would require a world of his own, and there would be no universe. And clearly man's freedom is restricted by the conditions both of heredity and of environment. The range of his selection is limited by the experience which gives content to his life, as well as by the inherited tendencies which are his from the beginning of his career. These afford ample opportunity for freedom in the development of his activity, but not unrestricted openings for any and every kind of life. A man cannot at will choose to be a mathematician, an artist, a statesman, or even a millionaire. But there is one form of activity which is never closed, and that is the realisation of moral values; one choice before every man, the choice of good or evil.

This is the limitation of human freedom which applies to man as a part of nature; and it is such that the line which nature restricts least, and leaves most open to free determination, is that concerned with the production and increase of moral values. But the more important aspect of the limitation remains. Man's freedom must surely be limited from the side not of nature only, as the medium in which it is exercised, but also of God. How then are we to conceive this limitation without man being altogether absorbed by God? The world as a time-process has a certain unity through natural law, but this law fails to cover or to account for the volitions of free minds; it has a further unity in the moral order, but this unity is still an ideal and never in our experience completely realised. Its full unity must therefore come from the fact that it is a purposive system, in which nature is the medium of moralisation, and finite minds are the agents who, in free alliance and free struggle, work out this unity in achieving their own perfection. The purpose exists eternally in the divine mind, and the time-process is the scene on which finite minds bring it about. Their agency must therefore be somehow directed — or, as the theologians say, overruled — towards the attainment of this end.

But may not the time-process end, after all, simply in confusion, perhaps in disaster, and its purpose fail? This is indeed a suggestion that has found a place in many theologies, which have imagined a hostile spirit — a prince of this world — who, although of lower rank and power, can yet frustrate the designs of the Supreme Mind by his implacable enmity. This is only one of the ways in which the unity of nature and morality is denied. It presents a vivid picture of the world struggle, but no solution of the universal problem, beyond denying that there is a true universe. Short of this supposition, and on the lines of our own reflexion, may it not be imagined that the world-plan meets only with partial success tempered by partial failure, that multitudes of finite spirits fail for ever to realise the good that is in their power? Freedom is a dangerous gift, and is the danger only to the recipient? In conferring this gift on finite beings may not the Supreme Mind have called into existence a power which he can no longer control, in the only way in which free spirits can be controlled?

This suggestion, again, cannot be refuted by conclusive argument. It is less violent and imaginative than the previous suggestion, but it is equally inconsistent with any view of a complete unity of the universe. My argument has been all along that, ultimately, the unity of the universe must be conceived as ethical; and this conception would bring moral discord into the heart of things. Can we regard the Supreme Mind as having so little foresight as to be unable to see the result of his own purpose? It has usually been maintained that this must be so, if free will be admitted. It is said that foreknowledge is inconsistent with freedom, so that, if men are free, their volitions cannot be foreseen even by divine intelligence, and God must be frequently taken by surprise by their actions. This view calls for examination, for it seems to me that it tends to misinterpret the nature of free activity, and that it assumes that divine and human foreknowledge follow the same method.

A man's free actions proceed from himself, that is, from his character. But what is his character? It is not simply a combination of distinct factors whose growth may be traced separately. None of these factors has any reality except in the unity of the conscious life; and this unity is not open to the inspection of an observer. The latter's knowledge of another self is always external and therefore incomplete. He is thus liable to surprises, not because an incalculable force may irrupt here and there into the otherwise orderly processes of volition, but because there is something within the circle of a man's character and dispositions that can never be adequately known to another, and that something is its centre. But God's knowledge need not be external, like that of the human observer. To him man's mind must be known from within, and, at the same time, without the obscurity and imperfection with which the man knows himself.

Even this, it may be urged, does not show that a choice which is truly spontaneous can be foretold. Such a choice implies a real possibility of opposites, a real absence of pre-determination, so that it could not be foretold even by complete knowledge from within of a man's character. Perhaps this is so. But it does not follow that divine foreknowledge works by the same method as human anticipation. It need not be of the nature of an inference from character as the cause to action as the effect. We can conceive another way, though its use is not open to us. The event which we perceive is never strictly instantaneous; it has a certain duration, very short, indeed, but not infinitesimal. This is our time-span, and in it we see at a glance what is really a succession. If this time-span were considerably enlarged, we should have immediate knowledge of a longer series, for example, of a succession of actions in which a resolution is made and carried out. Within the time-span differences of past and future do not interfere with immediacy. Why then should not all time be seen as one by an infinite intelligence? Assuming that God's knowledge is not limited to a finite span of the time-process, the whole course of the world's history will be seen by him in a single or immediate intuition. The question how a particular event, such as the action of a man, comes about — whether by free will or by mechanical necessity — will make no difference to the immediacy of that intuition. What we call foreknowledge will be just knowledge: past and future, equally with present, lie open to the mind of infinite time-span.

For this reason it appears to me that freedom is not related to foreknowledge in the same way as it is to pre-determination. Universal determination contradicts freedom; universal knowledge does not. And we cannot suppose that God, to whose view all time lies open, would call into existence spirits whose activity would frustrate his purpose in their creation.

Apart, therefore, from solutions which limit either the power or the knowledge or the goodness of God, the theistic world-view must maintain not only that the moral purpose of the universe is eternally present in the mind of God, but also that it will attain actual fulfilment in the finite minds through whom it is being worked out. And for this reason God must be regarded as not far off from each individual spirit. In what way this divine providence, direction, or overruling actually operates is a problem which philosophy cannot undertake to solve without assistance from that range of experience which I have not taken into account — the facts of the religious consciousness.

But one result emerges. I have said before, and the assertion followed from the preceding argument, that, in interpreting the world, theism has to proceed by selection when it seeks in the world or in men traces of the divine. The principle of selection cannot be anything else than the moral order which has been taken as the ground from which we must explain the course of the world. In all goodness we must see the manifestation of the divine purpose, in all evil a temporary failure in its realisation. In so far as men strive for its realisation they are ethically at one with God; in so far as they lose sight of this end they are ethically at variance with him. And this principle is not arbitrary; it follows directly from the position given to the moral order and from the way in which the order of nature and finite minds is related thereto. The old moralists who explained "conscience" as meaning "knowledge with God," may have given a fanciful derivation of the word. But the idea which prompted the derivation was not far wrong. In the moral consciousness we have some apprehension of the value which gives meaning to the world and which has been interpreted as a divine purpose; and in moral practice we cooperate towards the fulfilment of this purpose.

The theistic view of the world which I have been considering is definitely an ethical view. It was led up to by an enquiry into the facts of value in the world and by the conception of a moral order of the world; and it issues in a view which finds the moral purpose of the world to be the purpose of a Supreme Mind and which regards finite minds as attaining unity with this Supreme Mind not by the absorption of their individuality but by the perfecting of their character in cooperating with the divine purpose. Other values than the ethical have dropped out of sight in the course of the argument. Yet the general view which has been reached might be extended so as to cover them also. Wherever there is intrinsic worth in the world, there also, as well as in moral goodness, we may see a manifestation of the divine. God must therefore be conceived as the final home of values, the Supreme Worth — as possessing the fulness of knowledge and beauty and goodness and whatever else is of value for its own sake.

This view has not been put forward on account of its religious importance.

That is a side of things which I have hardly ventured to touch. It is given as an interpretation of reality which takes equal account of existents and laws and moral values. And, as such, it is neither inadequate to cover the facts of experience, as any naturalistic theory is, nor does it betray the hopeless incongruity on fundamental points which we find both in pluralism and in monism. At the same time, it is not contended that the view solves all questions or that it does not raise problems of its own. The solutions it gives are for the most part general; they offer a principle of explanation rather than an explanation of each event in detail. If particulars can be explained by it, it is mostly by the help of the religious consciousness which claims a more intimate apprehension of God than morality can offer. And the conception of a unity which is not yet but is to be realised, and which when realised will be ethically complete, though individualities remain distinct, raises speculative problems. Is God the Absolute? it may be asked; and if not, is he not therefore finite, so that the universe is incompletely unified by the idea of God? It may be answered that, if by the Absolute is meant the sum-total of reality, then there are real events and real beings which do not as we see them manifest the divine nature, so that God and the Absolute will not be identical. But there is nothing outside God in the sense of being fully independent of his being and will. The independence of finite beings is a restricted independence communicated by the divine will. If we conceive God as unable to limit himself in this way, then this conception also limits his power. It appears to me that the idea of the self-limitation of God involves no greater difficulty than the idea of the manifestation or appearance of the Absolute in things and persons. And, on the most rigid theory of the Absolute, the diversity of its appearances must be admitted — even if they are held to be only the appearance of diversity. . . .

William James

William James (1842-1910) is one of the greatest figures in the history of American philosophy. The brother of the novelist Henry James, he was professor at Harvard, where he developed his philosophical pragmatism. Briefly, according to his view, we have a right to believe in God because such belief has a psychologically beneficial effect upon us, though there is no metaphysical or scientific certainty concerning it. His pragmatistic understanding of the problem of ethical values is reflected in the paper that follows.

A Pragmatic Approach to the Moral Life *

The main purpose of this paper is to show that there is no such thing possible as an ethical philosophy dogmatically made up in advance. We all help to determine the content of ethical philosophy so far as we contribute to the race's moral life. In other words, there can be no final truth in ethics any more than in physics, until the last man has had his experience and said his say. In the one case as in the other, however, the hypotheses which we now make while waiting, and the acts to which they prompt us, are among the indispensable conditions which determine what that "say" shall be.

First of all, what is the position of him who seeks an ethical philosophy? To begin with, he must be distinguished from all those who are satisfied to be ethical sceptics. He *will* not be a sceptic; therefore so far from ethical scepticism being one possible fruit of ethical philosophizing, it can only be regarded as that residual alternative to all philosophy which from the outset menaces every would-be philosopher who may give up the quest discouraged, and renounce his original aim. That aim is to find an account of the moral relations that obtain among things, which will weave them into the unity of a stable system, and make of the world what one may call a genuine universe from the ethical point of view. So far as the world resists reduction to the form of unity, so far as ethical propositions seem unstable, so far does the philosopher fail of his ideal. The subject-matter of his study is the ideals he finds existing in the world; the purpose which guides him is this ideal of his own, of getting them into a certain form. This ideal is thus a factor in ethical philosophy whose legitimate presence must never be overlooked; it is a positive contribution which the philosopher himself necessarily makes to the problem. But it is his only positive contribution. At the outset of his inquiry he ought to have no other ideals. Were he interested peculiarly in the triumph of any one kind of good, he would *pro tanto* cease to be a judicial investigator, and become an advocate for some limited element of the case.

* William James, "The Moral Philosopher and the Moral Life," *The International Journal of Ethics* (published by University of Chicago Press), I (April, 1891). Used by permission.

. . . So far as the casuistic question goes, ethical science is just like physical science, and instead of being deducible all at once from abstract principles, must simply bide its time, and be ready to revise its conclusions from day to day. The presumption of course, in both sciences, always is that the vulgarly accepted opinions are true, and the right casuistic order that which public opinion believes in; and surely it would be folly quite as great, in most of us, to strike out independently and to aim at originality in ethics as in physics. Every now and then, however, some one is born with the right to be original, and his revolutionary thought or action may bear prosperous fruit. He may replace old "laws of nature" by better ones; he may, by breaking old moral rules in a certain place, bring in a total condition of things more ideal than would have followed had the rules been kept.

On the whole . . . we must conclude that no philosophy of ethics is possible in the old-fashioned absolute sense of the term. Everywhere the ethical philosopher must wait on facts. The thinkers who create the ideals come he knows not whence, their sensibilities are evolved he knows not how; and the question as to which of two conflicting ideals will give the best universe then and there, can be answered by him only through the aid of the experience of other men. . . . The intuitional moralists deserve credit for keeping most clearly to the psychological facts. They do much to spoil this merit on the whole, however, by mixing with it that dogmatic temper which, by absolute distinctions and unconditioned "thou shalt nots," changes a growing, elastic, and continuous life into a superstitious system of relics and dead bones. In point of fact, there are no absolute evils, and there are no non-moral goods; and the *highest* ethical life — however few may be called to bear its burdens — consists at all times in the breaking of rules which have grown too narrow for the actual case. There is but one unconditioned commandment, which is that we should seek incessantly, with fear and trembling, so to vote and to act as to bring about the very largest total universe of good which we can see. Abstract rules indeed can help; but they help the less in proportion as our intuitions are more piercing, and our vocation is the stronger for the moral life. For every real dilemma is in literal strictness a unique situation; and the exact combination of ideals realized and ideals disappointed which each decision creates is always a universe without a precedent, and for which no adequate previous rule exists. The philosopher, then *quâ* philosopher, is no better able to determine the best universe in the concrete emergency than other men. He sees, indeed, somewhat better than most men what the question always is, — not a question of this good or that good simply taken, but of the two total universes with which these goods respectively belong. He knows that he must vote always for the richer universe, for the good which seems most organizable, most fit to enter into complex combinations, most apt to be a member of a more inclusive whole. But which particular universe this is he cannot know for certain in advance; he only knows that if he makes a bad mistake the cries of the wounded will soon inform him of the fact. In all this the philosopher is just like the rest of us non-philosophers, so far as we are just and sympathetic instinctively, and so far as we are open to the voice of complaint. His function is in fact indistinguishable from that of the best kind of statesman at the present day. His books upon ethics, therefore, so far as they truly touch the moral life, must more and more ally themselves with a literature which is confessedly tentative and suggestive rather than dogmatic, — I mean with novels and dramas of the deeper sort, with sermons, with books on statecraft and philanthropy and social and economical reform. Treated in this way ethical treatises may be voluminous and luminous as well; but they never can be *final*, except in their abstracted and vaguest features; and they must more and more abandon the old-fashioned, clear-cut, and would-be "scientific" form.

The chief of all the reasons why concrete ethics cannot be final is that they have to wait on metaphysical and theological beliefs. I said some time back that real ethical relations existed in a purely human world. They would exist even in what we called a moral solitude if the thinker had various ideals which took hold of him in turn. His self of one day would make demands on his self of another; and some of the demands might be urgent and tyrannical, while others were gentle and easily put aside. We call the tyrannical demands *imperatives*. If we ignore these we do not hear the last of it. The good which we have wounded returns to plague us with interminable crops of consequential damages, compunctions, and regrets. Obligation can thus exist inside a single thinker's consciousness; and perfect peace can abide with him only so far as he lives according to some sort of a casuistic scale which keeps his more imperative goods on top. It is the nature of these goods to be cruel to their rivals. Nothing shall avail when weighed in the balance against them. They call out the mercilessness in our disposition, and do not easily forgive us if we are so soft-hearted as to shrink from sacrifice in their behalf.

The deepest difference, practically, in the moral life of man is the difference between the easy-going and the strenuous mood. When in the easy-going mood the shrinking from present ill is our ruling consideration. The strenuous mood, on the contrary, makes us quite indifferent to present ill, if only the greater ideal be attained. The capacity for the strenuous mood probably lies slumbering in every man, but it has more difficulty in some than in others in waking up. It needs the wilder passions to arouse it, the big fears, loves, and indignations; or else the deeply penetrating appeal of some one of the higher fidelities, like justice, truth, or freedom. Strong relief is a necessity of its vision; and a world where all the mountains are brought down and all the valleys are exalted is no congenial place for its habitation. This is why in a solitary thinker this mood might slumber on forever without waking. His various ideals, known to him to be mere preferences of his own, are too nearly of the same denominational value: he can play fast or loose with them at will. This too is why, in a merely human world without a God, the appeal to our moral energy falls short of its maximal stimulating power. Life, to be sure, is even in such a world a genuinely ethical symphony; but it is played in the compass of a couple of poor octaves, and the infinite scale of values fails to open up. Many of us, indeed, — like Sir James Stephen in those eloquent "Essays by a Barrister," — would openly laugh at the very idea of the strenuous mood being awakened in us by those claims of remote posterity which constitute the last appeal of the religion of humanity. We do not love these men of the future keenly enough; and we love them perhaps the less the more we hear of their evolutionized perfection, their high average longevity and education, their freedom from war and crime, their relative immunity from pain and zymotic disease, and all their other negative superiorities. This is all too finite, we say; we see too well the vacuum beyond. It lacks the note of infinitude and mystery, and may all be dealt with in the don't-care mood. No need of agonizing ourselves or making others agonize for these good creatures just at present.

When, however, we believe that a God is there, and that he is one of the claimants, the infinite perspective opens out. The scale of the symphony is incalculably prolonged. The more imperative ideals now begin to speak with an altogether new objectivity and significance, and to utter the penetrating, shattering, tragically challenging note of appeal. They ring out like the call of Victor Hugo's alpine eagle, "qui parle au précipice et que le gouffre entend," and the strenuous mood awakens at the sound. It saith among the trumpets, ha, ha! it smelleth the battle afar off, the thunder of the captains and the shouting. Its blood is up; and cruelty to the lesser claims, so far from being a deterrent element, does but add to the stern joy with which it leaps to answer to the greater. All through history, in the periodical conflicts of puritanism with the don't-care temper, we see the antagonism of the strenuous and genial moods, and the contrast between the ethics of infinite and mysterious obligation from on high, and those of prudence and the satisfaction of merely finite need.

The capacity of the strenuous mood lies so deep down among our natural human possibilities that even if there were no metaphysical or traditional grounds for believing in a God, men would postulate one simply as a pretext for living hard, and getting out of the game of existence its keenest possibilities of zest. Our attitude towards concrete evils is entirely different in a world where we believe there are none but finite demanders, from what it is in one where we joyously face tragedy for an infinite demander's sake. Every sort of energy and endurance, of courage and capacity for handling life's evils, is set free in those who have religious faith. For this reason the strenuous type of character will on the battle-field of human history always outwear the easy-going type, and religion will drive irreligion to the wall.

It would seem, too, — and this is my final conclusion, — that the stable and systematic moral universe for which the ethical philosopher asks is fully possible only in a world where there is a divine thinker with all-enveloping demands. If such a thinker existed, his way of subordinating the demands to one another would be the finally valid casuistic scale; his claims would be the most appealing; his ideal universe would be the most inclusive realizable whole. If he now exist, then actualized in his thought already must be that ethical philosophy which we seek as the pattern which our own must evermore approach.[1] In the interests of our own ideal of systematically unified moral truth, therefore, we, as would-be philosophers, must postulate

[1] All this is set forth with great freshness and force in the work of my colleague, Professor Josiah Royce: "The Religious Aspect of Philosophy." Boston, 1885.

a divine thinker, and pray for the victory of the religious cause. Meanwhile, exactly what the thought of the infinite thinker may be is hidden from us even were we sure of his existence; so that our postulation of him after all serves only to let loose in us the strenuous mood. But this is what it does in all men, even those who have no interest in philosophy. The ethical philosopher, therefore, whenever he ventures to say which course of action is the best, is on no essentially different level from the common man. "See, I have set before thee this day life and good, and death and evil; therefore, choose life that thou and thy seed may live," — when this challenge comes to us, it is simply our total character and personal genius that are on trial; and if we invoke any so-called philosophy, our choice and use of that also are but revelations of our personal aptitude or incapacity for moral life. From this unsparing practical ordeal no professor's lectures and no array of books can save us. The solving word, for the learned and the unlearned man alike, lies in the last resort in the dumb willingnesses and unwillingnesses of their interior characters, and nowhere else. It is not in heaven, neither is it beyond the sea; but the word is very nigh unto thee, in thy mouth and in thy heart, that thou mayest do it.

Albert Schweitzer

Schweitzer's work at Lambaréné is very famous. Born in Alsace in 1875, he acquired high distinction at an early age in theology, medicine, and music, but gave up his academic career to devote his extraordinarily versatile genius to missionary work among the natives of French Equatorial Africa. Though some of his theological views have met with considerable opposition, his influence upon Protestant theology in both Europe and America has been enormous. The dominant note in his ethical teaching is "reverence for life." His work has brought him numerous honors, including the Nobel Peace Prize; but few men are as insensible as is he to such worldly recognition. His immense energy, intellectual capacity, and formidable powers of concentration, together with his simplicity of life and high regard for the dignity of manual labor, make him one of the most remarkable men of our age. The following passage sets forth his characteristic view of the nature of ethical responsibility.

Reverence for Life *

Ethics consist . . . in my experiencing the compulsion to show to all will-to-live the same reverence as I do to my own. There we have given us that basic principle of the moral which is a necessity of thought. It is good to maintain and to encourage life; it is bad to destroy life or to obstruct it.

As a matter of fact, everything which in the ordinary ethical valuation of the relations of men to each other ranks as good can be brought under the description of material and spiritual maintenance or promotion of human life, and of effort to bring it to its highest value. Conversely, everything which ranks as bad in human relations is in the last analysis material or spiritual destruction or obstruction of human life, and negligence in the endeavour to bring it to its highest value. Separate individual categories of good and evil which lie far apart and have apparently no connection at all with one another fit together like the pieces of a jig-saw puzzle, as soon as they are comprehended and deepened in this the most universal definition of good and evil.

The basic principle of the moral which is a necessity of thought means, however, not only an ordering and deepening, but also a widening of the current views of good and evil. A man is truly ethical only when he obeys the compulsion to help all life which he is able to assist, and shrinks from injuring anything that lives. He does not ask how far this or that life deserves one's sympathy as being valuable, nor, beyond that, whether and to what degree it is capable of feeling. Life as such is sacred to him. He tears no leaf from a tree, plucks no flower, and takes care to crush no insect. If in summer he is

* Albert Schweitzer, *The Philosophy of Civilization*, trans. C. T. Campion (New York: The Macmillan Co., 1955), pp. 309–318. Used by permission, A. C. Black, Ltd., 1932.

working by lamplight, he prefers to keep the window shut and breathe a stuffy atmosphere rather than see one insect after another fall with singed wings upon his table.

If he walks on the road after a shower and sees an earthworm which has strayed on to it, he bethinks himself that it must get dried up in the sun, if it does not return soon enough to ground into which it can burrow, so he lifts it from the deadly stone surface, and puts it on the grass. If he comes across an insect which has fallen into a puddle, he stops a moment in order to hold out a leaf or a stalk on which it can save itself.

He is not afraid of being laughed at as sentimental. It is the fate of every truth to be a subject for laughter until it is generally recognized. Once it was considered folly to assume that men of colour were really men and ought to be treated as such, but the folly has become an accepted truth. To-day it is thought to be going too far to declare that constant regard for everything that lives, down to the lowest manifestations of life, is a demand made by rational ethics. The time is coming, however, when people will be astonished that mankind needed so long a time to learn to regard thoughtless injury to life as incompatible with ethics.

Ethics are responsibility without limit towards all that lives.

As a general proposition the definition of ethics as a relationship within a disposition to reverence for life, does not make a very moving impression. But it is the only complete one. Compassion is too narrow to rank as the total essence of the ethical. It denotes, of course, only interest in the suffering will-to-live. But ethics include also feeling as one's own all the circumstances and all the aspirations of the will-to-live, its pleasure, too, and its longing to live itself out to the full, as well as its urge to self-perfecting.

Love means more, since it includes fellowship in suffering, in joy, and in effort, but it shows the ethical only in a simile, although in a simile that is natural and profound. It makes the solidarity produced by ethics analogous to that which nature calls forth on the physical side, for more or less temporary purposes between two beings which complete each other sexually, or between them and their offspring.

Thought must strive to bring to expression the nature of the ethical in itself. To effect this it arrives at defining ethics as devotion to life inspired by reverence for life. Even if the phrase reverence for life sounds so general as to seem somewhat lifeless, what is meant by it is nevertheless something which never lets go of the man into whose thought it has made its way. Sympathy, and love, and every kind of valuable enthusiasm are given within it. With restless living force reverence for life works upon the mind into which it has entered, and throws it into the unrest of a feeling of responsibility which at no place and at no time ceases to affect it. Just as the screw which churns its way through the water drives the ship along, so does reverence for life drive the man.

Arising, as it does, from an inner compulsion, the ethic of reverence for life is not dependent on the extent to which it can be thought out to a satisfying conception of life. It need give no answer to the question of what significance the ethical man's work for the maintenance, promotion, and enhancement of life can be in the total happenings of the course of nature. It does not let itself be misled by the calculation that the maintaining and completing of life which it practices is hardly worth consideration beside the tremendous, unceasing destruction of life which goes on every moment through natural forces. Having the will to action, it can leave on one side all problems regarding the success of its work. The fact in itself that in the ethically developed man there has made its appearance in the world a will-to-live which is filled with reverence for life and devotion to life is full of importance for the world.

In my will-to-live the universal will-to-live experiences itself otherwise than in its other manifestations. In them it shows itself in a process of individualizing which, so far as I can see from the outside, is bent merely on living itself out to the full, and in no way on union with any other will-to-live. The world is a ghastly drama of will-to-live divided against itself. One existence makes its way at the cost of another; one destroys the other. One will-to-live merely exerts its will against the other, and has no knowledge of it. But in me the will-to-live has come to know about other wills-to-live. There is in it a yearning to arrive at unity with itself, to become universal.

Why does the will-to-live experience itself in this way in me alone? Is it because I have acquired the capacity of reflecting on the totality of Being? What is the goal of this evolution which has begun in me?

To these questions there is no answer. It remains a painful enigma for me that I must live with reverence for life in a world which is dominated by creative will which is also destructive will, and destructive will which is also creative.

I can do nothing but hold to the fact that the will-to-live in me manifests itself as will-to-live which desires to become one with other will-to-live. That is for me the light that shines in the darkness. The ignorance in which the world is wrapped has no existence for me; I have been saved from the world. I am thrown, indeed, by reverence for life into an unrest such as the world does not know, but I obtain from it a blessedness which the world cannot give. If in the tenderheartedness produced by being different from the world another person and I help each other in understanding and pardoning, when otherwise will would torment will, the division of the will-to-live is at an end. If I save an insect from a puddle, life has devoted itself to life, and the division of life against itself is ended. Whenever my life devotes itself in any way to life, my finite will-to-live experiences union with the infinite will in which all life is one, and I enjoy a feeling of refreshment which prevents me from pining away in the desert of life.

I therefore recognize it as the destiny of my existence to be obedient to this higher revelation of the will-to-live in me. I choose for my activity the removal of this division of the will-to-live against itself, so far as the influence of my existence can reach. Knowing now the one thing needful, I leave on one side the enigma of the universe and of my existence in it.

The surmisings and the longings of all deep religiousness are contained in the ethics of reverence for life. This religiousness, however, does not build up for itself a complete philosophy, but resigns itself to the necessity of leaving its cathedral unfinished. It finishes the chancel only, but in this chancel piety celebrates a living and never-ceasing divine service.

The ethic of reverence for life shows its truth also in that it includes in itself the different elements of ethics in their natural connection. Hitherto no system of ethics has been able to present in their parallelism and their interaction the effort after self-perfecting, in which man acts upon himself without outward deeds, and activist ethics. The ethics of reverence for life can do this, and indeed in such a way that they not only answer academic questions, but also produce a deepening of ethical insight.

Ethics are reverence for the will-to-live within me and without me. From the former comes first the profound life-affirmation of resignation. I apprehend my will-to-live as not only something which can live itself out in happy occurrences, but also something which has experience of itself. If I refuse to let this self-experience disappear in thoughtlessness, and persist in feeling it to be valuable, I begin to learn the secret of spiritual self-realization. I win an unsuspected freedom from the various destinies of life. At moments when I had expected to find myself shattered, I find myself exalted in an inexpressible and surprising happiness of freedom from the world, and I experience therein a clarification of my life-view. Resignation is the vestibule through which we enter ethics. Only he who in deepened devotion to his own will-to-live experiences inward freedom from outward occurrences, is capable of devoting himself in profound and steady fashion to the life of others.

Just as in reverence for my own will-to-live I struggle for freedom from the destinies of life, so I struggle too for freedom from myself. Not only in face of what happens to me, but also with regard to the way in which I concern myself with the world, I practise the higher self-maintenance. Out of reverence for my own existence I place myself under the compulsion of veracity towards myself. Everything I might acquire would be purchased too dearly by action in defiance of my convictions. I fear that if I were untrue to myself, I should be wounding my will-to-live with a poisoned spear.

The fact that Kant makes, as he does, sincerity towards oneself the central point of his ethics, testifies to the depth of his ethical feeling. But because in his search for the essential nature of the ethical he fails to find his way through to reverence for life, he cannot comprehend the connection between veracity towards oneself and activist ethics.

As a matter of fact, the ethics of sincerity towards oneself passes imperceptibly into that of devotion to others. Such sincerity compels me to actions which manifest themselves as self-devotion in such a way that ordinary ethics derive them from devotion.

Why do I forgive anyone? Ordinary ethics say, because I feel sympathy with him. They allow men, when they pardon others, to seem to themselves wonderfully good, and allow them to practise a style of pardoning which is not free from humiliation of the other. They thus make forgiveness a sweetened triumph of self-devotion.

The ethics of reverence for life do away with this crude point of view. All acts of forbearance and of pardon are for them acts forced from one by sincerity towards oneself. I must practise unlimited forgiveness because, if I did not, I should be wanting in sincerity to myself, for it would be acting as if I myself were not guilty in the same way as the other has been guilty towards me. Because my life is so liberally spotted with falsehood, I must forgive falsehood which has been practised upon me; because I myself have been in so many cases wanting in love, and guilty of hatred, slander, deceit, or arrogance, I must pardon any want of love, and all hatred, slander, deceit or arrogance which have been directed against myself. I must forgive quietly and unostentatiously; in fact I do not really pardon at all, for I do not let things develop to any such act of judgment. Nor is this any eccentric proceeding; it is only a necessary widening and refining of ordinary ethics.

We have to carry on the struggle against the evil that is in mankind, not by judging others, but by judging ourselves. Struggle with oneself and veracity towards oneself are the means by which we influence others. We quietly draw them into our efforts to attain the deep spiritual self-realization which springs from reverence for one's own life. Power makes no noise. It is there, and works. True ethics begin where the use of language ceases.

The innermost element then, in activist ethics, even if it appears as self-devotion, comes from the compulsion to sincerity towards oneself, and obtains therein its true value. The whole ethics of being other than the world flow pure only when they come from this source. It is not from kindness to others that I am gentle, peaceable, forbearing, and friendly, but because by such behaviour I prove my own profoundest self-realization to be true. Reverence for life which I apply to my own existence, and reverence for life which keeps me in a temper of devotion to other existence than my own, interpenetrate each other.

Because ordinary ethics possess no basic principle of the ethical, they must engage at once in the discussion of conflicting duties. The ethics of reverence for life have no such need for hurry. They take their own time to think out in all directions their own principle of the moral. Knowing themselves to be firmly established, they then settle their position with regard to these conflicts.

They have to try conclusions with three adversaries: these are thoughtlessness, egoistic self-assertion, and society.

To the first of these they usually pay insufficient attention, because no open conflicts arise between them. This adversary does, nevertheless, obstruct them imperceptibly.

There is, however, a wide field of which our ethics can take possession without any collision with the troops of egoism. Man can accomplish much that is good, without having to require of himself any sacrifice. And if there really goes with it a bit of his life, it is so insignificant that he feels it no more than if he were losing a hair or a flake of dead skin.

Over wide stretches of conduct the inward liberation from the world, the being true to oneself, the being different from the world, yes, and even self-devotion to other life, is only a matter of giving attention to this particular relationship. We fall short so much, because we do not keep ourselves up to it. We do not stand sufficiently under the pressure of any inward compulsion to be ethical. At all points the steam hisses out of the boiler that is not tightly closed. In ordinary ethics the resulting losses of energy are as high as they are because such ethics have at their disposal no single basic principle of the moral which acts upon thought. They cannot tighten the lid of the boiler, indeed, they do not ever even examine it. But reverence for life being something which is ever present to thought, penetrates unceasingly and in all directions a man's observation, reflection, and resolutions. He can keep himself clear of it as little as the water can prevent itself from being coloured by the dye-stuff which is dropped into it. The struggle with thoughtlessness is started, and is always going on.

But what is the position of the ethics of reverence for life in the conflicts which arise between inward compulsion to self-sacrifice, and the necessary upholdings of the ego?

I too am subject to division of my will-to-live against itself. In a thousand ways my existence stands in conflict with that of others. The necessity to destroy and to injure life is imposed upon me. If I walk along an unfrequented path, my foot brings destruction and pain upon the tiny creatures which populate it. In order to preserve my own existence, I must defend myself against the existence which injures it. I become a persecutor of the little mouse which inhabits my house, a murderer of the insect which wants to have its nest there, a mass-murderer of the bacteria which may endanger my life. I get my food by destroying plants and animals. My happiness is built upon injury done to my fellow-men.

How can ethics be maintained in face of the horrible necessity to which I am subjected through the division of my will-to-live against itself?

Ordinary ethics seek compromises. They try to dictate how much of my existence and of my happiness I must sacrifice, and how much I may preserve at the cost of the existence and happiness of other lives. With these decisions they produce experimental, relative ethics. They offer as ethical what is in reality not ethical but a mixture of non-ethical necessity and ethics. They thereby bring about a huge confusion, and allow the starting of an ever-increasing obscuration of the conception of the ethical.

The ethics of reverence for life know nothing of a relative ethic. They make only the maintenance and promotion of life rank as good. All destruction of and injury to life, under whatever circumstances they take place, they condemn as evil. They do not keep in store adjustments between ethics and necessity all ready for use. Again and again and in ways that are always original they are trying to come to terms in man with reality. They do not abolish for him all ethical conflicts, but compel him to decide for himself in each case how far he can remain ethical and how far he must submit himself to the necessity for destruction of and injury to life, and therewith incur guilt. It is not by receiving instruction about agreement between ethical and necessary, that a man makes progress in ethics, but only by coming to hear more and more plainly the voice of the ethical, by becoming ruled more and more by the longing to preserve and promote life, and by becoming more and more obstinate in resistance to the necessity for destroying or injuring life.

In ethical conflicts man can arrive only at subjective decisions. No one can decide for him at what point, on each occasion, lies the extreme limit of possibility for his persistence in the preservation and furtherance of life. He alone has to judge this issue, by letting himself be guided by a feeling of the highest possible responsibility towards other life.

We must never let ourselves become blunted. We are living in truth, when we experience these conflicts more profoundly. The good conscience is an invention of the devil.

Martin Buber

Buber, who was born in Vienna in 1878, is one of the most important of modern Jewish thinkers. In early life he took an active part in Zionism; then he devoted himself to religious philosophy, taking a particular interest in Chasidism, whence some of his later ideas were derived. Chasidism is a mystical movement within Judaism, having an eighteenth-century eastern European origin. Cultivated Jews in western Europe had tended to disparage it as narrow and primitive. Buber found it deserved greater appreciation. In 1923 he published a small book, Ich und Du, *an English translation of which appeared in 1937. The impact of this book on Christian theologians has been enormous: The relationship between persons and things (the "I-it" relationship) is distinguished from the relationship between persons and persons (the "I-Thou" relationship). The notion that God is to be addressed rather than discussed is abundantly familiar in Christian thought. St. Augustine's* Confessions *is the first known example of a sustained work written entirely as an address or prayer to God. The Scottish divine Thomas Erskine (1788-1870) wrote: "All religion is in the change from He to Thou. It is a mere abstraction as long as it is He. Only with the Thou we know God." The following passage is characteristic of Buber's thought on religion and moral responsibility.*

The Response of Man to Man *

The idea of responsibility is to be brought back from the province of specialized ethics, of an "ought" that swings free in the air, into that of lived life. Genuine responsibility exists only where there is real responding.

Responding to what?

To what happens to one, to what is to be seen and heard and felt. Each concrete hour allotted to the person, with its content drawn from the world and from destiny, is speech for the man who is attentive. Attentive, for no more than that is needed in order to make a beginning with the reading of the signs that are given to you. For that very reason, as I have already indicated, the whole apparatus of our civilization is necessary to preserve men from this attentiveness and its consequences. For the attentive man would no longer, as his custom is, "master" the situation the very moment after it stepped up to him: it would be laid upon him to go up to and into it. Moreover, nothing that he believed he possessed as always available would help him, no knowledge and no technique, no system and no programme; for now he would have to do with what cannot be classified, with concretion itself. This speech has no

* Martin Buber, *Between Man and Man,* trans. R. G. Smith (London: Routledge & Kegan Paul, Ltd., 1947), pp. 16–18. Used by permission of The Macmillan Co., New York.

alphabet, each of its sounds is a new creation and only to be grasped as such.

It will, then, be expected of the attentive man that he face creation as it happens. It happens as speech, and not as speech rushing out over his head but as speech directed precisely at him. And if one were to ask another if he too heard and he said he did, they would have agreed only about an experiencing and not about something experienced.

But the sounds of which the speech consists — I repeat it in order to remove the misunderstanding, which is perhaps still possible, that I referred to something extraordinary and larger than life — are the events of the personal everyday life. In them, as they now are, "great" or "small," we are addressed and those which count as great, yield no greater signs than the others.

Our attitude, however, is not yet decided through our becoming aware of the signs. We can still wrap silence about us — a reply characteristic of a significant type of the age — or we can step aside into the accustomed way; although both times we carry away a wound that is not to be forgotten in any productivity or any narcotism. Yet it can happen that we venture to respond, stammering perhaps — the soul is but rarely able to attain to surer articulation — but it is an honest stammering, as when sense and throat are united about what is to be said, but the throat is too horrified at it to utter purely the already composed sense. The words of our response are spoken in the speech, untranslatable like the address, of doing and letting — whereby the doing may behave like a letting and the letting like a doing. What we say in this way with the being is our entering upon the situation, into the situation, which has at this moment stepped up to us, whose appearance we did not and could not know, for its like has not yet been.

Nor are we now finished with it, we have to give up that expectation: a situation of which we have become aware is never finished with, but we subdue it into the substance of lived life. Only then, true to the moment, do we experience a life that is something other than a sum of moments. We respond to the moment, but at the same time we respond on its behalf, we answer for it. A newly-created concrete reality has been laid in our arms; we answer for it. A dog has looked at you, you answer for its glance, a child has clutched your hand, you answer for its touch, a host of men moves about you, you answer for their need.

Responsibility which does not respond to a word is a metaphor of morality. Factually, responsibility only exists when the court is there to which I am responsible, and "self-responsibility" has reality only when the "self" to which I am responsible becomes transparent into the absolute. But he who practises real responsibility in the life of dialogue does not need to name the speaker of the word to which he is responding — he knows him in the word's substance which presses on and in, assuming the cadence of an inwardness, and stirs him in his heart of hearts. A man can ward off with all his strength the belief that "God" is there, and he tastes him in the strict sacrament of dialogue.

Yet let it not be supposed that I make morality questionable in order to glorify religion. Religion, certainly, has this advantage over morality, that it is a phenomenon and not a postulate, and further that it is able to include composure as well as determination. The reality of morality, the demand of the demander, has a place in religion, but the reality of religion, the unconditioned being of the demander, has no place in morality. Nevertheless, when religion does itself justice and asserts itself, it is much more dubious than morality, just because it is more actual and inclusive. Religion as risk, which is ready to give itself up, is the nourishing stream of the arteries; as system, possessing, assured and assuring, religion which believes in religion is the veins' blood, which ceases to circulate. And if there is nothing that can so hide the face of our fellow-man as morality can, religion can hide from us as nothing else can the face of God. Principle there, dogma here, I appreciate the "objective" compactness of dogma, but behind both there lies in wait the — profane or holy — war against the situation's power of dialogue, there lies in wait the "once-for-all" which resists the unforeseeable moment. Dogma, even when its claim of origin remains uncontested, has become the most exalted form of invulnerability against revelation. Revelation will tolerate no perfect tense, but man with the arts of his craze for security props it up to perfectedness.

SECTION SEVEN

The Mystery of Evil

Job

The locus classicus in the Bible on the problem of evil is the Book of Job, to which the student is referred. Since it is so accessible in the Bible it is not reproduced here.

The Book of Job was written between the fifth and second centuries B.C.; *the exact date is uncertain. The traditional view was that suffering is the result of sin, and this view Job rejects. His deep piety in face of tribulation is eventually vindicated, and it is held to exhibit the purpose of his suffering. From a philosophical point of view this is perhaps the most profoundly interesting book in the Hebrew Bible.*

Boethius

For about two and a half centuries before the crowning of Charlemagne in the year 800, the intellectual life of Europe was at its lowest ebb. The social conditions attending political anarchy and inclusive wars were unfavorable to the pursuit of learning or the development of that culture which was to become the glory of a later period in the Middle Ages. Anicius Manlius Torquatus Severinus Boethius (ca. 480-ca. 524) is important because of his influence as the last Christian philosopher before the onset of the darkness that was for so long to prevail. Though it is now generally recognized that Boethius was not only a Christian but a champion of orthodoxy, his most notable work is not at all specifically Christian in tone, reflecting, rather, a Stoic heritage. It is from this work, the De Consolatione Philosophiae, *which Boethius wrote in prison, that the following excerpt is taken. The Lady Philosophy appears to Boethius in a vision to solace him in his misfortunes, and in the course of their imaginary conversation the problem of evil is raised, in the form of a discussion on Chance and Providence. Boethius, having declared that the existence of divine Providence is becoming clearer to him, goes on to inquire whether Chance plays any part at all in the life of men and the arrangement of the world.*

Chance and Providence *

Here she made an end and was for turning the course of her speaking to the handling and explaining of other subjects. Then said I: "Your encouragement is right and most worthy in truth of your name and weight. But I am learning by experience what you just now said of Providence; that the question is bound up in others. I would ask you whether you think that Chance exists at all, and what you think it is?"

Then she answered: "I am eager to fulfil my promised debt, and to shew you the path by which you may seek your home. But these things, though all-expedient for knowledge, are none the less rather apart from our path, and we must be careful lest you become wearied by our turnings aside, and so be not strong enough to complete the straight journey."

"Have no fear at all thereof," said I. "It will be restful to know these things in which I have so great a pleasure; and when every view of your reasoning has stood firm with unshaken credit, so let there be no doubt of what shall follow."

* Boethius, *The Consolation of Philosophy* (New York: Random House, Modern Library Series, 1943), pp. 101–120. Used by permission of I. M. Dent & Sons, Ltd., London.

"I will do your pleasure," she made answer, and thus she began to speak:

(*Philosophy discusses "chance."*)

"If chance is defined as an outcome of random influence, produced by no sequence of causes, I am sure that there is no such thing as chance, and I consider that it is but an empty word, beyond shewing the meaning of the matter which we have in hand. For what place can be left for anything happening at random, so long as God controls everything in order? It is a true saying that nothing can come out of nothing. None of the old philosophers has denied that, though they did not apply it to the effective principle, but to the matter operated upon — that is to say, to nature; and this was the foundation upon which they built all their reasoning. If anything arises from no causes, it will appear to have risen out of nothing. But if this is impossible, then chance also cannot be anything of that sort, which is stated in the definition which we mentioned."

"Then is there nothing which can be justly called chance, nor anything 'by chance'?" I asked. "Or is there anything which common people know not, but which those words do suit?"

"My philosopher, Aristotle, defined it in his *Physics*[1] shortly and well-nigh truly."

"How?" I asked.

"Whenever anything is done with one intention, but something else, other than was intended, results from certain causes, that is called chance: as, for instance, if a man digs the ground for the sake of cultivating it, and finds a heap of buried gold. Such a thing is believed to have happened by chance, but it does not come from nothing, for it has its own causes, whose unforeseen and unexpected coincidence seem to have brought about a chance. For if the cultivator did not dig the ground, if the owner had not buried his money, the gold would not have been found. These are the causes of the chance piece of good fortune, which comes about from the causes which meet it, and move along with it, not from the intention of the actor. For neither the burier nor the tiller intended that the gold should be found; but, as I said, it was a coincidence, and it happened that the one dug up what the other buried. We may therefore define chance as an unexpected result from the coincidence of certain causes in matters where there was another purpose. The order of the universe, advancing with its inevitable sequences, brings about this coincidence of causes. This order itself emanates from its source, which is Providence, and disposes all things in their proper time and place.

"In the land where the Parthian, as he turns in flight, shoots his arrows into the pursuer's breast, from the rocks of the crag of Achæmenia, the Tigris and Euphrates flow from out one source, but quickly with divided streams are separate. If they should come together and again be joined in a single course, all, that the two streams bear along, would flow in one together. Boats would meet boats, and trees meet trees torn up by the currents, and the mingled waters would together entwine their streams by chance; but their sloping beds restrain these chances vague, and the downward order of the falling torrent

[1] Aristotle, *Physics*, ii. 3.

guides their courses. Thus does chance, which seems to rush onward without rein, bear the bit, and take its way by rule."

(*Philosophy asserts the existence of free will.*)

"I have listened to you," I said, "and agree that it is as you say. But in this close sequence of causes, is there any freedom for our judgment, or does this chain of fate bind the very feelings of our minds too?"

"There is free will," she answered. "Nor could there be any reasoning nature without freedom of judgment. For any being that can use its reason by nature, has a power of judgment by which it can without further aid decide each point, and so distinguish between objects to be desired and objects to be shunned. Each therefore seeks what it deems desirable, and flies from what it considers should be shunned. Wherefore all who have reason have also freedom of desiring and refusing in themselves. But I do not lay down that this is equal in all beings. Heavenly and divine beings have with them a judgment of great insight, an imperturbable will, and a power which can effect their desires. But human spirits must be more free when they keep themselves safe in the contemplation of the mind of God; but less free when they sink into bodies, and less still when they are bound by their earthly members. The last stage is mere slavery, when the spirit is given over to vices and has fallen away from the possession of its reason. For when the mind turns its eyes from the light of truth on high to lower darkness, soon they are dimmed by the clouds of ignorance, and become turbid through ruinous passions; by yielding to these passions and consenting to them, men increase the slavery which they have brought upon themselves, and their true liberty is lost in captivity. But God, looking upon all out of the infinite, perceives the views of Providence, and disposes each as its destiny has already fated for it according to its merits: 'He looketh over all and heareth all.'[2]

"Homer with his honeyed lips sang of the bright sun's clear light; yet the sun cannot burst with his feeble rays the bowels of the earth or the depths of the sea. Not so with the Creator of this great sphere. No masses of earth can block His vision as He looks over all. Night's cloudy darkness cannot resist Him. With one glance of His intelligence He sees all that has been, that is, and that is to come. He alone can see all things, so truly He may be called the Sun."[3]

Then said I, "Again am I plunged in yet more doubt and difficulty."

(*Boethius cannot reconcile God's foreknowledge with man's free will.*)

"What are they," she asked, "though I have already my idea of what your trouble consists?"

"There seems to me," I said, "to be such incompatibility between the existence of God's universal foreknowledge and that of any freedom of judgment.

[2] A phrase from Homer (*Iliad*, iii. 277, and *Odyssey*, xi. 109), where it is said of the sun.

[3] This sentence, besides referring to the application of Homer's words used above, contains also a play on words in the Latin, which can only be clumsily reproduced in English by some such words as "The sole power which can see all is justly to be called the solar."

For if God foresees all things and cannot in anything be mistaken, that, which His Providence sees will happen, must result. Wherefore if it knows beforehand not only men's deeds but even their designs and wishes, there will be no freedom of judgment. For there can neither be any deed done, nor wish formed, except such as the infallible Providence of God has foreseen. For if matters could ever so be turned that they resulted otherwise than was foreseen of Providence, this foreknowledge would cease to be sure. But, rather than knowledge, it is opinion which is uncertain; and that, I deem, is not applicable to God. And, further, I cannot approve of an argument by which some men think that they can cut this knot; for they say that a result does not come to pass for the reason that Providence has foreseen it, but the opposite rather, namely, that because it is about to come to pass, therefore it cannot be hidden from God's Providence. In that way it seems to me that the argument must resolve itself into an argument on the other side. For in that case it is not necessary that that should happen which is foreseen, but that that which is about to happen should be foreseen; as though, indeed, our doubt was whether God's foreknowledge is the certain cause of future events, or the certainty of future events is the cause of Providence. But let our aim be to prove that, whatever be the shape which this series of causes takes, the fulfillment of God's foreknowledge is necessary, even if this knowledge may not seem to induce the necessity for the occurrence of future events. For instance, if a man sits down, it must be that the opinion, which conjectures that he is sitting, is true; but conversely, if the opinion concerning the man is true because he is sitting, he must be sitting down. There is therefore necessity in both cases: the man must be sitting, and the opinion must be true. But he does not sit because the opinion is true, but rather the opinion is true because his sitting down has preceded it. Thus, though the cause of the truth of the opinion proceeds from the other fact, yet there is a common necessity on both parts. In like manner we must reason of Providence and future events. For even though they are foreseen because they are about to happen, yet they do not happen because they are foreseen. None the less it is necessary that either what is about to happen should be foreseen of God, or that what has been foreseen should happen; and this alone is enough to destroy all free will.

"Yet how absurd it is that we should say that the result of temporal affairs is the cause of eternal foreknowledge! And to think that God foresees future events because they are about to happen, is nothing else than to hold events of past time to be the cause of that highest Providence. Besides, just as, when I know a present fact, that fact must be so; so also when I know of something that will happen, that must come to pass. Thus it follows that the fulfilment of a foreknown event must be inevitable.

"Lastly, if any one believes that any matter is otherwise than the fact is, he not only has not knowledge, but his opinion is false also, and that is very far from the truth of knowledge. Wherefore, if any future event is such that its fulfilment is not sure or necessary, how can it possibly be known beforehand that it will occur? For just as absolute knowledge has no taint of falsity, so also that which is conceived by knowledge cannot be otherwise than as it is conceived. That is the reason why knowledge cannot lie, because each matter must be just as knowledge knows that it is. What then? How can God know beforehand these uncertain future events? For if He thinks inevitable the fulfilment of such things as may possibly not result, He is wrong; and that we may not believe, nor even utter, rightly. But if He perceives that they will result as they are in such a manner that He only knows that they may or may not occur, equally, how is this foreknowledge, this which knows nothing for sure, nothing absolutely? How is such a foreknowledge different from the absurd prophecy which Horace puts in the mouth of Tiresias: 'Whatever I shall say, will either come to pass, or it will not'?[4] How, too, would God's Providence be better than man's opinion, if, as men do, He only sees to be uncertain such things as have an uncertain result? But if there can be no uncertainty with God, the most sure source of all things, then the fulfilment of all that He has surely foreknown, is certain. Thus we are led to see that there is no freedom for the intentions or actions of men; for the mind of God, foreseeing all things without error or deception, binds all together and controls their results. And when we have once allowed this, it is plain how complete is the fall of all human actions in consequence. In vain are rewards or punishments set before good or bad, for there is no free or voluntary action of the mind to deserve them; and what we just now determined was most fair, will prove to be most unfair of all, namely to punish the dishonest or reward the honest, since their own will does not put them in the way of honesty or dishonesty, but the unfailing necessity of development constrains them. Wherefore neither virtues nor vices are anything, but there is rather an indiscriminate confusion of all deserts. And nothing could be more vicious than this; since the whole order of all comes from Providence, and nothing is left to human intention, it follows that our crimes, as well as our good deeds, must all be held due to the author of all good. Hence it is unreasonable to hope for or pray against aught. For what could any man hope for or pray against, if an undeviating chain links together all that we can desire? Thus will the only understanding between God and man, the right of prayer, be taken away. We suppose that at the price of our deservedly humbling ourselves before Him we may win a right to the inestimable reward of His divine grace: this is the only manner in which men can seem to deal with God, so to speak, and by virtue of prayer to join ourselves to that inaccessible light, before it is granted to us; but if we allow the inevitability of the future, and believe that we have no power, what means shall we have to join ourselves to the Lord of all, or how can we cling to Him? Wherefore, as you sang but a little while ago,[5] the human race must be cut off from its source and ever fall away.

"What cause of discord is it breaks the bonds of agreement here? What heavenly power has set such strife between two truths? Thus, though apart each brings no doubt, yet can they not be linked together. Comes there no discord between these truths? Stand they for ever sure by one another? Yes, 'tis the mind, o'erwhelmed by the body's blindness, which cannot see by the light of that dimmed brightness the finest threads that bind the truth. But wherefore burns the spirit with so strong desire to learn the hidden signs of

[4] Horace, *Satires*, II. v. 59.

[5] *Supra*, Book IV. Met. vi. p. 135.

truth? Knows it the very object of its careful search? Then why seeks it to learn anew what it already knows? If it knows it not, why searches it in blindness? For who would desire aught unwitting? Or who could seek after that which is unknown? How should he find it, or recognise its form when found, if he knows it not? And when the mind of man perceived the mind of God, did it then know the whole and parts alike? Now is the mind buried in the cloudy darkness of the body, yet has not altogether forgotten its own self, and keeps the whole though it has lost the parts. Whosoever, therefore, seeks the truth, is not wholly in ignorance, nor yet has knowledge wholly; for he knows not all, yet is not ignorant of all. He takes thought for the whole which he keeps in memory, handling again what he saw on high, so that he may add to that which he has kept, that which he has forgotten."

(*Philosophy tries to shew how they may be reconciled.*)

Then said she, "This is the old plaint concerning Providence which was so strongly urged by Cicero when treating of Divination,[6] and you yourself have often and at length questioned the same subject. But so far, none of you have explained it with enough diligence or certainty. The cause of this obscurity is that the working of human reason cannot approach the directness of divine foreknowledge. If this could be understood at all, there would be no doubt left. And this especially will I try to make plain, if I can first explain your difficulties.

"Tell me why you think abortive the reasoning of those who solve the question thus; they argue that foreknowledge cannot be held to be a cause for the necessity of future results, and therefore free will is not in any way shackled by foreknowledge. Whence do you draw your proof of the necessity of future results if not from the fact that such things as are known beforehand cannot but come to pass? If, then (as you yourself admitted just now), foreknowledge brings no necessity to bear upon future events, how is it that the voluntary results of such events are bound to find a fixed end? Now for the sake of the argument, that you may turn your attention to what follows, let us state that there is no foreknowledge at all. Then are the events which are decided by free will, bound by any necessity, so far as this goes? Of course not. Secondly, let us state that foreknowledge exists, but brings no necessity to bear upon events; then, I think, the same free will will be left, intact and absolute. 'But,' you will say, 'though foreknowledge is no necessity for a result in the future, yet it is a sign that it will necessarily come to pass.' Thus, therefore, even if there had been no foreknowledge, it would be plain that future results were under necessity; for every sign can only shew what it is that it points out; it does not bring it to pass. Wherefore we must first prove that nothing happens but of necessity, in order that it may be plain that foreknowledge is a sign of this necessity. Otherwise, if there is no necessity, then foreknowledge will not be a sign of that which does not exist. Now it is allowed that proof rests upon firm reasoning, not upon signs or external arguments; it must be deduced from suitable and binding causes. How can it possibly be that things, which are foreseen as about to happen, should not occur? That would be as though we were to believe that events would not

[6] Cicero, *De Divinatione*, II.

occur which Providence foreknows as about to occur, and as though we did not rather think this, that though they occur, yet they have had no necessity in their own natures which brought them about. We can see many actions developing before our eyes; just as chariot drivers see the development of their actions as they control and guide their chariots, and many other things likewise. Does any necessity compel any of those things to occur as they do? Of course not. All art, craft, and intention would be in vain, if everything took place by compulsion. Therefore, if things have no necessity for coming to pass when they do, they cannot have any necessity to be about to come to pass before they do. Wherefore there are things whose results are entirely free from necessity. For I think not that there is any man who will say this, that things, which are done in the present, were not about to be done in the past, before they are done. Thus these foreknown events have their free results. Just as foreknowledge of present things brings no necessity to bear upon them as they come to pass, so also foreknowledge of future things brings no necessity to bear upon things which are to come.

"But you will say that there is no doubt of this too, whether there can be any foreknowledge of things which have not results bounden by necessity. For they do seem to lack harmony; and you think that if they are foreseen, the necessity follows; if there is no necessity, then they cannot be foreseen; nothing can be perceived certainly by knowledge, unless it be certain. But if things have uncertainty of result, but are foreseen as though certain, this is plainly the obscurity of opinion, and not the truth of knowledge. For you believe that to think aught other than it is, is the opposite of true knowledge. The cause of this error is that every man believes that all the subjects, that he knows, are known by their own force or nature alone, which are known; but it is quite the opposite. For every subject, that is known, is comprehended not according to its own force, but rather according to the nature of those who know it. Let me make this plain to you by a brief example: the roundness of a body may be known in one way by sight, in another way by touch. Sight can take in the whole body at once from a distance by judging its radii, while touch clings, as it were, to the outside of the sphere, and from close at hand perceives through the material parts the roundness of the body as it passes over the actual circumference. A man himself is differently comprehended by the senses, by imagination, by reason, and by intelligence. For the senses distinguish the form as set in the matter operated upon by the form; imagination distinguishes the appearance alone without the matter. Reason goes even further than imagination; by a general and universal contemplation it investigates the actual kind which is represented in individual specimens. Higher still is the view of the intelligence, which reaches above the sphere of the universal, and with the unsullied eye of the mind gazes upon that very form of the kind in its absolute simplicity. Herein the chief point for our consideration is this: the higher power of understanding includes the lower, but the lower never rises to the higher. For the senses are capable of understanding naught but the matter; imagination cannot look upon universal or natural kinds; reason cannot comprehend the absolute form; whereas the intelligence seems to look down from above and comprehend the form, and distinguishes all that lie below, but in such a way that it grasps the very form which could not be known to any other than itself. For it perceives and knows the general kind, as does reason; the appearance, as does the imagination; and the matter, as do the senses, but with one grasp of the mind it looks upon all with a clear conception of the whole. And reason too, as it views general kinds, does not make use of the imagination nor the senses, but yet does perceive the objects both of the imagination and of the senses. It is reason which thus defines a general kind according to its conception: Man, for instance, is an animal, biped and reasoning. This is a general notion of a natural kind, but no man denies that the subject can be approached by the imagination and by the senses, just because reason investigates it by a reasonable conception and not by the imagination or senses. Likewise, though imagination takes its beginning of seeing and forming appearances from the senses, yet without their aid it surveys each subject by an imaginative faculty of distinguishing, not by the distinguishing faculty of the senses.

"Do you see then, how in knowledge of all things, the subject uses its own standard of capability, and not those of the objects known? And this is but reasonable, for every judgment formed is an act of the person who judges, and therefore each man must of necessity perform his own action from his own capability and not the capability of any other.

"In days of old the Porch at Athens[7] gave us men, seeing dimly as in old age, who could believe that the feelings of the senses and the imagination were but impressions on the mind from bodies without them, just as the old custom was to impress with swift-running pens letters upon the surface of a waxen tablet which bore no marks before. But if the mind with its own force can bring forth naught by its own exertions; if it does but lie passive and subject to the marks of other bodies; if it reflects, as does, forsooth, a mirror, the vain reflections of other things; whence thrives there in the soul an all-seeing power of knowledge? What is the force that sees the single parts, or which distinguishes the facts it knows? What is the force that gathers up the parts it has distinguished, that takes its course in order due, now rises to mingle with the things on high, and now sinks down among the things below, and then to itself brings back itself, and, so examining, refutes the false with truth? This is a cause of greater power, of more effective force by far than that which only receives the impressions of material bodies. Yet does the passive reception come first, rousing and stirring all the strength of the mind in the living body. When the eyes are smitten with a light, or the ears are struck with a voice's sound, then is the spirit's energy aroused, and, thus moved, calls upon like forms, such as it holds within itself, fits them to signs without and mingles the forms of its imagination with those which it has stored within.

(*Human reasoning, being lower than divine intelligence, can at best only strive to approach thereto.*)

"With regard to feeling the effects of bodies, natures which are brought into contact from without may affect the organs of the senses, and the body's passive affection may precede the active energy of the spirit, and call forth

[7] Zeno of Citium (342–270 B.C.), the founder of the Stoic school, taught in the Stoa Poekile, whence the name of the school. The following lines refer to their doctrine of presentations and impressions.

to itself the activity of the mind; if then, when the effects of bodies are felt, the mind is not marked in any way by its passive reception thereof, but declares that reception subject to the body of its own force, how much less do those subjects, which are free from all affections of bodies, follow external objects in their perceptions, and how much more do they make clear the way for the action of their mind? By this argument many different manners of understanding have fallen to widely different natures of things. For the senses are incapable of any knowledge but their own, and they alone fall to those living beings which are incapable of motion, as are sea shell-fish, and other low forms of life which live by clinging to rocks; while imagination is granted to animals with the power of motion, who seem to be affected by some desire to seek or avoid certain things. But reason belongs to the human race alone, just as the true intelligence is God's alone. Wherefore that manner of knowledge is better than others, for it can comprehend of its own nature not only the subject peculiar to itself, but also the subjects of the other kinds of knowledge. Suppose that the senses and imagination thus oppose reasoning, saying, 'The universal natural kinds, which reason believes that it can perceive, are nothing; for what is comprehensible to the senses and the imagination cannot be universal: therefore either the judgment of reason is true, and that which can be perceived by the senses is nothing; or, since reason knows well that there are many subjects comprehensible to the senses and imagination, the conception of reason is vain, for it holds to be universal what is an individual matter comprehensible to the senses.' To this reason might answer, that 'it sees from a general point of view what is comprehensible to the senses and the imagination, but they cannot aspire to a knowledge of universals, since their manner of knowledge cannot go further than material or bodily appearances; and in the matter of knowledge it is better to trust to the stronger and more nearly perfect judgment.' If such a trial of argument occurred, should not we, who have within us the force of reasoning as well as the powers of the senses and imagination, approve of the cause of reason rather than that of the others? It is in like manner that human reason thinks that the divine intelligence cannot perceive the things of the future except as it conceives them itself. For you argue thus: 'If there are events which do not appear to have sure or necessary results, their results cannot be known for certain beforehand: therefore there can be no foreknowledge of these events; for if we believe that there is any foreknowledge thereof, there can exist nothing but such as is brought forth of necessity.' If therefore we, who have our share in possession of reason, could go further and possess the judgment of the mind of God, we should then think it most just that human reason should yield itself to the mind of God, just as we have determined that the senses and imagination ought to yield to reason.

"Let us therefore raise ourselves, if so be that we can, to that height of the loftiest intelligence. For there reason will see what it cannot of itself perceive, and that is to know how even such things as have uncertain results are perceived definitely and for certain by foreknowledge; and such foreknowledge will not be mere opinion, but rather the single and direct form of the highest knowledge unlimited by any finite bounds.

"In what different shapes do living beings move upon the earth! Some make flat their bodies, sweeping through the dust and using their strength to make therein a furrow without break; some flit here and there upon light wings which beat the breeze, and they float through vast tracks of air in their easy flight. 'Tis others' wont to plant their footsteps on the ground, and pass with their paces over green fields or under trees. Though all these thou seest move in different shapes, yet all have their faces downward along the ground, and this doth draw downward and dull their senses. Alone of all, the human race lifts up its head on high, and stands in easy balance with the body upright, and so looks down to spurn the earth. If thou art not too earthly by an evil folly, this pose is as a lesson. Thy glance is upward, and thou dost carry high thy head, and thus thy search is heavenward: then lead thy soul too upward, lest while the body is higher raised, the mind sink lower to the earth.

(*Philosophy explains that God's divine intelligence can view all things from its eternal mind, while human reason can only see them from a temporal point of view.*)

"Since then all that is known is apprehended, as we just now shewed, not according to its own nature but according to the nature of the knower, let us examine, so far as we lawfully may, the character of the divine nature, so that we may be able to learn what its knowledge is.

"The common opinion, according to all men living, is that God is eternal. Let us therefore consider what is eternity. For eternity will, I think, make clear to us at the same time the divine nature and knowledge.

"Eternity is the simultaneous and complete possession of infinite life. This will appear more clearly if we compare it with temporal things. All that lives under the conditions of time moves through the present from the past to the future; there is nothing set in time which can at one moment grasp the whole space of its lifetime. It cannot yet comprehend tomorrow; yesterday it has already lost. And in this life of to-day your life is no more than a changing, passing moment. And as Aristotle[8] said of the universe, so it is of all that is subject to time; though it never began to be, nor will ever cease, and its life is co-extensive with the infinity of time, yet it is not such as can be held to be eternal. For though it apprehends and grasps a space of infinite lifetime, it does not embrace the whole simultaneously; it has not yet experienced the future. What we should rightly call eternal is that which grasps and possesses wholly and simultaneously the fulness of unending life, which lacks naught of the future, and has lost naught of the fleeting past; and such an existence must be ever present in itself to control and aid itself, and also must keep present with itself the infinity of changing time. Therefore, people who hear that Plato thought that this universe had no beginning of time and will have no end, are not right in thinking that in this way the created world is co-eternal with its creator.[9] For to pass through unending life, the attribute

[8] Aristotle, *De Cælo*, I.

[9] Boethius speaks of people who "hear that Plato thought, etc.," because this was the teaching of some of Plato's successors at the Academy. Plato himself thought otherwise, as may be seen in the *Timæus*, *e.g.* ch. xi. 38 B., "Time then has come into

which Plato ascribes to the universe, is one thing; but it is another thing to grasp simultaneously the whole of unending life in the present; this is plainly a peculiar property of the mind of God.

"And further, God should not be regarded as older than His creations by any period of time, but rather by the peculiar property of His own single nature. For the infinite changing of temporal things tries to imitate the ever simultaneously present immutability of His life: it cannot succeed in imitating or equalling this, but sinks from immutability into change, and falls from the single directness of the present into an infinite space of future and past. And since this temporal state cannot possess its life completely and simultaneously, but it does in the same manner exist for ever without ceasing, it therefore seems to try in some degree to rival that which it cannot fulfil or represent, for it binds itself to some sort of present time out of this small and fleeting moment; but inasmuch as this temporal present bears a certain appearance of that abiding present, it somehow makes those, to whom it comes, seem to be in truth what they imitate. But since this imitation could not be abiding, the unending march of time has swept it away, and thus we find that it has bound together, as it passes, a chain of life, which it could not by abiding embrace in its fulness. And thus if we would apply proper epithets to those subjects, we can say, following Plato, that God is eternal, but the universe is continual.

"Since then all judgment apprehends the subjects of its thought according to its own nature, and God has a condition of ever-present eternity. His knowledge, which passes over every change of time, embracing infinite lengths of past and future, views in its own direct comprehension everything as though it were taking place in the present. If you would weigh the foreknowledge by which God distinguishes all things, you will more rightly hold it to be a knowledge of a never-failing constancy in the present, than a foreknowledge of the future. Whence Providence is more rightly to be understood as a looking forth than a looking forward, because it is set far from low matters and looks forth upon all things as from a lofty mountain-top above all. Why then do you demand that all things occur by necessity, if divine light rests upon them, while men do not render necessary such things as they can see? Because you can see things of the present, does your sight therefore put upon them any necessity? Surely not. If one may not unworthily compare this present time with the divine, just as you can see things in this your temporal present, so God sees all things in His eternal present. Wherefore this divine foreknowledge does not change the nature or individual qualities of things: it sees things present in its understanding just as they will result some time in the future. It makes no confusion in its distinctions, and with one view of its mind it discerns all that shall come to pass whether of necessity or not. For instance, when you see at the same time a man walking on the earth and the sun

---

being along with the universe, that being generated together, together they may be dissolved, should a dissolution of them ever come to pass; and it was made after the pattern of the eternal nature that it might be as like to it as possible. For the pattern is existent for all eternity, but the copy has been, and is, and shall be, throughout all time continually." (Mr. Archer Hind's translation.)

rising in the heavens, you see each sight simultaneously, yet you distinguish between them, and decide that one is moving voluntarily, the other of necessity. In like manner the perception of God looks down upon all things without disturbing at all their nature, though they are present to Him but future under the conditions of time. Wherefore this foreknowledge is not opinion but knowledge resting upon truth, since He knows that a future event is, though He knows too that it will not occur of necessity. If you answer here that what God sees about to happen, cannot but happen, and that what cannot but happen is bound by necessity, you fasten me down to the word necessity, I will grant that we have a matter of most firm truth, but it is one to which scarce any man can approach unless he be a contemplator of the divine. For I shall answer that such a thing will occur of necessity, when it is viewed from the point of divine knowledge; but when it is examined in its own nature, it seems perfectly free and unrestrained. For there are two kinds of necessities; one is simple: for instance, a necessary fact, 'all men are mortal'; the other is conditional; for instance, if you know that a man is walking, he must be walking: for what each man knows cannot be otherwise than it is known to be; but the conditional one is by no means followed by this simple and direct necessity; for there is no necessity to compel a voluntary walker to proceed, though it is necessary that, if he walks, he should be proceeding. In the same way, if Providence sees an event in its present, that thing must be, though it has no necessity of its own nature. And God looks in His present upon those future things which come to pass through free will. Therefore if these things be looked at from the point of view of God's insight, they come to pass of necessity under the condition of divine knowledge; if, on the other hand, they are viewed by themselves, they do not lose the perfect freedom of their nature. Without doubt, then, all things that God foreknows do come to pass, but some of them proceed from free will; and though they result by coming into existence, yet they do not lose their own nature, because before they came to pass they could also not have come to pass.

" 'What then,' you may ask, 'is the difference in their not being bound by necessity, since they result under all circumstances as by necessity, on account of the condition of divine knowledge?' This is the difference, as I just now put forward: take the sun rising and a man walking; while these operations are occurring, they cannot but occur: but the one was bound to occur before it did; the other was not so bound. What God has in His present, does exist without doubt; but of such things some follow by necessity, others by their authors' wills. Wherefore I was justified in saying that if these things be regarded from the view of divine knowledge, they are necessary, but if they are viewed by themselves, they are perfectly free from all ties of necessity: just as when you refer all, that is clear to the senses, to the reason, it becomes general truth, but it remains particular if regarded by itself. 'But,' you will say, 'if it is in my power to change a purpose of mine, I will disregard Providence, since I may change what Providence foresees.' To which I answer, 'You can change your purpose, but since the truth of Providence knows in its present that you can do so, and whether you do so, and in what direction you may change it, therefore you cannot escape that divine foreknowledge: just as you cannot avoid he glance of a present eye, though you may by your free will turn yourself to all inds of different actions.' 'What?' you will say, 'can I by my own action change livine knowledge, so that if I choose now one thing, now another, Providence oo will seem to change its knowledge?' No; divine insight precedes all future hings, turning them back and recalling them to the present time of its own peuliar knowledge. It does not change, as you may think, between this and that lternation of foreknowledge. It is constant in preceding and embracing by ne glance all your changes. And God does not receive this ever-present grasp f all things and vision of the present at the occurrence of future events, but rom His own peculiar directness. Whence also is that difficulty solved which ou laid down a little while ago, that it was not worthy to say that our future vents were the cause of God's knowledge. For this power of knowledge, ver in the present and embracing all things in its perception, does itself contrain all things, and owes naught to following events from which it has reeived naught. Thus, therefore, mortal men have their freedom of judgment ntact. And since their wills are freed from all binding necessity, laws do not et rewards or punishments unjustly. God is ever the constant foreknowing verseer, and the ever-present eternity of His sight moves in harmony with he future nature of our actions, as it dispenses rewards to the good, and unishments to the bad. Hopes are not vainly put in God, nor prayers in ain offered: if these are right, they cannot but be answered. Turn therefore rom vice: ensue virtue: raise your soul to upright hopes: send up on high our prayers from this earth. If you would be honest, great is the necessity njoined upon your goodness, since all you do is done before the eyes of an ll-seeing Judge."

David Hume

In the following passage Hume (see also page 132) treats aspects of the problem of evil as it relates to his interpretation of religion.

Nature Neither Good Nor Evil *

There seem to be *four* circumstances, on which depend all, or the greates parts of the ills, that molest sensible creatures; and it is not impossible bu all these circumstances may be necessary and unavoidable. We know so littl beyond common life, or even of common life, that, with regard to the œconom of a universe, there is no conjecture, however wild, which may not be just nor any one, however plausible, which may not be erroneous. All that belong to human understanding, in this deep ignorance and obscurity, is to be sceptical, or at least cautious; and not to admit of any hypothesis, whatever; mucl less, of any which is supported by no appearance of probability. Now this assert to be the case with regard to all the causes of evil, and the circumstances on which it depends. None of them appear to human reason, in the leas degree, necessary or unavoidable; nor can we suppose them such, without th utmost licence of imagination.

The *first* circumstance which introduces evil, is that contrivance or œconom of the animal creation, by which pains, as well as pleasures, are employe to excite all creatures to action, and make them vigilant in the great work o self-preservation. Now pleasure alone, in its various degrees, seems to huma understanding sufficient for this purpose. All animals might be constantly i a state of enjoyment; but when urged by any of the necessities of nature, suc as thirst, hunger, weariness; instead of pain, they might feel a diminution o pleasure, by which they might be prompted to seek that object, which is necessary to their subsistence. Men pursue pleasure as eagerly as they avoid pain at least, might have been so constituted.[1] It seems, therefore, plainly possibl to carry on the business of life without any pain. Why then is any animal eve rendered susceptible of such a sensation? If animals can be free from it a hour, they might enjoy a perpetual exemption from it; and it required a particular a contrivance of their organs to produce that feeling, as to endow them with sight, hearing, or any of the senses. Shall we conjecture, that suc a contrivance was necessary, without any appearance of reason? and shall w build on that conjecture as on the most certain truth?

But a capacity of pain would not alone produce pain, were it not for th *second* circumstance, viz. the conducting of the world by general laws; an

* *Dialogues concerning Natural Religion,* Part XI, from *The Philosophical Work of David Hume* (Boston: Little, Brown & Co., 1854), IV, pp. 147–161. Used b permission.

[1] This phrase is obscure. Hume apparently means that human beings might hav been constituted with a capacity for pleasure yet without a capacity for pain. [Eds.]

this seems nowise necessary to a very perfect being. It is true; if every thing were conducted by particular volitions, the course of nature would be perpetually broken, and no man could employ his reason in the conduct of life. But might not other particular volitions remedy this inconvenience? In short, might not the Deity exterminate all ill, wherever it were to be found; and produce all good, without any preparation or long progress of causes and effects?

Besides, we must consider, that, according to the present œconomy of the world, the course of Nature, though supposed exactly regular, yet to us appears not so, and many events are uncertain, and many disappoint our expectations. Health and sickness, calm and tempest, with an infinite number of other accidents, whose causes are unknown and variable, have a great influence both on the fortunes of particular persons and on the prosperity of public societies: and indeed all human life, in a manner, depends on such accidents. A being, therefore, who knows the secret springs of the universe, mighty easily, by particular volitions, turn all these accidents to the good of mankind, and render the whole world happy, without discovering himself in any operation. A fleet, whose purposes were salutary to society, might always meet with a fair wind: Good princes enjoy sound health and long life: Persons, born to power and authority, be framed with good tempers and virtuous dispositions. A few such events as these, regularly and wisely conducted, would change the face of the world; and yet would no more seem to disturb the course of Nature or confound human conduct, than the present œconomy of things, where the causes are secret, and variable, and compounded. Some small touches, given to CALIGULA's brain in his infancy, might have converted him into a TRAJAN: one wave, a little higher than the rest, by burying CÆSAR and his fortune in the bottom of the ocean, might have restored liberty to a considerable part of mankind. There may, for aught we know, be good reasons, why Providence interposes not in this manner; but they are unknown to us: and though the mere supposition, that such reasons exist, may be sufficient to *save* the conclusion concerning the divine attributes, yet surely it can never be sufficient to *establish* that conclusion.

If every thing in the universe be conducted by general laws, and if animals be rendered susceptible of pain, it scarcely seems possible but some ill must arise in the various shocks of matter, and the various concurrence and opposition of general laws: But this ill would be very rare, were it not for the *third* circumstance, which I proposed to mention, viz. the great frugality with which all powers and faculties are distributed to every particular being. So well adjusted are the organs and capacities of all animals, and so well fitted to their preservation, that, as far as history or tradition reaches, there appears not to be any single species, which has yet been extinguished in the universe. Every animal has the requisite endowments; but these endowments are bestowed with so scrupulous an œconomy, that any considerable diminution must entirely destroy the creature. Wherever one power is increased, there is a proportional abatement in the others. Animals, which excel in swiftness, are commonly defective in force. Those, which possess both, are either imperfect in some of their senses, or are oppressed with the most craving wants. The human species, whose chief excellency is reason and sagacity, is of all others the most necessitous, and the most deficient in bodily advantages; without clothes, without arms, without food, without lodging, without any convenience of life, except what they owe to their own skill and industry. In short, Nature seems to have formed an exact calculation of the necessities of her creatures; and like a *rigid master*, has afforded them little more powers or endorsements, than what are strictly sufficient to supply those necessities. An *indulgent parent* would have bestowed a large stock, in order to guard against accidents, and secure the happiness and welfare of the creature, in the most unfortunate concurrence of circumstances. Every course of life would not have been so surrounded with precipices, that the least departure from the true path, by mistake or necessity, must involve us in misery and ruin. Some reserve, some fund would have been provided to ensure happiness; nor would the powers and the necessities have been adjusted with so rigid an œconomy. The author of Nature is inconceivably powerful: his force is supposed great, if not altogether inexhaustible: nor is there any reason, as far as we can judge, to make him observe this strict frugality in his dealings with his creatures. It would have been better, were his power extremely limited, to have created fewer animals, and to have endowed these with more faculties for their happiness and preservation. A builder is never esteemed prudent, who undertakes a plan beyond what his stock will enable him to finish.

In order to cure most of the ills of human life, I require not that man should have the wings of the eagle, the swiftness of the stag, the force of the ox, the arms of the lion, the scales of the crocodile or rhinoceros; much less do I demand the sagacity of an angel or cherubin. I am contented to take an increase in one single power or faculty of his soul. Let him be endowed with a greater propensity to industry and labour; a more vigorous spring and activity of mind; a more constant bent to business and application. Let the whole species possess naturally an equal diligence with that which many individuals are able to attain by habit and reflection; and the most beneficial consequences without any alloy of ill, is the immediate and necessary result of this endowment. Almost all the moral, as well as natural evils of human life arise from idleness; and were our species, by the original constitution of their frame, exempt from this vice or infirmity, the perfect cultivation of land, the improvement of arts and manufactures, the exact execution of every office and duty immediately follow; and men at once may fully reach that state of society which is so imperfectly attained by the best-regulated government. But as industry is a power, and the most valuable of any, Nature seems determined suitably to her usual maxims, to bestow it on men with a very sparing hand and rather to punish him severely for his deficiency in it, than to reward him for his attainments. She has so contrived his frame, that nothing but the most violent necessity can oblige him to labour; and she employs all his other wants to overcome, at least in part, the want of diligence, and to endow him with some share of a faculty, of which she has thought fit naturally to bereave him. Here our demands may be allowed very humble, and therefore the more reasonable. If we required the endowments of superior penetration and judgment, of a more delicate taste of beauty, of a nicer sensibility to benevolence and friendship; we might be told, that we impiously pretend to break the order of Nature, that we want to exalt ourselves into a higher rank of being, that the presents which we require, not being suitable to our state and condition, would only be pernicious to us. But it is hard; I dare to repeat it, it is hard, that being placed in a world so full of wants and necessities; where almost every being and element is either our foe or refuses us their assistance, . . . we should also have our own temper to struggle with, and should be deprived of that faculty, which can alone fence against these multiplied evils.

The *fourth* circumstance, whence arises the misery and ill of the universe, is the inaccurate workmanship of all the springs and principles of the great machine of nature. It must be acknowledged, that there are few parts of the universe, which seem not to serve some purpose, and whose removal would not produce a visible defect and disorder in the whole. The parts hang all together; nor can one be touched without affecting the rest in a greater or less degree. But at the same time, it must be observed, that none of these parts or principles, however useful, are so accurately adjusted, as to keep precisely within those bounds, in which their utility consists; but they are, all of them, apt, on every occasion, to run into the one extreme or the other. One would imagine, that this grand production had not received the last hand of the maker; so little finished is every part, and so coarse are the strokes, with which it is executed. Thus, the winds are requisite to convey the vapours along the surface of the globe, and to assist men in navigation: but how oft, rising up to tempests and hurricanes, do they become pernicious? Rains are necessary to nourish all the plants and animals of the earth: but how often are they defective? how often excessive? Heat is requisite to all life and vegetation; but is not always found in the due proportion. On the mixture and secretion of the humours and juices of the body depend the health and prosperity of the animal: but the parts perform not regularly their proper function. What more useful than all the passions of the mind, ambition, vanity, love, anger? But how oft do they break their bounds, and cause the greatest convulsions in society? There is nothing so advantageous in the universe, but what frequently becomes pernicious, by its excess or defect; nor has Nature guarded, with the requisite accuracy, against all disorder or confusion. The irregularity is never, perhaps, so great as to destroy any species; but is often sufficient to involve the individuals in ruin and misery.

On the concurrence, then, of these *four* circumstances does all, or the greatest part of natural evil depend. Were all living creatures incapable of pain, or were the world administered by particular volitions, evil never could have found access into the universe: and were animals endowed with a large stock of powers and faculties, beyond what strict necessity requires; or were the several springs and principles of the universe so accurately framed as to preserve always the just temperament and medium; there must have been very little ill in comparison of what we feel at present. What then shall we pronounce on this occasion? Shall we say, that these circumstances are not necessary, and that they might easily have been altered in the contrivance of the universe? This decision seems too presumptuous for creatures, so blind and ignorant. Let us be more modest in our conclusions. Let us allow, that, if the goodness of the Deity (I mean a goodness like the human) could be established on any tolerable reasons *a priori*, these phenomena, however untoward, would not be sufficient to subvert that principle; but might easily, in some unknown manner, be reconcilable to it. But let us still assert, that as this goodness is not antecedently established, but must be inferred from the phenomena, there can be no grounds for such an inference, while there are so many ills in the universe, and while these ills might so easily have been remedied, as far as human understanding can be allowed to judge on such a subject. I am Sceptic enough to allow, that the bad appearances, notwithstanding all my reasonings, may be compatible with such attributes as you suppose: But surely they can never prove these attributes. Such a conclusion cannot result from Scepticism; but must arise from the phenomena, and from our confidence in the reasonings, which we deduce from these phenomena.

Look round this universe. What an immense profusion of beings, animated and organized, sensible and active! You admire this prodigious variety and fecundity. But inspect a little more narrowly these living existences, the only beings worth regarding. How hostile and destructive to each other! How insufficient all of them for their own happiness! How contemptible or odious to the spectator! The whole presents nothing but the idea of a blind Nature impregnated by a great vivifying principle, and pouring forth from her lap without discernment or parental care, her maimed and abortive children!

Here the MANICHÆAN system occurs as a proper hypothesis to solve the difficulty: and no doubt, in some respects, it is very specious, and has more probability than the common hypothesis, by giving a plausible account of the strange mixture of good and ill, which appears in life. But if we consider on the other hand, the perfect uniformity and agreement of the parts of the universe, we shall not discover in it any marks of the combat of a malevolent with a benevolent being. There is indeed an opposition of pains and pleasure in the feelings of sensible creatures: but are not all the operations of Nature carried on by an opposition of principles, of hot and cold, moist and dry, light and heavy? The true conclusion is, that the original source of all things is entirely indifferent to all these principles, and has no more regard to good above ill than to heat above cold, or to drought above moisture, or to light above heavy.

There may *four* hypotheses be framed concerning the first causes of the universe: *that* they are endowed with perfect goodness, *that* they have perfect malice, *that* they are opposite and have both goodness and malice, *that* they have neither goodness nor malice. Mixed phenomena can never prove the two former unmixed principles. And the uniformity and steadiness of general laws seem to oppose the third. The fourth, therefore, seems by far the most probable.

What I have said concerning natural evil will apply to moral, with little or no variation; and we have no more reason to infer, that the rectitude of the Supreme Being resembles human rectitude than that his benevolence resembles the human. Nay, it will be thought, that we have still greater cause to exclude from him moral sentiments, such as we feel them; since moral evil, in the opinion of many, is much more predominant above moral good than natural evil above natural good.

William Temple

William Temple (1881-1944) was a very notable Anglican ecclesiastic whose concern for social and economic questions, not least while he was Bishop of Manchester (1921-1929), made him a renowned national figure. A few years before his death he became Archbishop of Canterbury, the See that had been held by his distinguished father, Frederick Temple. William Temple was also, moreover, a religious philosopher of considerable importance in the history of English religious thought. Trained under Edward Caird, whose thought provided the starting point and even the mold of his own thinking, Temple developed his position on independent lines. Nature, Man and God, *from which the following passage is taken, is one of his best and most important works.*

Finitude and Evil *

As we set ourselves to consider what may be the place of evil in a world regarded as divinely created and divinely governed, it is worth while to remind ourselves at the outset of this possible subordination of evil to good. Indeed, if that were all that could be said, it would be sufficient to save Theism in principle, supposing that on other grounds it could establish itself. But that would leave us still without any real understanding of the place of evil in experience, and it is this which we must now try to reach.

We have two questions to consider, which may or may not turn out to be identical — the cause of evil, and the justification of its occurrence. First we must enquire how evil finds a place in the world-process as we have conceived it, and secondly, whether, when its origin is so understood, its occurrence is compatible with the belief that the world is created and ruled by a God who is both infinite Goodness and infinite Power.[1]

In the first stages of its existence the world exhibits neither life nor consciousness. At a certain point of its development life appears in rudimentary vegetable form. This life is void of consciousness. But again at a certain point in its development, life exhibits consciousness. Consciousness supervenes upon an organic existence which has already established a habitual routine. That routine includes the process in which one organism becomes food for another. If there is no consciousness, that cannot be called evil. If the organism that becomes the food of another is conscious, there is perhaps already evil in that combination of facts. But this seems less than certain; for the merely conscious organism lives in the present, and an extremely constricted present, so that consciousness perishes almost if not quite simultaneously with the occurrence of the event which in combination with continued consciousness would be evil.

* William Temple, *Nature, Man and God* (London: Macmillan & Company, Ltd., 1934), pp. 358–367. Used by permission of Mrs. Temple and the publishers.

[1] We are here concerned only with the former question. . . .

At this level then there is perhaps a very little evil, perhaps none at all. Bu once more at a certain stage in development consciousness becomes self-con sciousness. The organism is now not only conscious of its environment a offering occasions for satisfying appetite, or for flight from danger. It is nov conscious also of itself as distinct from its environment, and of possible state of itself as distinct from its actual state. It is . . . a self-distinguishing an self-seeking consciousness. Its time-span is increased. The "present" is now fo it a longer stretch of clock-time, and it has memory of a past and anticipatio of a future. Events now have value for it, and it is become a centre of value judgements.

As we look back we see that at any stage which we choose to isolate, prior t the human, there was a possible balance or harmony comprising the best pos sible good at that stage. It was in principle possible that each self-consciou organism should pursue its own interest in such ways that the good of lif should on the whole at least outweigh the evil. There seems to be no doub that life in the jungle is, on balance, good. The larger beasts must kill th smaller to maintain themselves; but though this involves for the smaller beast moments of terror, it seems clear from the accounts of naturalists that even fo them enjoyment of life is the prevailing tone or colour of experience. An though there is already some problem concerning the occurrence of any evi at all, yet at this level there is reason to be satisfied with a balance of goo over evil. That is not all that we have to say about it. But it is all that arise at this stage; and at this stage it is enough. For the stage at which evil may b taken up into good and made part of its own excellence is the stage of definit moral values. If life at the animal stage is good on the whole, then as a whol it is good, and no question of its justification arises. If later developments ap pear to offer a justification of the subordinate element of evil which it con tains, that is to be welcomed in the interest of a completely rational interpreta tion of the world; but even without it we can safely pronounce that the bes understanding we can frame of the animal world offers no obstacle to reasonable Theism.

It is with the advent of man that the problem assumes proportions so ove whelming. Mind, as known in man, early achieves a certain detachment fro its basis in the physical organism by its use of "free ideas." But it actuall holds these ideas by means of its capacity as imagination. The mind cann think without either percept or image. The use of the Figure in Geometry more than a convenience; it is a necessity. But it need not be drawn on pap or on a blackboard. It can be constructed in imagination. The mind is no strictly thinking about the Figure — the triangle ABC, for example; it is thin ing about the universal triangle; but it can only do this by means of a pa ticular triangle, taking care to avoid reference to any peculiarity of the parti ular triangle. Now imagination, just because it exists to offer particular in stances of general qualities, offers to desire the stimulus which the appropria physical objects offer to appetite. Hence comes a great, and in principle u limited, expansion of the life of desire, which initially functions only as e pressive of the vital needs of the organism or as stimulated by appropria objects in the physical environment. Desire as so expanded may take the for of aspiration or of lust. No doubt it always takes in fact both forms at first, and one way of expressing the purpose of educational discipline is to say that it aims at directing the whole force of desire away from lust towards aspiration. When this process is corrective rather than preventive it is commonly called "sublimation."

From these considerations it is clear that so far as Evil is a product of exaggerated or misdirected desire, the condition of its occurrence is identical with the condition that makes possible all the higher ranges of human life. The ancient Hebrews had ample justification for tracing sin to the "evil imagination." But to imagination also must be traced the possibility of all forms of distinctively human excellence. All depends on how it is used. To take up the thought of our earlier discussion of Freedom, all depends on the direction of attention; and this is largely within the mind's own control.

But this gives us rather the mechanism of evil as known in men than its mainspring. If the mind can control the direction of its attention, why does it so often give it a bad direction? It is easy to answer by attributing this to perversion or sin in the mind. But that hardly helps us. What is the source and nature of this perversion of mind? That any man ever chose evil, knowing it to be evil *for him,* is to me quite incredible. He may say, under an impulse of defiance, "Evil, be thou my good"; but his pursuit of it is then due to the fact that he has adopted it as his good and not because it is evil. To desire evil strictly for its own sake is impossible. To hate the human race so as to desire as good for one's self what is evil for all others, and even because it is evil for all others, is possible; but this evil for others is still desired as supposedly good for him who desires it.

In other words, a man is governed by what effectively appears good to him, which we shall henceforth term "the apparent good." And what appears good depends on the condition of his mind. It is not a reflective judgement with which we are now concerned. No one, probably, *thinks* cruelty good — certainly not as a general proposition, and hardly in a particular instance. Yet men do cruel things; they do them because at the moment those things appear good through gratification of some lust for self-assertion, or through their power to allay some panic fear. A man's character determines his apparent good at any moment; his apparent good determines his conduct.

If this process is working out to a bad result it is because the apparent good is not the real good. Sometimes it is possible to change the apparent good by setting beside it some presentation of the real good. There are many who habitually gain control of evil desires by turning their attention to the Figure of Christ, in contrast with which the object of the evil desire appears no longer good but abhorrent. Sometimes again it is possible to think out the full implication of what presents itself as good, and to see that taken in its real completeness it is bad. But as a rule the real good will be impotent against the apparent good unless it can be made equally apparent; and this means that it must be presented to the mind in some form apprehensible by the senses or in imagination. A man may know as a matter of general principle that stealing is not only wrong but bad — bad, that is, for him. But if he sufficiently desires an object that is within his grasp, he may none the less take it unless there is also before him the sorrow of the person robbed, or the penalty which he is likely to bring upon himself. Most of us have been able to master our covetousness of possessions sufficiently to be free from these temptations. The force of temptation is more felt in the region of bodily appetites, or of personal resentments, or of professional or commercial ambition, or of political sentiment. But the principle is the same. There may be a genuine apprehension of the true good in conceptual form; but this will not prevail against the vivid attraction of an apparent good unless it is presented in a form that is as effectively apparent. Imagination is usually the connecting link between thought and volition, and if the apparent good is to be changed otherwise than by conversion of the character, it must chiefly be through the occupation of the imagination with the things — and the relevant things — that are "pure, honourable and of good report."

But we have not yet come to the heart of the problem. Why is there a difference between the apparent and the real good? or, to put the question more usefully, why are we such that what appears to us good is other than the real good? For there is here an unquestionable bias or tendency to evil in human nature. Theologians have called this Original Sin; and if those words mean that every human being has in one respect or another such a bias or tendency to evil, they do not stand for a mysterious doctrine but for an evident and vitally important fact. Our task is to relate that fact to belief in the divine government of the world; but it will assist us if we first enquire further into the ground of the fact in human nature and its place in the world process as our argument has led us to envisage this.

The point which here concerns us is this. Mind arises within the world process as one of its episodes; but it is a peculiar episode in two ways. First, it is peculiar because it is able to take the process in which it occurs within the embrace of its awareness and its comprehension. Viewed from one standpoint, a man is a trifling occurrence — a midget breathing and moving for a brief span in one corner of a universe overwhelmingly vast. Viewed from another standpoint, he is himself the master of that universe, able to comprehend it as it can never comprehend him, and bending the mighty forces of nature to serve his purposes. He tames the force of lightning, turning it on and off with a switch. He regulates the waves of ether, bidding them carry accounts of his very games round the globe. To his lightest whim the august energy of Nature must be subservient. There may be rational minds domiciled in other planets, or in stars and nebulae. On the planet called Earth such minds have appeared, and their achievements make even the suns look small. That is one way in which Mind is peculiar as an episode in the world process.

The other, which more concerns us now, is this. Till Mind appeared as an episode in the world process, all other episodes had value in potentiality only, not in actuality — so far at least as the process itself supplied the condition of its actualisation. In the sight of God, and it may be also of spirits other than those born in the world process, that process and its episodes had value. But with the coming of minds there came also for the first time episodes within the process supplying to other episodes the condition for the actualisation of their value. Here, even more than in the impressive achievements lately enumerated, is the supreme peculiarity and distinction of mind. *The human mind is a focus of appreciation. It has knowledge of good and evil. The winning of that knowledge is called the Fall of Man, because acts, which before he won it were merely instinctive reactions to environment, become through that knowledge sins against the light. Again, because they are done against the light, they are done with a new degree of self-assertion. And, once more, because imagination is so potent to stimulate desire, there is an additional impulse to those acts. Man in so far as he is evil is worse than any animal; and in every man there is the bias or tendency to evil.* We are now in a position to track this to its source.

Mind, as it occurs as an episode in the world-process, takes the form of finite minds. It is indeed confined within extremely narrow limitations. It cannot attain to any grasp of the true proportions and perspective of the world in which it is set. Certain things have a value for it and are its apparent good. There is no inherent and absolute necessity for this to be other than the real good; yet the probability of divergence is so great as to amount to certainty for all practical purposes. The finite, and indeed very narrowly limited, mind appreciates the gigantic fact of good and evil. But its limitations hinder it from apprehending the full significance of these, or the true nature of the various objects which present themselves as apparent goods. *The mind by a necessary tendency of its own nature attaches more importance to values which find their actualisation in itself than to those which find it elsewhere; or to put it crudely, each man cares more about what seems to be good for him than about goods which he does not expect personally to enjoy. Even so far as he knows of these, they take a second place for him; and about many of them he knows nothing. So he becomes not only the subject of his own value judgements, which he can never cease to be, but also the centre and criterion of his own system of values, which he is quite unfit to be.*

Accordingly, as man rose above sub-human forms of life through the development of mind within his psychophysical organism as an increasingly dominant factor, he found himself self-centred. The animal also is self-centred. But in the animal this is an innocent state, because it is merely a given fact of nature; the animal self does not compare its actual condition with a conceived or imagined ideal; it is a consciousness but not a "self-distinguishing and self-seeking consciousness." Consequently it is self-centred without being self-assertive. But as soon as consciousness advances to full self-consciousness, so that the self, distinguishing itself from its environment, not only chooses what appetites it shall satisfy but even what ends it shall pursue, self-centredness becomes self-assertion. The good-for-self is alone effectively apparent good, and good in a fuller sense, though recognised to be real, is relatively powerless as motive. It is not utterly necessary that this should be so; and therefore it is not true to say that God made man selfish, or predestined him to sin. But that it should be so was "too probable not to happen"; and it is true to say that God so made the world that man was likely to sin, and the dawn of moral self-consciousness was likely to be more of a "fall" than an ascent. Human sin was not a necessary episode in the divine plan; but was always so closely implicated in the divine plan that it must be held to fall within the divine purpose. To the problem thus presented we must return at a later stage.

The individual members of human society are not mutually exclusive atoms of consciousness. Each is a partly self-determining, self-integrating system of experience; but the content of that experience is derived from environment. The part of that content with which we are now concerned is derived from social environment. We are, in part, reciprocally determining beings. We make each other what we are. Therefore the existence of one self-centred soul would spread an evil infection through all who come within its range of influence. This happens both positively by suggestion and negatively by repulsion. If A is self-centred, B tends to become so by imitation; but also B becomes so in self-defence. The instincts of gregariousness and of fear combine to produce the same result. And this process continues, so that A and B perpetually develop their own and one another's self-centredness. Actual human society is to a large extent, though never completely, that network of competing selfishnesses, all kept in check by each one's selfish fear of the others, which Glaucon describes in Plato's *Republic* and which Hobbes made the basis of his political philosophy in the *Leviathan*.

This may, perhaps, be called an evolutionary account of the origin of moral evil. But it must be sharply distinguished from any theory of moral evil which accounts for it by reference to a survival of animal impulses into the rational stage of development. The centre of trouble is not the turbulent appetites, though they are troublesome enough, and the human faculty for imagination increases their turbulence. But the centre of trouble is the personality as a whole, which is self-centred and can only be wholesome and healthy if it is God-centred. This whole personality in action is the will; and it is the will which is perverted. Our primary need is not to control our passions by our purpose, but to direct our purpose itself to the right end. It is the form taken by our knowledge of good and evil that perverts our nature. We know good and evil, but know them amiss. We take them into our lives, but we mis-take them. The corruption is at the centre of rational and purposive life.

C. J. Ducasse

Professor Curt John Ducasse was born in 1881 in Angoulême, France, and became a naturalized citizen of the United States in 1910. A Fellow of the American Academy of Arts and Sciences, he was President of the American Philosophical Association in 1939, and is an emeritus professor of Brown University.

In the following passage, from one of his later works, he considers the problem of evil in relation to theism, taking the view that moral goodness, being definable without reference to the ways in which it may come to be possessed, could be bestowed by an omnipotent God. On this view the traditional Christian explanation of the relation between human lack of goodness and the omnipotence of God would fall.

The Problem of Evil and Some Attempted Solutions *

. . . If men and all other things in the world were created by an omnipotent, omniscient, and infinitely good God, then, because omniscient, he knew *ab initio* that there would be evil in the kind of world he was creating; because omnipotent, he could have prevented this evil and indeed could eliminate it even now; and, because perfectly good, he would not have willed to create the kind of world in which evil would exist, and he would not now allow it to persist. Yet evil is rampant on earth.

As so stated, the problem is evidently an intellectual, and more specifically a theoretical, problem, which arises at all only if one assumes *ab initio* that a God of the kind described exists and created the world. Without such an initial assumption, the existence of evil would no more give rise to a contradiction than would the existence of good or of anything else in particular. What would remain would be only the *practical* problem of evil, namely, what to do about the evil that exists — how to eliminate it or at least minimize it. *This* is the "problem of evil" in, for instance, Buddhism; or in Zoroastrianism, which conceives its god, Ahura Mazda, as limited in power and as engaged in struggle with its devil, Angra Mainyu — a struggle in which man can participate by aligning himself, as he chooses, with one side or the other. For contemporary Humanism too, which, being naturalistic, rejects orthodox monotheism, the only "problem of evil" is the purely practical one of doing whatever may be possible to remedy particular evils.

The theologians of orthodox monotheism have expended vast ingenuity on the attempt to dispose of the *prima facie* contradiction which constitutes their problem of evil. We shall consider some of the chief solutions of it which have

* C. J. Ducasse, *Philosophical Scrutiny of Religion* (New York: The Ronald Press Company, 1953), pp. 352–365. Used by permission.

been proposed. But we cannot judge of their merits with confidence unless we are first thoroughly clear as to what the words "evil" and "evils" denote.

What Evil Is

When we say of a medicine that it has an *evil* taste, what we mean is plainly that its taste is *unpleasant*. That the taste is evil in this sense to the person who is experiencing it is an absolute fact; that is, it is a fact no matter what the medicine may happen to consist of; no matter whether the unpleasantness of the taste to him is native or acquired; no matter whether the unpleasantness is permanent or disappears after habituation; no matter whether the medicine which has the evil taste is or is not a good remedy for whatever may be ailing him; and no matter also whether or not the memory of the unpleasantness of the taste of the cure, added to the unpleasantness of the ailment itself, eventually leads him to avoid the kind of occasion which caused the ailment and thus makes him a wiser man.

In the light of this example, we may introduce certain terms, the use of which is indispensable for clarity in any discussion of evil and of its opposite, good. The first of those terms is "intrinsically evil" or "an intrinsic evil." By speaking of a taste itself, for instance, or of any other immediate experience itself, as *intrinsically evil*, we shall mean simply that *it is found unpleasant in greater or lesser degree by the experiencing person*. If on the contrary he finds it pleasant, then we shall speak of it as intrinsically good or as an intrinsic good.

Further, wherever in the sequel we use the word "pain," we shall not mean by it, as do psychologists, a particular *sensory quality*, which, although generally unpleasant, may when of low intensity be mildly pleasant.[1] We shall instead take the word "pain" in its ordinary, nontechnical sense of *strong unpleasantness*. That is, by a "painful" experience, we shall mean one that is strongly unpleasant, whether perhaps not more so than a scratch or pin prick, or perhaps as much so as what would be called torture, bodily or mental.

Keeping in mind that to speak of an experience as intrinsically evil is to say that it is unpleasant or painful to the person having it, we then see that no contradiction is involved in supposing that, for a given person or perhaps for others, it is sometimes a *good* thing that he should have a particular *intrinsically evil* experience; for it means only that the fact of his having it, will, for himself or others, have or contribute to *consequences* which ultimately are intrinsically good. In such a case we shall say that the experience, although intrinsically evil (or perhaps even because intrinsically evil) is nonetheless *instrumentally good*.

This, of course, leaves wholly open the question whether the instrumental goodness of it is great enough, or on the contrary too small, to outweigh its intrinsic evilness; or, if on the contrary the experience is intrinsically good, whether its intrinsic goodness is great enough, or too small, to outweigh such instrumental evilness as it may have.

It goes without saying that a given experience may well be *both* intrinsically

[1] See E. B. Titchener, *Textbook of Psychology* (New York: The Macmillan Co., 1909), Part I, p. 115; or H. C. Warren and L. Carmichael, *Elements of Human Psychology* (Boston: Houghton Mifflin Co., 1930), p. 134.

and instrumentally evil; or *both* intrinsically and instrumentally good. In the majority of cases, however, an experience, or the situation which causes it, has a variety of consequences, some of them evil and some of them good. And the experience itself, if it is complex, may have both pleasant and unpleasant characters; for example, in the immediate experience generated by tasting a certain substance, the gustatory component of the experience might be pleasant but the olfactory component unpleasant.

These remarks make evident that the immediate experiences we call suffering, discomfort, pain, aches, anguish, misery, distress, unhappiness, pangs, uneasiness, etc., all of which are unpleasant whether intensely or mildly, are in so far evils — *intrinsic evils;* that whatever states of affairs cause or contribute to cause them are in so far evils — *instrumental evils,* i.e., sources of evil; and that those immediate experiences themselves, in so far as their consequences happen to be evil, are *instrumental evils* too, in addition to being intrinsic evils. The qualification, "in so far," is called for by the fact pointed out above that experiences, their causes, and their effects, have in most cases both some good and some evil features.

Of course, persons too — their dispositions, their thoughts, their feelings, their habits, their acts — are capable of being evil; but their evilness is analyzable in the terms already defined. The act of punishing a much loved child is painful — is an intrinsic evil — to the parent doing it; and experiencing the punishment is, for the child, also an intrinsic evil. Yet the act, performed as it is for the sake of its contributing to mold the child's moral character, can, if done intelligently, be instrumentally good. The forms of action called evil — lying, stealing, cheating, getting drunk, killing, and so on — are so because, under normal circumstances, they tend directly or indirectly to cause far more suffering than happiness. If drunkenness, for instance, in addition to such intrinsic pleasantness as it has, had regularly the effect of making the drunkard healthy instead of sick, and caused him to act intelligently and wisely instead of stupidly and disastrously, then drunkenness would be not a vice but a virtue. The kinds of thoughts or feelings commonly ranked as evil are those which, whether in themselves pleasant or unpleasant, tend to express themselves in courses of action generally productive of evil, that is, of gratuitous suffering. Evil dispositions or habits are those which predispose one to react in evil ways to given kinds of situations. And a person is evil in so far as his dispositions, habits, attitudes, moods, feelings, thoughts, or impulses are evil in the senses stated.

Four Classes of Evils

When one attempts to classify the evils to which sentient beings are subject, what are called *physical evils* are probably the first to suggest themselves. They comprise all the pains and discomforts which arise from disease, from accidents, or from duress upon the body — headaches, toothaches, neuralgias; the pains of cancer, of arthritis, of wounds, of bruises, broken bones, burns; of heat, cold, thirst, hunger; of exhausting labor; and so on. Some persons whether by virtue of an exceptionally healthy constitution, or by the exercise of intelligence, or by good fortune, live from birth to death with but little of any of those pains; whereas others are plagued with a long succession of them.

A second group of evils are those we may call *psychological evils*. They include the sufferings due to unrequited love; to separation from, or death of, the beloved; to anxiety, fear, frustration, loneliness; and to other unhappy psychological states not traceable to causes in or accidents to the body of the suffering person, nor to vices in him or wickedness in others.

Mention of vice and wickedness brings us to a third group — that of *moral evils*. They comprise all defects of moral character — traits such as malice, hatred, greed, jealousy, selfishness, cruelty, intemperance, and so on, which automatically tend to cause suffering to the persons who have them or to others.

Lastly, there are *intellectual evils* — stupidity, irrationality, insanity, poor judgment, defective perception, and the errors or ignorance these breed, which prevent a person from dealing effectively with many of the situations he faces.

Metaphysical Evil

The philosopher Leibniz, whose *Theodicy* gave currency to this name for treatises attempting to reconcile the existence of evil with the justice of God (*θεός*, God, + *δίκη*, justice), distinguishes three kinds of evil — metaphysical, physical, and moral. Physical evil, he says, consists in suffering. Moral evil he conceives in theological terms, as "sin," but we have seen that moral evil can be defined, less questionably, in terms purely of what observation and reason discloses; and that if this is done, the things termed sins, when they really are evil, are so simply in virtue of the suffering intrinsic to them, or of the sufferings they naturally tend to bring about, or in virtue of both of these together.

By "metaphysical" evil, Leibniz means the fact that finiteness, limitation, is an absolute condition of the existence of any world at all. Only God himself can be infinite, unlimited, perfect; hence, if anything besides God is to exist at all, it necessarily has to be limited, imperfect. It has to contain at least the minimum of evil which the inherent finiteness of created beings automatically entails. As Leibniz puts it, "there is an original imperfection in the creature before sin, because the creature is limited essentially, and hence could not know everything and may make mistakes and commit other faults . . . metaphysical evil consists simply in imperfection, physical evil in suffering, and moral evil in sin."[2]

Leibniz thus does not argue that there is really no evil, or not much evil in the world; but only that there is no more of it than follows necessarily from the finiteness of anything other than God himself. It is this which he means when he asserts that everything is for the best in the best of all possible worlds — an optimism which, as often has been pointed out, is quite compatible with the assertion of pessimists, or of merely realists, that the best of all possible worlds is then a pretty bad world.

Evidently, "metaphysical evil" is not really the name of another category of evil besides the four we have mentioned; it is only the name of the explana-

[2] Gottfried Wilhelm von Leibniz, "Théodicée, Essais sur la Bonté de Dieu et la Liberté de l'Homme," *Oeuvres de Leibniz* (Paris: Charpentier, 1842), §§20, 21.

tion Leibniz offers for the fact that evil, of whatever kind, exists notwithstanding the goodness of God, and notwithstanding God's power to create any possible world.

Commenting on Leibniz's assertion that the world which actually exists is the best that was possible, Schopenhauer contends that, on the contrary, "the world . . . is as bad as it possibly can be if it is to continue to be at all." He argues that if planetary disturbances, volcanic cataclysms, corruptions of the atmosphere, abnormalities of temperature, defects in the organization of living things, and so on, were even a little worse than they actually are, this earth and everything on it would perish. "Even of the human race," he says, "powerful as are the weapons it possesses in understanding and reason, nine tenths live in constant conflict with want, always balancing themselves with difficulty and effort upon the brink of destruction. Thus, throughout, as for the continuance of the whole, so also for that of each individual being, the conditions are barely and scantily given, but nothing more . . . this world is so arranged as to be able to maintain itself with great difficulty; but if it were a little worse, it could no longer maintain itself. Consequently a worse world, since it could not continue to exist, is absolutely impossible; thus this world is the worst of all possible worlds."[3]

No doubt, it is Schopenhauer's temperament, rather than any cool survey of facts, which speaks in these words. But Leibniz's optimism is hardly more objective. That finiteness necessarily entails evil, or as much evil as actually exists, is very far from evident, especially when, as we have done, one has purged the notion of evil of the vagueness, the ambiguities, and the resultant *quid pro quo*'s, which commonly infest it. For one then sees that finiteness or limitation, such as is inherent in man's being man at all, is not automatically an evil. It is so only when it is a source of pain. But men and other sentient beings, though finite, are free from pain during the many moments, hours, or days of their lives when their bodily and other limited capacities are yet adequate to deal felicitously with the tasks or situations that happen to come their ways. And such suitability of equipment to environment, or of environment to equipment, could, by an omnipotent God, have been made universal instead of only occasional.

Additional light will be thrown on the whole subject if we now examine the notion of *possibility* and its implications as to what it would be or have been possible or impossible for an omnipotent God to create.

Omnipotence, the Possible, and the Impossible

We need here first to distinguish between logical and natural possibility or impossibility.

That is *logically* impossible, the program of which contains a contradiction whether explicit or implicit. Any such program is automatically self-canceling; i.e., is really no program at all, since to say that it contains a contradiction means that it forbids what it prescribes and prescribes what it forbids. For

[3] Arthur Schopenhauer, *The World as Will and Idea*, trans. R. B. Haldane and J. Kemp (London: Kegan Paul, 1906), Vol. III, pp. 395–396.

example, to speak and at the same time not speak; or to be, in the very same respect and by the same standard, at once good and not good; or finite and not finite; or free and not free; or wise and not wise; etc., are programs logically impossible — self-nullifying — which, because they are thus pseudo-programs, neither man nor God can carry out or satisfy. Hence God is not omnipotent if "omnipotent" means capable of doing even the *logically* impossible.

On the contrary, that is *possible within Nature,* the program of which is not only free from contradictions, but also does not require that the "laws of Nature," i.e., the properties of whatever Nature comprises, be other than what they actually are.

Since the question now in view concerns what is or is not naturally possible *to God,* or *to man,* "Nature" has to be taken, not as inclusive of *all* that exists, but as comprising *whatever confronts a given purposive being, human or divine.* Hence, since a given purposive being is confronted not only by the inanimate parts of Nature but also by the other purposive beings that exist, Nature will have a slightly different content for each. This means that the question as to what is and is not possible within Nature is a "systematically ambiguous" one. That is, the answer to it is essentially relative to specification of some particular purposive being, and of the powers he happens to possess or lack; for obviously, what would be possible for one person to do might be impossible to another whose powers were different.

Now to say that a given man has a certain power P means that, under circumstances and with implements of given kinds, volition by him to make some event E occur is immediately or mediately sufficient to cause occurrence of E. For example, given the properties in fact possessed by ink, by pens, and by paper; also the fact that I now have at hand pen, ink and paper; also the fact that my arm is not now paralyzed; etc., then I now have the power to write: writing is one of the things it is now *naturally possible* for me to do at will. Obviously, many other things are in the corresponding sense *naturally impossible* to me; i.e., I do not have unlimited power — omnipotence — within Nature.

The God of orthodox monotheism, on the contrary, is conceived as having omnipotence in the very sense just described, not only *within* Nature, but in addition *over* Nature, in the sense that he can at will alter, or make exceptions to, the laws of now existing Nature; whereas men cannot do this, but can accomplish their purposes *only through discovery of those laws and application of them.* Thus, what is "naturally possible" to man means what, with the powers he has, he can do *within the kind of "Nature" which actually exists.* But what is "naturally possible" to an omnipotent God includes not only what he, with his complete knowledge of the laws of this particular kind of "Nature," could do within it by applying them; but includes also creating or having created *a different kind of "Nature"* — a world whose constituent objects and beings would behave according to laws, i.e., would have properties and capacities, as *different as he pleased from those which obtain in the present kind of world;* provided only that, in the program of a different such world, no logical contradiction was contained.

Because power *over* Nature as well as *within* Nature is thus an intrinsic part of the power of an omnipotent creator, it is far from evident either that the finiteness of any possible world necessarily entails existence in it of as much evil as there is in the present world, or indeed of any evil at all.

Some Attempted Solutions of the Problem

Let us now consider the chief forms which have been taken by attempts to dispose of the contradiction between the existence of evil and existence of a God having the attributes which orthodox monotheism postulates.

One proposed solution consists in denying that any evil at all really exists — in saying that evil only appears to exist, that in reality it is only an illusion, and that to believe it exists is an error.

This would-be solution of the problem has in our days gained a certain popularity in some of the neoreligions, but its naïveté becomes obvious as soon as one asks whether illusions and errors are themselves goods or on the contrary evils. Of course, only one answer is possible. Hence what this purported refutation of the existence of evil really does is only to mention one particular kind of evil — namely, illusion, error, delusion, false belief — and to assert that *all* evil is of that special kind. But even if it were true that all evil is of a single kind, the fact would remain that a toothache, for instance, or migraine, or neuralgia, and so on, *hurts*, is *painful*, that is, is intrinsically evil; and this no matter what particular names, such as "illusion" or "false belief" one may please to tag it with, and no matter also whether illusion or error should happen to be what generates the pain.

Conceivably, of course, migraine or any particular other pain might be exorcisable simply by calling it names — for instance by calling it "illusion" — or curable by dispelling the illusion which, supposedly, generated it. But even if this were feasible, to point it out would not be to show that there *are* no toothaches, headaches or neuralgia, but only to show that the world is less evil than it would be if these and other pains were beyond the possibility of cure.

These remarks apply equally to the variant of the purported solution just considered which, instead of saying that evil is an illusion, asserts that evil is "purely negative" — that it is nothing positive but only the absence of good; for however this may be, the fact remains that migraine and other such ailments do occur and are painful.

Another contention sometimes met with is that certain things which, if taken by themselves, would be evil, do, because they are in fact parts in an inclusive whole, actually enhance the good of the whole. The standard illustration is the fact that certain discords, skillfully woven into a musical composition, may give it greater beauty than it would have if it were free from them. Or again, a sharp condiment, such as red pepper, may enhance the taste of a dish in which it is present, although, if tasted by itself, it would be unpleasant. This, one is told, is exactly the situation as regards the evils of the world. Man, presumptuously and invalidly, views them in isolation from the whole in which they are the enhancing discords or condiments; but God, who apprehends the whole at once, perceives that they contribute to make it better than it otherwise would be. Indeed, it has even been maintained that a part of the bliss of the elect in paradise consists in the joy of beholding the damned writhing eternally in hell — a joy of which their heavenly happiness would be short if there were no wicked to be damned.

The obvious comment on this proposed solution of the problem of evil is that even if the evils in the world make it better as perceived from God's point of view, they make it worse as perceived from man's point of view. And there *is* such a point of view as man's. To call it invalid, arbitrary, presumptuous, or by other condemnatory names does not enable man to surrender it and to take up God's point of view instead. To tell someone that although *he* happens to be having a raging toothache, nevertheless somebody else, whether called God or John Doe, does not suffer from it — or even that it adds to the value of what that other person beholds — might conceivably be telling him something true. But still the man with the toothache is neither God nor John Doe but only himself; and he exists; and he is in pain.

Another consideration of which much is often made is that many evils are really blessings in disguise; that is, that although in themselves they are evils, yet in the more or less long run they work for good, and often for good far outweighing the evils which brought it about. William Blake, for instance, has among his Proverbs of Hell one to the effect that if the fool but persists in his folly, he eventually becomes wise. Again, it has been argued that private vices, or at least certain of them, redound to the public benefit. And again, although, as Franklin remarked, experience is a dear school but fools will learn in no other, yet the fact remains that they do learn in it, so that, if their run is long enough, they become wise.

On the other hand, the common saying that there is no fool like an old fool indicates that sometimes the fool's run is too short for him to harvest the golden wisdom his folly would otherwise have brought him. Thus, not all evils are blessings in disguise. Many appear to be completely unmitigated; and, that they are not really so but ultimately have redeeming good fruits is not in the least shown by pious phrases as to the mysteriousness of God's ways. Moreover, although some evils do turn out to have been blessings in disguise, so, equally, do some blessings turn out to have been evils in disguise.

But even if it should somehow be true that all evils ultimately work for good, and for good great enough to outweigh the evil that was the means to it, even then all that would be true would be that the world is less evil than it would be if evils never bred goods but only further evils.

Finally — and this is the crucial point — that wisdom is gained only by learning from mistakes; or, more sweepingly, that often the good which man does is done only at the cost of some suffering — that is, by means intrinsically evil even if instrumentally good; this state of affairs, let it be noted, is due to the fact that man has to use such means as are left at his disposal by the limitations of his intelligence, of his knowledge, and of his equipment; and by the particular positions in which he finds himself at given times. But, as already pointed out, the means open within Nature to an omnipotent and omniscient God would be free from these limitations. Nor would such a God be bound as man is to work by applying the laws of existing Nature, since he would have the power to change them or to make as many exceptions to them as he pleased. Such a God could make all men be born with the sound constitution, the resistance to disease, the intelligence, and the other precious native endowments which now only a few have. He could confer on man at the start the wisdom and the virtue which now — with luck — a man gains only in the end and only at the price of blood, sweat and tears. For it is *not* true, as some have contended, that moral goodness could not be created as such or implanted by God in his creatures, but has, by its very nature, to be earned.[4] The nature of moral goodness can be defined wholly without reference to the way or ways in which it may come to be possessed; hence, that it could not possibly be bestowed but must be earned cannot be deduced from its nature, and is not true. What is true is only that no *man* can implant it ready-made into another man, so that, as the world and men are actually constituted and placed, each has to earn it for himself. An omnipotent God, however, could have conferred it on all men.

[4] Cf. P. Bertocci, *The Empirical Argument for God* (Cambridge: Harvard University Press, 1938), p. 260.

Bruce Marshall

Bruce Marshall was born in Edinburgh in 1899. After serving in the British Army in World War I, during which he was seriously wounded, he became an accountant in Paris, where he lived for many years before the writing of novels such as Father Malachy's Miracle, The World, the Flesh and Father Smith, *and* Vespers in Vienna *brought him international fame, including the Wlodomiertz Pietrzak Prize from Poland. His liturgical sense together with his generous human sympathies give his novels a peculiar flavor of earthiness touched by the hand of God. Attention was drawn to the theological importance of* Father Malachy's Miracle *in 1951, in Geddes MacGregor's* Christian Doubt, *and, more recently, in the fourth volume of Karl Barth's* opus maximum, Kirchliche Dogmatik.

The excerpts selected here are from The World, the Flesh and Father Smith, *whose hero is a Roman Catholic priest in a Scottish slum. The scene opens with Father Smith serving as a wartime chaplain in the front line. These passages are selected to illustrate an aspect of the stark reality of the problem of evil and the moral force of the solution provided in Christian faith and life.*

"All Glorious Within" *

When at length they moved off, Father Smith found himself side by side with the boozy major, but at first they didn't talk much, perhaps because the night was so beautiful. The marching men looked beautiful, too, with their rows and rows of heads going on and on. From time to time they sang the secular psalms that seemed to soothe their spirit: "There's a long, long trail awinding into the land of my dreams"; "You called me baby doll a year ago; you told me I was very nice to know"; "At seventeen he falls in love quite madly with eyes of a tender blue." Although he knew that there was no harm in the songs, Father Smith could not help feeling how very much more appropriate it would have been if they had sung psalms like the nuns sang, especially since they were fighting a righteous war. To cheer himself he began singing to himself under his breath, "Montes exultaverunt ut arietes: et colles sicut agni ovium"; but somehow the words didn't rhyme to the rumble of "We are Fred Karno's army," and he gave it up. Instead, he let his thoughts slide along in lazy images and speculations. How very wonderful it would be, he thought, if he were to win the Military Cross. And the Distinguished Service Order. And the Victoria Cross. The colonel wouldn't ask him where the hell he'd been then. The colonel would respect him then. And the Bishop,

* Bruce Marshall, *The World, the Flesh and Father Smith* (Boston: Houghton Mifflin Company, 1944), pp. 71–79, 117–122. Used by permission.

how pleased the old man would be! And the nuns and Monsignor O'Duffy and Father Bonnyboat and all his parishioners. The send-off he got at the station would be as nothing compared with the welcome which he would receive at the same station when he arrived back with the three bright ribbons on his breast. They'd all be there to meet him and the Town Council as well, and the nuns' eyes would be shining, and Monsignor O'Duffy would wave his huge red handkerchief in the air and cry: "My lord Bishop and folks, I now have great pleasure in calling upon ye all for to give three cheers for that great hero, the Reverend Father Thomas Edmund Smith, V.C., D.S.O., M.C." Then with haste he chased the picturing from his mind, for he knew it to be sinful, because pride had made him seek honour and glory in dreams and because such visionings multiplied by a million produced much of the world's misery. He reminded himself of how he had vowed at his ordination that he would never seek advancement or preferment, but would be Christ's doormat all the days of his life. This oath he now repeated silently within himself. A great happiness rose in him because he knew again what Jesus had meant when He said, "He who loseth his life shall find it."

"I say, Father, do you mind if I ask you a rather theological question?" the boozy major suddenly asked. "Tell me: is it a sin to kiss a girl at a dance when you've no intention of proposing marriage to her?"

"That all depends on how the kissing's done," Father Smith answered.

"In other words, a chap mustn't get too much of a kick out of it?"

"I'm afraid not."

"That's what's laid down in the rubrics, is it?" The major didn't seem to expect an answer, for he added: "I must say, God's a bit hard on a chap at times. Still, in spite of what you say, I'm sure God's too much of a Sahib to run a fellow in for ever and ever just because he got messed up with a bit of fluff."

They didn't talk much after that, but Father Smith thought over what the major had said. Perhaps the major was right. Perhaps God didn't take the genial sins too seriously. After all, malice was necessary for the commission of mortal sin, and the majority of men who drank to excess and ran wild with the girls were at bottom decent fellows. Lying, cheating, stealing, underpaying employees, money-grubbing, and mouthing big phrases to hide little thoughts — these were the sins that cried to God for punishment, since they harmed others more than their perpetrators. And yet being a decent fellow wasn't enough. The practice of a more heroic virtue was required if society as well as the individual was to be saved; but now that men had learned to be heroic in war, perhaps they would learn to be heroic in peace. Father Smith hoped that they would. The glow of the stars on the helmets of the marching men made them look very beautiful and austere. The crunch, crunch, crunch, of their feet beat the priest's hope into certainty. After all, they were brave men and brave men could not possibly go back to the old cowardice. "Beatus vir qui timet Dominum," Father Smith murmured, and this time found no difficulty in going on with the psalm.

They were to attack at dawn three mornings later. Father Smith said Mass at three o'clock in the major's dugout. He wore the vestments which Mother de la Tour had embroidered for him. Cloth of gold on one side, because cloth of gold could be used on all feasts and ferial days, and black on the other, because there were always requiems to be said, with so many poor fellows being killed.

Most of the Catholics in the battalion came to Mass and holy communion. Father Smith heard their confessions first, because they hadn't all been as good as they should have been, what with the red wine in the estaminets and the girls and all that. As there were almost fifty of them, the priest had to start in quite early — at one-thirty, to be precise — which left only two minutes for each confession, so that mortal sins came spurting out at a fine rate and were as quickly polished off. The priest wanted to begin by hearing the boozy major's confession, but the major said that if Father Smith didn't mind he'd very much rather bat last, because there was no saying how many more sins he could commit in ninety minutes. So Father Smith sat on his packing cases and heard the old, old tales of human frailty, and the major was last man in, and he wasn't so very original either, but perhaps that was because he had scarcely had much opportunity since his last confession three days previously: bless him, Father, for he had sinned, and last morning at stand-to he had been dreaming that he had been talking to a pretty girl in green silk pantaloons and a blighter of a sergeant major had woken him up, and when he had gone back to sleep, he had tried to dream about her again because she really was a corker, bless him, Father, with eyes that were blue one moment and violet the next.

The priest used the packing case he had been sitting on to hear confessions for his altar, with his portable altar stone and two candles and a crucifix. As he turned and saw in the blur of the candlelight the men's stern faces sweetly praying, he knew that this was how Mass should always be said, in a great hush and near death. There was no bell to ring at the Sanctus, so the major beat a teaspoon against a tin mug and it sounded quite holy. It sounded even holier at the Elevation, with Christ again in the Host and trembling in the shadows of the wine. Praying on above the mystery, Father Smith thanked the great good God for this one safe sure little miracle which He had promised would endure for ever, that men might be drawn from their sins and fastened to the bright things of heaven. Then he was down among them, giving them communion, thrusting God under their roofs, that they might be cleansed from the great stinking abomination of the world and know Him again when He smiled at them in paradise.

Too soon was the magic over and the world back again with stark immediate things to be done. As soon as he had unvested, Father Smith went out to make his thanksgiving among the cold piled sandbags. As he stood on the parapet praying out across the invisible grasses, the sky began to lighten and the priest knew that it would soon be dawn. Slowly the blue was draining from the sky and the stars were going out and the earth hardening out again flat and unmysterious from its crenellation of huddle and hill.

Father Smith looked at the sentry standing a few feet away from him and wondered if he was being afraid to die. Then as the darkness lessened the man's aspect grew familiar, and with a start the priest recognized Angus McNab.

"Angus, my boy, what on earth are you doing here?" the priest cried.

"Heavens, Father Smith!" the young man exclaimed. "I never kent that it was you was the R.C. padre. I only got back two days ago. Been back in Blighty for three months. Got a nice little packet in the airm. Nothing much really, just a flesh wound, but enough to keep me out of this sort of thing, thank God."

The young man's tone and bearing frightened the priest.

"Angus, what's come over you?" he asked. "Why were you not at confession and holy communion just now?"

"Och, hell, Father, don't let's talk about religion if you don't mind," Angus said.

"My son, that's no way to speak to your old parish priest," Father Smith said sternly. "And we *are* going to talk about religion, because religion's the only thing that's really worth talking about, and you know that every bit as well as I do." He looked into the young man's eyes and away down the years back to when the boy had been his acolyte and had freckles on his nose and sometimes a dirty smudge round his mouth. "Angus, Angus, who's been getting at you?" he asked.

"Nobody's been getting at me, Father," the young man said. "I just ken that religion's all havers, that's all. And the people at home are all havers, too. They pretend to care an awful lot about what happens to us puir sods out here, but they don't really, not deep down in their hearts they dinna. They sing an awful lot about keeping the hame fires burning and loving you and kissing you when you come back again, but it's only words. All they want is to stay at hame and be safe and have a good time. I ken because I've been on sick leave, and the folks didn't want to listen at all to what I had to tell them about things out here at the front. I ken because their eyes got empty and they were awa' off talking about something else before I'd finished speaking. And when I got on the tram with my sair airm in a great muckle splint and a yelly plaister, the auld bitches let on they didna see me, but sat on their great muckle doups clavering away about the price of tea and Mary Pickford and me with ma puir sticking-oot airm getting in everybody's way and nearly being cowped every time the tram turned a corner like. And the young lassies were just as bad. Christians! yon's no Christians! And it's for the likes o' them that I'm expected to hae me belly blawn oot aboot ma heid and to die a sair, sair death." He suddenly clutched the priest. "Father, Father, make them stop it. Make them no make me go over again. Father, Father, I'm that feared."

The priest let the boy weep a little, because he knew that tears, if they flowed long enough, could float many a soul back to God.

"Angus, how old will you be now?" he asked at length.

"Twenty, Father," the boy answered.

"Twenty, Angus, and you think yourself wiser than all the saints and doctors of the Church. Shame on you, Angus. Now you just stand there and tell me all you've done since your last confession. No, you needn't kneel. Just look out across no-man's-land and be a sentry still, but get your sins quickly off your soul because the battle'll soon be beginning and we've no time to lose."

When he had confessed Angus and given him absolution, the sky began to pale rapidly, but Father Smith still went on talking to the boy, because he still had some ghostly counsel to give.

"Listen, Angus," he said, "you mustn't be afraid to die, because you're in a state of grace now and ready to appear before our Lord. And you mustn't worry too much about the people at home being thoughtless and not understanding about the war. It's just lack of imagination, that's all. They'll understand all right when peace comes and they'll see what kind of world we've won for them. For the world's going to be a very wonderful place after the war, Angus, much more the kingdom of our Blessed Lord than ever it's been before."

"You're sure of that, Father?" The young man's eyes were shining now and not with tears.

"I'm sure of it, Angus. The Bishop says so. Everybody says so. Besides, it's only common sense. Men aren't going back to being mean and petty and selfish after standing up for years and years to this sort of thing."

"What about the German and the Austrian Catholics, Father? Are they fighting for a better world too?"

"They've been misled by their temporal rulers in political matters, but once we've won our victory the scales will fall from their eyes and God's garment will be knit whole again," Father Smith said.

"I don't think I'd mind so much dying for that sort of world, Father," Angus said. "Thanks, Father, for helping me." He self-consciously shook hands with the priest. "I'm afraid I've been no end of a silly gowk," he said.

They couldn't talk at all after that, because the barrage began, and the men came streaming up into the trenches and stood crouching under the parapet in their steel helmets. Some of them were joking and some of them stood drawn into themselves and grave, but through all of them the same question ran: "Will it happen to *me*?" The noise of the guns and of the shells bursting was terrific. The priest wondered how the Germans were liking it and if they, too, were standing hammered into sanctity at the thought of the attack which they must know must be coming. He wondered, too, if there were Catholics among them and if a priest had just given them holy communion too, and how our Lord kept judging the Germans and the Britons that must for ever be trooping before Him, red and angry from the battlefield. Then he was afraid for himself, for he knew that he, too, might die at any moment, and he wanted to go on living among advertisements for cigarettes and soot and chemist shops and sin, which was foolish of him, because the next world must be ever so much pleasanter.

Then an officer was beside him looking at his watch, and Father Smith made the sign of the cross and murmured the words of the general absolution, and even some of those who weren't Catholics bowed their heads because they knew that Father Smith was a priest and that he was praying for them. Then their bayonets pointed again and their steel helmets were clamped down on their heads and they were all priests and victims together and had never invited pretty girls to cricket matches or listened to water lapping under a rowing boat. Then somebody shouted and they were all gone, over and up and forward into the blast.

Father Smith didn't see Angus go over the top, but when he went forward with his holy oils, he came upon the boozy major lying wounded in a shell hole, with a great bloody gape in his belly.

"It's all right, Father; I still think God is a Sahib," he said as the priest bent to anoint him.

. . . . .

[*Father Smith is now back in Scotland in his parish in the slums. He visits Angus, only to find that the latter has just murdered his faithless wife.*]

Thinking of one parishioner made Father Smith think of another, and so he decided that he would go and call on Angus McNab and see how the young man was getting on. He set out, therefore, along the mean streets which led to the slum where Angus and his wife lived. As he moved among the dirty children, he tried to smile at them as he thought Monsignor O'Duffy would have smiled at them, because he knew that it wasn't only clean children that God wanted priests to love, but dirty ones especially, because they had so much to be compensated for; but he hadn't the monsignore's manner, because the children didn't smile back, and some of their parents even scowled, as though they were bracketing the priests with the employers. Father Smith began to wish that he had come another day, when there hadn't been a general strike, but he knew that was weak and cowardly of him.

He arrived at the tenement just in time to give Annie conditional absolution when Angus flung her out of the window. Kneeling on the pavement beside her broken body, he muttered the holy words while around him the stupid hostile faces mooned. "Make an act of contrition," he exhorted the pulp and the blood and the matted hair. "Say: 'O my God, Who art infinitely good in Thyself . . .' "; but no words came back from the pulp and the blood and the matted hair, and the policemen were already upstairs to take Angus away.

They hanged Angus on the Feast of Saint Cyril of Jerusalem, 1927, so Father Smith had to wear white vestments when he went to say Mass and give him holy communion in his cell.

Angus's confession was like most other confessions Father Smith had heard, a long thread of repeated rebellions against God, the suck and swish and swirl of silly sins. At first, as he listened the priest was too moved to pay much attention, because he was thinking of the dreadful thing that was going to happen to the young man and how he himself was perhaps partly responsible, because he had told Angus in the trenches that the world was going to be a kind and just and holy place after the war; then he remembered that, as Cardinal Newman had pointed out, even the smallest of venial sins was, in the eyes of God, a greater evil than the destruction of the whole earth and the perishing of its inhabitants in agonies of torture, and he forced himself to listen carefully, so that when all had been said he might the more surely soothe with sacramental balm. For the world was "about" being good and being bad and not "about" trade winds and centres of depression and chemists' shops and the price of war loan, as deep down in their hearts most people knew, only they were afraid to say so out loud in case other people would laugh at them.

Outside, as he thought this, the early morning trams clanged in the meaninglessness of another material day, and an early milk boy sang "Charleston, Charleston, she told me that I couldn't dance the Charleston."

When he had given Angus absolution, Father Smith vested and began the Mass in front of the same little portable altar which he had used in France. Angus, who had insisted on serving, answering back with a great common Scots accent which lent pathos to his Latin: "Ad Deum, qui laetificat juventutem meam." And what joy had God given to Angus's youth? Father Smith wondered. Angus hadn't been happy at the war, and he hadn't been happy after the war, with no job and his trollop of a wife carrying on with other men as soon as his back was turned. But perhaps Angus had been happy as a boy running with bare feet about the streets of the town. Perhaps he had been happy selling chocolates and cigarettes in Signor Sarno's cinema house. Or perhaps a glimpse of beauty had soaked colour into his soul: the noise of the sea at night, the shine of the rain on a policeman's cape, the wreaths of incense still smudged about the altar when High Mass was over. A rage against the rich rose in the priest as he thought of how easy things had been for them and how difficult for Angus. It was so simple for them, with their green lawns and their limousines and their conservatories and their holidays at Dinard, to talk about what *they* would do if they were workingmen, but it wasn't so easy for the workingman, especially when he hadn't any work to do.

"Father, I'm that feared," Angus said when the Mass was over.

"Angus, when they come for you you will say: 'Into Thy hands I commend my spirit; Lord Jesus, receive my soul,' " the priest said.

"Father, it's no right," Angus said. "She was a dirty stravaiging whore and she deserved all she got and I'm not going to take it lying down."

"Angus, there'll be no peace in God's good world until taking things lying down become a contagion," the priest said.

"I'm no going to take things lying down, I tell you," Angus began to shout. "It's no right; it's no fair. I fought in the war, in the muck and the blood, aye for four lang years, with the wind cauld aboot ma belly, and my boots tramping on deid men's tripes and they stinking like sewer pipes. They'd won an immortal fame, their names'd be written on golden scrolls in great big red and purple letters, so the fellies that slept at hame in their beds said. And I'd won immortal fame too; my name ought to have been written on golden scrolls for folks to have a read at, because my guts might have been lying at the bottom of a trench too, all stretched oot and cauld and trampit doon. But folk had forgotten the war by the time I got hame, they'd forgotten the laddies that fought and died and bled oot their sair red blood for them, and the fellies that had stayed at hame were oot o' their beds now, rubbing their great randy bellies against the lassies in the paly de donces. And what did I get for risking my ain one life for them and what did I get for my poor sair arm? I didna get whooring aroond with the lassies, at least not with the stuck-up yins with their heids in the air and their silken doups that only farted lavender and eau-de-cologne, I didna; I got a job at thirty bob a week and Annie Rooney wi' a great muckle airse on her like Ben Nevis and a great cauld mooth, at least when I got pitten oot by yon Sarno for asking for forty bob instead of thirty it was. And yet I loved her, Faither, I loved her because I thought she was all my ain. That's why I went oot along the dreich clarty streets selling matches and bootlaces in the wind and the rain and the snaw. That's why I climbed all yon steep stane steps to try to sell pencils to scribbling writing men with wee peery eyes and great big nebs in their offices that didna care how many laddies' banes lay rotting in Flanders' fields so long as they were safe and alive and screwing oot their sneaky wee figures. And all the time the dirty bitch was lying with her stinking meat in other men's airms with her yelly, yelly hair all streakit oot across the pillow and saying the same hot loving words in their lugs she used to say in mine. It's no fair, I tell you." Suddenly the venom was out of him and he was sobbing in the priest's arms. "Faither, Faither, I'm that feared," he said.

"Angus, you mustn't talk like that," the priest said. "You're in a state of grace, remember, but you'll be out of it again before you know where you are if you go on like that. Don't forget the implications of Christianity, Angus. It was never intended to be an easy religion, but a difficult one. That's just what the world doesn't understand and yet it's precisely what our Blessed Lord came down from heaven to teach. And He didn't find it easy to die either. Try to model yourself on Him, Angus. Try to understand something of the law of mystical substitution." He spoke quickly because he knew that time was short. "Make an act of contrition for the sins of your whole life, Angus. Tell God that you are sorry for not having understood His purpose better. Say: 'Into Thy Hands . . . ,' " but already the warder was turning the key in the lock.

There were quite a few there to see Angus die: the governor, the magistrates, the doctor, the warders, the hangman, all neat and respectable in their boots, but the priest didn't look at them much because he was too busy holding up the crucifix to Angus and telling him to commend his soul to Jesus. When it was all over, he anointed the corpse because he had not been able to do so previously as Angus had been in no technical danger of death. Then he went out into the sad sunshine where a policeman was already pinning on the prison door the notice of Angus's death. The crowd of ghouls who had gathered on the pavement made way for him as they crammed forward to read the notice. Among them the priest noticed Councillor Thompson, who surprisingly raised his hat. Father Smith raised his hat back and then hurried home to the church where Canon Bonnyboat had promised to say the nine-o'clock Mass for the repose of Angus's soul.

. . . . .

[*The book ends with the following chapter describing the deathbed of the priestly hero of the story.*]

Canon Smith liked the lighted lamps the nuns carried when Canon Muldoon brought him holy communion in bed. He liked to think of the pools of amber they made on the polished floors of the corridors, because it was just the sort of reflection the Blessed Sacrament cast on men's souls as it was hoisted above the unhappiness of the world. He liked to think of the nuns' habits as they swept along through the convent and of bent old Canon Muldoon following behind with the humeral veil wrapped round his precious Burden, because it was the whisper of God's poetry trickling on.

He liked it, too, when he was anointed, with the sky outside the window and the trees still there. As Canon Muldoon traced the last mercies on his weary body, far away out along the bend of the railway line, at the junction of the golf course and Sir Dugald Ippecacuanha's estate, a puff of smoke appeared, and a miniature worm of train rolled tinily along the embankment. Canon Smith liked looking at it, because that seemed to be part of God's poetry too. He lay thinking of the rhythm of the seasons and how right Canon Bonnyboat had been when he had compared the liturgy of the Church to the flowers and the leaves, which God painted new every year.

"Buon giorno, reverendo padre mio, e come sta?" Elvira said as she came in in her junior subaltern's uniform and knelt beside the bed, but he knew from the way that she smiled at him that she didn't expect him to answer, and besides Canon Muldoon was praying out the great grim words on which his soul must shortly sail: ". . . in the name of angels and archangels; in the name of thrones and dominions; in the name of principalities and powers; in the name of virtues, cherubim and seraphim; in the name of patriarchs and prophets . . ." Reverend Mother was kneeling beside the bed, too, with her face all wrinkled and wise, and she took his hand in both of hers and pressed it and he knew that she was saying good-bye to him in Christ Jesus their Lord. The new young nuns were there as well, with lovely red shiny faces like apples and eyes that would never grow old, because they were Christ's brides. Lady Ippecacuanha was there, too, making great gobbling noises in her throat, and the Polish chaplain and the new Bishop and old dried-up Councillor Thompson who had used to say such dreadful things about God's Church.

". . . In the name of holy monks and hermits . . ." He would be seeing quite a lot of old friends soon, if God was merciful and he landed on the right side of the fence. Angus McNab and the Bishop and the boozy major and the old sailor and Monsignor O'Duffy and Mother de la Tour and Mother Leclerc and Annie Rooney and a host of others who had been studded in the calendar of his prayers. He wondered if there would be flowers in heaven for Mother de la Tour and whether Angus would be allowed to wear the ribbon of the D.C.M. and if Annie Rooney liked singing the *Magnificat* now that God had made all things plain to her. For that was what death really was: a making of things plain, a shining forth from behind bomber aeroplanes and advertisements for syrup of figs.

And suddenly as he lay there he knew the answer to it all: how the lame and the sick should be healed and how the poor should be rewarded and how God's saints might eat peas off their knives; how the banker might be last and the harlot first; how a priest's hands never failed however flat his words; how the Church was all glorious within because the freight she carried healed all her cracks; why God often chose ugly blunt men to do the task of angels; why God was patient and why priests must be patient too; how mighty was their calling and how certain their ointment; and how it was in the answer that each man gave to Christ in the silence of his soul that the fairness of tomorrow's meadows lay. It was all so simple really, and he wanted to tell them before he went, but already the shore of them lined along his bed was retreating and he had time only to cry out at the Polish chaplain.

"Don't forget to let them know there'll be Mass on Sunday in the fish market," he said.

SECTION EIGHT

Religious Language

A. J. Ayer

Empiricist tendencies are powerful in the British philosophical tradition, and the influence of Hume on all later thought has been pervasive. In the early years of the present century there were signs of an impending revolution among philosophers. The work of Bertrand Russell and Alfred North Whitehead in mathematical philosophy was epoch-making in England. In Vienna as early as 1910 there was a movement that was distinctly positivistic in its interests and tendencies. Ten years later, we find, the attention of a group of philosophers in Vienna was drawn to certain problems whose character and importance are exhibited in the work of Ludwig Wittgenstein (1889-1951). In 1929, this group, which came to be known as the Viennese Circle, was functioning under the presidency of Moritz Schlick (1882-1936). Schlick considered philosophy to be a reflection upon the sciences. Since its function is to clarify the fundamentals and the structure of scientific knowledge, it should have nothing to do with questions that are supposed to transcend such knowledge. It is the business of philosophers to make it clear that questions that are not susceptible of empirical verification are profitless to pursue, since they are essentially meaningless. This position, upheld by Schlick, Rudolf Carnap, and others of the Viennese Circle, came to be known as "Logical Positivism" or "Logical Empiricism." American and British philosophers whose thought tended in similar directions naturally took great interest in and entered into close rapport with the members of the Viennese Circle. In England the predominating expression of the tendency has been in linguistic analysis, and the work of Alfred Julius Ayer, Language, Truth and Logic, *was notably influential in making the revolution in philosophy effective in the English-speaking world. Published in 1936, it met with wide success, not least due to the exceptional simplicity and clarity of its presentation. In the Second Edition, which appeared in 1946, and from which the following selection is taken, certain affirmations made in the earlier edition were modified, without, however, diminishing the force of the basic contentions. According to the view Ayer expounds, statements about the existence of God and similar religious utterances cannot evoke a philosopher's agnosticism any more than they can elicit his belief or disbelief; for, since such statements are meaningless, they cannot properly be considered at all.*

Born in 1910 and educated at Eton and Christ Church, Oxford, Ayer held the Grote Chair of the Philosophy of Mind and Logic at the University of London from 1946 till his appointment in 1959 to his present position as Wykeham Professor of Logic at Oxford.

God *Is Meaningless* *

. . . Mention of God brings us to the question of the possibility of religious knowledge. We shall see that this possibility has already been ruled out by our treatment of metaphysics. But, as this is a point of considerable interest, we may be permitted to discuss it at some length.

It is now generally admitted, at any rate by philosophers, that the existence of a being having the attributes which define the god of any non-animistic religion cannot be demonstratively proved. To see that this is so, we have only to ask ourselves what are the premises from which the existence of such a god could be deduced. If the conclusion that a god exists is to be demonstratively certain, then these premises must be certain; for, as the conclusion of a deductive argument is already contained in the premises, any uncertainty there may be about the truth of the premises is necessarily shared by it. But we know that no empirical proposition can ever be anything more than probable. It is only *a priori* propositions that are logically certain. But we cannot deduce the existence of a god from an *a priori* proposition. For we know that the reason why *a priori* propositions are certain is that they are tautologies. And from a set of tautologies nothing but a further tautology can be validly deduced. It follows that there is no possibility of demonstrating the existence of a god.

What is not so generally recognised is that there can be no way of proving that the existence of a god, such as the God of Christianity, is even probable. Yet this also is easily shown. For if the existence of such a god were probable, then the proposition that he existed would be an empirical hypothesis. And in that case it would be possible to deduce from it, and other empirical hypotheses, certain experiential propositions which were not deducible from those other hypotheses alone. But in fact this is not possible. It is sometimes claimed, indeed, that the existence of a certain sort of regularity in nature constitutes sufficient evidence for the existence of a god. But if the sentence "God exists" entails no more than that certain types of phenomena occur in certain sequences, then to assert the existence of a god will be simply equivalent to asserting that there is the requisite regularity in nature; and no religious man would admit that this was all he intended to assert in asserting the existence of a god. He would say that in talking about God, he was talking about a transcendent being who might be known through certain empirical manifestations, but certainly could not be defined in terms of those manifestations. But in that case the term "god" is a metaphysical term. And if "god" is a metaphysical term, then it cannot be even probable that a god exists. For to say that "God exists" is to make a metaphysical utterance which cannot be either true or false. And by the same criterion, no sentence which purports to describe the nature of a transcendent god can possess any literal significance.

* A. J. Ayer, *Language, Truth and Logic,* pp. 114–120. Reprinted by permission of Dover Publications, Inc., New York 14, New York.

It is important not to confuse this view of religious assertions with the view that is adopted by atheists, or agnostics.[1] For it is characteristic of an agnostic to hold that the existence of a god is a possibility in which there is no good reason either to believe or disbelieve; and it is characteristic of an atheist to hold that it is at least probable that no god exists. And our view that all utterances about the nature of God are nonsensical, so far from being identical with, or even lending any support to, either of these familiar contentions, is actually incompatible with them. For if the assertion that there is a god is nonsensical, then the atheist's assertion that there is no god is equally nonsensical, since it is only a significant proposition that can be significantly contradicted. As for the agnostic, although he refrains from saying either that there is or that there is not a god, he does not deny that the question whether a transcendent god exists is a genuine question. He does not deny that the two sentences "There is a transcendent god" and "There is no transcendent god" express propositions one of which is actually true and the other false. All he says is that we have no means of telling which of them is true, and therefore ought not to commit ourselves to either. But we have seen that the sentences in question do not express propositions at all. And this means that agnosticism also is ruled out.

Thus we offer the theist the same comfort as we gave to the moralist. His assertions cannot possibly be valid, but they cannot be invalid either. As he says nothing at all about the world, he cannot justly be accused of saying anything false, or anything for which he has insufficient grounds. It is only when the theist claims that in asserting the existence of a transcendent god he is expressing a genuine proposition that we are entitled to disagree with him.

It is to be remarked that in cases where deities are identified with natural objects, assertions concerning them may be allowed to be significant. If, for example, a man tells me that the occurrence of thunder is alone both necessary and sufficient to establish the truth of the proposition that Jehovah is angry, I may conclude that, in his usage of words, the sentence "Jehovah is angry" is equivalent to "It is thundering." But in sophisticated religions, though they may be to some extent based on men's awe of natural process which they cannot sufficiently understand, the "person" who is supposed to control the empirical world is not himself located in it; he is held to be superior to the empirical world, and so outside it; and he is endowed with super-empirical attributes. But the notion of a person whose essential attributes are non-empirical is not an intelligible notion at all. We may have a word which is used as if it named this "person," but, unless the sentences in which it occurs express propositions which are empirically verifiable, it cannot be said to symbolize anything. And this is the case with regard to the word "god," in the usage in which it is intended to refer to a transcendent object. The mere existence of the noun is enough to foster the illusion that there is a real, or at any rate a possible entity corresponding to it. It is only when we enquire what God's attributes are that we discover that "God," in this usage, is not a genuine name.

It is common to find belief in a transcendent god conjoined with belief in

[1] This point was suggested to me by Professor H. H. Price.

an after-life. But, in the form which it usually takes, the content of this belief is not a genuine hypothesis. To say that men do not ever die, or that the state of death is merely a state of prolonged insensibility, is indeed to express a significant proposition, though all the available evidence goes to show that it is false. But to say that there is something imperceptible inside a man, which is his soul or his real self, and that it goes on living after he is dead, is to make a metaphysical assertion which has no more factual content than the assertion that there is a transcendent god.

It is worth mentioning that, according to the account which we have given of religious assertions, there is no logical ground for antagonism between religion and natural science. As far as the question of truth or falsehood is concerned, there is no opposition between the natural scientist and the theist who believes in a transcendent god. For since the religious utterances of the theist are not genuine propositions at all, they cannot stand in any logical relation to the propositions of science. Such antagonism as there is between religion and science appears to consist in the fact that science takes away one of the motives which make men religious. For it is acknowledged that one of the ultimate sources of religious feeling lies in the inability of men to determine their own destiny; and science tends to destroy the feeling of awe with which men regard an alien world, by making them believe that they can understand and anticipate the course of natural phenomena, and even to some extent control it. The fact that it has recently become fashionable for physicists themselves to be sympathetic towards religion is a point in favour of this hypothesis. For this sympathy towards religion marks the physicists' own lack of confidence in the validity of their hypotheses, which is a reaction on their part from the anti-religious dogmatism of nineteenth-century scientists, and a natural outcome of the crisis through which physics has just passed.

It is not within the scope of this enquiry to enter more deeply into the causes of religious feeling, or to discuss the probability of the continuance of religious belief. We are concerned only to answer those questions which arise out of our discussion of the possibility of religious knowledge. The point which we wish to establish is that there cannot be any transcendent truths of religion. For the sentences which the theist uses to express such "truths" are not literally significant.

An interesting feature of this conclusion is that it accords with what many theists are accustomed to say themselves. For we are often told that the nature of God is a mystery which transcends the human understanding. But to say that something transcends the human understanding is to say that it is unintelligible. And what is unintelligible cannot significantly be described. Again, we are told that God is not an object of reason but an object of faith. This may be nothing more than an admission that the existence of God must be taken on trust, since it cannot be proved. But it may also be an assertion that God is the object of a purely mystical intuition, and cannot therefore be defined in terms which are intelligible to the reason. And I think there are many theists who would assert this. But if one allows that it is impossible to define God in intelligible terms, then one is allowing that it is impossible for a sentence both to be significant and to be about God. If a mystic admits that the object of his vision is something which cannot be described, then he must also admit that he is bound to talk nonsense when he describes it.

For his part, the mystic may protest that his intuition does reveal truths to him, even though he cannot explain to others what these truths are; and that we who do not possess this faculty of intuition can have no ground for denying that it is a cognitive faculty. For we can hardly maintain *a priori* that there are no ways of discovering true propositions except those which we ourselves employ. The answer is that we set no limit to the number of ways in which one may come to formulate a true proposition. We do not in any way deny that a synthetic truth may be discovered by purely intuitive methods as well as by the rational method of induction. But we do say that every synthetic proposition, however it may have been arrived at, must be subject to the test of actual experience. We do not deny *a priori* that the mystic is able to discover truths by his own special methods. We wait to hear what are the propositions which embody his discoveries, in order to see whether they are verified or confuted by our empirical observations. But the mystic, so far from producing propositions which are empirically verified, is unable to produce any intelligible propositions at all. And therefore we say that his intuition has not revealed to him any facts. It is no use his saying that he has apprehended facts but is unable to express them. For we know that if he really had acquired any information, he would be able to express it. He would be able to indicate in some way or other how the genuineness of his discovery might be empirically determined. The fact that he cannot reveal what he "knows," or even himself devise an empirical test to validate his "knowledge," shows that his state of mystical intuition is not a genuinely cognitive state. So that in describing his vision the mystic does not give us any information about the external world; he merely gives us indirect information about the condition of his own mind.

These considerations dispose of the argument from religious experience, which many philosophers still regard as a valid argument in favour of the existence of a god. They say that it is logically possible for men to be immediately acquainted with God, as they are immediately acquainted with a sense-content, and that there is no reason why one should be prepared to believe a man when he says that he is seeing a yellow patch, and refuse to believe him when he says that he is seeing God. The answer to this is that if the man who asserts that he is seeing God is merely asserting that he is experiencing a peculiar kind of sense-content, then we do not for a moment deny that his assertion may be true. But, ordinarily, the man who says that he is seeing God is saying not merely that he is experiencing a religious emotion, but also that there exists a transcendent being who is the object of this emotion; just as the man who says that he sees a yellow patch is ordinarily saying not merely that his visual sense-field contains a yellow sense-content, but also that there exists a yellow object to which the sense-content belongs. And it is not irrational to be prepared to believe a man when he asserts the existence of a yellow object, and to refuse to believe him when he asserts the existence of a transcendent god. For whereas the sentence "There exists here a yellow-coloured material thing" expresses a genuine synthetic proposition which could be empirically verified, the sentence "There exists a transcendent god" has, as we have seen, no literal significance.

We conclude, therefore, that the argument from religious experience is altogether fallacious. The fact that people have religious experiences is interesting from the psychological point of view, but it does not in any way imply that there is such a thing as religious knowledge, any more than our having moral experiences implies that there is such a thing as moral knowledge. The theist, like the moralist, may believe that his experiences are cognitive experiences, but, unless he can formulate his "knowledge" in propositions that are empirically verifiable, we may be sure that he is deceiving himself. It follows that those philosophers who fill their books with assertions that they intuitively "know" this or that moral or religious "truth" are merely providing material for the psycho-analyst. For no act of intuition can be said to reveal a truth about any matter of fact unless it issues in verifiable propositions. And all such propositions are to be incorporated in the system of empirical propositions which constitutes science.

A. D. Ritchie

The son of a well-known Scottish philosopher, Arthur David Ritchie became a Cambridge scientist. Only later in life did he turn to philosophy as a professional avocation. After some years as Professor of Philosophy at Manchester, England, he succeeded Norman Kemp Smith in the Edinburgh Chair of Logic and Metaphysics, from which he retired in 1959. While Ritchie may be said to stand in the Greco-Christian tradition, he has brought to both his Christianity and his humanism the outlook and practical experience of a biochemist. In the selection reproduced here he offers a penetrating critique of Logical Positivism, repudiating the phenomenalism it implies, which he accounts the parent of many fallacies.

Errors of Logical Positivism *

Positivists have excelled at destructive criticism. This criticism has been useful for pruning away absurd and superfluous theories but it is liable to be used to prune away everything else. The latest exponents, the Logical Positivists, are no less adept at criticism than their predecessors. The doctrines of this school have been surrounded with an air of mystery and inquirers have been frightened off by alarming technical apparatus. We all know that the Logical Positivists had proved that everybody else talked nonsense, but we did not know what they themselves talked. Mr. A. J. Ayer's exposition of the doctrine, *Language, Truth and Logic,* is therefore welcome as it is simple, clear, and free from technical mystification. It gives the ordinary reader a chance of seeing what it is all about. When the fundamental assumptions of the theory are stated clearly, as they are by Mr. Ayer, it seems to me equally clear that they are wrong, so that it should not be surprising if some of the conclusions drawn from them turn out to be wrong too.

In what follows I shall be concerned only with the general statement of the doctrine and with its application to scientific theory; not with any other applications.

The first set of assumptions are, as the name of the school implies, logical. It is assumed that all alleged propositions, that is all sentences or linguistic forms which profess to convey information or to make assertions which could be either true or false, are of three kinds. These are (1) Factual Propositions or Empirical Hypotheses, (2) Tautologies or Definitions, (3) Meaningless or Metaphysical verbal forms. Only class (1) are significant or actually say anything about anything.

Class (1) are either themselves assertions as to matters of fact which can

* A. D. Ritchie, *Essays in Philosophy* (New York: Longmans, Green & Co., Inc., 1948), pp. 70–85. Used by permission of The Royal Institute of Philosophy and A. D. Ritchie.

be verified by experience or else they can by purely logical analysis without change of significance be translated into such propositions . . . A proposition is said to be verified by experience when it refers to or describes correctly actual or possible contents of somebody's sense experience. It is not clear whose experience is concerned, whether it is somebody specified, anybody, or only the speaker himself. I have put in "somebody," but I suspect that the upholders of this doctrine always mean themselves. There are difficulties connected with the method of verification, but Mr. Ayer deals with them and his treatment will be discussed later. One further brief comment may be put in here. Mr. Ayer recognises . . . that the same form of words may function as (1) a factual proposition and also as (2) a tautology, without apparently realising that this admission will get him into trouble. The purely logical analysis of propositions becomes impossibly difficult if such initial ambiguities are allowed.

Class (2), Tautologies, are analytic in the sense that their contradictories cannot be asserted. For that very reason they do not assert any fact or inform us about facts. They have a legitimate use as definitions, to indicate what linguistic symbols are to be used as equivalent to what others. Mathematics consists entirely of such propositions; for instance $2 + 2 = 4$ defines (in part) how the symbols 2 and 4 are to be used. According to the Logical Positivists, philosophy ought to consist of such propositions, because its function is to analyse common assertions by substituting for them others which will display their true structure and significance, if any. There are propositions tautological in form, like "Business is Business," which have an emotional significance but no literal significance. Mr. Ayer disapproves of them.

This brings us to Class (3). Some propositions which are ostensibly factual or similar to factual ones have reference to entities which cannot from the nature of the case be experienced themselves or be displayed as logically constructed out of elements of experience. Alleged propositions of this kind are held to be strictly meaningless or "metaphysical." "Metaphysical" in Mr. Ayer's vocabulary is a term of abuse; that is to say it is an epithet applied to things he dislikes and not applied to things he likes, though possibly equally applicable.

This classification of propositions is the logical basis of the theory and distinguishes the "logical" from other positivists.

Perhaps it is a minor point, but it should be noticed that the term tautology is used in a loose and possibly misleading sense. Strictly tautology ought to mean an equation of identities, e.g. $2 = 2$, or Business is Business. Such equations, if intended seriously, are asserted to show that the terms are to be understood strictly according to definition and not figuratively. In the equation $2 + 2 = 4$ the two sides are not identical; they contain distinct and different symbols. These can, however, be substituted for one another without error for all mathematical purposes. We may say "Two sheep and two goats, that makes four animals" as long as it is only the numbers we are interested in and can afford to neglect their special characters as sheep or goats. This brings me to the next and more important point.

Everything the Logical Positivists say about language is based upon a theory of the mathematical logicians about mathematical language. This is probably excellent within its own sphere, but can it be extended to apply to all kinds of communication by language, that is by signs? Granted that the symbols 2 + 2 and 4 can be substituted for one another absolutely without error or change of meaning in all mathematical propositions, that is because the use of mathematical propositions depends entirely upon their form or structure and not at all upon their matter or content — if they have any. In other words, the propositions are used as definitions. In all ordinary language, including non-mathematical scientific language, form and matter cannot be readily distinguished. Even when they are distinguished the use of language depends upon the matter as well as the form, because the assertions are material; they point to what happens to exist, and are not purely formal like those of mathematics. The legitimate logical transformations that can be applied are limited to the formal or structural elements of language; in ordinary language what is expressed by signs such as "and," "or," "not," "all," "any," "some." Even then there are limitations. To say "The Nile is a great river" is not exactly the same as to say "The Nile is not a small river." Nor even is "Edinburgh is north of London" quite the same as "London is south of Edinburgh" except for certain limited technical purposes such as map reading, when A and B could stand for Edinburgh and London, and the propositions are in effect mathematical.

It is only to a very limited extent that linguistic signs can be interchanged without alteration of meaning, as is seen from the notorious fact that every language possesses words and phrases that cannot be translated into a foreign language. As a lawyer once pointed out to me, Mr. Justice Stareleigh's dictum, that "What the soldier said is not evidence," cannot be translated into French, because in a French court everything is evidence, or into German, because in a German court it would be an insult to the army. Forms of words can be found in French and German which to the ignorant Englishman may seem equivalent. They are not equivalent for Frenchmen or Germans, because their different history and traditions have given their language signs different meanings; they are referred to a different background.

If it is objected that all this has to do with the emotional effects of language and not with its legitimate scientific use, I would point out first of all that the proposition just mentioned is a technical one used in a strictly technical sense and not for the purpose of exciting irrelevant emotions, quite the contrary. But even where emotions are aroused, why assume that the expression or arousing of emotions must be illegitimate and incompatible with the scientific use of language? When you make an assertion at least you desire (Emotion No. 1) your hearers to assent (Emotion No. 2). To express and arouse emotion is the essential and fundamental function of all linguistic intercourse between human beings, even mathematicians and logicians. If it were not for the emotions concerned nobody would say anything, and the emotions are as much a part of the meaning as anything else. Emotion of course may be and often is objectionable when it is misplaced or inappropriate, just as it is objectionable to tell lies or misunderstand what is said. The emotion is right and the proposition true when they fit the facts, wrong and false when they do not.

To give a general definition of language one would have to say something of this kind — Language symbolises primarily an attitude or type of behaviour of the speaker which is directed towards things or persons, and it is used for the purpose of modifying the attitude or behaviour of other persons or possibly himself. These attitudes or behaviours are the external expression of what is internally an emotion of some kind. A command is perhaps a more elementary kind of speech than an assertion. But language symbols are concerned secondarily with symbolising appearances which are themselves signs standing for the things or persons towards which the speaker's emotions, thoughts, or actions are directed. This applies to all types of language. Mathematical language is the limiting case where the symbols are emptied as far as possible of all content so as to apply to everything in general and nothing in particular. It is only in mathematics that terms are interchangeable absolutely without error. The Logical Positivists, however, treat the limiting case as though it were the typical case, with the results that might be expected.

So much for the logical part which seems to be simply a mistake; now for the positivist part which is a more serious affair. Mr. Ayer assumes that all valid propositions asserting matters of fact are logically equivalent to or can be reduced without change of meaning to propositions which assert nothing but that certain data of sense can be or are experienced under certain conditions. That is to say Positivists like Mr. Ayer are Phenomenalists. The chief use the Phenomenalists make of their assumption is to show that propositions they dislike cannot be so reduced and are therefore invalid. Propositions they like are treated more circumspectly. I am inclined to suspect that no proposition would come through the ordeal unscathed.

Consider an ordinary scientific law, say, "The boiling point of benzene is 80.4° C."[1] This is a straightforward empirical generalisation from experiment and can be verified (according to the scientific use of this term, not necessarily the positivist use) any day by anybody who can obtain the necessary apparatus and has the elementary knowledge and skill to use it properly. Let us see what this involves. In the first place Aristotle or Archimedes, though cleverer than you and I, could not do it. They could not obtain the necessary technical information and had no chance of acquiring the necessary technical skill. In the second place, Robinson Crusoe on his island could not do it even supposing he had the knowledge and skill. Though I say "could not," I am prepared to admit that if the necessary raw materials were present in the island and if he lived long enough and worked hard enough, it is just conceivable that he might manage it. He would not only have had to make glass and blow his apparatus — easy enough of course when you know how — he would have to construct a thermometer and a barometer. He would have to calibrate them and work out the various corrections to be applied to their use. Lastly he would have to prepare pure benzene.

You and I can buy the benzene in a bottle trusting to the knowledge, skill, and material equipment of the coal miners, gas workers, and chemical workers who prepare and purify it, and trusting too to the integrity of the people who

[1] The boiling point of benzene now available to chemists in the United States is between 80.093 and 80.094. The argument is, of course, unaffected by this. [G. MacG.]

bottle it and label it; whereas they might have filled the bottle at the nearest garage. We must either trust in its purity as purchased or else purify it ourselves. We shall buy our thermometer and probably trust to the maker's or somebody else's calibration; even if we calibrate it ourselves we shall do so against another thermometer taken as a standard and assumed to be trustworthy. Even if we read the barometer ourselves, we shall trust to somebody else for the accuracy of the scale and the corrections to be applied. The last and really the least part of the business is setting up the apparatus and distilling the benzene, but even here the complications are not at an end. In nine cases out of ten we shall not see the mercury thread in the thermometer creep up to the mark we have agreed to call 80.4 and remain steady there while the bulk of the liquid distils over, but we shall see it remain steady at some other mark. However, when we have applied corrections, which people have worked out and printed in books, for the barometric pressure at that time and place and for the cool portion of the thermometer stem, the corrected number will come to 80.4 or something very near. Still we may have the bad luck to do the experiment during a storm when the barometer is changing rapidly, and then the temperature will not keep steady at all and we may have to start all over again.

Positivists seem to imagine that all that happens is to read the name Benzene on the label and see the mercury thread coincide with 80.4 on the scale. If that was so, the assertion that benzene boils at 80.4° C. would be tautological. The name on the label is a linguistic sign; so also is the scale on the thermometer. If there was nothing else involved we should have to conclude that by definition "Benzene" was equivalent to "what boils at 80.4° C. as indicated by the position of the mercury thread on such and such a scale," and similarly that the significance of the 80.4 mark was that by definition it corresponded to the temperature of the vapour of boiling "Benzene."

There is a grain of truth in this notion that the law holds by definition, as can be seen from the result of a negative experiment. Suppose that when distillation began the thermometer reading was round about 60° C. and then gradually and steadily rose until by the end it had reached 120° C.; should I conclude that the law was false? Of course not, I should conclude that the stuff in the bottle was not benzene; in fact that it had been filled at the garage pump and the label was fraudulent. It is not fair to conclude, however, that the law is a tautology. We are not dealing here with mathematical terms which can be invented and defined at will, but with terms intended to described natural entities and processes, that are largely independent of human volition. It may be part of the definition of benzene that it boils at 80.4° C. but it is only part. There is no complete definition of benzene; something unexpected may . . . turn up. Moreover, something else may be found to boil at 80.4° C., in which case the definition would need to be modified.

For certain purposes scientific laws can be treated as equivalent to definitions, and so far as they are used in this way are not strictly true or false or liable to upset by observation. But the definition may always turn out to be inconvenient in use and have to be dropped and another put in its place. Moreover, the fact that for some purpose the same form of words is used as a definition does not prevent it being used in other ways simply as a summary of what has actually been found to happen. Every generalisation is both a summary of past events and a method of defining terms for future use; the two functions are distinct but related. The propositions of natural science must themselves be examined to see how they are actually used. It is a grave error to assume offhand that they are just like mathematical propositions.

I fear I am digressing and going back to matters of logic. The main point to be emphasized here is that the verification of so simple and obvious a generalisation as the boiling point of a substance is a matter of great complexity. It is not to be lightly dismissed as "an observer experiencing certain sense data under certain conditions." It is true that there are certain critical sense data which, if they are of one kind, verify the law, if of another, confute. But these critical sense data are a very small part of the whole story and they are meaningless by themselves without the rest of the story. The story even in this simple case is a long and complex one. It has behind it a vast structure of human effort and experience, a co-operative effort, and the experience of many generations. Countless men of science from Galileo on have worked out the knowledge needed for it. Cinnabar miners in Spain, coal miners in Yorkshire, and glass workers in Czechoslovakia have sweated for it. If the verification of this law really depended upon translating it into terms of a single man's sense experience, it would have to go by default; at the best his task would be insuperably complex and difficult, at the worst impossible. Can co-operative human effort be translated into sense data; and if so, whose? Berkeley would have had an answer to this question, but his modern imitators, who think they can have his phenomenalism without his God to hold it all together, have no answer.

No proposition that enters into the discourse of the natural sciences describes or refers directly to an immediate datum of sense experience. They refer to the general properties and relations of physical objects and in certain cases to general relations between physical objects and classes of sense data. (For confirmation of this, see any scientific textbook.) The classes of sense-data to which they refer are of a restricted and highly conventionalised type, mainly what Sir Arthur Eddington called "pointer-readings." The function of the data is purely symbolic; they are nothing by themselves. They symbolise causal relations among physical objects, more particularly the operations the observer carries out upon physical objects. In fact "the observer," that famous figure in philosophical discussion, is more correctly described as "the operator."

Nobody has ever reduced any scientific proposition to propositions referring to nothing but actual or possible data or contents of sense experience. Failure to do so is concealed under a smoke-screen of phrases like "the necessary conditions for observations" and "logical constructions from sense data." The conditions, the observer himself, and the reason for logically constructing remain unexplained. The logical constructions are never constructed in any specific case; we are merely told they could be. In fact the positivist or phenomenalist account of the process of scientific verification is pure myth or, if you like, metaphysics. I should prefer to say that any possible account of the process of verification is metaphysical and the phenomenalist account is bad metaphysics.

This point is so important that perhaps I may be permitted to labour it further. The physical sciences as expounded by the investigators themselves have never been positivist. The positivists have always been armchair critics or else mathematicians. Meyerson has repeatedly emphasized this in his historical discussions of the matter, and it is no reply to Meyerson to say that though scientific investigation actually took this road, it ought to have taken another and positivist road. Science is what the investigators have actually done, and there is no "ought" about it. As Whitehead has pointed out . . . , if investigators had been positivists, they would in many cases have failed to make the discoveries they did. Physical science has always been based upon a belief, possibly "metaphysical," that there are causal processes operating in a physical universe which does not consist entirely of sense data. This belief may give rise to difficulties but its abandonment gives rise to worse ones.

If sense data are the only things that exist, then the existing ones must be actual sense data somebody is experiencing. Possible sense data without something to render them actual are nothing, and what renders them actual cannot be other sense data unless we attribute to sense data hitherto unsuspected "metaphysical" properties. Again, the positivist to fill his universe has to resort to logical constructions from sense data, but these are not sense data themselves, any more than a class is one of its members. The theory that scientific entities are logical constructions from sense data is intended to provide a logical bridge between immediate experience and scientific theory. It cannot bear the additional burden of the doctrine that scientific entities are "nothing but" sense data. The plausibility of the positivist case rests upon his apparently appealing to actual sense data; the possibility of its being valid rests upon a concealed appeal to what are not actual sense data.

It is worth noticing that certain psychologists (e.g. D. Katz; *The World of Colour*) have endeavoured to describe the actual character of sense data, have found the task singularly difficult and are not all agreed as to the results. On the other hand, their difficulties and disagreements have no obvious relevance to the propositions of physical science, and throw no doubt upon them.

Admittedly there are difficulties on any theory in accounting for the relations between sense experience and the supposed real world, but ordinary common sense and most realist or idealist philosophies do not stultify themselves at the outset. They allow, for instance, for the existence of some machinery by which possible sense data may become actual even if they find it hard to give a coherent account of the machinery. Possible sense data without machinery to actualise them are myths. Berkeley's phenomenalism, as I have said before, was reasonable. You can say of the material world "*esse est percipi*" if there is some being whose *esse est percipere* always and everywhere. A world can be built out of actual sense data if they are all actual always. Otherwise it must be built out of sense data and other things which are not sense data.

Phenomenalism therefore seems to me to be definitely wrong. It is not so much that it asserts what is false as that it neglects what is true. Nevertheless, there does appear to be something of value in positivist criticism, and positivism is perhaps not necessarily bound up with phenomenalism. Before discussing this point, however, there are some further aspects of Mr. Ayer's exposition to be mentioned.

In discussing the process of verification by observation Mr. Ayer decides, for reasons that appear to me sound, that absolute certainty is unattainable for any type of factual assertion and that probability is all that can be expected. As to the notion of probability, he does not attempt (perhaps wisely) to give a logical account of it, but contents himself with a pragmatic one. He says . . . , "Roughly speaking, all that we mean by saying that an observation increases the probability of a proposition is that it increases *our confidence* in the proposition, as measured by our *willingness to rely on it in practice* as a forecast of our sensations and to retain it in preference to other hypotheses in face of an unfavourable experience." Then he goes on to develop this notion of probability in more detail, and says later that what he says applies to all empirical propositions without exception, whether singular, particular, or universal. The whole of the discussion could hardly be bettered, but it introduces a terrible serpent into the positivist Eden. Notice the words I have italicized, whereby the truth or probability of factual assertions is made to depend upon value judgments based upon our emotional response. This conclusion will not worry most people, but it should worry Mr. Ayer, because in the next chapter he dismisses all ethical and aesthetic value judgments as mere expressions of emotion, of no factual significance and strictly meaningless. He holds . . . that to say (1) "you acted wrongly in stealing that money" adds nothing to the literal meaning of the assertion (2) "you stole that money." It merely shows that the expression of it is attended by certain feelings in the speaker. If this is so, he cannot also say that to assert his feelings of confidence in a proposition or his willingness to rely on it in practice add anything to its literal meaning. If to say that something is good, bad, right, wrong, beautiful, or ugly, is to say nothing, so also to say that something is probable is to say nothing.

It is worth noticing that the example is not quite fair because an ethical judgment is already implied in the word "stole." The origin of the curious dogma that sensations are essential constituents of factual propositions but emotions are not, is easily seen. It is the theory that the "subject" or "observer" is a purely passive recipient and not an agent or operator.

The sources of the dilemma are the fundamentally false logical theory of propositions and the positivism from which Mr. Ayer starts, and not his eminently reasonable views on probability and verification. Any theory of verification would be placed in the same difficulty given the same assumptions. Any type of assertion about truth, falsity, or probability is an assertion of value and will be meaningless if assertions of value are meaningless. I understand that some who incline to logical positivist views would admit that assertions about the truth of propositions are meaningless, but if so they had better give up philosophy and take vows of silence.

It is perhaps necessary to insist further that there is no escape from the difficulty by saying that assertions about the truth or falsity of propositions are definitions of terms or tautologies, because that is what they are not. They are either statements of fact or nothing. If you want to explain the meaning of "It is true that . . ." you can do so by substituting "It is a fact that, . . ." "It happens that, . . ." or "I expect that, . . ." or "I am confident that . . ." It must be some phrase indicating an attitude of mind, or emotional state directed towards alleged facts or events. This is simply another way of saying what I have said already in defining language.

There is another dilemma for Mr. Ayer. It is not so vital perhaps, and I am not at all clear where the fallacy lies. He has an interesting argument . . . against the common view that the contents of a person's sensations are entirely private and inaccessible to anybody else and that it is only the structure that is accessible. This is an argument which I should gladly subscribe to, but it involves the assumption explicitly stated by Mr. Ayer that it is a mistake to draw a distinction between the structure and content of sensations. But if the only factual propositions are propositions about sensations, how can it be legitimate to distinguish between structure and content in propositions? According to any theory, it must be admitted that there is some correspondence between propositions and what propositions are about; so that the difficulty is a real one. I do not profess to be able to see the way out.

The Logical Positivists have drawn attention to the problems of the character and functions of language and have shown that in some way the structure of language is or ought to be related to the structure of the world. We should be grateful to them for raising the question, even though their answers are wrong. They are wrong, as I have tried to show, in respect both of their logic and their phenomenalism. Their logic is a fallacious extension of theories applicable only to mathematics. In fact, the linguistic problems they raise cannot be solved by logic but need psychology too. To these fallacies they add the older one of phenomenalism.

Like Lucretius, the positivists conceive their role as that of destroyers of superstition. Most people are superstitious, and superstition takes many different forms, so that there is no lack of dragons for the slaying. To consider only scientific superstitions, there has been a tendency to include in scientific theory hypotheses or hypothetical entities which are superfluous in so far as no specific observable consequences can be deduced from them, or, at least, no consequences that cannot be deduced on other grounds. Criticism of such theories is a useful service, for they may be worse than superfluous, they may hinder the progress of knowledge by setting up barriers to observation.

Positivist criticism has, however, often been misdirected and ineffective because it was based upon misapprehensions as to the methods of scientific investigation, and because it was mixed up with phenomenalism. It has been assumed that science consisted of two parts, theories and facts. The theories were conceived as the most important part. They were essentially things written in books and capable of being criticised independently apart from "facts." It was forgotten that all statements of theory are metaphors (this statement is not a metaphor) and that metaphors are good or bad, helpful or unhelpful for purposes of communicating knowledge, rather than true or false simply. It was also assumed that the "facts" were simple collections of actual and possible sense data.

A correct statement is not easy to make in any simple way. The following is as near as I can get. Science is what scientifically trained persons do. Scientific training consists in acquiring technical skill, becoming a craftsman, as well as in learning what others are doing and have done by means of similar technique. The "facts" of science are not easy to disentangle from the theories because the ascertaining of facts depends upon the use of instruments, the construction and use of which depends in turn upon theory. It is, however, possible to make a rough distinction between the minimum of theory that is needed for experimental operations and the immediate results of the operations on the one hand, methods and data one might say, and theory in the stricter sense on the other, that is to say the formulation of abstract schemes intended to generalise the data as far as possible. These abstract schemes will by preference be expressed in mathematical form.

There is a tendency among theoretical physicists to say that the terms that are used for theoretical formulation need not have any "meaning" provided that all variables in the theoretical formulation can be translated into variables capable of direct observation by the use of appropriate methods. This tendency implies a partial acceptance of positivism.

Opposed to this modern tendency is an older one, still popular among experimental physicists and perhaps universal among experimentalists in biological science, the tendency to construct models as theoretical formulations. The models may be conceived in mechanical terms or be merely diagrams describing hypothetical geometrical relations. The experimentalist is generally not a mathematician by nature though he may have acquired mathematical technique, but is something more like a mechanic. That is to say he is good at handling things, and he likes to picture the world of scientific theory after the fashion of the things he handles. The model-making tendency has led sometimes to serious fallacies, because it allowed people to think the ultimate small-scale entities, atoms, electrons, protons, etc., were endowed with the same familiar properties as the instruments they handled and the things they looked at. The notion will not, of course, bear examination, for the familiar properties of what we see and handle depend upon the fact that these are aggregates of vast numbers of the ultimate units, which must themselves have quite different properties. As a parallel, the average age of the whole population of the British Isles remains constant (or nearly so), but that does not prevent each one of us growing older from year to year. It is easy to understand that an atom cannot be coloured and that colour is a property of aggregates. It is perhaps less obvious but equally certain that an atom has strictly no shape or size, because whatever has shape and size must have a surface, and only a large aggregate can have a surface. In fact, if Descartes was right in saying that the essential property of matter is extension, then atoms are not material.

An atom is best described as something happening round a centre. Sets of these centres tend to oscillate about certain mean distances when considered over long enough time intervals. To call this shape and size is at the best a figure of speech. That in fact is just the trouble; everything that is said about atoms must be said in terms borrowed from our knowledge of gross matter and must be metaphorical. These metaphors are liable to be taken literally. The formulae of the mathematician are also metaphors, but fortunately they have no literal meaning to deceive us.

In so far as theories depending upon models are liable to abuse, positivist criticism is justified. But there is no justification for sweeping them away altogether, because they have undoubtedly been useful. It may be instructive in this respect to consider the history of the atomic theory.

The atomic theory is one of those very general theories such that all possibilities can be stated as a simple dichotomy — either matter is infinitely divisible or not; if not, then there are atoms. No recent physicist, I believe, has ever taken infinite divisibility seriously. It is a difficult conception and its consequences obscure; but as far as any consequences can be made out it seems to contradict certain elementary facts, such as the expansion of gases, the reflection of light at surfaces, the existence of chemical elements and compounds. All these things are easy to understand on the atomic theory. It is true that classical hydrodynamic theory appears to assume that fluids are infinitely divisible, but this means no more than that their structure, if any, must be very fine relative to the volumes actually considered. At any rate, seventeenth- and eighteenth-century physicists seem to have been atomists simply because the theory clarified their ideas. There were in those days no consequences that could be deduced from and directly checked by observation. On these grounds contemporary positivists might have condemned the theory. The fault, however, lay with the lack of the technique needed to make the right kind of observations. As soon as the technique developed, the deductions were made and verified by observation. Scientific observation does not consist, as many seem to believe, in sitting with your mouth open waiting for things to happen. It consists in going about and interfering with things. What needed to be discovered were the methods of quantitative analysis of chemical compounds, begun by Lavoisier and continued by his successors. The last necessary step was taken by Dalton, who deduced from the atomic theory and the law of conservation of weight in chemical changes that, whenever two kinds of atom combine, they must combine in constant proportions by weight. Further, if two can combine in different proportions to make different compounds, the ratios of these proportions must be as simple whole numbers. These deductions he tested by experiment and found to be about right in the small number of cases he could try and as far as his very crude methods would allow. Very soon others took the matter up and it was found that the deductions held in every case examined. The more the methods of analysis improved the more exact the agreement became.

Since then other types of deduction from the atomic theory have been made and confirmed. Nevertheless, even towards the end of the nineteenth century there were philosophers of positivist views who looked with suspicion at the theory, largely, I believe, because it had been abused. Because, as mentioned already, atoms were supposed to be literally hard round things, like billiard balls, only smaller and less highly coloured. Nowadays the atomic theory is very firmly established, even though atoms are not quite so hard and round. At any rate, the old fallacies are avoided and even positivist philosophers no longer murmur against them. They have discovered that after all atoms are only "logical constructions" and quite respectable.

I think we must agree to the "Principle of Observability"; namely that no hypothetical entity or process is to be admitted to scientific theory unless it leads to consequences verifiable by experiment or other kind of observation; though two provisos should be added. The first has been mentioned already, namely that what can at any stage of progress be verified by observation depends upon the technique available for the purpose. No observational consequences of a hypothesis may be immediately apparent, but it may be a good hypothesis all the same, though obviously not so good as if they were apparent and verified.

The second proviso is rather more complicated. The most general hypotheses of physics that cover all entities or processes whatsoever are often such that both from the hypothesis and its contradictory observable consequences follow, so that each is a definite hypothesis; the contradictory is not a mere blank. Thus, either matter is infinitely divisible or it is atomic; either there is absolute motion or not; either there is no limit to the precision with which the position and velocity of electrons can be determined or there is a limit. In each case observable consequences follow from either alternative, and if one is false the other is true. This is not so with more special hypotheses, from the contradictories of which nothing can as a rule be deduced. If the structural formula of a chemical compound is so and so, then the compound will have such and such properties. It does not have those properties, therefore its formula is not so and so. Here there is only blank negation except on the unlikely assumption that there is one and only one positive alternative formula. There may be no alternative thought of; there may be far too many. There are cases where it is best to compromise. A hypothesis may fail in some respects, but it may be better than nothing. Something unexpected may always turn up to solve the difficulty.

In conclusion, if positivism in its scientific aspect meant nothing more than this kind of critical attitude towards hypotheses, there would be nothing to say against it. But positivism has always meant much more. In fact it has meant phenomenalism too; the theory that the material world consists of nothing but sense data. Whatever the truth may be, this theory I am sure is false and the mother of a great family of fallacies. It is plausible because it appeals to what we imagine to be immediate, certain, and actual, and because we do not realize that the possible sense data it has to drag in are purely mythical.

A. C. Ewing

Alfred Cyril Ewing holds an important place among contemporary English philosophers. Past President of the Aristotelian Society and, since 1941, a Fellow of the British Academy, Dr. Ewing has taught philosophy at the University of Cambridge since 1931. Among his numerous published writings is a long and important article that appeared in Mind *in 1937. Dr. Ewing has provided, as a personal contribution to the present anthology, a very much abbreviated form of this article, with a note written in 1961 that takes account of the changes that have taken place in the intellectual scene over the intervening years.*

Meaninglessness *

In this article I shall use the term *positivist* for short to mean simply "upholder of any of the verification theories which I shall consider." I shall first take the extremer form of the [verification] theory, according to which a statement is said to be verifiable, and therefore to have meaning, if and only if its truth could be conclusively established by sense-experience. "Sense-experience" is used to include (*a*) sense-perception, (*b*) introspection of images and emotions. Positivists would not usually admit that the occurrence of "mental acts" could be verified by experience, and would presumably have either to regard these as logical constructions out of sense-data and images, or deny their existence altogether. Still less would the term cover apprehension of "non-natural" properties or relations. Now I should have thought the first duty of any advocate of a verification theory of meaning would be to inquire how his theory itself was to be verified, and I propose to be a good positivist in this one case at least and put the question myself. How could we verify the statement that all meaningful statements are verifiable?

The first difficulty is that it is a universal proposition and therefore can never be conclusively established merely by experience; but we shall relax the condition, as probably most positivists themselves would, so far as to allow of progressive and incomplete verification, and count the verification theory of meaning as verified for all practical purposes if an adequate number of samples of all the different kinds of meaningful statements we can think of are found on examination to be verifiable and we are unable to think of any which are not verifiable. I doubt the consistency of this but I will be as charitable as possible and let it pass. . . . But I do not see how the positivists could establish the truth of their view even in a single case merely by sense-experience. For how can we ever know by sense-experience that there is not a part of the meaning of a statement that we cannot verify? The fact that we do not have any sense-experience of such a part proves nothing, since the point at issue

* *Mind,* XLVI (1937), 347–364.

is whether there is something in what we mean beyond sense-experience; and how can we know by sense-experience that there is not?

It therefore seems impossible that the verification theory could be verified in the way suggested, and I cannot conceive what other way there could be of verifying it. For according to the fundamental principles of those who hold the theory it could not be established by any sort of *a priori* argument, and therefore it must presumably be established, if at all, by the empirical examination of particular cases. Now, not merely is it the case that it has not in fact been verified in that way; we have just seen that it is logically impossible that it could be so verified. The statement that all meaningful statements are verifiable is therefore not itself verifiable. It follows that if it is true it is meaningless. But a sentence cannot possibly be both true and meaningless. Therefore the sentence in question cannot be true, but must be either meaningless or false. According to my view it is the latter.

Perhaps it will be said that, although the verification theory is nonsense, it is important and useful nonsense, while the kind of nonsense I talk is unimportant and useless nonsense. But if the statement that it is important and useful nonsense is to be accepted, this statement in turn ought to be verified by sense-experience, and how that could possibly be done puzzles me. It might be held that it is useful because it helps to solve philosophical problems; but how can we tell by sense-experience whether a philosophical problem is solved or not? The mere fact that we do not feel an emotion of puzzlement does not prove that we have reached a solution. Otherwise unlettered peasants would have solved all philosophical problems far better than philosophers, and persistent neglect to think would be the golden mothod for attaining success in philosophy. Also the method prescribed might easily remove the emotion of puzzlement in some men but not in others, and be useful for some philosophical problems but misleading for others.

It might be suggested that the statement of the verification theory should be regarded as a tautology and therefore as meaningless only in the comparatively innocuous sense in which all correct *a priori* statements are meaningless according to the theory. But, if this line were taken, it would be necessary to show that some formal contradiction was committed by denying the theory; and this is not claimed. The only *a priori* propositions that the theory admits are analytic tautologies, if these indeed can be called propositions, but the statement of the theory itself is essentially synthetic. It gives new information, and information not capable of formal proof. The theory therefore cannot, if it is true, be known *a priori*. No *a priori* arguments for it are possible on its own showing since it is synthetic, and it therefore cannot be meaningful even in the modified sense in which a positivist might admit analytic *a priori* statements to be so. . . .

The positivist is thus debarred from giving *a priori* reasons for his theory because it is synthetic, and also from giving empirical reasons because it cannot be based on an empirical inspection of meaning. His only refuge is to make his theory a purely arbitrary convention, which therefore requires no justification. But, if this is allowed, a philosopher may assert anything whatever he pleases. The positivist is excused from having to prove his theory, but only at the expense of admitting that there is no more ground for accepting it than there is for accepting any theory whatever. Even such an argument as that it is simpler than other accounts or more useful for establishing deductive systems would be an appeal to a criterion conformity with which certainly cannot be discovered by sense-experience. And it remains true that his theory could mean nothing on its own showing, being neither an *a priori* analytic proposition nor one verifiable by sense-experience. . . .

Let us now turn to the milder form of the theory which was sponsored by Mr. Ayer. According to this a statement is meaningful if and only if it is logically possible that observations might be made which would be relevant to its truth or falsehood, *i.e.*, make its truth more or less probable. Now this formulation of the theory does not give Mr. Ayer nearly so much as he wants. For, with the possible exception of the ontological proof, which I do not wish to defend, it is doubtful whether any philosophers have ever asserted a proposition to the truth of which they did not think some experience or other was relevant. What I mean may be made clear by taking a few examples from among the most abstract of metaphysical arguments. The cosmological proof, for instance, starts with the premise that something or other exists, this being regarded as given in experience; the argument for an Absolute Mind including all human minds professes to start from the incomplete and incoherent character of our experience, which is held therefore to point to a more complete experience, and to be supported by citing the empirical facts of co-operation and love; the realist view of physical objects claims to be based on the experience of perception either as in itself a proof of their existence (the direct theory of perception) or as a premise from which causal inferences can be made showing that they probably exist. No doubt in some of the cases I have mentioned the metaphysician may be wrong in thinking that experience renders his conclusion probable, but we can only decide whether this is so after we have examined and refuted his argument. Since he claims that experience is relevant we cannot dismiss his theory as meaningless without examination, as the positivist would like to do, merely on the ground that its probability cannot be affected by any experience. Most metaphysical arguments may be hopelessly wrong, but I do not see how we can tell whether they are except by examining them separately on their own merits, to see whether they can really be supported by experience. We cannot nonsuit all of them *en masse* by the positivist criterion without begging the whole question. Again, take the statement that the whole universe was created by a morally perfect God. This would be held by Mr. Ayer to be meaningless, and would be generally admitted to be a metaphysical doctrine if anything is. Yet it is quite clear that empirical facts regarding the amount and distribution of suffering in the world will affect its probability. If we came to the conclusion that there was much more suffering in the world than we had thought and that there were hardly any empirical cases of suffering producing any good result, it would obviously make the truth of the belief in some degree less probable. Further, the truth of the belief would increase the probability of some propositions about the future being true. For it would certainly at least increase the probability of the proposition that I shall survive bodily death being true. Now the latter is a proposition which clearly could be verified and presumably will in fact be verified, if it is true. For if it is true I shall verify it by having experiences after bodily death. The metaphysical proposition about God is therefore one which is relevant to experiential propositions and to which experiential propositions are relevant. . . .

Mr. Ayer has, therefore, not succeeded in giving a criterion which rules out metaphysics any more or less than the propositions he wishes to admit. Further, in its second, as in its first, form it remains highly doubtful whether the verification theory can itself be verified. For we could only verify it by examining all the different kinds of meaningful statements and seeing whether sense-experience was relevant to their truth, *i.e.*, whether they could be proved or refuted by sense-experience or rendered more or less probable. But once a positivist has admitted, as Mr. Ayer has now done, that a statement may have meaning, even if it asserts something which cannot be directly experienced, provided only there could be experiences from which we might make legitimate inferences to the effect that its probability is increased or diminished, he is open to the objection that we cannot possibly learn from sense-experience alone whether an inference is legitimate or not. That B follows from A is not anything that can be sensed, and mere sense-experience cannot justify us even in thinking it probable that it will follow from A unless the sense-experience is accompanied by some principles of probable inference which are not themselves objects of the senses.

If I am right the verification theory is completely suicidal, because, if it succeeds, it shows itself to be meaningless, and therefore not true. But, even if you are not willing to go so far as this with me, you must remember that philosophers have no right to assert a theory without reasons, at least unless they seem to themselves to see quite clearly that it is self-evident; and this cannot be so in the present case, for the positivist would certainly reject self-evidence as a criterion of truth and therefore cannot use it in defence of his own doctrine. Further you must remember that, unless a theory is proved with complete certainty, part of its criterion lies in the consequences which can be deduced from it, and if these are very unplausible they will cast doubt on the theory itself. To refuse to reconsider a theory of yours because it leads to absurd consequences is, unless the theory has been proved with certainty, not to deserve praise for being logical but to deserve blame for being prejudiced. . . .

It is sometimes asserted that the verification theory ought to be accepted because it is the only theory which provides a definition of meaning. But how do the positivists know that meaning is not indefinable? Some terms must be indefinable, and such a fundamental term as meaning is surely one of the most likely terms to be so. Further, can the mere absence of an alternative definition of meaning be any possible justification for giving a definition of meaning which would make meaningless many statements that prior to the definition were held by everybody to have meaning?

Further, this reminds me that I have not stated the verification doctrine in its most common form, simply because this form seemed to me even less plausible than the others and I wished to give my opponents a fair run for their money. As most usually stated, however, the theory asserts not only that no meaningful statements are unverifiable but that the meaning of a statement just is its verification (or its method of verification). And if we use the argument that we must have a definition of meaning and the verification theory is the only definition that has ever been suggested, we must conclude not merely that all meaningful statements are verifiable but that their verification (or method of verification) is identical with their meaning. Otherwise the theory would not be giving a *definition* of meaning. To this extremer form of the theory there seem to me to be two objections that are not applicable to the milder forms, which do not actually equate verification with meaning but only use it as a test of meaning. The first objection is that verification presupposes something which is verified, and this cannot itself be the verification but must be a proposition which cannot be reduced without residuum to its own verification. To say that what I mean in asserting a proposition is its verification seems to me parallel to saying "I lie" when what is said to be a lie is not a previous proposition but the proposition "I lie" itself. There is nothing to which the "it" in "its verification" refers unless there is a proposition to be verified over and above the verification of it. For what has to be verified is never the sentence but what it means. The sentence is a mere set of noises or black marks which occur and are experienced whether it is true or false, meaningful or meaningless.

Secondly, the belief in the occurrence of an event is very often verified by observing not it but its effects and concluding from them to the event as cause. It will follow that in these cases, if the meaning is identical with its verification, the event will be its own effects. Positivists abominate the entailment view of causation, but, if they were consistent with this definition of meaning, they would have to hold not only that the cause entails but that it analytically entails its effect. I think that an entailment view of causation is true, but even if I am right in this it is quite certain that the entailment, if present, must be synthetic, not analytic. . . .

This rejection of metaphysics comes from the unwarranted narrowing down of "justification" to "justification by sense-experience." If we want a criterion to determine when a statement has meaning, it is arguable that "verifiability" will do if we mean by this that a statement to have a meaning must be such that we can think of some conceivable method by which it might be supported (I think it is too strong to say "proved") or refuted. But, even so, we are not justified in assuming that the only way of supporting a proposition must be by sense-experience or by inductive argument from sense-experience. . . .

The positivists claim to settle once for all by a consistent use of their verification doctrine all the great philosophical issues of the past — the issues between empiricism and rationalism, realism and idealism, pluralism and monism, naturalism and theism; but before they have the least right to do this the verification doctrine must itself be justified. My aim in this paper has been to show both that it cannot be true, because if it were true, it would be meaningless, which is self-contradictory, and that even if *per impossibile* it could be true there is no more ground for believing it than there is for believing the damnatory clauses of the Athanasian creed.

Addendum

The foregoing article was written at a time when verificationists were inclined to be much more dogmatic than they are today, and it was not fair to all of them even then. The usual reply to my argument that the verification principle is on its own showing meaningless is that it does not apply to itself because it is intended as a criterion of the meaningfulness only of factual statements purporting to describe what exists, and that it is not a factual statement. Great emphasis is now laid on there being other kinds of meaning besides "factual meaning." However, I think my article still has some value in dispelling the widespread popular notion that metaphysics has somehow been proved impossible by means of the verification principle and in showing that the principle, even if not meaningless, is incapable of justification. Indeed, criticisms of this type have been so successful that the verification principle is now generally described, even by its adherents, not as an established proposition but as a methodological assumption or postulate. But even philosophers who are prepared to admit, if pressed, that the principle is only a methodological assumption, and therefore not asserted as true, still often seem to slip into regarding it in their own thoughts as if it had been shown to be true, or at least talk as if they do so. This is the case when they use it as a premise to establish a conclusion, e.g., when they argue that philosophical differences, which do not concern empirically verifiable propositions, are differences about language and not about facts.

A point which I ought to have discussed is Ayer's second definition of "verifiable" in the weak sense, which is roughly that a statement has factual meaning only if it could be used in making detailed directly verifiable predictions.[1] This suggests a good way of distinguishing between science and philosophy; but it cannot be proved that sentences which do not conform to the principle have no factual meaning and the process of making the predictions itself presupposes principles of inference which are not verifiable.

[1] A. J. Ayer, *Language, Truth and Logic* (London: Victor Gollancz, Ltd., 1946), 11 ff., 38–9.

A. J. Ayer and F. C. Copleston

Alfred Jules Ayer (see also page 304) and Frederick Charles Copleston are contemporary English philosophers representing radically different positions in their interpretation of religion.

Father Copleston, Professor of the History of Philosophy at Heythrop College, England, and at the Gregorian University, Rome, is a distinguished English Jesuit. Born in 1907 and educated at Marlborough and St. John's College, Oxford, he entered the Roman Catholic Church in 1925 and in 1930 the Society of Jesus, in which he was ordained priest in 1937. His extensive publications include Existentialism and Modern Man *and a six-volume history of philosophy.*

The dialogue, which took place in 1949, is reproduced here as it was recorded and without any attempt to recast it in a more literary form that would alter its tone of conversational spontaneity.

Logical Positivism: Discussion between Professor Ayer and Father Copleston *

AYER: Well, Father Copleston, you've asked me to summarize logical positivism for you, and it's not very easy. For one thing, as I understand it, logical positivism isn't a system of philosophy; it consists, rather, in a certain technique, a certain kind of attitude towards philosophical problems. Perhaps one thing which those of us who are called logical positivists tend to have in common is that we deny the possibility of philosophy as a speculative discipline. We should say that if philosophy was to be a branch of knowledge as distinct from the sciences it would have to consist in logic or in some form of analysis; and our reason for this would be somewhat as follows.

We maintain that you can divide propositions into two classes — formal and empirical. Formal propositions, like those of logic and mathematics, depend for their validity on the conventions of a symbol system. Empirical propositions, on the other hand, are statements of observation — actual or possible — or hypotheses from which such statements can be logically derived; and it is they that constitute science insofar as science isn't purely mathematical. Now our contention is that this exhausts the field of what we may call speculative knowledge. Consequently we reject metaphysics, if this be understood — and I think it commonly has been — as an attempt to gain knowledge about the

* Transcribed from a telediphone recording and used by permission of the British Broadcasting Corporation and of the participants, Professor Ayer and Father Copleston.

world by non-scientific means. Inasmuch as metaphysical statements are not testable by observation, we hold they're not descriptive of anything; and from this we should conclude that if philosophy is to be a cognitive activity, it must be purely critical. It would take the form of trying to elucidate the concepts that were used in science or mathematics or in everyday language.

COPLESTON: Well, Professor Ayer, I can quite understand, of course, philosophers' confining themselves to logical analysis if they wish to do so, and I shouldn't dream of denying or of belittling in any way its utility; I think it's obviously an extremely useful thing to do, to analyze and clarify the concepts used in science. In everyday life, too, there are many terms used that practically have taken on an emotional connotation — "progressive," or "reactionary," or "freedom," or "the modern mind." To make clear to people what's meant — or what *they* mean — by those terms, or the various possible meanings, is a very useful thing. But if the logical positivist means that logical analysis is the *only* function of philosophy, that's the point at which I should disagree with him; and so would many other philosophers disagree, especially, I think, on the Continent.

Don't you think that by saying what philosophy is one presupposes a philosophy or takes up a position as a philosopher? For example, if one divides significant propositions into two classes — namely, purely formal propositions and statements of observation — one is adopting a philosophical position, one is claiming that there are no necessary propositions which are not purely formal. Moreover, to claim that metaphysical propositions to be significant should be verifiable as scientific hypotheses are verifiable is to claim that metaphysics — to be significant — should not be metaphysics.

AYER: Oh, I agree that my position is philosophical, though not that it's metaphysical, as I hope to show later. To say what philosophy is is certainly a philosophical act, but this I mean is itself a question of philosophical analysis. We have to decide, among other things, what it is we're going to call philosophy — and I've given you my answer. It is not, perhaps, an obvious answer, but it at least has the merit that it rescues philosophical statements from becoming either meaningless or trivial.

But I don't suppose you want to quarrel about how we're going to use the word so much as to discuss the points underlying what you've just said. You would hold, I gather, that in the account I gave of the possible fields of knowledge, something's left out.

COPLESTON: Yes.

AYER: And that which was left out is what people called philosophers might well be expected to study?

COPLESTON: Yes, I should hold that philosophy at any rate meant a physical philosophy — begins in a sense where science leaves off. In my personal opinion one of the chief functions of metaphysics is to open the mind to the transcendent — to remove the ceiling, as it were, the room being the world as amenable to scientific handling and investigation. But this is not to say that the metaphysician is *simply* concerned with the transcendent. Phenomena themselves, objects of what you would probably call experience, can be considered from the metaphysical angle. The problem of the universals, for instance, is not, I should say, a purely linguistic problem, but a metaphysical problem. I'd say that metaphysical philosophy begins *in a sense* where science leaves off because I don't mean to imply that the metaphysician cannot begin until science has finished its work; if this were so, the metaphysician would be quite unable to start. I mean that he asks other questions than those asked by the scientist, and pursues a different method.

AYER: To say that philosophy begins where science leaves off is perfectly all right if you mean that the philosopher takes the results from the scientist, analyzes them, shows the logical connection of one proposition with another, and so on; but if you say it leaps into a quite different realm, the realm which you describe as the transcendent, then I think I cease to follow you. And here I can explain *why* I cease to follow you: I hold the principle — known as the principle of verification — according to which a statement intended to be a statement of fact is meaningful only if it's either formally valid, or some kind of observation is relevant to its truth or falsehood. My difficulty with your so-called transcendent statements is that their truth or falsehood doesn't, it seems to me, make the slightest difference to anything that anyone experiences.

COPLESTON: Well, I don't care for the phrase "transcendent statements." I think myself that some positive descriptive statements *about* the transcendent are possible, but, leaving that out of account, I think that one of the possible functions of the philosopher — a function which you, presumably, exclude — is to reveal the limits of science as a complete and exhaustive description and analysis of reality.

AYER: Limits of science? You see, I can quite well understand that you say science is limited insofar as many more things may be discovered. You may say, for example, that the physics of the seventeenth century was limited insofar as the physicists of the eighteenth, nineteenth, and twentieth centuries have gone very much further.

COPLESTON: No, I didn't mean that at all. Perhaps I can illustrate what I mean in reference to — anthropology. The biochemist can describe man within his own terms of reference, and up to a certain extent; but although biochemistry may doubtless continue to advance, I see no reason to suppose that the biochemist will be able to give an exhaustive analysis of man. The psychologist certainly wouldn't think so.

Now one of the possible functions of the philosopher is to show how all these scientific analyses of men — of man — the analysis of the biochemist, the empirical psychologist, and so on — are unable to achieve the exhaustive analysis of the individual human being. Karl Jaspers, for example, would maintain that man as a free — that is, precisely as free — being cannot be adequately handled by any scientist who presupposes the applicability of the principle of deterministic causality, and conducts his investigations with that presupposition in mind. I'm not a follower of Karl Jaspers, but I think that to draw attention to what he calls "existence" is a legitimate philosophical procedure.

AYER: I don't say that you can know a priori that human behavior is inexplicable. The most you can say is that our present stock of psychological hypotheses isn't adequate to explain certain features of it, and you may very well be right. But then what more is required is better psychological investigation; we need to form new theories, and test the theories by further observation — which is again the method of science. It seems to me that all you've said when you've talked of the limits of science is simply that a given science cannot explain things, or explain so much as you would like to see explained. But that, which to me seems to be perfectly acceptable, is only a historical statement about a point which science has reached at a given stage. It doesn't show that there's room for a quite different type of discipline, and you haven't made clear to me what that different kind of discipline which you reserve for the philosopher is supposed to be.

COPLESTON: Well, I still think that one of the possible functions of the philosopher is to consider what is sometimes called the non-empirical or intelligible self. There is an obvious objection from your point of view against the phrase "non-empirical self" — I agree. But I would like to turn to metaphysics in general. The scientist can describe various particular aspects of things, and all the sciences together can give, it is true, a very general description of reality. But the scientist, precisely as scientist, does not raise, for example, the question why anything is there at all. To raise the problem of being is, in my opinion, one of the possible functions of the philosopher. You may say that the question cannot be answered. I think that it can, but if it could *not* be answered, I consider that it is one of the functions of the philosopher to show that there *is* such a problem. Some philosophers would say that metaphysics consists in raising problems, rather than in answering them definitely, and though I don't myself agree with the sheerly agnostic position, I think that there *is* value in raising the metaphysical problems, quite apart from the question whether one can or cannot answer them definitely. That is why I said earlier on that one of the functions of the philosopher is to open the mind to the transcendent, to take the ceiling off the room, to use a rather crude metaphor.

AYER: Hm. Yes, there's a peculiarity about these "why" questions. Suppose someone asks you, "Why did the light go out?" You may tell him, "The light went out because there was a fuse," and he then says, "Why does the light go out when it's fused?" Then perhaps you tell him a story about electrical connections — wires, and so on; that is the "how" story. Then, if he's not satisfied with that, you may give him the general theory of electricity, which is again a "how" story. And then, if he's not satisfied with that, you may give him the general theory of electromagnetics, which is again a "how" story; you tell him that things function this way at this level; then your "why" answers are deductions from that. So that in the ordinary sense of a "why" question, asking a "why" question is getting a "how" answer at a higher logical level, a more general "how" answer. Well now, if you raise the question as regards the world as a whole, you're asking for what? The most general possible theory?

COPLESTON: Nn-o. The metaphysical question I have in mind is a different sort of question. If I ask, for example, how the earth comes to be in its present condition, I do expect an answer which refers to empirical causes and conditions — there I quite agree with you. I go to the astronomer for an answer. And if one persists in asking such questions, I daresay one could in theory go back indefinitely — at least, I'm quite prepared to admit the possibility. But if I ask why there are phenomena at all, why there is "something" rather than "nothing," I'm not asking for an answer in terms of empirical causes and conditions. Even if the series of phenomena *did* go back indefinitely, without beginning, I could still raise the question as to why the infinite series of phenomena exists, how it comes to be there. Whether such a question can be answered or not is obviously another matter, but if I ask whether anything lies behind phenomena, whether anything is responsible for the series, finite or infinite, of phenomena, the answer — supposing that there *is* an answer — must, in my opinion, refer to the reality lying beyond or behind phenomena — but, in any case, to ask why any finite phenomena exist, why there is "something" rather than "nothing," is to ask a different sort of question from the question why water tends to flow downhill rather than uphill.

AYER: But my objection is that your notion of an explanation of *all* phenomena is self-contradictory.

COPLESTON: Well, what is the contradiction?

AYER: The contradiction is, I think, that if you accept my interpretation of what "why" questions are, then asking a "why" question is always asking for a more general description — and asking for the "why" of that is asking for a more general description still. And then you say, "Give me an answer to a 'why' which doesn't take the form of a description" — and that's a contradiction. It's like saying, "Give me a description more general than any description, which itself is not a description," and clearly nobody can do that.

COPLESTON: Well, that's not quite the question I'm asking. There would be a contradiction if I didn't distinguish between a scientific question and a metaphysical question, but a metaphysical question concerns the intelligible structure of reality, insofar as it is not amenable to investigation by the methods of empirical science. It seems to me that when I propose a metaphysical question you ask me to restate the question as though it were a scientific question; but if I *could* do that, the question would not be a metaphysical question, would it?

AYER: Well, what form would the metaphysical question take?

COPLESTON: Well, in my opinion, the existence of phenomena in general requires some explanation, and I should say that the explanation would be in terms of a transcendent reality. I maintain that this is a possible philosophical question. Whatever the answer may be, it obviously cannot insist on a further description of phenomena. Aristotle asserted that philosophy begins with wonder. If someone feels no wonder at the existence in a physical world, well, he's unlikely to ask any questions about its existence as such, that's true.

AYER: But if you say anything of that kind, it still means that you are feeling your transcendent reality, or, rather, the statements about your transcendent reality, in the same way as the scientific hypothesis; it becomes a very, very general scientific hypothesis, and you want to say it's not like a scientific hypothesis.

COPLESTON: Why not?

AYER: I suppose it's because you can't test it in any way. If you can't test it in any way, then you've not got an explanation, and you haven't answered my question.

COPLESTON: Well, at this point I should like to remark that you are presupposing that one must be able to test every hypothesis in a certain way. I do not mean to allow that every metaphysical statement is an hypothesis, but, even if it were, it would not be tested scientifically without ceasing to be a metaphysical statement. You seem to me to reject the beginning of the reflective work of the intellect on which rational metaphysics depends.

Neither Spinoza nor Fichte nor Hegel nor Thomas Aquinas supposed that one could investigate scientifically what they respectively believed to be metaphenomenal reality, but each of them thought that intellectual reflection can lead the mind to postulate that reality.

AYER: Well, I suppose you give a sense in which it could; for example, you could compare it with . . . It's something heavily camouflaged and you can understand its value even if you can't see it. But that's because you know what it would be like to see it independent of the thing you describe.

Now your kind of penetration is a very queer one, because you say you can discern things lying behind other things with simply no experience of stripping off the disguise and coming across the thing undisguised.

COPLESTON: It's not exactly a question of the disguise. I can strip off camouflage and see the camouflaged thing with my eyes, yes. But no metaphysician would pretend that one could see a metaphenomenal reality with the eyes. It can be apprehended only by an intellectual activity, though that activity must of necessity begin with the objects of sense experience and introspection. After all, you yourself reflect on the data of experience; your philosophy doesn't consist in stating atomic experiences.

AYER: No, indeed, it doesn't. Since I hold that philosophy consists of logical analysis, it isn't combined in the act of stating experiences at all — if by taking experiences, you mean just describing them.

COPLESTON: Well, perhaps we are discussing my particular brand of metaphysics rather than logical positivism. However, I should maintain that the very ability to raise the question of the existence of the world or of a series of phenomena implies a dim awareness of the non-self-sufficiency of the world. Then this awareness becomes articulate and finds expression; it may be to a less physical speculation, to a contradistincting of contingent existence as such. And I should maintain that an intellectual apprehension of the nature of what I call "contingent being" as such involves an apprehension of its relatedness to self-grounded being. Some philosophers — Hegel among them, I think — would hold that one cannot think of finite being as such without implicitly thinking of the infinite. The words as such are, I should say, important. I can perfectly well think of a cow, for example, without thinking of any visible reality, but if I abstract from its characteristics as a cow, and think of it merely as contingent being, then I pass into the sphere of its physics.

AYER: But it's precisely questions like this question about the world as a whole, and about finite being as such, if you like, that I think we should rule out. Supposing you ask a question like: "Where do all things come from?"

Now that's a perfectly meaningful question as regards any given event. Asking where it came from is asking for a description of some event prior to it. But if you generalize that question it becomes meaningless. You are then asking what event is prior to all of them. And clearly no event can be prior to all of them, because if it is a member of the class of all of them it must be included in it, and therefore can't be prior to it.

Let me give another instance; it will take the same point. One can observe only one perception of an hallucination, meaning by this that it isn't corroborated by one's own further perceptions of other people, and that makes sense.

Now some people, and philosophers too I am afraid, want to generalize this, and say with a profound air: "Perhaps all our experiences are hallucinatory." Well, that of course becomes meaningless. In exactly the same way, I should say that this question of where does it all come from isn't meaningful.

COPLESTON: It isn't meaningful if the only meaningful questions are those which can be answered by the methods of empirical science, as you presuppose. In my opinion you are unduly limiting the "meaningfulness" to a certain restricted kind of meaningfulness. Now, the possibility of raising the question of the absolute seems to depend largely on the nature of relations. If one denies that one can discern any implication or internal relation in the existing phenomenon, considered as such, then a metaphysic of the absolute becomes an impossible thing. If the mind can discern such a relation, then I think a metaphysic of the absolute is possible.

AYER: Metaphysic of the absolute? I am afraid my problem is still what questions are being asked. Now supposing one says: "Is the world dependent on something outside itself?" Would you maintain that as a possible question?

COPLESTON: Yes, I think it's a possible question.

AYER: But then you are using a very queer sense of causation, aren't you? Because in the normal sense in which you talk of one event being dependent, or consequent, on another, you'd be meaning that they had some kind of temporal relation to each other. In fact, normally if one uses the word causation, one is saying that the later event is dependent upon the earlier, in the sense that all cases of the earlier are also cases of the later. But now, you can't be meaning that, because if you were you'd be putting your causes in the world.

COPLESTON: It would bring the world into relation with the reality; and personally I shouldn't dream of adopting any metaphysics which did not start with experience of this world. But the relating of the world to a Being outside the world would not bring that Being into the world. Incidentally, I have just used the word "outside." Well, that illustrates admirably the inadequacy of language for expressing metaphysical ideas. "Outside" suggests distance in space; "independent" would be better.

But I should like to make some remarks about this use of the word "cause." I am very glad you brought the question up. First of all, as far as I understand the use of the term by scientists, causal laws would mean to them, I suppose, statistical generalizations from observed phenomena. At least that would be one of the meanings, I think.

AYER: That makes it rather more genetic than it need be. I mean the question isn't really where the scientific expressions have come from, but what use they are put to. Let us say that they are generalizations which refer to observable events — phenomena, if you will.

COPLESTON: Well, I agree, of course, that one cannot use the principle of causality, if it is understood in a sense which involves reference to phenomena exclusively in order to transcend phenomena. Supposing, for example, that I understood by the principle of causality the proposition that the initial state of every phenomenon was determined by a preceding phenomenon or by preceding phenomena, I could not use such a principle to transcend phenomena, quite apart from the fact that it may not even apply to all phenomena. But what I understand by the philosophic principle of causality is the general proposition that every being which has not in itself its reason of existence depends for its existence on an extrinsic reality that I call cause. This principle says nothing as to the character of the cause. It may be free or not free. Therefore the principle cannot be "refuted" by infra-atomic indeterminism, if there is such a thing, any more than it is refuted by the free acts of men. Some philosophers would probably say that the principle is only subjective necessity. I don't hold that view myself, nor do I see any very cogent reason for holding it. Moreover, though the principle is, in a sense, presupposed by the scientist when he traces the connection between a phenomenal effect and a phenomenal cause, the principle mentions not phenomenal causes but an extrinsic reality. If one is speaking of all beings which have not in themselves the reason for their existence, the "extrinsic reality" in question must transcend them. To my way of thinking the philosophic principle of causality is simply an implication of the intelligibility of phenomena, if these are regarded as contingent events.

AYER: Well, then, again I think I should accuse you of the fallacy of misplaced generalization. You see, what is the intelligibility of phenomena? You can understand sentences, you can understand an argument. They can be intelligible or not. But what is the understanding of phenomena, even a particular one, let alone all phenomena?

Well, I think you could give a sense to understanding a particular phenomenon. You would recognize some description of it as an accurate description, and then understanding the phenomenon would be a matter of explaining this description — that is, of deducing it from some theory. Now, you say, are all phenomena intelligible? Does that mean that you are looking for a single theory from which every true proposition can be deduced? I doubt if you could find one, but even if you did you'd want that theory again, wouldn't you, to be explained in its turn? — which gives you an infinite regress. You see, phenomena just happen, don't they? Is there a question of their being intelligible or not intelligible?

COPLESTON: No, phenomena don't "just happen." I didn't "just happen." If I did, my existence would be unintelligible. And I'm not prepared to acquiesce in the idea that the series of phenomena just happened even if infinite existence is such. Whether it's an answerable question or not is another pair of shoes.

AYER: Well, I agree that many metaphysicians have supposed themselves to be asking and answering questions of this kind. But I still want to say that I don't regard these questions as genuine questions, nor do I regard the answers as intelligible. For example, let's take the case of someone who says that the answer is that really it's the absolute expressing itself. I say such an answer explains nothing, because I can do nothing with it, and I don't know what it would be like for such a proposition to be true. I should say the same about all statements of this kind.

COPLESTON: And why should it be necessary to do anything with a proposition?

AYER: Because you put this up as a hypothesis, and a hypothesis is supposed to explain.

COPLESTON: An explanation is meant to explain, certainly. What I meant was that there is no reason why we should be able to deduce "practical" consequences from it.

AYER: Well, if you don't get what you call practical answers, what kind of answers do you get?

COPLESTON: Theoretical answers, of course. I should have thought, as a simple-minded historian of philosophy, that one has been given a good many metaphysical answers. They cannot all be true; but the answers are forthcoming all the same.

AYER: Yes, but the trouble with these theoretical answers is that they are given not as explanations of any particular event, but of all events. And I wonder if this notion of an explanation of all events isn't itself faulty. When

I explain something by telling you that *this* is the way it works, I thereby exclude other possibilities — so that any genuine explanation is compatible with one course of events, and incompatible with another. That, of course, is what distinguishes one explanation from another. But something which purposed to explain all events, not merely all events that did occur, but any event that could occur, would be empty as an explanation because nothing would disagree with it. You might explain all events as they do occur, provided you allowed the possibility that if they occurred differently your explanation would be falsified. But the trouble with those so-called metaphysical explanations is that they don't merely purport to explain what does happen, but to serve equally for anything that could conceivably happen. However you changed your data, the same explanation would still hold; but that makes it as an explanation absolutely vacuous.

COPLESTON: I think that what you are demanding is that any explanation of the existence of phenomena should be a scientific hypothesis. Otherwise you will not recognize it as an explanation. This is to say: "All explanations of facts are of the type of scientific hypothesis or they are not explanations at all." But the explanations of all finite beings cannot be a scientific explanation, i.e., in the technical sense of the use of the word "scientific." But it can, I think, be a rational explanation all the same. After all, "rational" and "scientific" are not equivalent terms; and to my way of thinking it is a prejudice to say that they are equivalent.

AYER: But does a non-scientific explanation explain anything? Let me take an example. Supposing someone said that the explanation for things' happening as they did was that it answered the purposes of the deity. Now I should say that would be meaningful only if you could show that events going this way rather than that way answered his purpose. But if you're going to say that whatever happens is going to answer his purpose then it becomes useless as an explanation. In fact it's not an explanation at all. It becomes empty of significance because it's consistent with everything.

COPLESTON: I know it seeks the explanation of the world. I am considering ontological questions and what I am looking for is an ontological explanation, not simply a logical principle — abstract.

AYER: Even so, aren't you asking something contradictory? You see, so long as the explanation is contingent — that is, something that might be otherwise, logically — you're going to say it's not a sufficient explanation. So that you want for your proposition something that is logically necessary. But of course, once your proposition becomes logically necessary, it is a purely formal one, and so doesn't explain anything. So that what you want is to have a proposition that is both contingent and necessary — contingent — contingent insofar as it's got to describe the world, necessary insofar as it's not just something happening to be, but something that must be. But that's a contradiction in terms.

COPLESTON: There is a contradiction if one grants an assumption of yours which I deny. A proposition which is applicable to a contingent thing or event is not, however, necessarily a contingent proposition. Nor is the proposition that it *is* contingent an analytic or self-evident proposition. In any case, I'm not seeking the ontological explanation of the world simply in a proposition.

AYER: But shouldn't you be?

COPLESTON: Why should one be?

AYER: Well, what is explanation except a matter of deriving one proposition from another? But perhaps you prefer to call your ontological principle a fact. Then what you're asking for is a fact that is at one and the same time contingent and necessary, and you can't have it.

COPLESTON: Why should it be at one and the same time contingent and necessary?

AYER: It's got to be contingent in order to do for an explanation. It's got to be necessary because you're not satisfied with anything contingent.

COPLESTON: I shouldn't admit that it's got to be contingent in order to do its work of explanation. I'd say that it didn't do its work of explanation if it was contingent.

AYER: But how possibly could you derive anything empirical from a necessary proposition?

COPLESTON: I am not attempting to derive an empirical thing from a necessary proposition. I do attempt, however, to render empirical things intelligible by reference to an absolute or necessary being.

AYER: But surely a necessary being can only be one concerning whom the proposition that it exists is necessary.

COPLESTON: The proposition would be necessary, yes, but it doesn't follow that one can discern its necessity. I'm not holding, for instance, the ontological argument for the existence of God, though I do believe, myself, that God's existence is the "ultimate" ontological explanation of phenomena.

AYER: Well, now, ultimate in what sense? In the sense that you can't find a more general proposition from which it can be deduced?

COPLESTON: An ultimate principle or proposition is obviously not deducible if you must speak of propositions instead of beings.

AYER: Well, that is so, I think.

COPLESTON: Well, the world doesn't consist of contingent propositions, though things may be expressed in contingent propositions. Nor should I say that a necessary being consists of necessary propositions.

AYER: No, of course, I shouldn't say the word "proposition" — it's very bad grammar, bad logical grammar; but the words "necessary" and "contingent," which you introduced, do apply to propositions in their ordinary logical acceptance.

COPLESTON: Yes, certainly they do apply to propositions, but I do not accept the position that all necessary or certain propositions are tautologies. I think that there are necessary or certain propositions which also apply to things.

AYER: Yes, but not in any different sense. A statement to the effect that a thing is necessary could be translated into a statement that a proposition referring to that being was necessary. Now you've got into the difficulty, for from a logically necessary proposition — which I would say meant a formally valid proposition and therefore a materially empty proposition — you want to derive a proposition with material content. You do want to have it both ways; you want to have statements — facts, if you like — which are both contingent and necessary, and that, of course, you can't have — and a metaphysician can't have it either.

COPLESTON: But, you see, I don't believe that all certain propositions are only formally valid, in the sense of being tautologies. I am not saying that there are propositions which are both necessary and contingent; what I'm saying is that there are, in my opinion, propositions which are certain and which are yet applicable to reality. If the reality in question happens to be contingent, that doesn't make the proposition contingent, if by contingent you mean an uncertain empirical hypothesis.

AYER: Well, then, I must protest I *don't* understand your use of the word "necessary." You see, it seems to me we've got a fairly clear meaning for "logically necessary" — that is to say, propositions that are formally valid, that in technical terms are analytic, I should call logically necessary; and I can understand "causally necessary." I should say that events are linked by causal necessity when there is some hypothesis, not itself logically necessary, from which their connection is reducible. Now you want to introduce a third sense of necessity, which is the crucial sense for you, which isn't either of these, but is — what?

COPLESTON: By a necessary proposition I mean a *certain* proposition. You may say that there are no certain propositions which are applicable to reality; but that's another matter. Earlier in our discussion I distinguished at least two senses of the principle of causality, and the philosophic version I should regard as certain. In other words, besides purely logical propositions and what you would, I think, call empirical hypotheses, I believe that there are metaphysical propositions which are certain. Now take the principle of contradiction. I think there is a metaphysical version of the principle which is not simply what is sometimes called, unfortunately, I think, "a law of thought," but is, rather, imposed on the mind by its experience of being — or, better, by its reflection on its experience of being. But I presume that you would say that the principle is only formal. Well, it seems to me that if it's purely formal, then I ought to admit there's a possibility of this piece of paper being white and not white at the same time. I can't think it, but I ought, I think, on your assumptions, to admit the abstract possibility of it . . . But if I can't think it, I can't admit its abstract possibility.

AYER: Well, if you tell me that the paper is both white and not white, of course, you don't tell me anything about fact, do you?

COPLESTON: Well, no; and I should say that it is because one can't admit the possibility of its being both white and not white at the same time.

AYER: You can't admit that possibility, given existing conventions, about the use of the word "not," but of course you could perfectly well introduce the convention by which it would be meaningful — that is to say, supposing you chose, when the paper was grey, to say it was both white and not white, you would have altered your logic. But given that you're using a logic in which you exclude "*p* and not *p*," then of course you exclude the paper white and not white.

COPLESTON: A logic in which you don't exclude "*p* and not *p*" may have uses; but I don't see that any significant statement can be made about this piece of paper in such a logic. It seems to me that, if the principle of contradiction is purely formal and tautological, I ought to admit the possibility of the paper being white — what I *call* white — of being white and not white at the same time; but I can't think that.

AYER: No, of course you can't. You shouldn't be expected to, because to think that would be to use symbols in a way not in accordance with the conventions under which that particular group of symbols is to be used. But, of course, you could describe the same experience in a different sort of logic; you could introduce a different grammar of color classification, which allowed you to say that the paper was and was not a certain color — for example, in the case where the color is changing — certain Hegelians want to do that and we have no call to stop them. There's no particular advantage in doing it, because you can equally well describe that phenomenon in the Aristotelian logic; but if in the case where it's changing its color you like to say that it's both white and not white — well, that's all right, as long as it's understood how your terms are being used.

COPLESTON: It seems to me that it would be the nature of the thing itself that forced me to speak in a certain way. If I have before me Smith and Jackson, I can't think of Smith-and-Jackson at the same time. I should say that it's not merely a law of thought or an analytic tautology that forces me to say that, but the nature of the things themselves.

AYER: I agree that such conventions are based on empirical formulae, the nature of your experiences, and adapted to meet them; but you can again quite easily imagine circumstances in which you would be inclined to change your logic in that respect. Certain neurotic phenomena might very well incline one to say that Smith had acquired some of Jackson's personality, and then, if such things were very common, you might get a new usage of person, according to which you could have two different persons inhabiting one body or one person inhabiting different bodies.

COPLESTON: Well, I can agree to speak about things, using any terms I like, I suppose. I can agree to call that paper red, when I know that it's white, but that in no way alters the nature of the paper.

AYER: No, I'm not claiming that it does. The fact is that the paper looks as it looks; if you have a symbol system which you use to describe those facts, then that symbol system will itself have certain conventions governing the use of certain symbols in it. Now, I think in any given symbol system I could separate what I call the logical expressions from the descriptive expressions. Now, words like "not" I should say were logical expressions.

COPLESTON: Supposing one had another logical system. Is there any rule of speaking within that system? And suppose now you're using a three-valued logic. You could perfectly well use that to describe what you now describe, could you?

AYER: Yes; the difference would be that you couldn't make certain inferences that you now make. Thus from the fact that the paper was *not* not white you couldn't then infer that it was white; you could only infer that it was either white or the intermediate stage, which you would choose to describe, not by a separate word, which brings you back to your two-value system, but by saying both white and not white.

COPLESTON: Well, I still think that there are certain propositions which are founded on an experience of reality and which are not, therefore, simply formal propositions or tautologies. If one wishes to keep within the sphere of purely formal logic, one can perhaps on this understanding employ a three-valued logic. But purely formal propositions are not likely to help one in metaphysics. No doubt you would say, "Hear, hear." But I admit, and you don't, propositions which are certain and yet not purely formal. Some people would call such propositions "synthetic a priori propositions." I'm not particularly fond of the phrase myself, on account of its association with the philosophy of Kant. However, the issue between us, in any case, is whether or not there are propositions which are certain and which yet apply to reality; and I don't think that the introduction of the three-valued logic really affects the point very much. I have no wish to deny that there may be propositions which are purely formal. I am convinced of the existence of valid metaphysical propositions. However, I should like to raise another question, in order to get your views on it. Perhaps you'd help me to obtain clarity in the matter. I'm not quite certain about it. My question is this. Within a three-valued system of logic, would you say there is any rule of consistency at all?

AYER: Yes, otherwise there would be no logic.

COPLESTON: Then does it not seem that there is at least one proposition which governs all possible systems of logic?

AYER: No, that doesn't follow.

COPLESTON: Well, supposing, in a system without the principle of contradiction, one simply disregarded the principles of consistency within the system. Would you say then that one was contradicting oneself?

AYER: No, because in that sense the notion of contradiction as you understand it wouldn't apply.

COPLESTON: Well, would you say that one was at variance with the rules of the game?

AYER: Yes; you wouldn't be playing that game.

COPLESTON: Then there are some laws — if one likes to speak in that way — that govern all games?

AYER: No, there are no laws that govern all games, but each game has a certain set of laws governing it.

COPLESTON: Well, consistency, or observation of laws, within a game — whatever these laws may be — is itself, I would suggest, a kind of protoprinciple.

AYER: What's common to all of them is if the game is conducted in accordance with certain rules — then if you don't observe those rules you're not playing that game, though possibly some other.

COPLESTON: Well, are you producing unintelligible statements?

AYER: Whether the statements were intelligible or not would depend on whether they could be interpreted as counters in some other game.

COPLESTON: Ah, but within the game itself —

AYER: No, they wouldn't be.

COPLESTON: Well, then, it does seem to me that there is, at any rate, a principle of consistency, which seems to be a kind of protoproposition governing all reasoning.

AYER: Well, take it this way. Take it in the case of chess or bridge. Now you might play bridge and revoke.

COPLESTON: Yes.

AYER: And if it's done once, occasionally, that's considered to be a slip and you haven't stopped playing bridge. But supposing now you make revoking a general habit and nobody worries, you're allowed to revoke when you please, then you're playing some different game. Now possibly you might be able to determine the rules of that game too.

COPLESTON: Yes.

AYER: Well, now, exactly the same with logic, you see. In an ordinary, say, Aristotelian logic, certain moves were allowed.

COPLESTON: Necessitated I should say, yes.

AYER: And certain moves, including not admitting contradictions, are disallowed.

COPLESTON: Well?

AYER: Now, supposing you have a game which breaks those rules, then you have a different game.

COPLESTON: Granted. But I don't admit that all logics are games, in the sense that no logic applies to reality or that all possible logics apply equally well. I don't see any reason to say that. If one did say it the statement would be a philosophical, even a metaphysical, statement, and therefore, I suppose, according to your view technically meaningless. However, supposing that they are games, there is, I should suggest, a certain architectonics governing the playing of those games.

AYER: No, all you can say is, not that there's any given rule that must be observed in any game, because there isn't, but that in any game there must be some rules. And it's an empirical question which logic is the most useful. Compare the case of alternative geometries.

COPLESTON: Observance of consistency seems to me to mean something more than "Unless you observe the rules of the game, you don't observe the rules of the game." It seems to me to mean "If you contradict yourself — that is, if you contradict your premises and definitions — you don't reason significantly." That is not an arbitrary or conventional principle, I should suggest.

AYER: But surely all that you're saying is that in language — namely, the one we're now using, where one of the principles of correct reasoning is the observance of the law of non-contradiction — then anyone who violates this law isn't reasoning correctly. That is certainly a valid statement, but it is conventional.

COPLESTON: I should like to know, Professor, what you, as a logical positivist, think about the relation of language to philosophy. Would you say that philosophy depends on language in the sense that philosophical ideas depend on grammatical and syntactical structure?

AYER: Not quite in that sense, but I think philosophy can be said to be about language.

COPLESTON: Do you think that to some extent it depends on the language you use to do it in?

AYER: That which you can imagine to be possible depends very much upon what kind of symbol system you're using, yes.

COPLESTON: Can you give me an illustration of the way philosophy depends on language?

AYER: Well, I should say, for example, that the belief of Western philosophers in substance is very much bound up with the subject-predicate relationship in most sentences in Western languages.

COPLESTON: In that case it's a question of intelligent investigation, is it? I mean as to whether that is the case or not. We should find, if the theory is true, that if the grammatical and syntactical structures of the different languages are different, philosophical problems raised in those languages are different.

AYER: But, surely, you can translate the Western philosophical problems into some quite primitive, non-European languages, and where difficulty in doing so arises it's not owing to the grammatical and syntactical structure of the language in question so much as to the absence of the abstract expression which will correspond to the Western ideas.

COPLESTON: It seems to me that the idea has come before the expression. To say that the expression governs the idea and the formation of the ideas is rather to put the cart before the horse.

AYER: The idea comes before the expression. An image or something of that sort.

COPLESTON: Sometimes, of course, it will be an image, though I'm a little doubtful as to whether all ideas are accompanied by images. But if you take your concrete example, substance, presumably the Greeks had an idea of substance before they applied the word οὐσία to it.

Well, let's take a test case. Aristotle wrote in Greek, Avicenna and Averroës in Arabic, Maimonides, partly at least, in Hebrew. Well, if the theory of the dependence of philosophy on language is true, it ought, I think, to be empirically provable that the difference between the philosophies of Aristotle, Avicenna, Averroës, and Maimonides were due to differences in the grammatical and syntactical structure of the languages they respectively employed. As far as I know that's never been shown. It seems to me that the difference is due to quite other causes, partly theological causes.

AYER: Maybe. But I shall still maintain that philosophers have been influenced by language. Of course, the interesting thing now is not to find out why they said what they did, but to evaluate what it was they were saying, and how far it was significant or true, and I do think it rather queer that people have been so inclined to believe in substance with no empirical evidence about it whatsoever. I think that the grammatical distinction of subject and predicate may be one cause, but I admit that I haven't made the empirical investigation. This is only a conjecture. Similarly, I should expect people with ideographic languages to be less concerned about the problems of universals, for example, not being easily able to isolate abstract words.

COPLESTON: Yes, in some cases I should think it would be due not to deficiency of language so much as to direction of interest.

AYER: And then you get things like the tendency to treat all words as names.

COPLESTON: Yes, I know. I mean I'm not trying to adopt an extreme position. I should question any such extreme position, which I understand you don't hold, such as that philosophical problems are simply due to the form of the language in which the philosophers have been misled by language. For example, if one supposes that for every word there is a corresponding thing. To "redness," for example, to the word to correspond to redness, which is difficult from the redness of a rose or any other particular red thing. Then I should say that the philosopher was mistaken by language — misled by language. What I would emphasize would be that this question of the influence of language on philosophy is simply a question for an empirical investigation in any given case. The dogmatic a priori statement concerning influence of language on philosophy should, I think, be studiously avoided.

AYER: I agree that it's an empirical question how our own philosophical problems have grown up. That doesn't affect my contentions that the method of solving these problems is that of linguistic analysis.

COPLESTON: Yes. Well, perhaps we'd better attend to your principle of verifiability. You mentioned the principle of verification earlier. I thought possibly you'd state it. Professor, would you?

AYER: Yes, I'll state it in a very loose form; namely, that to be significant a statement must be either on the one hand a formal statement — one that I should call analytic — or on the other hand empirically testable. I should try to derive this principle by an analysis of understanding. I should say that understanding a statement meant knowing what would be the case if it were true. Knowing what would be the case if it were true means knowing what observations would verify it. And this in turn means being disposed to accept some situations as warranting the acceptance or rejection of the statement in question. From which there are two corollaries. One — which we've been talking about to some extent — : The statements to which no situations are relevant one way or the other are ruled out as non-factual. And, secondly, the contents of the statement, the cash value, to use James' term, consists of a range of situations, experiences, that would substantiate or refute it.

COPLESTON: Thank you. Now I don't want to misinterpret your position, but it does seem to me that we're supposing a certain philosophical position. What I mean is this. If you say that any factual statement, in order to be meaningful, must be verifiable, and if you mean, by verifiable, verifiable by sense experience, then surely you are presupposing that all reality is given in sense experience. If you are presupposing this, you are presupposing that there can be no such thing as metaphysical reality, and if you presuppose this you are presupposing a philosophical position which cannot be demonstrated by the principle of verification. It seems to me that logical positivism claims to be what I might call a neutral technique, whereas in reality it presupposes the truth of positivism. And please pardon my saying so, but it looks to me as though the principle of verifiability was cogitated partly in order to exclude metaphysical propositions from the range of meaningful propositions.

AYER: Even if that were so it doesn't prove anything, really. But to go back. I certainly shouldn't make any statement about all reality. That's precisely the kind of statement I use my principle in order not to make. Nor do I wish to restrict experience to sense experience. I shouldn't at all mind counting what might be called introspectable experiences or feelings; mystical experiences, if you like.

It would be true then that people who haven't had certain experiences won't understand propositions which refer to them, but that I don't mind either. I can quite well believe that your experience is different from mine. Let's assume, which is after all an empirical assumption, that you even have a sense difference from mine. I should then be in the position of a blind man, and I should admit that statements that are unintelligible to me might be meaningful to you. But I should then go on to say that the factual content of your statement was determined by your experiences — which contents are verifiers or falsifiers.

COPLESTON: Yes, you include introspection, and just assumed it, but my point is that you assumed that a factually informative statement is significant only if it is verifiable — at least in principle — by direct observation. Now obviously the existence of a metaphysical reality is not verifiable by direct observation unless you're willing to recognize a purely intellectual intuition as observation. I'm not very keen on appealing to intuition, though I see no compelling reason to rule it out from the beginning. However, if you mean, by verifiable, verifiable by direct sense observation, and/or by introspection, you seem to me to be ruling out metaphysics from the start. In other words, I suggest that acceptance of the principle of verification, as you appear to understand it, implies the acceptance of philosophical positivism. I think I should probably be prepared to accept the principle if it were understood in a very wide sense — that is, if verifiable by experience is understood as including intellectual intuition, and also as meaning simply that some experience, actual or conceivable, is relevant to the truth or falsity of the proposition concerned. But what I object to is any statement of the principle which tacitly assumes the validity of the definite philosophical position. Now you've made a distinction, I think, between the analytic statements, on the one hand, and the empirical statements, and the metaphysical and ethical statements on the other. Or at any rate the metaphysical statements — let's leave ethical out of it. You call the first group cognitive statements and the second emotive. Is that so?

AYER: I think the word "emotive" isn't very happy, though I've used it in the past, and I suggest I make it "emotion," which isn't necessarily the case. But I accept what you say if you mean by emotive simply not cognitive.

COPLESTON: Very well, I accept, of course, your substitution of non-cognitive for emotive, but my objection still remains that by cognitive statements I presume that you mean statements which satisfy the criterion of meaning — that is to say, the principle of verifiability; and by non-cognitive statements I presume you mean statements which do not satisfy that criterion. If this is so, it seems to me that when you say that metaphysical statements are non-cognitive you are not saying much more than that statements which do not satisfy the principle of verification do not satisfy the principle of verification. In this case, however, no conclusion follows as to the significance or non-significance of metaphysical propositions, unless, indeed, one has previously accepted your philosophical position — that is to say, unless one has assumed that they are non-significant.

AYER: It's not so simple as that. My procedure is this. I shall claim that the account I have given you of what understanding a statement is . . . does apply to ordinary common-sense statements and scientific statements. So I'd give a different account of how a mathematical statement functions, and a different account again of value judgment.

COPLESTON: Yes.

AYER: I then say that statements which don't satisfy these conditions are not significant, not to be understood; and I think you can quite correctly object that by putting my definitions together all I come down to saying is that statements that are not scientific or common-sense statements are not scientific or common-sense statements. But then I want to go further and say that I totally fail to understand — and, again, I'm afraid I'm using my own sense of understanding; what else can I do? — I fail to understand what these other non-scientific statements and non-common-sense statements, which don't satisfy these criteria, propose to be. Someone may say he does understand them, in some sense of understanding other than the one I've defined. I reply: It's not clear to me what that sense of understanding is, nor, a fortiori, what it is he understands, nor how these statements function. But of course you may still say that in making it a question of how these statements function I'm presupposing my own criterion.

COPLESTON: Well, then, in your treatment of metaphysical propositions you are either applying the criterion of verifiability or you are not. If you are, then the significance of metaphysical propositions would seem to be ruled out of court a priori, since the truth of the principle, as it seems to be understood by you, inevitably involves the non-significance of metaphysical propositions. In this case the application of the criterion to concrete metaphysical propositions constitutes a proof neither of the non-significance of metaphysical propositions nor of the truth of the principle. All that is shown, it seems to me, is that metaphysical propositions do not satisfy a definite assumed criterion of meaning. But it does not follow that one has to accept that criterion of meaning. You may legitimately say, if you like, "I will accept as significant factual statements only those statements which satisfy these particular demands or conditions." But it doesn't follow, does it, that I or anybody else has to make those particular demands before we are prepared to accept a statement as meaningful?

AYER: What I do is to give a definition of certain related terms: "understanding," "meaningful," and so on. I can't possibly accept them, either. But I can perhaps make you unhappy about the consequences of not accepting them. What I should do is this. I should take any given proposition, and show

how it functions. In the case of a scientific hypothesis, I would show that it had a certain function — namely, that, with other premises, you could deduce certain observational consequences from it. I should then say this is how this proposition works. This is what it does, this is what it amounts to. I then take mathematical propositions and play a slightly different game with them, and show that they function in a certain way, in a calculus, in a symbolic system. You then present me with these other statements, and I say: On the one hand, they have no observational consequences. On the other hand, they aren't statements of logic. All right. So you understand them. I have given a definition of understanding according to which they are not, in my usage of the term, capable of being understood. Nevertheless, you reject my definition; you are perfectly entitled to, because you can give understanding a different meaning if you like. I can't stop you. But now I say: Tell me more about them. In what sense are they understood? They are not understood in my sense. They aren't parts of a symbolic system. You can't do anything with them in the sense of deriving any observational consequences from them. What do you want to say about them? Well, you may just want to say they're facts or something of that sort. Then again I press you on your use of the word "facts."

COPLESTON: You seem to me to be demanding that in order for a factual statement to be significant, one must be able to deduce observational consequences from it. But I don't see why that should be so. If you mean directly observable consequences, you appear to me to be demanding too much. In any case, are there some propositions which are not verifiable, even in principle, but which would yet be considered by most people to have meaning and to be either true or false. Let me give an example. I don't want to assume the mantle of a prophet, and I hope the statement is quite false. But it is this. "Atomic warfare will take place and it will blot out the entire human race." Now, most people would think that this statement has meaning. It means what it says. But how could it possibly be verified empirically? Supposing it were fulfilled; the last man could not say with his last breath, "Coplestone's prediction has been verified," because he would not be entitled to say this until he was dead — that is, until he was no longer in a position to verify the statement.

AYER: It is certainly practically unverifiable. You can't be a man surviving all men. On the other hand, there's no doubt it describes a possible situation. Putting the observer outside the story, one knows quite well what it would be like to observe devastation and fail to observe any men. Now it wouldn't necessarily be the case that, in order to do that, one had to observe oneself. Just as, to take the case of the past, there were dinosaurs before there were men. Clearly, no man saw that, and clearly I, if I am the speaker, I can't myself verify it, but one knows what it would be like to have observed animals and not to have observed men.

COPLESTON: The two cases are different. In regard to the past, we have empirical evidence. For example, we have fossils of dinosaurs. But in the case of the prediction I mentioned, there would be nobody to observe the evidence and so to verify the proposition.

AYER: In terms of the evidence, of course, it becomes very much easier for me. That would be too easy a way of getting out of our difficulty, because there is also evidence for the atomic thing.

COPLESTON: Yes, but there would be no evidence for the prediction that it will blot out the human race, even if one can imagine the state of affairs that would verify it. Thus by imagining it, one's imagining oneself into the . . .

AYER: No, no.

COPLESTON: Yes, yes. One can imagine the evidence and one can imagine oneself verifying it; but in point of fact, if the prediction were fulfilled, there would be no one there to verify it. By importing yourself imaginatively into the picture, you are canceling out the condition of the fulfillment of the prediction. But let us drop the prediction. You have mentioned imagination. Now, what I should prefer to regard as the criterion of the truth or falsity of an existential proposition is simply the presence or absence of the asserted fact or facts, quite irrespective of whether I can know whether there are corresponding facts or not. If I can at least imagine or conceive the facts, the existence of which would verify the proposition, the proposition has significance for me. Whether I can or cannot know that the facts correspond is another matter.

AYER: I don't at all object to your use of the word "facts" so long as you allow it to be observable facts. But take the contrary case. Suppose I say, "There's a drogulus over there." And you say, "What?" and I say, "Drogulus," and you say, "What's a drogulus?" "Well," I say, "I can't describe what a drogulus is because it's not the sort of thing you can see or touch; it has no physical effects of any kind; it's a disembodied being." And you say: "Well, how am I to tell if it's there or not?" And I say: "There's no way of telling. Everything's just the same if it's there or it's not there. But the fact is it's there. There's a drogulus there standing just behind you, spiritually behind you." Does that make sense?

COPLESTON: It seems to me to do so. I should say that a drogulus in the room or not is true or false, provided that you can — that you at any rate, I have some idea of what is meant by a drogulus, and if you can say to me it's a disembodied spirit, then I should say that the proposition is either true or false whether one can verify it or not. If you said to me: "By 'drogulus' I merely mean the word 'drogulus' and I attach no other significance to it whatsoever," then I should say that it isn't a proposition any more than if I said "piffle" was in the room.

AYER: That's right. But what is "having some idea" of something? I want to say that having an idea of something is a matter of knowing how to recognize it. And you want to say that you can have ideas of things even though there's no possible situation in which you could recognize it because nothing would count as finding it. I would say that I understand the words "angel," "table," "clock," "drogulus" if I'm disposed to accept certain situations as verifying the presence or absence of what the word is supposed to stand for. But you want to admit these words without any reference to experience, whether the thing they are supposed to stand for exists, and everything is to go on just the same.

COPLESTON: No. I should say that you can have an idea of something if there's some experience that's relevant to the formation of the idea, not so much to its verification. I should say that I can form the idea of a drogulus or a disembodied spirit from the idea of body and the idea of mind. You may say that there's no mind and there's no spirit, but, at any rate, there is, as you'll admit, certain internal experience of thinking and so on which at any rate accounts for the formation of the idea. Therefore I can say I have an idea of a drogulus or whatever it is, even though I'm quite unable to know whether such a thing actually exists or not.

AYER: You would certainly not have to know that it exists, but you would have to know what would count as its existing.

COPLESTON: Yes, well, if you mean by count as its existing that there must be some experience relevant to the formation of the idea, then I should agree.

AYER: Not to the formation of the idea, but to the truth or falsity of the propositions in which it is contained.

COPLESTON: The word "metaphysics" and the phrase "metaphysical reality" can have more than one meaning, but when I refer to a "metaphysical reality" in our present discussion I mean a being which in principle (and not merely in fact) transcends the sphere of what can be sensibly experienced. Thus God is a metaphysical reality. Since God is, *ex hypothesi*, immaterial, he cannot, in principle, be apprehended by the senses.

May I add two remarks? My first remark is that I do not mean to imply that no sense experience is in any way relevant to establishing or discovering. I certainly do believe that metaphysics must be based on experience of some sort, but metaphysics involves intellectual reflection on experience. No amount of immediate sense experience will disclose the existence of a metaphysical reality. In other words, I should say, there is a halfway house between admitting only the immediate data of experience and, on the other hand, leaping to the affirmation of a metaphysical reality without any reference to experience at all. You yourself reflect on the data of experience. The metaphysician carries that reflection a stage further.

My second remark is this. Because one cannot have sense experience of a metaphysical reality it doesn't follow that one couldn't have another type of experience of it, and if anybody had such experience it does not seem to me that the metaphysical reality is deprived, as it were, of its metaphysical character and become non-metaphysical. I think that's an important point.

AYER: Yes, but asking are there metaphysical realities isn't like asking are there still wolves in Asia, is it? It looks as if you've got a clear usage for metaphysical reality and then ask does it occur or not, does it exist or not, as if I'm arbitrarily denying that it exists. My difficulty is not in answering the question — are there or are there not metaphysical realities? — but in understanding what usage is being given to the expression "metaphysical reality." When am I to count a metaphysical reality? What would it be like to come upon a metaphysical reality? That's my problem. It isn't that I arbitrarily say there can't be such things, already admitting the use of the term, but that I'm puzzled about the use of the term. I don't know what people who say there are metaphysical realities mean by it.

COPLESTON: Well, that brings us back to the beginning — the function of philosophy, I think. I should say that one can't simply raise in the abstract the question: Are there metaphysical realities? Rather, one asks: Is the character of observable reality of such a kind that it leads one to postulate a metaphysical reality, a reality beyond the physical sphere? If one grants that it is, even then one can only speak about that metaphysical reality within the framework of human language. And language is, after all, primarily developed to express our immediate experience of surrounding things, and therefore there's bound, I fully admit, to be inadequacy in any statements about a metaphysical reality.

AYER: But you're trying to have it both ways, you see. If it's something that you say doesn't have a meaning in my language, then I don't understand it. It's no good saying: "Oh, well, of course, it really has a meaning," because what meaning could it have except in the language in which it is used?

COPLESTON: Well, let's take a concrete example. If I say, for example, God is intelligent — well, you may very well say to me, "What meaning can you give to the word 'intelligent'? — because the only intelligence you have experienced is the human intelligence, and are you attributing that to God?" and I should have to say no, because I'm not. Therefore, if we agree to use the word "intelligent" simply to mean human intelligence, I should have to say God is not intelligent. But when I say that a stone is not intelligent I mean that a stone is less than intelligent; when I say God is intelligent I mean that God is more than intelligent, even though I can't give an adequate account of what that intelligence is in itself.

AYER: Do you mean simply that he knows more than any given man knows? But to what are you ascribing this property? You haven't begun to make that clear.

COPLESTON: It's a point, of course. But what you are inviting me to do is to describe God in terms which will be as clear to you as the terms in which one might describe a familiar object of experience or an unfamiliar object which is yet so like familiar objects that it can be adequately described in terms of things which are really familiar to you. But God is *ex hypothesi* unique; and it's quite impossible to describe him adequately by using concepts which normally apply to all ordinary objects of experience. If it were possible, then God wouldn't be God. So I think you're really asking me to describe God in a manner possible only if he weren't God.

I freely admit that all human ideas on God are inadequate. I also affirm that this must be so, owing to the finitude of the human intellect and to the fact that we can come to a philosophical knowledge of God only through reflection on the things we experience. But it doesn't follow that we can have no knowledge of God. It does follow, though, that our philosophical knowledge of God cannot be more than analogical.

AYER: Yes, but in the case of an ordinary analogy when you say that something is like something else you understand what both things are. But in this case, if you do say something is analogical I say: Analogical of what? And you don't tell me of what. You merely repeat the first term of analogy. Well, I get no analogy. It's like saying that something is "taller than," and I say, "Taller than?" and you repeat the first thing you say. Then I understand it's taller than itself, which is nonsense.

COPLESTON: I think that one must distinguish physical analogy and metaphysical analogy. If I say that God is intelligent, I don't say so simply because I want to call God intelligent, but either because I think that the world is such that it must be ascribed, in certain aspects at least, to a Being which can be described in human terms only as intelligent or because I am satisfied by some argument that there exists an absolute Being and then deduce that that Being must be described as intelligent. I am perfectly well aware that I have no adequate idea of what that intelligence is in itself. I am ascribing to God an attribute which, translated into human terms, must be called intelligence. After all, if you speak of your dog as intelligent, you are using the word in an analogous sense, and it has some meaning for you, even though you don't observe the dog's physical operations. Mathematicians who speak of multidimensional space have never observed, I suppose, such a space, but presumably they attach some meaning to the term. Or when we speak of "extrasensory perception" we are using the word "perception" analogously.

AYER: Yes, but mathematical physicists do test their statements by observation, and I know what would count as a case of extrasensory perception. In the case of your statement I don't know what counts. Of course, you might give it an empirical meaning; you might say that by "God is 'intelligent' " you meant that the word had certain features. Then we'd inspect it to see if it had the features or not.

COPLESTON: Well, of course I do argue from the world to God. I must start from the world to God. I wouldn't wish to argue from God to the features of the world. But to keep within your terms of reference of empiricism, I should say that if God is personal then he's capable, for example, of entering into relationship with human beings. Then it's possible to find human beings who claim at any rate they have a personal intercourse with God.

AYER: Then you've given your statement a perfectly good empirical meaning. But it would then be like a scientific theory, and you would be using it in exactly the same way as you might use a concept like "electron" — to account for, explain, predict a certain range of human experience — namely, that certain people did have these experiences which they described as "entering into communion with God." Then one would try to analyze it scientifically, find out in what conditions these things happened. Then you might put it up as a theory. What you'd done would be psychology.

COPLESTON: Well, as I said, I was entering into your terms of reference. I wouldn't admit that when I was saying God is personal I merely meant that God could enter into intercourse with human beings. But I should be prepared to say that he was personal even if I had no reason for supposing that he entered into intercourse with human beings.

AYER: No, but it's only in that case one has anything one can control. The facts are that these human beings have these experiences. They describe these experiences in a way which implies more than that they're merely having them. But if one asks what more, then what answer does one get? Only, I'm afraid, repetition of the statement that was questioned in the first place.

COPLESTON: Well, let's come back to this religious experience. However you subsequently interpret the religious experience, you'd admit, then, that it was relevant to the truth or falsity of the proposition that God existed.

AYER: Relevant only insofar as the proposition that God existed is taken as a prediction or description of the occurrence of their experiences. But not, of course, that one has any inference you might want to draw, such as that the world was created, or anything of that kind.

COPLESTON: No. We'll leave that out. What I'm trying to get at is that you'd admit the proposition "God exists" could be a meaningful form of metaphysical proposition.

AYER: No, it wouldn't then be a meaningful metaphysical proposition. It'd be a perfectly good empirical proposition, like the proposition that the unconscious mind exists.

COPLESTON: The proposition that people have religious experience would be an empirical proposition, I quite agree. And the proposition that God exists would also be an empirical proposition, provided that all I meant by saying that God exists was that some people have a certain type of experience. But actually that's not all I mean by it. All I originally said was that if God is personal then one of the consequences would be that he could enter into communication with human beings. If he does so that doesn't make God an empirical reality in the sense of not being a metaphysical reality, but God can perfectly well be a metaphysical reality — that is, independent of physics or nature even if intelligent creatures have a non-sensible experience of him. However, if you wish to call metaphysical propositions empirical propositions, by all means do so. It then becomes a question of terminology, I think.

AYER: Oh, no. I suggest that you're again trying to have it both ways. You see, you allow me to give these words, these shapes, or noises an empirical meaning. You allow me to say that the test . . . [of whether] what you call

God exists or not is to be that certain people have certain experiences, just as the test whether the table exists or not is that certain people have experiences. Only the experiences are a different sort. Having got that admission, you then shift the meaning of the words "God exists"; you no longer make them refer simply to the possibility of having these experiences, and so argue that I have admitted a metaphysical proposition, but of course I haven't. All I've admitted is an empirical proposition, which you've chosen to express in the same words as you also want to use to express your metaphysical proposition.

COPLESTON: Pardon me. I didn't say that the test . . . [of whether] what I call God exists or not is that certain people have certain experiences. I said that if God exists one consequence would be that people could have certain experiences. However, even if I accept your requirements, it follows that in one case at least you are prepared to recognize the word "God" as meaningful.

AYER: Of course I recognize it as meaningful if you give it an empirical meaning, but it doesn't follow there's any empirical evidence for the truth of your metaphysical proposition.

COPLESTON: But then I don't claim that metaphysical propositions are not in some way founded on reflection on experience. In a certain sense I should call myself an empiricist, but I think that your empiricism is too narrow.

AYER: My quarrel with you is not that you take a wider view of experience than I do, but that you fail to supply any rules for the use of your expressions. Let me try to summarize. I'm not asking you for explicit definitions: All that I require is that some indication be given of the way in which the expression relates to some possible experience. It's only when a statement can't be interpreted as referring even indirectly to anything observable that I wish to dismiss it as metaphysical. It's not necessary that the observation should actually be made; there are cases, as you've pointed out, where for practical, or even for theoretical, reasons, the observation couldn't, in fact, be made, but one knows what it would be like to make it. The statements which refer to it would be said to be verifiable in principle, if not in fact. To put the point more simply, I understand a statement of fact, I know what to look for on the supposition that it's true. My knowing what to look for is itself a matter of my being able to interpret the statement as referring, at least, to some possible experience.

Now you may say — indeed, you have said — that this is all entirely arbitrary. The principle of verifiability is not itself a descriptive statement; its status is that of a persuasive definition. I am persuaded by it, but why should you be? Can I prove it? Yes — on the basis of other definitions. I have in fact tried to show you how it can be derived from an analysis of understanding. But if you're really obstinate you'll reject these other definitions, too, so it looks as if we reach a deadlock. . . . I claim for my method that it does yield valuable results in the way of analysis, and with this you seem disposed to agree. You don't deny the importance of the analytic method in philosophy, nor do you reject all the uses to which I put it; therefore you accept in the main the account that I give of empirical propositions. You have indeed objected to my treatment of the propositions of logic, but there I think that I'm in the right. At least I'm able to account for their validity, whereas on your view it is utterly mysterious.

The main difference between us is that *you* want to leave room for metaphysics. But now look at the result that you get. You put forward your metaphysical statements as ultimate explanations of fact, yet you admit that they're not explanations in any accepted sense of the term, and you can't say in what sense they *are* explanations. You can't show me how they're to be tested, and you seem to have no criterion for deciding whether they are true or false. This being so, I say they're unintelligible. You say no, you understand them; but for all the good they do you — I mean cognitively, not emotionally — you might just as well abandon them.

This is my case against your metaphysical statements. You may decline to be persuaded by it, but what sort of case can you make *for* them? I leave the last word to you.

COPLESTON: Well, I've enjoyed our discussion very much. I've contended that a metaphysical idea has meaning if some experience is relevant to the formation of that idea, and that a rational metaphysic is possible if there are — as I still think there are — principles which can express an intellectual apprehension and a nature of being. I think that one *can* have an intellectual experience — or intuition, if you like — of being. A metaphysical proposition is testable by rational discussion, but not by purely empirical means. When you say that metaphysical propositions are meaningless because they are unverifiable in your sense, I don't really think that this amounts to more than saying that metaphysics are not the same thing as empirical science.

In short, I consider that logical positivism, apart from its theory of analytic propositions, really embodies the notion of nineteenth-century positivism; that the terms "rational" and "scientific" have the same extension. This notion certainly corresponds to a popularly held prejudice, but I don't see any adequate reason for accepting it. I still find it difficult to understand the status of the principle of verification. It must be, I should have thought, either a proposition or not a proposition. If it is a proposition it must be, on your premises, either a tautology or an empirical hypothesis. If it's a tautology, then no conclusion follows as to metaphysics; if it's an empirical hypothesis, then the principle itself would require verification. But the principle of verification cannot itself be verified. If, however, the principle is not a proposition, it should be, on your premises, meaningless. In any case, if the meaning of an existential proposition consists, according to the principle, in its verifiability, it is impossible, I think, to escape an infinite regress, since the verification will itself need verification, and so on indefinitely; and if that is so, then all propositions, including scientific propositions, are meaningless.

David Cox and Thomas McPherson

The methods of the logical empiricists plainly exclude discussion of empirically unverifiable propositions, such as those which affirm the existence of a transcendent deity. It would seem therefore that they are entirely alien to Christian theology. Nevertheless, it is natural and proper to raise the question: Can Christian theologians use the methods of the logical empiricists, and, if so, what results may be expected to ensue? In 1950, in the British periodical Mind, *this possibility was entertained in an article by David Cox, to which Thomas McPherson made reply. The article, reproduced here under (A), and the reply, (B), furnish an illustration of the kind of discussion that such a question may provoke.*

Can the Verification Principle Be Applied to Christian Doctrines? *

(A)

I propose to recommend the method of logical positivists to Christian theologians. Logical positivists offer a methodology, and not a scheme of philosophy, but they do not hesitate to show that the method which they offer has implications for metaphysics and ethics. Christianity is a way of living, but theologians rarely hesitate to claim that that way of living also has implications for metaphysics and ethics. Thus the method of the logical positivists and the Christian way of living have points of contact: theologians should not be indifferent to the logical positivists — they should consider their position, and define their attitude to it. I shall argue that theologians can and should accept the method which logical positivists offer.

The point of contact between Christianity and logical positivists is that at which theologians make statements which purport to be "metaphysical" or "ethical." There has always been considerable difficulty in pointing to any ethical system and saying "there you have the Christian ethic," and for this and other reasons I do not intend to discuss ethical statements. I shall consider those statements made by theologians which are supposed to be "metaphysical": that means that I shall discuss Christian doctrine. It is important for my argument that "Christian doctrine" cannot be divorced from the way of living which is Christianity: this fact is often forgotten or ignored. I shall consider what change of attitude to "Christian doctrine" would be necessary if Christians were to accept the method of logical positivists, and I shall claim

* *Mind,* LIX, 209–218, 545–550. Essays "The Significance of Christianity," by David Cox, and "The Reply," by Thomas McPherson, used by permission of *Mind* and David Cox.

The parenthetical page references in Mr. McPherson's article have been changed to conform to the pagination of this book.

that it would be a return to the attitude of the early church. I do not suggest that the attitude which I shall recommend was explicit or formulated, but that it lay behind the doctrinal controversies of the first two or three centuries of the church's life.

In effect my argument will be that Christians should accept "the verification principle," and it will be well to make one comment on that principle here. There is at least one form in which it is sometimes stated that is unacceptable to Christians: this form contains an addition to the primary method of logical positivists, and is not essential to their method. The verification principle can be stated adequately without it. When they realise this I believe that Christians should be able to accept the verification principle without difficulty.

The Verification Principle

According to logical positivists all statements which are worth while making are either "formal rules" or "empirical hypotheses." Formal rules define the use of symbols in a science, and, in particular, the use of words in a language, or jargon. Empirical hypotheses are, in the main, what the common man would call "statements of fact" — but not all ostensible statements of fact are empirical hypotheses. Logical positivists say something like this: when we are confronted with an ostensible statement of fact there are two questions which we may ask about it; we may ask "is it true?" or we may ask "what does it mean?". We usually assume that if a statement is grammatically correct the answer to the second question is *never* "nothing" — that is, that it means something. We rarely bother to ask the second question unless we suspect a misunderstanding. If this assumption is mistaken, then the second question is of major importance: if the answer should happen to be "nothing," then it is stupid to ask "is the statement true?". Logical positivists ask us to consider whether, because a statement is grammatically correct, it *must* mean something. Their first principle is "a statement that is grammatically correct is not, therefore, significant," that is, does not therefore mean something. If we accept their method we have to begin by asking of every ostensible statement of fact "is it significant?"

We can accept this much of their method without committing ourselves to anything. Nothing that I have said closes the possibility that all grammatically correct statements are significant. It is the positive proposal which logical positivists make which causes controversy. Logical positivists offer a test of significance, and this test is the "verification principle": it may be stated —

> an ostensible statement of fact is significant if, and only if, it can, in principle, be verified by human experience.

Logical positivists claim that they know what is meant by "understanding" statements which can be verified by experience, and they argue that those who wish to make use of statements which cannot be verified in this way should explain in what sense they "understand" them. If we accept the principle, then, to show that an ostensible statement of fact is significant, we have to show how it is related to human experience — we have to show that there are experiences (actual or possible) which would take place in one way if the statement were true, and in another way if it were false. If we demonstrate the significance of a statement we show, at the same time, how we can test its truth.

I propose to recommend the verification principle to Christian theologians: I should make it clear what accepting it would involve. It would mean confining Christian doctrines to —

1. Formal rules: that is, statements which indicate in what ways the terms of theological jargon are to be used.

I shall not discuss this class of statements in detail, partly because I see no reason why it should cause theologians any trouble with regard to accepting the method of logical positivists, and partly because I conceive that they will have the greatest trouble in deciding which doctrines are to be regarded as formal rules, and which are to be regarded as

2. Empirical hypotheses: that is, significant statements which can be verified by human experience.

This implication of the verification principle is one which theologians may find it hard to accept: it implies two things which are contrary to the common theological approach:

(*a*) Overhauling the whole body of Christian doctrine, with the intention of restating it in accordance with the verification principle: that is, with the intention of showing how their doctrines are related to human experience. *And*, as a consequence of such an overhaul, rejecting those doctrines (if any) which cannot be shown to be "significant."

(*b*) When they have done this theologians must admit that they are not left with a body of doctrine consisting of "statements of fact," but with a number of "empirical hypotheses." Empirical hypotheses may be more or less probable, but they can never have the status of "dogma": they are always, in principle, liable to modification, or contradiction by subsequent experience.

It may not be easy for theologians to accept such an attitude to Christian doctrine: in the next section I shall try to show why such an attitude would be less revolutionary than it may appear. But there is a form in which the verification principle is sometimes recommended which Christians cannot accept. This form is "an ostensible statement of fact is significant if, and only if, it can be verified, in principle, by sense-experience." If the principle, in this form, is an integral part of the method of logical positivists, then their method is quite impossible to Christians. I give three reasons for thinking that it is not an integral part of their method —

1. If this is the form of the principle that logical positivists recommend, then they cannot claim that they recommend a bare methodology. In this form the principle contains a metaphysical statement to the effect that all human experience can be analysed in terms of sense-experience.

2. The statement that all human experience can be analysed in terms of sense-experience is properly an empirical hypothesis: if logical positivists include it in their principle they raise it to the status of "dogma," which contradicts their own method. It is not an hypothesis with a particularly high probability.

3. Professor Ayer, in a broadcast discussion with Fr. Copleston, admitted two things:

(*a*) That there are human experiences which are not sense-experiences.

(*b*) That there *may* be human experiences which can only be known by those who enjoy them.

For these reasons I do not see how the introduction of the word "sense-" can be an essential part of the logical positivists' method, and I recommend the verification principle to Christians in the form "an ostensible statement of fact is significant if, and only if, it can be verified, in principle, by human experience."

Christian Doctrine

Originally Christian doctrine was not intended to provide a description of what might be called "transcendent reality." When we study Christian doctrines we often forget this, but it is not forgotten in the study of the history of doctrine. In textbooks and in lectures it is asserted that the Christian church was compelled to formulate her doctrines in order to "safeguard Christian experience." The church only defined doctrines unwillingly, when forced to do so by some real need. So long as doctrines are no more than is sufficient for the purpose of safeguarding experience they will be significant by the test of the verification principle. They will, in fact, perform just those two functions which logical positivists claim to be the functions of all significant statements — they will lay down formal rules for the use of theological terminology, and they will indicate the possibility, or the probability, of the occurrence of certain experiences. If Christian doctrines do no more than safeguard Christian experience, then they will be significant in the sense that logical positivists use the term. Two things follow —

1. Such doctrines can be restated in such a way that their significance is apparent, without their essential content being affected.

2. This sort of restatement would provide a means of finding out how far doctrines fulfil their original function.

There is no doubt that Christian doctrines which go beyond the needs which called them forth have been promulgated, nor that, sometimes, they have been generally accepted by the church. The question to theologians is whether the existence of such doctrines is due to a necessary and essential development of Christian thought, or whether it is due to unnecessary elaboration. I believe that it is the result of unnecessary elaboration, and I think that there are three main reasons why such elaboration has taken place —

1. If the primary purpose of those who formulated Christian doctrines was to safeguard certain experiences, then their chief care was to see that the formulae which they offered were sufficient to do this. If their formulae should happen to be more than sufficient, they would not be unduly concerned, unless they conflicted with other Christian experiences. If this happened the doctrine was corrected in course of time: the doctrinal controversies show how a definition of doctrine which was more than sufficient might lead to a new heresy (*e.g.*, the history of Nestorianism and Eutychianism). If the too great sufficiency of a doctrine consisted of non-significant statements, however, it would not lead to a new heresy, and would not be corrected — just because non-significant statements do not have bearing upon experience.

2. When the first doctrines were formulated the philosophical temper was

such that it was natural to formulate them in "metaphysical statements," however closely they might be related to experience. If the doctrines of the church are compared with those of gnostic philosophers, the restraint of the former is apparent: at the same time the gnostic systems also indicate the sort of statements natural to philosophers. (I doubt whether the ramifications of gnosticism were as far divorced from the experience of their originators as they are from ours in the twentieth century — I believe that the implications of language have changed considerably in the interval.)

3. The church has, from time to time, baptised men whose minds had a "metaphysical" interest: it was natural that such men should try to build "metaphysical" systems in which Christianity was prominent: such men introduced doctrines which were explicitly "metaphysical."

In these ways (and probably in other ways as well) Christian doctrines divorced from Christian experience have arisen: a good case can be made for removing accretions from that core of doctrine which fulfills its function of safeguarding Christian experience. It seems to me that the method of the logical positivists is the instrument which the theologian requires to do this. It should be remembered that the restraint of the creeds is notorious, and I do not believe that there are any statements in the creeds which cannot be restated in such a way that their significance is apparent.

I have already mentioned some of the implications of accepting the verification principle: the most practical is that theologians should restate their doctrines. There is no harm in this even for those who do not accept the verification principle. Three comments may be added —

1. The Christian teacher to-day is confronted with a real problem. To many people the doctrines of the church seem to be out of touch with everyday life: attempts to show the relevance of Christianity to daily life are often indirect, and sometimes unconvincing. A random illustration follows: "God is your father; He is also John Smith's father; therefore you and John Smith are brothers, and you ought to return the book you borrowed from him two years ago." That is by no means the best we can do, but I do not think that the best, along those lines, is satisfactory. The sort of restatement involved in accepting the verification principle would force theologians to elaborate the *direct* application of doctrine to experience: we might, for example, hear more about what it means to "know God as our father," and less about the "implications of the universal fatherhood of God." I believe that the sort of restatement of doctrine which I suggest would be a valuable contribution to Christian apologetics.

2. The fact that a doctrine could be restated so that its significance was apparent would be a reason to reassert the traditional form, and not a reason to dispense with it. While the restatement would justify it, the traditional statement would still have uses which the restatement did not have, and it might well remain the most convenient *expression* of the doctrine.

3. Until a serious attempt to restate Christian doctrine with reference to the verification principle has been made, we can have no idea how much or how little is apt to such restatement. To accept the verification principle is not to reject any specific doctrine, although it is to accept the possibility that

some doctrines may be non-significant. Whether this is so or not cannot be known until the attempt has been made. I give two illustrations of the way that I imagine restatement would be attempted.

Two Illustrations of Restatement

I am going to give two illustrations of what I mean by "restating Christian doctrine in the light of the verification principle." I want to give some idea of the sort of thing that would have to be done, and also to try to show that it is possible. Some who do not accept the verification principle may accept the restatements which I suggest, with the reservation "the doctrine means this, but it means something else as well"; some who accept the verification principle may not admit that my restatements are adequate — but those who accept it must admit that an adequate restatement, similar to that which I suggest, would exhaust the meaning of the doctrine. I certainly make no claim to be able to give wholly adequate restatements of the two doctrines which I shall discuss: the work of restatement, if it is seriously undertaken, is a complicated task. All I wish is to illustrate the sort of thing that would have to be done. The two doctrines which I shall attempt to restate are "God exists" and "God created the world from nothing": I choose the first because of its central importance, and the second because it is, at first sight, a particularly non-significant statement.

If the work of restatement were to be carried out fully from the beginning, we should have to begin with the formal rules governing the use of the theological terminology. Before we could attempt to restate the doctrine "God exists" we should have to state the rules governing the use of the word "God." I shall not do that here, but there is one comment which is necessary: I do not think that the word is rightly to be used except in such phrases as "meeting God," or "encountering God," or "knowing God." I suggest that the rules governing the use of the word "God" will be rules which describe the human experiences which are to be called such names as those I have mentioned: I think that there may be some difference of opinion as to the necessary characteristics of such experiences — for example, "God is loving" could be restated as a formal rule "no experience of meeting a person who is not someone who loves you can be rightly called 'an experience of meeting God,'" but it could also be stated as an empirical hypothesis "some experiences called 'meeting God' will probably be experiences of meeting a person who loves you." The decision as to which is the correct way to deal with such a statement is a problem for theologians. What I have said leads to the sort of restatement which is required to reveal the significance of the doctrine "God exists."

The problem of restating the doctrine is made easier if we consider the sort of experiences which it was originally intended to safeguard, and which led to the statement being made. I suggest that they were experiences so like that of meeting another human being that they could most easily be described as a "personal encounter"; and, at the same time, that they were not usually marked by the sense-experiences which we commonly associate with meeting a person; also, I suggest, they would be such that, if they were regarded as encounters with a person, then they must be regarded as encounters with a person having certain definite characteristics — the precise delineation of those characteristics would, of course, depend upon the formal rules governing the use of the word "God." Once the phrase "meeting God" has been given content by these rules the doctrine "God exists" can be stated —

> "some men and women have had, and all may have, experiences called 'meeting God.' "

The doctrine "God created the world from nothing" is more complicated. This is because it involves three terms instead of two — God, man, and the world, instead of God and man. It will be found that every restatement involves the introduction of one extra term — the human being(s) whose experience we consider. The doctrine "God made the world from nothing" connects two classes of experience: the experiences called "meeting God," and the everyday experiences of "the material order." Once again, the original purpose of the doctrine will help the restatement: the doctrine has always been asserted against those who are disposed to regard the material order as "evil" or "indifferent"; it has been intended to assert that the world is God's world, and that nothing in it is opposed to Him if it is properly used. Now if we assert that the experience called "meeting God" can be regarded as the encounter with a person who has a concern for the well-being of men, then we can state the doctrine "God created the world from nothing" "everything which we call 'material' can be used in such a way that it contributes to the well-being of men." I put this forward as a possible statement of the doctrine, I can well believe that it could be improved if other aspects of the experience "meeting God" are taken into account: but I believe that any restatement of it which reveals its significance must be something like the one I suggest.

I believe that this sort of restatement of all Christian doctrines is of first importance to-day: it is incumbent upon any theologian who accepts the verification principle. Those who wish to retain doctrines which cannot be stated in a verifiable form have to explain in what sense they "understand" such doctrines.

Verification and Truth

In the second section I said that we might ask two questions about a statement — "what does it mean?" and "is it true?". I have tried to show that theologians should ask the first question about their doctrines, and I have also tried to show how, in principle, the meaning of their doctrines should be made clear. At the same time I have attempted to vindicate Christian doctrine from the charge of being "non-significant" — that is, to preserve it from the limbo to which metaphysics is being exiled (rightly, as I believe) by the logical positivists. If Christians can defend their doctrines as "significant" the second question still remains — are they true?

In the restated form Christian doctrines appear as "empirical hypotheses," and the restatement will indicate in what way they can be shown to be probable or improbable. They can never have greater probability than, for instance, the statement "if I jump out of the window I shall fall downwards," but, since Christianity is primarily a way of living, it hardly seems necessary that they should. When theologians have restated their doctrines, then those who consider that any importance attaches to the question "are they true?" will be able to see how they can be tested in experience. Since Christians claim that Christianity is the most satisfactory and adequate way of living for men and women, Christian teaching has some *a priori* right to be regarded as important: but there are serious difficulties confronting anyone who would test the empirical hypotheses which theologians put forward.

(*a*) The experiments to be made are not quiet, objective experiments that we sit back and watch: they involve every moment of everyday life.

(*b*) They require perseverance over long periods when no result is obtained either way.

(*c*) They may require real heroism, and they will certainly be arduous.

(*d*) If they don't come off, the experimenter can never be quite sure that it was not his fault.

(*e*) Christianity has no thought of time — there is no question of saying "if you really try to be a Christian for ten years you will know that Christianity is true": a whole lifetime of real effort may leave the question still unanswered.

Reasoning, persuasion, and discussion may convince others that Christian teaching is significant: it may convince that it is important: nothing but experience of the Christian life can convince that it is true. For this reason the only ultimate appeal that Christians can make is that made by a Jewish poet: "taste and see how good the Lord is" — it is an empirical appeal that should appeal to an avowedly empirical school of philosophy.

(B)

Mr. David Cox ("The Significance of Christianity," MIND, April, 1950) tries to restate two "Christian doctrines" in a way in which they shall be verifiable, in principle, "by human experience." These two restatements he offers as a sample of what might be done to reconcile theological doctrine with the verification principle. He chooses to demonstrate on "God exists" and "God created the world from nothing."

What I want here to show is that Mr. Cox's restatement of the first proposition neither represents it adequately nor is verifiable. I discuss only the first restatement because the second is made to depend on the first and falls with it. Mr. Cox is very disarming. He is quite prepared to admit that there may be something wrong with his restatement; but suggests that someone else should do better. I hope to show both what *is* wrong with his restatement of "God exists" and also that no-one *could* do better — along *these* lines.

Mr. Cox's restatement of "God exists" is "Some men and women have had, and all may have, experiences called 'meeting God.' "

1. "God exists" is not adequately translated by this statement. Something or somebody could exist without anyone's ever having "met" it or him (more later about "meeting"), and even without its being possible that anyone *could* ever meet it or him. Lots of things existed before men existed. Probably lots of things will exist after men have ceased to exist. And there is nothing wrong with saying that on a planet attached to a star in a galaxy untold distances

beyond our Galaxy a single wonderful being came into existence Melchizedek-ly at the moment I began to write this sentence, and will cease to exist at the moment I make the coming semi-colon, leaving no trace of himself whatever; so that no matter if a magnificent space-ship were built *now,* and set off through space *now,* with Mr. Cox in it, it would arrive too late for Mr. Cox to meet the wonderful being. We just do not *mean* by "X exists" "some men and women have had, and all may have, the experience of meeting X." (But, of course, these two sentences are related. The second entails the first, though not *vice versa.*)

But does Mr. Cox perhaps mean that *God's* existence, unlike that of other things and persons, *does* somehow depend on at least the possibility of men and women's meeting Him? Perhaps he means this. But then did God not exist at all before men existed? Or, if He existed, was He not truly God before He created men and women? This is a hard saying. (Or are angels "men and women," and did angels exist from the beginning?)

Perhaps Mr. Cox's disarmingness is intended to get him out of answering difficulties like these I have raised. He writes as if he would not greatly care if it were objected that his restatement restates only part of what is meant by the original proposition (p. 361). Perhaps his own criterion of an adequate translation would be: preservation of essential content (p. 359) and the making of this explicit; and this evidently has something to do with "safeguarding Christian experiences." But by "essential" content Mr. Cox seems to mean verifiable content (p. 361). (It is its verifiability that is for him the thing to be most insisted on about the basic "Christian experience" of "meeting God.") This looks almost analytic. "God exists" is seen to be verifiable if we restate it so as to make its essential content explicit. What is its essential content? That part of the "meaning" of "God exists" that is verifiable.

But, anyway, it *isn't* verifiable, as we are now to see.

2. Mr. Cox himself says (p. 362): "Those who wish to retain doctrines which cannot be stated in a verifiable form have to explain in what sense they 'understand' such doctrines." But what is to be understood by Mr. Cox's restatement? In particular, how is "meeting" used in it (cf. "encountering God" and "knowing God" on p. 361)? I know what it would be like to meet Mr. Cox, but not what it would be like to meet God. In a way I do see what Mr. Cox wants to say; but I don't think he ought to have said "meet." We don't use "meet" except where the senses are involved. We must *see* someone when we meet him (or if we are blind must hear him speak to us and feel his hand shake ours). In general, if we are not blind, sight is essential and no other sense will do. Take introducing and being introduced. If two people stand back-to-back and are introduced to each other by a third person, and each says "How do you do," but neither looks round at the other, have they "met"? I think it is doubtful whether we would say they had. If two people have only spoken on the telephone have they met? No, for this is just the sort of situation where we say, "Well, I've never actually *met* him, but we once discussed something on the 'phone," etc. And this doesn't apply only to "meet" in the sense of "be introduced to." If we "meet someone in the street" whom we know already this involves *seeing* him, and perhaps stopping to talk to him

(at least acknowledging him by nodding, smiling, or scowling, etc. — otherwise we say we have merely "seen" him in the street, or "passed" him in the street, and not that we have "met" him in the street). Mr. Cox says that meeting God is, or is like, meeting a person. But in what way like? Do we *see* God, let alone nod to Him when we pass in the street? Surely not. But this is how we use "meet." Until Mr. Cox says what the likenesses and differences are between *his* use of "meet" and its common use, his phrase "meeting God" is, for me at least, not meaningful, and so his restatement is not verifiable.

Mr. Cox wants a kind of verification that is not verification by "sense experience." The "experience of meeting God," he would say, is a "human experience" but not a "sense experience." He says (p. 361) that meeting God is "not usually marked by the sense-experiences which we commonly associate with meeting a person." This is surely a very inverted-comma'd kind of meeting. It is misleading to use "meet" here, for "meet" is so closely tied to sense experience. It is incongruous to use "meet" and yet exclude sense experience (especially sight). That is one reason why we smile when we read in anthologies of comic verse:

> "As I was going up the stair
> I met a man who wasn't there.
> He wasn't there again today —
> I wish to God he'd go away!"

But if not "meet" what else? Mr. Cox is in a dilemma that anyone else would be in who tried to do what he has tried to do. If he wants a restatement of "God exists" that shall be verifiable he is bound to use words like "meet." But no such word could satisfy him (I leave him to try others for himself — like his own suggestions of "encounter" and "know"). The trouble is that statements using words like "meet" are all verifiable, but only in the way Mr. Cox does not want, *i.e.* they are verifiable by *sense* experience. Either he must take this kind of verification, or give up using words like "meet." But I don't see how he *can* give up using words like "meet," if he also wants to speak of God as a *person* (or "like" a person — *sufficiently* like); for then words like "meet" and no others are the words he must have.

3. Another point about verification. I wonder whether Mr. Cox has done what he intended to do. I think he has in mind the view that "God exists" is itself verifiable, and is verifiable *because* "some men and women have had, and all may have, experiences called 'meeting God.'" But the view that he in fact puts forward is not that the situation described by this second proposition is the verification of the first proposition, but that the second proposition is a restatement (in verifiable form) *of* the first, and that *it* (the second proposition) is what is *to be* verified. But, at best, to verify this second proposition would be only a second-hand kind of verification of "God exists." (Roughly, we would know that God exists not by meeting Him but by meeting someone who has met Him.) And things are worse even than this. Take the part of the restatement that runs: "Some men and women *have* had experiences called, etc." What would it be to verify this? By asking someone who was present and saw them meeting God? But no-one could see them, for sense experience

is ruled out. I imagine Mr. Cox would agree with the view that, to put it in his terminology, "the experience of meeting God" is a *private* thing. He himself says — p. 359 — reporting, or paraphrasing, Professor Ayer: "There *may* be human experiences which can only be known by those who enjoy them." And "meeting God" may well be such a case. Of course, "experience" is anyway an unfortunate word; for we often use "experience" *meaning* by it something quite private. I am not sure whether this is the kind of privacy that the experience of meeting God is supposed to have.

But, it may be said, suppose the verifier is himself one of the men and women who "have had the experience, etc.": what then? But surely one does not "verify" one's own experiences (or, better, *that* one has oneself had certain experiences) in the "private" sense of "experience"; one just *has* them, and either remembers having had them or forgets. But I shall not press this: perhaps I am exploiting the ambiguity of "experience."

Now take the other part of the restatement — the part that runs: "All *may* have experiences, etc." This is surely not verifiable. I can understand what it would be to "verify" that something *has* happened or *is* happening, but not what it would be to "verify" that something *may* happen. Surely one "verifies" actualities, not possibilities (except, of course, in the sense in which one "verifies" someone's statistical calculations about the probability of an average so-and-so being such-and-such).

4. Mr. Cox's difficulties arise because he is trying to do what cannot be done. And I confess I do not see why he wants to do it. Theological propositions have their own meaning. I think it is more valuable to examine them and find out what their meaning is, than to work on them to make them fit a philosophical view that divides all propositions up according to a rigid principle. Theology needs a great deal of clarification. It is a subject-matter to which contemporary techniques in philosophy have not yet been applied. In what follows I offer a few remarks (there is no space in a short Note to give details) of what results we may get from applying such techniques to "God exists." My interest in this proposition is not in pulling it about to make it verifiable, but in the preliminary business of leaving it alone for a while and looking at what sort of proposition it is.

In ordinary life we usually make existential statements only about (and ask existential questions only about) things that we know or think *don't* exist. We say "Fairies exist (don't exist)," "Ghosts exist (don't exist)," "Unicorns exist (don't exist)"; or we ask "Do ghosts, etc. exist?" But we don't say (but see exception below) "Chairs exist," "Tables exist"; or ask "Do chairs exist?" We are quite happy with talk about chairs and tables, but talk about their *existence* worries us, because it seems to be putting them into the class of things that we know or think don't exist, or anyway into the class of things of whose members it *makes sense* to say either that they exist or that they don't exist. We are inclined to feel that if anything exists chairs exist; for chairs, and things like chairs, are precisely what *do* exist: only we do not *say* this, for it sounds odd; as if by saying it we are admitting that it is capable of being doubted. Children, to whom unreal things are sometimes as familiar as apples and chairs and tables, can be badly upset by being told that "there aren't really any fairies"; as upset as we should be if told — and convinced — that there are no chairs and tables. The statement "God exists," because sometimes made and significant-sounding — as "ghosts exist" is significant-sounding — seems somehow to carry the suggestion that God does *not* exist, or *may* not exist, or is anyway the sort of thing or being talk about whose existence "makes sense" as talk about the existence of chairs and tables does not. Does God then belong to the fairy-world or ghost-world and not to the chair-world? It seems so.

This distinction that I am drawing between the fairy-world and the chair-world is a pretty sharp one. Naturally, when one draws sharp distinctions one expects border-line cases to pop up suddenly and confront one. Here, the border-line case is exemplified by "electrons exist." And this, as we can see on looking at it, is a border-line case because we are not quite sure how to use "electron." (Is an electron something "really out there," or only a concept worked with in physical calculations?) Electron is a new concept, not yet legislated for. This, of course, is typical of border-line cases. There is no need to assign electrons to *either* world until we are more sure what we *mean* by "electron." Another interesting case is that exemplified by "moas exist" (the moa is a very large New Zealand bird now extinct), said by someone who means "moas *still* exist" or "there still are some moas in the unexplored mountain country of South Westland." This kind of case (like "another planet exists on which there is life like ours") belongs to the chair-world, and someone saying something like this is saying something empirically testable. It is an interesting border-line case because the fact that "exists" tacked on to, say, "moas" is significant-sounding, gives it in one way a likeness to "fairies exist" rather than to "chairs exist"; though we do also want to say that moas belong to the chair-world rather than to the fairy-world. Of course, there are differences between God and fairies — notably that the existence of the first is maintained much more vehemently than the existence of the second; but all I want to do here is to make the general point as strongly as I can — ignoring qualifications — that the significance of "God exists" suggests that God is the same sort of *thing* as fairies and unicorns, and not the same sort of *thing* as chairs and tables. We say something "exists" when it is in another place (or "place") from that where we are, or is unfamiliar to us (unexperienced by us); and the things that belong in these classes are pre-eminently things that *don't* exist (like fairies and unicorns).

Now suppose someone *were* to ask (though only a person spoiled by philosophy would ask) "Do chairs exist?" We should think it an odd question, but if we saw that the questioner was serious we should perhaps, by way of answering him, point out a couple of chairs and say: "That's a chair, and so is that; look at them and feel them, and you'll find that they certainly exist. So that at least two chairs exist. Does that prove to you that chairs exist?" If he said he was not satisfied we could discuss with him further and try to find out what more he could possibly want, and whether he was really wanting anything that could be given. But it is not possible in this way to point to God and say: "That's God; look at Him and feel Him, and you'll see that He certainly exists." A Moorean answer will not do here. There isn't any empirical answer to the question. This, as I pointed out, we recognise in the fact of our talking in the natural way we do about "the existence of God." The things whose existence it makes sense to talk about are, in that way, different from the things whose existence it does not make sense, in general, to talk about. (The "existence" of the things whose existence it sounds odd to talk about is our *standard* for the use of "exists"; and this is just *why* it sounds odd to *talk* about their existence.)

We *may* sometimes want to say "Chairs exist," but only, I think, as a way of pointing out how "exist" is used. If someone asked "What does 'exist' mean?" we might answer: "Well, chairs exist and ghosts don't." In this use we should not think it strange to couple "chairs" and "exist," because we were not ourselves *saying* that chairs exist, but using the odd phrase "chairs exist" as a way of helping to point out the use of "exist."

But does God perhaps have a special "kind" of existence, like Meinongian and Russellian subsistence? This is not Mr. Cox's view, though it is a view often held. The interest of Mr. Cox's position is, indeed, in his not wanting to say this. The familiar view is: God exists, but He has a special "kind" of existence. This is to cut the string binding God to "ordinary experience" at the beginning, and, provided we are willing to agree to this special kind of existence, it kills our questions. God is just *different*, and so our "experience" of Him must be different from our "experience" of things (or beings) that exist in the "ordinary" way, like chairs and tables and Mr. Attlee. But Mr. Cox tries the novelty of cutting the string further away. He wants to say: God exists in the "ordinary" way (like Mr. Attlee), but meeting Him is a different "kind" of *meeting*. He might have cut it still further away and said: God exists in the ordinary way, and we meet Him in the ordinary way, but the sense experiences we have in meeting Him are a different "kind" of *sense experience*. The further away you cut the string the more words you must use in special "senses."

It is an uneasy half-way position that Mr. Cox is trying to balance in. His attempt to have it both ways is interesting. But I do not think it will do.

Ernst Cassirer

Cassirer (1874-1945), who was born in Breslau, taught in Berlin and Hamburg for many years before his exile in 1933, which took him to Swedish and American universities. A Neo-Kantian of the Marburg school, Cassirer displayed predominantly epistemological interests, which so developed as to draw him to a study of conceptualization in the physical and chemical sciences and in mathematics. Cassirer accounted all modes of man's consciousness to be aspects of the different ways of symbolizing. Man is a symbolific (symbol-making) animal. In the following passage Cassirer discusses the nature of metaphor in relation to language and myth.

The Power of Metaphor *

It has frequently been noted that the intellectual link between language and myth is metaphor; but in the precise definition of the process, and even in regard to the general direction it is supposed to take, theories are widely at variance. The real source of metaphor is sought now in the construction of language, now in mythic imagination; sometimes it is supposed to be speech, which by its originally metaphorical nature begets myth, and is its eternal source; sometimes, on the contrary, the metaphorical character of words is regarded as a legacy which language has received from myth and holds in fee. Herder, in his prize essay on the origin of speech, emphasized the mythic aspect of all verbal and propositional conceptions. "As all nature sounds; so to Man, creature of sense, nothing could seem more natural than that it lives, and speaks, and acts. A certain savage sees a tree, with its majestic crown; the crown rustles! That is stirring godhead! The savage falls prostrate and worships! Behold the history of sensuous Man, that dark web, in its becoming, out of *verbis nomina* — and the easiest transition to abstract thought! For the savages of North America, for instance, everything is still animate; everything has its genius, its spirit. That it was likewise among Greeks and orientals, may be seen from their oldest dictionary and grammar — they are, as was all nature to their inventor, a pantheon! A realm of living, acting creatures. . . . The driving storm, the gentle zephyr, the clear fountain and the mighty ocean — their whole mythology lies in those treasure troves, in *verbis* and *nominibus* of the ancient languages; and the earliest dictionary was thus a sounding pantheon."[1]

The romantics followed the way indicated by Herder; Schelling, too, sees in language a "faded mythology," which preserves in formal and abstract dis-

* Ernst Cassirer, *Language and Myth* (New York: Dover Publications, Inc., 1946), pp. 84–97. Used by permission.

1 "Ueber den Ursprung der Sprache," *Werke* (ed. Suphan), V, pp. 53 f.

tinctions what mythology still treats as living, concrete differences.[2] Exactly the opposite course was taken by the "comparative mythology" that was attempted in the second half of the nineteenth century, especially by Adalbert Kuhn and Max Müller. Since this school adopted the *methodological* principle of basing mythological comparisons on linguistic comparisons, the *factual* primacy of verbal concepts over mythic ones seemed to them to be implied in their procedure. Thus mythology appeared as a result of language. The "root metaphor" underlying all mythic formulations was regarded as an essentially verbal phenomenon, the basic character of which was to be investigated and understood. The homonymity or assonance of denotative terms was supposed to break and direct the way for mythic fantasy.

"Let us consider, then, that there was, necessarily and really, a period in the history of our race when all the thoughts that went beyond the narrow horizon of our everyday life had to be expressed by means of metaphors, and that these metaphors had not yet become what they are to us, mere conventional and traditional expressions, but were felt and understood half in their original and half in their modified character. . . . Whenever any word, that was at first used metaphorically, is used without a clear conception of the steps that led from its original to its metaphorical meaning, there is danger of mythology; whenever those steps are forgotten and artificial steps put in their places, we have mythology, or, if I may say so, we have diseased language, whether that language refers to religious or secular interests. . . . What is commonly called mythology is but a part of a much more general phase through which all language has at one time or other to pass."[3]

Before one can attempt any decision between these antagonistic theories, this battle for the priority of language over mythology or myth over language, the basic concept of metaphor requires scrutiny and definition. One can take it in a narrow sense, in which it comprises only the *conscious* denotation of one thought content by the name of another which resembles the former in some respect, or is somehow analogous to it. In that case, metaphor is a genuine "translation"; the two concepts between which it obtains are fixed and independent meanings, and betwixt them, as the given *terminus a quo* and *terminus ad quem,* the conceptual process takes place, which causes the transition from one to the other, whereby one is semantically made to stand proxy for the other. Any attempt to probe the generic causes of this conceptual and nominal substitution, and to explain the extraordinarily wide and variegated use of this sort of metaphor (i.e., the conscious identification of avowedly diverse objects), especially in primitive forms of thinking and speaking, leads one back to an essential attitude of mythic thought and feeling. Heinz Werner, in his study of the origins of metaphor, has presented a very plausible argument for the supposition that this particular kind of metaphor, the circumlocution of one idea in terms of another, rests on quite definite motives arising from the

[2] Schelling, "Einleitung in die Philosophie der Mythologie," *Sämtliche Werke,* 2nd div., I, p. 52.

[3] Max Müller, *Lectures on the Science of Language,* second series (New York: Scribner, Armstrong & Co., 1875), pp. 372–376.

magical view of the world, and more especially from certain name and word taboos.[4]

But such a use of metaphor clearly presupposes that both the ideas and their verbal correlates are already given as definite quantities; only if these elements, as such, are verbally fixed and defined can they be exchanged for one another. Such transposition and substitution, which operate with a previously known vocabulary as their material, must be clearly distinguished from that genuine "radical metaphor" which is a condition of the very formulation of mythic as well as verbal conceptions. Indeed, even the most primitive verbal utterance requires a transmutation of a certain cognitive or emotive experience into sound, i.e., into a medium that is foreign to the experience, and even quite disparate; just as the simplest mythical form can arise only by virtue of a transformation which removes a certain impression from the realm of the ordinary, the everyday and profane, and lifts it to the level of the "holy," the sphere of mythico-religious "significance." This involves not merely a transference, but a real *μετάβασις εἰς ἄλλο γένος*; in fact, it is not only a transition to another category, but actually the creation of the category itself.

If, now, one were to ask which of these two types of metaphor begets the other — whether the metaphorical expressions in speech are produced by the mythic point of view, or whether, on the contrary, this point of view could arise and develop only on the basis of language — the foregoing considerations show that this question is really specious. For, in the first place, we are not dealing here with a temporal relation of "before" and "after," but with the logical relation between the forms of language and of myth, respectively; with the way the one conditions and determines the other. This determination, however, can be conceived only as reciprocal. Language and myth stand in an original and indissoluble correlation with one another, from which they both emerge but gradually as independent elements. They are two diverse shoots from the same parent stem, the same impulse of symbolic formulation, springing from the same basic mental activity, a concentration and heightening of simple sensory experience. In the vocables of speech and in primitive mythic figurations, the same inner process finds its consummation: they are both resolutions of an inner tension, the representation of subjective impulses and excitations in definite objective forms and figures. As Usener emphatically said: "It is not by any volition that the name of a thing is determined. People do not invent some arbitrary sound-complex, in order to introduce it as the sign of a certain object, as one might do with a token. The spiritual excitement caused by some object which presents itself in the outer world furnishes both the occasion and the means of its denomination. Sense impressions are what the self receives from its encounter with the not-self, and the liveliest of these naturally strive for vocal expression; they are the bases of the separate appellations which the speaking populace attempts."[5]

Now this genesis corresponds precisely, feature for feature, with that of the

[4] Heinz Werner, *Die Ursprünge der Metapher* (Leipzig, 1919), esp. chap. 3, pp. 74 ff.

[5] Usener, *Götternamen*, p. 3.

"momentary gods." Similarly, the significance of linguistic and mythic metaphors, respectively, will reveal itself, so that the spiritual power embodied in them may be properly understood, only as we trace them back to their common origin; if one seeks this significance and power in that peculiar concentration, that "intensification" of sense experience which underlies all linguistic as well as all mythico-religious formulations.

If we take our departure once more from the contrast which theoretical or "discursive" conception presents, we shall find indeed that the different *directions* which the growth of logical (discursive) and mythic-linguistic conception, respectively, have followed, may be seen just as clearly in their several *results.* The former begins with some individual, single perception, which we expand, and carry beyond its original bounds, by viewing it in more and more relationships. The intellectual process here involved is one of *synthetic supplementation,* the combination of the single instance with the totality, and its completion in the totality. But by this relationship with the whole, the separate fact does not lose its concrete identity and limitation. It fits into the sum total of phenomena, yet remains set off from them as something independent and singular. The ever-growing relationship which connects an individual perception with others does not cause it to become merged with the others. Each separate "specimen" of a species is "contained" in the species; the species itself is "subsumed" under a higher genus; but this means, also, that they remain distinct, they do not coincide. This fundamental relation is most readily and clearly expressed in the scheme which logicians are wont to use for the representation of the hierarchy of concepts, the order of inclusion and subsumption obtaining among genera and species. Here the logical determinations are represented as geometric determinations; every concept has a certain "area" that belongs to it and whereby it is distinguished from other conceptual spheres. No matter how much these areas may overlap, cover each other or interpenetrate — each one maintains its definitely bounded location in conceptual space. A concept maintains its sphere despite all its synthetic supplementation and extension; the new relations into which it may enter do not cause its boundaries to become effaced, but lead rather to their more distinct recognition.

If, now, we contrast this form of logical conception by species and genera with the primitive form of mythic and linguistic conception, we find immediately that the two represent entirely different *tendencies* of thought. Whereas in the former a concentric expansion over ever-widening spheres of perception and conception takes place, we find exactly the opposite movement of thought giving rise to mythic ideation. The mental view is not widened, but compressed; it is, so to speak, distilled into a single point. Only by this process of distillation is the particular essence found and extracted which is to bear the special accent of "significance." All light is concentrated in one focal point of "meaning," while everything that lies outside these focal points of verbal or mythic conception remains practically invisible. It remains "unremarked" because, and in so far as, it remains unsupplied with any linguistic or mythic "marker." In the realm of discursive conception there reigns a sort of diffuse light — and the further logical analysis proceeds, the further does this even clarity and luminosity extend. But in the ideational realm of myth and language there are always, besides those locations from which the strongest light proceeds, others that appear wrapped in profoundest darkness. While certain contents of perception become verbal-mythical centers of force, centers of significance, there are others which remain, one might say, beneath the threshold of meaning. This fact, namely, that primitive mythical and linguistic concepts constitute such *punctiform* units, accounts for the fact that they do not permit of any further *quantitative* distinctions. Logical contemplation always has to be carefully directed toward the *extension* of concepts; classical syllogistic logic is ultimately nothing but a system of rules for combining, subsuming and superimposing concepts. But the conceptions embodied in language and myth must be taken not in extension, but in intension; not quantitatively, but qualitatively. Quantity is reduced to a purely casual property, a relatively immaterial and unimportant aspect. Two logical concepts, subsumed under the next-higher category, as their *genus proximum*, retain their distinctive characters despite the relationship into which they have been brought. In mythico-linguistic thought, however, exactly the opposite tendency prevails. Here we find in operation a law which might actually be called the law of the leveling and extinction of specific differences. Every part of a whole is the whole itself; every specimen is equivalent to the entire species. The part does not merely represent the whole, or the specimen its class; they are identical with the totality to which they belong; not merely as mediating aids to reflective thought, but as genuine presences which actually contain the power, significance and efficacy of the whole. Here one is reminded forcefully of the principle which might be called the basic principle of verbal as well as mythic "metaphor" — the principle of *pars pro toto*. It is a familiar fact that all mythic thinking is governed and permeated by this principle. Whoever has brought any part of a whole into his power has thereby acquired power, in the magical sense, over the whole itself. What significance the part in question may have in the structure and coherence of the whole, what function it fulfills, is relatively unimportant — the mere fact that it is or has been a part, that it has been connected with the whole, no matter how casually, is enough to lend it the full significance and power of that greater unity. For instance, to hold magical dominion over another person's body one need only attain possession of his pared nails or cut-off hair, his spittle or his excrement; even his shadow, his reflection or his footprints serve the same purpose. The Pythagoreans still observed the injunction to smooth the bed soon after arising so that the imprint of the body, left upon the mattress, could not be used to the owner's detriment.[6] Most of what is known as "magic of analogy" springs from the same fundamental attitude; and the very nature of this magic shows that the concept in question is not one of mere analogy, but of a real identification. If, for instance, a rain-making ceremony consists of sprinkling water on the ground to attract the rain, or rain-stopping magic is made by pouring water on red hot stones where it is consumed amid hissing noise,[7] both ceremonies owe their true magical sense to the fact that the rain is not just represented, but is

[6] Jamblichos, *Protreptichos*, p. 108, 3, quoted after Deubner, *Magie und Religion* (Freiburg, 1922), p. 8.

[7] See Parkinson, *Thirty Years in the South Seas*, p. 7; quoted by Werner, *Die Ursprünge der Metapher*, p. 56.

felt to be really present in each drop of water. The rain as a mythic "power," the "daemon" of the rain, is actually there, whole and undivided, in the sprinkled or evaporated water, and is thus amenable to magical control.

This mystic relationship which obtains between a whole and its parts holds also between genus and species, and between the species and its several instances. Here, too, each form is entirely merged with the other; the genus or species is not only represented by an individual member of it, but lives and acts in it. If, under the totemistic conception of the world, a group or clan is organized by totems, and if its individual members take their names from the totem animal or plant, this is never a mere arbitrary division by means of conventional verbal or mythical "insignia," but a matter of genuine community of essence.[8] In other respects, too, wherever a genus is involved at all, it always appears to be wholly present and wholly effective. The god or daemon of vegetation lives in each individual sheaf of the harvest. Therefore, an ancient but still popular rural custom demands that the last sheaf be left out in the field; in this remnant, the power of the fertility-god is concentrated, from which the harvest of the coming year is to grow.[9] In Mexico and among the Cora Indians the corn-god is supposed to be present, fully and unrestrictedly, in every stalk and even every grain of corn. The Mexican corn-goddess Chicomecoatl in her maidenhood is the green stalk, in her old age the corn harvest; but she is also each separate kernel and each particular dish. Likewise, there are several deities among the Coras who represent certain kinds of flowers, but are addressed as individual flowers. The same is true of all the Coras' demoniac creatures: the cicada, the cricket, the grasshopper, the armadillo are simply treated as so many individual wholes.[10] If, therefore, ancient rhetoric names as one of the principal types of metaphor the substitution of a part for the whole, or vice versa, it is easy enough to see how *this* sort of metaphor arises directly out of the essential attitude of the mythic mind. But it is equally clear that for mythic thinking there is much more in metaphor than a bare "substitution," a mere rhetorical figure of speech; that what seems to our subsequent reflection as a sheer transcription is mythically conceived as a genuine and direct identification.[11]

[8] Cf. my study, *Die Begriffsform im mythischen Denken* (Leipzig, 1922), pp. 16 ff.
[9] Cf. Mannhardt, *Wald- und Feldkulte,* 2nd ed. (Berlin, 1904–1905), I, 212 ff.
[10] See Preuss, in *Globus,* Vol. 87, p. 381; cf. esp. *Die Nayarit-Expedition,* Vol. I, pp. 47 ff.
[11] This is the more obviously valid if we consider that for mythic and magical thought there is no such thing as a *mere* picture, since every image embodies the "nature" of its object, i.e., its "soul" or "daemon." Cf., for example, Budge, *Egyptian Magic,* p. 65: "It has been said above that the name or the emblem or the picture of a god or a demon could become an amulet with power to protect him that wore it and that such power lasted as long as the substance of which it was made lasted, if the name, or emblem, or picture was not erased from it. But the Egyptians went a step further than this and they believed that it was possible to transmit to the *figure* of any man, or woman, or animal or living creature the soul of the being which it represented, and its qualities and attributes. The statue of a god in a temple contained the spirit of the god which it represented, and from time immemorial the people of Egypt believed that every statue and figure possessed an indwelling spirit." The same belief is held to this day among all "primitive" peoples. Cf., for instance, Hetherwick,

In the light of this basic principle of mythic metaphor we can grasp and understand, somewhat more clearly, what is commonly called the metaphorical function of language. Even Quintilian pointed out that this function does not constitute any *part* of speech, but that it governs and characterizes all human talk; *paene quidquid loquimur figura est*. But if this is indeed the case — if metaphor, taken in this general sense, is not just a certain development of speech, but must be regarded as one of its essential conditions — then any effort to understand its function leads us back, once more, to the fundamental form of verbal *conceiving*. Such conceiving stems ultimately from that same process of concentration, the compression of given sense experiences, which originally initiates every single verbal concept. If we assume that this sort of concentration occurs by virtue of several experiences, and along several lines, so that two different perceptual complexes might yield the same sort of "essence" as their inner significance, which *gives* them their meaning, then at this very point we should expect that first and firmest of all the connections which language can establish; for, as the nameless simply has no existence in language, but tends to be completely obscured, so whatever things bear the *same* appellation appear absolutely similar. The similarity of the aspect fixed by the word causes all other heterogeneity among the perceptions in question to become more and more obscured, and finally to vanish altogether. Here again, a part usurps the place of the whole — indeed, it becomes and is the whole. By virtue of the "equivalence" principle, entities which appear entirely diverse in direct sense perception or from the standpoint of logical classification may be *treated* as similars in language, so that every statement made about one of them may be transferred and applied to the other. Preuss, in a characterization of magic-complex thinking, says: "If the Cora Indian classes butterflies, quite absurdly, as birds, this means that all the properties which he notes in the object are quite differently classified and related for him than they are for us from our analytical, scientific point of view."[12] But the apparent absurdity of this and other such classifications disappears as soon as we realize that the formation of these primary concepts was guided by language. If we suppose that the element emphasized in the name, and therefore in the verbal concept of "bird," as an essential characteristic was the element of "flight," then by virtue of this element and by its mediation the butterfly does belong to the class of birds. Our own languages are still constantly producing such classifications, which contradict our empirical and scientific concepts of species and genera, as for instance the denotation "butterfly" (Dutch *botervlieg*), in some Germanic tongues called a "butterbird." And at the same time one can see how such lingual "metaphors" react in their turn on mythic metaphor and prove to be an ever-fertile source for the latter. Every characteristic property which once gave a point of departure to qualifying conceptions and qualifying *ap-*

"Some animistic beliefs among the Yaos of British Central Africa" . . . : "The photographic camera was at first an object of dread, and when it was turned upon a group of natives they scattered in all directions with shrieks of terror . . . In their minds the *lisoka* (soul) was allied to the *chiwilili* or picture and the removal of it to the photographic plate would mean the disease or death of the shadeless body."

[12] Preuss, *Die geistige Kultur der Naturvölker* (Leipzig, 1914), p. 10.

pelations may now serve to merge and identify the *objects* denoted by these names. If the visible image of lightning, as it is fixed by language, is concentrated upon the impression of "serpentine," this causes the lightning to *become a snake*; if the sun is called "the heavenly flier," it appears henceforth as an arrow or a bird — the sun-god of the Egyptian pantheon, for instance, who is represented with a falcon's head. For in this realm of thought there are no abstract denotations; every word is immediately transformed into a concrete mythical figure, a god or a daemon. Any sense impression, no matter how vague, if it be fixed and held in language, may thus become a starting point for the conception and denotation of a god. Among the names of the Lithuanian gods which Usener has listed, the snow-god Blizgulis, the "Shimmerer," appears beside the god of cattle, the "Roarer" Baubis; also in relation to these we find the god of bees, Birbullis the "Hummer," and the god of earthquake, the "Thresher" Drebkulys. Once a "Roarer God" in this sense was conceived, he could not but be recognized in the most diverse guises; he was naturally and directly *heard*, in the voice of the lion as in the roaring of the storm and the thunder of the ocean. Again and again, in this respect, myth receives new life and wealth from language, as language does from myth. And this constant interaction and interpenetration attests the unity of the mental principle from which both are sprung, and of which they are simply different expressions, different manifestations and grades.

Ronald W. Hepburn

The passage that follows is a critical study of Rudolf Bultmann by the contemporary British philosopher Ronald W. Hepburn.

In modern Biblical criticism methods were devised by certain German scholars for assessing the historicity of passages by a close analysis of their structural forms. The methods they used in this process, called Formgeschichte, *were carried by Bultmann to an extreme that led to radical historical skepticism, which, partly in the manner of another European theologian, Karl Barth, he both separated from and yet coupled with faith. The process Bultmann came to advocate is called "demythologization." It is the basis of this process that is critically considered in the following passage.*

Demythologizing and the Problem of Validity *

The Definition of Myth

Any instability in the concept of myth itself would be found to imperil the discussion at point after point. Yet Bultmann neither offers a satisfactory definition, nor abides by the definition he does offer. "Mythology," he writes (p. 10),[1] "is the use of imagery to express the other worldly in terms of this world and the divine in terms of human life, the other side in terms of this side." By his own test this definition itself is partly couched in mythological language, which is cause enough for bewilderment. And it is sufficiently wide in its scope to include all pictorial, analogical and symbolical speech whatever. Now in another place Bultmann concedes that *all* utterance about God is analogical, and therefore (if the first definition is to stand) irreducibly mythological. Bultmann cannot mean this. For if it were true, it would make demythologizing a logically impossible task; and the contrast he constantly wishes to make between "mere mythology" and authentic existentialist interpretation would be robbed of its basis. Perplexity does not end here: in a discussion on the expression "act of God" (p. 196 f.) Bultmann decides against calling this "mythological language," on the ground that "mythological thought regards the divine activity . . . as an interference with the course of nature," and "acts of God," to Bultmann, are not of this sort. Therefore to speak of such acts is not to speak mythologically, but *analogically*. This conclusion, however, violates his original definition of myth in two ways at once:

(1) Bultmann is saying: "the expression 'act of God' is not mythological language, but analogical," whereas on his definition this antithesis

* R. W. Hepburn, "Demythologizing and the Problem of Validity," *New Essays in Philosophical Theology* (New York: The Macmillan Co., 1955), pp. 229–262. Used by permission of The Macmillan Co. and Student Christian Movement Press, Ltd.

[1] References are to pages in *Kerygma and Myth*, edited Bartsch (S.P.C.K., 1953).

could not be made, since "myth" is there plainly the "genus" word, with "analogy," "pictorial image," etc., as species.

(2) The mythological has been redefined as that which depicts God as "interfering in the course of nature"; while the first definition concerned itself only with myth as a form of language and said nothing at all about the *content* of any particular myths.

The contrast mentioned a moment ago between "just mythology" and "existentialist interpretation" (p. 110) reminds us that Bultmann frequently uses "myth" and its cognates as pejoratives. For example: Bultmann may well be right when he claims that the New Testament myths are *in origin* Jewish and Gnostic. But he goes on to say that they are also Jewish and Gnostic "in essence" — a very different claim (pp. 3, 15). "Identical in essence with X" implies "containing no more than X," "of the same value as X." Part of Bultmann's failure to justify his transition from "in origin" to "in essence" may be due to just this pejorative innuendo carried by "myth" which militates against the scrutiny and evaluation of each individual myth (and modification of myth) on its own merits.

Here, then, in the definition of "myth," is one point at which greater logical rigour is urgently required, if the discussion is to be set on a secure foundation.

The Flight from the Evidential

Bultmann's reluctance to face problems of validity manifests itself in a recurrent pattern of argumentation, which could be schematized in roughly the following way:

(*a*) A fact or argument appears, which *prima facie* is hostile to validity of the Christian position;

(*b*) Bultmann turns aside from its negative evidential implication; and

(*c*) transforms the hostile fact in such a way as to make it yield positive support for a modified and freshly secured theological view.

The suspicion grows, as one reads, that no evidence at all would be admitted as finally detrimental to Bultmann's position. If he actually believes this (and it is not an *absurd* belief to hold), it ought to be clearly exhibited as the crucial tenet it undoubtedly would be, and argued for as such.

Two simple examples may bring out this pattern of thought.

(1) On page 11 of *Kerygma and Myth* Bultmann describes how antinomies are generated by conflicting imagery in the New Testament. "The virgin birth is inconsistent with the assertion of [Christ's] pre-existence," so is the creation doctrine with talk about the "rulers of this world," and the law as God-given with the statement that it came from the angels. To Bultmann all this implies, "Rise, therefore, *above* the mythological."

(2) Christ failed to return in the way the disciples had at first expected. We ought, says Bultmann, to profit from their mistake; recognizing that the Last Things are mythological conceptions, not historical.

In both cases a difficulty is metamorphosed into a theologically acceptable "truth." But in each case too Bultmann has side-stepped an equally important sceptical option — without giving adequate reasons for so doing. In the first case we might say: "Conflicting views? then so much the worse for the reliability of the documents!"; and in the second case: "Jesus did not come, because the disciples were simply and tragically wrong about him." Plausibility can be given to evasive moves like these in individual instances, but only so long as the by-passed sceptical options are never gathered together and faced *cumulatively* as a challenge, more or less formidable, to the Christian position.

One may go further: the whole category of the evidential is repeatedly pushed aside by Bultmann as of no importance, or, worse, as a snare. He speaks scornfully of the "provable": "It is precisely its immunity from proof which secures the Christian proclamation against the charge of being mythological" (p. 44). The language of myth is concrete and pictorial, concerned with stones rolling away and men rising into the sky, suggesting in many cases events that might be captured by the camera. Not so the truths of non-mythological Christian belief: for to Bultmann the removal of Christianity from the realm of myth up-grades it in value. So much so, that the reader is prepared to accept, if he is off-guard, that to remove it from the realm of the "provable" must also be an act of up-grading, to be welcomed like a release from a long-standing bondage. But in this way Bultmann has again omitted to argue for a vital proposition, namely that absence of evidence does not disqualify a religion from being acceptable by reasonable men, or that "unprovable" here is not equivalent to "baseless" or "unfounded," as it undeniably is in many contexts.

In speaking of faith Bultmann makes this turn of thought particularly plain: "It is impossible to prove that faith is related to its object . . . it is just here that its strength lies" (p. 201). Once more the absence of evidence is taken as a commendation. For if the relation of faith to God *were* provable, then, says Bultmann, God would be reduced to the status of one item among others in the furniture of the universe: and only "in that realm [are we] justified in demanding proof." Unfortunately this latter sentence begs the question. It assumes that we know already — have had convincingly shown to us — that there are in fact two "realms" — a belief which should surely appear as part of the end-product, not as the initial presupposition of a reasoned theology. Again, a sceptical option demands attention but does not receive it; that is, "If God's being cannot be established, there *may* be no God."

The furthest Bultmann goes in this extraordinary and fascinating flight from the evidential is to transform the failure to obtain proof into an aggressive refusal to accept any *possible* proof. Thus he rejects I Cor. 15.3–8 as evidence for the resurrection, not explicitly on critical grounds, but in his own words — "that line of argument is fatal *because* it tries to adduce a proof for the *Kerygma*" (p. 112; my italics).

This trend of thought, yoked with his critical standpoint, leads Bultmann to speak evasively and ambiguously of the Biblical narratives. As Schleiermacher could say of the ascension only that "something happened," so Bultmann says of the resurrection with similar cloudiness, "I have no intention whatever of denying the uniqueness of the first Easter Day" (p. 111), selecting a vocabulary which permits the retention of a reverent attitude but leaves altogether unclear the nature of the event towards which the attitude is adopted, and therefore leaves equally unclear what procedure could show whether the attitude was an *appropriate* one or not.

An avowed historical agnosticism about the events of Jesus' life would be quite unexceptionable. What one finds in Bultmann, however, is something more positive and dogmatic. At many crucial points he casts about in his mind for an interpretation of an event which he thinks adequate to the existential seriousness of Christianity and proceeds to *read back* his interpretation into the original documents however these may resist the treatment, and however many critical questions may be begged. It is one thing to say, "I have no idea what happened at the ascension, but it provides an excellent symbol for Christ's oneness with the Father": quite another thing to say, "The ascension did not happen — *could* not have happened: it is an excellent symbol, etc., etc." To speak of the "unique and final revelation of God in history" may be misleading as Bultmann claims, in its tendency to lead to thinking of that revelation as a *revelatum,* an event which happened once in the remote past, to which we have access only by historical documents; in Bultmann's words, "something which took place in the past and is now an object of detached observation" (p. 111). But anxiety on this score has gone too far when it results in a fight against history itself; and it cannot be invoked as justification for abandoning the evidential as such.

It is hardly an exaggeration to say that Bultmann would feel an *embarrassment* at the very possibility that certain events might after all have taken place just as the documents narrate them. Doubtless a Christian ought not to see a miracle as a divine conjuring trick, but should interpret the miraculous in personal and moral categories. But that does not give Bultmann warrant to say, "the God of revelation is the God of judgment and forgiveness, *not* the Cause of abnormal phenomena" (p. 121; my italics). It may also be true that in the believer's passage from death into life "outwardly everything remains as before, but inwardly his relation to the world has been radically changed" (p. 20), but Bultmann is over-eager to make this inner invisible event the paradigm not only of conversion but of the New Testament message in its entirety, for the most momentous divine activity still leaves "undisturbed" the "closed weft of history" (p. 197). Can he also consistently say, "It is indeed part of the *skandalon* that . . . our salvation is One who is involved in all the relativity of history" (p. 111)? For he is as anxious to *escape* the level of the verifiable as the logical positivists were to remain within it, in making verifiability the touchstone of meaningfulness. Both are guilty through excess of zeal: the positivists in their belief that any simple verification procedure could prove adequate to every possible experience, Bultmann in refusing to make plain what states of affairs would be incompatible with Christian belief, or just how different the world would have to be before belief would have to be declared senseless.

The historian's task would be impossible, were he forbidden to fill out imaginatively the reconstruction of events to which his sources bear witness. Yet at what point legitimate interpretation fades into fanciful and irresponsible refashioning of the past is often a hard question. We have no guarantee that any ingenious device we may introduce into a production of Shakespeare was actually present in the poet's mind when he wrote his play; how much more uncertain is the assurance of Bultmann that the demythologized, existentialist account of the New Testament proclamation does not in fact distort that proclamation, for all its philosophical attractiveness.

Fact and Language

A theology which aims at being logically transparent must carefully distinguish issues of fact from matters of linguistic convenience. Now, the very word "demythologize" strongly suggests a venture in translation, the substitution of more literal language for pictorial and symbolic language. Yet this is thoroughly deceptive. If the ascension, say, is amenable to demythologizing, that is to say something not only about the language in which the "event" is described, but to decide also about the actual status of the event itself, to deny that Jesus did in fact rise into the air. And no linguistic investigation could lead by itself to such conclusions. Put it differently: to qualify for mythhood a statement must be (on Bultmann's definition) actually about "the other world" or "the other side." The process of demythologizing must accordingly consist of at least two phases, of which the first is the recognition that the scriptural account concerned is mythological in nature; while the second phase re-interprets its substance non-mythologically. But the question whether any particular narration *is* mythical cannot be settled by Bultmann or anyone else while acting in the capacity of *translator*. An event such as a piece of prophetic symbolism may be historical (Jesus did enter Jerusalem in triumph, did curse the fig tree) and at the same time be mythological in Bultmann's sense. Or the alleged event may not have happened and the narrative still retain mythological value. What one must insist is that whether or not the imagery, etc., of the narrative yields itself to translation into existentialist terms, this does nothing to tell us which of those possibilities is more likely to be true. Yet Bultmann repeatedly suggests that "X is described in mythological terms" implies "X cannot have happened as narrated," and does not make it plain that the latter judgment requires a quite distinct investigation.[2]

Two brief examples of this may be hazarded. First, the expression "the cross" is indispensable in devotional language; but the very reasons which make it valuable there make it a dangerous and slippery term in a theology like Bultmann's — namely its conflation of two distinguishable conceptions, the actual crucifixion of Jesus at Calvary and the "meaning" that event can have for the Christian. This span of meaning permits a theologian to keep his reader in a state of sustained uncertainty about exactly what historical claim, if any, he is making when he speaks of "the cross."

Second, "Take . . . the case of a child being sacrificed in order to ensure the success of an enterprise or to avert misfortune. Such a practice implies a 'crude mythological conception of God' " (p. 108). Here the rejection of a

[2] An analogy with Political Theory presents itself here. The idea of a Social Contract may be a valuable one in justifying political obedience under certain circumstances. To speak of it as a "myth" is neither to assert nor to deny the historicity of such an original Contract. . . .

primitive view of sacrifice (as in the stories of Iphigenia and Jeptha's daughter) appears to be part and parcel with Bultmann's general impatience with the mythological: its repudiation is represented as involved in the passage from myth to non-myth. But is this not misleading in the extreme? What is "crude" about the sacrifice theory is not its mythological nature, but its *moral* inadequacy. Abandoning it is not a piece of linguistic spring-cleaning but a value-judgment, logically quite different.

There may be at least a hint of this fact-language conflation on page 7 of *Kerygma and Myth* where Bultmann says: "The only criticism of the New Testament which is theologically relevant is that which arises *necessarily* out of the situation of modern man" (Bultmann's italics). One such "necessity" is disbelief in the miraculous as interference in the order of nature. Now, as Austin Farrer remarks in the same volume, some modern men do not find such a belief impossible. But Bultmann whisks his reader past the possible objection, aided by this word "necessarily" which is always ready to take on the logician's sense of "analytically, logically necessary," therefore not falsifiable by any matter of fact. Again the controversial is made to seem less controversial, and objections on the score of validity are glided over by the hint that the truth of the statement is guaranteed by linguistic convention, that its denial involves contradiction.

Myth and Oblique Language

The project of demythologizing raises in an acute form the general problem of the religious use of language, the logical nature of statements about God. We may start with Bultmann's crucial statement, ". . . there are certain concepts which are fundamentally mythological, and with which we shall never be able to dispense — e.g. the idea of transcendence. In such cases, however, the original mythological meaning has been lost, and they have become mere metaphors or ciphers" (pp. 102 f.). "*Mere* metaphors," note; the phrase suggests that these concepts are "as near literal as makes no difference." But in fact it makes a great deal of difference. The gulf between literal (or direct) and oblique language cannot be bridged so lightheartedly. For if propositions about God are irreducibly oblique — that is, symbolical, analogical and so on, then to demythologize is not to remove all obliqueness, but only obliqueness of certain sorts: on the other hand, if it is possible to speak literally of God, then demythologizing is quite a different activity, not one of translation out of one code into another, but rather of *de*coding altogether. The question which should be of greatest concern to the theologian is not whether this or that myth may be re-expressed in language less flagrantly pictorial, more abstract in appearance, but whether or not the circle of myth, metaphor and symbol is a closed one: and if closed then in what way propositions about God manage to *refer*. Bultmann's first definition of "myth" gave the word a sense sufficiently extended to include every kind of oblique language; yet in practice he gives very little scrutiny indeed to this general issue, and even (as we have noticed) contrasts the mythological with the analogical — a procedure for which his definition gives no warrant. That is to say: the nature of demythologizing as an enterprise must remain logically obscured so long as we leave unsettled the question "Is any direct talk of God possible, or can one talk only obliquely of him?" How inattention to this question can enfeeble the debate can be brought out as follows.

Bultmann's critics have often pointed out that his existentialist terminology is no less mythological than the New Testament ideas from which he wishes to deliver us. Bultmann is prepared to admit this: even "transcendence" is a mythological concept, but one (he is assured) in which myth is merely vestigial, neutralized, reduced to the harmless status of "mere metaphor or cipher." But the more searching objection can still be made that this *appearance* of directness and abstract sterility can be (logically) a menace. If the demythologized talk of God is still oblique, then it should display its obliqueness overtly, for to carry it surreptitiously may be rather like treating measles by hiding the rash with face-powder. For all we know, the suppressed picture, the latent myth, may still be doing the work in the expression concerned; and the "cashing" of it may be impossible without once more reverting to the concealed, but active, myth.

The importance of this may be made plainer by referring to a perceptive article by Ian Crombie, where he considers the challenge to religious belief presented recently by certain linguistic philosophers. In particular, it had been argued that a proposition like "God loves me" appears at first sight to be rich in meaning but is in fact qualified out of existence as soon as we attempt to describe in detail what precisely it claims. Although there are certain sorts of behaviour which give good grounds for denying that one human being loves another, the Christian is expected to go on saying "God loves me" even when his child is born blind and he himself succumbs to an incurable disease. Even the proposition "God exists" is eroded away to emptiness by successive qualifications: "he exists — *but* is invisible, inaudible, intangible, not *in* the world nor a name for the world as a whole. . . ." Now, in his article, Crombie granted that any attempt to speak literally, directly, of God was indeed bound to fail. Nevertheless, we can still speak of him — in "parable" (using the word in an extended sense). We say "God loves us"; what this is like as an experience in God's own being we have not the least idea (nor, without taking in the hereafter, can we exhaustively verify or falsify it): for to predicate "loving" or "acting" or "suffering" of One who infinite and unconditioned is at once to snap the links with every intelligible use of these words. But if we think of "God loves us" as a parable, an oblique utterance, the word "loves" is being used not in a stretched sense but with its everyday familiar meaning. Without knowing what it is like for God to love, we do know now what thoughts of God and what sorts of behaviour are appropriate and what not. We accept one parable about God, rather than another, on the authority, primarily, of Jesus Christ. The parabolic is only one of the two "parents" of religious belief: the other is what might be called "undifferentiated theism," and springs from a sense of the contingency (or beauty, etc.) of the world, giving a "direction" in which the revealed parable can be referred.

Professor Tillich, in a conversation, once pointed out to me how closely this analysis followed the pattern of his own treatment of the same problem, however different his starting-point. Tillich maintains that all propositions about

God are symbolic, except one: for without one direct proposition the oblique language, despite its internal coherence, would have no anchor in reality; the flotilla of symbols would be adrift, unpiloted. To Tillich this one direct proposition is "God is Being — itself," and its resemblance to Crombie's "undifferentiated theism" is obvious enough.

Neither Crombie nor Tillich was engaged on a project of demythologizing. None the less, my point is that demythologizing is only an artificially broken off segment of the problem with which they *were* grappling, and that both of them permit the logical structure of their enterprise to shine through with a clarity impossible to the close disciple of Bultmann. Thus Crombie's presentation, if acceptable, makes it at once plain what sort of procedure is relevant to establishing its truth: each "parent" of belief requires a separate justification. With the theistic, for instance, we must ask how far it is exposed to the general difficulties of the classical arguments of natural theology despite its prelinguistic character: with the parabolic we must investigate the grounds on which we accept Jesus' authority in uttering the parable.

The Existentialist Interpretation

So far I have been trying to lay bare some of the pitfalls which beset Bultmann's enterprise, ways in which the problem of validity tends to be sidestepped in demythologizing and the logic of religious statements obscured rather than clarified. Something must be said in conclusion (however briefly), about the other half of the total programme — the revision of the *Kerygma* in existentialist terms. Do existentialist modes of thought, as Bultmann adopts them, help or hinder the fashioning of a theology whose logical structure reveals itself through its presentation and terminology?

In the first place, there is an undeniable advance from a sentimentalist analysis of belief (as in Schleiermacher) to an existentialist analysis. The advance is comparable to that recent progress from the positivist's dichotomy between "descriptive and emotive" language to the recognition of the variety of actual linguistic functions as seen in the writing of philosophers like Wisdom and Austin. Existentialism provides the theologian (the poet and novelist too) with a rich vocabulary in which to express important elements of the human situation — decision, commitment, dereliction, anguish and many more. Indeed, its theological adaptability is not matter for surprise, since the roots of existentialism go back as far as Pascal and Augustine.

But the adoption of a twentieth-century existentialist terminology is not without its dangers. Certain of these were admirably discussed in Christopher Evans' broadcast review of *Kerygma and Myth*. It is as a tentative supplement to what he said there that I hazard these three additional criticisms.

The first is the most formidable, but space will permit only its bare statement. Overwhelmingly concerned with the phenomenology of faith and the life of faith, existentialist thought is in continual peril of failing to emerge from the subjectivist circle at all. A subjectivist account can provide an informative description of what it is like to think and act as *if* there were a God, of the "inward" metamorphosis which accompanies belief. But it is unable to go further (and it is only here that the question of validity becomes relevant), unable to say whether the belief is justified or unjustified, whether or not there exists a Being before whom the believer has taken up the attitude of faith.

A second danger arises from the almost unlimited hospitality which existentialist thought gives to the paradoxical. Even granting that there are situations in which one is forced to say, "This is a paradox — an enigma, a mystery," there are others in which the proper response is, "This is paradoxical, contradictory and nonsensical." The more cautious a theologian is of paradox, the less he revels in it for its own dramatic sake — the less likely he will be to revere the nonsensical and the invalid when he ought to be dismissing them. His ideal language is one which (by its reluctance to resort to paradox in all but unavoidable contexts) reduces the risk of such confusions as far as possible. Again, it is not an insensitivity to the value of metaphor and analogy in exposition that prompts the suspicion that existentialist language is frequently over-tolerant also of those. In sentences like "we possess the present through encounter" (p. 116, *K.a.M.*) the adoption of the language of drama in the field of general philosophy has begotten a metaphorical mode of speech in which cogent argumentation or criticism is desperately hard. Distortion is inevitable when all relations come to be conceived on the model of interpersonal encounter.

Finally, an existentialist dramatic vocabulary tends on occasion illicitly to prescribe to the theologian what questions he should or should not pursue, where his inquiry should start and (worse still) where it should end. Bultmann writes: "It is not for us to question [the] credentials" of the "word of preaching," "It is we who are questioned" (p. 41). Perhaps: but this alluring language of drama cannot justify the theologian's evasion of that abiding and ultimate question — "*on what grounds* ought I to assume an attitude of obedience before the New Testament and not before, say, the Koran?" On another page we read: "I think I may take for granted that the right question to frame with regard to the Bible — at any rate within the Church — is the question of human existence" (pp. 191 f., *ibid.*), as if by the weightiness of existential utterance itself one could smother the thousand and one *other* questions — of historicity, integrity of text, interpretation — which likewise clamour for their answer, and concern Churchmen as much as unbelievers. Here existentialism has become Bultmann's master, not his servant. So long as it provides the means of expressing what without its terms would be inexpressible, theologians can do nothing but respect it: but it is time to protest when it proceeds arbitrarily to impose limits upon critical examination, whether of doctrine or document.

The quest for a language that is adequate to describe our experience in all its multifariousness is the common task of philosophers and theologians. They must resist equally the artificial truncation of language on dogmatic positivist lines and any language ("inflationary" language, Isaiah Berlin would call it) which is given to the multiplication of metaphysical or theological entities beyond necessity, and from crying mystery where there is not always mystery but sometimes only muddle. In each case a defective linguistic instrument is an obstacle not only to clarity in exposition but also to the attainment of validity.

F. W. Dillistone

Frederick William Dillistone, who has been Dean of Liverpool, England, since 1956, was born in 1903 and educated at Oxford, of which he is a Doctor of Divinity.

In the following passage from his Christianity and Symbolism, *Dr. Dillistone considers problems of symbol and metaphor in religious language, with reference not only to the Christian claim and in the light of the Christian "Word" as* Logos *and as* Kerygma, *but also to the aesthetic reflections of the contemporary poet Stephen Spender.*

The Function of Metaphor *

In man's recurrent attempts to resolve conflicts, the primary form which the symbol takes is the *metaphorical*. The basic function of a metaphor is to provide a *transference* from the expected to the unexpected, from the usual to the surprising. There must always be some element of unlikeness, even incongruity, in the employment of a word or a group of words in a metaphorical way. This does not mean that no elements of likeness remain; if such were the case the metaphor would lose its power. It does mean that when a metaphor is first presented, we recognise at once that language is being employed in an unusual way. We are surprised, even shocked, by the fact that this word does not really belong to the situation in which it is being used.[1] We are compelled to ask ourselves why the word is being used in this particular context and in this particular way. Some, it may be assumed, will come to the conclusion that language is being grievously mishandled; others, however, may well find in this new departure the unlocking of a gate into a wholly new dimension of existence.

Just as the analogy has certain links with the simile, so the metaphor has links with the *contrast*. The contrast indicates that a pattern of relations in one context is markedly different from a pattern of relations in another—though there must be some elements in common in the two situations for the contrast to have point. Now the establishment of a contrast can be a highly important act. It invites attention to the variety and openness of reality, which is neither a deadpan uniformity nor a jumble of totally unconnected parts. At the same time, the contrast never does more than link two patterns together; it points out their dissimilarity, which is more striking than their similarity, but it goes no further. It reveals a conflict; it does nothing to resolve it.

* F. W. Dillistone, *Christianity and Symbolism* (London: Wm. Collins Sons & Co., Ltd., 1955), pp. 160–168. Used by permission.

[1] It could, indeed, be claimed that this is also true of the analogy but in that case the transition is so gentle and so natural that we are not shocked: we are only conscious of a feeling of general approval and satisfaction.

The metaphor, on the other hand, not only uncovers conflicting elements in reality but holds them together in a tentative resolution. The resolution is not final, for there are ever wider areas of conflict to embrace. But every metaphor which holds together two disparate aspects of reality in creative tension assumes the character of a prophecy of the final reconciliation of all things in the kingdom of God. It is the favourite tool of all the great poets — in fact, as Lewis says, it is "the life-principle of poetry, the poet's chief test and glory." Through it the imagination performs its task, the task which Coleridge describes as dissolving, diffusing, dissipating in order to re-create, as reconciling opposite and discordant qualities, as struggling to idealise and to unify. Through it the prophet leaps outside the circle of present experience, the realm of the factual and the commonsense, the typical and the regular. He parts company with those who are travelling the surer and steadier road of analogical comparison. By one act of daring he brings into creative relationship the apparently opposite and contrary and, if his metaphorical adventure proves successful, gains new treasure both for language and for life.

It has been the special merit of Martin Foss in his book about symbol and metaphor, to show that it is altogether too limited a use of the word metaphor to confine it, as books on grammar usually do, to the direct application to some object of a name which does not properly belong to it.[2] We are often told that whereas a simile asserts that a certain man is like a lion in his acts of strength and courage, a metaphor applies to him straight away the name, "lion," leaving it open to the imagination to conceive in what ways the title is most appropriate. But this is only a minor example of a much more comprehensive process. Metaphor, as Foss suggests, challenges us at the very place where we seem to be secure in our familiarity and understanding and bids us look again. Are we sure that we have seen rightly? Are we certain that we have taken everything into consideration? Is our present universe of discourse capable of embracing all the discordant elements of reality? Metaphor, in other words, is the process of the continuous enlargement of man's symbolic world and this process comes to its clearest manifestation in the activity of speech.

In the realm of speech it is the task of the metaphor "to oppose the tendency of the word toward smooth and expedient fixation in familiar fences, and to draw it into the disturbing current of a problematic drive. In a way every sentence is metaphorical, conveying to the single word a meaning beyond its dictionary sense. Every word loses in the setting of the sentence something of its 'general' character, becomes more concrete; but in doing this it gains another kind of generality, the generality of context, difficult to define, a lawfulness which is very individual. This seems paradoxical, and it is this paradox which the mere comparison avoids. But in order to avoid it, the comparison simplifies, becomes one-sided and unfair to the concrete object. It loses too much and gains too little. Therefore we do not compare where we are vitally concerned, that is where we love. The metaphorical process of speech does not enhance the kind of generality which is systematic, i.e. which is an addition of parts to a whole. It is the unique generality of the intentional process to

[2] Martin Foss, *Symbol and Metaphor in Human Experience* (Princeton, N.J.: Princeton University Press, 1949).

which the terms are sacrificed, and it is their mutual destruction in this process out of which a new and strange insight arises. . . . In blasting the symbols and shattering their customary meaning the dynamic process of the searching, striving, penetrating mind takes the lead and restores the truth of its predominant importance. It is what Aristotle aims at when he calls the metaphor energy."[3]

This explosion of energy will normally be made through the individual. It is the individual who suddenly sees the new possibility, the new reconciliation; it is the individual who struggles with conventional language to make it express his own insight; it is the individual who flashes the word of communication which makes all things new. Let us examine in more detail how exactly this takes place.

In dealing with the analogical symbol I pointed out that men need symbolic frameworks within which to live and worship and think: hence the systems of ethics, of liturgies and of myths which human history contains. A code of ethics, as we saw, is always in danger of becoming rigid and unyielding but it can be preserved from this fate if the method of analogy continues to be vigorously employed. But the very phrase "vigorously employed" brings us to the heart of a new problem. Whence is the required vigour and energy to be obtained? A community tends always to settle down into familiar patterns; the products of abstract thought tend to become stereotyped and uninteresting. The influx of new energy, then, must come from the creative individual who through an intense emotional experience of tension and reconciliation discovers the new word. This word (which need not be limited to a single term) is charged with dynamic energy and when it is brought into contact with any pattern of regularity it immediately disturbs and unsettles it. But it is through creative encounters of this kind that human language is renewed and the process of constant re-interpretation carried forward.

In the realm of ethics it is *the moral reformer* who suddenly draws together aspects of human experience which had formerly been kept strictly apart. In the days of Amos the prophet the people of Israel regulated their communal life by a recognised code of conduct but other peoples were regarded as outside the pale — they had no part nor lot in the righteousness of Israel. And the result was, as the book of Amos makes abundantly clear, that the closed system of Israel's moral life was steadily deteriorating. It was the supreme achievement of Amos that he suddenly related the conduct of his own people to that of the neighbouring nations and held them firmly together under the same standard of judgment. To ignore existing distinctions and to forge a new unity of moral judgment was shocking and absurd; but it was the occasion of one of the great creative advances in ethical theory and judgment.

In the days of Jesus of Nazareth a basic legal code had been expanded and extended until it seemed that every possible contingency of human conduct had been provided for. But still the great division existed between those who acknowledged the supremacy of the Law and those who were outside its orbit. The latter were heathen, enemies, aliens, without God and without hope; the former were a chosen people, instructed in the law, heirs of the covenant of promise. It was not surprising that men's attitudes were governed by the gen-

[3] *Ibid.*, p. 59 f.

eral rule: "Thou shalt love thy neighbour and hate thine enemy." This was the recognised framework within which a stable community life could be established. But it was an altogether revolutionary message that Jesus proclaimed when He bade men love their enemies and pray for their persecutors. The coupling together of "love" and "enemy" was the startling new conception. The very foundations of morality seemed to be in jeopardy and yet it was the beginning of perhaps the greatest advance in morals that the world has ever known.

In the realm of worship it is the *liturgical reformer* who leads the way to the resolving of conflicts which arise through the attempt to relate old forms of worship to new conditions of life. Ritual-forms gradually take shape within the context of Nature's regularities and the rhythmic response of human societies. The words of the liturgy, though at first experimental and variable, gradually flow into regular sequences which correspond to the general character of the life of the society which employs them. So long as no revolutionary event occurs the liturgy can be adapted and extended to include mention of new needs which may arise in the course of ordinary historical development. But when critical tensions and conflicts develop within any society and the process of communication between different sections or different generations within the society breaks down, the situation calls for a reformer to initiate a radical break with ancient word-forms and to provide new cult-forms bearing some relation to the actual breach in the historical situation. Cranmer with his new Order of Communion, Luther with his new congregational hymns, Calvin with his new provision for the proclamation of the Word of God — each in his own way was seeking to provide a liturgical form which would hold together within a common worship those who had broken with the old yet were feeling the strain and the pain of an existence from which the old supports seemed to have been snatched away. Novel concepts such as the priesthood of all believers and the doctrine of justification by faith needed to be powerfully expressed in new liturgical forms so that the conflict between the old and the new might be resolved within a new creation. The final outcome of such a process is a new burst of energy springing from the new resolution or reconciliation and revitalising the whole of the liturgical context within which it is set.

Finally, in the realm of thought, there is a general mythical framework within which the thought-life of a society normally moves. It is governed by its view of the universe and of the processes of Nature, and it must be capable of continuous growth and extension as man's knowledge of these processes develops. But once again the slow and patient work of myth-makers and scientists and philosophers is not enough. There must also be the daring leap of the pioneering man of genius — the adventurer in ideas, the poet, the storyteller, the prophet. The product of his imagination may be expressed in poetry or in prose, depending upon the nature of his genius and the particular circumstances of his time. But the all-important quality of his contribution will be the metaphorical tension which characterises it. He will link together words, events, situations, patterns of life in a way which has never been attempted before. The combination will startle, surprise and even repel. Men's first reaction is to cling to the familiar. Even if they are willing to advance a short distance into the unknown they prefer to be able to return to their base whenever the spirit moves them. But the man of faith and imagination insists on coupling together the immediate and the remote, the present and the future, the material and the spiritual, the ugly and the beautiful, the evil and the good. He takes a new step, utters a new word, and this, says Dostoevski, is what men fear most to do. He creates a new tension, sets up a new suspense and thereby breaks through all recognised patterns and leads the way to a complete renewal of human thought.

There is a revealing section in Stephen Spender's *World Within World* which illustrates the nature of the process of which I have been speaking. He tells how at first he looked upon poetry as word-pictures or word-music outside everyday life. "You look out of a window on to a lawn; beyond the lawn there is a stream running parallel with the house and the horizon, and, barring the horizon, rising like a pillar whose top is dark against the fiery wheel of the moon, is a poplar tree whose leaves, absorbing the darkness, are filled with the music of nightingales. My idea of a poem was the imitation of some such picture." (That there is a place for poetry made up of musical phrases and word-pictures Mr. Spender would not presumably deny.) But then his ideas began to change. "I began to realise that unpoetic-seeming things were material for poetry. What seemed petrified, overwhelming and intractable could be melted down again by poetry into their symbolic aspects. The fantasy at the back of actuality could be imagined, and the imagination could create its order. What excited me about the modern movement was the inclusion within new forms of material which seemed ugly, anti-poetic and inhuman. The transformation of the sordid scene and life of the Dublin of Stephen Daedalus and Bloom into the poetic novel whose title, *Ulysses*, sets its aim beside that of the most timeless epic; the juxtaposition of scenes of European decline with ones recalling the greatest glories of the past tradition, in Eliot's *The Waste Land*; these showed me that modern life could be material for art, and that the poet, instead of having to set himself apart from his time, could create out of an acceptance of it." And so he began writing poems containing references to gas works, factories and slums!

Instances could be multiplied. It is as the poet, the prophet, and the storyteller become the creators of the encounter that great advances are made. It may be the encounter of the past with the present or of the present with the future or of the familiar with the foreign — it is in true meeting that life is renewed. The encounter is never a flat and uninteresting event. It involves tension, excitement, suspense, fear, hope, sorrow, joy, but it is the door to eternal life and the kingdom of God.

Two final reflections arise out of this discussion. In the first place it is worth pointing out that only within the context of a wide historical perspective is it possible to envisage the full process of which I have been speaking. In the history of the development of man's moral life we see the constant interplay between the systems of ethics built upon the framework of the law of nature and the challenges of prophets and reformers; in the history of man's religious development we see the dialectic between systems of communal rites and the dramatic creations of heroic individuals; in the history of human thought we see the movement to and fro between systems of mythology and the new adventures of men of genius. It can be claimed, therefore, that of all verbal forms *history* is the greatest and most important. Obviously history can become limited in its vision and narrow in its scope but where there is the honest attempt to see the whole picture, to avoid no unpleasant facts, to hold together the society and the individual, to give full place to new developments as well as to established patterns, to include man's symbolic adventures in the realms of art, ethic and religion, history can become the most comprehensive of all symbolic word-structures and the most significant guide-post towards the fulfilment of human destiny.

In the second place it may be claimed that the Christian faith and tradition gives full recognition both to the Word as *Logos*, as related to the structure of creation, as groundwork and pattern of the developing organism of the Body of Christ, *and* to the Word as *Kerygma*, as proclaiming the event of redemption, as constituting the leap of a living flame between God and man, eternity and time, holiness and sin. The divine meaning or principle (Logos) which existed from all eternity in the being of God, which formed the ground and the energy of all created existence and which sustains the created order and in-forms itself within the growing Body of Christ — this Logos received its supreme manifestation in the life of Jesus. This life, through its gathering together of the diverse elements both of the natural order and of human life into an unceasing movement of aspiration towards a true integration in God, became the supreme example of a living analogical symbol. The record of this life constitutes a word-symbol of determinative significance. Here is revealed a proportion, a meaning, a principle of organic development, which cannot be paralleled elsewhere. The Eternal Word takes the flesh of temporal words and moulds them to its own pattern of self-oblation within the life of the Godhead itself.

But God's Word is also Kerygma, the Gospel of Judgment and Salvation. God comes to man in a crisis of destruction and re-creation. Old forms, old words, old symbols, are crossed out; but mysteriously and paradoxically the crossed-out word reveals a startling new symbol of power and life. And the central, determinative symbol within this series of critical events is the crucifixion of the Word of God. The Kerygma, the witness to this pivotal event, tells how the promised Messiah was taken and by wicked hands was crucified and slain. Yet in reality it was not He Who was destroyed — it was the images of messianic promises and the covenant-symbols of the chosen people of God. Out of His tomb there sprang forth a new Word, a metaphorical symbol of unique significance. Here is revealed a promise, an assurance, a proleptic disclosure of the true reconciliation which nothing can destroy. Out from the event of the Death and Resurrection of the Servant of God a cry has gone forth to the ends of the earth: "God was reconciling the world to Himself in Christ: we pray you in Christ's stead, be ye reconciled to God."

W. Fraser Mitchell

In the following selection Fraser Mitchell (see also page 20) considers some aspects of the nature of religious language from the point of view of an educationist of deeply religious instincts.

The Language of Religion *

Poetry, according to Plato, "is Love talking musically"; it is experience of a certain sort expressed in a recognizable manner. Poetry, according to Wordsworth, "is the breath and finer spirit of all knowledge," and it can be communicated by the use of the everyday speech of the common man; it is the "grace" or "virtue" which gives all human activity lasting worth, and because it is resident in and distributed throughout all human activity it finds its expression in the terms employed by men and women as they go about their daily work. What is true of poetry is true also of religion. It is experience of a certain quality, but it is not experience set over against the ordinary and customary activities of mankind; and because it is bound up with the whole round of human activity — whether that activity is regarded as things done or things suffered (which T. S. Eliot has shown to be one) — it must strive to express itself in terms connected with what men do or suffer. If poetry, to quote Wordsworth again, "sheds no tears such as angels shed, but natural human tears," religion employs no celestial notation to which the harps of heaven are tuned, but takes the common materials with which men are familiar and uses them to communicate with other men. Thus religion, as distinct from theology or mysticism, or any particular field for the study of religious experience, has no language of its own, because religious experience is not a separate experience from other possible experiences, but a particular way of experiencing or regarding all human activity. It is not an epiphenomenal *plus.* It is neither the foam on the wave nor the salt in the water. It is the totality and immediacy of the impact the wave makes upon each one of us, presenting us with something that embraces both knowledge and sensation but is more than both, so that we attain an enhanced personality. We do not only receive and accept and assimilate, but we come to a realization that we are able to receive and engage in the variety of human activity because we are parts of a living whole, which renders such experience possible but does not spread it uniformly over all of us like icing on a cake. When we have had our experiences we are not left like a mass of solid rock with various fossils inside it; we are like trees of a forest with an infinite variety of branch formation. We know because we are known; and we are made aware of the systole and diastole of Being not because once, as Matthew Arnold wrote,

* W. Fraser Mitchell, "The Language of Religion." Used by permission of the author.

"the heavenly house *we* trod
And lay upon the breast of God,"

but because we still enjoy this privilege, and we can still see the universe *sub specie aeternitatis,* and recognize the "something far more deeply interfused" that combines human activity and Divine activity — which, indeed, makes all activity one.

Finding terms to express such religious apprehension did not mean primarily finding words or employing language as we understand it. Religious expression had a hoary antiquity long before the origin and organization of human speech. The awe of barely human creatures before such recurrent phenomena of nature as day and night, summer and winter, rain and drought, found expression in ritual and probably pictorial representation long before ritual began to be accompanied by words, or pictorial art found a counterpart in story. Myth, as Schelling showed, is not a deliberate exercise of human ingenuity dependent on story-telling or the existence of words. "Mythology is essentially active and self-moving in accordance with an indwelling law."[1] It is a way of regarding life direct. It is not the making of stories but is what primitive man experiences. His experiences could be mimed long before man achieved secondary expression in words. The dance and other forms of "doing," the re-creation of circumstances by architectural means, including effects of light and shade, the recapitulation of sounds, pictorial and plastic representation — all alike have been employed to express religious apprehension, to try and retain it or to convey it to those who have not had it direct The importance of this field of expression was made plain once and for all by Otto in *Das Heilige,*[2] where he showed that "the basic impulse underlying the entire process of religious evolution" is the awareness of "something" rather than of "someone" in one's surroundings or circumstances which fills a human being with awe, as before *mysterium tremendum,* but which also attracts him, so that he wants to have a repetition of the experience, even if in the process he should be utterly destroyed. Outstanding experiences of this nature recorded in the Old Testament are those of Jacob at Bethel and of the prophet Isaiah when he had his vision of God, high and lifted up, with a train of worshiping cherubim and seraphim. Jacob had his vision at nightfall in a lonely place. For Isaiah the sanctity and perhaps the mural decorations of the Temple in Jerusalem prepared the way for his experience; in his case expression almost certainly led to further experience. In both accounts we are reminded of the greatness and "otherness" of God; but, terrifying as the experience in either case must have been, it left with the man who underwent it the assurance that God existed and had a purpose for him. The vision itself abased and overwhelmed the man, but it also assured and attracted him. Here we are face to face with the beginning

[1] Friedrich von Schelling, *Philosophie der Mythologie,* as quoted in Ernst Cassirer, *The Problem of Knowledge* (London: Oxford University Press, 1950), p. 297.

[2] Rudolf Otto, *Das Heilige,* First Edition, 1917, trans. into English as *The Idea of the Holy* by J. W. Harvey (London: Oxford University Press, 1923). Edition cited here is that of The Oxford Bookshelf, 1936.

of the long process by which fearful and trembling worship became communion with God.

Primitive man is fascinated by the sense of "the mysterious," and, as Otto points out, this fascination becomes for him "an untiring impulse" leading to creativity of one kind or another. At times his inventiveness is directed to architecture and manifests itself in the arrangement of light and shadow, as in the pillared temples of Egypt and Greece, or in the carefully manipulated vistas and aerial prospects of Gothic cathedrals. The direct impact of awareness of the deity is evident in the familiar episode of the boy Wordsworth, in the midst of his nutting expedition, suddenly made conscious of "a Presence" by the interruption he had occasioned in the silence and arrangement of the place.

The effects of an artificially ordered environment, whose purpose was the educative one of inducing and perpetuating religious consciousness, as they wrought upon the boy Walter Pater, may be studied in his sensitive account of a young priest, Gaston Latour, in his book *Gaston Latour.* Of this lad Pater recalls that he found in the "perpetual twilight" of the Cathedral of Chartres a correspondence with that part of his nature which recoiled from the too precise definitions of the intellect. Pater notes further how the "ritual order" of a medieval cathedral, whose various "offices devout imagination had elaborated from age to age with such a range of spiritual colour and light, with so much poetic tact in quotation, such a depth of insight into the Christian soul," presents us with an educational method once familiar to the greater part of Christendom. By this method doctrine was permeated with Spirit, and men's intellectual formulations, alike with their emotional experiences, expressed in a multiple language their all-pervasive religious apprehension of Reality. But expression acted at the same time as suggestion (in the technical psychological meaning of that term), and, as was true centuries later with the singing of the Wesleys' hymns by their adherents, possessed an almost magical power to reproduce in others the "high moment" experienced by those already religiously aware.[3]

The incident of the young Wordsworth breaking down the beech-tree branches and by so doing breaking also the customary quiet of the wood — scattering the silence, one might almost say, as another lad might have disturbed a still pond by agitating it with the branch of a tree — reminds us that silence itself may be not only a condition for religious experience but essential to it. It may also be the seal and expression of that experience at its deepest. As Otto says, "There is the plainest inward kinship between the two forms of worship which, viewed externally, seem to stand at the opposite poles of religious development" — the Quaker meeting and the Roman Catholic Mass. In the Mass at the moment of transubstantiation there comes the silence of realization. The silence of waiting, which is commonly regarded as characteristic of Friends' worship, leads, as does the former kind of silence, to the final

[3] Sydney G. Dimond, *Psychology of the Methodist Revival* (London: Oxford University Press, 1926), pp. 121–123, 124.

or sacramental silence of communion with God and fellowship with other worshipers.

All the way from primitive man's "doing" to the attainment of "being" by modern people of varying levels of intellectual, aesthetic, and moral attainment, expression of experiences which carry religious significance can manage without words. For this reason the ritualist and the Quaker have much in common. It is when the expression of religious experience is attempted through language that difficulties begin to arise. These depend to some extent on differing theories of the origin and development of language — a subject too vast to be discussed in the present context. No educated person is likely to identify the word with the thing denoted, but the relationship between the word and the thing denoted has for centuries been a topic for debate, and seldom more so than in recent decades. Is any specific word merely a "sign," a convenient or conventional way of representing a "thing," and is it of no importance what the sign word is? If we have attended one of Dr. Frank Laubach's literacy campaigns, we have been shown a picture of an object whose sign word in our mother tongue we immediately think of, and alongside of it the word used for the object in a language strange to us; and in a matter of minutes we have acquired the new word. But an idea or emotion cannot be represented in this simple manner, and as we move further from the simple pictorial reference to concrete objects we shall meet with increasing difficulties of how to express our notions and sensations verbally. Moreover, ever since the fifth century B.C., as a result of the pervasive influence of Greek thought, men, first in Europe and now in all the continents, tend to expect words to provide logical meaning. And about "meaning," and whether "meaning" exists in the universe or is a persistent "vulgar error," and if it does exist, what precisely we should intend by it, there is still further debate.

This is extremely awkward when we turn to the actual experiences which men and women undergo and which are the occasions of their awareness of a unitary and interpretive element in existence, since if "meaning" is non-existent words are meaningless, while if we define meaning in any one specific manner we are limiting the possible interpretation of Reality. Shelley, in *A Defence of Poetry,* warned his readers against the "presumption" of those who assumed that poetry was composed according to the rules of logic and was an act of the conscious will. In our day, in spite of abundant lip service paid to the functioning of the unconscious, and in spite of the recognition accorded to both prose writers and poets who have followed the psychologists into new regions of awareness and have employed language in ways appropriate to their adopted theories, the strangle hold of logical meaning still largely prevails. The experiences of men and women are not allowed to speak for themselves and to convey, either to those who have them or to those who hear them at second hand, data which is *sui generis.* Instead, they are interpreted in terms of logical or psychological theory.

This is the paramount sin of the "liberal" or "modernist" theologian, against which what is loosely and often inaccurately described as Fundamentalism is a justifiable protest. Either there is a psychology of the Word of God deducible from a careful and consistent study of Holy Writ or there is a Christian psychology derivable from the consensus of all branches of the Christian Church, in spite of occasional disagreement in certain areas, and such a psychology provides the clue to human nature. Temporary fashions in psychology cannot be made touchstones to approve or disallow, to explain or explain away religious experience. The nature of man is to be derived from the experience of Christian man — or, more widely, of man as he embraces a religious view of life — and cannot be deduced from some other standpoint. Religion cannot be thought of as relevant to some given situation. On the contrary, every situation as it presents itself is either relevant or irrelevant to religion, and if it is irrelevant it must be pronounced of no importance. It is not necessarily deliberately false, or wrong, or ugly, but if it does not permit and actively promote in men who are involved in it a sense of oneness with the whole of existence, so that they feel assured that their lives have significance and themselves "status" in respect to a universal purpose, it is not a worthwhile situation.

To say this is to remind ourselves that, while religion does not exist apart from normal human life, and, therefore, must speak to us through the situations of the common life, it must not derive its vocabulary exclusively from any one department of that life. Logic, psychology, art, a particular science — none of these can wholly supply the language which is to express the realization of the interrelation of individual experience with social experience and ultimately with cosmic experience; neither can the varying *Weltanschauungen* of particular countries or periods.

Hegel's theory that each generation of philosophers is bound to reinterpret Reality in terms of the knowledge made available in their time is inapplicable in the sphere of religion, for religion, being concerned with the abiding constituents of the human make-up, cannot accommodate itself to the almost certainly temporary hypotheses of any period. The range of human sentiment and sympathy, it is true, changes from century to century, and varies greatly from place to place, but the fundamental needs of man as man remain constant. During the nineteenth century men hoped persistently that some one science would emerge which would be seen to hold the clue to the interpretation of Reality and which could succeed to the place formerly occupied by religion. That scientists today no longer make such a claim is clear from Joseph Needham's statement that:

> In order to correct the distortion of vision which we must necessarily suffer when we apply the scientific method, we must have recourse to other methods of human perception, we must philosophise, appreciate beauty, and make use of the faculty of mystical experience.[4]

This is to take what Merz well called the "synoptic view of the inner life," a view which reminds us of both the fundamental condition of our existence and the essential nature of religion.[5] We exist as organisms, and we are ever

[4] Joseph Needham, "Mechanistic Biology and Religious Consciousness," in Joseph Needham (ed.), *Science, Religion and Reality* (London: Sheldon Press, 1926), p. 249.

[5] *Ibid.*, p. 256.

striving after a greater perfection organically, whether by purely biological means or by achieving what we recognize as a more complete harmony with that in our environment with which the conservation of values appears to be bound up. We know ourselves to be citizens of the universe and not aliens driven hither and thither by blind force from the urge to unity and organization on which not only our existence but our possibilities or personality-formation or self-affirmation depend. As Macmurray writes: "Belief in God, whatever else it may involve, at least includes the capacity to live as part of the whole of things in a world which is unified."[6] Theism implies Holism; we need not only a universal language but a language capable of expressing the whole gamut of human experience, and this religion alone can supply.

In our time, as Dr. E. L. Allen believes, the world is moving forward from the ecumenicity of particular churches to the ecumenicity of the higher religions.[7] This attitude, if indeed it should prevail, would resolve the difficulties that have overtaken all attempts to reach a synthesis or amalgam of the best that is to be found in different systems of religion by calling attention not to the identities or similarities in each but to the fresh insights and different emphases in each. The vocabulary of religious experience would be enlarged and the range of religious apprehension extended.

This, in a way, connects with the later and more fully developed thought of the late Karl Mannheim, whose use of the term "Christian paradigmata"[8] to express the stimulus and example Christianity can afford mankind illustrates once again the appropriateness of linguistic analogies to express the contemporary action of One who was himself the "Word" of God. If for "Christian" we substitute "religious," Mannheim and Allen will be found to advocate a similar procedure. According to Mannheim, we can take a statement or a story charged with religious significance — above all, the narrative of the life and death of Jesus — and seek guidance from it how to act — "act" in this context including "think" and "feel" — in a specific situation of contemporary living. To use the parables of Jesus, for example, in this way can give clarity and precision to our own lives such as is given in speech or writing by employing the varying forms of words.

He who "declines" the divine archetype inevitably comes to reproduce the divine activity. Human conduct becomes expressive of collaboration with God; for, while there remain grounds for argument how individuals are led to make the attempt, the results are beyond dispute. On the contrary, if men ignore the religious paradigmata their conduct will be alien to the Divine Will for mankind or actively hostile to that Will. If, as a third possibility, they treat the paradigmata as rigid and unalterable regulations for the conduct of life, they are ignoring the living and developing nature of religious language, which Dr. F. W. Dillistone has shown to be inescapable,[9] inasmuch as such language — and, indeed, he would claim, all language — originates not in the

[6] John Macmurray, *Creative Society* (London: Student Christian Movement Press, 1935), p. 22.

[7] E. L. Allen, *Christianity Among the Religions* (London: Allen & Unwin, 1960).

[8] *Diagnosis in Our Time* (London: Kegan Paul, 1943), pp. 117 *et seq.*

[9] *Christianity and Symbolism* (London: Wm. Collins & Sons, Ltd., 1955), p. 159.

need for improved communication but belongs to that range of "doings" which we have heard Otto describing, whereby men recapitulate their experiences with a view to enjoying their renewal.[10] And because what is being expressed are the dealings of the living God with his creature, there is necessarily present a constant creative or re-creative element.

Dangerous as Brunner's statement may become if employed as an argument for differential treatment of those who respond to the divine calling and those who do not or who have never heard the call, for the Christian

> man becomes man only in hearing the Word of God. To be a person is not a condition or state; it is not a fact of nature, like being a European or a Negro; to be a person is an act.[11]

It is the "act" by which a man responds to what he hears God saying to him, for, as Brunner says elsewhere: "The creation of the new creature is indeed a miracle of God, but not magic. God's spirit is no magical stream of power, but always speaking spirit."[12] "Speaking" is the key word here; how the metaphor of speech is to be understood is partly elucidated in Harriet Auber's hymn:

> "He came in tongues of living flame,
> To teach, convince, subdue;
> All-powerful as the wind He came,
> As viewless too."

It is surely an aspect of man's persistent tendency to anthropomorphism to demand, as many do, some message from God in terms of human speech; "a sunset-touch,/A fancy from a flower-bell, someone's death" are as clearly intimations of the Divine as "A chorus-ending from Euripides" or a page of Holy Writ. It was no pantheism, as Dr. S. C. Carpenter reminds us, but a deep "Cross-centered theology" reaching out thence into a "mysterious region of cosmic faith," which led Joseph Plunkett — shot in Dublin at Easter, 1916 — to write:

> "The thunder and the singing of the birds
> Are but his voice — and, carven by his power,
> Rocks are his written words."[13]

God still speaks to men in "many and various ways," because in all these he is still speaking to them by his Son, who is "the first-born of all creation, for in him all things were created, in heaven or on earth, visible and invisible."

[10] *Ibid.*, p. 139.

[11] Emil Brunner, *The Word and the World* (London: Student Christian Movement Press, 1931), p. 32.

[12] Emil Brunner, *God and Man*, trans. D. Cairns (London: Student Christian Movement Press, 1936), p. 86.

[13] S. C. Carpenter, *Supernatural Religion and its Relation to Democracy* (London: Ivor Nicholson, 1932), p. 60.

H. D. Lewis

Professor H. D. Lewis of the University of London, one of the most outstanding contemporary religious philosophers in the English-speaking world, has here personally assembled from his book Our Experience of God *a series of excerpts so as to provide a concise summary of his position. To his work in this field Professor Lewis brings, on the one hand, his native Welsh fervor and Celtic genius for imaginative insight into the nature of religion and, on the other, the rigorous caution and intellectual precision of a well-trained philosophic mind.*

*Expression of the Experience of God **

Experience and Images

Religion begins in wonder — this has often been said, and I think it is profoundly true, but we have also to consider carefully how such a statement must be understood and what sort of wonder is involved. For we could very properly use the word "wonder" today in many ways that have no specially religious import. (Page 104.)

The wonder which is basic to religion, and in which it begins, comes with the realization, usually sharp and disrupting, that all existence as we know it stands in a relation of dependence to some absolute or unconditioned being of which we can know nothing directly beyond this intuition of its unconditioned nature as the source of all other reality. This may seem a highly sophisticated statement to associate with the primitive and rude origin of religion, and it would certainly be out of place if it implied the slightest ability on the part of primitive man to formulate his new-found conviction in such terms as I have just used. Philosophy comes late with a high and sophisticated state of culture. But certainties which we may recognize best perhaps today in their philosophical garb, or which need some infusion of philosophy into ordinary thought for us to acquire and recognize them, may nonetheless be obtainable more simply, if also in some respects more dimly, at much more naïve and less reflective levels of experience. (Page 107.)

It would be wrong, however, to assume that the consciousness of an absolute or unlimited reality, which lies "beyond" the world as we normally apprehend it, comes in the first place, or indeed at any time, in clear detachment from other experiences and the attitudes they engender. That would be peculiarly unlikely to happen to naïve or untutored minds not habituated to abstract thought; but an additional reason, and one more important for us,

* H. D. Lewis, *Our Experience of God* (London: George Allen and Unwin, 1959). Used by permission of the author and the publishers.

for expecting the apprehension of a supreme reality beyond finite life to have special association with other kinds of experiences is that the former is almost certain to be prompted by situations which make a deep impression in other ways. Some crisis will precipitate the leap which takes the mind beyond finite things, and the nature of this will have much to do with the shaping of the total religious experience and its subsequent development.

Crises of the sort mentioned will be of various kinds. Some will turn on conditions more external to the agent himself than others, extraordinary or alarming natural occurrences for example — tremors of the earth, eclipses, thunder and lightning, whirlwinds, sandstorms, volcanic eruptions, drought, plagues, floods. Disturbances due to human agencies, such as migrations or battles or extensive social change, will have a similar role. In other instances the crisis will be more personal — exile, solitude, failure or frustration, loss of prestige or possessions, defeat, punishment and shame, triumph or great good fortune. The distinction between these two sorts of conditions of disturbance must not be exaggerated. It is in virtue of their influence upon our own destinies, as well as by the immediate impact they make upon us, that natural disturbances excite and impress. Lightning is not merely an impressive and extraordinary spectacle, it is alarming and destructive. Turns of personal fortune will also have their significance deepened and emotionally toned by physical surroundings, most of all for imaginative minds likely to make a new mental advance. A case where the conditions seem to be nicely balanced as between what is more internal and the course of external events is the changing of periods and seasons in nature. For here we have events likely on their own account to arouse deep reactions but which have also much to do with survival and prosperity. The physical entities which figure most prominently in these, the resplendent sun and the pale, waxing or waning moon, impress in the same double way. We thus find features of nature or of personal history through which individuals are apt, by close interaction of what lies more without the individual and distinctive events in his own life, to be sharply confronted with their own limitations and the power and impressiveness of what lies beyond themselves in their environment; and these will be also the factors most likely to prompt reflection about what lies altogether beyond themselves and their environment, the infinite or unconditioned.

The situations to which I have alluded will not always take the form of disturbance and upheaval. The reverse of these may be equally potent. Calm after storm, the gentleness of the onset of a new season, the stillness of remote and secluded places, ease of fortune after turmoil and trouble, accommodation with one's enemies and the serenity of age after the wildness of youth, may also set the mind in the mood where it is induced to pass beyond its present transitory setting and awaken to the new notion of what lies altogether beyond all its limitations. God may be found by "the gentle waters" and in "green pastures" as well as in the flood and the storms of the desert, and he may be heard in "the still, small voice." Quite likely, the interaction of peace and storm, of upheaval and normality, and of the emotional and other reactions these induce, has an outstanding role in the development of religion at all stages, and there is certainly much in the history of peoples especially prominent in religious history, such as the Hebrews, to suggest this. The eruption at Sinai, and events connected with it, which undoubtedly affected them deeply, are offset by the influence of periods of settlement after nomadic roamings.

The importance of these considerations lies for us at the moment in their bearing on the question of the filling of the content of religious awareness. For it seems to me that this begins to be formed from the first onset of any properly religious life through the way the first apprehension of finite being as having a supreme and infinite source, and the emotional and other accompaniments of this awareness which we have also in mind in designating it "wonder," impress themselves into the situation which prompts them by lending to that situation something of their own quality and aura of mystery. Certain features of initial religious situations acquire a particular prominence or sharpness of outline in this process, through which secular parts of a total experience are toned by their association with religious insight, and those come to constitute for us in this way the first formulations of the "Word of God."

This works in two directions, first inwardly into the more personal experience and history of the agent himself; and, secondly, outwardly into the external situation in which he finds himself. The nerve of the first movement is found in the reactions directly elicited by initiation into the mystery of dependent being and its absolute source. There is no reason to suppose, as some views of early religion might suggest, that these reactions are bound to be violent, at least in their outward manifestations. On the contrary, they may be very sober, and that, it seems to me, is certainly what we should expect them to be at first. To find that the edges of things are not where we take them to be, that they merge, not only into one another in the unities we can understand, but into an entirely different background, rich and inexhaustible and giving them a character totally different from what we normally find in them, to be strained to the limit of understanding and confronted with absolute novelty at the same time as the basic uncertainties are eased and the sense of faltering in an insecure, impermanent world yields to the completest of all assurances and the guarantee of reason by what goes beyond and completes it — all this is more likely to induce a bating of breath and stilling of the mind into quiet wonder than immediate demonstration of excitement. Is not this the attitude of the scientist when problems that have long baffled him yield to an obvious solution by a new way of looking at things, perhaps overwhelmingly simple, or of the artist when all falls easily and obviously into place; is there not here a suspension of all activity that might compete with the process that is so strangely fulfilling itself of its own accord, and is it not in a similar integrating of all activity into a meditative mood of suspended animation that a man becomes inwardly silent before the greatest mystery of all? As the tension is eventually relieved, the pent-up energies summoned up and arrested in the first moment of wondering awareness will find release in various ways, according to temperament and circumstance, and in the course of this much in the original experience may lose its purity. But it seems to me that the note of stillness rather than violence is that most likely to govern the first dawning of true religion and its main moments at all times.

This stillness of mind is not, however, numbness or quietism, but, on the contrary, an alerting and concentration of all the powers of the mind, the more especially as "the beyond" is apprehended, not in detachment but as involved in facts of the world which are most sharply presented "here and now." There will thus be a heightening of perceptiveness and sensitivity, but qualified by the selectiveness by which attention is directed mainly to matters most consonant with the new experience through which we are passing and the new perspective into which all things are cast when viewed in the light of our altered notions of their boundaries. We may thus in one sense be taken "out of ourselves" or lifted to a "seventh heaven" and feel that we have left behind the more mundane and drabber affairs of our normal existence; but we never quite do this, any more than the poet does so in moments of intense creativity. The world as we normally think of it may be forgotten and our impressions of it effaced, but it will be nonetheless very much with us in another guise. We may be impervious to much that goes on around us, and certain events may fail to make any impression that we notice on our senses. But we may be all the more sharply aware of our environment in other regards, as the poet, to continue what seems the aptest analogy here, may have much in his poem conditioned, directly or indirectly, by things he notices, the color and shape of a leaf or the gleam of light on a wall or the tinted clouds in a sky, out of the corner of his mind, as it were, not reflectively and self-consciously, but yet acutely and vividly and taken up subtly in some fashion into what he writes or says. The world as remembered will be present in the same way. A poet or a mystic may thus seem quite unaware of some features of present environment; both may fail to observe what happens about them or to be conscious of physical sensations which are normally most obtrusive. But they have at the same time a heightened consciousness of their environment in other ways, and while they may well declare themselves, in some extreme cases, to have been "out of the body," they are not so in fact, but, on the contrary, more than ever within the body and within the ordinary world differently perceived. In the moment of live religious experience we will thus be more than usually perceptive of certain things in our present environment and responsive to them, although not perhaps the things we would notice most obviously at other times; and this holds as much for what is occurring within ourselves as for features of the external situation.

Alertness of this kind will be heightened and directed also by a profounder consciousness of unity in things communicated to us by our apprehension of its transcendent source and guarantee. This reduces the proclivity we have to heed events more as they enter into the orbit of our particular interests and spheres of activity, or to take a romantic view of the world and whatever it holds for us of good or ill. Events which are remote from spheres in which their significance is most evident are thus accorded their due importance and seen to have essential affinity with the matters which impinge more insistently and inescapably upon us. Our judgments are thus corrected and made objective and we incur a discipline which should deepen in every regard our devotion to the truth. How consistent this is with what we know of religion in its living and undefiled forms is easily perceived, and it may readily be confirmed by inspection of the progress of religion from its humblest to its most exalted modes. The language and symbols of religion are rich with encomiums of truth, whether it concern God or man, this world or another. Its censure of deceit and hypocrisy is heavy and some of its sublimest and most impressive praise is reserved for those who have no deception in them, either for themselves or for others. Debased religion has often obstructed the search for truth and won for religion the enmity and suspicion of inquiring minds, but it is not hard to see that where religion thrives on dogmatism and intolerance the energies which it has released are being exploited in ways not consistent with the insight which generated them. The long chapter of religious persecution and narrowness needs more explaining than can be accorded it here; although views already advanced about corrupt forms of religion suggest the course which such explanation should take. But I think few who study the main sources of religious inspiration and the utterances which typify best its course in the past will question the extent to which undefiled religion puts a premium on integrity and love of truth. This, I submit, is most consistent with what we must think of religious awareness as involving a reinforcement of our sense of objectivity and bringing comprehensiveness into our apprehension of our environment, and that is a characteristic of religious insight which it exhibits from the start and retains at its core so long as it is able to be true to itself.

Nowhere is this more evident than in our grasp of ethical truth. Values and obligations are markedly external to ourselves; they are not our own creations and do not depend directly on what we feel and think ourselves. We acknowledge and recognize what we deem of worth and owe it to comply with our duties whether that pleases us or not. But in having our thought directed to what is so completely "beyond" or "other than" ourselves as the absolute source of being which wholly eludes comprehension, we find ourselves also better disposed to appreciate fairly the standards of worth and the obligations which confront us directly, not, it may be, in some abstract form, but as qualifying some situation in which we are placed.

The relation of ethics and religion at this point is in fact twofold, for just as the apprehension of a transcendent reality bordering all that we otherwise know induces a sharper and truer appreciation of ethical distinctions, so our sensitivity to those distinctions predisposes us in turn to have our minds guided beyond the sphere in which they naturally function to what is more completely external or "beyond." There is for this reason a close and persistent interaction of ethics and religion, which we may also readily trace in the history of their progress and which has often been made the subject of comment and speculation by students of both.

To the extent that our apprehension of the ultimate mystery which surrounds our own existence (and all other finite being) has the effect of heightening and correcting our perceptiveness of the world about us and ourselves, and to the extent that it makes us more appreciative of ethical distinctions and their objective or external quality, it will much affect our understanding of ourselves and of our present environment in the situation in which that apprehension is vividly awakened in us. This is one distinctive characteristic of the general enlightenment which religion brings and which gives to religion a content peculiarly its own and yet made up of features of finite experience. (Pages 110–116.)

By means of the emotional accompaniments or effects of our initial discernment of all finite reality, but more expressly of what is present as here and now, as having a transcendent source of whose particular nature we can have no direct comprehension, and even more, and more importantly, by the sharpening of moral sensitivity and the alerting of the faculties by which we take note of our environment, certain features of the situation in which this discernment or apprehension occurs acquire a distinctiveness and prominence which they would not normally exhibit. Independently of this, such situations are likely to be exceptional and to represent some climax or crisis in our own personal history or in the course of the events which make the biggest impact upon us. In this way the significance we attach to certain secular or finite features of some situations in which we find ourselves, a significance which is itself furthermore finite or secular throughout, has a special connection with our apprehension of the transcendent. The course of such experiences in one's own life and the life of one's society will yield results of distinctive importance for our understanding of our environment and the reactions to it which are fitting for us. If, furthermore, the features of those distinctive and critical situations which are thus specially highlighted for us have, as religious people claim, a compelling and insistent character, which rivets attention upon them, then we are disposed to conclude, and are justified in doing so it seems to me, that we are here being afforded a clue to the importance the transcendent has specifically for us in our present existence and to the expectations we may form on the basis of our dependence upon it; and this, moreover, over the continuous history of ourselves and our society will present itself increasingly as a "dealing" with us of that which is beyond the sphere of finite existence altogether, which, along with various reactions or responses of our own, builds itself up into a relationship of intimate and fairly sustained communion which is already presupposed in all but the most initial and incipient awakening of religious apprehension and causes us to think immediately in personal terms of the situations in which this particular process of illumination occurs. (Pages 118–119.)

It must not therefore be supposed that, in attributing very peculiar qualities to religious experience and distinguishing sharply between it and other experience, I wish to circumscribe religious experience closely. On the contrary, just as I have urged that the transcendent becomes immanent when the consciousness of it is led to associate itself with certain features of finite existence and put on these the imprint of what is altogether beyond them, so the live religious experience in which this consists extends itself into yet other experiences by lending them something of its own quality. (Page 124.)

The point to be stressed is that, while the distinctiveness of the "live" religious experience, as I have called it, must not be overlooked or underestimated, we must not regard it as the intrusion of a wholly unusual factor into the normal occasions of life, or something peculiar which happens to us oddly now and again, but, normally at least, as the renewal of a formative influence by which the remainder is deeply affected and which, in consequence, the latter is more and more predisposed to receive. And the more we are enabled to regard the renewal of insight and power in this way, in vital relation to the fullness of a religious life which it animates and out of which it arises, the more we shall appreciate how there will be extensions of meaning or significance in religion, not only as distinctive religious experiences are viewed in relation to one another, but also in respect of the whole of what comes about in consequence of them, in the way of further insights or changes of attitude, for us and for other members of society; and this may also be regarded as part of the story of the way the transcendent enters into vital and intimate relation to us within our own lives.

Much in the course of this story will remain imprecise; the spread of the difference which it makes to us cannot be carefully mapped, but will, rather, have very uncertain and fluid edges. Much will pass into total oblivion, just as a friendship may be sustained and extended in innumerable ways of which it would be quite impossible to give a detailed account. It is the general impression which stays as a rule. But while it will not be possible to note and record precisely the part which distinctive religious experiences play in our lives, or to determine exactly when they arise and fade again into others, we are able to recognize in a general way not only the more direct impact of one religious occurrence on others and the pattern of the course such occurrences take, but also the manifold accretions of meaning and importance as this process immerses itself in our life as a whole; and this gives a further reach and dimension as it were to the distinctive media or symbols from which we detect, in the indirect way which alone is possible to us, what are the particular ways in which the transcendent may come to count for us and be, in this manner, disclosed.

Of this process there will be two forms we need to distinguish. There will be in the first place, as again in the case of friendship or love, a general or over-all impression of the way the relationship builds itself up. We may find, for example, that the moments of religious insight are sharper and more pointed in their significance on occasions of grave and outstanding need, in grief, perplexity or doubt for example, and there may thus be produced the general impression of an ever present help in trouble. We may find comfort when comfort is especially needed by the new breadth that is given to our mental or spiritual outlook, and we may find sources of strength when despair would otherwise overwhelm us by finding ourselves feeling and thinking in ways that are superior to our normal lot, and there may be marked accretions of strength to our personalities in these ways. Occurrences of this sort may of course be easily travestied as we think of them in retrospect or generalize about them, and we may come to think of them in more mechanical ways as a more explicit intervention in the outward course of the difficulties which beset us;

and when men are at a primitive stage of development and apt to rationalize their experience in the ways that are more amenable to their understanding and call for the least effortful response, unusual turns of events, an unexpected deliverance for example, may be seized upon to confirm or exemplify superstitious beliefs in magic or totem for which the facts provide no justification. But this is another issue, and I postpone for the moment any observations to be made on the question of a possible divine intervention in external events as it appears in the light of the views advanced in this book. The point is that we may have distinctively religious occasions in the course of which we may have the impression of being helped or solaced or strengthened.

In a similar way we may find that the more distinctively religious moments are also apt to occur on occasions of deviation on our part from the course we believe we ought to be following; they stand as it were athwart our path and may arrest our course in a way which we can regard as a peculiarly spiritual deliverance, in which our own personalities, and not merely our particular circumstances, have been preserved from disaster and degradation. Alternatively, we may find, in yielding to a temptation, that we have an accuser other than our own conscience, an accuser which speaks with yet greater gravity from within the heightening of our own sense of worth and dignity in the clearer illumination which religious experience brings and the association of moral values with the general intervention of the transcendent in our lives. We shall then be disposed to conclude that in religion we are confronted with a specially righteous power and that the intervention from outside our finite experience, which is also within it, has to do especially with the moral quality of our lives. God will be a God of righteousness and justice and he will search out our hearts.

This again admits of travesty and misrepresentation according to the stage of moral enlightenment we may have reached and the play of our imagination. But that need not trouble us here. And just as we may find in the livelier moments of religious experience a terrible accuser deepening the accents of our own conscience and making us sensitive to moral distinctions we might have overlooked or considered trivial, so we may also find an eventual healer, a healer whose ministrations may be costing and humbling and whose cures may not always be immediate, but who provides in the last resort the only balm that will work by presenting in the world at large a sustaining of moral and kindred values which gives us confidence in taking them into our hearts again and renewing their hold by identifying them more closely with the religious interventions by which they are extended and deepened. In the same context we may find also that the blunting of our religious awareness, and the relapse into less elevated attitudes towards the world, is countered by unexpected renewal of moods of religious sensitivity, that God, in the simpler language of live religion, does not "abandon us wholly" or "leave himself without witness," and we may come to know of ways in which we may facilitate this process and make ourselves more open to its influence. And here we may see the germ of our thought of God as the restorer of right relations with himself, as renewer of life and healer, as redeemer and God of grace.

There may be much more than this to a mature conception of grace, and

Christianity has, in my opinion, a proper claim to a particular ministry of grace and redemption. But I think we must start from the sort of experience I have just described and which is far from being a monopoly of any religion. And if we find, in the manner of which I have only given an indication in outline here, that there are certain general impressions, such as those instanced, to be obtained of ways in which the alleged divine intervention in human experience occurs, then we have certain general pointers or counters by which to sum up and sustain the faith we acquire, and for which we come to have a special regard.

This will hold also for very different kinds of total impression which we may acquire of the process of divine disclosure. For we may find not only that there are recurring patterns or modes which the process usually exhibits, but also that it has taken a particular course in a particular history, our own or that of our community. This will be linked up of course with the shape our own destiny has taken at the secular level, but if we find that, at distinctive and outstandingly significant interludes in our own story, the course of our lives has been modified in some fashion such as to give us an altered conception of its nature as a whole, and that this modification takes the religious form we have been discussing, or even if we merely find that the primary religious occurrences in our lives, considered in relative detachment from the remainder, build up into a special shape or story of their own, then we are presented with a very special way in which religious experience is the medium of divine disclosure, a particular revelation in history. And while this again is not the exclusive monopoly of any community or period or religion, it may well be more evident in some situations and periods than others, and there may well be a distinctive form of it which may yield the tenets of a particular faith and substantiate the claim to uniqueness to be made on its behalf.

But of processes of this sort again certain general impressions may be obtained, blending with the more basic and universal over-all impressions of the process of revelation already noted. The God who succors and preserves, and who restores the erring to right relations to himself, may be found to have done this in outstanding ways which have given shape to our affairs over a particular period, and especially perhaps some period of importance in the story of a people or community; and this will present itself to us, in our total impression of the process, in close and specific identification of God's activity with the particular occurrences in which it has thus been made especially evident to us. God will be the God of Abraham, Isaac and Jacob, the God who led his people out of captivity, who revealed himself especially to their leader in ways which left their pronounced and indelible mark on the whole of their subsequent story at all its levels, and who created within them the expectation, often marred by crudities and distortions of interpretation, of some triumphant culmination of this process of his dealing with them. And for such a people God will be the living God who discloses himself to them in this distinctive shaping of their history.

Those who are most sensitive to this process, and they will normally include those who have participated most prominently in it, will moreover have represented the process, both in its general scope and in the particular way in which it impinges most closely upon them and on any part they may be playing in the affairs of their community at the time, in significant and expressive terms peculiar to their age and circumstances; and the more their imaginative and artistic propensities are inflamed, as it is very natural for them to be, by the tensions of the events in which they take part, the more will colorful metaphors and parables appear giving further particularity and concretion to the process of revelation. God will be the great king, the patient, long-suffering tender of the vineyard, the husband who never forsakes his beloved however she offends but draws her with "bonds" of love, and, in due course, as profound insight supervenes upon superstition and distortion, the blameless victim by the shedding of whose blood the guilty are redeemed and the demands of righteousness and sanctity met.

In this process, also, God himself will be given more specific representation in easily recognizable forms; the "arm of the Lord" will be found encompassing men, his throne will be in the skies, and his voice will be heard. In moments of religious exaltation and excitement men will be prone, moreover, to have colorful visions and abnormal experience of other sorts which will lend their own imagery to the more permanent representations of God. There will be perpetuated certain established ways of designating him and these will be such familiar and common accompaniments of religious living and aids to its maintenance that the distinction will be largely blurred in many minds between what is real and what is figurative in such representations. Religion will live in its inspired images, and at less sophisticated stages, where the sense of the religious molding of life is also marked and vivid; the domination of experience by its more creative and life-giving images will be considerable. (Pages 125–130.)

The religious imagery to which I have just referred, however vivid and indispensable it may be at certain stages, does not represent the truth about God and his activity directly, but only at a certain remove; for the warrant for the images comes from certain experiences and the total significance of these in our experience as a whole. What the images gather together and represent are the patterns and recurrences of certain distinctive events, which, in their significant patterns or sequences especially, are themselves the ultimate and irreducible ingredients of our knowledge of God. (Page 131.)

This reflection is prompted also by consideration of the way imagination works. We must not lapse into the error of what is sometimes known as "faculty psychology." The imagination is not a thing apart, but a feature of a total experience, and it has its material on which to work. It is not some odd separate gift of imagination that Shakespeare had, but imaginative insight into what life is like, and the more there is insight of this kind in the exercise of imagination, in distinction from the sheer precipitation of one image by another, the finer it is. Possibly it is by this test that many modern artists and poets — Dylan Thomas perhaps? — are found lacking. But however that may be, imagination never works quite in a vacuum, and the rightful stress today on the importance of "image thinking" will become one-sided unless we bear in mind also the need for imagination to be duly integrated with living.

The moral of this for our theme is that the images which figure in religious belief have their proper significance in relation to the experiences which they sum up and reflect and whose life they help to sustain. Images must thus be anchored in experience and never allowed to take wing very far on their own. But subject to this qualification, and bearing in mind that the qualification must not be understood too mechanically or allowed to become a curb on enterprising exercises of the religious imagination, we must award a very prominent place to the work of imagination in giving sharp and impressive delineation of the course which religious experiences take, both in themselves and as a leaven of life as a whole, for the individual and his society. Nor must we crudely and slickly attempt to unpack this imaginative presentation of the truth into its ultimate elements in experience. For the particular merit of images lies in the fact that they enable us to gain a total or over-all impression of certain presentations and occurrences in such a way that the contribution of each to the total impression is not explicitly noticed, and in this way we can also retain an over-all impression of the character of certain occurrences when the memory of them individually has passed into oblivion. This does not preclude the control of images and the vetting of them on the basis of experience. But it does mean that such work requires to be skillfully and patiently carried out by remaining sensitive to the inherent dynamic of the image and sufficiently conversant in a general way with the facts out of which it arises to be informed by the images and not misled. Sanity and wisdom in living turns much on the skill we exercise here and the ease with which it comes to us by custom. We need to be imaginatively at home in the real world. (Pages 138–139.)

In substance, what we find in art as in religion is that the new forms are not thrust upon us wholly unannounced in a totally unqualified newness, much less are they deliberately manufactured to meet a contemporary need; they grow out of earlier forms, not in a random way which calls for no particular tending, but with a subtlety which makes its own most exacting demands on attention. And this, in both cases, involves much besides the spontaneous generation of form out of form. For the latter activity cannot proceed effectively, even if it can occur at all, apart from the novel apprehensions or experience of a further content which they mediate. A lack, in modern art, parallel to the one noted, is the absence of new insight and effective relevant new experience of the world. We are all realists in a sense, forced to be so in the exigencies of new and alarming situations thrust upon us; and yet we may view the changing scene obtusely and be stunned by its crudities and clamor, so that we do not draw our new experiences together into the perspectives which can make them artistically and religiously significant. We need, in art, to live in a certain way in the present, without evasions and undaunted; and at the same time to cherish and sustain the art of the past, not in a dilettante fashion but as a rounded way of experiencing the world by people not afraid of the impact of the world. In this way the art of the past is enabled to pierce the present and produce within it new art forms by which the world of today is illumined.

These resemblances of art and religion are not accidental. There is much affinity of substance between the two. In art as in religion there is an alertness of mind by which we became aware of features of our mental or physical environment which we would not otherwise notice. Objects and situations acquire a starkness and character which they do not normally exhibit, they are placed in new perspectives and thrust into contexts which give them new interest and significance. Ideas and things are coaxed out of their normal background and made to impress us more in this way on their own account, while at the same time being put in suggestive juxtaposition to others. The world is viewed thus without the gloss which habit and personal interest put upon it and assessed more objectively on its own account; the worth and interest it ought properly to have for us are better displayed, and in this respect the artist, however averse to the title in some moods, is bound to be a moralist. He is not the teacher of precepts, and in the matters which fall outside his main or immediate purview his own practice may be lax, although much less so in essentials, I suspect, than is often assumed in many cases; the morality he inculcates need not be conventional, and it may not be coordinated. As a creator and innovator in his proper role, he may be unduly attracted to novelty in manners and morals, and not be appreciative enough of established practice and humdrum, but often indispensable, services of the normal round. But when every allowance of this sort is made — and the finer the artist the less in the main is there need for it — the artist, in the particular illumination he brings *qua* artist, presents the world in a way which exhibits better its worth and claims. In the process which engages our interests and emotions more completely, we are also enabled to view things in greater detachment from ourselves, in more arresting outline and truer perspectives.

The artist accomplishes this by various devices, exploiting the links of association, comparing and contrasting and following out partial resemblances in novel situations by simile or metaphor or unusual allusion. But when these and kindred devices, and subtle variations of these, on which the artist hits by living in the world of art, and on which he need not reflect in an abstract way — when these yield the images which give us the appropriate new impressions of things, these images generate others out of themselves and add to the available store or repertoire of the artist on which he may draw in further disclosures of reality. The immediate generation of image out of image must, however, be checked, as we have seen, and subdued to the process of producing the patterned imagery which continues to be revelatory of experience and the world. Images will thus expand and merge into others, not merely by their own momentum but under the impact of new experience which they help to make possible and direct.

This happens in religion also, but this *and more.* For there the merging of symbol into symbol and the patterning of imagery has a basic principle of its own which is not present in art as such. In art we need only the insights and appropriate symbolism which provide best on their own account a peculiar disclosure of what some facts or situations are like, together with the fusion and extension of the experiences in which this happens, and their sustaining symbols, into others in a way which is naturally required or inherent in this process in itself. There is mystery here and newness, but only that which is involved in coming to know our finite environment in this extraordinary way. The artistic devices are effective in themselves and combine in their own ways under the impact of fresh experience. But this is not what happens initially in religion.

In religion, as we have seen, we have a new impression of our environment due to the apprehension we acquire of the world as a created world and all that is within it as deriving from an unconditioned source quite different in nature from all finite being, complete or perfect in the most absolute way and irreducibly mysterious to us. This awareness, the shock it administers to us and the sense that all things are made new to us in consequence of it, does not depend essentially or in the first place on special techniques, as in art, or require familiarity with the techniques of art, least of all in their more cultivated form. It comes about in its own way, and there is inherent to it as a rule an insistent or summoning character of its own, not derived, as in art, from the content disclosed and our interest. This is bound up with the situation in which we find ourselves, but with a sense, not wholly derived from the situation, of there being something radically irresistible in our having this experience here and now, of its being imposed even if also sought, and imposed more from outside ourselves than in the compulsions to which the artist is subject. The inherent character of this experience points also in its own way to the appropriate focusing of it and predisposes it to a certain representation. This is where art is taken up into religion and serves to give firmer form and continuity to the religious insights, just as it may also predispose us to have them by the character it gives to the antecedent situation.

The similarities of art and religious experience make it easy to confuse them, as they also make it hard to disentangle the properly religious process from any artistic activities, incipient perhaps or unsophisticated, which may be included within it. This also makes it hard to determine how far some kind of art is indispensable in religion. The vision which the artist has is, moreover, always on the point of passing over into a religous one, for in having the individual character of things displayed in the strangeness and mystery of their being just what they are, in being caught up in their finality in the impact they make in art, we are impinging closely on the ultimate mystery of all things in the inevitability of their having a transcendent source. The reference "beyond" which objects have is not something around them, or attached to them; they wear it in being what they are. In his own exhibition of the world, to himself and others, the artist comes thus very close to the religious visionary or prophet, and the one role may thus the more easily and imperceptibly pass into the other. Through misunderstanding, as indicated earlier, this may not always be evident to artists or to religious persons; both may affix to themselves wrong labels. But in point of fact art is made all the more readily available to the religious process it serves because it is always on the point of transmuting itself into religion proper; the associations it sets up vibrate in close harmony with those of religion and help the transmutation of artistic symbols into religious ones.

Kindred affinities are present in the patterning of religious experiences. This is again determined in the first instance by the inherent nature of those experiences and the occasions on which they occur; they are merged into one another and are renewed and extended and take on their own account some significant course determined by the transcendental reference at the center. This is quite different from the spontaneous interweaving of artistic images at their own level. The controlling factor, the drive or impulse, is different in the two cases, and the meaning we cull from a religious course of events is an expressly religious one. But art may not only help to focus individual items of this, it also brings its own momentum and the confluence of its terms to help in exhibiting and sustaining the inherent patterns of the religious occurrences; and here again the affinities of art and religion are important, for they help to keep the former subservient to the latter and ensure its more effective absorption into the inherent dialectic of the religious process itself.

There are then these close affinities of art and religion, and art in the service of religion, most of all at the level of shaping the creative religious images, has been of extreme importance and contributed extensively to religion out of what it is in itself; it has merged into the religious process, but it has not dominated it. The danger is indeed always present, as stressed, that the artistic imagery should pull religion out of its proper course into other paths, or become an end in itself in religion and corrupt the whole. But one of the marks of great prophecy, and of the religious life which is closest to it, is its avoidance of this danger and the triumphant absorbing of creative artistic activity into its own processes. Religion has in turn provided a corrective to the proneness of art to lapse from its own course. (Pages 200–204.)

Index

A

Abraham, 103, 176, 177, 407
Absolute: Hegel on the, 6, 232; Sorley on the, 240
Academy, Plato's, 268[9]
Actuality: Aristotle on, 72ff
Addams, Jane, 17
Adoration, Kierkegaard on, 127
Agape, 178ff
Ahura Mazda, 283
Albertus Magnus, St., 81
Al Hallaj, faith of, 218[2]
Allegory, Origen's use of, 44
Allen, E. L., 397
Ambrose, St., 46
Amos, 388
Anaxagoras, 70, 72
Angels, Loyola on the sin of the, 145
Angra Mainyu, 283
Angst, Kierkegaard on, 117[7]
Animals, Hume on endowments of, 272f
Animism, 375[n]
Anselm, St.: on ontological argument, 75ff; on man, 76; on desolation of man's heart, 77; on faith and understanding, 77, 78; reply to Gaunilon, 78ff; on existence, 78; mentioned, 75, 81
Apollo, 44
Apostles' Creed, 122
Aristotle: on Prime Mover, 28ff; on motion, 68ff; on motion and time, 68f; on imperishability of motion, 70; on finite and infinite, 70; on love and strife, 70f; on kinds of substance, 71; on actuality, 72ff; on final cause, 73ff; on love and friendship, 226ff; on the friendship of good men, 227; on friendship and utility, 228; on good character, 229; on friendship and bad fortune, 230; Farrer on view of human nature, 187ff; mentioned, 49[6], 68, 81, 153, 160, 180, 187, 203, 226, 260[1], 268, 268[8], 333, 340, 342, 344, 388
Arnold, Matthew, 392
Art, H. D. Lewis on, 409ff
Artemis, 44
Asashananda, Swami, 218[3]
Aspiration, Emerson on, 16
Ataraxia, 180
Athanasian Creed, 326
Atheism, Ayer on, 306
Athens, 68
Auber, Harriet, 398
Augustine, St.: on creation, 46ff; on the Trinity, 47; on evil, as privation of good, 47; on good and evil, 47ff; on good without evil, 48; on good and evil as coexisting, 49; on logic, 49; mentioned, 21, 26, 46, 209, 253
Averroës, 344
Avicenna, 344
Ayer, A. J.: on *God* as a meaningless term, 305ff; on proofs for God's existence, 205; on atheism and agnosticism, 306; on the moralist, 306; on God as a transcendent object, 306f; on religion and natural science, 307; on religious feeling, 307; on religious knowledge, 307ff; on sense experience, 308; on intuition and mysticism, 308; on religious experience, 309; debate with Copleston, 328–355; summary of logical positivism, 328; on metaphysics, 329ff, 347ff, 350ff; on limits of science, 330f; on problem of transcendent, 33f; on hypothesis, 336; on causality, 335; on contingent and necessary propositions, 337ff; on tautologies, 339; on symbols, 340f; on logic, 341ff; on language, 343f; on meaningful propositions, 345ff; on emotive statements, 346; on verification, 347ff; on factual statements, 348f; on religious experience, 353; mentioned, 304, 310, 311, 313, 317, 318, 324, 325, 327, 366

B

Baghdad, 218[2]
Barrès, 158
Barnes, William Ernest, 18
Barrett, Sir William, 202[3]
Barth, Karl, 75, 292, 377
Bartsch, Hans W., 377[1]
Bayle, Pierre, 98[10], 101[26]
Beatific Vision, the, 218ff, 393ff
Beauty, Royce on, 52
Belief: evidence for, 15; and understanding, 77

Bereavement, agony of, 223
Berkeley, George, 50, 52, 53, 99[16], 315, 316
Berlin, 369
Bernières, 161
Bertocci, P., 291[4]
Bethel, 393
Bethlehem, 170
Biblical criticism, 377
Bodies: as first-beginnings of things, 37; natural inertia of, 96
Boethius: on chance and providence, 259ff; on free will, 260ff; on the freedom of the human spirit, 261; on foreknowledge and free will, 261ff; on reconciliation of foreknowledge and free will, 264ff; on human reasoning, 266f, 268ff; on God's foreknowledge of all things, 268ff; on God's eternal present, 269; on kinds of necessity, 270; on foreknowledge and necessity, 270f
Bonaventure, St., 81
Bosanquet, Bernard, 5
Bossuet, Jacques Bénigne, 95
Boston, 202[4]
Bourdelot, 104
Bourignon, Antoinette, 98[10]
Bradley, F. H., 5
Bravery, in a civilized state, 137[2]
Bremond, Henri: on "the rationalist obsession," 158ff; on mysticism, 159ff
Buddhism, 283
Budge, Sir Ernest A. T. W., 374[11]
Brunner, Emil, 412
Buber, Martin: on the response of man to man, 253ff; on responsibility, 253; on morality, 254; on life of dialogue, 254; on religion and morality, 254f; on dogma, 255
Bultmann, Rudolf: Hepburn on, 377ff; mentioned, 377, 378, 379, 380, 381, 382, 383, 384, 385

C

Caird, Edward, 5, 277
Caird, John, 5
Calculus, 95
Calvin, John, 104, 389
Campion, C. T., 246[n]
Caner, Sarah Ann, 158[n]
Caritas, 178
Carlyle, Thomas, 5
Carmichael, L., 284[1]
Carnap, Rudolf, 304
Carpenter, S. C., 398
Cassirer, Ernst: on the power of metaphor, 369ff; on mythology, 370f; on metaphor, 370; on types of metaphor, 371ff; on the development of a concept, 372; on logic, 372f; on mythic thought, 373; on magic, 373; on relationship of the whole to its parts, 373ff; on metaphorical function of language; mentioned, 393[1]
Catherine of Genoa, St., 212
Cause: Comte on fruitless search for, 65; Aristotle on first, 73; Aristotle on final, 73ff; Descartes on first, 93; Hume on, 133; Copleston on, 335
Celsus, 43, 44, 45
Certitude: Pascal on, 106; Newman on, 149
Chadwick, Henry, 43
Chance, Boethius on, 259ff
Character, Aristotle on, 229
Charlemagne, 259
Chartres, 394
Chasidism, 253
Christianity and Symbolism, Dillistone, 386[n], 397[9]
Christianity: as a Person, 126; as a unique force, 181
Christian Church, 11, Kierkegaard's attack on the, 128[24]
Christian Discourses, Kierkegaard, 115[4]
Christian doctrine, Cox on, 359ff. *See also* Dogma
Christian faith, as solution to problem of evil, 292ff
Christian Doubt, MacGregor, 292
Christology, Kierkegaard on, 115
Chrysippus of Soli, 44
Cicero, 264, 264[6]
City of God, Augustine, 47[3]
Cleanthes, 98[12]
Coleridge, Samuel T., 5, 387
Cogito, ergo sum, 84
Commitment, Kierkegaard on necessity of, 126[20]
Compassion, Schweitzer on, 247
Comte, Auguste: on positivism and religion, 64; on monotheism, 64; on demonstrable necessities, 65; on social life, 65; on love, 66; on worship of humanity, 66
Concept of Dread, Kierkegaard, 121[12], 128[23]
Concept, Cassirer on development of, 372
Concluding Unscientific Postscript, Kierkegaard, 115[3]
Confessions, Augustine, 47[3], 253
Conscience, Lewis on, 406
Consciousness, modes of, 84ff

Consolation of Philosophy, Boethius, 259n
Contra Celsum, Origen, 43n
Conversion, of Pascal, 103
Copernicus, 99[15]
Copleston, F. C.: debate with Ayer, 328ff; on metaphysics, 329ff; on role of philosophy, 329; on limits of science, 330f; on intelligible structure of reality, 332; on problem of transcendent, 333f; on self-sufficiency of the world, 334; on causality, 335; on contingent and necessary propositions, 337ff; on tautologies, 339; on symbols, 340f; on logic, 341ff; on language, 343f; on meaningful propositions, 345ff; on emotive statements, 346; on verification, 347ff; on metaphysical propositions, 347ff; on factual statements, 348f; on philosophic knowledge of God, 351; on religious experience, 353f; mentioned, 358
Cosmological argument: 81, 95[2], 115
Cox, David: on theology and logical positivism, 356ff; on metaphysics, 356; on verification principle, 357f; on empiricism, 357; on "sense"-experience, 359; on Christian doctrine, 359ff; on need for restatement of Christian doctrine, 360ff; on applying the verification principle to Christian doctrine, 361ff; on truth and verification, 362f; on religious experience, 362ff; on verifying existence of God, 362ff; McPherson's reply to, 363–367
Cranmer, Thomas, 389
Creation: Augustine on, 46ff; Leibniz on, 100; Hocking on, 235
Creativity, Hocking on, 214
Crises, and the religious response, 400
Crombie, Ian, 384; Hepburn on, 383
Cromwell, Oliver, 59, 61
Crucial Situations, Kierkegaard, 120[10,11]
Cultus and religious doctrine, 9, 10
Culture-religion, Kierkegaard on, 113

D

Dalton, John, 320
Dante, 207, 209
Das Heilige, Otto, 173n, 393, 393[2]
David, 164
Deane, S. N., 75n
Death: and belief in God, 15; as the ruin of life, 15; Royce on, 59; Plato on, 197f; Hocking on, 216; MacKinnon on, 221ff; and the language of religion and poetry, 222
De Caelo, 72[4], 268[8]
Deism, 7, 234
Deity in Time, The, Johnson, 112n
Democritus, 70, 71
Demythologization and the problem of validity, 377ff
Denmark, Church of, 128[24]
Descartes, René: on the ontological argument, 84ff; on perception, 84; on consciousness, 84ff; on external world, 85; on ideas, 86ff; on ideas and objects, 87; on the nature of God, 90; on perfection, 90ff; on man, 92; on first cause, 93; mentioned, 95[1], 97, 97[9], 98[12], 160, 319
Determinism, Farrer on, 183f
Deus ex machina, 10[26]
Dialogue, Buber on life of, 254
Dillistone, F. W.: on function of metaphor, 386ff; on metaphor and reality, 386ff; on language and metaphor, 387; on analogical symbol, 388; on moral reformers, 388; on liturgical reformers, 389; on mythical framework of thought, 389f; on poetry, 390; on history, 391; on Christian theology and symbol, 391; mentioned, 397
Divine: Mitchell on union of human and, 393; Lewis on nature of, 407
Dogma: Unamuno on, 22, 25; Buber on, 255. *See also* Christian doctrine.
Donne, John, 26
Dostoevski, Feodor Michaelovitch, 390
Doubt, Descartes on, 84ff
Ducasse, C. J.: on evil, 283ff; on nature of evil, 284f; on pain, 284; on good and evil, 284f; on classes of evil, 285f; on metaphysical evil, 286f; on Schopenhauer, 287; on logical and natural possibility, 287f; on omnipotence of God, 287ff; on monotheism, 288; on laws of nature, 288; on attempted solution of the problem of evil, 289–291
Duns Scotus, 81, 98[9]
Duty: as resignation to laws of nature, 150; Newman on, 153f

E

Earth, as one of the four elements, 38
Ecstasy, divine and human, 211
Eddington, Sir Arthur, 315
Efficient cause, argument from, 82
Egypt, 376
Either/Or, Kierkegaard, 117[6]
"Either/or," Kierkegaard on, 118
Élan vital, 216

Eliot, T. S., 406; *The Waste Land*, 390
Emanation, Leibniz on, 98[12]
Emmanuel, 166, 172
Emerson, Ralph Waldo, 16
Emotions, and language, 312
Emotive statements, Ayer and Copleston on, 346
Empedocles, 70, 71, 72
Empiricism, Cox on, 357
Enchiridion, Augustine, 46
Epicurus, 32, 43, 44, 232
Epistemology, Cassirer's interest in, 369
Eros, 178, 215
Erskine, Thomas, 253
Essays and Addresses on the Philosophy of Religion, von Hügel, 208[n]
Essays in Philosophy, Ritchie, 310[n]
Essence: Leibniz on, 97; as object of God's understanding, 97[7]; Plato on knowledge of, 196
Ethics: Nygren on relationship to the religious question, 180; and final truth, 241; James on relationship to metaphysics, 243; relation to obligation, 244; Schweitzer on, 247, 251; Lewis on, 403ff
Ethics, Spinoza, 99[16]
Ethics, Nichomachean, Aristotle, 203[5], 226[n]
Euripides, 412
Evans, Christopher, 384
Evidential, Hepburn on Bultmann's flight from, 378ff
Evil: and the ordering of the whole, 45; Augustine on, as privation of good, 47; as source in the good, 49; Leibniz on origin of, 96[5], Ducasse on, 284f; Kant on man's natural propensity toward, 136f; Kant on the ground of, 138; Kant on overcoming man's propensity toward, 140; Kant on origin in man of, 141f; Sorley on the problem of, 232ff; Job and the problem of, 258; Hume on natural, 276; Hume on moral, 276; Temple on, 277; and finitude, 277ff; as misdirected desire, 279; Ducasse on problem of, 283ff; Ducasse on nature of, 284f; classes of, 285f; Ducasse on metaphysical, 286f; Ducasse on attempted solution of, 289–291
Evolution: as spendthrift of life, 17; as divine plan, 18
Ewing, A. C.: on logical positivism, 322ff; on theory of verification, 324f; on metaphysics, 324f; on the problem of meaning, 325f; on sense-experience, 326
Exercises, Loyola, 145
Existential thinking, Kierkegaard on, 114
Existentialism: Farrer on, 185; Hepburn on, 384ff
Experiment, Hume on relationship to probability, 133

F

Fabri, Honoratus, 97[7]
Fact, Hepburn on relationship to language, 381ff
Factual propositions: Ritchie on, 310f; Ayer and Copleston on, 348ff
Faith: and reason, 12, 43f; as postulates, 12; and understanding, 77; as a leap, 116, 118; James on, 244; Bultmann on, 379
Farrer, Austin: on freedom of the will, 183ff; on determinism and libertarianism, 183f; on existentialism, 185; on freedom and responsibility, 185f; on need of respect for humanity, 186; on the Greek view of man, 187; on Aristotle's view of human nature, 187ff; on positivism, 189; on theology, 191
Fear, and belief in divine power, 32
Feeling, Hocking on, 214
Fellowship, Nygren on, 180
Finite: and the infinite, 70; restricted independence of, 240
Finitude, and the problem of evil, 277ff
Five Ways, the, St. Thomas on, 81ff
Flaubert, Gustave, 17
Foreknowledge: and free will, 261ff, 264ff; and necessity, 270f
Forgiveness, Schweitzer on, 249f
Formgeschichte, 377
Foss, Martin, on metaphor, 387
Fragments, Kierkegaard, 117[6], 122[13], 126[16], 126[20]
Francis of Sales, St., 158, 163
Freedom: and responsibility, 185f; and moral values, 233; Sorley on, 236; and determinism, 236; on human, 237; and foreknowledge, 238; Schweitzer on, 249; and the human spirit, 261
Freedom of the Will, Farrer, 183[n]
Frege, Gottlob, 3
Freud, Sigmund, 165
Friendship: Aristotle on kinds of, 226ff; of good men, 227; and utility, 228; truest, 229; and bad fortune, 230; as a partnership, 231

G

Galileo, 315
Galloway, George: on philosophy and re-

ligion, 6, 8; on philosophy and the philosophy of religion, 8; on Christian philosophy, 8; on theology, 9; on cultus and religious doctrines, 9f; on science and religion, 10; on the Christian Church, 11; on faith and reason, 12
Gaunilon, St. Anselm's reply to, 78
Genesis, 143
Gilson, Étienne, 75
Glaucus, 200
Gnosticism, 378
God: Origen on unity of, 43; as unmoved mover, 68; as actuality, 74f; Descartes on the nature of, 90; origin of the idea of, 93; Leibniz on the nature of, 96ff; as *actus purus*, 96[6], 99[16]; in relationship to the Monads, 98[12]; Kierkegaard on belief in, 116; Kierkegaard on love of, for man, 123; Kierkegaard on appearing of, in time, 124; Kierkegaard on the God-Man, 127; Nygren on the nature of, 182; von Hügel on the nature of, 210; as transcending the natural order, 234; and human freedom, 237f; self-limitation of, 240; Boethius on, 268ff; Ducasse on omnipotence of, 287ff; Ayer on, 305ff; Copleston on uniqueness of, 351; Ayer and Copleston on philosophical knowledge of, 352ff; Cox and McPherson on verifying the existence of, 362ff; H. D. Lewis on experience of, 399ff
Goethe, Johann Wolfgang von, 112
Good: and evil, 47; as coexisting, 49; Nygren on, 179ff; beatific vision of, 215; Schweitzer on, 246; condition of mind and, 279; Ducasse on, 284ff
Grace: Kierkegaard on relationship to ethics of, 128; Kierkegaard on need for, 113; Loyola on the will as soliciting, 146
Grammar of Assent, A, Newman, 149
Green, T. H., 5
Guilloré, 161
Guilt: Kierkegaard on, 119; Kant on, 140
Gupta, N. N., 216
Guyon, Mme. (Jeanne Marie Bouvier de la Mothe), 160

H

Haldane, R. B., 287[3]
Hall, Norman, 216
Hamlet, 52, 53, 54
Harris, Charles R., 199
Harvey, J. W., 393[2]
Heard, Gerald, 217
Hearne, Samuel, 137[1]
Heart; Unamuno on, 23; man's longing, 51; desolation of, 77; Pascal on, 111; Kant on evil nature of, 140; Lewis on God as the searcher of the, 406
Hegel, G. W. F.: mentioned, 5, 6, 7, 112, 114, 116[5], 232, 334, 340, 396
Heidegger, Martin, 128[24]
Hepburn, Ronald W.: on Bultmann's demythologization, 377ff; on Bultmann's flight from the evidential, 378ff; on miracles, 380; on fact and language, 381ff; on myth and historicity, 381[2]; on myth and oblique language, 383ff; on Crombie, 383; on existentialism, 384ff; on paradox, 385
Herder, Johann Gottfried von, 369
Heaven and hell, von Hügel on, 208ff
Heythrop College, England, 328
Hind, Archer, 269[9]
Hinduism, 218
Histoire littéraire du sentiment religieux en France, Bremond, 158[n]
Hobbes, Thomas, 282
Hocking, William E.: on living and dying, 214ff; on feeling, creativity, and love, 214; on immortality, 215ff; on creative aspect of love, 215f; on death, 216; on will-to-live, 217; on will-to-death, 217; on beatific vision, 218, 220; on union of vision and time, 219
Holmes, Oliver Wendell, 17
Holy, the, Otto on the nature of, 173ff
Homer, 207, 261[2], 261[3]
Hominism, 14
Horace, 143[10], 263[4]
Harvard University, 3, 50, 241
Hügel, (Baron) Friedrich von: on heaven and hell, 208ff; on purgatory, 208, 212; on the final destination of man, 209; on spiritual nature of man, 209; on the nature of God, 210; on divine and human ecstasy, 211; on saved and lost spirits, 211f; on pain, 213
Hugo, Victor, 244
Human Enterprise, The, Otto, 14
Humanism: Kierkegaard on, 118, 283
Humanity: religion of, 64; worship of, 66; need for respect for, 186; ideal, 187
Hume, David: on miracles, 132ff; on the Christian religion, 132; on cause and effect, 133; on reliability of human testimony, 134f; on nature as neither good nor evil, 272ff; on animals, 272; on nature's laws, 272f; on capacity of man for pleasure, 272; on industry and labor, 274; on ills of man, 274; on hypotheses concerning first causes, 276; on natural

and moral evil, 276; mentioned, 99[16], 304
Huxley, Thomas H., 18
Hypothesis, Ayer on, 336

I

Ich und Du, Buber, 253
Idea: Royce on relationship of, to object, 59; Descartes on, as image, 86
Ideal, in ethical philosophy, 241
Idea of the Holy, The, Otto, 173
Idealism: Royce as a representative of, 50; Berkeley's, 53f; synthetic, 61
Ideas: in relationship to facts, 50; Royce on, 51ff; and the function of our world, 51; world of, 57ff; and reality, 63; and objects, 87; as pictures and images, 88
Ignatius Loyola, St.: on the sin of the angels, 145; on methods of meditation, 145ff; on grace, 146; on recommendations for meditation, 147
Iliad, 261
Illative sense: Newman on, 149ff; concerning the nature of, 153; range of, 156
Illumination, Masefield on, 219
Images: Lewis on, 399ff; on religious, 408
Imagination: Descartes on, 84; Lewis on, 408f
Immortality: Schiller on, 199ff; in relationship to knowledge in our present life, 203; on rejecting supernatural character of, 205; on theory of psychological continuity, 206; Hocking on, 215ff; MacKinnon on, 221ff; MacKinnon on traditional arguments for, 222; in relationship to the way man speaks of death, 223
Iphigenia, 382
Isaac, 103, 407
Isaiah, 48[4], 166, 169
Israel, 388

J

Jacob, 22, 103, 393, 407
James, Henry, 241
James, William: on pragmatic approach to the moral life, 241ff; on ethics and final truth, 241; on ethical science, 242; on metaphysics, 243; on obligation, 244; on religious faith, 244; on a moral universe, 244; mentioned, 50, 117, 177[1], 199, 202, 203[4]
Jansenism, 103, 104, 108, 110, 111
Jaspers, Karl, 330, 331
Jeptha, 382
Jerusalem, 381
Jesuits. *See* Society of Jesus.
Jesus: Kierkegaard on the ethical teachings of, 121; the parents of, 167; as Saviour, 169; Jury on, 166ff, 170ff; mentioned, 388
John of the Cross, St., 161, 163
Job, the Book of, 258
Johnson, Howard A., 112
Jowett, Benjamin, 194
Joseph, 168, 169
Judaism, 114
Julian of Norwich, Mother, 209
Jupiter, 97[9]
Jury, Paul: on Jesus, 166ff; on Jesus as Emmanuel, 168ff; on Jesus as Saviour, 169; on Christian mythology, 169; on Jesus of Nazareth, 170ff
Justification, by grace through faith, 128

K

Kant, Immanuel: on evil in man, 136ff; on miracles, 136; on mysticism, 136; on bravery, 137[2]; on war, 137[3]f; on man's natural propensity toward evil, 136ff; on freedom of the will, 138; on self-love, 139; on overcoming evil, 140; on guilt, 140; on transgression of the moral law, 143; on state of innocence, 143; on good will, 144; mentioned, 23, 57, 60, 137[1], 173, 209, 232, 249
Karma, law of, 218
Katz, D., 316
Kemp, J., 287[3]
Kerygma, 386, 391
Kerygma and Myth, Bultmann, 377[1], 378, 384, 385
Kierkegaard, Søren Aabye: on man, 112, 117, 125; on culture-religion, 113; on grace, 113; on "Progress," 113; as a prophet, 114; on theodicy, 115; on ontological argument, 115; on cosmological argument, 115; on Christology, 115; on belief, 116; on "life's way," 117; on tragedy, 117[6]; on *Angst*, 117[7]; on humanism, 118; on renunciation, 119; on guilt, 119; on self-determination, 120; on the ethical teachings of Jesus, 121; on redemption, 122; on paradox, 122[13], 124f; on God's love, 123; on suffering servant, 124; on commitment, 126[20]; on Christ, 127[20]; on justification, 128; mentioned, 21

Kingdom of God in America, The, R. Niebuhr, 113[2]
Kuhn, Adalbert, 370

L

Labor, Hume on, 274
Language: Ritchie on, 313; Ayer and Copleston on, 343f; Cassirer on, 375; Hepburn on, 381ff; Dillistone on metaphor in, 387; Mitchell on, 395
Language and Myth, Cassirer, 369[n]
Language, Truth and Logic, Ayer, 304, 305[n], 310, 327
Latour, Gaston, 394
Lambaréné, 246
Latta, Robert, 95
Lavoisier, Antoine Laurent, 320
Law, Kierkegaard on, 121
Laws, Plato, 72[6]
Leibniz, G. W.: on monadology, 95ff; on cosmological proof, 95[2]; on the nature of God, 96ff; on substance, 95f; on inertia of bodies, 96; on evil, 96[5]; on God as *actus purus*, 96, 99[16]; on essences, 97[7]; on laws of nature, 97[9]; on sufficient reason, 98[11]; on God in relationship to monads, 98[12]; on the Trinity, 99[13]; on pre-established harmony, 100[11], 101[26]; on moral necessity, 100[20]; on non-spatial character of monad, 101[24], 101[27]; on perfection, 101[25]; mentioned, 95, 96[3], 97[8], 98[9], 185, 286, 287
Leo XIII, Pope, 149
Leucippus, 72
Leviathan, Hobbes, 282
Lewis, H. D.: on experience of God, 399ff; on images, 399ff; on philosophy, 399; on experiences of crisis, 400; on peace of spirit, 400f; on content of religious awareness, 401f; on effect of the environment in the religious response, 401f; on ethics, 403ff; on types of religious experience, 404f; on love, 405f; on conscience, 406; on the nature of the divine disclosure, 407; on religious images, 408; on imagination, 408; on art, 409ff
Libertarianism, Farrer on, 183f
Life: Kierkegaard on, 117; Schweitzer on reverence for, 246ff; and death, Hocking on, 214ff
Living Thoughts of Pascal, The, Mauriac, 103
Logic: not applicable to the contraries good and evil, 49; Newman on the function of, 157; Ayer and Copleston on, 341ff; Cassirer on, 372f
Logical positivism: Farrer on, 189; Ritchie on errors of, 310ff; Ewing on, 322ff; Ayer's summary of, 328; Ayer-Copleston debate on, 328ff; mentioned, 64, 304, 356, 357
Logos, 386, 391
Lotze, Hermann, 50
Louis XIV, 167
Love: Comte on, 66; and strife, 70f; as a fundamental Christian motif, 178; Hocking on, 214; creative aspect of, 215f; Aristotle on, 226ff; Schweitzer on, 247; Lewis on, 405f
Lowrie, Walter, 116[5]
Lucretius: on nature, 32ff; on matter, 34ff; on void, 35ff; on void and bodies, 36f; on time, 36; on bodies and first-beginnings, 37; on earth, air, fire, and water, 38; on matter as indestructible, 39; on limitless universe, 40ff; on ceaseless motion, 40; on ether, 41f; on infinite space, 42; mentioned, 318

M

MacGregor, Geddes, 161[4], 165, 292, 313[1]
MacKinnon, Donald: on death, 221ff; on traditional arguments for immortality, 222; on the agony of bereavement, 223; on the Christian emphasis on the resurrection, 224
Macmurray, John, 397
Magic, Cassirer on, 373
Maimonides, Moses, 344
Malaval, 161, 162
Man: Anselm on, 76; Descartes on, 92; Kierkegaard on contradiction within, 111; predicament of, 117; sorrow of, 120; on humiliation of, 125; Kant on nature of, 136ff; on the good will within, 144; Newman on the nature of, 151; Farrer on, 187; von Hügel on, 209; Schweitzer on, 246; Buber on response of man to, 253ff; Hume on capacity for pleasure, 272; on ills of man, 274; Temple on fall of, 281
Manicheanism, Hume on, 276; mentioned, 46
Mannheim, Karl, 397
Manning, Henry Edward (Cardinal), 149
Mauriac, François, 103
Marshall, Bruce, 292
Masefield, John, 219
Matter: Lucretius on, 34ff; Royce on, 56ff

Matthew, St., 48[5], 49[7], 170ff
McKeon, Richard, 68, 226
McPherson, Thomas: on problem of verification, 363ff; reply to David Cox, 363ff; on religious experience, 364; on verifying existence of God, 365; on meaning of theological propositions, 366
Mean, between good and evil, 141[7]
Meaning: Ewing on, 322ff; Cassirer on, 372
Meaning of God in Human Experience, The, Hocking, 219
Meaning of Immortality, The, Hocking, 214
Meditation, Loyola on rules for, 145ff
Meinong, Alexius, 368
Memmius, 41
Mendel, Alfred O., 103
Méré, Chevalier de, 110
Metaphor: Cassirer on the power of, 369ff; Cassirer on types of, 371ff; Dillistone on, 386ff; Foss on, 387
Metaphysics: Nygren on the relationship of, to philosophical analysis, 179; Ritchie on, 311; Ewing on, 324f; Copleston on, 329ff; Ayer on, 329; Ayer and Copleston on, 330ff, 347ff; Cox on, 356
Metaphysics, Aristotle, 68, 263[5]
Meynell, Sir Francis, 26[n]; Wilfred, 26
Michel, André, 165, 166[1], 170[1]
Mill, John S., 55
Milton, John, 110, 207
Mind: Royce on priority of, 56; and the real world, 58; Newman on laws of, 152; and values, 236ff; Temple on, 278ff; and the religious response, 402
Miracles: Hume on, 132ff; Kant on, 136; Hepburn's analysis of Bultmann on, 380
Mitchell, W, Fraser: on language of religion, 392ff; on religious experience, 392; on union of the divine and human, 393; on myth, 393; on vision, 393f; on the mysterious, 394f; on the nature of worship, 394ff; on religious language, 395; on religious experience and other types of experience, 396; on the nature of religion, 396ff; mentioned, 20
Monadology, The, Leibniz, 95, 96[6]
Monads: "claims and aspirations" of, 96[4]; Leibniz on the nature of, 98ff; non-spatial character of, 101[24], 101[27]
Montaigne, Michel de, 110
Monotheism: Comte on, 64; Ducasse on, 288
Moral law, Kant on, 143
Moral life, pragmatic approach to, 241ff
Moral necessity, Leibniz on, 100[20]
Moral order, and the natural order, 235
Moral universe, James on, 244
Moral Values and the Idea of God, Sorley, 232
Moralism, Kierkegaard on, 118; Ayer on, 306
Motion: Lucretius on, 40; Aristotle on, 68ff; and time, 69, 70; argument from, 81; Plato on, 194
Mozart, Wolfgang Amadeus, 216
Müller, Max, 370
Munro, H. A. J., 32
Multiverse, 235
Myers, F. W. H., 202[4]
Mystery: basis for hope and consolation, 23; primitive man's response to, 394f
Mystical Element in Religion, The, von Hügel, 208
Mysticism: Kant on, 136; Bremond on, 159ff; Ayer on, 308
Myth: and legend, 44; Christian, 169; Cassirer on, 370f; Bultmann's definition of, 377; in relationship to history, 381[2]; Hepburn on, 382ff; Mitchell on, 393

N

Napoleon, 167
Natura incorruptibilis, 48
Nature: origin of, 32ff; Lucretius on, 34ff; Leibniz on laws of, 97[9]; Hume on, 272ff; Ducasse on laws of, 288
Nature, Man and God, Temple, 277
Nazarene and Nazareth, 170ff
Necessity: Comte on demonstrable, 65; Boethius on kinds of, 270; and foreknowledge, 270
Needham, Joseph, 396
Neighbor, Nygren on love of, 182
Neo-Platonism, 46, 47[3], 68
New Essays in Philosophical Theology, Antony Flew and Alastair MacIntyre, 377[n]
Newman, John Henry (Cardinal): on illative sense, 149ff; on certitude, 149; on certainty, 149; on duty, 150, 153f; on man, 151; on laws of the mind, 152; on range of the illative sense, 156; on function of logic, 157; mentioned, 297
Nicholas of Cusa, 101[23], 102[29]
Nicole, Pierre: anti-mystic rationalism of, 158; on contemplation, 162; mentioned, 109, 159, 160, 161
Niebuhr, H. Richard, 113
Nirvana, 218

Nonexistence of God, Max Otto on, 14ff
Numinous, the, 173ff, 177
Nygren, Anders: on *agape*, 178ff; on Plato, 179; on metaphysics, 179; on the ethical question, 180; on the religious question, 180f; on the uniqueness of Christianity, 181; on the nature of God, 182; on the Good, 179, 182; on love of neighbor, 182

O

Objectivity, Lewis on sense of, and religious awareness, 403
Objects, Descartes on external, 85
Occasionalism, 101[26]
Odyssey, 109[2]
O'Neill, Eugene E., 216
On the Nature of Things, Lucretius, 32[n]
Ontological argument: Anselm on, 75ff; Descartes on, 84ff; Kierkegaard on, 115
Origen: on inspiration of Scriptures, 43; on unity of God, 43; on faith and reason, 43f; on allegory, 44; on myths and legends, 44; on evil, 45; mentioned, 209
Otto, Max: on nonexistence of God, 14ff; on human mortality, 15; on theism, 15; on evolution, 17f
Otto, Rudolf: on the numinous, 173ff, 177; on religious experience, 175; on worship, 175; on Schleiermacher, 175ff; mentioned, 393, 394, 398
Original sin, 280
Our Experience of God, Lewis, 399[n]
Outler, Albert D., 46

P

Pain: von Hügel on, 213; Ducasse on, 284
Pantheism, Sorley on, 234
Paradox: Unamuno on, 23; Kierkegaard on, 122[13], 124f; Hepburn on, 385
Parmenides, 68
Pascal, Blaise: conversion of, 106; on certitude, 106; on salvation, 107; on purity, 108; on the contradictions within man, 111; on the heart of man, 111; mentioned, 21, 103
Pater, Walter, 394
Paul, St., 26, 45, 121
Peano, Giuseppe, 3
Pegis, A. C., 81[n]
Pentecost, Kierkegaard's parable for, 128f
Perfection: Descartes on, 90f; Leibniz on, 101[25]
Perplexities and Paradoxes, Unamuno, 21
Perrier, Gilberte, 107, 108, 109
Phaedo, 194
Phaedrus, 72[6], 194
Phenomenalism, Ritchie on, 313ff
Philebus, 44
Philosophical Scrutiny of Religion, Ducasse, 283
Philosophy: and philosophy of religion, 6; Schiller on, 199ff; and ethical problems, 242; Copleston on, 329; Lewis on relationship to the religious response, 399
Philosophy of Civilization, The, Schweitzer, 246
Philosophy of religion: and philosophy, 6; and Christian philosophy, 8; dependence of, upon philosophy, 8; and theology, 9; and authority, 11
Philosophy of Religion, Galloway, 5
Physics, Aristotle, 68, 260[1]
Piper, Leonore E. (Mrs.), 202[4], 204, 206
Plato: Leibniz on, 97[8]; Nygren on, 179; on the immortality of the soul, 194ff; on motion, 194; on soul as self-moving, 194; on soul and body, 195; on knowledge of the essence of things, 196; on man's desire for truth, 196; on the soul, 197; on death, 197f; mentioned, 5, 20, 43, 44, 68, 69, 70, 72, 199, 200, 209, 214, 268[9], 268, 269, 282, 392
Plotinus, 209, 220
Plunkett, Joseph, 398
Pluralism, Sorley on, 232
Poetry, Dillistone on, 390
Potency, in relationship to actuality, 72
Poiret, Pierre, 98
Pope, Alexander, 185
Positivism. *See* Logical positivism.
Possibility: St. Thomas on, 82; as germinal reality, 100[21]; Ducasse on logical and natural, 287f
Postscript, Kierkegaard, 115[4], 119[8], 119[9], 120[11], 121[12], 125[17], 125[18], 126[19], 126[20]
Pragmatism: Schiller on, 199; James on, 241
Predestination: Pascal on, 104; Temple on, 281
Pre-established harmony, 100[17], 101[26]
Preuss, Konrad Theodor, 374[10], 375[12]
Price, H. H., 306[1]
Prime Mover, Aristotle on, 68ff
Progress: medical, 14; Kierkegaard on, 113; human, 125
Proofs for God's existence, 81ff; Kirkegaard on, 115; Kant on, 136

Propositions: Ritchie on types of, 310ff; Ayer and Copleston on contingent and necessary, 337ff; Ayer and Copleston on meaningful, 345ff
Protarchus, 44
Psychical research, Schiller on, 201f
Purgatory, 208, 212
Pythagoreanism, 74, 194

R

Reality: Royce on, and the world of sense, 52ff; as ideal, 54ff; spiritual nature of, 233; Copleston on the intelligible structure of, 332; Ayer and Copleston on the problem of transcendent, 333f; Ayer and Copleston on metaphysical, 350ff; Dillistone on function of metaphor in relation to, 386ff
Reason: and social life, 65; Boethius on, 268ff
Redemption: Kierkegaard on, 122
Religion: Whitehead's definition of, 3; as doctrine, 4; and social fact, 4; Unamuno on, 21; and morality, 254f; and natural science, 307; Mitchell on language of, 392ff; Mitchell on essential nature of, 396f
Religious experience: Whitehead on, 4; explication of in theology, 12; Otto on, 175; Ayer on, 309; Ayer and Copleston on, 353f; Cox and McPherson on, 362ff; Lewis on, 399ff; and other types of experience, 404f; and art, 411f; Mitchell on, 392, 395f
Religiousness: Kierkegaard on, 120ff; Schweitzer on, 248
Renunciation, Kierkegaard on, 119
Republic, 200[2], 282
Responsibility, Buber on, 253
Resurrection and immortality, 224
Revelation, Unamuno on, 23
Rilke, Rainer Maria, 216
Ritschl, Albrecht, 8
Ritchie, A. D.: on the errors of logical positivism, 310ff; on types of propositions, 310–312; on emotions and language, 312; on language, 313; on physical science, 316, 319; on value judgments, 317; on scientific observation, 320f
Roannez, Duc de, 105
Royce, Josiah: and absolute idealism, 50; on the larger self, 50ff; on ideas and reality, 50ff; and the formation of our world, 51; on the world of sense, 52ff; on world-spirit, 53; on ideal truth, 54; on space, 54; on matter, 56ff; on death, 59; on the self, 60ff; on synthetic idealism, 61; mentioned, 244[1]
Russell, Bertrand, 3, 304, 368

S

Sacy, Samuel Silvestre de, 110
Samos, 44
Sanskrit, 217
Sartre, Jean-Paul, 185
Sassoon, Siegfried, 219
Satires, Horace, 143[11], 263[4]
Satisfactions, Kirkegaard on finite, 119
Saturn, 97[9]
Schelling, Friedrich Wilhelm Josef von, 369, 370[2], 393[1]
Schiller, F. C. S.: on immortality, 199ff; on philosophers and scientists, 199f; on philosophy, 200f: on psychical research, 201f; on immortality and our knowledge of this life, 203; on rejecting supernatural character of immortality, 205; on psychological continuity, 206
Schlick, Moritz, 304
Schleiermacher, Friedrich Daniel Ernst, 175ff, 379, 384
Schopenhauer, Arthur, 50, 210, 287[3], 287
Schubert, Franz Peter, 218[2]
Schweitzer, Albert: on reverence for life, 246ff; on good and evil, 246; on ethical man, 246; on ethics, compassion, suffering, 247; on will-to-live, on destructive will, 248; on freedom, 249; on forgiveness, 249f; on relative ethics, 251
Science: and religion, 10; Schiller on, 199f; Ritchie on, 319ff; Ayer and Copleston on, 330ff
Scotland, 297
Scripture, Origen on, 43
Self: the larger, 50; and knowledge of the object, 60; infinite, 62; Temple on, 281
Self-determination, Kierkegaard on, 120
Self-love, Kant on, 139
Sénancour, Étienne Pivert de, 118
Sense-experience: Hume on, 132; Ayer on, 308; Ritchie on, 316; Ewing on, 326; Cox on, 359
Sermon on the Mount, Farrer on, 186
Shelley, Percy B., 395
Simmias, 194, 195, 196, 197
Smith, Norman Kemp, 310
Smith, R. G., 253
Society for Psychical Research, 202[3], 207
Society of Jesus, 109, 145, 158, 165, 328

Socrates, 18, 186, 195ff
Solomon, 164
Sorley, W. R.: on theism and moral values, 232ff; on monism and pluralism, 232; on problem of evil, 232ff; on spiritual nature of reality, 233; on moral values and freedom, 233; on pantheism, 234; on deism, 234; on natural order and moral order, 235; on creation and the idea of God, 235; on mind and values, 236; on freedom, 236ff; on freedom and foreknowledge, 238; on the absolute, 240; on mind and values, 239; on finite things, 240; on the self-limitation of God, 240
Soul: Plato on immortality of, 194ff; as self-moving, 194; and the body, 195; as beholding things in themselves, 197
Space: Lucretius on, 42; Royce on, 54
Spender, Stephen, 390
Spinoza, Benedict, 96[3], 98[12], 209
Spirit of Modern Philosophy, The, Royce, 50
Stalin, Joseph, 187, 188
Stareleigh, Justice, 312
Stephen, Sir James, 243
Stirling, James H., 5
Stoicism, 43, 44, 180, 209, 259, 266[7]
Substance: Aristotle on kinds of, 71; Leibniz on, 95f
Suffering, Schweitzer on, 247
Symbol: Ayer and Copleston on, 340f; Dillistone on, 388ff

T

Tautologies: Ritchie on, 311; Ayer and Copleston on, 339
Teleological argument, 81
Temple, Frederick, 277
Temple, William: on finitude and evil, 277ff; on evil and the world-process, 277; on mind, 278ff; on evil as misdirected desire, 279; on temptation, 280; on original sin, 280f; on the self, 281; on predestination, 281
Tertullian, 209
Theism: Unamuno on proofs for, 22; Kierkegaard on ethical humanistic, 118; and moral values, 232ff; mentioned, 15
Théodicée, Leibniz, 96[5], 99[13], 101[22], 101[24], 286
Theology: Galloway on, 9f; and Christian dogmatics, 10; and metaphysics, 12; Farrer on, 191; Cox on, 356ff; McPherson on, 366
Theresa of Avila, St., 161, 162, 163, 164
Thomas Aquinas, St.; on God's existence, 81ff; argument from motion, 81; argument from efficient cause, 82; argument from possibility and necessity, 82; on gradation of things, 82; on governance of the world, 83; mentioned, 68, 95[1], 98[9], 160
Thomas, Dylan, 408
Thought: Cassirer on mythic, 373; mythical framework of, 389f
Timaeus, 70[2], 72[5], 72[7], 268[9]
Time: existing not by itself, 36; and motion, 69f
Titchener, E. G., 284[1]
Tolstoy, Leo, 217
Training in Christianity, Kierkegaard, 122[13], 125[15], 126[2]
Transcendence and immanence, 397
Trent, Council of, 81
Trinity: St. Augustine on, 47; Leibniz on, 99[13]
Truth: Royce on ideal, 54; and ideas, 56; Plato on man's desire for, 196; unified moral, 244; Cox on, and verification, 362f

U

Ulysses, Joyce, 390
Unamuno, Miguel de: on skepticism, 21; on religion, 21ff; on dogmas, 22, 25; on theistic proofs, 22; on the heart, 23; on mystery, 23; on paradox, 23
Universe: Lucretius on, 40ff; perfection and order of, 101; first causes of, 276
Usener, Hermann Karl, 371[5], 376

V

Valéry, Paul, 109
Value: as an ideal realm, 234f; and judgments, 317
Vanzetti, Bartolomeo, 16
Varieties of Religious Experience, James, 176[1]
Veitch, John, 84
Vergil, 167
Verification: Ewing on, 324ff; Ayer and Copleston on, 347ff; Cox on, 357f; on applying the principle of, to Christian doctrine, 361ff; McPherson on, 363ff
Void: Lucretius on, 35ff; unfathomable, 40

W

Wallace, W., 5
Walpole, Sir Robert, 141[4]
Wasserman, Jacob, 113
Waste Land, The, Eliot, 390
Werner, Heinz, 370, 371[4], 373[7]
Wesley, Charles, 394
Whitehead, Alfred North: on definition of religion, 3; on religion as belief, 4; on religion as doctrine, 4; on religion as solitariness, 4; mentioned, 304, 316
Will, freedom of the: Kant on, 138; Farrer on, 183ff
Will-to-die, Hocking on, 217[1]
Will-to-live, Hocking on, 217; Schweitzer on, 248
Windelband, W., 14
Wisdom, John, 384
Wittgenstein, Ludwig, 304
Wonder, as basic to religion, 399
Wordsworth, William, 392, 394
World as Will and Idea, The, Schopenhauer, 287[3]
World: governance of, 83; Ayer and Copleston on, 334f
Worship: Otto on, 175; Mitchell on nature of, 394ff

Y

Yaos, 375[n]
Yoga, 216

Z

Zeno of Citium, 266[7]
Zeus, 44
Zionism, 253
Zoroastrianism, 283